The **Rough Guide** to

St Petersburg

written and researched by

Dan Richardson

ROUGH GUIDES

NEW YORK • LONDON • DELHI

www.roughguides.com

△ The Grand Cascade, Peterhof

Introduction to

St Petersburg

Where were you born?
St Petersburg.
Where did you go to school?
Petrograd.
Where do you live now?
Leningrad.
And where would you like to live?
St Petersburg.

St Petersburg, Petrograd, Leningrad and now, again, St Petersburg (in Russian, Sankt Peterburg) – as this tongue-in-cheek catechism suggests, the city's succession of names mirrors Russia's history. Founded in 1703 as a "window on the West" by Peter the Great, St Petersburg was for two centuries the capital of the Tsarist Empire, synonymous with hubris, excess and magnificence.

During World War I the city renounced its Germanic-sounding name and became Petrograd, and as such was the cradle of the revolutions that overthrew Tsarism and brought the Bolsheviks to power in 1917. Later, as Leningrad, it epitomized the Soviet Union's heroic sacrifices in the war against Fascism, withstanding almost nine hundred days of Nazi siege. Finally, in 1991 – the year that the USSR collapsed – the change of name, back to St Petersburg, was deeply symbolic, infuriating the wartime generation but delighting those who pined for a pre-revolutionary golden age; a dream kept alive throughout the years of Stalinist terror, when the poet Osip Mandelstam (who died in a labour camp) wrote:"We shall meet again in Petersburg . . ."

St Petersburg's sense of its own identity owes much to its origins and the interweaving of myth and reality throughout its history. Created by the will

▽ "Walruses" swimming in the icy Neva

of an autocrat, on a barren river delta on the same latitude as the southern tip of Greenland, the Imperial capital embodied Peter the Great's rejection of Old Russia – represented by the former capital, "Asiatic" Moscow – and his embrace of Europe. The city's architecture, administration and social life were all copied or imported, the splendid buildings appearing alien to the indigenous forms and out of place in the surrounding countryside. Artificiality and self-consciousness were present from the beginning and this showpiece city of palaces and canals soon decreed itself the arbiter of Russia's sensibility and imagination. Petersburgers still tend to look down on the earthier Muscovites, who regard them in turn as snobbish. As the last tsar, Nicholas II, once remarked, "Remember, St Petersburg is Russian – but it is not Russia."

For all that, the city is associated with a host of renowned figures from Russian culture and history. It was here that Tchaikovsky, Stravinsky and Shostakovich composed; Pushkin, Dostoyevsky and Gogol wrote their masterpieces; Mendeleyev and Pavlov made their contributions to science; and Rasputin, Lenin and Trotsky made history. So, too, are various buildings and sites inseparable from their former occupants or visitors: the amazing Imperial palaces outside St Petersburg, where Peter and Catherine the Great led the field in exuberant living; the Yusupov Palace, where Rasputin was murdered; Finland Station, where Lenin returned from exile; and the Winter Palace, the storming of which was heralded by the guns of the cruiser

> As the last tsar once remarked, "St Petersburg is Russian – but it is not Russia."

Aurora, now moored along the embankment from the Peter and Paul Fortress – itself a Tsarist prison to generations of revolutionaries.

Today, "Piter" (as it's affectionately known) casts itself as Russia's cultural capital. For its three hundredth anniversary in 2003, much of the centre was facelifted and President Putin (a Leningrader by birth) hosted a G8 summit to raise St Petersburg's profile abroad. While the city has never looked finer or been so tourist-friendly as now, homelessness, alcoholism and poverty are all too visible reminders of the human cost of Russia's transition to capitalism. Yet the city has endured far worse in its history, and there are plenty who anticipate a brighter future.

What to see

St Petersburg is Russia's second largest city, with a population of five million and an urban sprawl of over 1400 square kilometres, across islands and peninsulas delineated by the **River Neva** and its tributaries. The metro covers most parts of the city of interest to visitors, but the historic centre is best explored on foot – easily done with a decent map, given the abundance of landmarks.

The Venice of the North

For once, the sobriquet is justified. Built on mud and water, St Petersburg is every bit as grandiose, decrepit and vulnerable to flooding as Venice is. Rivers and canals make up one tenth of its area; most parts of the city are only 3m above sea level. On granite embankments, ornate bridges and wrought-iron fences, dolphins, tritons and nymphs mingle with armorial and Soviet motifs. The stucco facades of its palaces, painted in cool blues and yellows or rich hues of apricot or crimson, are reflected in the dark waters. St Petersburg's beauty is suffused with melancholy; bygone glories and tragedies are evoked at every turn.

St Petersburg's major islands and "mainland" districts are juxtaposed in the magnificent panorama of the Neva Basin. On the south bank of the Neva, the golden dome of St Isaac's Cathedral and the needle-spire of the Admiralty loom above the area **within the Fontanka** (Chapter 1), whose vibrant main axis, **Nevskiy prospekt**, runs past a slew of sights culminating in the Winter Palace. The seductive vistas along the Moyka and Griboedov waterways entice you to wander off in search of the Mariinskiy ballet, the spot where Rasputin was murdered, or the setting for *Crime and Punishment*.

▽ The Bronze Horseman

Two museums here rate a chapter each. The **Hermitage** (Chapter 2) boasts superlative collections of Rembrandt, Spanish masters, French Impressionists and Post-Impressionists; treasures from Siberia, Central Asia, India, Persia and China – plus the sumptuous state rooms of the Winter Palace, which forms part of the complex. If homegrown art is lacking there, that's because it's in the **Russian Museum** (Chapter 3), running the gamut from folk art and icons to Futurism and Socialist Realism.

Opposite the Admiralty, on the spit or Strelka of **Vasilevskiy Island** (Chapter 4), the Rostral Columns and Naval Museum proclaim a maritime heritage bequeathed by Peter the Great. Nearby is the Kunstkammer of anatomical curios founded by Peter as Russia's first museum and still the city's most ghoulish tourist attraction. Farther along the embankment stand the Academy of Arts and the palace of Prince Menshikov.

Completing the panorama is the **Peter and Paul Fortress** (Chapter 4), its bastions surrounding a soaring cathedral where the Romanov monarchs are buried, and a Prison Museum attesting to the dark side of its history. Beyond its moat, the city's zoo and mosque mark the onset of the residential **Petrograd Side**, with its Art Nouveau buildings and flat-museums commemorating the opera singer Chaliapin and the Bolshevik "martyr" Kirov, whose name was given to the archipelago that forms its hinterland. The **Kirov Islands** are the city's summer playground, with boating lakes, the Kirov Stadium and Yelagin Palace.

> St Petersburg's beauty is tinged with melancholy.

Back on the "mainland", the area beyond the Fontanka is designated **Liteyniy, Smolniy and Vladimirskaya** (Chapter 6), after the three localities that define its character. Its finest sights are the Smolniy

Cathedral, near the Institute from where the Bolsheviks orchestrated the October Revolution, and the Alexander Nevsky Monastery, in whose cemeteries many of the city's most famous personages are buried. However, don't neglect the atmospheric Vladimirskaya district, where Dostoyevsky's apartment and the Pushkinskaya 10 artists' colony are located, along with an assortment of odd museums.

Further out, the industrial **Southern Suburbs** (Chapter 7) are dignified by grandiose Soviet architecture such as the House of Soviets and the Victory Monument, and Tsarist triumphal arches that were re-erected in the euphoria of the Soviet Union's victory over Nazi Germany. Aside from these, there's the lovely Art Nouveau Vitebsk Station, an Outdoor Railway Museum, and an atmospheric cemetery, the Literatorskie mostki.

The **Vyborg Side** (Chapter 8) of the Neva is similarly industrial but noteworthy in other ways. Anyone interested in the city's revolutionary past should visit Finland Station, where the first ever Lenin statue still stands, and the cruiser *Aurora*, preserved as a relic of 1917, is moored. Kresty Prison and the Piskarov Cemetery are sombre reminders of the victims of Stalin's purges and the hundreds of thousands who died during the Blockade. Only the Buddhist temple strikes a lighter note.

Just outside the city, the **Imperial palaces** (Chapter 9) are among Russia's premier attractions, particularly Peterhof with its magnificent fountains, and the Catherine Palace at Tsarskoe Selo with its fabled Amber Room. Though both deserve a full day each, it's possible to combine Tsarskoe Selo with another palace, Pavlovsk, if you're willing to dash around.

The island naval base of **Kronstadt** (Chapter 10) is best known today for an annual rave staged in an offshore sea fort. While the **Gulf coast** has several beach resorts that come alive in summer, the real draw for city dwellers are the forests, lakes and weekend *dachas* (cottages) of the

△ The Catherine Park, Tsarskoe Selo, in February

Karelian Isthmus. This region once belonged to Finland and was previously contested by Russia and Sweden, as is evident at **Vyborg**, near the Finnish border.

On Lake Ladoga, the prison-fortress of **Shlisselburg** (Chapter 11) is a poignant reminder of those who suffered there in Tsarist times and its resistance to the Nazi Blockade, while the **Valaam** archipelago attests to the centuries-old monastic tradition in Russia's northern lakes, whose isolation gave rise to the amazing wooden churches of **Kizhi** Island in Lake Onega.

Ladoga is linked to the great inland waterways of Russia, which once enriched **Novgorod** (Chapter 12). Its medieval Kremlin, parish churches and outlying monasteries merit a full day's exploration, while local hotels are cheap enough to make an overnight excursion from St Petersburg quite feasible.

When to go

St Petersburg lies on the same latitude as the Shetland Islands and Anchorage, Alaska, but its **climate** is less harsh than you'd imagine. Summers are hot and while winters may be cold by Western European standards, they rarely compare with the cold of winter in Moscow, let alone Siberia.

New Year and January is the best time to come. The city looks magical covered in snow and days can be gloriously sunny. Arts and music lovers will find plenty to enjoy; party animals can revel in the nightlife; and visitors needn't queue to get into the Hermitage or the Imperial palaces (though they'll have to forgo seeing the fountains at Peterhof). New Year occasions shopping and merrymaking, much as Christmas in the West, and it's worth sticking around to catch the traditional Russian Orthodox Church celebrations of both holidays, in early January.

Spring is chiefly rewarding for the rituals and candle-lit processions marking Orthodox **Easter**, when cathedrals are so packed that people wait for hours to get in. (Christmas services are as splendid yet not nearly so crowded.) Whereas Easter is a moveable feast whose date can be foretold, the amazing sight of **ice floes** grinding their way down the Neva may not occur until April or even early May, depending on the spring thaw.

The most popular time is **summer**, especially during the intoxicating "**White Nights**" (mid-June to mid-July). While it's hard to resist nights turned to days and weeks of festivities, there's a downside to visiting then. Accommodation is scarce; there are queues for the Hermitage and Imperial palaces; and the ballet dancers at festivals are rarely top class. Days are baking hot and nights sultry with the occasional downpour providing relief from the humidity. In August, everyone who can afford to leaves the city, if only to stay in a *dacha* (cottage) in the surrounding countryside.

By mid-September **autumn** is under way, with cloudy skies and falling temperatures. In October theatres reopen and the Mariinskiy starts its new season, making this one of the best times for ballet and opera lovers prepared to risk the first frosts (and sometimes snowfalls), though there can also be warm and sunny days, when the city looks especially beautiful in the soft northern light. It's best to **avoid** coming in November, December or February, when the weather is uncertain and cultural offerings are patchy.

Finally, make sure you **bring** the right gear. Lots of layers, a hat and waterproof footwear with non-slip soles are essential for winter. A compact rainproof jacket will protect you from showers in spring or autumn. Shorts and T-shirts are fine for summer, but pack long trousers or a skirt for visiting churches, the ballet, or dining out – and a mosquito net to drape over your bed if you're unsure that your lodgings have screens on the windows.

Monthly temperatures and average monthly rainfall in St Petersburg

	Jan	Feb	Mar	Apr	May	June	July	Aug	Sept	Oct	Nov	Dec
Max. temp. (°C)	-7	-5	0	8	15	20	21	20	15	9	2	-3
Min. temp. (°C)	-13	-12	-8	0	6	11	13	13	9	4	-2	-8
Rainfall (mm)	35	30	31	36	45	50	72	78	64	76	46	40

25

things not to miss

It's not possible to see everything that St Petersburg has to offer on a short trip – and we don't suggest you try. What follows is a subjective selection of the city's highlights, shown in no particular order, ranging from the peerless art collection of the Hermitage to the sumptuous palaces on the outskirts, all arranged in colour-coded categories to help you find the very best things to see, do and experience. All entries have a page reference to take you straight into the guide, where you can find out more.

01 Peter and Paul Fortress Page **175** • The kernel from which the city developed, the fortress contains a cathedral where the Romanovs are buried and a prison museum denouncing their tyranny.

02 Mariinskiy Theatre

Page **376** • World-class ballet and opera performed in a magnificent auditorium under the baton of maestro Gergiev, by the company better known abroad as the Kirov.

04 Dvortsovaya ploshchad (Palace Square)

Page **73** • The boldest of St Petersburg's public spaces juxtaposes the rampant triumphalism of the General Staff building and the Alexander Column with the Baroque effusions of the Winter Palace.

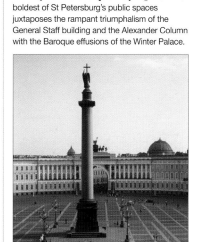

03 Russian Museum

Page **141** • The world's largest collection of Russian art runs the gamut from medieval icons, such as this one of saints Boris and Gleb, to abstract art by Malevich and Kandinsky.

05 Soviet retro

Page **356** • Firmly tongue-in-cheek, *Lenin's Mating Call* features bar girls in Komsomol uniforms (pictured here), while *Purga* (see p.369) invites customers to celebrate New Year every night with the Soviet anthem and the Kremlin clock chiming midnight.

06 Ice Hockey Page **399** • Watch SKA St Petersburg – one of the top teams in Russia – in action at the Ice Palace or the Yubileyniy Sports Palace during the hockey season.

07 Banya Page **395** • A quintessential Russian experience, the banya is a sauna with a masochistic twist that leaves you gasping for more and feeling wonderfully relaxed afterwards.

08 Shlisselburg Page **304** • The Tsarist Alcatraz, where generations of revolutionaries once suffered, it later withstood 500 days of bombardment during the Nazi Blockade of Leningrad and remains a sombre memorial to human courage.

09 Georgian cuisine Page **348** • The healthiest and tastiest of Russia's diverse culinary traditions, owing to its emphasis on fresh herbs, vegetables, pulses, nuts and garnishes such as pomegranate seeds – but Georgian food has plenty to offer carnivores, too.

10 Pavlovsk Page **276** • Created for Tsar Paul, Pavlovsk Palace is surrounded by a vast Romantic park, full of Antique follies and especially lovely in autumn.

11 Church of the Saviour on the Blood Page 82 • A standing rebuke to foreign architecture and revolutionary ideas, built on the spot where Alexander II was fatally injured by a nihilist's bomb; its onion domes evoke St Basil's Cathedral in Moscow, and its interior is entirely covered in gilded mosaics.

12 Peterhof Page 247 • The most dramatic element of Peterhof, the first of the Imperial palaces outside the city, is the Grand Cascade.

13 St Isaac's Cathedral Page 97 • Decorated inside with 14 kinds of marble, jasper, malachite, gilded stucco and mosaics, the cathedral's golden dome offers a stunning view of the inner city.

14 Orthodox choral music Page 203 • Inseparable from the Byzantine rituals of the Orthodox faith, this is best heard at the Preobrazhenskiy Church, whose choir includes many singers from the State Kapella.

15 **The Hermitage** Page **118** • This stupendous museum boasts masterpieces by artists from Rembrandt to Matisse, prehistoric Siberian mummies and curios such as the Kolyvan Vase, displayed in a complex incorporating the Winter Palace, with its fabulously ornate decor.

17 **White Nights** Page **50** • Several weeks in midsummer when twilight is as dark as it gets, and half the city stays up partying, toasting the Neva bridges as they rise to let ships sail upriver in the small hours.

16 **Cruiser Aurora** Page **186** • The warship whose guns heralded the October Revolution has been preserved as a museum – though some say that a sister ship was substituted for the original. Decide for yourself.

18 Fort Dance Page **370** • A mid-summer rave party in an abandoned plague laboratory and naval fort, way out in the Gulf of Finland. How cool can you get?

19 Yusupov Palace Page **110** • A waxworks tableau of Rasputin's murder in the cellar where it happened, as well as sumptuous apartments mirroring generations of aristocratic taste, make the Yusupov Palace irresistible.

20 Valaam Page **307** • Sheer cliffs and bays, limpid lakes and forests full of mosses, bog flowers, berries and mushrooms, make this monastic archipelago a natural arcadia.

21 Kunstkammer Page **162** • Peter the Great's collection of grotesqueries was Russia's first museum and remains one of the city's most popular tourist attractions.

22 Novgorod Page **317** • This medieval city celebrates its pagan roots with bonfires and revelry on the Night of Ivan Kupala (July 6).

24 Kizhi Page **312** • Built entirely of wood, the amazing Church of the Transfiguration is twice the height of St Basil's in Moscow, and sited on a remote island in Lake Onega.

23 Tsarskoe Selo Page **264** • The Catherine Palace at this Imperial suburban estate contains the mirrored Great Hall and the fabled Amber Room.

25 Nevskiy prospekt Page **62** • This imperial thoroughfare through the heart of the city is the nexus for sightseeing, shopping, café society and much else, and is thronged until the small hours, especially during the White Nights.

Contents

Using this Rough Guide

We've tried to make this Rough Guide a good read and easy to use. The book is divided into nine main sections, and you should be able to find whatever you want in them.

Front section

The front **colour section** offers a quick tour of St Petersburg. The introduction aims to give you a feel for the place and tells you the best times to go. Next, the author rounds up his favourite aspects of St Petersburg in the **things not to miss** section – whether it's fantastic architecture, great day-trips or a special café. Right after this comes the Rough Guide's full contents list.

Basics

The Basics section covers all the **pre-departure** nitty-gritty to help you plan your trip, and the practicalities you'll want to know once you're there. This is where to find out how to get there, what paperwork you'll need, what to do about money and insurance – in fact just about every piece of **general practical information** you might need.

The City

This is the heart of the Rough Guide, divided into user-friendly chapters, each of which covers a city district or major museum. Every chapter starts with an **introduction** that helps you decide where to go, followed by a tour of the sights.

Out from the city

This section covers **day-trips** to the Imperial palaces outside the city and **overnight excursions** to more distant destinations such as Vyborg, Valaam and Novgorod, including details of transport, local accommodation and restaurants.

Listings

Listings contains all the consumer information you need to make the most of your stay in St Petersburg, with chapters on **accommodation**, places to **eat and drink**, **nightlife** and **culture** spots, **shopping** and **sports** in the city.

Contexts

Read Contexts to get a deeper understanding of what makes St Petersburg tick. We include a brief **history** and a review of **books** relating to the city.

Language

The **language** section offers useful guidance for speaking Russian and pulls together all the vocabulary you might need on your trip, including a comprehensive **menu reader**. Here you'll also find a **glossary** of words, terms and acronyms peculiar to Russia.

Small print + Index

Apart from a full **index**, this section covers publishing information, credits and acknowledgements, and also has our contact details in case you want to send in updates, corrections or suggestions for improving the book.

Colour maps

The back colour section contains four maps and plans, showing St Petersburg, its central districts and the metro, for an overview of the city.

Map and chapter list

Contents

Listings

Contexts

Language

Small print and Index

Colour maps

1. St Petersburg
2. Central St Petersburg

3. St Petersburg metro

Basics

Basics

Getting there

St Petersburg's peripheral location in northeastern Europe means that, unless you're coming from Helsinki or Tallinn, the quickest and easiest way to get there is by flying. There are direct flights from almost every European capital; the flight time from London is three hours. If you have more time, then travelling overland from Finland, the Baltic States, Germany or Poland (accessible by low-cost airlines) becomes an attractive option, with approaches by train, bus or car and ferry. While St Petersburg still lies beyond the scope of low-price airlines or rail passes, and the need to obtain a visa makes it hard to take advantage of last-minute offers, you should be able to save money on both tickets and Russian visas by booking months ahead of time. For short visits to St Petersburg, a package tour may well be cheaper than doing things independently, once you've taken the cost of accommodation and visas into account.

Booking flights online

Many airlines and discount travel websites offer you the opportunity to book your tickets online, cutting out the cost of agents and middlemen, and often giving you a discount at the same time. Good deals can often be found through discount or auction sites, as well as through the airlines' own websites – though some can't distinguish between St Petersburg in Russia and its Florida namesake, even if you input the right airport code, LED. Another thing to bear in mind is that many online deals permit little or no flexibility, so your flight dates need to mesh with the dates of your Russian visa, which may take several weeks to obtain (see p.23).

Online booking agents and general travel sites

ⓦ **www.travel.yahoo.com** Incorporates a lot of Rough Guides material in its coverage of destination countries and cities across the world, with information about places to eat, sleep and other practicalities.
ⓦ **www.cheapflights.com** Flight deals, travel agents, plus links to other travel sites (US only: for the UK and Ireland, ⓦwww.cheapflights.co.uk).
ⓦ **www.cheaptickets.com** Discount flight specialists.
ⓦ **www.etn.nl/discount.htm** A hub of consolidator and discount agent web links, maintained by the nonprofit European Travel Network.
ⓦ **www.expedia.com** Discount air fares, all-airline search engine and daily deals (US only; for the UK,

ⓦwww.expedia.co.uk; for Canada, ⓦwww.expedia.ca).
ⓦ **www.flyaow.com** Online air travel info and reservations site.
ⓦ **www.gaytravel.com** Gay online travel agent, offering accommodation, cruises, tours and more.
ⓦ **www.geocities.com/thavery2000** Has an extensive list of airline toll-free numbers (from the US) and websites.
ⓦ **www.hotwire.com** Bookings from the US only. Last-minute savings of up to forty percent on regular published fares. Travellers must be at least 18 and there are no refunds, transfers or changes allowed. Log-in required.
ⓦ **www.in-russia.com** Discount flight and hotel bookings in Russia, from the US only.
ⓦ **www.lastminute.com** Offers good last-minute holiday package and flight-only deals (UK only; for Australia, ⓦwww.lastminute.com.au).
ⓦ **www.priceline.com** Name-your-own-price website that has deals at around forty percent off standard fares. You cannot specify flight times (although you do specify dates) and the tickets are non-refundable, non-transferable and non-changeable (US only; for the UK, ⓦwww.priceline.co.uk).
ⓦ **www.skyauction.com** Bookings from the US only. Auctions tickets and travel packages using a "second bid" scheme. The best strategy is to bid the maximum you're willing to pay, since if you win you'll pay just enough to beat the runner-up regardless of your maximum bid.
ⓦ **www.smilinjack.com/airlines.htm** Lists an up-to-date compilation of airline website addresses.
ⓦwww.travelocity.com. Destination guides, hot web

fares and best deals for car rental, accommodation and lodging as well as fares. Provides access to the travel agent system SABRE, the most comprehensive central reservations system in the US.

ⓦ **www.travelshop.com.au** Australian website offering discounted flights, packages, insurance and online bookings.

Flights from Britain and Ireland

The Russian airline Aeroflot and British Airways (BA) between them operate up to nine scheduled **direct flights** a week from London to St Petersburg. Aeroflot flies from Heathrow and Gatwick; BA from Gatwick only. Leaving aside special offers from BA – such as the £199 return being promoted at the time of writing – Aeroflot's fares are generally lower, ranging from around £210 to £320 during low season, £230 to £370 in high season. You can book flights with Aeroflot on ⓦwww.aeroflot.online.com; their official website, ⓦwww.aeroflot.co.uk, is fit only for checking schedules. Other good sources of direct flight tickets are ⓦwww.cheapflights.co.uk and ⓦwww.expedia.co.uk.

The alternatives involve an **indirect flight** via another European city, eg Lufthansa via Frankfurt, KLM via Amsterdam, Air France via Paris, Austrian Airlines or Lauda Air via Vienna, CSA via Prague, SAS via Stockholm, SN Brussels via Brussels, or Finnair via Helsinki. Some airlines offer connections from cities other than London: Lufthansa from Birmingham and Manchester; SN Brussels from Manchester, Newcastle, Glasgow and Edinburgh; SAS and Finnair from Manchester; and KLM from all of them. It's also worth investigating **low-cost airlines** such as easyJet and Ryanair, which sometimes offer amazingly low fares to cities from where cheap onward connections to St Petersburg are available, such as Ryanair from Glasgow to Frankfurt or Paris, and from London to Stockholm or Frankfurt; and easyJet to Amsterdam from Edinburgh or Liverpool.

If you have more time for the journey, it's feasible to use Finland, Estonia or Latvia as jumping-off points for overland travel to St Petersburg. Return flights to Helsinki cost as little as £50–70 from BA. Fares to Rīga and Tallinn start at £100; the best deals are usually from Glasgow or Manchester. Although the cost of onward travel to St Petersburg is quite reasonable, any savings on the flight are likely to be wiped out by the cost of spending time in Helsinki, Rīga or Tallinn – each of which has plenty for visitors to see and do. Overland transport from these cities to St Petersburg is detailed on p.19.

There are **no direct flights** to St Petersburg **from Ireland**, so the best you can hope for is an indirect flight via another hub city. Dublin offers more choice of routings and lower prices than Belfast, so travellers from the North may do better by flying to London or Manchester for an onward connection. For departures from Dublin, the cheapest routing is usually CSA via Prague (for about €420), which tends to be well below fares on Aeroflot, Air France or BA.

Airlines

Aeroflot UK ☏020/7355 2233, ⓦwww.aeroflot.co.uk, though you'll get better results from ⓦwww.aeroflotonline.com.
Air Baltic UK ☏020/7393 1207, ⓦwww.airbaltic.com.
Air France UK ☏0845/0845 111; Ireland ☏01/605 0383; ⓦwww.airfance.com.
Austrian Airlines UK ☏0845/601 0948 or 020/7434 7350, ⓦwww.aua.com.
British Airways UK ☏0845/733 33 77; Ireland ☏1800/626 747; ⓦwww.ba.com.
British Midland UK ☏0870/6070 555, ⓦwww.flybmi.com.
Czech Airlines (CSA) London ☏020/7255 1898; Manchester ☏0161/489 0241; Ireland ☏01/407 3036; ⓦwww.csa.cz.
easyJet ☏0870/600 0000, ⓦwww.easyjet.com.
Estonian Air UK ☏020/7333 0196, ⓦwww.estonian-air.com.
Finnair UK ☏0870/241 4411; Ireland ☏01/844 6565; ⓦwww.finnair.com.
KLM ☏08705/074 074, ⓦwww.klm.com.
Lufthansa UK ☏0845/7737 747; Ireland ☏01/844 544; ⓦwww.lufthansa.co.uk.
Ryanair UK ☏0871/246 0000; Ireland ☏01818/303 030; ⓦwww.ryanair.com.
SN Brussels Airlines UK ☏0870/735 2345; Ireland ☏01/844 5440; ⓦwww.brussels-airlines.com.
SAS UK ☏0845/607 2772; Ireland ☏01/844 5440; ⓦwww.sas.se.
Swiss UK ☏0845/601 0956, ⓦwww.swiss.com.

Transaero ☎0870/8507 767,
Ⓦwww.transaero.ru/english

Discount ticket agents in the UK and Ireland

Airborn Travel ☎020/8498 1212,
Ⓦwww.airborn.co.uk. General discount flight agent.
Benz Travel ☎020/7462 0000,
Ⓦwww.benztravel.co.uk. Discount flight agent.
Eastways Travel ☎020/7247 2424,
Ⓦwww.aeroflotonline.com. UK discount agent for Aeroflot.
Joe Walsh Tours Ireland ☎01/676 0991,
Ⓦwww.joewalshtours.ie. General budget fares agent.
North South Travel ☎01245/608 291,
Ⓦwww.northsouthtravel.co.uk. Friendly, competitive travel agency, offering discounted fares worldwide – profits are used to support projects in the developing world, especially the promotion of sustainable tourism.
STA Travel UK ☎0870/1600 599,
Ⓦwww.statravel.co.uk. Worldwide specialists in low-cost flights and tours for students and under-26s, though other customers welcome.
Trailfinders UK ☎020/7628 7628; Ireland ☎01/677 7888; Ⓦwww.trailfinders.com. One of the best-informed and most efficient agents for independent travellers.

Package tours

Given the price of flights to and hotels in St Petersburg, there's a strong incentive to look for a **package tour** – an easy way of cutting the cost and trouble of organizing a trip. There are all kinds of possibilities, from city breaks to Trans-Siberian tours and luxury cruises. Unless otherwise stated, all prices below are for one person in a twin share; where two prices are given, these refer to low- and high-season rates.

While Interchange can arrange homestay (£34 a night) or hotel accommodation (from £42) for travellers making their own way to St Petersburg, a **city break** makes sense if you have just a few days. Voyages Jules Verne offers four nights for £295–375, including flights and tours; unescorted breaks are available from Intourist (£419–489), Interchange (from £525) and Worldchoice (from £608). Several firms take in **Moscow with St Petersburg**; the cheapest eight-day package comes from Intourist

(£592–839). The two cities can be combined with historic towns on the **Golden Ring**, such as Kostroma, Uglich, Suzdal and Novgorod; an eight-day coach tour from Intourist costs £869, eleven days from Cosmos Tourama, £1069–1120. St Petersburg is also visited on **multi-country coach tours** by Cosmos (£1159–1219) and Wallace Arnold Holidays (£1099) – the latter also features Moscow and Novgorod on its sixteen-day itinerary.

A more leisurely approach is a Volga **cruise** between Moscow and St Petersburg (or vice versa). Cosmos, for example, offers a twelve-day tour (£1019–1059) spending three days in each city with stopovers at Kostroma, Uglich and Yaroslavl, plus the wooden churches of Kizhi (see p.312). Alternatively, Intourist does an eight-day tour (£1039) focusing on St Petersburg and Kizhi, which is reached by hydrofoil from Petrozavodsk, rather than by cruise boat. St Petersburg also features on Voyages Jules Verne's twelve-day cruise of Baltic cities, starting and finishing in Dover (£695–845).

The other main area of tourism are **Trans-Siberian Railway packages** and "soft adventure" spin-offs in Siberia or Mongolia. The Russia Experience offers numerous land-only trips starting in Moscow or St Petersburg and ending up in China, Mongolia or Vladivostok; they run, for example, a twelve-day trip to Beijing that includes staying in a felt tent on the Mongolian steppes (£899); forays into Buryatia or Tuva to witness Buddhist and shamanistic traditions; and whitewater rafting in the Altay Mountains. GW Travel operates private "nostalgia" trains from Moscow to Mongolia for the Naadam festival (£3295), and along the Silk Road from Beijing to Moscow (£4515), likewise priced land-only. You can even see volcanoes, geysers and bears in Kamchatka (£2499) or visit a Siberian tiger reserve (£1499) with Russian Gateway UK; both these packages include return flights from the UK.

Specialist travel agents and tour operators in the UK

Abercrombie and Kent ☎0845/ 0700 610,
Ⓦwww.abercrombiekent.co.uk. Tailor-made de luxe city breaks in St Petersburg and Moscow.

BSI (UK) Ltd ☏020/7224 4678,
🌐www.bsi.uk.com. Flights, hotel bookings and
visas for Russia; tailor-made itineraries.
Cosmos Tourama ☏0880/298 0171,
🌐www.cosmostourama.co.uk. Mainstream tour
operator with two Moscow/St Petersburg tours, one
featuring Kizhi and the Volga towns, the other
Novgorod and Suzdal.
GW Travel ☏01565/754 540, 🌐www.gwtravel
.co.uk. Tours in private trains from Moscow to St
Petersburg and Vladivostok; to Mongolia; and from
Beijing to Moscow via the Silk Road.
Inntel-Moscow Travel Co ☏020/7495 7555,
🌐www.inntel-moscow.co.uk. Visa support, flights
and hotel bookings within the CIS.
Interchange UK ☏020/8681 3612,
🌐www.interchange.uk.com. Tailored short breaks,
flights, hotel and homestay bookings in St Petersburg
and Moscow; escorted tours to Georgia and Armenia.
Intourist ☏020/7538 8600, 🌐www.intourist.co
.uk. Moscow and St Petersburg city breaks, twin-
centre and Golden Ring tours; tailor-made Trans-
Siberian and adventure holidays.
Norvista ☏020/7409 7334, 🌐www.norvista
.co.uk. Scandinavian and Baltic specialists, acting as
ferry and rail agents in the region, which also does
St Petersburg and Moscow city breaks.
Russian Gateway (UK) Ltd ☏0750/803 160
📧travel@russiangateway.co.uk, 🌐www
.russiangateway.fsnet.co.uk. Tours of St Petersburg,
Moscow, the Golden Ring, Lake Baikal and the
Russian Far East (including volcano- and bear-
watching in Kamchatka).
Scott's Tours ☏020/7383 5353,
🌐www.scottstours.co.uk. Specialists in discount
flights to Russia and the CIS, visa support,
accommodation and other services.
The Russia Experience UK ☏020/8566 8846,
🌐www.trans-siberian.co.uk. Trans-Siberian
specialists in individual and small group travel in
Russia, Mongolia, China and Tibet. Operates the
Beetroot Backpackers Bus between Moscow and St
Petersburg over the summer (see p.22).
The Russia House Ltd ☏020/7403 9922,
🌐www.therussiahouse.co.uk. Visa support, hotel
bookings and other services, mainly for business
travellers.
Travel for the Arts ☏020/ 8799 8350,
🌐www.travelforthearts.co.uk. De luxe tours for
music lovers, scheduled for the Russian Orthodox
Easter and the Stars of the White Nights festival.
Voyages Jules Verne ☏020/7616 1000,
🌐www.vjv.co.uk. City breaks, twin-centre tours and
a Baltic cruise visiting St Petersburg.
Wallace Arnold Holidays ☏020/8686 9833 or
011/3231 0739, 🌐www.wallacearnold.com. St

Petersburg, Moscow and Novgorod feature on its
coach tour of seven European countries.
Worldchoice ☏0870/0100 429,
🌐www.worldchoice.co.uk. Mainstream operator
with Moscow and St Petersburg city breaks.

Flights from the USA and Canada

There are **no direct flights** to St Petersburg
from the US or Canada. Russia's national
carrier, Aeroflot, flies from Montreal and five
US cities to Moscow and has several same-
day onward flights to St Petersburg (about
ten hours flying time in all), but at $860 year-
round, you may well do better with other
one- or two-stop flights offered by the
major European carriers, that allow you to
depart from any number of US gateways.
Fares from Eastern gateways range from
$650–950 in low season to $860–1600 during summertime; from the West Coast,
upwards of $800/$1500 during low/high
season. From Canada, Air Canada's fare of
C$2000/C$2400 in high/low season is often
undercut by British Airways or Air France.

Alternatively, you may wish to travel to a
European city and make your way **overland**
from there. Helsinki is the closest foreign
capital to St Petersburg, just seven hours
away by train; Berlin is a cheaper, but more
distant (36 hours by train or coach), gateway. If St Petersburg is part of a longer
European trip, you'll also want to check out
details of the Eurail pass (see p.17).

Airlines in the US and Canada

Aeroflot US ☏1-888/340-6400; Canada
☏416/642-1653, 🌐www.aeroflot.com. Note,
however, that this site is good only for checking
schedules; you'll get better results from their US
consolidator, 🌐www.amadeus.net.
Air Canada ☏1-888/247-2262,
🌐www.aircanada.ca.
Air France US ☏1-800/237-2747,
🌐www.airfrance.us; Canada ☏1-800/667-2747,
🌐www.airfrance.ca.
Austrian Airlines ☏1-800/843-0002,
🌐www.aua.com.
British Airways ☏1-800/247-9297,
🌐www.ba.com.
Czech Airlines (CSA) US ☏1-877/359-6629 or
212/765-6022; Canada ☏416/363-3174,
🌐www.csa.cz.

Delta Air Lines ✈ 1-800/241-4141,
💻 www.delta.com.
Finnair ✈ 1-800/950-5000, 💻 www.finnair.com.
KLM/Northwest Airlines ✈ 1-800/447-4747,
💻 www.nwa.com, 💻 www.klm.com.
Lauda Air ✈ 1-800/843-0002,
💻 www.laudaair.com.
Lufthansa US ✈ 1-800/645-3880; Canada
✈ 1-800/563-5954; 💻 www.lufthansa-usa.com.
Scandinavian Airlines (SAS) ✈ 1-800/221-
2350, 💻 www.scandinavian.net.
Swiss ✈ 1-877/359-7947, 💻 www.swiss.com.
United Airlines ✈ 1-800/538-2929,
💻 www.ual.com.
US Airways ✈ 1-800/622-1015,
💻 www.usair.com.
Virgin Atlantic Airways ✈ 1-800/862-8621,
💻 www.virgin-atlantic.com.

Discount agents in the US and Canada

Council Travel ✈ 1-800/226-8624,
💻 www.counciltravel.com. Nationwide organization
that mostly, but by no means exclusively, specializes
in student travel.
New Frontiers/Nouvelles Frontières
✈ 1-800/677-0720, 💻 www.newfrontiers.com.
French discount-travel firm based in New York City.
Other branches in LA, San Francisco and Quebec
City.
Skylink US ✈ 1-800/247-6659 or 212/573-8980;
Canada ✈ 1-800/759-5465;
💻 www.skylinkus.com. Consolidator.
STA Travel ✈ 1-800/777-0112 or 1-800/781-
4040, 💻 www.sta-travel.com. Worldwide specialists
in independent travel; also student IDs, travel
insurance, car rental, rail passes, etc.
Travac ✈ 1-800/872-8800, 💻 www.thetravelsite
.com. Consolidator and charter broker with offices in
New York and Orlando.
Travel Avenue ✈ 1-800/333-3335, 💻 www
.travelavenue.com. Full-service travel agent that
offers discounts in the form of rebates.
Travel Cuts Canada ✈ 1-800/667-2887; US
✈ 1-866/246-9762; 💻 www.travelcuts.com.
Canadian student-travel organization.

Package tours

Package tours from the US to Russia may
be land-only or include flights; some let you
choose, and the land-only price is often the
same all year round. For an eight-day **city
break** in St Petersburg (the shortest period
on offer), the Russian National Group

charges from $1914 to $2259 (including
flights); Mir Corp from $2995 to $3495 (land-
only from $2595). Many operators offer an
eight-day **St Petersburg and Moscow
tour**, with an overnight train journey between
them. The cheapest of such tours are
offered by Mir Corporation, starting at $610,
and Adventure Center ($810). The Russian
National Group runs a mid-priced tour
($1969–2299 flights included), while Exeter
International's de luxe package costs
$4000–4700 for ten days, flights included.

To see more of Russia, you can visit the
Golden Ring of historic towns and monasteries beyond Moscow. Mir Corporation
charges from $3495 ($2595 land-only) for a
twelve-day tour of Moscow, St Petersburg
and the Golden Ring, while an eight-day
package from Geographic Expeditions costs
from $4295 (including flights). Or you can
combine the Golden Ring with neighbouring
capitals on a fifteen-day coach tour of
Tallinn, Moscow, Suzdal, Kostroma, St
Petersburg and Helsinki (from $1440 land-
only with the Adventure Center). Other packages take in the **Trans-Siberian Railway** or
the **Silk Road** through Central Asia – Mir
Corporation offers Beijing to Moscow by the
Silk Road in a luxurious private train for
$6995 (land-only).

Another option is **cruising**. A typical cruise
from Moscow to St Petersburg (or vice
versa) involves three or four days in each
city, and three or four days visiting the
ancient Volga towns of Yaroslavl, Kostroma
and Uglich – and is sometimes extended to
thirteen days to include Kizhi (see p.312).
You can get such a tour from the Russian
National Group for $1899–2149 including
flights, or $1110 land-only; General Tours'
twelve-day cruise costs from $2209 (includ-
ing flights); while Exeter International's de
luxe sixteen-day cruise starts at $4600
(flights included). Price differentials are
reflected in the standard of hotel accommodation, meals and excursions, rather than
the cruise boats. More unusual itineraries
include from St Petersburg to Solovki (see
p.305) and Arkhangelsk, with Mir
Corporation (from $2195 land-only) or the
Russian National Group; "In the Footsteps of
the Cossacks", starting and ending in Kiev,
offered by General Tours (from $2289 with

flights, $2159 land-only); and Explorer's Norway and Russia Arctic cruise featuring Svalbard Island, Solovki and Arkhangelsk (from $7450).

Tour operators in the USA and Canada

Abercrombie and Kent ☎1-800/554-7016, ⊛www.abercrombieandkent.com. Luxury cruises from Moscow to St Petersburg, and around the Baltic capitals. Tour departures from US and Canada; prices include flights.

Adventure Center ☎1-800/227-8747, ⊛www.adventure-center.com. Moscow–St Petersburg; and a coach tour of Tallinn, Moscow, Suzdal, Kostroma, St Petersburg and Helsinki.

Affordable Tours ☎1-866/265-2651, ⊛www.affordable-abercrombie-and-kent-tours .com. Agent for Abercrombie and Kent and other luxury cruise operators; packages include a Norway and far northern Russia cruise inside the Arctic Circle.

Exeter International US ☎800/633-1008 or 813/251-5355, ⊛www.exeterinternational.com. De luxe St Petersburg-Kizhi-Moscow cruises, and tours of the Imperial palaces led by author Suzanne Massie (see p.276). Flights from the US included.

General Tours ☎1-800/221-2216, ⊛www.generaltours.com. Cruises from St Petersburg to Moscow via Kizhi, and from Kiev to Odessa, Sevastopol and the River Dnieper, plus a Jewish heritage tour of Moscow and St Petersburg. Flights from the US included.

Geographic Expeditions ☎1-800/777-8183 or 415/922-0448, ⊛www.geoex.com. Adventure tours of Far Eastern Siberia (including reindeer trekking), and a Moscow-Golden Ring-St Petersburg package. Flights from the US included.

Intours Corporation Canada ☎1 416/766-4720, ⊛http://canada.intourist.com. Canadian affiliate of Intourist, with tours of St Petersburg, Moscow, the Golden Ring, Siberia and the Russian Far East. Their website carries general info but not prices.

Mir Corporation US ☎800/424-7289, ⊛www.mircorp.com. Small group tours on themes such as Siberian shamanism and the Gulag Archipelago; the Silk Road by private train; St Petersburg, Moscow and Golden Ring. Mostly priced land-only.

Pioneer Tours and Travel ☎1-800/369-1322, ⊛www.pioneerrussia.com. Customized individual tours, special-interest and educational tours to Russia and the CIS. It's best to phone for information, as their website is useless.

Russian National Group Inc ☎877/2211-7120 or 212/575-3431, ⊛www.russia-travel.com.

Affiliated to the Russian National Tourist Office in New York. All kinds of tours, including cruises to Solovki. Visa support, accommodation and flight bookings in Russia.

Russia House ☎202/986-6010, ⊛www.russiahouse.org. Arranges visas, tickets and accommodation in Russia, mainly for business travellers.

Saga Holidays ☎1-800/343-0273, ⊛www.sagaholidays.com. Specialists in group travel for seniors, with several Baltic cruises that visit St Petersburg, starting and finishing in England (flights from US included).

Scantours Inc ☎1-800/223-7226, ⊛www.scantours.com. Scandinavian ferry agent selling cruises and land-only Russian city breaks.

VisitRussia.com ☎1-800/755-3080, ⊛www.visitrussia.com. Online Russian travel agency with a sales office in New York.

Flights from Australia and New Zealand

Flight time **from Australia and New Zealand** to St Petersburg is over twenty hours, and can be longer depending on routes. Some entail touching down in Asia, and all involve changing planes at a European gateway for the last leg to St Petersburg. Given the length of the journey, you might be better off including a night's stopover in your itinerary – some airlines include one in the price of the flight. Finnair, Cathay Pacific, Emirates, Aeroflot, Korean Air, Scandinavian Airlines and Lauda seem to offer the best deals, in tandem with Qantas, BA or KLM. There's a plethora of airline combinations online, so shop around and be flexible.

Fares vary from low (mid-Jan, Feb, Oct & Nov) to high (June–Sept, Christmas & New Year) season. Average return **fares** to St Petersburg from eastern gateways are A$2100–2300 in low season, A$2300–2600 in high season. Fares from Perth or Darwin cost around A$200 more. From Auckland you can fly to Seoul with Korean Airlines and then on to Moscow and St Petersburg from NZ$6200. Alternatively, you could fly into Moscow instead – it costs A$300–600 less than to St Petersburg and is feasible with two flights rather than three. For the best results online, input the code for Moscow's Domodedovo airport (DME).

Airlines in Australia and New Zealand

Aeroflot Australia ☏ 02/9262 2233,
🖰 www.aeroflot.com. No NZ office.
British Airways Australia ☏ 1300/767 177;
New Zealand ☏ 0800/274 847 or 09/356 8690;
🖰 www.ba.com.
Cathay Pacific Australia ☏ 13 17 47,
🖰 www.cathaypacific.com/au; New Zealand
☏ 09/379 0861 or 0508/800 454;
🖰 www.cathaypacific.com/nz.
Czech Airlines (CSA) Australia ☏ 02/9247 7706,
🖰 www.csa.cz/en.
Emirates Australia ☏ 02/9290 9700 or 1300/303
7777; New Zealand ☏ 09/377 6004;
🖰 www.emirates.com.
Finnair Australia ☏ 02/9244 2299; New Zealand
☏ 09/308 3365; 🖰 www.finnair.com.
Garuda Indonesia Australia ☏ 02/9334 9970;
New Zealand ☏ 09/366 1862; 🖰 www
.garuda-indonesia.com.
KLM Australia ☏ 1300/303 747,
🖰 www.klm.com/au_en; New Zealand ☏ 09/309
1782, 🖰 www.klm.com/nz_en.
Korean Air Australia ☏ 02/9262 6000;
New Zealand ☏ 09/914 2000;
🖰 www.koreanair.com.au.
Lauda Air Australia ☏ 1800/642 438 or 02/9251
6155; New Zealand ☏ 09/522 5948;
🖰 www.aua.com.
Qantas Australia ☏ 13 13 13, 🖰 www.qantas
.com.au; New Zealand ☏ 0800/808 767,
🖰 www.qantas.co.nz.
Scandinavian Airlines (SAS) Australia
☏ 1300/727 707; New Zealand agent: Air New
Zealand ☏ 09/357 3000; 🖰 www.scandinavian.net.
Singapore Airlines Australia ☏ 13 10 11; New
Zealand ☏ 0800/808 909;
🖰 www.singaporeair.com.
Sri Lankan Airlines Australia ☏ 02/9244 2234;
New Zealand ☏ 09/308 3353; 🖰 www.srilankan.lk.
Swiss Australia ☏ 1800/221 339,
🖰 www.swiss.com. No NZ office.
Thai Airways Australia ☏ 1300/651 960; New
Zealand ☏ 09/377 0268; 🖰 www.thaiair.com
Virgin Atlantic Airways Australia ☏ 02/9244
2747; New Zealand ☏ 09/308 3077;
🖰 www.virgin-atlantic.com.

Package tours

The **package tours** to Russia available in
Australia and New Zealand don't usually
include flights, as it's assumed that travellers
will be making their own way there via Asia

or Europe. However, most tour operators
can arrange flights if required. All prices
quoted below are without flights unless stated otherwise, and for a single person at
twin-share rates.

The most popular tours involve the **Trans-
Siberian Railway**, linking Beijing, Ulan Bator
(in Mongolia) and Vladivostok (on Russia's
Pacific coast) with Moscow, the gateway to
St Petersburg. Besides their different starting
points, the three routes can offer diverse
experiences such as staying in a Mongolian
nomad's tent, as part of the package or
optional extras – so it's worth carefully studying what's on offer, as well as prices.

China-based Moonsky Tours Ltd arranges
no-stopover trips from Beijing to Moscow, via
Manchuria (from A$534) or Mongolia (from
A$477), excluding the cost of visas. Passport
Travel offers the same routes with stopovers
for A$796 and A$851 respectively, with three
days homestay in Moscow, and the same in
St Petersburg for A$264 extra. Gateway
Travel's multi-stopover trip costs A$4057 and
includes hotel accommodation in Moscow,
plus St Petersburg for A$878 more. Other,
longer itineraries such as Sundowners' twen-
ty-day Beijing-to-St Petersburg odyssey feature side trips to Buddhist monasteries and
Lake Baikal, while **Silk Road** tours visit the
ancient cities of Kashgar, Bukhara and
Sammarkand, en route to Moscow and St
Petersburg. Passport Travel's Silk Road tour
costs A$1953; Adventure World charges
NZ$5500.

Twin-centre packages are aimed at visi-
tors flying directly to Russia or coming from
Western Europe. They typically offer three
nights in Moscow and three nights in St
Petersburg plus an overnight train journey,
with homestay or hotel accommodation.
Passport Travel quotes A$454; Gateway
Travel from A$1283; Eastern European
Travel Bureau A$1940; and Adventure
World, from NZ$1940. These operators also
do two- and three-day city breaks in St
Petersburg or Moscow, starting from A$297.
Or you can **cruise** between the two cities via
the historic Volga towns; Abercrombie and
Kent has a de luxe twelve-day tour from
A$8990 (including flights). Short cruises from
St Petersburg to Valaam and Kizhi can be
booked through Gateway.

Travel agents and tour operators in Australia and New Zealand

Abercrombie and Kent Australia ℡03/9536 1800; New Zealand ℡0800/441 638; ✆www.abercrombiekent.com.au. An upmarket cruise featuring Moscow, St Petersburg, Uglich, Kostroma and the Imperial palaces. Includes flights.

Adventure World Australia ℡02/9956 7766 or 1300/363 055; New Zealand ℡09/524 5118; ✆www.adventureworld.com.au. Trans-Siberian and Moscow/St Petersburg packages, sold on a land-only basis.

Australians Studying Abroad ℡02/9509 1955, ✆www.asatravinfo.com.au. Cultural and historical tours; its Heritage Cities of the Baltic includes St Petersburg.

Bentours Australia ℡02/9241 1353, ✆www.bentours.com.au. Scandinavian specialists with a luxury cruise that visits St Petersburg, acting as agents for SAS, Viking Line and Scanrail.

Budget Travel New Zealand ℡09/366 0061 or 0800/808 040, ✆www.budgettravel.co.nz. Long-established agent with budget air fares and accommodation packages.

Eastern European Travel Bureau Australia ℡02/9262 1144 ✆www.eetbtravel.com. Trans-Siberian and twin-centre packages, homestays in St Petersburg and Moscow, and river cruises.

Flight Centres Australia ℡13 31 33 or 02/9235 3522, ✆www.flightcentre.com.au. Promises to beat any other discount fare quoted online.

Gateway Travel Australia ℡02/9745 3333, ✆www.russian-gateway.com.au. Russia/CIS specialists offering Trans-Siberian packages, air and rail deals, and cruises from St Petersburg to Valaam and Kizhi.

Moonsky Tours Ltd Beijing ℡8610/6591 6519; Hong Kong ℡852/2723 1376; ✆www.monkeyshrine.com. Reliable, low-cost Trans-Siberian operator, based in China. Agent for the Beetroot Bus in Russia (see p.22).

Passport Travel Australia ℡03/9867 3888, ✆www.travelcentre.com.au. Trans-Siberian itineraries and Moscow-St Petersburg packages, based on homestay accommodation (hotel upgrades are available).

Silke's Travel Australia ℡1800 807 860 or 02/83472000, ✆www.silkes.com.au. Gay and lesbian specialist travel agent.

STA Travel Australia ℡1300/733 035, ✆www.statravel.com.au; New Zealand ℡0508/782 872, ✆www.statravel.co.nz. Fare discounts for students and under-25s as well as student cards, rail passes and accommodation.

Student Uni Travel Australia ℡02/9232 8444, ✆www.sut.com.au; New Zealand ℡09/379 4224; ✆www.sut.co.nz.

Sundowners Australia ℡03/9672 5300 or 1300/133 447; New Zealand ℡0800/174 073; ✆www.sundowners.com.au. Various Trans-Siberian and Silk Road itineraries.

Trailfinders Australia ℡02/9247 7666 or 03/9600 3022, ✆www.trailfinders.com.au. Discounted flights, car rental, tailor-made tours, rail passes and RTW tickets.

Top Deck Australia ℡07/3839 7877, ✆www.connectionsadventures.com. Its budget coach tour of five European countries visits St Petersburg and Moscow.

By train

Travelling by train from London to St Petersburg takes three days and three nights, and for those not entitled to student or youth discounts, costs as much as flying. There isn't a direct train, and going by rail only really makes sense if you're planning to visit St Petersburg as part of an extensive European odyssey. The city's main international rail gateways are Berlin, Warsaw and Prague (see below), Helsinki and Tallinn (see p.19).

The route

To reach St Petersburg **from Britain** without stopping, you must leave on Monday, Thursday or Saturday, to catch a night train from Brussels to Berlin that connects with an onward service to Russia. The 6.11pm Eurostar from London Waterloo to Brussels Midi arrives two hours before the departure of the night train to Berlin at 11.30pm. Arriving at Ostbahnhof or Zoo Station at 8am next day, you change trains or take the U-Bahn to Berlin-Lichtenberg, where the train to St Petersburg departs at 1.30pm on Tuesdays, Fridays and Sundays, arriving at St Petersburg's Vitebsk Station two days later at 6.30am.

The **route** goes through Germany, Poland and Belarus. Be sure to have **visas** for Poland (if required), Belarus (see box on p.20) and Russia (p.23) before leaving. None is issued at border crossings, and visa-less passengers may be forced off at Brest on the Polish-Belarus border, where trains are jacked up in order to change to the wide-gauge Russian tracks (meant to make it difficult for invaders to use the network). Bring food and drink for the whole journey, since there's nothing available in Russian wagons except hot water from the samovar, and the odd can of beer.

Starting **from Warsaw or Prague** is another possibility. There's a nightly train from Warsaw's Gdansk Station to St Petersburg (27hr) and another from the Central Station via Moscow, which connects with a train from Prague (Fri & Sat). The Prague–Warsaw train has a bad reputation for robberies.

Tickets and passes

Because of Russian Railways' sporadic refusal to honour return bookings made in Britain, and problems interfacing with their computer system, some UK rail agents are unable to sell through-tickets to St Petersburg, and only European Rail is able to book a full **return** journey. Their cheapest return fare (£342; £165 if you're 26 or under) commits you to a fixed return date; a flexible ticket costs £47 extra. International Rail and German Railways will sell only **one-way** tickets for the outward journey, making the cost of a return trip far higher; International Rail quotes £404 (£304 youth rate); prices for the Berlin–St Petersburg stretch can't be obtained from German Railways. There are also specialist travel agents such as Russian Gateway UK (see p.12), which quotes £750/£650 for a return journey via Brussels and Cologne, with a first/second class coupe from Germany onwards.

There are various European rail passes, but none covers Russia, Belarus or the Baltic States. With **InterRail**, for example, you'll need a one-month three-zone pass (£320; £225 youth rate) to get as far as Warsaw or Helsinki; the onward fare to St Petersburg is about the same from either city (around £35/$60), but the journey from Helsinki is much quicker and doesn't require a transit visa for Belarus. Note that InterRail isn't valid in the UK, though you're entitled to discounts in Britain and on Eurostar and cross-Channel ferries. To qualify for the pass you must have been resident in Europe for six months.

North Americans, **Australians** and **New Zealanders** who don't qualify for InterRail can obtain a **Eurail** pass, which comes in various forms, and must be bought before leaving home. For more information, and to reserve tickets, contact Rail Europe in North America (US ☎1-877/456-7245; Canada ☎1-800/361-7245; ⊛www.raileurope.com); and CIT World Travel (☎02/9267 1255 or 03/9650 5510, ⊛www.cittravel.com.au) or Rail Plus (☎1300/555 033 or 03/9642 8644, ⊕info@railplus.com.au) in Australia.

Rail contacts

European Rail ☎020/7387 0444, ⊛www.europeanrail.com. Rail specialists that offer competitive international railway tickets from anywhere in the UK to most European cities, including St Petersburg.

Eurostar ☎0870/160 6600, ⊛www.eurostar.com. Latest fares and youth discounts (plus online booking) on the London–Paris and London–Brussels Eurostar service, and competitive add-on fares from the rest of the UK.

German Railways (Deutsche Bahn) UK ☎0870/243 5363, ⊛www.bahn.de. Competitive discounted fares for any journey from London across Europe, with very reasonable prices for those journeys that pass through Germany. Their website can't give prices for tickets to St Petersburg, but does allow journey-planning.

International Rail ☎08701/201 606, ⊛www.international-rail.com. Agent for all European railways and rail passes. Sells outward-bound tickets to St Petersburg.

Joe Walsh Tours Ireland ☎01/676 0991, ⊛www.joewalshtours.ie. General budget fares agent.

Rail Europe UK ☎0870/584 8848, ⊛www.raileurope.co.uk. SNCF-owned information and ticket agent for all European passes, and journeys from London as far as Warsaw.

By coach

Unlike to Prague or Budapest there are no cheap, direct services from Britain to St Petersburg, and although you can get there by **coach** from Berlin or Frankfurt (both readily accessible from the UK by low-cost airlines), the journey will probably cost as much as flying once hidden costs are taken into account – so this approach is better suited if you're travelling around or based in Central Europe and you'd like to visit Russia and the Baltic States, but don't fancy using (or qualify for) an InterRail or Eurail pass.

Services **from Germany** to St Petersburg are operated by Eurolines Russia, an affiliate of the European-wide bus consortium Eurolines. Their English-language website (🌐www.eurolines.ru) is informative but doesn't allow online booking. Coaches leave the central bus stations in Frankfurt and Berlin on Tuesdays, Fridays, Saturdays and Sundays, and arrive outside St Petersburg's Baltic Station two days later. It's cheaper to travel from Berlin (£46/$84/€66 one-way, £79/$144/€113 return) than from Frankfurt (£64/$117/€92 one-way, £111/$203/€159 return). Tickets can be booked through BEX (☎030/3022 5294) in Berlin's central bus station, or DTG (☎069/790 3250) at Mannheimerstr. 4, in Frankfurt.

Another, more roundabout, route is to go from Germany **via Estonia**. Eurolines Estonia (🌐www.eurolines.ee) runs coaches to Tallinn from Berlin (daily; 26hr; £61/$111/€87 one-way), Munich (Sun; 35hr; £77/$140/€110), Frankfurt (Mon–Fri; 34hr; £75/$137/€107), Cologne (Thurs, Wed & Sat; 35hr; £75/$137/€107) and Stuttgart (Mon–Fri; 38hr; £77/$140/€110). From Tallinn, you can continue on to St Petersburg by Eurolines Russia coach or by train (see "Travelling from Finland, Estonia or Latvia", p.19).

A still longer route is from Germany **via Latvia**, using the Eurolines Estonia service to Rīga from Berlin (Wed & Fri; 22hr; £50/$92/€72 one-way), Frankfurt (Wed & Fri; 32hr; £61/$111/€87), Munich (Wed; 32hr; £61/$111/€87), Cologne (Thurs; 33hr; £61/$111/€87) or Stuttgart (Wed & Fri; 34hr; £64/$115/€90). From Rīga there's a Eurolines Russia coach to St Petersburg (see "Travelling from Finland, Estonia or Latvia", p.19).

Although coach fares are extremely cheap, you have to consider the cost of transit visas for Poland and/or Belarus (see "Visa requirements for overland travel" on p.20). You'll also need to obtain a Russian visa in advance (see p.23).

By car and ferry

It doesn't make sense to **drive** from Britain to St Petersburg unless you're also touring Scandinavia and the Baltic States. The easiest route on the outward journey is **via Sweden and Finland**; from Helsinki it's equally straightforward to reach either St Petersburg or Tallinn, and visit the other city on the way back to Helsinki before heading home. Ferries run all year round; fares are highest in July and August. Be sure to book as far ahead as possible to ensure places on the different lines and get the lowest rates on offer.

The first stage involves taking a DFDS Seaways car ferry from Newcastle to Gothenburg (Mon & Fri; 24–26hr). As with low-cost airlines, fares vary according to demand at the time of booking. Expect to pay from £138 per person in high season, £124 off-season, plus the car fare (£144/£122 in high/low season); rates increase the nearer the time of departure you book the tickets.

From Gothenburg you drive to Stockholm to board one of the huge, lavishly equipped Silja or Viking ferries to Helsinki (daily 9am & 5pm; 16–17hr). The high-season one-way fare for a single person sharing a four-berth cabin is £33/$60; a car costs £19/$35. **From Helsinki** to St Petersburg there are two (or three) options. **By road**, you can cover the 350km in about six hours, allowing for an hour or so stuck in a queue of vehicles on both the Russian and Finnish sides of the border, which has several checkpoints along 15km of road, before you reach Vyborg (see p.298). Alternatively, there's Silja Line's new *Fantasia* car ferry, sailing from Helsinki's West Terminal every other day at 4pm, which docks at Tallinn for 45 minutes before sailing on to St Petersburg, arriving at 9am next day. The service was inaugurated just as this book went to press, with special introductory rates from £36/$65/€55 per person. It's mainly aimed at tourists making a short return cruise, travelling on a Russian cruise visa (see p.19) for €32; if you want to stay on in St Petersburg you'll need to get a regular Russian visa before you board the vessel.

A more roundabout way is to go **via Estonia** – if only to see the stunning medieval centre of Tallinn. There are regular Viking (2 daily; £10–13/$18–24 one-way, car £10/$18) and Tallink (2–3 daily; 4hr;

£10–14/$15–22, car £8–12/$15–22) ferries from Helsinki to Tallinn throughout the year, and from spring till mid-autumn Tallink's Express Autocatamarans zip across in only one hour forty minutes (3–4 daily; Sun–Wed £8–13/$14–24/€12–20 one-way, car £8–11/$14–20/€12–17; Thurs–Sat £13–14/$24–26/€20–22, car £8–13/$14–24/€12–20).

Driving licence and insurance requirements in Russia are covered on p.37.

Ferry companies and agents

DFDS Seaways ☎08705/333000 or 08705/333111, ⊛www.dfds.co.uk. Newcastle to Gothenburg ferries.
Emagine UK Ltd ☎01942/262662, ⊛www.emagine-travel.co.uk. Agents for Viking ferries from Stockholm to Helsinki.
Norvista UK ☎0870/744 7315; Ireland ☎01/677 9944; ⊛www.norvista.co.uk Agents for Silja and Viking ferries.
Tallink ⊛www.tallink.fi/en/ Ferries and catamarans from Helsinki to Tallinn; online booking facility.

Travelling from Finland, Estonia or Latvia

Travelling **from Helsinki** to St Petersburg offers the widest choice of transport, and was for many years the most popular approach with those travelling around Europe **by train**. Although none of the European rail passes is valid for services to St Petersburg, the second-class fare (£33/$62/€50 one-way, return is double) isn't exorbitant, and easily available in Helsinki. There are two trains daily: the Finnish *Sibelius* (early in the morning) and the Russian *Repin* (in the afternoon) – both are comfortable and do the 350-kilometre journey in seven hours, stopping at Vyborg (see p.298) en route to St Petersburg's Ladoga Station. Work upgrading the line to a high-speed service has just begun. Details can be obtained from Finnish Railways' website ⊛www.vr.fi.

Alternatively, there are two daily **coaches** operated by Finnord and Ardis. These two companies share offices in Helsinki's main bus station and at Vyborg and St Petersburg, have identical fares, routes, stopovers and coaches (with airconditioning,

toilets and videos) – the only difference is the colour of their vehicles. They leave Helsinki at 9am and 11pm, arriving in St Petersburg eight hours later, where they stop at Finnord's office before terminating at the *Pulkovskaya Hotel*. Tickets should be booked one or two days ahead; the one-way fare to St Petersburg is about £28/$40/€42; returns cost double.

One last option is a short return **cruise** from Helsinki. Kristina Cruises (☎05/211 4230, ⊛www.kristinacruises.com) offers two full days in St Petersburg aboard the *Kristina Regina* (weekly June–Aug; from £571/$1000/€825 per person), while Silja Line (☎09/180 4555, ⊛www.silja.com) operates the de luxe *Opera* (Tues mid-August to early Jan which spends one day (departing Sat & Mon, from £173/$308/€260) or two days (Wed, from £259/$463/€390) in St Petersburg. Prices for Kristina Cruises include full board, tours and excursions; Silja's none of these. On both cruises, EU citizens travel on a special Russian cruise visa (€15 per person from Silja; included in Kristina Cruises) that permits them to disembark in St Petersburg only as a group; other nationalities must get a regular Russian visa before joining the cruise, but can come and go as they wish.

Travelling **from Tallinn**, the Estonian capital, is increasingly popular with backpackers and a major route for commercial travellers and smugglers, so most vehicles are packed with luggage and the border formalities are long and rigorous. Eurolines Russia (see p.18) runs five **coaches** daily from Tallinn (8–9hr; one-way from £6/$10/€8), terminating outside St Petersburg's Baltic Station, near their office on ulitsa Shkapina. For bookings in Tallinn, contact MootoReisi AS, Lastekadu 46 (☎372/601 0700). Alternatively, there's the daily EVR express **train** leaving just before midnight and arriving at St Petersburg's Baltic Station at 8.30am next day. A second-class sleeper costs £16/$28/€24 one-way. Tickets are sold by EVR Ekspress Reisid, Toompuiestee 37 (☎315/615 6722, ⊛www.evrekspress.ee).

Travelling **from Rīga**, the Latvian capital, is the longest of the three journeys to St Petersburg. It takes at least fourteen hours on a Eurolines Russia (☎371/750 3135) or Latvian Ecolines (☎371/721 4512, ⊛www.ecolines.lv) **coach** (2–3 daily); the one-way fare is £9/$17/€13. The overnight **train** is less prone to delays (14hr) and a lot comfier; a one-way coupe costs £33/$60/€47. Details can be found on the Latvian Railways website (⊛www.ldz.lv).

Anyone approaching St Petersburg via Finland, Estonia or Latvia should be sure to obtain a **Russian visa** beforehand, as they are not issued at border crossings, and may not be easily available from the Russian consulates in Helsinki, Tallinn or Rīga either.

Citizens of some nationalities might also require an Estonian or Latvian visa, again obtainable only in advance.

Coach and ferry agents in St Petersburg

Ecolines in the main ticket hall of Vitebsk Station ☎326 45 93, ⊛www.ecolines.lv. Operates a daily bus to/from Rīga.
Eurolines Russia ul. Shkapina 10 ☎168 27 40, ⊛www.eurolines.ru. Coach operators to the Baltic States and Germany. Sales manager Elena Moiseeva speaks English and is very helpful (☎252 70 70, ✉eltickets@eurolines.ru).

Visa requirements for overland travel

The following list covers requirements for citizens of the EU, the US, Canada, Australia and New Zealand. Nationals of other countries should consult the relevant embassy (see list below).

Belarus
All foreigners require visas, plus medical insurance. If not on a transit visa, you must also have medical insurance from a state-approved insurer (available at the border for about $15).

Australia/New Zealand No embassies or consulates; Belarus visas may be applied for online at ⊛www.visatorussia.com.
Canada 130 Albert St, Suite 600, Ottawa, ON K1P 5G4 ☎613/233-9994, ✉belamb@igs.net, ⊛www.belarusembassy.org.
Single-entry transit visa CDN$50, double-entry CDN$90 (allow 5 working days).
UK 6 Kensington Court, London W8 5DL ☎020/7938 3677 or 020/7937 3288, ⊛www.belembassy.org/uk. Single/double-entry transit visa £15/£50 (allow 5–10 working days).
US 1619 New Hampshire Ave NW, Washington, DC 20009 ☎202/986-1604, ✉consul@belarusembassy.org, ⊛www.belarusembassy.org. Downloadable form. Single/double-entry tourist/transit visa $100/$200 (allow 5 working days).

Estonia
Visa required by Canadians.

Australia/New Zealand 86 Louisa Rd, Birchgrove, NSW 2141 ☎02/9810 7468, ✉eestikon@ozemail.com.au.
Canada 958 Broadview Ave, Toronto ON M4K 2R6 ☎416/461-0764, ✉estcosu@ca.inter.net; 260 Dalhousie St, Suite 210. Ottawa, ON K1N 7E4. ☎613/789-4222; 1199 West Hastings St, 5th floor, Vancouver, British Columbia VGE 3TS ☎604/408-2673, ✉hjaako@discoverycapital.com; ⊛www.estemb.ca. Single/double-entry tourist visa CDN$22/CDN$34.
UK 16 Hyde Park Gate, London SW7 5DG ☎020/7589 3428, ⊛www.estonia.gov.uk.
US 2131 Massachusetts Ave NW, Washington, DC 20008 ☎202/588-0101, ⊛www.estemb.org.

Latvia
No visas required. All nationalities must have medical insurance.

Ferry Centre/GR-Travel ul. Vosstaniya 19 ☎275 45 20, ✉info@paromy.ru, ⊛www.paromy.ru. Russian agents for Silja, Viking, DFDS and other Scandinavian lines.

Finnord/Ardis Italyanskaya ul. 37 ☎314 89 51.Ticket agents (and the point of departure) for both coach lines to Helsinki.

Coming from Moscow

Visitors taking the Trans-Siberian Railway or InterRailing around Europe will almost inevitably reach St Petersburg **from Moscow**. Of the fourteen trains from Moscow's Leningrad Station, the fastest are the evening *Nevskiy Express* (daily) and train #164 (Mon, Tues, Thurs, Fri), which take just under five hours, arriving shortly after 11pm. However, most people prefer an **overnight train** (8–9hr) arriving between six and nine o'clock next morning, namely the *Smena*, *Nikolaevskiy Express*, *Krasnaya Strela*, *Express* or *Afanasiy Nikitin*, which depart around midnight with the city hymn playing on the platform and smartly uniformed guards waving batons. Their unisex two- or four-berth coupes are overheated, but otherwise quite comfortable; secure the door handle with the plastic device provided, or

Australia/New Zealand Melbourne: PO Box 23, Kew, Victoria 3101 ☎03/9499 6920; Adelaide: 8 Barr-Smith St, Tusmone, SA 5064 ☎08/8333 3123; Canberra: Box 457, Strathfield, NSW 2135 ☎02/9744 5981.

Canada 280 Albert St, Suite 300, Ottawa, ON K1P 5G8 ☎613/238-6068; consulates in Toronto and Victoria can be found on ⊛www.ottawa.am.gov.lv.

UK 45 Nottingham Place, London W1U 5LR ☎020/7312 0125; Wales: Lulworth House, Monk St, Abergavenny NP7 5NP ☎1873/857 177.

US 200 West 79th St, Apt 6E, New York 1004 ☎212/496-2295; consulates in LA, Houston and Cincinnati can be found on ⊛www.latvia-usa.org.

Lithuania
No visa required.

Australia/New Zealand No embassy.

Canada 130 Albert St, Ottawa ON K1P 5G4 ☎613/567-5458.

UK 84 Gloucester Place, London W1H 3HN ☎020/7486 6401.

US 2622 16th St NW, Washington, DC 20009 ☎202/234-5860, ⊛www.ltembassyus.org.

Poland
Canadians, Australians and New Zealanders require visas.

Australia 7 Turrana St, Yarralumla, Canberra, ACT 2600 ☎02/6272 1000; 10 Trelawney St, Woollahra, Sydney ☎02/9363 9816; Box 128, 4000 Brisbane ☎07/324 9564; Level 12, 20 Collins St, 3000 Melbourne ☎03/9654 5180; ⊛www.poland.org.au. Single/double entry transit visa A$21/41.

Canada 443 Daly Ave, Ottawa, ON K1N 6H3 ☎613/789-0468, wwww.polishembassy.ca. Single/double entry transit visa C$20/38.

Ireland 5 Ailesbury Rd, Dublin 4 ☎01/283 0855, ⊛www.polishembassy.ie.

New Zealand 17 Upland Rd, Kelburn, Wellington ☎04/475 9453; 51 Granger Rd, Howick, Auckland 1705 ☎09/534 4670; ⊛www.poland.org.au. Single-entry tourist visa NZ$72, double-entry visa NZ$96.

UK 73 Cavendish St, London W1W 6LS ☎0870/744 2700; 4 Palmerston Rd, Sheffield S10 2TE ☎0114/276-6513; 19 Whiteladies Rd, Clifton, Bristol BS8 1PB ☎0117/973 2333; ⊛www.poland.org.uk.

US 2640 16th St NW, Washington, DC 20009 ☎202/234-3800; 12400 Wilshire Blvd, Suite 555, Los Angeles, CA 90025 ☎310/442-8500; a list of other US consulates can be found on ⊛www.polandembassy.org.

insert a wedge into the flip-lock in the upper left corner of the door. Shortly after leaving Moscow an attendant will come around dispensing sheets and offering tea to passengers in first class. Mineral water, sweets and paper towels are provided gratis.

While the journey is easy enough, buying **tickets** in Moscow is another matter, as speculators sometimes scoop the lot and booking offices can be bewildering. The least crowded and most helpful one is at Leningradskiy pr. 1, beside Belarus Station, which sells domestic and international tickets and has some English-speaking staff. Bring your passport, since tickets are sold to named individuals only, and conductors make identity checks before allowing passengers on board. Foreigners no longer pay more than Russians (for whom fares have doubled), nor need pay in hard currency. Tickets may be ordered through Infinity Travel (Komsomolskiy pr. 13, ☎095/234 65 55) or any of Moscow's hostels or hotels, for a surcharge.

Alternatively, you could consider a more leisurely journey to St Petersburg, with stopovers en route, aboard the Beetroot Bus.

The Beetroot Bus

The **Beetroot Bus** is an enjoyable compromise between packaged and independent travel, which enables visitors to Moscow or St Petersburg to sample Russia's provincial heartland. Since you can join the bus in either city, it's ideal for people arriving in Moscow on the Trans-Siberian, or in St Petersburg from the Baltic States, who plan to visit the other city later. From July to September, the **classic** tour (£399) features three days sightseeing in each city, a day relaxing at Lake Mets with a barbecue and a sauna, and a day and a night in Novgorod, with its medieval Kremlin. A **Golden Ring** tour (£275), starting and finishing in Moscow, can be bolted on to this itinerary, while the Bolshevik Beetroot tour (£499) starting in St Petersburg focuses on Soviet sites and includes tickets for the ballet. There's even a tour for bladers, led by the 2003 European Rollerblade Slalom champion, Katya Voronicheva. In spring and autumn, the **Beet Train** tour (£359) involves an overnight train from Moscow to Novgorod, and a bus to St Petersburg. All tours include airport or station transfers and superior budget accommodation. Details appear on ⊛www.beetroot.org. For bookings contact The Russia Experience in London (see p.12) or Moscow (☎095/453 43 68,✉info@trans-siberian.co.uk); booking three to four weeks ahead is advisable to obtain a visa, but it can be arranged sooner if you're prepared to pay more.

Red tape and visas

Bureaucracy has always been the bane of Russia, and visas are the greatest deterrent to would-be visitors; the system seems designed to make you spend money to get round the obstacles it creates. Visas must be obtained in advance from a Russian embassy or consulate abroad. If you're not on a package tour, this requires some kind of visa support, which is available from B&B agencies, hostels and hotels in St Petersburg for their guests, or from specialist travel agents or visa brokers abroad (at greater expense). Then there's the fee for the visa itself – which varies from country to country according to type of visa and the speed at which it's issued – plus an extra sum if you pay an agency to deliver and collect your documents at the consulate rather than applying by post and allowing more time for the process. All in all, you'll be lucky to obtain a visa for much less than £60/$100, and could spend a lot more if you're in a hurry.

Your passport must be valid for at least six months after your intended date of departure from Russia, and contain at least one blank page for the visa to be stuck into place. In some countries they insist on two or three blank pages. Why is unfathomable, a sign of the Byzantine nature of the system.

Visas

There are several types of visa available, so it's important to know which one you want. The most common is a **tourist visa**, valid for an exact number of days up to a maximum of thirty (29 for US citizens), covered by proof of pre-booked accommodation in Russia for the entire period. If you're going on a package tour, the formalities can be sorted out for you by the travel agency, though they may charge extra for this. If you're travelling independently, **visa support** can be provided by specialist travel agents in your own country (see "Getting There") or by some B&B agencies, hostels and hotels in St Petersburg (fees vary; see Chapter 13, "Accommodation"). You have to email or fax them the following information: nationality, date of birth, passport number and date of expiry, length of stay at the hotel or hostel, date of arrival and departure from Russia, and credit card details. The visa support documentation should be faxed or emailed to you the following day. If you are applying through a tourist agency in your own country, the procedure is essentially the same.

A **business visa** is valid for three, six or twelve months; the first two can be either single- or double-entry; the last is a multiple-entry visa that involves vetting by the Russian FSB security service (a time-consuming formality). The main advantage of a business visa is that you're not obliged to pre-book accommodation, so you can rent a flat or stay with friends, as you wish. You don't have to be doing business in order to get one; you simply need to provide the consulate with a stamped letter of invitation (or fax, in some cases) from an organization in Russia that's accredited to the MID (Ministry of Foreign Affairs). There are lots of foreign and Russian travel agencies and visa brokers that can provide an invitation for a fee. Travel agencies may charge a lower rate for the service if you also book a tour and/or accommodation with them.

If you don't have a business visa, and wish to stay with Russian friends, you'll need a **private individual visa**, which is the hardest kind to obtain. This requires a personal invitation (*izveschenie*) from your Russian host – authorized by the local PVU (see p.25) – guaranteeing to look after you for the duration of your stay. A faxed copy is not acceptable, so the original has to be posted from St Petersburg to your home country, and the whole process can take three or four months to complete.

If you are planning only to pass through Russia en route to another country, you can apply for a **transit visa**, valid for a 72-hour stopover in one city. You'll need to show a ticket for your onward journey from Russia, and a visa for the destination country if required.

All these visas are in the form of a page-sized sticker with a tear-off exit visa that's collected when you leave Russia; travellers with a double- or multi-entry visa subsequently receive exit and entry stamps in their passports. Additionally, you should receive in advance or on arrival an **Immigration Card** (*Immigratsionaya karta*), supposedly introduced to keep closer tabs on people entering Russia, though in practice the Border Guards don't seem so concerned with collecting it when you leave. However, you will face difficulties if you lose your visa (and passport). You must report the loss to the main PVU office and your consulate in St Petersburg (see p.26 and p.403), which should eventually issue you with a replacement. Russian exit visas issued within the country cost $150, and your consulate will also charge a sum to replace your passport. It's a wise precaution to make photocopies of your passport, Russian visa, Immigration Card and currency declaration (see p.42).

Note that if you intend to travel between Russia and any other republics of the former Soviet Union, you need a separate visa for each independent state, and also a multiple-entry visa to get back into Russia. By law, foreigners wishing to stay in Russia for longer than three months must obtain a **doctor's letter** certifying that they are not HIV-positive, and bring it with them to Russia (the original, *not* a photocopy) – but most visa brokers and specialist travel agents seem to be able to sidestep this requirement when applying on your behalf for a six- or twelve-month business visa.

Russian embassies and consulates abroad

Australia 78 Canberra Ave, Griffith, Canberra, ACT 2603 ☎02/6295 9474; 7–9 Fullerton St, Woollahra, Sydney, NSW 2025 ☎02/9326 1866; ⓦwww.sydneyrussianconsulate.com.
Canada 52 Range Rd, Ottawa, Ontario K1N 8J5 ☎613/236-0920 or 613/336-7220, ⓦwww.rusembcanada.mid-ru.

Ireland 186 Orwell Rd, Rathgar, Dublin 14 ☎01/492 3492, ⓔrussian@indigo.ie.
New Zealand 57 Messines Rd, Karori, Wellington ☎04/476 6742 or 04/481 3101, ⓔeor@netlink.co.nz or embassyofrussia@xtra.co.nz.
UK 5 Kensington Palace Gdns, London W8 4QS ☎020/7229 8027, ⓕ020/7229 3215; 58 Melville St, Edinburgh EH3 7HF ☎0131/225 7098, ⓔvisa@edconsul.demon.co.uk.
US 2641 Tunlaw Rd, NW, Washington, DC 20007 ☎202/939-8907 or 202/939-8913, ⓔwasconsru@prodigy.net; 9 East 91st St, New York, NY 10128 ☎212/348-0926, ⓔnymail@ruscon.com; 2790 Green St, San Francisco, CA 94123 ☎415/928-6878, ⓔconsulsf@ix.netcom.com; 2323 Westin Bldg, 2001 6th Ave, Seattle, WA 98121 ☎206/728-1910, ⓔconsul@consul.seanet.com; ⓦwww.russianembassy.org.

Applying for a visa

Supplying Russian visas is a business, as the address of the official World Wide Web list of Russian embassies and consulates implies (ⓦwww.russianembassy.biz). There are many quasi-official sites that are linked to **visa brokers**, such as ⓦwww.russialink.org (in the UK), ⓦwww.russianvisas.org or ⓦhttp://russia-visa.com (in the US), and will give details of prices only through these brokers. However, other sites allow you to download a visa **application form** for free, which you can submit by post following the instructions given, having double-checked the visa fee with the embassy – thereby eliminating the agency fee, which is likely to be around £40–60/$80–100.

With all applications, you need to submit a photo (signed on the back) and your passport. Applying to the consulate rather than through a travel agent or visa broker, you'll also need to include the fee (cash or money order only, no cheques), plus a prepaid SAE envelope (preferably registered) for postal applications. Postal applications are preferable to delivering or collecting in person, when you may have to queue for ages outside the consulate, but will add at least a week to the visa-processing times below, which assume that all the visa support documentation is already there. Moreover, it's important to follow the procedure exactly, since it differs from country to country in certain minor yet crucial respects.

In Britain, the Edinburgh consulate is more helpful than the London one, so better for applications by post (or in person, if you live in Scotland). Application forms can be faxed to you by the consulate on request, or downloaded from the website of the Russian embassy in the US or Canada (UK-based sites charge for this privilege). When applying for a tourist, business or transit visa, it's acceptable to enclose a fax or photocopy of your accommodation voucher, invitation or ticket for onward travel. The visa fee is directly related to the speed of processing your application: £30 for six to fourteen working days; £60 for three to five working days; £80 for next day issue; £90 for the same day; and £120 for one hour.

In the US, you can download the application form from the embassy website, ⓦwww.russianembassy.org, as well as Form 95, which American males aged 16–45 must now submit as a tit-for-tat for US immigration controls on Russians since 9/11. It's left to the consulate's discretion whether applicants can send a fax or photocopy of their invitation or travel voucher, or must submit the original – it's wiser to follow the latter course if the consulate hasn't specified. There's a flat fee of $100 for any kind of visa in six working days. Otherwise, the cost of a single/double-entry tourist or business visa is $150/200 in three working days; $200/250 next day; and $300/350 for same-day issue. For a multi-entry visa the rates are $300, $350 and $450. By way of comparison, visa brokers ⓦrussia-visa.com quote $180 for a visa in six days; $240 for a double-entry visa in eighteen days; and $350 for a multi-entry one in 22 working days.

In Canada the form is downloadable at ⓦwww.rusembcanada.mid.ru. Canadians must have three blank pages in their passport and include a photocopy of the page with their personal details. A fax or photocopy of the invitation or voucher is OK for single-entry visas, but for a double- or multi-entry the originals must be supplied. Fees again depend on processing time. A single/double-entry tourist or business visa costs CDN$75/100 in fourteen working days; CDN$150/175 in seven days;

CDN$180/205 in three days; and CDN$210/235 next day. Respective rates for a multi-entry visa are: CDN$200, CDN$275, CDN$305 and CDN$335.

In Australia a tourist visa (allow twelve working days) and a business visa (fifteen working days) both cost A$85.

Citizens of the **Schengen countries** (Austria, Belgium, France, Germany, Holland, Italy, Portual and Spain) must also submit an **Insurance Card** with their visa application, which can be downloaded at ⓦwww .russianvisas.org.

Registration and the PVU

By law, all foreigners are supposed to **register** within three working days of arrival at the Passport and Visa Service or **PVU** (*Passport i Viza Upravlenie* – still universally known by its old acronym, **OVIR**) and obtain a stamp on their exit visa to that effect. Large **hotels** will automatically register guests for the duration of their hotel stay, however they obtained their visa support, but visitors who opt for **homestay** or **flat rental** should realize that only the company that issued their visa invitation can legally register them, so it's vital that it has an office (or accredited partner) in St Petersburg. Similarly, **hostels** may register only guests who got their visa support from the hostel (or its partner). The Way to Russia website (ⓦhttp://waytorussia.net) spells out the **current regulations** in all their Kafkaesque complexity.

While not registering within the 72-hour limit is technically an infringement merely penalized by a $2 fine, Militia officers may try to extort more, and attempting to leave Russia without a registration stamp renders you liable to a fine of $200. The easiest way to get belatedly registered is to check into a hotel for one night. This might not cover your whole time in Russia, but at least you'll have a stamp on your exit visa. The *Neva*, *Morskaya* and *Rus* hotels (see pp.336–340) may be willing to register you for however long you require, in return for one night's payment, while the Tais agency specializes in "virtual" hotel registrations (see listings overleaf).

The opening hours of PVU offices are short and change frequently. Staff are surly and lackadaisical. Bring a Russian to help out if at all possible. See below for the addresses of the main and district PVU offices.

Registration agencies and PVU offices in St Petersburg

Tais Kazanskaya ul. 8/10 (in the yard), ☎312 80 37, ⓦwww.tais.spb.ru. Agency that can register anyone on a tourist or business visa for a fictitious stay at the *Morskaya Hotel* for $20 (even after the deadline has expired).

PVU Head office Kirochnaya ul. 4 ☎278 34 86; open Mon, Wed & Fri 10am–noon. Get there at least an hour before opening to have any hope of processing your registration. Touts may sell places in the queue. See map on p.201.

PVU Admiralteyskiy district Sadovaya ul. 55/57 ☎310 74 21.

PVU Frunzenskiy district nab. Obvodnovo kanala 48 ☎166 14 68.

PVU Kalinskiy district Mineralnaya ul. 3 ☎540 39 87.

PVU Kirovskiy district ul. Avtovskaya 22 ☎183 44 14.

PVU Krasnogvardeyskiy district Zanevskiy pr. 22 ☎528 67 67

PVU Moskovskiy district Blagodatnaya ul. 34 ☎298 18 27.

PVU Nevskiy district ul. Sedova 86 ☎262 20 70.

PVU Petrograd Side district ul. Grota 1/3 ☎230 83 60.

PVU Primorskiy district ul. Savushkina 83 ☎430 15 09.

PVU Tsentralniy district per. Krylova 5 ☎315 79 36.

PVU Vasilevskiy Island district 19ya Liniya 12 ☎321 75 24.

PVU Vyborg Side district Lesnoy pr. 20 ☎542 21 72.

Customs and allowances

Border controls have relaxed considerably since Soviet times. Bags are no longer searched for subversive literature, but simply passed through an X-ray machine. However, it is still prudent to declare all foreign currency that you bring into the country, plus any laptops or mobile phones, and you may be asked to do the same when you leave (see p.34 for details). If you're travelling with hypodermic needles, bring a prescription for them and declare them under "Narcotics and appliances for use thereof". GPS devices may not be brought into Russia.

Export controls are more of a problem, as the rules change so frequently that even customs officials aren't sure how things stand. The main restriction is on exporting antiques and contemporary art, though it's unclear where they draw the line between artwork and souvenirs (which aren't liable to controls). However, you can be fairly sure of encountering problems if you try to take out antique icons, samovars, porcelain or jewellery. You can export 250 grams of black caviar and any amount of red, and there are no limits on alcohol or cigarettes – though the last two are subject to allowances set by other countries.

Permission to export contemporary art and antiques (anything pre-1960, in effect) must be applied for to the Ministry of Culture at Malaya Morskaya ul.17 (Mon–Fri 11am–2pm; ☎ & ⒻR311 03 02), but you would be advised to ask the seller to do the paperwork for you, if possible. If the export is approved, you can be liable for tax of up to one hundred percent of the object's value. Pre-1960 books must be approved by the Russian National Library, using the entrance on Sadovaya ulitsa by the crossroads with Nevskiy prospekt (Tues 3–6pm, Thurs 4–6pm & Fri 10am–noon).

Insurance

Medical insurance is obligatory for citizens of Australia and the Schengen states (Austria, Belgium, France, Germany, Netherlands, Portugal and Spain), and is strongly advisable for other nationalities, even if covered by reciprocal state health-care agreements. Before taking a new policy, however, it's worth checking whether you're already covered: some all-risks home insurance policies may cover your possessions when overseas, and many private medical schemes include cover when abroad. In Canada, provincial health plans usually provide partial cover for medical mishaps abroad, while holders of official student/teacher/youth cards in Canada and the US are entitled to meagre accident coverage and hospital in-patient benefits. Students will often find that their student health coverage extends during the vacations and for one term beyond the date of the last enrolment. Bank and credit cards often have certain levels of medical or other insurance included and you may automatically get travel insurance if you use a major credit card to pay for your trip.

After exhausting the possibilities above, you might want to contact a specialist travel insurance company, or consider the travel insurance we offer (see box). A typical travel insurance policy usually provides cover for the loss of baggage, tickets and – up to a certain limit – cash or cheques, as well as cancellation or curtailment of your journey. Most of them exclude so-called dangerous sports unless an extra premium is paid. Many policies can be chopped and changed to exclude coverage you don't need. Read the small print and benefits tables of prospective policies carefully; coverage can vary wildly for roughly similar premiums.

With medical coverage, ascertain whether benefits will be paid as treatment proceeds or only after return home, and whether there is a 24-hour medical emergency number. When securing baggage cover, make sure that the per-article limit – typically under £500 equivalent – will cover your most valuable possession. If you need to make a claim, you should keep receipts for medicines and medical treatment, and in the event you have anything stolen, you must obtain an official statement from the police (see p.54).

Rough Guides travel insurance

Rough Guide offers its own low-cost travel insurance, especially customized for our statistically low-risk readers by a leading British broker, provided by the American International Group (AIG) and registered with the British regulatory body, GISC (the General Insurance Standards Council). There are five main Rough Guides insurance plans: **No Frills** for the bare minimum for secure travel; **Essential**, which provides decent all-round cover; **Premier** for comprehensive cover with a wide range of benefits; **Extended Stay** for cover lasting four months to a year; and **Annual multi-trip**, a cost-effective way of getting Premier cover if you travel more than once a year. Premier, Annual Multi-Trip and Extended Stay policies can be supplemented by a "Hazardous Pursuits Extension" if you plan to indulge in sports considered dangerous, such as scuba-diving or trekking. For a policy **quote**, call the Rough Guide Insurance Line: toll-free in the UK ☎0800/015 09 06 or ☎+44 1392 314 665 from elsewhere. Alternatively, get an online quote at ⓦwww.roughguides.com/insurance

Health

Visitors to St Petersburg are advised to get booster-shots for diphtheria, polio and tetanus, but there's no need to be inoculated against typhoid and hepatitis A unless you're planning to visit remote rural areas. Though there's no danger of malaria, mosquitoes can be fierce during the summer months, so a mosquito net or a locally available repellent is advisable. The most likely hazard for a visitor, however, is an upset stomach or the disruption of their biorhythms during the midsummer White Nights.

Giardia and heavy metals

St Petersburg's water supply is extracted from the polluted River Neva, and its anti-quated filtration plants are unable to deliver tap water free of the parasitic bacteria **Giardia lamblia** (to which the locals are largely immune). To avoid giardia, use only bottled water for drinking and cleaning your teeth, or use tap water that has been boiled for fifteen minutes. If ingested, giardia may cause acute diarrhoea, which should be treated with 200mg of Metronidazole (Flagyl) three times daily for fourteen days. In Russia this drug is called Trikapol and comes in 250mg tablets; it's used by Russians for treating body lice, so you may get a funny look when you ask for it.

Also present in the water supply are **heavy metals** such as lead, cadmium and mercury. Brief exposure to these substances shouldn't do you any harm, but long-term residents may suffer from skin complaints and apathy as a result. Simply boiling the water is not enough: you need to leave it to stand for a day and avoid drinking the dregs. If you're staying for a long period of time, a proper water filter makes life easier; imported models are sold all over town. Alternatively, you can buy spring water in five-litre bottles from most food stores, and bottled mineral water is available everywhere.

Mosquitoes and ticks

St Petersburg's waterlogged basements are an ideal reservoir for **mosquitoes**, present throughout the year in most buildings and particularly noxious in summer. The best solution for a good night's sleep is to bring a mosquito net, but, failing that, you should invest in a mosquito-zapping device known as an Ezalo, taking tablets under the generic name of Raptor, both of which are sold at local pharmacies, supermarkets and house-hold goods shops.

More seriously, forested areas such as the Karelian Isthmus beyond St Petersburg are potentially infested with encephalitis-bearing **ticks** (*kleshy*) during May and June. Russians take care to cover their heads, shoulders and arms at this time of year when walking in forests, so you should do the same or, failing that, check all over your body (particularly your neck and shoulders) for signs of burrowing ticks. If you find them, press around the tick's head with tweezers, grab it and gently pull outwards; avoid pulling the rear of the body or smearing chemicals on the tick, which increases the risk of infection and disease.

White Nights, bootleg liquor and sexually transmitted diseases

Anyone coming in June or July is liable to be affected by the famous **White Nights**. The sun barely dips below the horizon for a few hours, so the sunlight is still strong at ten in the evening and a pearly twilight lasts through the small hours of the night, playing havoc with your body clock. Locals are used to it and revel in the annual shift to a 24-hour consciousness, but newly arrived foreigners often find it hard to pace themselves when the general attitude is "Let's party!" If you're here for only a few days it's OK to burn the candle at both ends, but anyone staying for a week or longer will inevitably make deep inroads into their sleep-account. This particularly applies to young children, who may find it impossible to sleep when they should, with sunlight streaming in through the thin curtains of hotels or flats.

If you drink alcohol, it's hard to avoid the national drink, vodka – and frankly, you can't hope to relate to Russia without at least one vodka-fuelled evening with Russians. Getting drunk and speaking *dushe po-dushe* (soul-to-soul) goes with the territory. Unfortunately, so does **bootleg liquor** – a hazard that can be avoided by following the advice on p.350.

Torrid White Nights, vodka and a rampant sex industry make St Petersburg one of the most hedonistic cities on earth (a would-be governor recently pledged to promote this as the city's selling point). Just keep in mind that the large number of intravenous drug users and prostitutes has made it Russia's worst nexus of **AIDS/HIV**, so you would be rash to have any sexual encounter without using a condom. In the event of being found to be HIV-positive or carrying an infectious disease such as syphilis or hepatitis, you risk being incarcerated in a locked isolation ward and treated like a subhuman. If you suspect you're infected, seek treatment outside Russia.

Pharmacies, doctors and hospitals

For minor complaints, it's easiest to go to a high-street **pharmacy** (*aptéka*), which stocks a wide range of Western and Russian products; most are open daily from 8am to 9pm and identifiable by the green cross sign. It goes without saying, however, that if you are on any prescribed medication, you should bring enough supplies for your stay. This is particularly true for diabetics, who should ensure that they have enough needles.

The standard of **doctors** varies enormously, so seek recommendations from friends or acquaintances before consulting one. Some Russian specialists are highly skilled diagnosticians who charge far less for a private consultation than you'd pay in the West,

while private **dentistry** is so much cheaper that savvy foreigners often get their teeth fixed while they're here.

If your condition is serious, public **hospitals** will provide free emergency treatment to foreigners on production of a passport (but may charge for medication). However, standards of hygiene and care are low compared with those in the West and horror stories abound. Aside from routine shortages of anaesthetics and drugs, nurses are usually indifferent to their patients unless bribed to care for them properly. Long-term expats advise, "Get an interpreter first, then a doctor." On the whole, however, foreigners rely on special clinics with imported drugs and equipment, and American-standard charges – a powerful reason to take out insurance. As a last resort, Helsinki is only an hour's flight or six hours' drive from St Petersburg. Many foreign clinics have their own ambulances, and can arrange medical evacuations. For a regular public **ambulance phone** ☏01 and demand "*Skoraya pomosh*" – the more urgent you sound, the better the chance of a speedy response.

Clinics in St Petersburg

American Medical Clinic nab. reki Moyki 78 ☏140 20 90. All medical and dental services; medical evacuation. Open 24hr.

British-American Family Practice Grafskiy per. 7 ☏327 60 30. Open 24hr.

Euromed Suvorovskiy pr. 60 ☏327 03 01, ⊕www.euromed.ru. Family practice, dental and emergency. Direct billing to all Scandinavian and Japanese and major European insurance companies. Open 24hr.

Eye Trauma Clinic Liteyniy pr. 25 ☏272 59 55. Open 24hr. Little English spoken.

Medi Chain of dental clinics The one at Moskovskiy pr. 79 is open 24hr (☏324 00 05); all other branches daily 8am–10pm. Accepts all credit cards except Union Card.

International Clinic ul. Dostoyevskovo 19/21 ☏320 38 70, ⊕www.icsb.com. Full medical services. Direct billing to insurance companies; 25 percent discount for students. Open 24hr.

Information, websites and maps

Although St Petersburg has yet to become as tourist-friendly as Prague or Budapest, the city has a fairly efficient tourist office and there are several useful listings magazines available. Russian tourist offices abroad are few in number and poorly stocked with maps and brochures. If you want to do some research or whet your appetite for the city before you go, it's worth checking out the various websites below.

Information

St Petersburg's main tourist office is the **City Tourist Information Centre** (Mon–Fri 10am–7pm, Sat 10am–6pm; summer also Sun 10am–6pm; ☎311 28 43 or 315 21 53, Ⓦwww.ctic.spb.ru), at Nevskiy pr.41, through the doorway of the Beloselskiy-Belozerskiy Palace furthest from Anichkov bridge over the River Fontanka (see map on p.41). Although their website is in Russian only and they seldom respond to email (Ⓔservice@ctic.spb.ru or info@ctic.spb.ru), their limited stock of free leaflets is supplemented by ledgers of useful information that you can peruse on the premises. The staff are kind enough to warn visitors not to buy the St Petersburg **Guest Card** that's on sale (a waste of money, since few places that signed up for the scheme now observe it), and if asked nicely can make phone enquiries and hotel (but not hostel or homestay) reservations on your behalf. In summer they also have a branch in the lobby of the *Oktyabrskaya Hotel*, opposite Moscow Station, that supposedly works the same hours, but is less reliable.

Alternatively, there's the old standby of using the service desks at such hotels as the *Astoria, Pribaltiyskaya, Pulkovskaya* and (best of all) the *Grand Hotel Europe* – or their counterparts at St Petersburg's hostels (for addresses, see Chapter 13) – which are usually willing to help out even if you're not staying there. For those who speak Russian, there's the *Znak Otveta* telephone enquiry service (☎326 96 96), which can give general tourist information such as opening hours and transport information.

Certain **publications** are also useful. If you're staying a while, it's worth investing in the pocket-sized *St Petersburg Traveller's Yellow Pages* ($7–10), which lists all kinds of businesses and services, with lots of maps and advice on diverse aspects of life in the city. It's annually updated and is sold in leading hotels and Pulkovo-2 airport; the Russian-language version, *Lucshee v Sankt Peterburge*, is sometimes available as a free promotional offer at foreign medical clinics in St Petersburg, and there is also a free online English version (see p.31). For reviews of restaurants, clubs, concerts and exhibitions, check out the free English-language bi-weekly *St Petersburg Times*, and the free monthly magazines *Pulse* and *Where St Petersburg* (see p.48) – available in the tourist office and hotels, restaurants, bars and shops frequented by foreigners.

Russian friends or acquaintances are often generous with their help and time, and know their city well. News of good places to eat, shop or have fun was traditionally spread by word of mouth rather than the media, and old habits die hard, despite there being far less need for a grapevine today. Alternatively, visitors can hire guides or interpreters from most of the tour and travel agencies listed in the *St Petersburg Traveller's Yellow Pages*.

Websites

There are myriad **websites** about Russia; the trick is finding ones that are up to date, relevant and accurate. Official tourist sites are notably lacking in all these respects. The City Government site (Ⓦwww.spb.ru) is partly available in English, but the only festivals listed since St Petersburg's 2003 anniversary bash are trade fairs, while the snazzy jubilee site (Ⓦwww.300.spb.ru) set up for the event hasn't been updated at all since then (though it's still worth a visit for its live-cam views and the chance to hear the city's hymn). The city's official tourist website (㉫www.ctic.spb.ru) is fairly up to date but in Russian only, and thus useless for most foreign visitors. This leaves the field clear to sites belonging to tourist agencies, hotels and hostels (see below), which have more of an interest in providing up-to-date info – though this can't be taken for granted. Details of what's currently on in the city can be obtained from the *St Petersburg Times* website. See below for some of the most useful sites; a list of Russian media websites is given on p.48, while other sites are given in the text as appropriate.

Useful websites

Accommodation ㉫www.all-hotels.ru, ㉫www.hotels.spb.ru or ㉫www.waytorussia.net. Three good sites for booking hotel rooms at discount rates; the last two also handle B&B, homestays and flat rental in St Petersburg. Other sites where you can book accommodation are listed under "Tourism" below, and on p.332.
Classical music ㉫www.classicalmusic.spb.ru. Links to local orchestras and venues. The site carries some news of coming events, but its festivals listings are way out of date.
Ballet ㉫www.mariinsky.spb.ru. Official site of the world-famous Mariinsky (Kirov) Ballet, with news, features, schedules of performances, and online booking.
Gay & Lesbian ㉫www.gay.ru. Advice, listings and contacts for gay and lesbian visitors to Russia.
Hermitage ㉫www.hermitagemuseum.org. Official site of the Hermitage Museum, featuring highlights of the collection, news of events and temporary exhibitions, and online-booking to beat the queues in summer (see p.120).
Literature ㉫www.kiosek.com/dostoyevsky is a research site for everything about Dostoyevsky, including texts of his works. ㉫www.other.spb.ru has excerpts from John Nicholson's entertaining book *The Other St Petersburg*.
Palaces ㉫www.alexanderpalace.org is a lavishly illustrated historical site devoted to the Imperial palaces and the Romanov dynasty.
㉫www.peterhof.org, ㉫www.eng.tzar.ru and ㉫www.pavlovskart.spb.ru are the official sites of Peterhof, Tsarskoe Selo and Pavlovsk Palace respectively.
Russian Museum ㉫www.rusmuseum.ru. Skimpier than the Hermitage website, it provides a peek at the world's premier collection of Russian art, and notice of temporary exhibitions in the Benois Wing.
St Petersburg Times ㉫www.sptimes.ru. Bi-weekly English-language paper with local and national news and weekly listings, linked to its sister-paper the *Moscow Times*. Access to the archives is limited to subscribers.
Tourism ㉫www.ryh.ru, ㉫www.saint-petersburg .com, ㉫www.travelto.spb.ru and ㉫www .travel-labs.co. The four best commercial sites. None is perfect, but by visiting them you can get an idea of the city, panoramic views, practical info, hotel discount rates, special offers, weather reports, and diverse links.
Yellow Pages ㉫www.infoservices.com. *Traveller's Yellow* Pages for St Petersburg, Moscow, Novgorod and Vyborg. Comprehensive listings for each city, plus theatre seat-plans and maps of the towns surrounding the Imperial palaces.

Maps

The **maps** in this guide should be sufficient for most purposes, but if you need more detail, or are staying outside the centre, it's worth investing in a detailed street plan. If you can read the Cyrillic alphabet, it's best to buy a locally produced map once you arrive. The fold-out *Polyplan Map of St Petersburg* is updated annually, features all major sights and covers the whole city; it costs about $3 from local bookshops or kiosks (considerably more in map shops abroad). These outlets also sell a pocket-sized *Atlas S-Peterburg S kazhdym domom*, which identifies the street number of every building (making it invaluable for locating clubs, restaurants and residential blocks), but few museums and monuments; and an annually updated map of all the minibus routes in the city, called *Vse Marshrutnye Taksi na karte Sankt-Peterburga* (both costing $3).

Foreign maps in English sold abroad include a detailed, laminated *Lonely Planet* map ($6); an *Insight Map* ($9) that confusingly gives the names of sites in Russian, in the Latin alphabet; and outdated, unwieldy *Falk plan* or *Freytag & Berndt* maps – only the last two are commonly found in St Petersburg. At a pinch, visitors can also use the English colour maps in the free magazine *Where St Petersburg*.

Serious map buffs who intend to make a lot of trips outside the city might also buy the Cyrillic *Polyplan Map of St Petersburg's Environs*, featuring plans of the towns surrounding the Imperial palaces, Kronstadt and Shlisselburg – or you can download useful, if somewhat dated, maps of Vyborg, Novgorod, Strelna and Gatchina from the *Traveller's Yellow Pages* (ⓦ www.infoservices.com). The website ⓦ www.300.spb.ru features historical maps of St Petersburg in the eighteenth and nineteenth centuries.

Map outlets

UK and Ireland

Easons Bookshop 40 O'Connell St, Dublin 1 ☎ 01/873 3811, ⓦ www.eason.ie.
Stanfords 12–14 Long Acre, London WC2E 9LP ☎ 020/7836 1321, ⓦ www.stanfords.co.uk, ⓔ sales@stanfords.co.uk. Maps available by mail, phone order or email. Other branches ⓔ sales@stanfords.co.uk; plus branches in British Airways offices at 156 Regent St, London W1R 5TA ☎ 020/7434 4744, and 29 Corn St, Bristol BS1 1HT ☎ 0117/929 9966.

USA and Canada

Rand McNally ☎ 1-800/333-0136, ⓦ www.randmcnally.com. Around thirty stores across the US; dial ext 2111 or check the website for the nearest location.
World of Maps 1235 Wellington St, Ottawa, ON K1Y 3A3 ☎ 1-800/214-8524, ⓦ www.worldofmaps.com.

Australia and New Zealand

Mapland 372 Little Bourke St, Melbourne, Victoria 3000 ☎ 03/9670 4383, ⓦ www.mapland.com.au.
Specialty Maps 46 Albert St, Auckland 1001 ☎ 09/307 2217, ⓦ www.ubdonline.co.nz/maps.

St Petersburg

Anglia nab. reki Fontanki 40 ☎ 279 82 84, ⓔ info@anglia-books.spb.ru.
Dom knigi Nevskiy pr. 28, 2nd floor ☎ 318 64 02. Has the largest selection of tourist maps in the city.

Addresses

In Russian usage, the street name is written before the number in **addresses**. When addressing letters, Russians start with the country, followed by a six-digit postal code, then the street, house and apartment number, and finally the addressee's name; the sender's details are usually written on the bottom of the envelope. The number of the house, building or complex may be preceded by *dom*, abbreviated to *d*. Two numbers separated by an oblique dash (for example, 16/21) usually indicate that the building is on a corner; the second figure is the street number on the smaller side street. However, if a building occupies more than one number (for example, 4/6), it is also written like this; you can usually tell when this is the case as the numbers will be close to each other and will both be even or odd. *Korpus* or *k.* indicates a building within a complex, *podezd* (abbreviated to *pod.*), an entrance number, *etazh* (*et.*) the floor and *kvartira* (*kv.*) the apartment. **Floors** are numbered in American or Continental fashion, starting with the ground floor, which Russians would call *etazh 1*. To avoid confusion we have followed the Russian usage throughout this book.

The main **abbreviations** used in St Petersburg (and in this book) are: ul. (for *ulitsa*, street); nab. (for *naberezhnaya*, embankment); pr. (for *prospekt*, avenue); per. (for *pereulok*, lane) and pl. (for *ploshchad*,

---

Cyrillic addresses

alleya	аллея	*naberezhnaya*	набережная
bulvar	бульвар	*pereulok*	переулок
dom	дом	*ploshchad*	площадь
dvor	двор	*podezd*	подъезд
etazh	этаж	*prospekt*	проспект
kvartira	квартира	*sad*	сад
korpus	корпус	*shosse*	шоссе
most	мост	*ulitsa*	улица

square). Other common terms include *most* (bridge), *bulvar* (boulevard), *shosse* (highway), *alleya* (alley) and *sad* (garden). In the city centre most of the streets now have **bilingual signs** (Cyrillic and Latin script), which make it easier to find your way around.

Visitors should be aware of the quintessentially St Petersburg distinction between the **main entrance stairway** (*paradnaya* *lesnitsa*) of an apartment building, and the subsidiary entrances off the **inner courtyard** or *dvor*. Traditionally the former was for show, with handsome mirrors and carpets, while the real life of the apartments revolved around the *dvor*. In Soviet times the grand stairways were gradually reduced to the darkened, shabby stairwells of today, but the *dvor* never lost its role as the spiritual hearth of St Petersburg life.

Arrival

Most visitors arrive by air and enter the city via one of the grand Stalinist thoroughfares that whets your appetite for the historic centre. If you're not being met at the airport, the taxi ride will be your first introduction to Russian-style haggling and manic driving. Arriving by coach from Helsinki, you'll cross Petrograd Side and the River Neva – another scenic curtain-raiser. The sea approach holds some appeal, with vistas of shipyards as you steam towards the Sea Terminal on Vasilevskiy Island, or the Neva basin in the heart of the city. Arriving by train, you'll be pitched straight into things.

Airports

St Petersburg's **international airport**, Pulkovo-2 (☎104 34 44), is 17km south of the city centre. In the baggage reclaim hall of the Arrivals building there's a hard-currency duty-free shop and an exchange machine that takes US dollars and euros, while the lobby beyond customs contains car rental desks and a bureau de change (daily 10.30am–9.30pm). If you arrive after the latter has closed, there's another exchange in the nearby Departures building that's open until later. BCL phonecards (see p.45) are sold from the trolley-rental point in the luggage hall.

There are several ways of getting into the city. A cheap **bus** service (#13) and a slightly more expensive **minibus** (#K-13) run every twenty minutes or so to Moskovskaya ploshchad, from where you can continue your journey by metro. For both the bus and minibus, you'll need rubles to buy a ticket once on board. Services depart from outside the Arrivals building and the journey to Moskovskaya ploshchad takes about twenty minutes.

If you have a lot of luggage or don't feel up to dealing with public transport immediately, there are always plenty of **taxis** waiting outside – both licensed and unofficial (see p.37). You're expected to pay in hard currency (or in rubles at a poor exchange rate), and the price is negotiable: $20 is fair for a ride into the centre, but drivers usually open the bidding at $60. Package tourists and guests with reservations at the *Astoria Hotel, Hotel Pribaltiyskaya* or *Grand Hotel Europe* will be met by the particular hotel's own minibus.

Should you fly to St Petersburg from Moscow or somewhere else in the Russian Federation, you'll arrive at the **domestic airport**, Pulkovo-1, 15km south of the city, from where buses #39 and #339 run regularly to Moskovskaya metro station. Taxi fares are much the same as from Pulkovo-2.

Leaving St Petersburg

When leaving St Petersburg, allow plenty of time to get to the international airport in order to arrive at least an hour and a half before your flight is scheduled to depart. Using public transport, give yourself at least an hour from the centre: catch bus #13, or one of the minibuses that depart from outside Moskovskaya metro, but make sure that the latter is going to Pulkovo *mezhdunarodniy aeroport* (the international one).

Check-in opens ninety minutes before take-off for Western airlines and two hours before for Aeroflot flights; be aware that check-in desks close forty minutes before departure. Passengers often have to queue for thirty minutes in order to pass through the only working metal detector, before they can submit their baggage for inspection and then join a queue at check-in. Beyond that lies passport control and a final customs check, where the customs officer will ask to see your original currency declaration (see p.42) and a duplicate form detailing what you're taking out of the country (forms are available in the hall).

Train stations

St Petersburg's train stations are linked to the city centre by a fast, efficient metro system, and named after the direction from which trains arrive. Trains from Moscow pull into **Moscow Station** (Moskovskiy vokzal), halfway down Nevskiy prospekt, one stop from the downtown area by way of the metro interchange Ploshchad Vosstaniya/Mayakovskaya. Coming from Tallinn or Rīga you'll arrive at the **Baltic Station** (Baltiyskiy vokzal) beside the Obvodniy Canal and Baltiyskaya metro, while trains from Berlin or Warsaw end up at **Vitebsk Station** (Vitebskiy vokzal), near Pushkinskaya metro. Trains from Helsinki and Northern Russia now terminate at the new **Ladoga Station** (Ladozhskiy vokzal)

east of the Neva – linked to the centre by Ladozhskaya metro – but may still stop at their former terminus, the historic **Finland Station** (Finlyandskiy vokzal), served by Ploshchad Lenina metro. All these mainline stations have exchange offices and/or ATMs.

Bus terminals

Eurolines Russia coaches from Berlin, Frankfurt, Tallinn and Rīga drop passengers on the square outside the Baltic Station (Baltiyskaya metro), near the Eurolines office, while **Finnish coaches** from Helsinki drop them at the Finnord office on Italyanskaya ulitsa, and the *Pulkovskaya Hotel* in the southern suburbs. In the unlikely event of you arriving on a coach run by a different company, from the Baltic States or another Russian city, you could arrive at the **Bus Station** (Avtovokzal) near the Obvodniy Canal. To reach the centre from there, walk a few blocks west (left) along the canal to catch any bus or tram up Ligovskiy prospekt, alighting either at the metro station of the same name, or further north at Ploshchad Vosstaniya metro, beside Moscow Station.

Cruise boat moorings

Finnish "booze cruise" vessels usually dock at the **Sea Terminal** (morskoy vokzal) on the Gulf coast of Vasilevskiy Island, some 4km west of the centre. Other than taking a taxi (you're likely to be charged at least $10, though Russians pay only $4), the best way of getting into the centre is to catch a #K-128 minibus to Vasileostrovskaya metro station on Bolshoy prospekt, and then continue by metro. More upmarket Baltic cruise ships moor in the **Neva basin** instead – usually within fifteen minutes' walk of the Winter Palace, off the Angliyskaya naberezhnaya to the west of the Admiralty, or near the Mining Institute on the other side of the Neva.

City transport and tours

St Petersburg is a big city, which means that sooner or later you're going to want to make use of its cheap and relatively efficient public transport system. As well as the fast metro network, there are minibuses, buses, trolleybuses and trams (in that order of usefulness). Newspaper kiosks sell fold-out maps of minibus routes across the city for about $3.

Tickets

In an effort to stamp out fare evasion on buses, trams and trolleybuses, the authorities have replaced the old system whereby passengers were trusted to buy tickets in batches of ten and punch them using a gadget aboard the vehicle, with conductors selling individual tickets (*talony*). As there is a **flat fare** on all routes there's no need to state your destination. On minibuses you simply pay the driver; no ticket is issued.

Unless you're going to be in St Petersburg for a long time and make regular use of particular services, it's not worth buying a one- or three-month pass for any combination of the above vehicles, though you might purchase a one-month **yediniy bilet**, valid for up to seventy journeys on buses, trolleybuses, trams and the metro, simply to avoid buying *talony* or metro tokens all the time. The *yediniy bilet* goes on sale in metro stations and kiosks towards the end of the calendar month, for a few days only; there is also a half-monthly version that goes on sale during the middle of the month.

The system on the **metro** is different, insofar as you can either buy metro **tokens** (*zhetony*) from the cashier (each token is valid for one journey, with as many changes of line as you wish), or various kinds of machine-readable **tickets**. There is a *prisnoy bilet* valid for ten, twenty or sixty journeys within a thirty-day period, or a one-month *prisnoy bilet* valid for up to seventy journeys. Alternatively, you can buy a **transport card** (*transportnaya karta*) valid for an unlimited number of journeys within a one-month (*na mesats*) or three-month (*tri mesyatsa*) period, or even an entire year (*na god*), starting from the date of issue. With all of these, you feed the ticket or card into the slot of the turnstile, wait for the light to switch from red to green, and retrieve it from the other slot. If you're using a *yediniy bilet*, you simply show it as you walk past the guardian at the end of the row of turnstiles.

Although the **price** of tickets and passes is liable to increase in line with inflation, public transport is still affordable for the locals and amazingly good value for tourists. A metro *zheton* costs about $0.25, a minibus ride in town $0.30–0.50 and a trip to Peterhof and other suburban destinations $1.

The metro

The metro's former name, "The Leningrad Metro in the name of Lenin with the Order of Lenin", gives you an idea of the pride that accompanied its construction, which began in the 1930s. There are four **lines** in operation (see the colour map at the back of this book), though further construction is hampered by a lack of funds and the sheer difficulty of tunnelling through St Petersburg's marshy subsoil. Stations are marked with a large "M" and have separate doors for incoming and outgoing passengers.

All **signs and maps** on the metro are in the Cyrillic alphabet; the colour metro map in this book gives the Cyrillic characters for each station and the common signs you will come across. Although each metro line is numbered and colour-coded, the shade of colour varies widely according to which map you buy. The colours on our map are as representative as any.

The metro covers most parts of the city you're likely to visit, except for the Smolniy district and the western end of the downtown area within the Fontanka. Depending on the line, trains run daily from about

5.45am till midnight or slightly later, with **services** every one to two minutes during peak periods (8–10am and 5–7pm), and every three to five minutes at night. Note, however, that certain underground walkways linking crucial **interchange stations** may close earlier – in particular, between Mayakovskaya and Ploshchad Vosstaniya, or Gostiniy Dvor and Nevskiy Prospekt. Where two lines intersect, the station may have two **separate names**, one for each line, or, alternatively, be numbered (as at Tekhnologicheskiy Institut or Ploshchad Aleksandra Nevskovo stations).

Owing to the city's many rivers and swampy subsoil, most of the lines were built extremely deep underground, with vertiginous **escalators** that almost nobody walks up, although the left-hand side is designated for that purpose. The older lines also boast a system of "horizontal lifts", whereby the **platforms** are separated from the tracks by automatic doors that open in alignment with those of the incoming trains – a bit of Stalinist wizardry that's been abandoned on the newer lines. Many of the station vestibules and platforms are notable for their **decor**, especially those on the downtown section of the Kirovsko–Vyborgskaya line, adorned with marble, granite, bas-reliefs and mosaics. It's worth travelling almost to the end of the line to see the glass columns at Avtovo station.

Since the platforms carry few signs indicating which station you are in, it's advisable to pay attention to the Tannoy **announcements** (in Russian only) in the carriages. As the train pulls into each station, you'll hear its name, immediately followed by the words *Sléduyushchaya stántsiya* – and then the name of the *next* station. Most importantly, be sure to heed the words *Ostorózhno, dvéry zakryváyutsya* – "Caution, doors closing" – since they slam shut with great force. Should anyone ask if you are getting off at the next stop – *Vy vykhodíte?* – it means that they are, and need to squeeze past.

Minibuses

The biggest improvement to the transport system in recent years has been the spread of **minibuses** (*marshrutnoe taxi*, or *marshrutki*). Besides being faster than buses, trolleybuses or trams, they usually carry only as many passengers as there are seats, and can be flagged down or drop you off at any point along their route, making them both comfortable and convenient. There are **flat fares** on all routes, which are slightly higher than on other forms of surface transport. The services running to outlying points of interest such as Peterhof, Tsarskoe Selo and Pavlovsk may be the fastest and easiest way of getting there providing there aren't any road works holding up the traffic.

Minibuses are usually numbered, with the prefix K, and carry a Cyrillic **signboard** listing their termini and the main points (and metro stations) along the route. You should never assume that this is the same as the one followed by buses or trolleybuses with the same route number, although in some cases it is. The most useful *marshrutka* routes are listed where appropriate in the text.

Buses, trams and trolleybuses

Since there are few destinations of interest to tourists that can't be reached by minibus, visitors have less reason than they did to use the city's antiquated, overcrowded **buses**, **trolleybuses** and **trams** – the last being the slowest of the lot, though many visitors enjoy riding them at least once, purely for the experience. While foreigners are often discouraged by pushing and shoving, Russians rarely take this personally.

As a rule, the system is supposed to operate daily from 5.30am to 1am, although cutbacks may see these **hours** reduced on some lines after 9pm. Some buses operate only during peak periods (daily 6–9am and 4–7pm), though these generally serve outlying factories and are of little use to visitors. **Trolleybuses #1, #7 and #10** offer a sedate sightseeing trip up Nevskiy prospekt and on to the Strelka; catch one from opposite Ploshchad Vosstaniya metro. Even better for sightseeing are **trams #2 and #54**, which run along Sadovaya ulitsa, past the Engineer's Castle and across the Neva to the Peter and Paul Fortress, with wonderful views all the way. During summer, **antique**

trams run from Finland Station, along Liteyniy prospekt and through the centre to ploshchad Turgeneva.

Stops are relatively few and far between, so getting off at the wrong one can mean a lengthy walk. Bus stops are marked with an "A" (for *avtobus*); trolleybus stops with what resembles a squared-off "m", but is in fact a handwritten Cyrillic "t" (for *trolleybus*). Both are usually attached to walls, and therefore somewhat inconspicuous, whereas the signs for tram stops (bearing a "T", for *tramvay*), are suspended from the overhead cables above the road.

In addition to the services outlined above, there are **express buses** (*ekspress*) on certain routes prefixed by an э. These tend to leave from metro or mainline stations and serve the airport and other outlying destinations. Passengers pay the driver and the fares are double those on regular buses.

Taxis

Registered taxis are run by many different companies. They are usually Volgas or Fords, painted bright yellow with a chequered logo on the doors. If the domed light on the roof is on, the taxi is unoccupied. At the time of writing, taxis no longer use meters, so if you don't agree on a price first you're liable to pay whatever the driver demands at the end of the journey. Some drivers are happy to make opening bids of $20 or more, before coming down a bit; others refuse to bargain at all. Though obviously open to abuse, this *laissez faire* system is kept within bounds by strong competition from ordinary vehicles acting as taxis (see below), except at airports and major hotels, where the "taxi mafia" has a stranglehold and drivers have agreed on fixed rates for certain journeys. At the airport it can be difficult to avoid their clutches, but at hotels you can always walk a block or two away and then look for an ordinary car.

Most Russians eschew taxis in favour of **hitching rides in private vehicles**, which enables ordinary drivers to earn extra money

Taxis can be called out 24 hours on ☎312 00 22.

as *chastniki* (moonlighters). You simply stand on the kerb and flag down any likely looking vehicle heading in the right direction. When one stops, state your destination and what you're willing to pay ("*Mozhno* [say the destination] *za* [say the sum in rubles] *rubley?*"); the driver may haggle a bit, but there's so much competition that it's a buyer's market. As a rule of thumb, one pays the ruble equivalent of $3 for a fifteen-minute journey, which should get you to most places in the city centre. Foreigners may be asked for more, but can usually get the same price by remaining firm – though if travelling with Russian friends, it's best not to speak until the deal is concluded.

As the above system is unregulated, it's as well to observe some **precautions**. Don't get into a vehicle which has more than one person in it, and never accept lifts from anyone who approaches you, particularly outside restaurants and nightclubs. Instances of drunken foreigners being robbed in the back of private cars are not uncommon, and women travelling alone would be best advised to give the whole business a miss.

Driving

You don't really need a **car** in St Petersburg, since the public transport system is cheap and efficient. Traffic is relatively heavy and many Russian motorists act like rally drivers, swerving at high speed to avoid potholes and tramlines, with a reckless disregard for pedestrians and other cars. Bear in mind also that some drivers are likely to have purchased their licence, rather than passed a test. Driving yourself, therefore, requires a fair degree of skill and nerve.

To drive a car in St Petersburg you are required to carry with you all of the following **documents**: your home driving licence and an international driving permit with a Russian-language insert (available from motoring organizations); an insurance certificate from your home insurer, or from your travel company; your passport and visa; the vehicle registration certificate; and a customs document asserting that you'll take the car back home when you leave (unless, of course, you rented it in St Petersburg).

Petrol (*benzin*) is easy to come by, and cheaper than in Western Europe. Foreign cars require 95 octane (4-star) or 98 octane (premium), but most Russian models use 92 octane (3-star) fuel. **Lead-free petrol** and high-octane fuel suitable for cars fitted with catalytic converters are sold at Neste-Petro and BP service stations, which take major credit cards as well as rubles. At all gas stations, you pay before filling up. If you **break down**, 24-hour emergency repairs or tow-away is provided by A24 (☎320 90 00), LAT (☎001) or Veho (☎115 97 79).

Rules of the road – and the GIBDD

Rules and regulations are often ignored unless there are traffic cops around. Traffic coming from the right, or onto roundabouts, has **right of way**, while **left turns** are only allowed in areas indicated by a broken centre line in the road, and an overhead sign. If you are turning into a side street, pedestrians crossing the road have right of way. **Trams** have right of way at all times, and you are not allowed to overtake them when passengers are getting on and off, unless there is a safety island.

Unless otherwise specified, **speed limits** are 60km (37 miles) per hour in the city and 80km (50 miles) per hour on highways. It is illegal to drive after having consumed *any* **alcohol** – the rule is stringently enforced, with heavy fines for offenders. **Safety-belt use** is mandatory (though many Russians only drape the belt across their lap, and drivers may be insulted if you belt up), and **crash helmets** are obligatory for motorcyclists. Take extra care when driving in **winter** (between Oct and March), when snow and ice make for hazardous road conditions.

Rules are enforced by the **GIBDD**, a branch of the Militia (see p.55) recognizable by their white plastic wands tipped with a light, which they flourish to signal drivers to pull over. Empowered to levy on-the-spot fines, they're notorious for regarding drivers as a source of income. If you're unlucky enough to get fined, it's easier to pay there and then: if not, you'll have to surrender your licence and reclaim it when you pay at the local police station. Unless your Russian is fluent it's better not to argue, but concentrate on negotiating a lower fine. As a rule of thumb, you pay the ruble equivalent of $1–3 if you don't think you've done anything wrong but an officer insists that you have, and $6 if you've really committed an offence.

Vehicle crime is on the increase and Western cars are a favourite target – never leave anything visible or valuable in your car. Guarded parking (*avtostoyanka*) is available at all top hotels (free for guests) and in many locations around the city centre.

Car rental

If you have Russian friends or acquaintances, asking around may well get you a car with a driver for a lot less than you'd pay for self-drive hire at a car rental agency. Daily rates start at $49 for a VW, Skoda or Renault from Biracs; $80 for a Ford Escort from Hertz. A foreign car is preferable to a Russian one if you're driving yourself. Many rental agencies insist on payment by credit card and require the full range of documentation (see p.37) for self-drive rental. The only international agency represented in St Petersburg is Hertz. Local Hertz and Svit agencies offer a 24-hour service, which you can reserve through the *Grand Hotel Europe* or the *Moskva Hotel*.

Rental agencies abroad

Hertz Australia ☎13 30 39; Canada ☎1-800/263-000; Ireland ☎01/676 7476; New Zealand ☎0800/654 321; UK ☎0870/844 8844; US ☎1-800/654-3001; ⊛www.hertz.com.

Rental agencies in St Petersburg

Astoria-Service Borovaya ul. 11/13, office 65, room 1 ☎112 15 83. Cars, limos and minibuses with drivers only.
Biracs per. Boytsova 8 (☎310 53 56) and Pulkovo-1 airport; ⊛www.biracs.ru. VW, Toyota and Skoda cars.
Hertz Malaya Morskaya ul. 23 (☎324 32 42) and Pulkovo-2 airport. Cars with or without driver. CCs only (Amex, Visa, MC, DC, JCB).
Rex Konyushennaya pl. 2, office 206 ☎320 66 62, ⊛www.relux.spb.ru. Mercedes cars and minibuses with drivers.
Svit ul. Korabelstroiteley 14, V.O. ☎325 93 29. Fords with or without drivers. Open 24hr. Takes CC.

Beware of the bridges

Whether travelling by car or on foot, you should always bear in mind that, between April and November, the **Neva bridges** are raised late at night to allow ships to pass through, severing the islands from the mainland. It's a spectacular sight as they swing open, and one that draws many spectators to the embankments during the White Nights. Should you inadvertently get stuck on the wrong side of the Neva, you can either wait for the bridge to reopen or look for a small boat prepared to take you across. Given that you're in no position to haggle, this is likely to cost you a packet – unless you happen to find a second boatman who's willing to undercut the first.

The following opening times apply only when the Neva is navigable; in **winter**, when the river is frozen over, the bridges remain permanently lowered. Always allow an extra five minutes if aiming to get across a bridge, as they can open or close early and there is invariably a crush of cars waiting to race wildly across during the brief interval that some of them come down again around 3am. Conversely, they may stay open all night if there's a naval holiday or too many ships. For up-to-date **information** on bridge opening hours (in Russian), phone ☎063 (9am–8pm).

Dvortsoviy most 1.55–3.05am & 3.15–4.45am.
Birzhevoy most 2.25–3.20am & 3.40–4.40am.
Troitskiy most 2–4.40am.
Most Leytenanta Shmidta 1.55–4.50am.
Liteyniy most 2.10–4.35am.
Kamennoostrovskiy most 2.15–3am & 4.05–4.55am.
Most Petra Velikovo 1.25–5.05am.
Most Aleksandra Nevskovo 2.35–4.50am.
Sampsonievskiy most 2.10–2.45am & 3.20–4.25am.
Tuchkov most 2.20–3.10am & 3.40–4.40am.
Grenaderskiy most 2.45–3.45am & 4.20–4.50am.
Volodarskiy most 2–3.45am & 4.25–5.45am.
Most Svobody 2.10–2.45am & 3.20–4.25am.

Cycling

In Russia, **cycling** is seen as more of a leisure activity than a means of transport. St Petersburg has a handful of intrepid cyclists, but the combination of potholed roads, manic motorists, tramlines and air pollution is enough to put most people off. However the Kirov Islands (see Chapter 5) are relatively car-free and a pleasure to cycle around, and riders with enough stamina might also consider cycling to Tsarskoe Selo (25km), which is agreeably rural once you get beyond Pulkovo airport. You can carry your bike aboard the train for the journey back to St Petersburg. If you're leaving your bike somewhere, be sure to secure it with a Kryptonite or other U-shaped lock, rather than just a chain and padlock. To be inspired for longer journeys, read Dan Buettner's *Sovitrek: A Journey by Bicycle Across Russia* (1994) or contact the Bicycle Club of Russia (@www.bigfoot .com/~rctc), which organizes cycling expeditions. About the only **repair** outlet for foreign bikes in St Petersburg is Motolyubitel (Apraksin dvor, korpus 1 ☎310 01 54).

Tours

There are heaps of tours available in St Petersburg, covering all the main attractions inside and outside the city, plus more esoteric themed tours on sociological or cultural aspects of Russian life. Price-wise, there's generally a big difference between the regular scheduled tours aimed at Russian tourists – which are OK for sightseeing the city or reaching one of the Imperial palaces if you've got a guidebook on your lap – and the excursions arranged for foreigners, which are usually a lot dearer, and booked for groups or individuals on an ad hoc basis.

Coach tours

Numerous local tourist agencies offer **coach tours** of the city and its environs, with commentary in Russian. The most accessible firms have kiosks outside Gostiniy dvor on Nevskiy prospekt (see p.68), where you can buy tickets and check schedules. Davranov Travel (☏311 01 60 or 311 86 94, ⊛www.davranov.ru in Russian only) is the largest operator and its tours are partly translated into English. They do day-trips ($5–8) to four of the Imperial palaces, plus Novgorod, Kronstadt and Shlisselburg – destinations also offered for a similar price by Eclectica (☏279 05 53, ⊛www.eclectica.ru in English), which also does over a hundred themed tours, available in foreign languages if you give enough notice. Russian-only tours are provided by Tur Servis (☏314 87 40), whose destinations include Vyborg ($7) and Oranienbaum ($6). Note that none of these prices includes admission to the palace or fortress that is the object of the excursion. More off-beat coach tours on sociological themes such as Russian child-rearing or law enforcement are available from Monomex Tours (☏445 01 59, ⊛www.2russia.com).

Boat tours

One of the pleasures of St Petersburg in summer is **cruising on the canals and rivers**, navigable from May till mid-October. The cheapest trips are aboard the large, enclosed boats that Russians call **kater** (cutters) – their disadvantage is that you have to endure a non-stop commentary in Russian. The main operator is Bark (☏315 56 06), with departures every half hour from the pier at nab. reki Fontanki 44, near the Anichkov most on the River Fontanka. Tours last just over an hour, taking in the Fontanka, the Kryukov Canal, the River Moyka and the Neva basin, and cost $4 per person. Bark also does two-hour **night cruises** (1am–3am; $8 per person). Alternatively, Neva Cruises' tours (10am–10pm; $4 per person) depart from the pier outside the Hermitage and cruise up and down the Neva for an hour. If you fancy hosting your own private boat party, you can rent larger and more luxurious vessels from Mir (☏311 83 20; ask for Yelena Krashnikova).

It's also possible to rent a small motorboat, advertised as **"water-taxis"**, from the moorings alongside the Politseyskiy most, where Nevskiy prospekt crosses the Moyka. You hire the entire boat (plus driver) for a negotiable price in hard currency; $45 an hour for a four-seater is standard, but a ten-seater is better value at $55 if you can get a group together. The route is pretty much the same as the tours mentioned above, though you can combine elements of the two if desired. The advantage of the water-taxis is that there's no commentary, the itinerary is much more flexible, and you can bring along champagne and caviar to complete the experience, particularly during the White Nights, when the boats work into the small hours. Call ☏230 77 47 to book in advance or go down to the bridge and pay a small deposit. If you do go boating at night, stick to the canals rather than cruising around the Neva basin, where collisions with larger ships are possible, especially in the not completely unlikely event that your motorboat captain happens to be drunk.

Walking tours

Peter Kozyrev of Peter's Walking Tours (⊛info@peterswalk.com, ⊛www.peterswalk.com) does a range of excursions on foot covering the city's highlights in five (daily; $11) or three hours (Mon, Wed, Thurs & Fri; $11), and themed tours relating to Dostoyevsky (Wed & Fri; $11), Rasputin (Thurs; $11), the Bolshevik Revolution (Sat; $14), the Blockade of Leningrad (Sun; $17) and the city's Communist legacy (Tues; $11) – plus especially intriguing tours of the city's rooftops or criminal neighbourhoods (by arrangement). Tours depart from the *St Petersburg International Hostel* (see p.344) or *Café Max* on Nevskiy prospekt (p.47). Another enthusiastic and well-informed guide is Sasha Bogdanov (☏322 75 00 or 314 57 05), who specializes in providing off-the-beaten-track experiences of the city, and charges about $20 per day.

While walking is by far the best way to enjoy the historic city centre, there are few pedestrian zones and you should always be aware of traffic. Cars may cut across the pavement en route to (or emerging from) the courtyards of buildings, and motorists pay no attention to pedestrian crossings without a traffic light. Even when the green man is showing, cars can turn in from side streets.

Helicopter tours

St Petersburg's layout is best appreciated from the air, though helicopters can't fly directly over the centre, but range over the river from the Peter and Paul Fortress to the Smolniy. Flights leave from behind the Golovkin Bastion of the fortress at weekends (April–Oct) and last about fifteen minutes ($35 per person). Seats can be booked on the spot or through Baltic Air (Nevskiy pr. 7/9, office 12 ☎238 45 20). Balloon trips over the city have long been suspended for security reasons, but in the event that they resume, the firms to contact are Aerotour Balloons (☎265 50 18) or Oparin Balloons (☎264 63 58).

Costs, money and banks

Russia's economy has been on a rollercoaster for over a decade. Russians have lost their money so often that cynicism runs deep; the colossal fortunes made by so-called oligarchs are the other side of the coin. At the time of writing, inflation was under control and the economy growing. St Petersburg's boom in property, retailing and services (with rising wages in these sectors) has given it a wider spread of people with disposable income than any other city in Russia except Moscow, which enjoys the lion's share of the nation's wealth.

For visitors, **costs** in general terms compare well with major cities in Western Europe; you can eat, drink, travel and go to concerts or clubs for less than in Paris or London. The chief exception is **accommodation**, with relatively few decent hotels for under £55/$100 a night; even B&B can cost £16–22/$30–40 per person. If you're staying longer than a few weeks, renting a flat works out much cheaper, about £5–8/$10–15 daily – less than you'd pay for a bed in a hostel. Another factor is discriminatory ticket pricing at museums, palaces, the Mariinsky Theatre and other major attractions, whereby foreigners pay up to sixteen times what Russians do. While the Hermitage or Russian Museum charges seem fair enough, anyone hoping to see all the interiors at Peterhof would need to spend £22–27/$40–50, unless they have a student card entitling them to a fifty percent discount.

Package tourists with prepaid accommodation including full- or half-board really only need money for tickets to museums and palaces, buying gifts and the odd snack or drink. Unless you go overboard in expensive places, £30/$55 a day should suffice. Independent travellers will of course have to add accommodation costs and food on top of this figure. Staying in a modest hotel and sticking to inexpensive bars and restaurants, you could get away with a total daily budget of £80/$150, but patronizing fancier establishments will easily triple or quadruple this figure. Alternatively, if you rent a flat and live as Russians do, you could spend £30/$55 a day or less on the whole works, including lodging, food and drink.

Russian currency

Russia's currency, the **ruble**, has been relatively stable since the crash of 1998.

Currency reform saw rows of zeros vanish from banknotes and the reappearance of the kopek (though at 100 kopeks to one ruble, it's virtually worthless). The denominations in circulation are coins of 5, 10 and 50 kopeks and 1, 2 and 5 rubles; and notes of 5, 10, 50, 100, 500 and 1000 rubles. Counterfeiting isn't unknown, but limited to 100 ruble notes (fakes are recognizable by their thick paper, dull serial numbers and unclear watermarks), owing to the security features on higher denomination notes – so you needn't worry much about it.

Given that many hotels and museums still peg their prices to some figure in foreign currency, and that anything might happen to the ruble during the lifetime of this edition, **all prices in this book are quoted in US dollars**, calculated at the rate of exchange at the time of writing (about 30 rubles to the dollar). However, Russia is increasingly influenced by the **euro**, so fluctuations in the relative value of both currencies can affect real costs on the ground. Though almost everywhere specifies prices in rubles, some restaurants, bars, clubs and hotels quote them in so-called **"standard units"** (*uslovnye yedenitsy*, abbreviated to УЕ), which can mean dollars, euros or some midway point between the two – whichever is most advantageous for them, basically. So far as restaurants go – and sometimes hotels and bars as well – this is often an indication that the establishment is overpriced, and best avoided.

In all cases, you'll be expected to pay in rubles at the exchange rate (*kurs*) set by the Central Bank or the establishment, unless the transaction is with a private individual, such as a landlord, who may well prefer to receive hard currency. To find out the Central Bank rate, check in the financial section of the *St Petersburg Times*, or on the currency converter websites ⓦ www.xe.com and ⓦ www.oanda.com. The designation code for Russian rubles is "RUR". Inside Russia, ruble prices are written with a Cyrillic p or py, followed by a decimal point and a к for kopeks – so that 12p.50к means twelve rubles and fifty kopeks.

Currency declaration

Despite the relaxation of the system, visitors arriving in Russia should still take the trouble to fill in a **currency declaration form** stating how much money they are carrying and listing valuables such as gold jewellery, video cameras, laptop computers and mobile phones (the latter under the heading "high-frequency radio-electronic devices and means of communication"). Forms are often handed out on the plane shortly before landing, and can be obtained at Pulkovo-2 airport or any border crossing. Show the form as you go through customs and you should get a stamp (it doesn't matter if you don't).

Upon **leaving Russia**, you're supposed to fill in a duplicate form stating how much currency you're taking out of the country, and submit both for comparison to a customs official. However, for amounts of up to $3000 this is only required for "statistical reasons", and in theory you can take out up to $10,000 (and 50,000 rubles) without any difficulties, so it isn't a problem if you lose the original form. Rather, the reason for having it is to provide cover during your stay against ID checks by the Militia, who might find the lack of a declaration a pretext for hassling you (see p.54).

Changing money

Changing money with street hustlers is a sure way to be cheated, and there's no reason to exchange money anywhere other than in a proper **bank** or a **currency exchange bureau** (*obmen valuty*). These can be found all over St Petersburg, including inside shops and restaurants (usually open the same hours as the host establishment). Most banks set fairly similar rates, but it's worth seeking out the best one if you're changing a lot of cash at once. Rates are

bank	Банк
currency exchange	обмен валюты
convertible currency	СКВ
standard units	УЕ
ruble	рубль
buying rate	покупка
selling rate	продажа
exchange rate	курс

listed in the financial section of the *St Petersburg Times*. Commission should be negligible. You may need to show your passport.

Since the majority of banks and exchange bureaux want only US dollars or euros, bringing any other currency will limit your options as to where you can change money. Moreover, owing to counterfeiting as many places insist on new-style US dollars in good condition – notes in other currencies may also be refused if they're in a dodgy state. Likewise, guard against receiving any torn ruble notes in return. Surplus rubles can be converted back into hard currencies at most banks.

Banking hours are usually Monday to Friday 9am to 6pm, often with a break at lunchtime. Outside these times, you may find the odd bank open, but will otherwise have to rely on exchange outlets and international hotels.

Traveller's cheques and bank cards

Traveller's cheques (TCs) are no longer the cheapest or the most convenient way to carry funds – bank cards are better, see below – and the only brand that's readily replaceable if lost or stolen in St Petersburg is **American Express** (Malaya Morskaya ul. 23, ☎326 45 00, ✆www.americanexpress .ru; Mon–Fri 9am–5pm). Amex TCs can otherwise be cashed at branches of Bank Moskvy, Baltiyskiy Bank, Guta-Bank and Vneshtorgbank, which also accept Thomas Cook and Visa, and in the case of the last two, Citi Corp cheques. Commission charges range from 1 to 4 percent. The usual fee for purchasing TCs is 1 or 2 percent, though this fee may be waived if you buy them through a bank where you have an account. Be sure to keep the purchase agreement and a record of the cheques' serial numbers separate from the cheques themselves. In the event that cheques are lost or stolen, the issuing company will expect you to report the loss forthwith to their office in St Petersburg (only Amex has an office there) or overseas.

A **debit card** is best for **ATM** (*bankomat*) withdrawals, as the flat transaction fee is usually quite small (£1.50/$2.80), and there

are no interest payments. Make sure that you have a personal identification number (PIN) that's designed to work overseas – your bank will be able to advise on this. **Credit cards** are an easy way of carrying your funds, and can be used either in ATMs or over the counter. Almost all banks and many exchange bureaux will give cash advances in rubles on Visa, MasterCard or Maestro; Guta-Bank and Gazprombank accept Union Card, and Baltiyskiy Bank, Diners Club. Cash advances are treated as loans, with interest accruing daily from the date of the withdrawal, plus a 1–4 percent commission charge. You can **pay** by credit card in most hotels and restaurants and quite a few shops, though not all cards are accepted widely, and in shops it may depend on whether the single member of staff who knows how to swipe cards is working that day. Always keep the **receipts** from ATM withdrawals or card transactions, and be sure to know the overseas hotline number for reporting **lost or stolen** cards. However, it's worth phoning their Moscow offices first: ☎095/933 66 36 for Amex, ☎095/956 48 06 for Diners Club, MasterCard, JCB or Visa.

Wiring money

Having money wired from home using one of the companies listed below is never cheap, and should be considered as a last resort. The fastest **transfer** (10–15 minutes) is with an Amex MoneyGram (3–30 percent commission on the sum), but Western Union (4–15 percent commission) has more local branches in St Petersburg. With any transfer you should check beforehand exactly how much it'll cost in fees. If you're in really dire straits, get in touch with your **consulate** in St Petersburg (see p.403), who will usually let you make one phone call home free of charge, and will – in worst cases only – repatriate you, but will never, under any circumstances, lend you money.

Money-wiring companies

American Express MoneyGram Australia ☎1800/230 100; New Zealand ☎09/379 8243 or 0800/262 263; UK and Republic of Ireland ☎0800/6663 9472; US and Canada ☎1-800/926-9400; ✆www.moneygram.com.

Thomas Cook Britain ☏01733/318 922; Canada ☏1-888/823-4732; Northern Ireland ☏028/9055 0030; Republic of Ireland ☏01/677 1721; US ☏1-800/287-7362; ⊚www.us.thomascook.com.

Western Union Australia ☏1800/649 565; New Zealand ☏09/270 0050; Republic of Ireland ☏1800 /395 395; UK ☏0800/833 833; US and Canada ☏1-800/325-6000; ⊚www.westernunion.com.

Post, phones and email

Telecommunications has been one of the fastest growing sectors of the economy for over a decade, with a massive improvement in international and domestic phone services and Internet access, and widespread use of mobiles (cell phones). Only the postal system lags behind.

Post

The Russian **postal system** is notoriously inefficient. Incoming international mail takes up to three weeks to arrive, while the outbound service is even less reliable. As a result, most Russians entrust letters to someone travelling abroad, for safer postage there, while foreigners either emulate them, employ an express mail or courier firm, or communicate by email instead (see p.46).

To **post a letter**, your best bet is to try the *Grand Hotel Europe* or the *Nevsky Palace Hotel*, both of which offer a service dispatching letters only, via Finland, for around $1.50 to Europe and $2 for the US. They take around four days to arrive. EMS Garantpost, Post International and Westpost offer an express delivery service via Finland or Sweden, which can take anything from three to five days, or there are international courier services, whose rates are still higher. With all of these services it pays to shop around for the best deal (see listings below).

St Petersburg's **main post office** (*glavniy pochtamt*) is at Pochtamtskaya ul.9 (Mon–Sat 9am–7.45pm, Sun 10am–5.45pm ☏312 83 02), a few blocks from St Isaac's Cathedral. **District post offices** (*pochta*) are generally open from 9am to 2pm and 3pm to 7pm and can be identified by the blue and white sign depicting a postman's horn and the frigate emblem of the city. **Parcels** *must* be taken unwrapped to the main post office, where they'll be inspected and

wrapped for you, though you can then send them off from any post office. If you want only stamps, it's easier to go to the postal counters in a big **hotel** such as the *Astoria* or *Pulkovskaya*, rather than queue in a post office, although there's a heavy mark-up on the price.

If you're staying a while and expecting to receive mail, it's worth buying a few American Express traveller's cheques simply to use their **client mail service**, which is more reliable than the **poste restante** in public post offices.

International express mail and courier services

DHL Nevskiy Palace Hotel ☏380 20 01; Izmaylovskiy pr. 4 ☏326 64 00; ⊚www.dhl.ru. **EMS Garantpost** Konnogvardeyskiy bulvar 4 ☏325 75 25, ⊚www.garantpost.ru. **Federal Express** nab. kanala Griboedova 16 ☏311 98 31; pr. Yuriya Gagarina 34 ☏327 04 80. **Post International** Nevskiy pr. 34, 2nd floor ☏318 44 72. **TNT** Sofiyskaya ul.14 ☏118 33 30, ⊚www.tnt.ru. **UPS** Shpalernaya ul. 51 ☏327 85 40. **Westpost** Nevskiy pr. 86 ☏327 30 92.

Phones

Public phonecard phones have largely superseded the old-style payphones that used *zhetony* (tokens). The most common are the green-and-white **SPT phones**, which can be used for local, intercity and international calls.

Signs

Communications centre	Переговорный пункт
Fax	Факс
Email	Электронная почта
Intercity telephone	Междугородный телефон
Internet	Интернет
Local telephone	Таксофон *or* телефон
Post office	Почта
Poste restante	До Востребования

They sometimes take coins as well, although this is only really practical for local calls. SPT **phonecards** (*telefonaya karta*) are sold in metro stations, post offices and banks in various denominations of units, costing from $4 upwards. The cheapest ones may not allow you to call abroad.

The big hotels and flashier restaurants also have **BCL card phones**, which use satellite links for international connections. These sometimes have an echo and are expensive, although still cheaper than in your **hotel room or business centre**, where the cost of an international call can be anything from $5 to $30 a minute. Another way to make an international call is to go to a **communications centre** (*peregovorny punkt*) – there's one in every district. If you're lucky enough to have access to a **private phone**, you'll find that local calls are still free, while rates for intercity and international calls are about as low as you'll get in Russia without buying an international discount phonecard or signing up for IP telephony (see below).

To **make a direct international call** dial 8, wait for the tone to change and then dial 10, followed by the country code, city code (omitting the initial zero if present) and subscriber number. To call anywhere in Russia, or most of the former Soviet republics (except the Baltic States), dial 8, pause, and then the city code (including any zeros). Calls placed through the international operator (☎079/☎073 for outside/inside the CIS) cost twice as much and may take time to come through.

If you have access to a touch-tone phone you can choose between a plethora of **discount phonecards** (from phone dealers and kiosks; the Nevskiy prospekt/Sadovaya ulitsa underpass offers most choice) that let you call selected countries at reduced rates – though you'll need some knowledge of the language or help from Russian friends to check out what's on offer. Visitors with their own phone who are staying for a while may prefer using a local company providing web-based, or **IP**, **telephony**, such as Comset (⌨www.comset.net), Delta Telecom (⌨www.deltatelecom.ru) or WestCall (⌨www.westcall.spb.ru). Calls to the US or Western Europe cost about $0.80 per minute, but call quality can vary depending on web traffic.

Mobile phones are wildly popular in St Petersburg. Europeans using the GSM system can use their own phones in the city, but Americans must rent a special phone from their cellular dealer before leaving; in either case calls will be expensive. Anyone intending to use a mobile extensively, or over several months, will save money by buying or renting a *mobilnik* from a local dealer and using a Russian network. Shopping around is essential, but it's better to pay more for a reliable service with MTS (⌨www.spb .mts.ru) or MegaFon (⌨www.nwgsm.com) than suffer the spotty coverage of cut-price operators such as Tele2. MTS can also provide **WAP** services, enabling those with a WAP phone to use it to go online for $0.20 a minute.

Always bear in mind the **time difference** when calling Russia from abroad. Lines are at their busiest during UK or US office hours, but you'll have fewer problems getting through at, say, 7am in the UK – which is 10am in St Petersburg. Conversely, should you phone St Petersburg after 3pm UK time, everyone will have already left the office (it's acceptable to call people at home up until 11pm or midnight, local time).

Direct dialling codes

To St Petersburg
From Britain ☎00 7 812
From Ireland ☎00 7 812
From the US and Canada
☎011 7 812
From Australia and New Zealand
☎0011 7 812

From St Petersburg
Australia ☎8 (pause) 10 61
Finland ☎8 (pause) 10 358
Ireland ☎8 (pause) 10 353
New Zealand ☎8 (pause) 10 64
UK ☎8 (pause) 10 44
US and Canada ☎8 (pause) 10 1

Email

One of the best ways to keep in touch while travelling is to sign up for a **free Internet email address** that can be accessed from anywhere, for example YahooMail or Hotmail – accessible through ⊛www.yahoo.com and ⊛www.hotmail.com. Once you've set up an account, you can use these sites to pick up and send mail from any Internet café, or hotel with Internet access.

You can go online at numerous **cafés** in the centre of St Petersburg, many of which are open 24 hours. Hourly rates vary, but are rarely more than $3 at peak times and as little as $1 after midnight, with premium rates for higher-speed and broadband links. At most places the staff speak some English and can reset the on-screen language format so that you don't have to grapple with instructions in Cyrillic. The Russian word for @ is *sobachka* (literally "dog"); a dot is a *tochka*.

If you bring your own computer to Russia make sure you write it in your customs declaration and avoid putting it through X-ray scanners (insist on a hand examination). If you need to connect to the Internet, you'll require an (American) Bell lead for your modem that can connect directly to a five-pin Russian telephone plug, or a UK/Russian adaptor. For details, plus information on electrical systems in different countries, check out the useful website ⊛www.kropla.com. Since AOL and Compuserve closed down their Russian gateways, the field has been dominated by home grown ISPs such as Russia Online (⊛www.rol.ru), Matrix (⊛www.mns.ru), Peterlink (⊛www.peterlink.ru) and Metrokom (⊛www.metrocom.ru). Clients must open an account and choose between prepaying or buying Internet scratch-cards, valid for a set number of hours' use. With these, you call up the ISP, give your account number and then the PIN that's on the back, every time you go online. When using a computer in Russia be wary

Cyrillic script and the Internet

One difficulty with accessing websites and receiving emails in Cyrillic is that there are two different systems for representing Cyrillic letters. One is the so-called **WIN encoding** (officially CP-1251), the other is the **KOI-8** system, favoured by Russians among themselves. PCs with Windows 98 or later have everything needed to handle either system, providing you activate your machine by following the simple instructions on ⊛http://ourworld.compuserve.com/homepages /PaulGor/. This enables Outlook Express users to set up both their browser and email for Cyrillic, and Hotmail and Yahoo users to read and write emails in Cyrillic. For Macs or PCs with Windows 95 or earlier, you need to install Cyrillic fonts from ⊛http://funet.fi/pub/culture/russian/comp/fonts/fonts.html or ⊛http://babel.uoregon.edu/yamada/fonts/russian.html, by changing the default font in your email programme. For web page access, PC users with Windows 98 and Internet Explorer version 5.0 or later should follow the first site's instructions. With other browsers or any Mac software you need to replace the existing default font by KOI-8 or WIN Cyrillic. If you receive a document composed of question marks you've been sent it in an unreadable "ornamental" Cyrillic font, and need to ask for it to be re-sent in Arial, Courier or some other standard font.

of the fluctuations in the electricity current. If you need help, there are computer dealers all over town – though warranty agreements on hardware or software bought abroad don't apply within Russia. Pirated software is widely available in shops and markets.

Internet cafés in St Petersburg

Arka Internet Club nab. kanala Griboedova 7, ⓦwww.arka.spb.ru. Hourly rates $1 (midnight–8am), $2 (10am–1pm) or $2.50 (1–11pm). Mon–Thurs 10am–11.30pm, Fri–Sun 24hr.

Café Max Nevskiy pr. 90/92, 2nd floor ☏273 66 55, ⓦwww.cafemax.ru. The city's largest Internet café is the starting point for Peter's Walking Tours

(see p.40), and also runs the Internet café in the Hermitage Museum (p.121). All-night use for $4.50.

Consay Ligovskiy pr. 63 ☏164 57 452, ⓦwww.consay.sp.ru. Open 24hr.

Cro-Magnon Nevskiy pr. 81, on the right side of the courtyard on the second floor ☏279 57 26. Open 24hr.

5.3GHZ Internet Center Nevskiy pr. 63, 2nd floor ☏314 60 69. $2 per hour. Open 24hr.

Quo Vadis? Nevskiy pr. 24 ☏311 80 11, ⓦwww.quovadis.ru. Features a bar, library and design studio. $2 per hour. Open 24hr.

Red Fog Internet Centre Kazanskaya ul. 30–32. Internet $1.20 per hour; cheap rate 11.30pm–8.30am. Open 24hr.

Tetris ul. Chernyakhovskovo 33 ☏164 48 77, ⓦwww.netcafe.spb.ru. Daily 10am–11pm.

The media

The city's major hotels sell a limited range of foreign newspapers, generally a day or more old. Local English-language papers are useful for finding out what's on, and the *St Petersburg Times* features some national and international news, but to keep up with world events it's better to go online at an Internet café, or tune into foreign radio or satellite TV.

Russian TV is partially accessible to those with a limited grasp of the language: game show formats are familiar and news broadcasts gorily explicit. The press requires a real knowledge of the language. Besides sensationalism, its main flaw is peddling propaganda for business and political ends. While glasnost and the collapse of Soviet power led to almost total media freedom, it wasn't long before Russia's new financial oligarchs were bundling TV stations and newspapers into media empires. Most journalists shared the oligarchs' aim of getting Yeltsin re-elected, for fear of what a Communist victory would mean for their own careers; having colluded in one campaign to mould opinion, it was natural to go along with the wave that swept Putin into power, and then acquiesce when he stripped three oligarchs of their media

empires, and control passed into the hands of others, closer to the Kremlin.

The press

If you can understand the language, the **Russian press** holds some surprises for those who remember it from olden days. *Pravda*, the Communist Party daily, fell into the hands of "Greek swindlers who claimed to be Communists" in the mid-1990s, and now only a rebel version exists in cyberspace. *Izvestiya*, once the organ of the Soviet government, and the erstwhile Young Communists' daily, *Komsomolskaya Pravda*, are now respectively a pro-business sheet and a popular tabloid, both owned by the oligarch Potanin. The elite peruse *Kommersant*, a liberal paper that's the last remnant of Berezovsky's media empire, or *Nezavisimaya Gazeta*, independent by name and allegiance. Russia's angry dispossessed buy *Sovetskaya Rossiya* or *Zavtra*, both unashamedly far right, xenophobic hate-sheets. A more amusing read, *Limonka*, published by the National Bolshevik Party, is a vehicle for the ego of its leader, Limonov.

The best-selling **local papers** in St Petersburg are *Smena*, *Sankt-Peterburgskie Vedomosti* and *Chas Pik*, the last having the fullest listings of **what's on** (augmented on Fridays by a separate supplement, *Pyatnitsa*), and strong connections with the security forces and the Governor's office. *Afisha*, *Sobaka* and *Pulse* are cooler, lifestyle-listings magazines, which, like the more family-oriented, pocket-sized *Vash Dosug*, are published every month, staggered to overlap each other.

Foreign newspapers aren't widely available, but you're sure to find the *International Herald Tribune*, *Newsweek*, *The Times* and *The Guardian* in the *Grand Hotel Europe*, *Nevsky Palace* and *Astoria* hotels, heavily marked-up. Many foreigners prefer the **local English-language press**, which is better distributed, free and will tell you what's going on locally. The doyen of the pack is the *St Petersburg Times* (published Tues & Fri), which is good for local news and features, and has a useful listings and reviews section in the Friday edition. While the monthly *Neva News* is seldom worth reading, the style magazine *Pulse* carries excellent club and exhibition reviews, and the glossy magazine *Where St Petersburg* contains tourist-related features, news and listings. All are free and available from hotels, shops and restaurants frequented by foreigners. The *St Petersburg Times* was one of the first papers in the world to go online, followed by its big sister the *Moscow Times* and its local rival *Pulse* (see below).

Russian media online

Afisha ⊛ www.spb.afisha.ru. Monthly style and listings magazine with good reviews and listings, in Russian only.

Gateway2Russia ⊛ www.gateway2russia.com. News and information portal, run in partnership with the UK *Financial Times*.

Gazeta.Ru ⊛ www.gazeta.ru/english. Online news and features magazine.

Moscow Times ⊛ www.themoscow.times.com. The paper isn't distributed in St Petersburg, but is worth reading if you're going to Moscow, or for its national news. Linked to the *St Petersburg Times* website.

NTV ⊛ www.ntv.ru. News, features and schedules for the NTV channel. Some of the website is in English.

Pravda.ru ⊛ http://english.pravda.ru. English-language edition of the erstwhile Communist Party paper, in cyberspace.

Pulse ⊛ www.pulse.spb.ru. Monthly St Petersburg style and listings magazine, produced in English and Russian. The online version is a shadow of the printed magazine.

RIA Novosti ⊛ www.rian.ru. Multilingual, state-owned Russian International News Agency.

Russian Media ⊛ www.media-run.com. Links to Russian news agencies, newspapers, magazines, TV and radio stations.

Russia Journal ⊛ www.russiajournal.com. Daily version of the Moscow-based weekly, rumoured to be sponsored by the CIA.

St Petersburg Times ⊛ www.sptimes.ru. The city's oldest English-language newspaper; archives accessible by subscription.

TV and radio

Television in the Yeltsin era was outrageously biased, yet rivalry between media moguls made for some plurality and criticism. Putin ended that by using the financial giants Gazprom and LUKoil to prise the networks from their owners, ensuring that the Kremlin no longer needs favours to get its message across nor has much to fear from critical coverage. **ORT** (Channel 1) is the nation's favourite for its soaps, game shows and classic Soviet films. Its former owner Berezovsky was the *éminence grise* of Russian politics until he fled abroad to avoid being jailed on suspicion of fraud like his rival Gusinsky, whose **NTV** (Channel 3) angered the Kremlin with its reportage of the war in Chechnya, till Gazprom took over. While NTV news has since lost its edge, the station's slick thrillers, drama and documentaries make better viewing than **Channel 4**'s equivalents and are streets ahead of the wholly state-owned **RTR** (Channel 2), whose mix of soaps, tedious state events and servile news gives its the lowest rating of the lot.

Their local counterparts are **Kultura** (Channel 5), whose highbrow profile suffered under Governor Yakovlev; **STS** (Channel 6), a light entertainment channel founded with the help of Ted Turner; several secondary channels, available only with the aid of a subsidiary aerial, which are heavy on game shows and US, Brazilian and Mexican films and soaps; and local cable TV stations delivering **OTV** (European news and documentaries), MTV-Russia, and Sky.

As far as **radio** goes, most cafés and bars tune into one of the many FM music stations. The most popular are Europa Plus, which dishes out "the best of the West" on 100.5 FM, and the equally mainstream Radio Maximum (102.8). Russkoe Radio (107.8) and Radio Retro (88) are devoted to Russian music of the 1960s, 1970s and 1980s, and Radio Chanson (104.4) offers a mixture of easy listening from France and Russia. For classical music, tune in to Klassika Petersburg (88.9). Should you have a short-wave radio, it's also possible to pick up the BBC World Service (see ◍www.bbc .co.uk/worldservice for frequencies).

Opening hours, holidays and festivals

Twenty-four-hour food and liquor stores exist in most residential areas of the city (many take an hour's break in the morning), alongside bakeries and other food shops, open Monday to Saturday from 9am to 6pm or 7pm (with an hour or two's break between 1pm and 4pm). Retailers in the downtown area keep similar hours, while malls and department stores may stay open until 9pm or later, even on Sundays. Kiosks near metro stations close by mid-evening or work all night, depending on what they're selling.

Museums, galleries and churches

Opening hours for **museums and galleries** tend to be from 10am or 11am to 5pm or 6pm. They are closed at least one day a week, but there are no hard and fast rules as to which. In addition, one day in the month will be set aside as a *sanitarniy den* or "cleaning day", and it's not unusual to find museums unexpectedly closed "for repairs" (*na remont*) or "technical reasons" (*po tekhnicheskim prichinam*), usually owing to staff shortages. Full opening hours are detailed in the text.

Ticket prices to museums are higher for foreigners than for Russians; minor museums charge $3–5 and major attractions such as the Hermitage and the Imperial palaces demand $10–15. A **student card** entitles you to a fifty-percent discount at all museums, and free admission to the Hermitage. If you're going to visit a lot of museums, it's tempting to purchase a student card at the *RST Hostel* (see p.405) or, if you're with Russians, let them buy the tickets and keep silent till you're past the *babushka* on ticket control. Many museums require you to buy a permit for **photography** (cameras $1–3; video up to $5; no discounts) or leave your camera in the cloakroom (*garderob*), and some make visitors put on felt or plastic overshoes (*tapochki*) to protect their parquet floors.

At some museums you can rent an **audioguide** (*player*) at the ticket desk (*kassa*), or arrange a **guided tour** (*beseda*) through the excursions bureau in English or other foreign languages. There are no hard and fast rules about how far in advance you should book a tour, and a lot may depend on the museum's staffing rosters. Some museums have set rates for guided tours, others prefer to negotiate on an ad hoc basis.

Churches and other places of worship are open for services, if not all day. It often depends on how valuable their icons are and whether there are enough parishioners, since few churches can afford to hire guards. In Soviet times, many were converted into museums, swimming pools, cinemas or workshops. Most have now reverted to their former purpose but many are still being repaired or redecorated, which may limit access. Orthodox churches celebrate the Divine Liturgy (*Bozhestvennaya Liturgia*) at 8am, 9am or 10am Monday to Saturday, and at 7am or 10am on Sunday and saints' days; most also hold services at 5pm or 6pm daily, some with an *akafist* or series of chants to the Virgin or saints. Both services last about two hours. Additional services are held on saints' days (*Prestolniy prazdnik*). Orthodox believers cross themselves with three fingers (first the head, then the stomach, followed by the right shoulder and then the left).

Details of services in other Christian, Muslim, Jewish and Buddhist places of worship appear in the Friday edition of the *St Petersburg Times*.

National holidays

National holidays (*prazdnik*) have been a contentious issue since the end of Communism. All the major Soviet ones are still observed, but **May Day**, once a nationwide compulsory march, nowadays sees only die-hard Communists, skinheads and anarchists take to the streets, while the anniversary of the Bolshevik Revolution on **November 7** has been wishfully renamed the Day of Reconciliation and Accord. The only holidays celebrated as in Soviet times are **New Year**, always a family and friends affair; International Women's Day on **March 8**, when Russian men give flowers to their spouses and female acquaintances and make a big fuss of doing the housework for one day of the year; and Victory Day on **May 9**, marked by military parades. Defenders of the Motherland Day on **February 23** was reinstated by Yeltsin as a national holiday, but is more low-key, while Russian Independence Day on **June 12** – the anniversary of Russia's secession from the Soviet Union – has become a feel-good event that tries to please everyone, called Russian Flag Day. And, of course, the

Russian Orthodox Christmas on **January 6–7** is once again a national holiday, although Good Friday is still a working day, much to the Church's annoyance. As Easter is a moveable feast according to the Orthodox calendar, it may coincide with public holidays in May, giving rise to an extended holiday period of three to four days. If public holidays fall at the weekend, a weekday will often be given off in lieu. Some holidays and festivals are celebrated by fireworks, or by the lighting of the flames on the Rostral Columns on the Strelka.

Festivals

No publication or website gives the full rundown of the city's festivals throughout the year. Some events are sure to occur at a certain time, but others drift across the calendar, or vanish in some years. The best you can usually hope for is a month's notice in *Where St Petersburg*, *Pulse* or the *St Petersburg Times*. Nearer the time, events are advertised by posters and banners on the streets.

There are numerous **music festivals**, from jazz (March, April & Nov) to indie or avant-garde (April) – but classical music, ballet and opera claim centre stage during the ten-day **St Petersburg Spring** (May), the **Stars of the White Nights** and the **Palaces of St Petersburg** festivals. These last two run from early June to the end of July or August, through the famous **White Nights** (*Belye nochy*) when the city parties into the small hours, with revellers thronging Nevskiy prospekt and the Neva embankment, where the raising of the bridges from 1.55am onwards occasions much popping of champagne corks. You can rely on nights being short and celebratory for at least two weeks on either side of the "official" White Nights between June 11 and July 2, with a one-day carnival sometime during that period. Other events around the same time include the **Festival of Festivals** international **film** bash, a two-day **beer festival** on Dvortsovaya ploshchad (first weekend in June), the ceremonial opening of the Fountain Season at Peterhof (first Sat or Sun), and the Tsarskoe Selo Carnival at Pushkin (last Sat in June).

St Petersburg celebrates its own foundation on **City Day** (May 27) with brass bands and jolly games at various locales, especially the Peter and Paul Fortress, from which the traditional fireworks display is launched. **May Day** parades went out of fashion during the 1990s but are coming back, while **Victory Day** (May 9), commemorating the surrender of the Nazis in 1945, is still fervently marked by the older generation, with a parade of war veterans down Nevskiy prospekt and wreath-laying ceremonies at the Piskarov Cemetery. The **Siege of Leningrad Day** (Sept 8) and the **anniversary of the breaking of the Blockade** (Jan 27) are also big days for World War II veterans, but not public holidays, while the approach of **Navy Day** (last Sun in July) is heralded by the appearance of warships and subs in the Neva basin. On the day itself, motorboats ferry families out to open days on the warships, while their crews drink and brawl ashore (not a time to wander the streets), and the Rostral Columns are lit at night, augmented by a fireworks display. **Airborne Forces Day** (first Sat in Aug) sees parachute displays, benefit concerts and veterans wearing stripy uniform vests zooming around town in armoured cars. Thankfully, **Defenders of the Motherland Day** (Feb 23) is limited to wreath-laying ceremonies at selected sites, while **Russian Independence Day** (June 12) is enlivened by a pop concert on St Isaac's Square, followed by fireworks.

St Petersburg's vibrant counter-culture is manifest in a **Love Parade** inspired by its Berlin namesake. Some years it takes the form of a parade along Nevskiy; other years there may be cruises to Fort Alexander, off the coast of Kronstadt (see p.370), for a rave with fireworks (mid or late August). Another, still newer, event is the **bikers' festival**, or rival festivals of St Petersburg and Moscow bikers' clubs, on the islands or outside the city, in early August.

The **sports** calendar revolves around soccer, ice hockey and sailing. Depending on how well local **football** teams Lokomotiv and Zenit (see p.192) do in the qualifying and semi-final rounds of the Russian Championship (starting in March and ending in November) and the Russian Cup (starting and finishing in May), there may be more or less action at the Petrovskiy and Kirov stadiums, or the Yubileyniy Sports Palace in the

case of the indoor CIS Cup finals (January). **Ice hockey** comes a close second in popularity: SKA St Petersburg is often a favourite in the run-up to the Spartak Cup in August, in matches at the Yubileyniy Sports Palace or the Ice Palace in Malaya Okhta – even if Russia rarely does so well in the World Championships in July. **Sailing** competitions occur in July and August, with Big Ships coming to St Petersburg every few years. Other festivals focus on **rock-climbing** (early May), **motor racing** (early July), **windsurfing** (late July), **golf** (August) and **tennis** (September).

Despite all the Christmas trees and bunting, Russians ignore the Western Christmas in the rush to prepare for **New Year** (*Noviy God*). This remains a family occasion until midnight, when a frenzied round of house-calling commences, getting steadily more drunken and continuing until dawn. As you cross the Neva, watch out for the blazing torches atop the Rostral Columns. In residential areas, you may see people dressed as *Dyed Moroz* (Grandfather Frost, the Russian equivalent of Father Christmas) and his female sidekick, *Snegurochka* (Snow Maiden), who do the rounds wishing neighbours a Happy New Year (*s Novim Godom!*).

The **Russian Orthodox Christmas** (*Rozhdestvo*) starts at midnight on January 6 and goes on until dawn the following day. The choir, the liturgy, the candles and the incense combine to produce a hypnotic sense of togetherness, or *sobornost*. Despite their emotional charge and Byzantine splendour, Orthodox services are come-and-go as you please, allowing non-believers to attend without embarrassment, but women should cover their heads and wear a skirt. The high point of the Orthodox calendar, though, is **Easter** (*Paskha*), when worshippers exchange triple kisses and the salutation "Christ is risen!" – "Verily He is risen!" For both Easter and Christmas celebrations, the principal churches and the Alexander Nevsky Monastery are packed to the gills.

Less obviously, the **festivals of other faiths** are celebrated in their places of worship. The synagogue on Lermontovskiy prospekt comes alive at Rosh Hashana,

Calendar of holidays, festivals and events

Note: National holidays are marked with an asterisk.

January
New Year's Day (January 1)*.

Orthodox Christmas (January 6–7)*.

Russian Christmas Folklore Festival at the Museum of Wooden Architecture in Novgorod (January 7).

Old New Year (night of January 13/14) according to the Julian calendar, celebrated by traditionalists.

CIS Cup indoor finals or semi-finals, if any St Petersburg team is in the running (sometime in January).

February and March
Defenders of the Motherland Day (February 23)*.

Maslenitsa Traditional feast of pancakes, celebrated at Shuvalovka and Novgorod (one week before the beginning of Lent, usually in late Feb).

Buddhist New Year (late February/early March).

International Women's Day (March 8)*.

International Festival of Jazz Dance and Music (early March).

Prokofiev Young Violinists contest at the Kapella (second half of March).

April and May
Russian Championship and Russian Cup qualifying matches at the Petrovskiy Stadium (early April onwards).

Festival of Russian Theatres from all over the CIS (mid-April).

SKIF festival of indie and avant garde music, DJs and performance artists from Russia and abroad (April).

Orthodox Easter – not a public holiday, but a major celebration (date varies).

International Labour Day/Spring Festival (May 1 and 2)*.

Climbing for Everybody festival on the Karelian Isthmus (early May).

Victory Day (May 9)*.

Sonorous Nightingale children's festival at Vyborg (early or mid-May).

St Petersburg Spring international festival of classical music (mid-May).

Religious procession by water to the St Nicholas Skit on Valaam (May 19).

Day of Slav culture at Novgorod (May 24).

City Day (May 27).

June–August
Stars of the White Nights international festival of ballet, opera and classical music (early June till early August).

Fountain season at Peterhof ceremonially opens (first Sat or Sun in June).

Folklore Festival at Novgorod's Museum of Wooden Architecture (first Sun in June).

Beer festival on Dvortsovaya ploshchad (first weekend in June).

International Arts Festival of music, graphics and poetry at Peterhof and Oranienbaum (early June).

Festival of Festivals international film festival (throughout June).

Russian Independence Day or Russian Flag Day (June 12)*.

Yom Kippur, Hanukkah and other Jewish festivals; the mosque on the Petrograd Side is the focus for Ramadan celebrations (dates vary); and the Buddhist temple across the

Tsarskoe Selo Carnival at Tsarskoe Selo/Pushkin (see p.268), outside the city (last Sat in June).

Sand Sculptures festival on the beach beside the Peter and Paul Fortress (end of June/early July).

Palaces of St Petersburg chamber music and fireworks at Peterhof, Tsarskoe Selo and Pavlovsk (June and July).

LUKoil Cup Formula 1600 racing at the Kirov Stadium (first Sun in July).

Night of Ivana Kupala revels at Lake Ilmen near Novgorod (June 6/7).

White Nights Swing international jazz festival (early July).

Open View (or Open Look) festival of modern dance (early July).

Baltic Cup windsurfing championships at Zelenogorsk on the Gulf of Finland (second half of July).

Musical Olympics for visiting soloists (second half of July).

Baltic Regatta international sailing week, at the Central/River Yacht Club on Petrovskiy Island (second half of July).

Love Parade and **Fortdance** (last week in July).

Knights' Tournament at Vyborg Castle (last weekend in July).

Navy Day (last Sun in July).

Russian Cup matches between current contenders for the cup at the Petrovskiy Stadium (June/August).

Airborne Forces Day (first Sat in August).

Golf National Cup at Solechnoe (first week in August).

Bikers' festivals (early August).

Sailing Week (August).

Consecration of the water at Valaam (August 14).

Festival of the Kizhi Volost on Kizhi (August 23).

Window on Europe film festival at Vyborg (throughout August).

September
Siege of Leningrad Day (September 8).

St Petersburg Open international tennis tournament, at the SKK.

Ice hockey season begins.

Sacred Music Festival in Novgorod (late September).

Early Music Festival at the Kapella and the Menshikov and Sheremetiev palaces (late September till mid-October).

October and November
Baltic House Festival of drama (October).

Fountain season at Peterhof closes (first or second week in October).

Festival of Spanish Music at the Hermitage Theatre (first half of October).

Day of Reconciliation and Accord (November 7)*.

Autumn Rhythms international jazz festival (mid-November).

December
Winter folklore festivities at Shuvalovka, near Strelna (last week in December).

New Year's Eve Carnival at Novgorod (December 31).

river from Yelagin Island is at the heart of events during the sixteen-day Tibetan New Year festival, *Tsagaalgan* (late Feb/early March).

Trouble and the police

St Petersburg's lurid reputation for mafia killings and police corruption is based on fact, but exaggerates its effect on everyday life for most people. Personal security is generally in inverse proportion to personal wealth; those with most to fear are local politicians or rich businessmen. The average citizen – or visitor – is no more likely to be a victim of crime than in any other large European city. Pickpockets are the main hazard, on Nevskiy prospekt and around the major tourist sites.

Avoiding trouble is mostly commonsense. Keep your money in a money-belt under your clothing, and don't carry cameras or other valuables in a bag on your back. Most street robberies involve gangs of child-pickpockets rather than stick-ups or muggings. Sensible precautions include making photocopies of your passport and visa, and noting down traveller's cheque and credit card numbers. If you have a car, don't leave anything in view when you park it, and take the cassette/radio with you. Luggage and valuables left in cars make a tempting target and foreign or rental cars are easy to spot. Vehicles get stolen, too; use guarded parking lots, or park in the inner courtyards of buildings.

Changing money with street hustlers is a sure way to get ripped off, and the Militia couldn't care less about these instances. Getting blind drunk or going back to strange flats with prostitutes is asking for trouble, and neither the Militia nor foreign consulates have much sympathy in such cases. If you're unlucky enough to be robbed you'll need to **go to the police**, if only because your insurance company will require a police report. Few Militia speak any language but Russian; try the phrase *Menya obokrali* – "I've been robbed". There are Militia posts in every metro station.

Generally, the law in Russia is Janus-faced. Bribery is widespread, and few Russians expect cops or judges to be honest. Many regard the police as a predatory force with links to organized crime – a suspicion confirmed in St Petersburg in 2003 with the arrest of two dozen senior detectives, dubbed "Werewolves" by the local press for having "gone over to the dark side". Police corruption at a lower level is manifest in petty **shakedowns**. In a neat Catch-22, you're not obliged to carry **identification** by law, but the police can demand ID and, if not satisfied, take you to a Militia station. Some use this as a licence to hassle people, especially those with darker skins (on grounds of "security") or tourists who might pay a "fine" when something is found to be "wrong" with their documents. It's best to carry your passport and Immigrant Card at all times and be ready to point out that your visa, registration stamp and currency declaration are all in order – which makes it hard for them to find a pretext. If you have a mobile (cell) phone, pull it out and tell the officer you'd like to call your consulate (see p.403) to have somebody meet you at the police station. Do not surrender your passport. In a funnier case of cops on the take, police are known to wait in the Mikhailovskiy Gardens for nocturnal revellers to relieve themselves; they then pounce, threatening arrest unless a "fine" is paid (100 rubles suffices).

Sexual harassment and racism

Sexual harassment is no worse than in Western Europe, but the tendency of Russian men to veer between extreme

Emergencies

The emergency number for the police, ambulance and fire services is ☏01 gallantry and crude chauvinism – and of Russian women to exploit their femininity – makes for misunderstandings when foreigners are involved. Russian women feel secure enough to flag down cars as taxis (see p.37), but foreign women shouldn't risk it. At some clubs and hotels, unaccompanied women are liable to be viewed as prostitutes, hassled by security guards or even by pimps, mistaking them for freelance operators. **Prostitution** is not illegal under Russian law, and most upmarket hotels, bars and nightclubs have prostitutes who'll proposition foreign males and even married couples.

Russians of both sexes regard striptease acts as normal entertainment. Political correctness has barely a toehold in Russian society. **Racism** is a casual and common phenomenon, sometimes expressed violently, mostly against Roma, Chechens, Azerbaijanis and Central Asians, but also Africans and Arabs. Anyone dark-skinned can expect to be stopped by the Militia on a regular basis.

The police

The Ministry of the Interior (MVD) maintains several law-and-order forces, all of them armed and with a high profile on the streets. Foremost are the regular police, or **Militia** (*Militsiya*), in blue-grey uniforms with red bands on their caps, or jumpsuits and parkas in shades of grey. Militiamen are much in evidence around metro stations, where they often conduct spot ID checks.

The other main branch of the Militia is the **GIBDD**, or traffic police – still universally known by its former title, the GAI – who you're likely to run into only if you're driving or happen to be involved in an accident (see p.38). They wear Militia uniforms emblazoned with a badge, armband or large white letters reading ДПС (standing for *Dorozhno*

Patrulnaya Sluzhba, or Highway Patrol Service).

Some checkpoints are also manned by the **OMON**, a paramilitary force charged with the responsibility of everything from riot control to counter-insurgency. In St Petersburg, they guard important state buildings, patrol crowds and lend muscle to Militia crackdowns on Mafia gangs. Dressed in green or grey camouflage and toting Kalashnikovs or pump-action shotguns, they look fearsome but are unlikely to bother tourists unless they get caught up in a raid of some kind. Should you be so unlucky, don't resist in any way – even verbally. The same goes for operations involving **RUOP**, the smaller Regional Force Against Organized Crime, whose teams wear civilian clothes or paramilitary uniforms like the OMON's, only the patch on the back reads РУОП instead of ОМОН.

Aside from maybe having your passport scrutinized by a plainclothes agent at Pulkovo airport, you shouldn't have any contact with the once-feared KGB in its post-Soviet incarnation as the **Federal Security Service** (FSB) unless you get involved in environmental activism or high-tech acquisitions. The FSB has now regained the powers of the KGB in the 1970s, thanks to its former boss, President Putin, but it no longer intervenes in the lives of ordinary Russians, who are happy to ignore it. Visitors are free to do likewise, or saunter past the Bolshoy dom (see p.205) out of curiosity (taking photos is not advised).

You're far more likely to encounter **private security guards** in banks, stores, clubs or restaurants. They are allowed to carry guns, but have no powers of arrest and you're not legally obliged to show them ID. However, since many wear paramilitary garb, you may find it hard to distinguish them from the OMON (who have full police powers); private guards usually wear an ОХРАНА badge.

Travellers with disabilities

The needs of disabled citizens in Russia were largely ignored in the past, and the chronic shortage of funds has hindered progress even now in places where attitudes have changed. Wheelchair access to most of the major international hotels in St Petersburg is possible with some assistance, but only the *Grand Hotel Europe* and the *Nevsky Palace* (the city's most expensive hotels) are fully wheelchair-accessible. Of the city's museums, only the Hermitage and the Russian Museum have ramps or lifts for wheelchairs.

Transport is a major problem, since buses, trams and trolleybuses are virtually impossible to get onto with a wheelchair, and the metro and suburban train systems only slightly better. Of the theatres and museums, only the Teatr na Liteynom is wheelchair-accessible. It's worth noting that disabled customers (along with war veterans) are permitted to jump the queues in all shops.

Contacts for travellers with disabilities

UK and Ireland

Access Travel 6 The Hillock, Astley, Lancashire M29 7GW ☎01942/888 844, ✆www.access-travel .co.uk. Tour operator that can arrange flights, transfers and accommodation, personally checked out before recommendation.
Holiday Care 2nd floor, Imperial Building, Victoria Rd, Horley, Surrey RH6 7PZ ☎01293/774 535, Minicom ☎01293/776 943, ✆www.holidaycare .org.uk. Provides free lists of accessible accommodation abroad. Information on financial help for holidays available.
Irish Wheelchair Association Blackheath Drive, Clontarf, Dublin 3 ☎01/833 8241, ✉iwa@iol.ie. Useful information provided about travelling abroad with a wheelchair.
Tripscope Alexandra House, Albany Rd, Brentford, Middlesex TW8 0NE ☎0845/758 5641, ✆www.justmobility.co.uk/tripscope, ✉tripscope@cabinet.co.uk. This registered charity provides a national telephone information service offering free advice on UK and international transport for those with a mobility problem.

US and Canada

Access-Able ✆www.access-able.com. Online resource for travellers with disabilities.
Directions Unlimited 123 Green Lane, Bedford Hills, NY 10507 ☎1-800/533-5343 or 914/241-1700. Tour operator specializing in custom tours for people with disabilities.
Mobility International USA 451 Broadway, Eugene, OR 97401, voice and TDD ☎541/343-1284, ✆www.miusa.org. Information and referral services, access guides, tours and exchange programmes. Annual membership $35 (includes quarterly newsletter).
Society for the Advancement of Travelers with Handicaps (SATH) 347 5th Ave, New York, NY 10016 ☎212/447-7284, ✆www.sath.org. Non-profit educational organization that has actively represented travellers with disabilities since 1976.
Travel Information Service ☎215/456-9600. Telephone-only information and referral service for disabled travellers.
Twin Peaks Press Box 129, Vancouver, WA 98661 ☎360/694-2462 or ☎1-800/637-2256, ✆www .twinpeak.virtualave.net. Publisher of the *Directory of Travel Agencies for the Disabled* ($19.95), listing more than 370 agencies worldwide; the *Directory of Accessible Van Rentals* ($12.95); and *Wheelchair Vagabond* ($19.95), loaded with personal tips.
Wheels Up! ☎1-888/389-4335, ✆www.wheelsup.com. Provides discount air fare, tour and cruise prices for disabled travellers, publishes a free monthly newsletter and has a comprehensive website.

Australia and New Zealand

ACROD (Australian Council for Rehabilitation of the Disabled) PO Box 60, Curtin, ACT 2605 ☎02/6282 4333; Suite 103, 1st floor, 1-5 Commercial Rd, Kings Grove 2208 ☎02/9554 3666. Provides lists of travel agencies and tour operators for people with disabilities.
Disabled Persons Assembly 4/173–175 Victoria St, Wellington ☎04/801 9100. Resource centre with lists of travel agencies and tour operators for people with disabilities.

The City

The City

Within the Fontanka

T he heart of St Petersburg is circumscribed by the seven-kilometre-long River Fontanka and the broader River Neva, which separates it from Vasilevskiy Island and the Petrograd Side. Concentrated on this oval of land **within the Fontanka** are some of the city's greatest monuments – the Winter Palace, the Admiralty and the Bronze Horseman, the Engineers' Castle, the Summer Palace and Garden, and the cathedrals of St Isaac and Our Lady of Kazan – as well as the art collections of the Hermitage and the Russian Museum; the Mariinskiy Theatre (better known as the Kirov); the Gostiniy and Apraksin bazaars; and a whole host of former palaces associated with the good, the bad and the downright weird.

The area is defined by a fan of avenues, chief among them Nevskiy prospekt, which radiate from the Admiralty, interwoven with canals spanned by elegant bridges. The area's historical associations practically peel off the walls: here, unbridled rulers and profligate aristocrats once held sway, poets were driven to suicide, murderers wept in remorse and revolutionaries plotted assassinations. Nowadays, fronds of algae floating beneath the surface of the jet-black or mildew-green water enhance the general air of dereliction, confirmed in the backstreets by stray cats, scrawny crows and gaggles of drunks.

There are enough sights within the Fontanka to keep you busy for days – as well as most of the city's restaurants, theatres, concert halls, banks, airline offices and swankiest hotels. All in all, you're likely to spend much of your time in this area, and largely judge St Petersburg on the strength of it.

Canals and bridges

All the waterways in the centre of St Petersburg resemble **canals** whether they're man-made or not, having been lined with granite **embankments** (*naberezhnaya*) during the reign of Catherine the Great. Their beauty is enhanced by **bridges** whose charms are conveyed by names such as the "Bridge of Kisses" (Potseluev most) and the "Singer's Bridge" (Pevcheskiy most): for a view at water-level, take one of the **cruises** from Anichkov most on the Fontanka, Kazanskiy most on the Griboedov Canal, or Politseyskiy most on the Moyka. As for **addresses**, remember that even numbers are always on the south side of the canal or river, odd numbers on the opposite (north) embankment. On Nevskiy prospekt, however, even numbers are on the north side of the avenue, and buildings are numbered starting from the Admiralty.

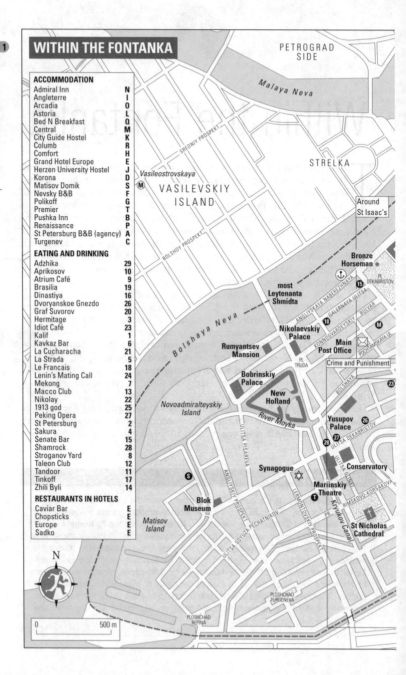

WITHIN THE FONTANKA

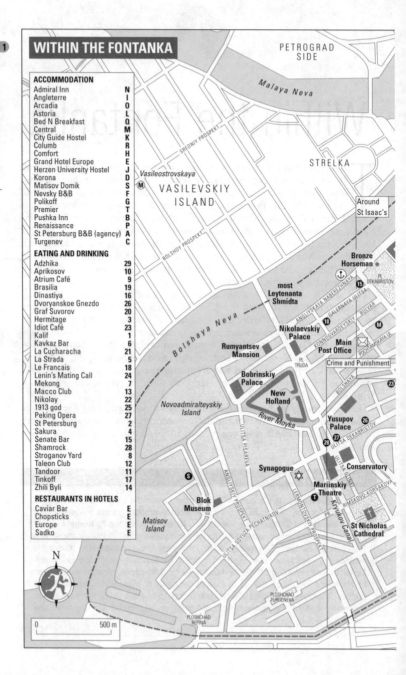

ACCOMMODATION

Admiral Inn	N
Angleterre	I
Arcadia	O
Astoria	L
Bed N Breakfast	Q
Central	M
City Guide Hostel	K
Columb	R
Comfort	H
Grand Hotel Europe	E
Herzen University Hostel	J
Korona	D
Matisov Domik	S
Nevsky B&B	F
Polikoff	G
Premier	T
Pushka Inn	B
Renaissance	P
St Petersburg B&B (agency)	A
Turgenev	C

EATING AND DRINKING

Adzhika	29
Aprikosov	10
Atrium Café	9
Brasilia	19
Dinastiya	16
Dvoryanskoe Gnezdo	26
Graf Suvorov	20
Hermitage	3
Idiot Café	23
Kalif	1
Kavkaz Bar	6
La Cucharacha	21
La Strada	5
Le Francais	18
Lenin's Mating Call	24
Mekong	7
Macco Club	13
Nikolay	22
1913 god	25
Peking Opera	27
St Petersburg	2
Sakura	4
Senate Bar	15
Shamrock	28
Stroganov Yard	8
Taleon Club	12
Tandoor	11
Tinkoff	17
Zhili Byli	14

RESTAURANTS IN HOTELS

Caviar Bar	E
Chopsticks	E
Europe	E
Sadko	E

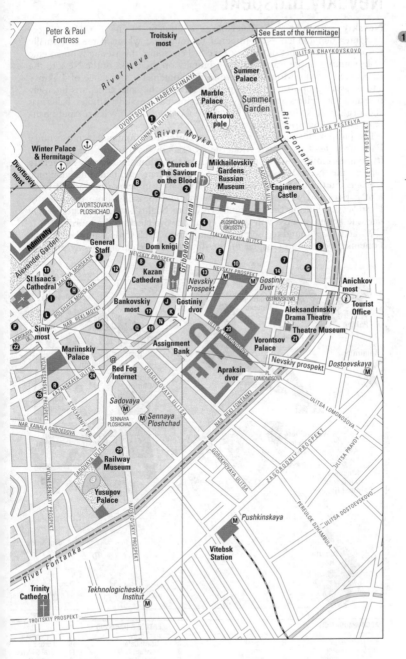

Peter & Paul
Fortress

See East of the Hermitage

ULITSA CHAYKOVSKOVO

Troitskiy
most

River Neva

Summer
Palace

Marble
Palace

DVORTSOVAYA NABEREZHNAYA

MILLIONNAYA ULITSA

River Moyka

Summer
Garden

River Fontanka

ULITSA PESTELYA

LITEYNIY PROSPEKT

Winter Palace
& Hermitage

Mársovo
pole

Dvortsoviy
most

Church of
the Saviour
on the Blood

Mikhailovskiy
Gardens
Russian
Museum

SADOVAYA ULITSA

DVORTSOVAYA
PLOSHCHAD

Canal

PLOSHCHAD
ISKUSSTV

ITALYANSKAYA ULITSA

Engineers'
Castle

Admiralty

Alexander Garden

General
Staff

Dom knigi

Griboedov

NEVSKIY PROSPEKT

NEVSKIY PROSPEKT

Nevskiy
Prospekt

St Isaac's
Cathedral

MALAYA MORSKAYA

Kazan
Cathedral

Gostiniy
Dvor

Anichkov
most

BOLSHAYA MORSKAYA

Bankovskiy
most

Gostiniy
dvor

OSTROVSKOVO

Tourist
Office

NAB. REKI MOYKI

Assignment
Bank

Aleksandrinskiy
Drama Theatre

Theatre Museum

Siniy
most

MORSKAYA UL.

ULITSA ZODCHEGO ROSSI

Vorontsov
Palace

Mariinskiy
Palace

VOZNESENSKIY PROSPEKT

Red Fog
Internet

GOROKHOVAYA ULITSA

Apraksin
dvor

Nevskiy prospekt

Dostoevskaya

KAZANSKAYA ULITSA

STOLYARNIY PER.

Sadovaya

SENNAYA
PLOSHCHAD

Sennaya
Ploshchad

NAB. REKI FONTANKI

LOMONOSOVA

ULITSA LOMONOSOVA

NAB. KANALA GRIBOEDOVA

SADOVAYA ULITSA

Railway
Museum

MOSKOVSKIY PROSPEKT

GOROKHOVAYA ULITSA

ZAGORODNIY PROSPEKT

ULITSA PRAVDY

Yusupov
Palace

PEREULOK DZHAMBULA

ULITSA DOSTOEVSKOVO

Pushkinskaya

River Fontanka

Vitebsk
Station

Trinity
Cathedral

Tekhnologicheskiy
Institut

TROITSKIY PROSPEKT

VOZNESENSKIY PROSPEKT

Nevskiy prospekt

Nevskiy prospekt is St Petersburg's equivalent of the Champs Élysées or Unter den Linden – an Imperial thoroughfare whose name is virtually synonymous with that of the city. Like St Petersburg, the avenue is on an epic scale, running all the way from the Admiralty on the banks of the Neva to the Alexander Nevsky Monastery beyond the Fontanka – a distance of 4.5km – and measuring up to 60m wide in places. Yet, at the same time, it is intensely human in its foibles and failings, juxtaposing palaces and potholes, ballerinas and beggars – as Gogol wrote in *Tales of Good and Evil*, "What a rapid phantasmagoria passes over it in a single day!"

The prospekt manifests every style of **architecture** from eighteenth-century Baroque to *fin-de-siècle* Style Moderne (Russia's own version of Art Nouveau), its skyline culminating in the golden spire of the Admiralty. Nevskiy's **streetlife** reflects the New Russia: bemedalled war veterans promenading alongside teenagers in the latest fashions; cadets linking arms in beery camaraderie; barefoot gypsies and wild-eyed drunks like *muzhiks* (peasants) from the pages of Dostoyevsky. During the midsummer "White Nights", when darkness barely falls, the avenue is busy with people, even at two o'clock in the morning.

While you're bound to use public transport to reach some sights beyond the Fontanka (covered in Chapter 6), the downtown stretch of Nevskiy prospekt

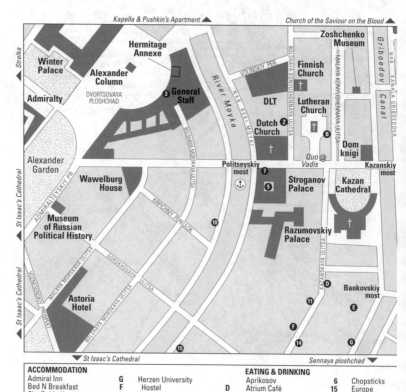

ACCOMMODATION				EATING & DRINKING	
Admiral Inn	G	Herzen University		Aprikosov	6	Chopsticks
Bed N Breakfast	F	Hostel	D	Atrium Café	15	Europe
City Guide Hostel	E	Korona	B	Brasilia	14	Graf Suvorov
Grand Hotel Europe	A	Polikoff	C	Caviar Bar	A	Hermitage

can really only be appreciated on foot. The least demanding approach involves taking the **metro** to Gostiniy Dvor or Nevskiy Prospekt station, and **walking** the 1.5km to Dvortsovaya ploshchad (Palace Square) – an itinerary with Kazan Cathedral and two stunning canal vistas as its highlights. A longer (2.4km) but even more rewarding option is to start from Mayakovskaya metro station, 600m beyond the River Fontanka, then catch a **bus** (#22), **trolleybus** (#1, #5, #7, #10 or #22) or **minibus** (#K-47, #K-147, #K-187) or walk up to Anichkov most and proceed from there. Whichever approach you choose, the chief **landmarks** are the glass cupola and globe of Dom knigi; the green dome of Kazan Cathedral; and the gilded spire of the Admiralty.

This account progresses from Anichkov most on the Fontanka towards the Winter Palace and the Admiralty. To describe Nevskiy prospekt's sights roughly in the order in which they appear, it switches from one side of the road to the other more often than you're likely to do in practice, and merely alludes to various **turn-offs** that receive fuller coverage later in the text.

Some history

Like so much in the city, the prospekt was built during the reign of Peter the Great under the direction of a foreigner, in this case the Frenchman Jean-Baptiste Le Blond, who ploughed through 4km of forests and meadows to connect the newly built Admiralty with the Novgorod road (now Ligovskiy

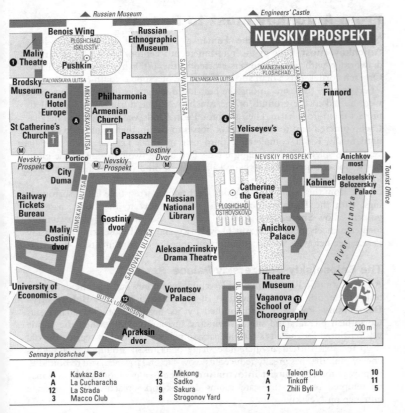

A	Kavkaz Bar	2	Mekong	4	Taleon Club	10
A	La Cucharacha	13	Sadko	A	Tinkoff	11
12	La Strada	9	Sakura	1	Zhili Byli	5
3	Macco Club	8	Strogonov Yard	7		

prospekt). It was constructed by Swedish prisoners of war (who then had to clean it every Saturday), and the prospekt's grand view suggested its original title, the "Great Perspective Road", changed in 1738 to Nevskaya perspektivnaya ulitsa, after the River Neva to which it leads, and shortened to its present name twenty years later. The Bolsheviks renamed it "25 October Avenue" (after the date of the Revolution), but this was effectively ignored by the city's inhabitants, and in 1944 the avenue officially reverted to its previous name.

The contrast between Nevskiy's past and present state is illuminating. During the nineteenth century, its pavements were kept clean by the simple expedient of forcing all the prostitutes arrested during the night to sweep the street at 4am. On every corner stood a wooden box housing three policemen, who slept and ate there, and the prospekt's length was festooned with pictorial store signs, depicting the merchandise for the benefit of illiterate passers-by. All traffic was horse-drawn, a "wild, bounding sea of carriages" which sped silently over the snow in winter. The impact of war and revolution was brought home to British agent Sidney Reilly when, returning after the tsar's overthrow, he found the Nevskiy almost deserted, unswept for weeks and strewn with the bodies of horses that had starved to death. Today, Nevskiy looks as prosperous and thriving as it did in Russia's so-called "best year" – 1913 – when the Empire celebrated the tercentenary of the Romanov dynasty, blissfully unaware of the disasters to come.

From Anichkov most to Passazh

Nevskiy prospekt crosses the Fontanka by way of the 54-metre-long **Anichkov most**, built in the mid-nineteenth century to replace a narrow drawbridge with wooden towers erected in the 1700s by Colonel Anichkov. On each corner rears a dramatic bronze statue of a supple youth trying to tame a fiery steed – these are among the best-loved sculptures in St Petersburg, and were buried in the grounds of the Anichkov Palace during World War II to protect them from harm. Their sculptor, Pyotr Klodt, was plagued by Nicholas I, who ordered him to send a pair of horses to Berlin, then another to Naples, until finally, Klodt completed a third pair in 1850. Legend has it that he vented his spleen by depicting the tsar's face in the swollen veins of the groin of the horse nearest the Anichkov Palace (or, in other versions, his own wife's lover, or Napoleon).

Aside from this wonderfully sly dig, the bridge is irresistible for its surroundings, with the Fontanka curving majestically away to the north, past the golden-yellow **Sheremetev Palace** (see p.199). South of the bridge two more former princely piles – the Anichkov Palace and the Beloselskiy-Belozerskiy Palace (see below) – vie for attention on opposite embankments.

The Beloselskiy-Belozerskiy Palace

An anachronistic Rococo masterpiece built by Andrey Stakenschneider in the mid-nineteenth century heyday of Neoclassicism, the **Beloselskiy-Belozerskiy Palace** is distinguished by its bearded, muscled atlantes, its Corinthian pilasters and sinuous window surrounds. Sadly, when the facade was repainted for the city's tercentenary, somebody decided to replace the old deep red that turned an incredible shade of crimson around sunset with a cheesy pink that has greatly reduced its wow-factor. However, you're bound to stop by at the city **tourist information office** (see p.30 for details) and may be tempted to visit the state rooms or waxworks, reached by a separate entrance on Nevskiy.

Of the many waxwork shows in St Petersburg, those in the Beloselskiy-Belozerskiy Palace are the best. They are arranged into two exhibitions (daily 11am–6pm; $3 each), between them spanning a thousand years of Russian history and featuring tableaux depicting significant historical events. The figures are unusually lifelike; some of the faces were modelled on the actual skulls or death masks of the personages they represent. Two surprising inclusions are Casanova and Baron Münchhausen, both of whom visited St Petersburg in the days of Catherine the Great.

The upstairs **state rooms** (11am–6pm; $3) are sometimes closed on Saturday or Sunday, or for concerts, and you may have to wait for enough visitors to form a group for a tour in Russian. The palace's last residents were Grand Duke Sergei and Elizabeth of Hesse. After Sergei was killed by Nihilists in 1905, Elizabeth retired from society, founded a convent and became its abbess – which didn't dissuade the Bolsheviks from throwing her down a mineshaft in 1918. She was canonized as a saint of the Russian Orthodox Church, and her body now rests in Jerusalem.

On the **grand staircase**, note the strategically placed mirror that enabled Elizabeth to observe guests arriving and prepare to greet her favourites. A series of reception rooms culminates in an audience hall and a ballroom (used for concerts). The palace's original **concert hall** has splendid oak panelling, filigree work and a ceiling with pendentive flowers and stucco traceries in the Eclectic style of the 1880s.

The Anichkov Palace

Across the Fontanka lies a larger, Neoclassical ensemble comprising the **Kabinet**, or Chancellery, established by Alexander I, and the cream-coloured **Anichkov Palace**, named after the colonel who set up an encampment here when the city was founded. In 1741, the site was purchased by Empress Elizabeth to build a palace for her lover, Alexei Razumovsky, a Ukrainian chorister whom she may have secretly married (his nickname was "the night-time Emperor"), while Catherine the Great subsequently presented the palace to her own favourite, Potemkin. In 1817, the future Nicholas I moved in, setting a precedent for the rest of the century, during which it was home for heirs to the throne. In Soviet times the building became the Palace of Pioneers and Youth, now renamed the **Palace of Youth Creativity**. The palace is usually only open for concerts and other special events; the entrance is through the wrought-iron gates on Nevskiy prospekt.

Ploshchad Ostrovskovo

A little further up Nevskiy comes the first of the set-piece squares opening off the prospekt. Laid out by Carlo Rossi in 1828–34, the square is now called **ploshchad Ostrovskovo** after the dramatist Nikolai Ostrovsky, but some still refer to it by its pre-revolutionary name of Aleksandrinskaya ploshchad (after Nicholas I's wife, Alexandra). Locals, however, have always called it "Katkin sad" ("Katya's Garden"), after the **statue of Catherine the Great** that was erected here in 1873. Matvey Chizhov and Alexander Opekushin sculpted the ermine-robed empress almost twice as large as the figures of her favourites and advisers clustered around the pedestal, including Prince Potemkin – who grinds a Turkish turban underfoot as he chats to Marshal Suvorov – and Princess Dashkova, the first female president of the Russian Academy of Sciences. Somewhat surprisingly, this is the only statue of Catherine in St Petersburg.

Catherine the Great

Catherine the Great of Russia (1729–96) always disclaimed that sobriquet, insisting that she was merely Catherine II, but posterity has insisted upon it. She was born Princess Sophie of Anhalt-Zerbst, in northern Germany, on May 2, 1729, and married at the age of 15 to the 16-year-old Russian heir apparent, Peter. The marriage was a dismal failure, and the belated birth of a son and heir, Paul, probably owed more to the first of Catherine's lovers than to her husband, the future Tsar **Peter III**. Notwithstanding this, Catherine strove to make herself acceptable to the Russian court and people, unlike her husband, who made his contempt for both – and her – obvious, until their worsening relations made conflict inevitable. On July 28, 1762, with the assistance of the Orlov brothers and the support of the Guards, Catherine staged a coup, forced Peter to abdicate, and proclaimed herself ruler; Peter was murdered by the Orlovs a few days later.

Her reign was initially characterized by enlightened absolutism: under Catherine's patronage, works of philosophy, literature and science were translated into Russian; hospitals, orphanages, journals and academies founded; roads, canals and palaces built. The Crimea was annexed to Russia, in which quest she was greatly assisted by Prince Potemkin, who planted the Tsarist flag on the shores of the Black Sea, having beaten back the forces of the Ottoman Empire.

Later, however, Catherine's reactionary instincts surfaced, as the French Revolution turned her against any hint of egalitarianism and towards the Orthodox Church. Meanwhile, she gradually lost her taste for older, masterful lovers such as Orlov and Potemkin, opting for ever younger, more pliable "favourites". Estimates of their number range from 12 to 54, and although Catherine was probably no more promiscuous than the average male European sovereign, she was judged by the standards set by the self-righteous Habsburg Empress Maria Theresa, the so-called "Virgin of Europe". For more about Catherine's life, see the accounts of the Winter Palace (p.76), Peterhof (p.255), Tsarskoe Selo (p.264) and Oranienbaum (p.261).

Along the right-hand side of the square is the dove-grey Ionic facade of the **Russian National Library** (Mon–Fri 9am–9pm, Sat & Sun 11am–7pm), crowned with a figure of Minerva, goddess of wisdom, and garnished with statues of philosophers. This Rossi-built extension of Petersburg's first public library, opened in 1814, holds such treasures as Voltaire's library (purchased by Catherine the Great) and a postage stamp-sized edition of *Krylov's Fables*, so clearly printed that it can be read with the naked eye. A plaque on the Nevskiy side of the library attests that Lenin was a regular visitor between 1893 and 1895. His predilection for its weighty tomes is commemorated by a joke involving his wife, Krupskaya, and his lover, Inessa, in which he tells each that he will be seeing the other so that he can slope off to read in the library.

Behind the statue of Catherine stands Rossi's *tour de force*, the **Aleksandriinskiy Drama Theatre**, its straw-coloured facade decorated with a columned loggia topped by a statue of Apollo in his chariot, and flanked by niche-bound statues of the muses Terpsichore and Melpomene. Renamed the Pushkin Theatre on the centenary of the poet Alexander Pushkin's death in 1937, the theatre once again bears its original title, though the facade has two plaques, one with each name. The theatre company here can trace its history back to 1756, making it the oldest in Russia. While Gogol's *The Government Inspector* caused a sensation at its first staging in 1836, Chekhov's *The Seagull* was so badly received at its premiere in 1896 that he fled the theatre to wander anonymously among the crowds on Nevskiy.

The Theatre Museum and Vaganova School of Choreography

Behind the theatre, at pl. Ostrovskovo 6, a small **Theatre Museum** (Mon & Thurs–Sun 11am–6pm, Wed 1–7pm; closed Tues & the last Fri of each month; $2) exhibits items belonging to the opera singer Fyodor Chaliapin, the choreographer Marius Pepita and other stars of the Russian stage; Rimsky-Korsakov's annotated scores and Tchaikovsky's letters; costume sketches by Bakst and a half-life-sized replica of a Constructivist stage set designed for the Moscow Theatre in the early 1920s. Ask an attendant to open the **ballet room**, holding costumes from the first production of *The Sleeping Beauty*. From September to May, weekly **concerts** are held in the museum, employing the piano on which Tchaikovsky once played.

Next door stands the **Vaganova School of Choreography**, probably the world's finest classical ballet school, which has produced dancers such as Anna Pavlova, Tamara Karsavina, Vaslav Nijinsky, Galina Ulanova, Rudolf Nureyev and Mikhail Baryshnikov. Its origins go back to 1738, when J.B. Landé began to train the children of palace servants to take part in court entertainments, though it wasn't until 1934 that a modern curriculum was implemented by the Russian choreographer Agrippina Vaganova (1879–1951), nicknamed the "Empress of Variations". Over two thousand young hopefuls apply to the school every year, of which only ninety are chosen to undergo its gruelling regime.

The school is located on **ulitsa Zodchevo Rossi** (Master-builder Rossi Street). Of all the architect's creations, this street is the most perfectly proportioned: exactly as wide as the height of its buildings (22m) and ten times as long, with every facade, paving stone and lamppost exactly mirroring those on the opposite side of the street. At the far end is the crescent-shaped **ploshchad Lomonosova**, another of Rossi's designs, whose severe buildings used to house the Tsarist ministries of the Interior and Public Instruction.

Malaya Sadovaya, Yeliseyev's and Passazh

Returning to Nevskiy, you can cross the avenue by an **underpass** at the junction with Sadovaya ulitsa, where teenage **musicians** play to their friends and passers-by into the small hours of the night. Turn right up the ramp on the far side and you'll emerge by the 24-hour café *Zhili Byli*, followed shortly by **Malaya Sadovaya ulitsa**, running north off Nevskiy. This trendy pedestrianized street has several outdoor beer dens and cute little **statues**. Cast your eyes to the second-floor ledges of the houses 20m off Nevskiy, to espy a male **black cat**, destined never to meet the female **white cat** across the way. At street level there's a bronze memorial to **Karl Bulla**, whose photos of St Petersburg in the last decade of the Tsarist era are classics. Also check out the **courtyards** of no. 3 and no. 4; the former has a statue of the deceased **dog** of a local artist, while the latter has a nice **kids' playground** and Style Moderne ironwork, showing what can be done if the tenants pool their funds and keep the courtyard neat and clean.

On the corner of Malaya Sadovaya and Nevskiy stands the St Petersburg branch of the famous pre-revolutionary food store, **Yeliseyev's** (Mon–Fri 10am–9pm, Sat & Sun 11am–9pm), baldly designated "Gastronom No. 1" during the Soviet period. Designed by Yuri Baranovsky in 1902–3, it's one of the most stunning Style Moderne buildings in the city. The interior, at its best in the delicatessen to the left of the entrance passage, has been preserved more or less intact. Intricate gold filigree work adorns the high ceiling, which is festooned with crystal fairy lights, while from the walls wrought-iron flowers burst forth, culminating in a gracefully drooping chandelier.

Returning to the underpass and crossing Sadovaya ulitsa, you'll find the northern side of Nevskiy rife with hoardings advertising two emporiums on the same block. At no. 48, **Passazh** (Mon–Sat 10am–9pm, Sun 11am–9pm) is a 180-metre-long, galleried shopping arcade built in 1846 for St Petersburg's upper classes, selling porcelain, antiques, shoes and cosmetics. Its canary-yellow walls are offset by maroon marble surrounds, topped by a glass canopy like that of GUM in Moscow. More opulent but less elegant is the newly opened **Grand Palace** (daily 11am–9pm) at no. 44, a quadruple-level marbled mall of French and Italian designer stores, aimed at "New Russians" who can afford to spend $500 on a pair of shoes. (A New Russian joke goes like this: two guys buy identical ties at different shops, and one brags to the other that his cost twice as much.) Both malls exit on Italyanskaya ulitsa, off ploshchad Iskusstv, so can be used as shortcuts to the Russian Museum (p.141).

Gostiniy dvor to the Griboedov Canal

On the other side of Nevskiy, the eighteenth-century **Gostiniy dvor** (daily 10am–10pm) is a central point of reference, its columned arcades dominating the junction with Sadovaya and extending for 230m along the prospekt. It took over sixty years to complete, and derived its name and inspiration from the *gostiniy dvory*, or "merchants' hostels", of Old Russia, offering lodgings and storage space, besides serving as a bazaar where each product was allocated a specific area – there was even one for the sale of stolen goods, which buyers entered at their peril. Nineteenth-century visitors were also warned that the average merchant reckoned that "the worse his wares, the sooner will his customers want to renew their stock", while the doormen were "by no means content with verbally inviting the stranger to walk in", but grabbed their "arm, or coat-tails, without ceremony". The **interior** is nearly a kilometre in circumference and its upper level nowadays mostly contains boutiques selling furs and designer clothes, while the gallery around the outside offers fine views of the area and features several cafés. During maintenance work on the gallery in 1965, the authorities discovered over 300 pounds of gold hidden by merchants.

Outside the dvor on Nevskiy, you'll see "**Red Grannies**" selling far-left and far-right newspapers, and people touting **coach excursions** around St Petersburg and to the Imperial palaces, run by several tourist companies with **kiosks** near Dumskaya ulitsa (see p.40 for details).

Dumskaya ulitsa and the Portico

Dumskaya ulitsa, on the western side of Gostiniy dvor, is one of the few downtown locations that rates a **warning**, as short-change artists and other crooks lurk outside the exchange offices and Luigi Rossa's elegant Neoclassical **Portico** (now a theatre booking office), refreshing themselves at the basic 24-hour street **café** out front. Nearby is the entrance to an underpass leading to Nevskiy Prospekt metro station – look out for the excellent blind accordionist and the groups of old ladies singing Russian folk songs in the traditional harsh *gortan* style.

The street is named after the former seat of the **City Duma**, or pre-revolutionary municipal government, one of the few elected institutions in Petrograd until it was suppressed by the Bolsheviks in October 1918 – an event deemed worthy of a plaque in Soviet times. The Duma's triple-tiered red-and-white **tower** was erected in 1804 to give warning of fires, and later adapted for semaphore and heliograph signalling between St Petersburg and the Imperial palaces outside the city; ironically, it caught fire in 2000 and has yet to be repaired – billboards mask the damage.

From the Armenian Church to St Catherine's

In Tsarist times Nevskiy prospekt was dubbed the "Street of Tolerance", owing to the variety of non-Orthodox denominations that were allowed to build their churches here. Across the road from Gostiniy dvor stands the **Armenian Church** (Armyanskaya tserkov), an azure Neoclassical edifice, built in the 1770s by the German-born architect Felten, and set back from the street in its own courtyard. Converted into a workshop during Soviet times, it has now been restored as a place of worship, with a simple yet elegant decor of pastel colours and fake marble. Notice the fountain in the yard, resembling a silvered bouquet of pomegranates and grapes.

Near the church, the broad, tree-lined **Mikhailovskaya ulitsa** forms a grand approach to ploshchad Iskusstv and the Mikhailovskiy Palace (which contains the Russian Museum; see p.141) beyond. The whole of the western side of the street is occupied by the de luxe **Grand Hotel Europe** (Yevropeyskaya), built in 1873–75 but greatly altered by the Art Nouveau architect Fyodor Lidval. Turned into an orphanage after the Civil War, it was totally refurbished in the 1980s by a Swedish-Russian joint venture. The hotel's bar-restaurant, *Sadko*, is a comfortable place to sit and watch the world go by on Nevskiy.

Further up the prospekt, amid the next block and set back slightly from the street, **St Catherine's Church** (Kostyol Svyatoy Yekateriny) was St Petersburg's main Roman Catholic church. Its steps have now been taken over by street artists, and inside it harbours the tombs of **General Moreau**, a Frenchman who fought on the Russian side against Napoleon and died after losing his leg in the Battle of Dresden (1813), and **Stanislaw Poniatowski**, the last king of Poland. Enthroned by his erstwhile lover, Catherine the Great, Poniatowski subsequently died fighting the Russians near Leipzig, but was buried in St Petersburg. In 1938, his remains were repatriated and secretly interred in eastern Poland, before being dug up yet again and transferred to Warsaw's Royal Castle, where they remain to this day, stashed away in a coffin out of sight and still denied a decent burial, since many Poles regard him as a traitor.

At the end of the block, on the corner of the Griboedov embankment, **Nevskiy Prospekt metro station** is a focal point for teenagers, old women selling cigarettes, and boozers, who dub it "the climate" (*klimat*), because of the warm air blowing from its vestibule – a blessing during the Russian winter.

Crossing the Griboedov Canal: Dom knigi

The wide expanse of **Kazanskiy most** (Kazan Bridge) carries Nevskiy prospekt across the **Griboedov Canal** (kanal Griboedova). Originally called the "Krivushchy" ("twisting river"), it was canalized and embanked under Catherine the Great and henceforth nicknamed the "Katinka Kanavka", or "Catherine's Gutter", flowing as it did through the heart of the notorious Haymarket district, until the Soviets renamed it after the writer Alexander Griboedov (see p.220). It's worth lingering to admire the superb **views** along the canal. To the left, beyond the colonnades of Kazan Cathedral, you might be able to glimpse **Bankovskiy most** (Bank Bridge), with its gilded griffons (see p.103), while to the right are the multicoloured onion domes of the **Church of the Saviour on the Blood** (p.82). If the view tempts you onto the water, private **motorboats** can be rented from the northeastern embankment in summer for trips along the canals (see p.40 for details).

Looming above the northwestern corner of Kazanskiy most is the former emporium of the American sewing-machine company, Singer, now St Petersburg's largest bookstore, **Dom knigi** (Mon–Sat 9am–11pm, Sun till 10pm). Designed by Pavel Syusor and completed in 1904, its Style Moderne exterior is distinguished by a conical tower topped by the Singer trademark: a giant glass globe, which used to light up at night. Now an established and well-loved landmark, it was thought to be in bad taste at the time – an Imperial decree stating that all secular buildings had to be two metres lower than the Winter Palace thwarted Singer's plan for an eleven-storey structure, but failed to scotch the entire project. Before the Revolution, women used to work at sewing machines in the windows to pull in the crowds. Although the interior has been greatly altered since then, some of the original ornamentation survives, notably the brass ivy entwined around the wrought-iron banisters.

Kazan Cathedral

Kazan Cathedral (Kazanskiy sobor) is one of the grandest churches in the city, its curvaceous colonnades embracing Nevskiy prospekt like the out-stretched wings of a gigantic eagle. The cathedral was built between 1801 and 1811 to house a venerated icon, Our Lady of Kazan, reputed to have appeared miraculously overnight in Kazan in 1579, and brought by Peter the Great to St Petersburg, where it resided until its miraculous disappearance in 1904. Although the cathedral was erected during the reign of Alexander I, its inspiration came from his father Paul, and it was his idea that the cathedral should be designed and executed by Russian artists, despite being modelled on St Peter's in the Vatican.

During the Soviet period, the cathedral housed the infamous **Museum of Atheism**, whose foundation in 1932 coincided with a period of anti-religious repression in Leningrad, when scores of churches were closed and clergy arrested. Containing over 150,000 exhibits, from Egyptian mummies to pictures of monks and nuns copulating, it was used to prove Marx's famous maxim that "religion is the opium of the people". Renamed the Museum of Religion during perestroika, it was moved out in 1999 and is now located near St Isaac's Cathedral (see p.97). There are daily **services** in the cathedral, which at **Easter** overflows with believers greeting each other with the salutation *Kristos voskres!* (Christ is risen!) and replying with the traditional answer *Voistine voskres!* (Verily, He is risen!)

The exterior

The semicircular **colonnade** is made up of 96 Corinthian columns hewn from Karelian granite, but unlike in the city's other great nineteenth-century cathedral, St Isaac's, sculptural decoration was kept to a minimum: it's easy to miss the **bas-reliefs** at either end of the colonnade – depicting *Moses Striking the Rock* and *The Adoration of the Brazen Serpent* – and the bronze **statues** hidden in the porticoes of (from left to right) St Vladimir, John the Baptist, Alexander Nevsky and St Andrew. The bronze **doors** facing the prospekt are worth inspecting at close quarters: an exact copy of Ghiberti's doors for the Florentine Baptistery, which Michelangelo allegedly described as "splendid enough to serve as the gates of paradise".

In 1837, two **statues** by Boris Orlovsky were erected at either end of the colonnade: to the west, **Michael Barclay de Tolly**; to the east, **Mikhail**

Kutuzov, the hero of Tolstoy's *War and Peace*. The Scottish-born General de Tolly's contentious policy of strategic retreat before Napoleon's armies prompted his replacement by the one-eyed Field Marshal Kutuzov, who used to close his good eye and pretend to sleep so that his aides could express their opinions freely. Public opinion forced Kutuzov to engage the vastly superior French troops at the Battle of Borodino (1812), which produced no clear winner despite horrendous casualties on both sides.

The interior

The cathedral is **open** to sightseers (Mon, Tues, Thurs & Fri 11am–5pm, Sat & Sun noon–5pm, closed Wed; free) outside prayer times, but visitors should behave with decorum. Depending on which part of the interior is being refurbished, the entrance may be on the left or the right of the colonnades facing Nevskiy, and the first sight you might see is the **tomb of Marshal Kutuzov**, overhung with captured Napoleonic banners. He was buried here with full honours, on the spot where he had prayed before setting off to war. The object of his prayers was the icon **Our Lady of Kazan**, or *Derzhavnaya* (Sovereign), which reputedly disappeared in 1904, to reappear miraculously in Moscow on the day of Nicholas II's abdication, where the woman who found it dreamt of being told that the divine power vested in the tsars had now returned to the Mother of God. In the latest chapter of this long-running mystery, Our Lady of Kazan is now thought to be one and the same as an icon currently in the possession of the Prince Vladimir Cathedral on the Petrograd Side (see p.192). Kazan Cathedral's own iconostases were ripped out in the 1930s, so makeshift versions now serve until new ones can be carved, in contrast to the solemnity of its granite columns and the grisaille frescoes around its central cupola and barrel-vaulted wings.

On towards the Moyka

A number of lesser sights are distributed on either side of Nevskiy prospekt as it heads to the River Moyka, 250m to the northwest. Diagonally opposite the cathedral, set back behind a summer beer garden, is the mid-nineteenth-century **Lutheran Church** (Lyuteranskaya tserkov), built in a vaguely neo-Romanesque style unusual for St Petersburg. After being converted into a swimming pool (complete with diving boards and spectators' stands) in the late 1950s, it has now been returned to the Lutherans, who are slowly restoring it, as related by an exhibition in the lobby (Mon–Fri 10am–2pm & 3–6pm). During the late 1840s, Mussorgsky was a pupil at the eighteenth-century **Peterschule** (officially School No. 222) next door.

At no. 20, further on past Bolshaya Konyushennaya ulitsa, the former **Dutch Church** occupies a much larger building, but is unlikely to revert to its original function, of which the only hint is a small dome peeping over the portico, and two sculpted angels holding open the Book of Enlightenment. The House of Chess (the city's main chess club) and various shops are now ensconced here.

The Stroganov Palace

Across the prospekt, the pink-and-white facade of the **Stroganov Palace** (Stroganovskiy dvorets) overlooks the intersection of Nevskiy and the River Moyka. Built by Rastrelli in 1753, it's a fine example of Russian Baroque, paying homage to the carved window-frames of traditional peasant cottages, whilst flaunting its owner's status with Doric columns and pediments emblazoned with the Stroganov coat of arms. Although from street level it's hard to make it out, this features a bear's head flanked by sables – the Stroganovs owned vast tracts of Siberia, and earned a fortune from salt trading (their chef also invented the dish beef stroganoff). The palace now belongs to the Russian Museum and its (poorly) restored state rooms exhibit **Tsarist porcelain** from the Gardner and Lomonosov factories (Wed–Sun 10am–6pm; $8). Downstairs is a separate **waxworks exhibition** (daily 11am–7pm; $3) of figures from Russian history, inferior to the one in the Beloselskiy-Belozerskiy Palace. The courtyard contains a glassed-in restaurant (see p.356) and an expensive shop masquerading as a Chocolate Museum (p.386).

The adjacent **Politseyskiy most** (Police Bridge), spanning the River Moyka, was the first iron bridge in St Petersburg, constructed in 1806–8 to the design of Scotsman William Hastie. Originally called the "Green Bridge" after the colour of its outer walls, it was subsequently renamed the "Police Bridge" and then, after the Revolution, the "People's Bridge", before reverting to its second name in 1992. Moored beside the northeast embankment are small, private motorboats that can be rented for **canal trips** (p.40).

Beyond the Moyka

Immediately across the river stand two buildings ripe with faded good looks and historical significance. On the left-hand side, occupying the entire block between the embankment and Bolshaya Morskaya ulitsa, is a salmon-pink edifice nicknamed the "House with Columns", now containing the **Barrikada Cinema**. The site was originally occupied by a wooden palace belonging to Empress Elizabeth, which was replaced in the late eighteenth century by a mansion for St Petersburg's chief of police. The nineteenth-century Italian architect Giacomo Quarenghi, who designed several buildings in and around St Petersburg including the Hermitage Theatre, lived on the second floor when he arrived in Russia.

Across the prospekt stands the yellow-and-white building with colonnaded arcades at either corner which formerly housed the fashionable *Café Wulf et Béranger*, frequented by the poet Pushkin, who met his second here en route to his fatal duel with D'Anthès in 1837. It later became the *Restaurant Leiner*, where Tchaikovsky is supposed to have caught cholera. Today, it contains the shamelessly touristic **Literaturnoe Café** and an excellent antique bookshop.

At this point, you'll probably be lured off Nevskiy towards the Winter Palace by the great arch of the General Staff building (see p.74), leaving behind the **Wawelburg House** – now the headquarters of Aeroflot – which dominates the corner of Nevskiy and Malaya Morskaya ulitsa. This massive greystone pile evinces virtually every style of masonry, with an abundance of armorial reliefs, floral swags and Aztec heads. Its architect, Peretyatkovich, designed it to resemble both the Doge's Palace in Venice and the Palazzo Medici-Riccardi in Florence; the stone was imported from Sweden by the banker Wawelburg, whose initials appear on the shield crowning the pediment and above the service entrance on Malaya Morskaya ulitsa.

If you stick with the prospekt all the way to the needle-spired Admiralty (see p.94), it's worth watching out for a couple of buildings on the right-hand side as you go. Outside the 1930s secondary school at no. 14 is a stencilled **warning sign**, in blue and white, which reads: "Citizens! In the event of artillery fire, this side of the street is the most dangerous!" During the siege of Leningrad (1941–44), such signs were posted on the northwestern sides of the city's main thoroughfares after ballistic analysis determined that they were most at risk from Nazi shellfire. A little further on, at nos. 8 and 10, stand the oldest houses on the prospekt, dating from the early 1760s and adorned with decorative griffons and medallions.

To the Winter Palace

The best way of **approaching the Winter Palace** (which houses the Hermitage – see Chapter 2) is to turn right off Nevskiy prospekt at Bolshaya Morskaya ulitsa, whose northern end was designed by Rossi to lie along the Pulkovo meridian (the Tsarist equivalent of the Greenwich meridian), so that at midday, the houses cast no shadow. The beauty of this approach becomes obvious as the street curves beneath the triple arch of the General Staff building – also designed by Rossi – and you first glimpse Dvortsovaya ploshchad, its towering Alexander Column set against the facade of the Winter Palace – it's been called "the greatest compliment ever paid by one architect to another", so eloquently does Rossi's design introduce and frame the open space and buildings of Dvortsovaya ploshchad beyond.

Dvortsovaya ploshchad (Palace Square)

The theatrical expanse of **Dvortsovaya ploshchad** (Palace Square) is inseparable from the city's turbulent past. Here, the Guards hailed Catherine as empress on the day of her coup against her husband Peter III, while later rulers revelled in showy parades. Fittingly, it was also the epicentre of the mass demonstration on what became known as "**Bloody Sunday**", which marked the beginning of the 1905 Revolution. On January 9, 1905, Father Gapon, head of a workers' society sponsored by the secret police, led thousands of strikers and their families to the square. Unarmed and bearing religious banners and portraits of the tsar and the tsaritsa, they sought to present a petition to Nicholas II – who was actually at Tsarskoe Selo. The Preobrazhenskiy Guards opened fire on the crowd without warning, killing hundreds (the police figure was "more than thirty"). Gapon himself was later accused of being a traitor, and hanged by revolutionaries in a Finnish lake resort in 1906. At the outbreak of World War I, however, much of the hostility felt towards "Bloody Nicholas" after the massacre was submerged in a wave of patriotic fervour, and hundreds of thousands of people sank to their knees and bellowed "God save the tsar" as he emerged from the Winter Palace.

Despite this, within three years Tsarism had been swept away in the **February Revolution** of 1917. The determination of Kerensky's Provisional Government to continue the war enabled the Bolsheviks to mobilize support by promising "Peace, Bread, Land" and launch a second revolution. On October 25, 1917, the square witnessed the famous **storming of the Winter Palace**, immortalized (and largely invented) in Eisenstein's film *October* – ironically, more people were injured during the making of the film than in the event itself. Having taken over all the key installations, Lenin (rather prematurely) announced the resignation of the Provisional Government at 10am. In fact, the first real exchange of fire didn't take place until 9.40pm, followed by blank shots from the cruiser *Aurora*, anchored down-river. Sporadic gunfire continued until around 10pm, when the three hundred-odd Cossacks defending the palace deserted en masse, leaving only a few-score officer cadets and members of the shaven-headed Women's Battalion to continue resistance. They were persuaded to lay down their arms and, in the early hours of the morning, a large group of Bolsheviks entered by a side entrance and made their way through the palace's interminable rooms to arrest the Provisional Government.

Eisenstein's version of events was filmed in 1928, but by then the myth of the dramatic mass charge across the square was already part of Soviet folklore, thanks to the spectacles staged in honour of the **first anniversary of the October Revolution**. In 1918, a group of artists including Nathan Altman and Marc Chagall transformed the square by covering the Alexander Column, the facades of the Winter Palace, and the General Staff with sculptures and more than 5000 square metres of canvas plastered with avant-garde art. For the **third anniversary** (1920), under the glare of giant arc lights, a battalion of Red Army troops and thousands of citizens pretended to storm the palace, while fifty actors dressed as Kerensky (who was, in fact, absent at the time of the assault) made identical speeches and gestures, on a stage backed by Futurist designs.

In 1991, the square was at the centre of events during the referendum on the city's name, when groups of people congregated to argue the merits of Leningrad or Petersburg. During the attempted **putsch** in August of the same year, Mayor Sobchak addressed some 150,000 citizens who assembled here in support of Boris Yeltsin and to protest against the coup. Though political rallies still occur here, the square is more used to tourists, skateboarders and people offering horse-and-carriage rides or coach excursions to the Imperial palaces outside the city – plus the occasional beer or music festival.

The Alexander Column

Napoleon had hardly begun his 1812 retreat from Moscow when it was decided that a triumphal column should be erected in the middle of the square. However, work on the **Alexander Column** (Aleksandrovskaya kolonna) didn't begin until 1830, when Auguste de Montferrand, the inexperienced architect in charge of building St Isaac's Cathedral, landed the job. Crowned by an angel, whose face is supposedly modelled on Alexander I's, the monument is 47.5m high, one of the tallest of its kind in the world. The **bas-relief** facing the Winter Palace depicts two figures representing the Niemen and Vistula, the two great rivers that Napoleon crossed on his march to Moscow, together with the simple inscription, "To Alexander I from a grateful Russia".

Its construction entailed Herculean efforts, rewarded by a faultless climax. After two years spent hewing the 600-tonne granite monolith from a Karelian rock face, and a year transporting it to St Petersburg, the column was erected in just forty minutes using a system of ramps, pulleys and ropes, pulled by two thousand war veterans. More than a thousand wooden piles had to be driven into the swampy ground to strengthen the foundations and, so the story goes, Montferrand insisted the mortar be mixed with vodka to prevent it from freezing. But the most disconcerting aspect of its construction is that the column isn't attached to the pedestal at all, but stays there simply by virtue of its immense weight.

The General Staff building

To complete the architectural ensemble around the square, Alexander I purchased (and demolished) all the private houses that faced the Winter Palace, and in 1819 commissioned Carlo Rossi to design a new headquarters for the Russian Army **General Staff** (Generalniy shtab) building. The edifice frames one side of the square in a gigantic yellow arc, its sweeping facade interrupted by a colossal **arch** commemorating the Patriotic War against Napoleon. The underside is covered in armorial bas-reliefs; above the arch, Victory rides her six-horsed chariot, while two Roman soldiers restrain the horses from leaping over the edge. The whole structure was so large, rumours spread that it would collapse, prompting Rossi to declare, "If it falls, I fall with it" – he proved his point by standing on top of the arch as the scaffolding was removed. At one time the General Staff building also served as a prison: Griboedov spent four months here in 1826 as a suspected Decembrist, and Lermentov was held for five days before being exiled to the Caucasus for having written his *On the Death of a Poet* about Pushkin.

As diplomat Samuel Hoare observed, "true to Russian type, the facade was the best part of the building", concealing "a network of smelly yards and muddy passages that made entrance difficult and health precarious". At the outbreak of World War I, work often came to a standstill "owing to a perfect covey of saint's days and national anniversaries", while the quartermaster general "made a common habit of arriving in his office about eleven at night, and of working until seven or eight the next morning". Confusion also prevailed at the Foreign Ministry, housed in the eastern wing of the building, where, following the Bolshevik seizure of power, the head of the Petrograd Cheka (forerunners of the KGB), Moses Uritskiy, was assassinated in August 1918.

The building has now been given to the **Hermitage**, and is ultimately intended to house its Impressionist and Post-Impressionist collections and contemporary art. At present, however, only two floors of the Foreign Ministry have been converted to exhibition space (10.30am–6pm, Sun till 5pm; closed Mon; $5.30). The second floor is used for temporary exhibitions, while the third is divided into two sections. One is devoted to the Post-Impressionists **Pierre Bonnard** and **Maurice Denis**, with nine huge decorative panels from Denis's *Story of Psyche* series, commissioned by the Muscovite millionaire Morozov. The other, entitled **Realms of the Eagle**, displays over six hundred examples of Empire Style decorative art – from dinner services to ceremonial regalia – in a series of rooms once occupied by Chancellor Count Nesselrohde. Don't miss the satirical prints of fashions and customs of the Empire period. As with the main Hermitage, admission is free for students and children.

The Winter Palace

The **Winter Palace** (Zimniy dvorets) is the finest example of Russian Baroque in St Petersburg, and at the time of its completion was the largest and most opulent palace in the city. Its 200-metre-long facade features a riot of ornamentation in the fifty bays facing the square, including two tiers of pilasters, a balustrade peppered with urns and statuary, and the prominent

The Winter Palace and the Hermitage

Although begun as separate buildings, the **Winter Palace** and the **Hermitage** are now effectively one and the same thing. Catherine the Great created the first Hermitage and its embryonic art collection, and though "respectable" citizens were admitted after 1852, it became fully accessible only following the October Revolution – its collection swollen with Old Masters, precious objects and dozens of Impressionist masterpieces confiscated from private owners. Originally occupying only the eastern annexe, today the Hermitage's paintings take up most of the rooms in the Winter Palace. For a full account of the Hermitage collection and state rooms, see Chapter 2.

The palace in history

The Winter Palace is as loaded with history as it is with gilt and stucco, having been a winter residence for every tsar and tsaritsa since **Peter the Great** (not to mention the court and 1500 servants). Though Peter always preferred to live at Monplaisir, he died in the second Winter Palace – the first of several Imperial demises of note associated with the building.

The first tsar to inhabit the present structure was **Peter III**, who lived with his mistress, Elizabeth Vorontsova, in the southeastern corner of the second floor, while his wife, the future **Catherine the Great**, resided on the other side of the courtyard. On assuming the throne, Catherine redecorated and took over Peter's quarters, giving her lover, Grigory Orlov, the rooms directly beneath her own. Decades later, following a visit by the last of her paramours, Platon Zubov, she was found unconscious on the floor in her bedroom and later died. Given that she was then 67, it's difficult to believe the scurrilous legend (probably a Prussian invention) that she died whilst attempting to copulate with a stallion (which supposedly crushed her when the harness suspending it from the ceiling broke).

Despite the choice of luxurious apartments available, **Nicholas I** picked himself one "no larger than a Bloomsbury dining room", furnished with barrack-like simplicity, where he worked, ate, slept and entertained his mistresses – and eventually died of influenza in the middle of the Crimean War. In contrast, his wife Alexandra ensured no expense was spared in the adornment of her state room – the emerald green and gold Malachite Drawing Room.

Alexander II also chose to reside in a remote corner of the palace, furnished not with the Rembrandts or Rubens at his disposal, but in the simple, tasteless, bourgeois fashion of the day. In 1880 a bomb was planted below the Imperial Dining Hall by a member of the revolutionary Narodnaya Volya; eleven soldiers died, but the tsar – who had taken a break between courses – survived. A year later, however, another attempt on his life succeeded, and he died of his wounds in his apartment in the southwestern corner of the palace.

Nicholas II lived in the apartments above the Malachite Room until 1904, when increasing unrest forced the Imperial family to retreat to Tsarskoe Selo, only returning to the capital for state functions. At the outbreak of World War I, he pledged before five thousand people in the palace's St George's Hall that he would "never make peace so long as the enemy is on the soil of the fatherland", just as Alexander I had when Napoleon invaded the country in 1812. For much of the war, the great state rooms on the second floor were occupied by a hospital for invalids established by the tsaritsa, and during the February Revolution, loyalist troops made a brief last-ditch stand there.

In July 1917, the **Provisional Government** made its fateful move from the Mariinskiy Palace (see p.101) to the Winter Palace. Kerensky took over the tsaritsa's old rooms, and even slept in her four-poster bed. His ministers conferred in the Malachite Drawing Room and were arrested by the Bolsheviks in an adjacent dining room in the early hours of October 26. Party activists quickly put a stop to looting, except in the Imperial wine cellars, where every unit on guard soon got roaring drunk – and twelve people drowned. By 1922, most of the palace had been given over to the Hermitage art collection, while another part housed the Museum of the Great October Socialist Revolution (p.185) between the wars.

vertical drains so characteristic of the city. From this ultimate symbol of power, the autocrat could survey the expanse of Dvortsovaya ploshchad or gaze across the Neva to the Peter and Paul Fortress. As the journalist Alexander Herzen wrote of the palace, "Like a ship floating on the surface of the ocean, it had no real connection with the inhabitants of the deep, beyond that of eating them."

The existing Winter Palace is the **fourth structure** of that name, all of them built within half a century of each other. The first two, created for Peter the Great on the site of the present Hermitage Theatre, reflected his penchant for Dutch architecture; their remains were discovered during recent restoration and are now open to the public. In 1730, Empress Anna commissioned a third version (on the site of today's west wing) by Bartolomeo Rastrelli, but her successor Elizabeth was dissatisfied with the result and ordered him to start work on a replacement. This was intended to take two years to build and cost 859,555 rubles, though in the event it took eight years and cost 2.5 million, obliging Elizabeth to open a network of beer halls to finance the excess. What you see now is not entirely what Rastrelli had in mind. Originally the **facade** was painted an icy turquoise blue with white trimmings; this was given a uniform coat of Venetian red in the nineteenth century, but is now sage-green and white. A fire in 1837 caused enormous damage but, in typically Russian fashion, "neither money, life nor health was spared" to restore it completely – the court was re-established there within fifteen months.

The Small and Large Hermitages and the Hermitage Theatre

Once Rastrelli had completed the Winter Palace, new buildings were gradually added to the east wing, becoming ever more austerely Neoclassical in style. The first addition was the long, thin annexe known as the **Small Hermitage** (Maliy Ermitazh). Directly inspired by Peter the Great's Hermitage at Peterhof, it was given the same, somewhat ironic, name – anything less "hermitic" would be difficult to imagine. It was built as a private retreat for Catherine the Great and it was here that she began the Imperial art collection that would eventually become the world's largest art gallery.

The **Large Hermitage** (Bolshoy Ermitazh), to the east, is made up of two separate buildings: the "Old Hermitage", facing the River Neva, was built to house the rapidly expanding Imperial art collection, and in the mid-nineteenth century this was augmented by the "New Hermitage", designed as Petersburg's first purpose-built public art gallery. Its best exterior features are the ten giant granite **atlantes** which hold up the porch on the south facade, their rippling, polished muscles glistening in the sunlight.

Beyond stands the **Hermitage Theatre** (Ermitazhniy teatr), built in 1775–84 by Quarenghi as a private theatre for Catherine the Great. Once a fortnight she would fill it with the capital's diplomats; otherwise, the average audience of private guests rarely reached double figures. The theatre was built directly over the **remains of Peter the Great's Winter Palace** (see below), and joined to the rest of the complex by a covered passageway which passes over the **Winter Moat** (Zimnaya kanavka), originally dug to surround Peter's palace. The views, as you look beneath the overhead passageway to the Neva beyond, and inland across the canal, are some of the loveliest in the city.

The Winter Palace of Peter the Great and Preobrazhenskiy Barracks

A sizeable remnant of the original **Winter Palace of Peter the Great**, sometimes known as "Peter's Hermitage", was rediscovered and unearthed between 1976 and 1986. Only accessible on a guided **tour** ($7), and reached by a separate entrance at Dvortsovaya nab. 32 (just beyond the Winter Moat), the remains consist of part of a courtyard flanked on two sides by arcaded galleries and small private apartments used by Peter and Catherine I. Though the flagstones and stucco look rather new, you can't help being charmed by the eagle-shaped gala sledge and open carriage used for masquerades, or by the reconstruction of Peter's turnery and other rooms, hung with Dutch still lifes and French landscapes purchased on his grand tour – not to mention a life-size wax figure of the tsar by Carlo Rastrelli, commissioned in 1725 by Peter himself.

Beyond the Winter Moat, on the south side of the Hermitage Theatre, are the former **Preobrazhenskiy Barracks**. As the first regiment of the Imperial Guard, whose colonel was always the tsar himself, the Preobrazhenskiy was the most powerful of the regiments established by Peter the Great – taking its name from Preobrazhenskoe, the summer estate where Peter spent his youth. During the uncertain decades following his death, the Guards became de facto kingmakers, whose allegiance was essential for any prospective ruler. This could be alienated by seemingly trivial matters – such as a change of uniform – as Peter III discovered when the Preobrazhenskiy cast off the Prussian-style garb introduced by him, and donned its old uniform of bottle-green and scarlet to salute Catherine's coup.

The view from the embankment

There are more magnificent views from **Dvortsovaya naberezhnaya** (Palace Embankment) across the widest part of the River Neva. To the north, the gilded spire of the Peter and Paul Cathedral soars above its island fortress; to the west, the rust-red Rostral Columns stand proudly on the Strelka; while to the east, the river curves around past the Summer Garden and runs beneath bridges to the Petrograd and Vyborg sides. In summer, this is also the place from which to catch **hydrofoils to Peterhof**, the great Imperial palace beside the Gulf of Finland (see p.250 for details).

In Tsarist times this spot was the scene of the **Blessing of the Waters** or "Jordan Feast" on January 6. The ceremony took place in a chapel erected for the occasion on the frozen Neva, and despite sub-zero temperatures, tradition required the court to appear in silk stockings and shoes, without winter coats:

Empress Anna and the Ice Palace on the Neva

Like many of the early Romanovs, **Empress Anna Ivanova** was extremely fond of practical jokes. In the winter of 1739–40, she press-ganged the middle-aged widower, Prince Golitsyn, into marrying an "extremely ugly" Mongol lady. Anna organized the whole event, beginning with a procession of goats, pigs, cows, camels, dogs and reindeer, pulling couples in national dress from each of the "Barbarous Races" of the empire. Bringing up the rear was an elephant with a cage on its back, containing Golitsyn and his bride. After a grotesque wedding feast the newlyweds were transported to Anne's *coup de théâtre*: a palace made entirely out of ice, erected on the frozen Neva.

The **Ice Palace** was incredibly beautiful, with Baroque balustrades, cornices and columns, and surrounded by flowers and trees. Everything inside, right down to the chairs, tables and chandeliers, was carved out of ice. Finally, there was a four-poster bed upon which the couple were forced to consummate their marriage. The empress stayed with them while they undressed and got into their icy bed, before retiring to watch their antics from the warmth of the Winter Palace.

While Golitsyn died shortly afterwards, fate reserved an odd comeuppance for Anna, who grew morbidly depressed under the malign influence of her lover, Count Biron. Legend has it that walking one evening in the blue twilight of her mirrored palace, she encountered an obese figure in full regalia, and – recognizing it as herself – died of apoplexy.

at one such event, Alexander I contracted frostbite in three of his fingers. As for ordinary folk, the most devout had their newborn babies baptized through holes in the ice. Sometimes the priest lost his grip, or the infant caught pneumonia, but the parents were generally ecstatic, believing that the child had gone straight to heaven. Most bizarre of all, however, is the story of the Ice Palace on the Neva (see box on p.78).

East to the Summer Garden and Palace

There are several possible routes from the Hermitage to Peter the Great's Summer Garden, the most direct being along either Millionnaya or the Neva embankment. Alternatively, you could follow the curve of the Moyka, taking in **Pushkin's Apartment** and the nearby church where he lay in state. Either

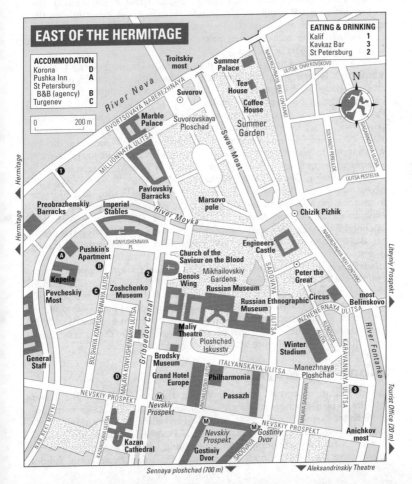

way, you can't avoid **Marsovo pole**, where the Imperial troops used to parade. On the far side of this, surrounded by water, is the **Summer Garden**, the most romantic of the city's parks and home to Peter's **Summer Palace**.

Along Millionnaya

The first private houses in St Petersburg were built across the Neva on Petrograd Side in 1704, followed shortly afterwards by an elegant street of houses on this side of the river, dubbed **Millionnaya ulitsa** (Millionaires' Street) after the members of the royal family and the wealthy aristocracy who made it their home during the nineteenth century. Today, a new generation of Russian millionaires are buying up the old palaces and knocking through the walls of communal flats to create huge luxury apartments, though they're outwardly indistinguishable from the shabby *kommunalki* that occupy the rest of the buildings.

Of the various **palaces** on Millionnaya, few are architecturally outstanding, but many were at the centre of the cultural and social life of the Russian aristocracy before the Revolution. The grandest buildings, predominantly on the left-hand side, have their main facades on the Neva, so to appreciate them fully (and to follow the account given below) you will need to walk along the embankment for part of the way.

The Italianate building at no. 26 on the embankment is **Grand Duke Vladimir's Palace**, easily identified by its griffon-infested portal. A notorious rake and hedonist, Vladimir was one of the most powerful public figures during the reign of his nephew, Nicholas II, but it was Vladimir's wife, Maria Pavlovna, who really set Petersburg talking. One of the tsar's most outspoken aristocratic critics, she hosted a popular salon, but left the city in the winter of 1916–17 vowing, "I'll not return until all is finished here" – and never did. It's worth trying to get inside the palace – now owned by the Academy of Sciences – to see its sumptuously gilded stairway, flanked by huge Chinese vases.

Further along is **Grand Duke Michael's Palace** (no. 18), an over-wrought neo-Baroque building that is so big that one of Michael's sons used a bicycle to visit his sister-in-law in another part of the palace. At **Putyatin's House**, Millionnaya no. 12, on March 3, 1917, another Grand Duke Michael – Nicholas II's brother and named successor following his abdication the previous day – renounced his right to the throne, formally ending the Romanov dynasty.

Next door at no. 10, the architect Stakenschneider took the opportunity to build himself a suitably majestic home, which hosted another popular salon in the mid-nineteenth century. The French writer **Balzac** stayed here in 1843 and met a Polish countess, Éveline Hanska, whom he had promised to marry back in 1832, once her husband died. Although the count had passed away in 1841, Balzac – a confirmed womanizer – managed to delay the marriage until 1850, just five months before he himself pegged out.

Along the Moyka

An alternative route east from the Winter Palace is to follow the **River Moyka**, which describes a graceful arc before joining the River Fontanka. Both rivers resemble canals, being embanked and adorned with handsome railings and flights of steps. The first bridge is **Pevcheskiy most**, or "Singer's Bridge", named for the nearby **Kapella** building, home of the Imperial Court Choir (now the Glinka Choir) established by Peter the Great. Various famous

Russian musicians, including Rimsky-Korsakov and, of course, Glinka, worked here, and the Kapella concert hall boasts some of the best acoustics in the city (see p.375 for concert information). On the other side of the river, a plaque on the facade of no. 31 commemorates the city's first mayor, **Anatoly Sobchak**, who lived there from 1960 until his death in 2000.

Pushkin's apartment

Just up from the Kapella, a little wooden doorway at no. 12 leads to the garden-courtyard of **Pushkin's apartment** (10.30am–5pm; closed Tues & the last Fri of each month; $1.25). The *kassa* on the left as you enter the yard rents an English audio guide ($2.75) to the second-floor apartment that Pushkin leased for his wife, their four children and her two sisters in the last unhappy year of his life (1836–37). The most evocative of its eleven rooms is the poet's **study**, containing a replica of his library of over 4500 books in fourteen

Alexander Pushkin

Among Russians, **Alexander Pushkin** (1799–1837) is probably the most universally esteemed of all the great writers: "In him, as if in a lexicon, have been included all of the wealth, strength, and flexibility of our language," wrote Gogol, shortly after the poet's death. However, the difficulty of translating Pushkin's subtle "poetry of grammar" means that he is rarely lauded with such passion outside Russia. Here, though, not only is he seen as the nation's greatest poet and the father of Russian literature, but his tragic death assured him the status of a national martyr.

Born in Moscow, Pushkin was educated at the Imperial Lycée in Tsarskoe Selo (see p.274), though he was an indifferent pupil, excelling only in fencing, French and dancing. His first major poem, *Ruslan and Lyudmila*, caused an enormous stir in 1820, as did his subsequent political poems, for which he was exiled to the southern provinces. Hard drinking, gambling and sex characterized his periods of exile, during which Pushkin wrote his romantic "southern cycle" of poems, which, as he himself admitted, "smack of Byron", to whom he is often compared. In 1826, the new tsar, Nicholas I, allowed Pushkin to return to St Petersburg and met him personally, appointing himself as the poet's censor. In 1831, Pushkin married **Natalya Goncharova**, one of the most beautiful women in St Petersburg. The tsar made him a *junker* (officer cadet), and as such he was able to attend court functions, which, preferring a more solitary existence, he disliked, unlike Natalya, who enjoyed them enormously.

Pushkin's untimely death at the age of 38 was due to a French officer called **D'Anthès**, the adopted son of the Dutch ambassador, Heeckeren. D'Anthès set tongues wagging with his advances towards Natalya; some believe he acted at the tsar's bidding, as an *agent provocateur* or a panderer. Pushkin received anonymous letters mocking him for being a cuckold, which he concluded had been sent by Heeckeren. He challenged D'Anthès to a duel (January 27, 1837) at Chernaya Rechka (see p.238), where the Frenchman was shot in the hand, and Pushkin was fatally wounded. The doctor posted notices outside the door of his apartment to keep his admirers informed about their hero's condition, until he died after several days in extreme agony.

Pushkin's second in the duel was an equerry, so his **funeral** took place around the corner in the Equerries' Church on February 1, 1837 (though it was misleadingly announced that it would be held at St Isaac's Cathedral). Since Pushkin was officially persona non grata at the time, a decree was issued forbidding university professors and students from attending. Nevertheless, the city's intelligentsia turned out in force, as did the diplomatic corps. Three days after the funeral, Pushkin's body was removed in secret and laid to rest at his country estate.

languages, and a portrait of his teacher and fellow poet, Vasily Zhukovsky, given to Pushkin on the publication of *Ruslan and Lyudmila*, with the dedication "To the victorious pupil from the vanquished master". Pushkin kept a "blackamoor" figure on his desk to remind him of his great-grandfather, Abram Hannibal, an Abyssinian prince whom he immortalized in his last, unfinished novel, *The Negro of Peter the Great*. In the Russian fashion, the clock in the study was stopped at the moment of Pushkin's death (2.45am), while in the nursery you can see the waistcoat that he wore at the duel (complete with bullet hole) and a candle from his funeral service (see below).

Konyushennaya ploshchad and the Church of the Saviour on the Blood

Pushkin's funeral service in the Equerries' Church at the Imperial Stables on **Konyushennaya ploshchad** drew such crowds that cab drivers needed no other directions than "To Pushkin!" Inside the church, souvenir hunters tore his frock coat to shreds and snipped curls from his hair and sidewhiskers. Under Communism, the stables were taken over by the state removals company and the square became little more than a turnaround for trams; now the church has been restored and the trams banished, while a stream of coaches brings tourists to admire the memorial to another untimely death.

The **Church of the Saviour on the Blood** (Khram "Spas na krovi"; 10am–8pm; closed Wed; $8.30; children under 7 free) was begun in 1882 on the orders of Alexander III to commemorate his father, Alexander II, who had been slain on the site the year before. It was decreed that the tabernacle should be on the spot where his blood had stained the cobblestones – hence the church's unusual name and the fact that it juts out into the Griboedov Canal. Architecturally, it was a slap in the face for Classicism, built in the neo-Russian style to resemble St Basil's in Moscow, with gilded, faceted onion domes like psychedelic pineapples, and a facade aglow with plaques recording the events of Alexander's reign, mosaic scenes from the New Testament, and 144 coats of

The assassination of Alexander II

The **assassination of Alexander II** (March 1, 1881) followed numerous previous attempts on the tsar's life by the revolutionary Nihilist organization, Narodnaya Volya (People's Will). Their original plan involved digging a tunnel from below what is now Yeliseyev's food store and packing explosives beneath Malaya Sadovaya ulitsa, along which the tsar was expected to drive to a review at the Imperial Riding School. Although he unintentionally avoided this attempt by taking a different route, the revolutionaries had learned from previous failures, and had posted a backup team of bombers. As the Imperial party returned along the Griboedov embankment, **Nikolai Rysakov** hurled his bomb, killing a Cossack and mortally wounding himself and a child, but only denting the axle of the tsar's carriage. Ignoring the coachman's urgings to drive on, Alexander began berating his would-be assassin, who – in response to the tsar's assurance that "I am safe, thank God" – groaned, "Do not thank God yet!" As Alexander turned back towards his carriage, another terrorist, **Ignaty Grinevitsky**, threw a second bomb, which found its target. The tsar was carried off bleeding to the Winter Palace, where he expired shortly afterwards; Grinevitsky himself died of his wounds a few hours later. Legend has it that Alexander had a plan for constitutional reforms in his pocket at the time of his murder; if it's true, the Nihilists scored a spectacular own goal, since his successors were utterly opposed to any change whatsoever.

arms representing the provinces, cities and towns of the Russian Empire – giving it the most flamboyant **exterior** of any building in St Petersburg.

Like so many churches, it was closed in the 1930s and turned into a storeroom, gravely damaging the interior; in 1970 it became a museum of mosaics, before being closed once again for over two decades. Since it reopened in 1997, the church has become one of the city's foremost tourist attractions, owing to its amazing **interior**, entirely covered in **mosaics** based on paintings by Nesterov, Vasnetsov, and other religious artists of the era. From Christ and the Apostles in the cupola to the images of saints and Biblical scenes on the walls and pillars, framed by wide decorative borders, the total area covered amounts to over seven thousand square metres. Despite the steep entry fee and long queue for tickets it would be a shame to leave St Petersburg without seeing it.

The site's visual drama is enhanced by the florid **Style Moderne railings** of the nearby Mikhailovskiy Gardens, cast from aluminium, which at that time was worth more than gold. You can have yourself photographed with people in eighteenth-century costumes or enjoy a five-minute ride around ploshchad Iskusstv in a horse-drawn carriage. Among the **buskers** in the vicinity, look out for the guy who plays a carpenter's saw with a violin bow; if you're after **souvenirs**, there's a host of stalls on the square between the church and the River Moyka.

Malaya Konyushennaya and the Zoshchenko Museum

Though something of a detour, it's worth sidetracking to **Malaya Konyushennaya ulitsa**, an attractive street between Konyushennaya ploshchad and Nevskiy prospekt which has been pedestrianized and adorned with a cast-iron **Metrological Pavilion**, built in 1997 according to the nineteenth-century designs of Nikolai Pansere. If nothing else, it provides an excuse to cross the Griboedov Canal by a footbridge from where there's an excellent – and photogenic – view of the Church of the Saviour on the Blood.

Also on Malaya Konyushennaya ulitsa is the **Zoshchenko Museum** (10.30am–6.30pm; closed Mon; $1), reached by entering the courtyard of no. 4/2, passing through a door on the left and up a stairway to the third floor, to find flat #119. This tiny two-room apartment was the last residence of the satirist Mikhail Zoshchenko (1894–1958), whose life mirrored the fortunes of many writers of that era. Born into an academic Petersburg family, he volunteered for the army in 1914 and was gassed at the front. Returning home after the February Revolution he tried many professions before starting to write in 1921, and won a wide following with his short stories, whose style was copied by generations of Soviet comedians and movie actors. His novel *Before the Sunrise* was an attempt to exorcise his depression through psychoanalysis. Although unscathed by the purges of the 1930s, Zoshchenko fell victim to the postwar *Zhdanovshchina* (see p.426); expelled from the Writers' Union for "hooligan representations", he was reduced to dire poverty. The museum contains a collage of humble personal effects and period artefacts, and preserves his bedroom, where his widow lived until 1981.

Around Marsovo pole

Back on the River Moyka, beyond Konyushennaya ploshchad, the **Marsovo pole** (Field of Mars) was a parade ground for the Imperial Guards from the earliest days but didn't acquire its name until the great military reviews of the nineteenth century. Its western side is flanked by an incredibly long yellow facade with three Doric porticoes, that was formerly the **Pavlovskiy Barracks**. Founded by Tsar Paul in 1796, the first recruits of the Pavlovskiy Guards regiment were allegedly chosen for their snub noses – Paul being so ashamed of his own pug nose that his face never appeared on coins ("My ministers hope to lead me by the nose, but I haven't got one," he once remarked). Nor was the selection of guards on the basis of physical appearance so unusual – all the Preobrazhenskiy and Semyonovskiy Guards were respectively blond and brunette.

Following the overthrow of Tsarism, Marsovo pole changed character completely. On March 23, the 180 people who had died in the February Revolution were buried in a common grave in the centre of the field, dignified two years later by the erection of a granite **Monument to Revolutionary Fighters**, one of the first such works of the Soviet era. Lofty epitaphs by Commissar Lunacharsky adorn the gravestones, and an **Eternal Flame**, lit on the fortieth anniversary of the Revolution, flickers at the centre – it's now a popular place for newlyweds to have their photo taken. Heroes of the October Revolution and the Civil War were buried here too, including the head of the Petrograd Cheka and the editor of *Krasnaya Gazeta*, both assassinated in 1918 by Socialist revolutionaries. Finally, in 1920, sixteen thousand workers took part in a *subbotnik* (day of voluntary labour), transforming the dusty parade ground – dubbed the "Petersburg Sahara" – into the manicured park that exists today.

The Marble Palace

As a retirement present for her former lover Count Grigori Orlov, who orchestrated her seizure of power, Catherine the Great built him the costliest palace in the city. Designed by Antonio Rinaldi, and faced with green and grey marble, which had recently been discovered in enormous quantities in the Urals, it quickly became known as the **Marble Palace** (Mramorniy dvorets; 10am–5pm, Mon till 4pm; closed Tues; $8). However, Orlov died before it was finished (he never lived there) and Catherine repossessed it for the crown, whereupon it gradually fell into ruin till it was refurbished in the late nineteenth century by Grand Duke Konstantin, its last resident. After the Revolution it was turned into the city's main Lenin Museum, with the famous armoured car from which Lenin spoke outside the Finland Station standing proudly in its courtyard, until the museum was closed after the 1991 coup.

Now, the courtyard contains a **statue of Alexander III** that once stood near the Moscow Station. The clodhopping horse and hulking rider were widely ridiculed in tsarist times; even their sculptor, Pavel Trubetskoy, reputedly said, "I don't care about politics. I simply depicted one animal on another". At first the Bolsheviks let the statue remain with a sarcastic inscription by poet Damian Bedniy – but in 1937 it was taken away and spent the next six decades in storage or buried underground, till it was exhumed and erected here in 1994.

Architecturally, the palace is a link between Catherine's Baroque city and Alexander I's Neoclassicism, with elements of both on the exterior. All that remains of Rinaldi's original interior are the main staircase of grey and blue marble with allegorical statues in niches, and the fabulous **Marble Hall**, featuring a dozen hues of stone, offset by gilded chandeliers and a parquet floor. Today, the palace is a branch of the Russian Museum, used to display a rotating selection of works from the **Ludwig Collection** of modern art, donated by the German chocolate king, Peter Ludwig. Picasso, Beuys, Rauschenberg, Warhol and Basquiat are among the foreign artists featured alongside the St Petersburg neo-Academist Olga Tobreluts and the Muscovites Ilya Kabakov and Erik Bulatov. On the floor above you'll find temporary exhibitions by contemporary artists, or antiques from the Russian Museum's storerooms.

If the cost of admission seems steep for what's on show, it's nothing compared to what foreigners are charged to see the **Konstantin Romanov Memorial Museum**, on the ground floor of a side wing. Its four rooms look as they did when the Grand Duke lived here, writing poems and plays and translating *Hamlet* into Russian under the *nom de plume* "KR". Albums of biblical scenes in his library and a secret chapel behind a bookcase in his study show his religiosity, while a Gothic Music Room, with dragons, bats and other creatures craning from the wainscoting, attests to his theatrical side. The music room and study are gorgeous, but hardly justify paying $25 – though if you have a student card issued in Russia, the tour costs only $1. **Tours** begin at the *kassa* in the lobby of the main building (Mon, Wed, Thurs & Fri at noon & 3pm).

Suvorovskaya ploshchad

At the northern end of the park, abutting Troitskiy most (Trinity Bridge), **Suvorovskaya ploshchad** is named for the Russian general **Alexander Suvorov** (1730–1800), whose bronze **statue** stands on a granite plinth at the centre of the square. Suvorov, a veteran of the Italian campaigns against Napoleon, was a portly man, though he is portrayed here as a slim youth in Roman garb, representing Mars, the god of war. Don't believe the urban myth (related as fact in one foreign guidebook) that the statue is made from recycled rods from Sosnovy Bor nuclear reactor – for this to be true, the reactor would had have to have been running in 1801, when the statue was cast.

On the east side, by the embankment, the late eighteenth-century building where the satirical writer Ivan Krylov once lived stands beside a green mansion which housed first the Austrian and later the **British Embassy**. In March 1918 the diplomatic corps followed the Soviet government to Moscow, leaving only a small contingent in Petrograd. Shortly after the attempt on Lenin's life in August, there was a shoot-out between the British naval attaché, Captain Cromie, and the Petrograd Cheka, who stormed the building looking for counter-revolutionaries. Cromie killed a commissar before being shot dead himself. The remaining British officials were arrested, but the ambassador was already in Vologda, courting White generals. Such intrigues were nothing new; two hundred years earlier, an English ambassador fostered the conspiracy to murder Tsar Paul at the Engineers' Castle (see p.90).

The Summer Garden

The **Summer Garden** (Letniy sad) is the city's most treasured public garden. Less than a year after founding the city in 1704, Peter the Great employed a Frenchman, Le Blond, to design a formal garden in the style of Versailles, with intricate parterres of flowers, shrubs and gravel, a glass conservatory, and orange and lemon trees. Sixty white marble statues of scenes from Aesop's *Fables* adorned the numerous fountains, their water drawn from the Fontanka. Unfortunately, a disastrous flood in 1777 wrecked the garden, uprooting trees and destroying the fountains. Reconstruction took place under Catherine the Great, who preferred the less formal, less spectacular, English-style garden that survives today.

Notwithstanding this – and the dress restrictions introduced during the reign of Nicholas I, which remained in force until the Revolution – the Summer

Garden has always been popular with Petersburgers. Amongst the Romantics drawn here were Pushkin, Gogol, Tchaikovsky and the Ukrainian poet Shevchenko, while the novelist Goncharov used the garden as a setting for a meeting between the ill-starred couple, Oblomov and Olga, in his book *Oblomov*. The garden's popularity with lovers dates back to the early nineteenth century, when **marriage fairs** took place here on Whit Monday. The participants were mostly from the lower classes, "dressed in a great deal of finery badly put on, and a great many colours ill-assorted," as one English traveller sniffily observed. The young hopefuls would line up facing each other, men on one side, women on the other, and behind them their parents, who would enter into negotiations once a mutual preference had been expressed.

The Summer Garden is scheduled to **close** for the whole of **2004**, for a total refurbishment and the installation of fountains – it isn't clear at the time of writing if this means that the Summer Palace will also be inaccessible, or if opening hours will revert to their old pattern (detailed below) once the park reopens.

Around the garden

Normally, the Summer Garden is **open** daily (May–Sept 10am–9.30pm; Oct–March 10am till dusk; $0.30) except during April, when the park is closed to dry out; the admission charge is waived over winter, when the statues are protected from cracking by insulated boxes, and making snow sculptures is a popular pastime. Surrounded on all sides by water, the garden is best approached from the Neva embankment, through the tall, slender wrought-iron grille, designed in 1770–84 by Yuri Felten, whose father had come to St Petersburg from Danzig as a master cook for Peter the Great. While Le Blond's fountains have disappeared, the northern half of the garden still features more than eighty **Baroque statues** (there were originally over two hundred). Few are of any great artistic merit, but together they evoke the romantic charm of eighteenth-century court life.

One of the most distinguished statues is that of **Cupid and Psyche**, on a platform that juts out into the Swan Moat, depicting the moment at which Psyche falls in love with Cupid, as she leans over his sleeping figure, holding a lamp to his face to catch her first glimpse. Alongside numerous other allegorical and mythological figures are several interesting historical statues, including a flattering bust of **Queen Christina of Sweden** (the fifth statue on the right as you walk straight ahead from the main gates): Christina ruled Sweden for just ten years (1632–42) before her secret conversion to Catholicism (which was proscribed in her homeland) was discovered, forcing her to abdicate. In the centre of the park is a large memorial to the popular satirical writer **Ivan Krylov** (1769–1844), paid for by public subscription. Like Aesop, Krylov used animals in his fables to illustrate human foibles, and many of his characters decorate the statue's pedestal, some of them playing musical instruments.

The Summer Palace

In the northeastern corner of the garden stands the **Summer Palace** (Letniy dvorets; May to mid-Nov 11am–6pm; closed Tues & the last Fri of each month; $2.60) that Domenico Trezzini began in 1710 for Peter the Great. A modest two-storey building of bricks and stucco – one of the first such structures in the city – the new palace was really only a small step up from the wooden cottage in which Peter had previously lived on the other side of the river. Its position, at the point where the Fontanka joins the Neva, suited

Court life in Petrine times

Along with Monplaisir at Peterhof, the Summer Palace is still faintly redolent of court life in Petrine times. Peter lived here with little pomp, preferring to lounge around in old clothes, attended only by a couple of servants and two valets (whose stomachs he used as pillows on long journeys). This informality nearly cost him dearly, as an attempt was made on his life by an Old Believer (religious dissident) during a meeting in the palace reception room. Peter's hospitality was legendary – and feared. The most important summer celebration was the anniversary of the Battle of Poltava (June 28), when Peter himself served wine and beer to his veterans. Sentries were posted at the gates to prevent guests from fleeing when the huge buckets of corn brandy were brought on for compulsory toasting, which wouldn't stop until all the guests were blind drunk – something the foreign ambassadors were particularly wary of. The only willing participants were the clergy, who "sat at their tables, smelling of radishes and onions, their faces wreathed in smiles, drinking toast after toast". Dancing and drinking would continue until dawn, though "many simply sank down where they were in the garden and drifted into sleep".

Peter's maritime bent; the seating area with benches, now laid out to the south side of the palace, was originally a small harbour.

The palace was equally divided between husband and wife: Peter occupied the first floor, while Catherine took over the top floor. Information on each room is posted in English and Russian and the decor, though not original, has been faithfully reproduced. The tsar's **bedroom** is typically modest; his four-poster bed is significantly shorter than he was, since in those days the aristocracy slept propped half upright on pillows. Next door is Peter's **turnery**, where he would don a leather apron and spend hours bent over his mechanical lathes, presses and instruments; he also liked to receive important guests here. The room is dominated by a huge metereological device, which is connected to the palace weather vane and measures the strength and direction of the wind.

In Petrine times, major banquets were held at the Menshikov Palace on Vasilevskiy Island (see p.165); the **dining room** here was used for less formal gatherings. Having taken his seat, Peter would blithely tell his guests, "Those of you who can find places may sit where you want. The rest of you can go home and dine with your wives" – prompting much "cuffing and boxing" which he enjoyed immensely. He also loved practical jokes, such as concealing dead mice in the soup, or having dwarves burst forth from mounds of pâté. Another source of pride, along with the turnery, was the palace's **kitchen**, which was unusually modern for its day, plumbed with running water from the nearby fountains, and – most importantly – opening directly onto the dining room: Peter liked his food hot, and in large palaces dishes would usually be lukewarm by the time they reached the table.

The **top floor** was the domain of Peter's wife, who became Empress Catherine I upon his death. She was one of the most unlikely people to end up ruling Russia, having started life as a Lithuanian peasant girl, but had a good influence on Peter – insisting that women be present (and remain sober) during his notorious drinking parties, and that the men could get drunk only after nine o'clock. She was also one of the few people unmoved by his violent temper. On one occasion, Peter smashed a Venetian mirror, shouting, "See, I can break the most beautiful object in my house," to which she replied, "And by doing so, have you made your palace more beautiful?"

△ Dvortsovaya ploschad seen through the arch of the General Staff building

The Tea House, Coffee House and Swan Lake

South of the Summer Palace stands the **Tea House** (Chayniy domik), a simple Neoclassical pavilion built in 1827. Damaged by fire in 1981, it has since been restored and is now an exhibition hall. Carlo Rossi's nearby **Coffee House** (Kofeyniy domik), on the site of an old grotto from Petrine times, is currently a souvenir shop and cafe. At the southern end of the garden is the **Swan Lake**, enlivened by said birds, and on its far side, at by the entrance/exit to the gardens, stands a giant red porphyry **vase**, a gift from the Swedish king Karl Johan to Nicholas I.

South of the Moyka

Across the Moyka from the Summer Garden looms the **Engineers' Castle** – a building forever associated with the murder of Tsar Paul, and now a branch of the Russian Museum. Its dramatic facade and spire lure sightseers onwards in the direction of the main **Russian Museum** on ploshchad Iskusstv, while the shady **Mikhailovskiy Gardens** behind the museum offer a respite from the traffic along Sadovaya ulitsa.

Crossing the road from the garden to the castle, you'll notice people peering over the embankment where the Moyka joins the Fontanka. They're paying homage to **Chizik Pyzhik**, a tiny statue of the Siskin bird whose green and yellow plumage was likened to the uniforms of law students in tsarist times, giving rise to the ditty: "*Chizhik Pyzhik, gde ty bil? Na Fontanke vodku pil*" ("Chizhik Pyzhik, where have you been? On the Fontanka drinking vodka"). The first monument to be erected in the glasnost era by an individual rather than an organization, it has since become a kind of good-luck talisman, at which Russians throw coins – even when the statue has been stolen, as it is from time to time.

The Engineers' Castle

The pensive poet casts a glance
At the palace buried in oblivion,
A tyrant's menacing memorial
Deserted in the mists of sleep.

Alexander Pushkin, *Freedom*

Few buildings in St Petersburg are so imbued with myths and the character of their original owner as the Mikhailovskiy or **Engineers' Castle** (Inzhenerniy zamok; for opening times see p.90). Tsar Paul commissioned this fortified residence shortly after he assumed the throne in 1796; to clear the site, he had the wooden palace that Rastrelli had built for Empress Elizabeth – in which he himself had been born and raised – burnt to the ground: an act pregnant with significance for a man plagued by rumours of illegitimacy, who wanted nothing more than to erase the memory of his hated mother, Catherine the Great.

Paul employed Vincenzo Brenna to construct the building (named the Mikhailovskiy Castle after the Archangel Michael appeared in a vision to one of Paul's guards) and, in a deliberate snub to Catherine's taste for a unified aesthetic, specified a different style for each facade. He happily plundered much of the building material (and most of the furniture) from the palaces his mother

The assassination of Tsar Paul

The origins of the **conspiracy** against Paul are murky. Count Pahlen, head of foreign affairs and the police, was ideally placed to prepare a coup and had good reasons for doing so, but the English ambassador, Lord Whitford, secretly gave money to buy support and may even have proposed the plot to Count Zubov – another key conspirator – under the cover of an affair with Zubov's sister, Olga (thereby fitting the description of a diplomat as a man sent abroad to lie for his country). However, animosity towards Paul ran so deep that almost everyone who was anyone ended up playing some kind of role in the conspiracy.

Paul had already alienated the nobility and the Guards by curtailing their privileges. His own diplomats were aghast at him sending a force of Cossacks to expel the British from India without consulting anyone, and inviting the sovereigns of Europe to settle their differences by hand-to-hand combat. His impulsiveness and erratic behaviour were the talk of St Petersburg; "the Emperor is literally not in his senses," Whitford reported to London. With the prospect of a European conflict looming, it was in both the Russians' interests and England's to have Paul replaced by a less bellicose monarch. Pahlen even obtained the consent of Paul's heir apparent, the future Alexander I, whose only proviso was that his father's life be spared.

At midnight, March 11–12, 1801, some sixty conspirators set off in the rain for the castle. En route they quenched their thirst with champagne, but were almost scared off by a flock of crows while creeping through the Summer Garden. Paul's false sense of security in the castle had led him to replace the guard of thirty well-armed men with just two unarmed hussars, a valet and a sentry. One of the hussars resisted but was quickly dealt with; the tsar, having vainly tried to hide, was arrested in his nightshirt and cap. Then several soldiers who had got lost burst into the room and lunged at him, upsetting the night-light and plunging the room into darkness. In the confusion, Paul was knocked unconscious and strangled with his own sash.

When Paul's death was officially ascribed to apoplexy – as his father's had been – Tallyrand quipped, "Really, the Russian government will have to invent another disease." Meanwhile, Alexander promised the Guards: "During my reign, everything will be done according to the principles of my beloved grandmother, Catherine the Great." All Paul's reforms and innovations were revoked – his mother had triumphed yet again, from beyond the grave. (See the box on p.280 for more about Paul's life.)

had built, and insisted that his monogram appear throughout the palace – over eight thousand times, according to one account.

Paul moved into the castle in February 1801, even before the paint was dry. To allay his fear of being murdered – as his father had been – it was surrounded by a moat with drawbridges protected by cannons, and had a secret passage for escaping in emergencies, reached by a trapdoor near his bedroom. In the event, he spent only forty days here before his worst fears were realized and he was strangled in his bedroom (see box above).

As the scene of a regicide the castle was subsequently shunned by the Imperial family and later given to a military engineering academy, where Dostoyevsky was enrolled at the age of sixteen. After the Revolution, it was used to house libraries, institutes and record offices. Restoration began in the 1980s, and the palace subsequently became a branch of the Russian Museum. *Objets d'art* from its vast collection are displayed in the restored state rooms which you can wander during **visiting** hours (Mon 10am–5pm, Wed–Sun 10am–6pm; $8). To see other parts of the palace such as the site of Paul's murder, you'll need to book a **guided tour** in Russian five days in advance (℡313 41 73; $30 group rate).

The castle's **exterior** was inspired by the chateau of the Prince de Condé, which Paul had seen on his European tour, and painted a distinctive apricot colour that matched his mistress's gloves. A holy woman is said to have foretold that Paul would live as many years as there were letters in the inscription above the portico on the south face – a prophecy fulfilled when he died at the age of 47. The octagonal inner courtyard contains a recently installed **statue of Paul** enthroned, wearing thigh-boots and holding the Imperial orb and sceptre – a pose that delighted him, but which cruelly underlines the futility of his ambitions.

Inside the museum you can see a model of the moats and drawbridges that originally defended the castle – and may be re-created in real life if funding materializes. A grand fake marble staircase graced with a copy of the *Dying Cleopatra* (the original is in the Hermitage) ascends to the **state rooms**. Gilding and caryatids abound in the burgundy throne room of his wife, Maria Fyodorovna, and in the state dining hall, where Paul ate supper two hours before his murder. In his day, the barrel-vaulted Antique Gallery boasted statues, now in the Hermitage, solid bronze doors and four tapestries based on Raphael's work that were a gift from Louis XVI and hung in the Raphael Gallery. Now, eighteenth- and nineteenth-century portraits, landscapes and allegorical paintings from the Russian Museum's collection are hung in these galleries and a suite of rooms that once belonged to Paul's son Konstantin.

Paul's own suite was long ago carved up into a warren of passages comprising the "backstage" of the museum, which can only be seen on a tour. Although his bedroom was converted into a chapel to efface the scene of the crime, you can still see the backstairs used by his assassins. One reason they got this far was that they included an officer charged with reporting urgent news to the tsar at any time of the day or night. Paul's fate was sealed by his final error – he ran to hide in his mistress's bedroom rather than making for the secret passage, and found his line of retreat blocked. The tour ends downstairs in a charming **church** with artificial marble columns, where the composer Glinka got married.

Beyond the Engineers' Castle

South of the castle, Rossi laid out the triumphal **Klenovaya alleya** (Maple Alley) on the site of Paul's former parade grounds. At the top end is an equestrian **statue of Peter the Great**, erected by Paul and sporting the pithy inscription *Pradyedu pravnuk* ("To great grandfather from great grandson"), intended to quell persistent rumours of his illegitimacy.

To the east, on Belinskovo ploshchad, St Petersburg's **State Circus** (Tsirk) occupies the late nineteenth-century premises of the Cinizelli Circus, whose traditions it maintains. To the south stand two **pavilions** designed by Rossi to house those members of Paul's *corps de gardes* who were on duty guarding the approach to the castle.

Across Inzhenernaya ulitsa, west of Klenovaya alleya, the **Winter Stadium** (Zimniy stadion) was originally the Mikhailovskiy Manège – an Imperial riding school built by Rossi in the 1820s. During the Revolution, the Manège served as the headquarters of the Armoured Car Detachment, a die-hard Bolshevik unit that sped around in Austin armoured cars, clad in black leather. From the triangular Manezhnaya ploshchad, outside the stadium, **Italyanskaya ulitsa** (Italian Street) leads west to ploshchad Iskusstv and the Russian Museum.

Ploshchad Iskusstv and the Mikhailovskiy Gardens

Early in the nineteenth century, Carlo Rossi designed a palatial square and thoroughfare off Nevskiy prospekt, every facade conforming to an overall Neoclassical plan. Both were originally named after the Mikhailovskiy Palace that dominates the square, but in Soviet times the latter was renamed **ploshchad Iskusstv** (Square of Arts) owing to the many artistic institutions located here, and is still known as such today. A **statue of Pushkin** reciting his poetry, by the city's leading postwar sculptor, Mikhail Anikushin, was erected in its centre in 1957.

Besides the Mikhailovskiy Palace you might consider visiting the **Brodsky Museum** (11am–6pm; closed Mon & Tues; $2) at pl. Iskusstv 3, in the former home of Isaak Brodsky, a leading Socialist Realist painter responsible for such gems as *Lenin in the Smolniy*. It displays his collection of 800 minor works by Repin, Levitan, Kramskoy and other "Wanderers" plus a few of his own pictures. Next door on the corner of Italyanskaya ulitsa stands a recreation of the **Stray Dog cabaret**, where Mayakovsky, Akhmatova and other Futurists and Acmeists hung out before the Revolution – nowadays just a tourist trap for coach parties.

The Mikhailovskiy Palace: the Russian Museum and Russian Ethnographic Museum

Amazingly, while Rossi was overseeing the General Staff building, he was also working on the **Mikhailovskiy Palace** (Mikhailovskiy dvorets). The two epitomize the Russian Empire style of Alexander I's reign, one rampantly martial and the other coolly Neoclassical, with a relentless parade of Corinthian columns across a pale yellow facade. Sadly, little remains of Rossi's interior, save the main staircase and the austere "White Room" inside what is now the **Russian Museum**, occupying the central and western wings of the palace. This vast repository of Russian art is a must-see for any visitor, and rates a chapter of its own (see pp.141–154).

In the early 1900s, the palace's east wing and stables were replaced by an annexe to house the museum's ethnographic collections, which eventually became the **Russian Ethnographic Museum** (10am–6pm; closed Mon & the last Fri of each month; $4; ⓦwww.ethnomuseum.ru). The museum is deeply Soviet (or Tsarist) in its inclusion of myriad peoples that once comprised the Soviet Union (or Tsarist Empire), some of them no longer in the Russian Federation, or fighting for independence – a treasure trove of folk art, costumes, tools, and reconstructed dwellings, from the shores of the Baltic to the grasslands of Mongolia. Its main hall is decorated with a giant **frieze** of peasants and workers from every nation of the former USSR. The museum proper kicks off in the west wing with the **Russian** people and traces their peasant life – the norm for ninety percent of the population until the 1900s. On the **second-floor** north balcony you'll find exhibits on the **Ingush** and **Ossetian** peoples of the North Caucasus – though while the war in Chechnya continues, the section on the **Chechens** has been turned to face the wall.

An adjoining room covers the numerous ethnic groups who live in the melancholy landscape of the Volga basin and the Ural mountains: the largest being the **Tatars**, followed by the **Bashkirs** and **Chuvash**, the last one of the few non-Muslim Turkic peoples. The **Mordvinians**, **Udmurty**, **Mari** and

Komi are also present here, Finno-Ugric peoples whose language is related to Estonian, Hungarian and Finnish. The south balcony covers the few remaining nomadic Siberian Lapps, such as the **Evenki** and **Nanaytsy**, whose movements are still dictated by the need to find pastures for their reindeer. The more numerous **Buryat** people remained nomads until after the Revolution, and traditionally practised shamanism, but have since settled more or less permanently around Lake Baikal and are now mostly practising Buddhists. The other main group represented here are the **Yakuts**, pastoralists whose language and culture continue to thrive.

The first floor of the **east wing** covers the more familiar Slav peoples, beginning with the two largest groups, the **Ukrainians** and **Belarussians**, and the Russians themselves. Both balconies on the upper floor are filled with examples of contemporary folk art, such as *matryoshka* dolls, Zhostovo trays and Palekh boxes. The southern rooms cover the **Kazakhs** and **Turkmenians**, and have a display of traditional Kazakh felt tents. There's also a **Children's Centre** (Sat & Sun 11am–5pm), where instructors teach handicrafts such as weaving, printmaking and pottery.

Behind the palace are the **Mikhailovskiy Gardens**, whose broad lawns and deep pools of shade are especially appreciated during the hot summer months, when the White Nights find people playing badminton here at three o'clock in the morning, and there are outdoor **concerts** during the day (as advertised by the entrance gates).

The Maliy and the Philharmonia

On the western side of ploshchad Iskusstv stands the **Maliy Opera and Ballet Theatre** (Maliy operniy teatr) – previously known as the Mikhailovskiy – the city's main opera house after the Mariinskiy. While the building appears to be part of Rossi's masterplan, it was actually designed by the architect Bryullov – although Rossi was responsible for the square's other great musical institution, the **St Petersburg Philharmonia**, on the corner of Mikhailovskaya ulitsa, which was originally the concert hall of the Salle des Nobles.

Of all the figures associated with these institutions, the one closest to the hearts of the city's intelligentsia is **Dmitri Shostakovich** (1906–75), whose opera, *Lady Macbeth of Mtsensk*, was premiered at the Maliy in 1934 to great critical acclaim, only to be denounced by *Pravda* as "Chaos instead of Music" less than two years later. After years during which his music swung in and out of official favour, Shostakovich scored his greatest public success with his Seventh Symphony – the "Leningrad Symphony" – during the Blockade of the city in World War II. He wrote the first three movements whilst serving as an air warden (breaking off composing whenever the sirens sounded), before being evacuated to Kuybyshev, where he completed the work, which was broadcast nationwide from here on August 9, 1942 (some of the orchestra wore uniform, having been recalled from the front for the event). Yet despite his commitment to the war effort, he was one of the first victims of the postwar cultural purge known as the *Zhdanovshchina*, being accused of "formalist perversions and anti-democratic tendencies" in his art, and his relations with the Soviet authorities remained uneasy until his death in 1975.

Other notable events at the Philharmonia have included the premieres of Beethoven's *Missa solemnis* (1824) and Tchaikovsky's Sixth Symphony – the latter conducted by the composer just a few days before his death in 1893. It was here, too, that the American dancer Isadora Duncan made her Russian debut a few days after "Bloody Sunday" in 1905.

The Admiralty and the Bronze Horseman

> The whimsical medusas cling angrily,
> anchors rust like discarded ploughs –
> and, lo, the bonds of three dimensions are all sundered
> and opened are the seas of all the world.

Osip Mandelstam, *The Admiralty*

Standing at the apex of Nevskiy prospekt, the **Admiralty** building (Admiralteystvo) is one of the world's greatest expressions of naval triumphalism, extending 407m along the waterfront from Dvortsovaya ploshchad to ploshchad Dekabristov. Marking the convergence of three great avenues that radiate across the city centre – Nevskiy prospekt, Gorokhovaya ulitsa and Voznesenskiy prospekt – its golden spire draws you naturally towards it on any walk along Nevskiy. Once there, you'll want to take the time to stroll in the **Alexander Garden** and explore the neighbouring ploshchad Dekabristov, which is dominated by the **Bronze Horseman**, the city's renowned statue of Peter the Great. This part of town is shown on the map on p.98.

The Admiralty

The **Admiralty** was originally founded by Peter the Great in 1704 as a fortified shipyard, with a primitive wooden tower and spire. A ban was placed on building in the vicinity to maintain a firebreak – hence the open spaces that still surround the edifice. As the shipyards moved elsewhere, and the Admiralty became purely administrative in function, Andreyan Zakharov was commissioned to design a suitable replacement.

Built in the early 1820s, the key feature of the existing building is a central **tower** rising through tiers and columns and culminating in a slender **spire** sheathed in gold. Like the spire of the Peter and Paul Cathedral, it asserted the city's European identity – differentiating its skyline from the traditional Russian medley of onion domes. It also enabled the tsar to scan the streets for miles around, using a telescope, to check whether they were being laid out according to plan. Topping the spire is a gilded **weather vane** shaped like a frigate, which has become the emblem of St Petersburg, appearing on everything from medals to shopping bags. Another piece of symbolism is encoded in the building itself, whose plan corresponds to the Greek and Cyrillic initial letter of Peter's name – П – as does the form of the arched tower facing the Admiralty Garden.

The Admiralty's **facade** swarms with Neoclassical sculptures and reliefs, glorifying Russia's maritime potency. The archway of the main entrance is flanked by trios of nymphs bearing globes, representing the triple aspects of the goddess Hecate. A frieze below the entablature shows Neptune bequeathing his trident to Tsar Peter, while statues of Achilles and other heroes embellish the ledge below the colonnade. This in turn is topped by statues of the four seasons, winds and elements, and the mythological patrons of shipbuilding and astronomy, Isis and Urania.

The **porticoes** of the 163-metre-long side wings are similarly adorned, with reliefs of deities rewarding Russian bravery or artistry with laurel wreaths. Two lesser archways on the **embankment** side feature the Genii of Glory, a pair of angelic figures blowing trumpets (a symbol of St Petersburg); sadly, the river-front facade is marred by a row of late nineteenth-century apartment buildings. The Admiralty building has been occupied by a naval college since 1925 and the only part that is open to the public is the rather expensive restaurant in the east wing, opposite the Winter Palace. North along the embankment towards Dvortsoviy most (Palace Bridge) you'll notice a statue of **Peter the Shipbuilder**, a gift from the city of Amsterdam, where Peter worked as a common shipwright to learn the skills needed to build a Russian navy.

The Alexander Garden and prospekt

Largely obscuring the Admiralty, the wooded **Alexander Garden** (Aleksandrovskiy sad) leads towards ploshchad Dekabristov, toddlers and lovers mingling with officers from the naval college. On Sunday afternoons in summer, a navy **brass band** plays near the Zhukovsky statue. Other Russians honoured with monuments here include Glinka, Lermontov and Gogol (near the fountain), but the most engaging of the statues commemorates General Nikolai Przhevalsky (1839–88), whose intrepid journeys in Central Asia are symbolized by a saddled camel. There's a bizarre legend that Przhevalsky was the real father of Iosif Dzhugashvili – better known to history as Stalin.

Admiralteyskiy prospekt, beside the park, rates a mention for two buildings. The grey-and-white Neoclassical pile at no. 6 was the headquarters of the Imperial secret police for over fifty years before the Revolution and, from December 1917 until March 1918, the headquarters of the Bolshevik Cheka, led by "Iron" Felix Dzerzhinsky. Since 1995 it has housed a small branch of the **Museum of Russian Political History** (Mon–Fri 10am–5.30pm; $2.75) covering the history of the secret police in three rooms on the second floor. The first room re-creates the interior as it was during the reign of Alexander III, with a curtained-off door through which agents could enter in secret to report to their chief. The others contain photographs of leading *Chekisti* and famous foreign spies like Reilly, plus memorabilia such as bulletproof vests and KGB medals – but unless you understand Russian, it will interest only hardcore espionage buffs.

Two blocks further along Admiralteyskiy prospekt is the **Lobanov-Rostovskiy House**, a massive wedge-shaped mansion built in 1817–20. The columned portico facing the prospekt is guarded by two stone **lions** immortalized in Pushkin's poem *The Bronze Horseman* (see overleaf).

Ploshchad Dekabristov

Ploshchad Dekabristov – an expanse of fir trees and rose beds merging into the Alexander Garden – is largely defined by the monuments that surround it, and known for the event recalled by its name, "Decembrists' Square". The **Decembrists' revolt** began on the morning of December 14, 1825, when a group of reformist officers marched three thousand soldiers into the square in an attempt to force the Senate to veto the accession of Nicholas I and proclaim a constitutional monarchy. Alas, the senators had already sworn allegiance to Nicholas and gone home, while the officers' leader, Prince Trubetskoy, never showed up. The revolt turned from farce to tragedy as the tsar surrounded the square with loyalist troops. When labourers on St Isaac's Cathedral started pelting them with bricks, Nicholas feared that the revolt could spread and ordered his troops to attack. By nightfall the rebellion had been crushed and interrogations were under way; Nicholas attended the trials and dictated the sentences. Five ringleaders were hanged and 130 officers stripped of their rank and exiled in fetters to Siberia. Although the soldiers had only been obeying orders, with little or no idea of the revolt's aims, dozens were forced to "run the gauntlet" of a thousand men twelve times – that is, to be clubbed twelve thousand times.

The Bronze Horseman

Once on the square, your eyes are inevitably drawn to the famous equestrian statue of Peter the Great, known as the **Bronze Horseman** (Medny vsadnik), which rears up towards the waterfront. Of all the city's monuments, none has been invested with such poetic significance: a symbol of indomitable will and ruthless vision. The statue made its literary debut in Pushkin's epic *The Bronze Horseman* (1833), an evocation of the Great Flood of 1824. In the poem, the only survivors are a poor clerk, Yevgeny, who climbs on top of one of the lions outside the Lobanov-Rostovskiy House to escape the floodwaters, and the statue of the Horseman itself, which comes to life and pursues him through the city. The radical journalist Herzen regarded the statue as a symbol of tyranny, whereas Andrei Bely likened it to Russia on the verge of the apocalypse: "Your two front hooves have leaped far off into the darkness, into the void, while your two rear hooves are firmly implanted in the granite soil."

Peter the Great

Peter the Great (1672–1725) was responsible for irrevocably changing Russia's character, turning it from an ultra-parochial, backward country to an imperial power to be reckoned with. In childhood, he had experienced at first hand the savagery of Old Muscovy, when several of his family were butchered by the Kremlin Guards during a power struggle between the Naryshkin and Miloslavskiy clans. Secluded in Preobrazhenskoe, outside Moscow, he began to form his own "toy" regiments and mingle with the isolated foreign community: unlike most Russians, he was anything but xenophobic (styling himself "Peter" rather than "Pyotr"). He also taught himself to sail, and his enthusiasm for maritime affairs and Western ways was given full rein after the death of his elder brother and co-tsar, the feeble-minded Ivan V.

In 1697–98, Peter embarked on a **grand tour** of Europe, travelling incognito to be free of the burdens of protocol, so that he might concentrate on studying shipbuilding in Holland and England, where he worked on the docks as an apprentice. His aim was to create a Russian navy in order to drive back Charles XII of Sweden and secure a Baltic "Window on the West" – the genesis of **St Petersburg** itself. Yet when he wasn't poring over plans, inspecting the navy, founding institutions or leading his armies into battle, Peter enjoyed a riotous lifestyle with cronies such as Menshikov (p.165) and Lefort. Together they formed the "Drunken Synod", whose parties parodied the rituals of the Orthodox Church, reflecting his crude sense of humour and his dislike of Old Russia – though the former was somewhat mitigated by his astute second wife, **Catherine I** (p.87).

Amongst Peter's innovations were the Kunstkammer, or "chamber of curiosities", Russia's first public museum (p.162), and the imposition of a tax on those who wore beards and caftans, after Peter proclaimed them backward and impractical. His westernizing reforms and lukewarm devotion to Orthodoxy alienated nobles and commoners alike – but the beheading of the Kremlin guard (1698) and the execution of his own son, **Tsarevich Alexei** (p.178), dissuaded further rebellions. Opinion remains divided over Peter's achievements. Whereas most Russians see him as a great ruler who advanced the nation, others blame him for perverting its true, Slavic destiny, or setting an autocratic precedent for Lenin and Stalin. Unlike them, however, Peter's sheer *joie de vivre* makes him hard to dislike, for all his brutality.

The statue was commissioned by Catherine the Great to glorify "enlightened absolutism" – an ideal that she shared with Peter the Great (see box on p.96), and which served to emphasize her place as his true political heir (she had, after all, no legitimate claim to the throne). Hence, the canny inscription, "To Peter I from Catherine II", which appears on the sides in Latin and Russian. The French sculptor, Étienne Falconet, was allocated the finest horses and riders in the Imperial stables, so that he could study their movements. Later, he sketched them held motionless on a special platform, while a cavalry general of similar build to Peter sat in the saddle. The statue wasn't completed until 1782 (Falconet complaining of arrears in his salary), with disaster narrowly averted during the casting stage, when a foundry man tore off his clothes to block a crack in the mould, preventing the molten metal from escaping. Its huge **pedestal** rock was brought from the village of Lakhta, 10km outside Petersburg; Peter had supposedly surveyed the city's environs from this 1600-tonne "Thunder Rock", sculpted by the waves over millennia. A trampled serpent (symbolizing evil) wriggles limply down the back of the pedestal.

As a visit on any sunny day will confirm, the statue is a customary spot for newlyweds to be photographed, before drinking a toast on the Strelka to celebrate their nuptials (see p.158). Don't even think of emulating the drunken foreigner who once climbed up onto the statue to sit behind Peter in the saddle, and was swiftly arrested and heavily fined. When he protested at the enormity of the fine, the police replied, "If you will ride with great people, you must pay great people's prices."

The Senate and Horseguards' Manège

The colossal ochre-and-white **Senate and Synod** building on the far side of ploshchad Dekabristov was constructed in the mid-nineteenth century to replace an old mansion that had formerly housed both institutions. Peter established the Senate (1711) to run Russia in his absence, and the Holy Synod (1721) to control the Orthodox Church, and both had assumed a more permanent role by the time that Rossi designed these new premises. Echoing the General Staff, a resplendent arch unites the twin buildings, which now contain historical archives.

Further south stands the former **Horseguards' Manège** (Konnogvardeyskiy manezh), built as an indoor riding school at the beginning of the nineteenth century. The architect Quarenghi felt that its prime location called for a temple-like portico fronted by the Sons of Zeus reining in wild horses, which was copied from a similar arrangement outside the Quirinale Palace in Rome. In 1840 the naked youths were removed after the Holy Synod objected to their presence within sight of St Isaac's Cathedral, and they were reinstated only in 1954. The Manège was used for concerts in tsarist times (Johann Strauss conducted here), but is now the **Central Exhibition Hall**, used for both modern art and trade exhibitions.

St Isaac's Cathedral and around

Looming majestically above the rooftops, **St Isaac's Cathedral** (Isaakievsky sobor) – one of the city's premier tourist attractions – is visible from way out in the Gulf of Finland, but is too massive to grasp at close quarters. It stands on its own square, **Isaakievskaya ploshchad** (St Isaac's Square), and it's from the

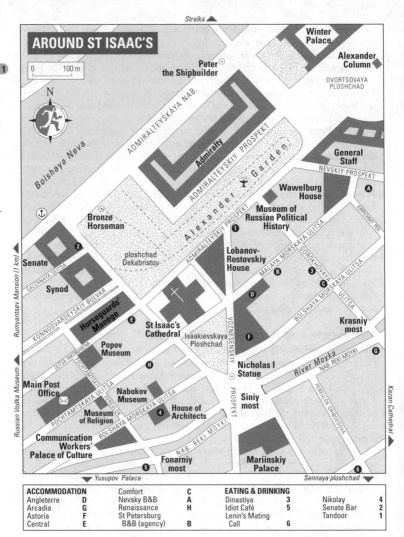

Rumyantsev Mansion (1 km) ◄

Russian Vodka Museum ◄

Kazan Cathedral ►

Sennaya ploshchad ▼

ACCOMMODATION		Comfort	**C**	EATING & DRINKING		Nikolay	**4**
Angleterre	**D**	Nevsky B&B	**A**	Dinastiya	**3**	Senate Bar	**2**
Arcadia	**G**	Renaissance	**H**	Idiot Café	**5**	Tandoor	**1**
Astoria	**F**	St Petersburg		Lenin's Mating			
Central	**E**	B&B (agency)	**B**	Call	**6**		

centre of this that you'll get the best view of the cathedral. By day, its gilded dome is one of the glories of St Petersburg's skyline; at night, its gigantic porticoes and statues seem almost menacing, like something dredged up from the seabed. Its opulent interior is equally impressive, as is the wonderful view from its colonnade.

During World War II, the cathedral appeared on Luftwaffe bombing maps as "reference point no. 1", and the park to the south was dug up and planted with cabbages to help feed the famished city. Today, the only hazard to be encountered on Isaakievskaya ploshchad is the traffic, zooming across from all sides, but worth braving for a bevy of interesting buildings around its edges.

The Cathedral

The **Cathedral** (10am–8pm; closed Wed; $8.30) is the fourth church in St Petersburg to have been dedicated to St Isaac of Dalmatia, a Byzantine monk whose feast day fell on Peter the Great's birthday (May 30). The previous one on this site was judged too small even before its completion, so a competition to design a replacement was announced after Russia's victory over Napoleon in 1812. By submitting no fewer than 24 designs in various styles, a young, unknown architect, Auguste de Montferrand, impressed Alexander I into giving him the commission, though he soon required help from more experienced architects. The tsar insisted that the walls of the previous church be preserved, causing huge problems until he relented three years later, at which point everything was demolished and work began again from scratch. Many reckoned that construction (1818–42) and decoration (1842–58) were deliberately prolonged, owing to the popular superstition that the Romanov dynasty would end with the cathedral's completion – a more likely explanation is that the delays were caused by Montferrand's incompetence.

During Soviet times the cathedral was a Museum of Atheism, where visitors could see an enormous Foucault's pendulum that supposedly proved the falsity of religion by demonstrating the earth's rotation; and although it has been reconsecrated as a place of worship it is still classified as a **museum**. Foreigners buy **tickets** inside the cathedral – the entrance is beneath the south portico – so you can decide if the interior is worth the expense or not. A separate ticket is required for the colonnade and the dome ($3), which closes one hour earlier.

The interior

The cathedral's vast **interior** is decorated with fourteen kinds of marble, as well as jasper, malachite, gilded stucco, frescoes and mosaics. An 800-square-metre painting by Karl Bryullov of the Virgin surrounded by saints and angels covers the inside of the cupola, while biblical scenes by Ivan Vitali appear in bas-relief on the huge bronze **doors** and as murals and mosaics elsewhere (all labelled in English). Malachite and lazurite columns frame a white marble **iconostasis**, decorated by Neff, Bryullov and Zhivago, its wings flanking the gilded bronze doors into the **sanctuary**. Only the monarch and the patriarch were admitted to the sanctuary, whose stained-glass window is contrary to Orthodox tradition (though perfectly acceptable elsewhere in an Orthodox church). At the back of the nave are vintage scale-models of the cathedral, its dome and the scaffolding used to erect the portico. Montferrand is remembered by an outsized cast-iron relief, copied from a figure on the extreme left of the western portico – which was all the honour that he received for dying on the job after forty years. His widow begged that he be interred in St Isaac's crypt, but the tsar refused to sully it with the tomb of a non-Orthodox believer and sent his coffin home to France.

The dome and colonnade

The cathedral's height (101.5m) and rooftop statues are best appreciated by climbing the 262 steps up to its **dome** – the third largest cathedral dome in Europe. This consists of three hemispherical shells mounted one inside the other, with 100,000 clay pots fixed between the outer and middle layers to form a lightweight vault and enhance the acoustics. Nearly 100kg of gold leaf was used to cover the exterior of the dome, helping push the total cost of the cathedral to 23,256,000 rubles (six times that of the Winter Palace). The sixty men who died from inhaling mercury fumes during the gilding process were not the only fatalities amongst the serf-labourers, who worked fifteen hours a day without any holidays, since Nicholas believed that "idleness can only do them harm". Dwarfed by a great **colonnade** topped with 24 statues, the dome's windswept iron gallery offers a stunning panoramic view of central St Petersburg. The *kolonada* has its own entrance beneath the south portico, so visitors must exit the cathedral on the Neva side and go back round again.

Around Isaakievskaya ploshchad

On the eastern side of Isaakievskaya ploshchad, the pinkish-grey **Astoria Hotel** is famous for those who have – and haven't – stayed there. Built in the early 1900s, its former guests include the American Communists John Reed and Louise Bryant, and the Russian-born Anarchists Emma Goldman and Alexander Berkman. It's said that Hitler planned to hold a victory banquet here once Leningrad had fallen, and sent out invitations specifying the month and hour, but leaving out the exact date. Adjacent to the Astoria is a smaller, butterscotch annexe named the *Angleterre*, where the poet Sergei Yesenin apparently slashed his wrists and hanged himself in December 1925, leaving a verse written in his own blood:

> See you again, my friend, I'll see you
> Good friend, you're here inside me
> The foretold parting is a promise to
> Be, one day, once more, beside me.
> See you again, my friend, no words, no hand
> Don't grieve, don't let your brow betray you
> In life there's nothing new in a dying man.

In 1998, however, Yesenin's niece pressed the authorities to reopen the investigation into his death, following allegations that Yesenin was killed by the secret police. The theory is that Trotsky ordered him to be beaten up, to dissuade Yesenin from planning to emigrate, but the *Chekisti* entrusted with the job killed him by accident, and faked a suicide to cover it up – the poem being written by the *Chekist* commander Yakov Blumkin.

At the centre of the square prances a haughty, bronze equestrian **statue of Nicholas I**, known to his subjects as "the Stick" (*Palkin*) and abroad as the "Gendarme of Europe". Sculpted by Klodt, its granite, porphyry and marble pedestal is adorned with figures representing Faith, Wisdom, Justice and Might – modelled, it's said, on Nicholas's daughters; bas-reliefs depict the achievements of his reign, and four lampstands flaunt screaming eagles.

Along the west side

Across the square from the *Astoria* and the tsar's statue are a trio of buildings with diverse antecedents. The **Myatlev House** (no. 9) is the oldest on the square, dating from the 1760s, its medallioned facade bearing a plaque attesting to the fact that the French encyclopedist Denis Diderot stayed here (Oct 1773 to March 1774) at the invitation of Catherine the Great. When Diderot fell on hard times, she bought his library but allowed him to keep the books and be paid for "curatorship" until his death. The house is named after a later owner, the poet Ivan Myatlev. Alongside stands a brown granite building that served as the German Embassy until the outbreak of World War I, when a mob tore down its statues, flung them in the Moyka and looted the building in an orgy of hysterical patriotism.

Since Soviet times the pilastered Doric edifice at no. 7 has housed the renowned **Vavilov Institute of Plant Breeding**. The institute is proud that it preserved its collection of 56,000 edible specimens throughout the Blockade – when 29 of its staff died of malnutrition – and equally proud of its founder, Nikolai Vavilov (1887–1943), Russia's greatest geneticist. The Brezhnev-era memorial plaque fails to mention that he was arrested, tortured, accused of heading a nonexistent underground opposition party, and died in prison during Stalin's time. Around the side of the building, on the Moyka embankment, a tetrahedral granite **obelisk** marks the level of the worst floods in the city's history – the five-metre watermark is at chest height, and a mark well above head level can also be seen.

Siniy most and the Mariinskiy Palace

Isaakievskaya ploshchad's southern end continues across **Siniy most**, the Blue Bridge, which is so wide that you hardly realize the Moyka is flowing beneath it. Like the Red and Green bridges further along the Moyka, the Siniy gets its name from the colour of its river-facing sides. Until Alexander II abolished serfdom in 1861, serfs were bought and sold here in what amounted to a slave market.

Beyond the bridge, the **Mariinskiy Palace** (Mariinskiy dvorets) now flies the tricolour and crest of the Russian Federation, but the palace's pediment still sports the five awards bestowed on Leningrad during the Soviet era – a schizoid heraldry reflecting the palace's colourful history. Built for Maria, the favourite daughter of Nicholas I, it later became the seat of the State Council; the Council of Ministers met here while Tsarism was falling, as did the Provisional Government before it moved into the Winter Palace. After 1948, the palace housed the Executive Committee of the City Council, which was effectively run by the Communist Party until the setting up of a mayoralty in 1991. During the putsch that year, thousands of citizens turned out to defend the democratically elected council and mayoralty, but the latter then transferred to the Smolniy Institute, leaving the palace to the City Legislative Council, which Yeltsin dissolved in 1993. The Council was eventually reconstituted in 1995, but still has an uneasy relationship with the Governor's office at the Smolniy, which has far more power. The area beyond the Mariinsky Palace is covered under "West of St Isaac's" (p.107) and "Between the Yusupov Palace and the Blok Museum" (p.110).

Between Nevskiy and Voznesenskiy prospekts

If you don't reach St Isaac's Cathedral by way of the Admiralty and ploshchad Dekabristov, you'll probably approach it along one of the streets or canals between Nevskiy and Voznesenskiy prospekts. These two avenues delineate a central wedge full of contrasts and vitality, encompassing the old financial district along Bolshaya and Malaya Morskaya, the faded beauty of the Moyka and Griboedov embankments, and the bustling lowlife of Sadovaya ulitsa and Sennaya ploshchad.

Malaya and Bolshaya Morskaya

Before the Revolution, financiers and aristocrats congregated in the banks and clubs of **Bolshaya Morskaya** and **Malaya Morskaya** (Great and Little Morskaya), a pair of streets dubbed "the City". In 1918, these were taken over or shut down, leaving only imposing facades as a reminder of their heyday – until an influx of foreign companies revitalized their prospects and sent property values soaring in the 1990s. As these streets are the nexus of downtown St Petersburg, you're bound to pass this way often.

Malaya Morskaya

Turning off Nevskiy prospekt at the Wawelburg House (see p.72), you find yourself on **Malaya Morskaya ulitsa**, with its many literary and artistic associations. Number 10, on the left-hand side, is known as the "**Queen of Spades' House**", having once been the residence of Princess N.P. Golitsyna, who is thought to have been the model for the countess in Pushkin's short story *The Queen of Spades*. A former society beauty, she was an old woman in Pushkin's day, when she was nicknamed "Princess Moustache". By a neat coincidence, *The Queen of Spades* was later turned into an opera by **Tchaikovsky**, who occupied the Empire-style block diagonally across the street at no. 13, on the corner of Gorokhovaya ulitsa. It was here that he died on October 25, 1893, most likely from cholera contracted from a glass of unboiled water that he consumed in the *Restaurant Leiner* on Nevskiy prospekt (the theory that he committed suicide to avoid a scandal over his love affair with his nephew is now discredited, following research showing that homosexuality was generally tolerated in Russian high society at that time).

A block further on, a plaque at no. 17 remembers **Gogol**, who lived there from 1833 to 1836, during which time he wrote such short stories as *The Nose*, *Nevskiy Prospekt* and *Diary of a Madman* – set in a St Petersburg where "everything breathes falsehood" – and his satirical drama *The Government Inspector*. Despite the play's success, Gogol felt misunderstood and victimized, and left the city two months after its premiere. His last years were marked by religious mania and despair: lapsing into melancholia, he ate only pickled cabbage and, suffering from cataleptic fits, died after being mistakenly buried alive in a Moscow cemetery in 1852 – as was discovered years later when his body was exhumed, and claw marks were found inside the coffin.

Bolshaya Morskaya

Running parallel to Malaya Morskaya a block to the northwest, the longer **Bolshaya Morskaya ulitsa** features a succession of grandiose facades interspersed with airline offices. At no. 15, on the right, stands the former **Russian Commercial and Industrial Bank**, sporting ornate bronze doors; across the road, the old **Fabergé** emporium (see box on p.103) at no. 24 is recognizable by its voluptuous brown granite pillars. Diagonally opposite at no. 29 is a Baroque mansion reminiscent of a miniature Winter Palace, containing the **Bank for Foreign Economic Affairs**. Beyond Gorokhovaya ulitsa, a statue of Mother Russia succouring a widow, child and pensioner crowns the former **Rossiya Insurance Company**. The further reaches of Bolshaya Morskaya beyond St Isaac's are covered on p.107.

Along the Moyka embankment

Walking along the **River Moyka embankment** (naberezhnaya reki Moyki) from Nevskiy prospekt to Isaakievskaya ploshchad takes longer, but its

Fabergé

Carl Fabergé (1846–1920) turned a small family jewellers in St Petersburg into a world-famous company with branches in Moscow, Kiev, Odessa and London. In 1884, Alexander III commissioned him to design a jewelled Easter egg for the empress – the first in a series of **Imperial Eggs** exchanged by the tsar and tsaritsa every year until the fall of the Romanovs. Although most reference books state that there were 56 eggs in total, art historian Valentin Skurlov believes that only fifty were made expressly for the Imperial family. Even more intricate was the **Grand Siberian Railway Egg**, produced to mark the completion of the line to Vladivostok. Its enamelled gold shell is engraved in silver with a map of the route, each station marked by a gem; inside is a tiny gold-and-platinum replica of the Trans-Siberian Express, which runs when the clockwork locomotive is wound up. After the Bolsheviks closed down his Russian branches in 1918, Carl fled the country, while many of his *objets d'art* were smuggled out or sold off by the state. The first Imperial Egg sold at Christie's in London fetched £85/$136 (in 1934); in 2004, nine eggs and 180 other Fabergé pieces from the Forbes collection were bought for $90 million by the oil magnate Viktor Vekselberg, after an appeal for the eggs to return to Russia made by the director of Moscow's **Kremlin Armoury**, which already has the world's biggest collection of Imperial Eggs (ten). The Virginia Museum of Fine Arts in the US owns five, and Queen Elizabeth II, three, while eight are unaccounted for. A few eggs and other Fabergé objects are usually on display in the Hermitage in room 307.

melancholy charm is hard to resist – the sooty tan, beige and grey facades like a Canaletto canal vista painted by L.S. Lowry.

Turning off Nevskiy prospekt by the Stroganov Palace (see p.71) brings you to the eighteenth-century **Razumovskiy Palace**, while further along is the old **Foundling House** (Vospitatelniy dom) for abandoned babies, which by 1837 was taking in 25,000 children a year, before farming them out to peasant families for "nursing". Today, both buildings belong to the Herzen Pedagogical Institute.

Immediately beyond, the Moyka is spanned by **Krasniy most**, or Red Bridge, carrying Gorokhovaya ulitsa across the river. Of the four similar wrought-iron bridges built across the Moyka in the early nineteenth century, it alone retains its original form, featuring four granite obelisks topped with gilded spheres. From Krasniy most, it's 400m along the embankment to Siniy most at the bottom of Isaakievskaya ploshchad (see p.101).

Along the Griboedov Canal

The winding **Griboedov Canal** (kanal Griboedova) makes a fairly indirect approach to St Isaac's, but the views are so lovely you hardly notice the distance. At the very least, you should walk as far as Bankovskiy most, the first footbridge off Nevskiy prospekt. Here, the south bank of the canal is thronged with students from the **University of Economics**, which is easily identified by the wrought-iron railings and curved wings of what was previously the Assignment Bank. The bank lent its name to the picturesque **Bankovskiy most**, or Bank Bridge, whose suspension cables issue from the mouths of four griffons with gilded wings – in ancient Greece, these mythical creatures were thought to be the guardians of gold. Its designer, Walter Traitteur, also built Lviniy most (Lion Bridge), further along the canal (see p.110 for a description of this and other sights beyond Voznesenskiy prospekt).

Beyond this point the canal runs beneath **Muchnoy most** – a wrought-iron footbridge – and the humped **Kamenniy most** (Stone Bridge), which carries

Gorokhovaya ulitsa across the canal. Looking north up the avenue from the bridge you can see the Admiralty spire; in the other direction, the Theatre of Young Spectators. In 1880, the Narodnaya Volya planted dynamite beneath the bridge in an attempt to kill Alexander II as he rode across, but the plan failed.

Soon after Kamenniy most the canal becomes tree-lined and veers left, passing beneath the arched, wrought-iron **Demidov most**. South of here the embankment opens on to **Sennaya ploshchad**, which was the setting for *Crime and Punishment* (see below). Thereafter, the canal switchbacks through a residential area, spanned by a pair of bridges with gilt finials, and under **Voznesenskiy most**, decorated with bundles of spears and gilded rosettes, which carries Voznesenskiy prospekt across the Griboedov Canal.

Sadovaya ulitsa

The longest of the routes between Nevskiy and Voznesenskiy prospekts is quite unlike the others. Thronged with people and traffic, the two-kilometre length of **Sadovaya ulitsa** is notable for its arresting **streetlife** and once palatial edifices standing cheek by jowl with seedy communal apartments. You can ride all the way along Sadovaya from Gostiniy dvor to Sennaya ploshchad and on to the St Nicholas Cathedral by tram (#54) or minibus (#K-19 or #K-212).

Originally bordered by country estates (hence its name, "Garden Street"), Sadovaya became a centre for trade and vice in the nineteenth century, when its markets and slums rubbed shoulders with prestigious institutions – much as they do today. The initial stretch is flanked by the Gostiniy dvor (p.68) and, further on, by the old **Vorontsov Palace**, set back from the south side of the street behind ornate railings. Built between 1749 and 1757 by Rastrelli, this later housed the elite *corps des pages*, an academy for boys from the highest ranks of the nobility, whose students included Rasputin's assassin Yusupov, the anarchist Prince Kropotkin, and several of the Decembrists. Today it serves as the Suvorov Military Academy, whose cadets cut a dash in their black-and-red uniforms.

On the next block stands the **Apraksin dvor**, a labyrinthine complex of shops fronting cul-de-sacs full of lockups and *ateliers*. Built by Corsini in the 1860s, it took its name from an earlier warren dedicated to Peter the Great's admiral, Fyodor Apraksin, which *Murray's Handbook* described in the 1870s as crowded with "a motley populace", all "bearded and furred and thoroughly un-European". At night, the yard nearest ulitsa Lomonosova rocks to the sound of bands playing at *Money Honey* (see p.368).

Sennaya ploshchad – and Dostoyevsky's "Crime and Punishment"

As Sadovaya ulitsa nears the Griboedov Canal it opens onto **Sennaya ploshchad** (Hay Square). Flanked by dour apartment blocks from the 1930s, when the square was remodelled and its eighteenth-century Church of the Assumption demolished to build a metro station – both optimistically called ploshchad Mira (Peace Square) – this St Petersburg equivalent of Skid Row was facelifted for the city's tercentenary and now has fancy spoked benches and shopping arcades instead of shabby kiosks, but retains more than a whiff of its disreputable past. In Dostoyevsky's time it was known, and functioned, as the **Haymarket**, embodying squalor, vice and degradation. Here, infants were sold to be mutilated by professional beggars, and ten-year-old prostitutes rented out for fifty kopeks a night. Thousands of people slept outdoors, huddled around

CRIME AND PUNISHMENT

Pl. Truda

River Moyka

Yusupov Palace

Mariinskiy Palace

Mariinskiy Theatre

Conservatory

KAZANSKAYA ULITSA

STREMVANAKA

GRAZHDANSKAYA ULITSA

KAZNACHEYSKAYA ULITSA

Griboedov Canal

Sadovaya (M)

SENNAYA PLOSHCHAD

(M) Sennaya Ploshchad

Nevskiy prospekt

SADOVAYA ULITSA

MOSKOVSKIY PROSPEKT

PR. RIMSKOVO-KORSAKOVA

Railway Museum

SADOVAYA ULITSA

VOZNESENSKIY PROSPEKT

BOLSHAYA PODYACHEVSKAYA ULITSA

PROSPEKT RIMSKOVO-KORSAKOVA

ULITSA OLINI

UL. PRZHEVALSKOVO

ULITSA DEKABRISTOV

TEATRALNAYA PL.

Yusupov Garden

St Nicholas Cathedral

SADOVAYA ULITSA

NAB. REKI FONTANKI

NEB. REKI FONTANKI

River Fontanka

IZMAYLOVSKIY PROSPEKT

Dostoyevsky Museum

ZAGORODNIY PROSPEKT

Pl. Turgeneva (500)

N

0   200m

Trinity Cathedral

Tekhnologicheskiy (M) Institut

SITES

Dostoyevsky's Flats	1,2 &3
Raskolnikov's Lodgings	4 &5
Sonya Marmeladov's Lodgings	6 &7
Moneylender's Flat	8
Police Station	9
Dostoyevsky's Mock Execution	10
Dostoyevsky's Wedding	11

fires, trading their shirt for a bite to eat or a gulp of vodka. Local tenement blocks provided lodgings for tradespeople, clerks, prostitutes and students, who thronged the pubs on every corner.

The Haymarket was the setting for *Crime and Punishment*, whose feverish protagonist, Raskolnikov, finally knelt in the square in atonement for his murder of the moneylender Alyona Ivanova. **Dostoyevsky** knew the area well, for he lived in several **flats** on nearby Malaya Meshchanskaya ulitsa (Petit-Bourgeois Street) – now Kaznacheyskaya ulitsa: at no. 1 from 1861 to 1863, before he took a spa-cure at Wiesbaden; at no. 9 in April 1864; and finally at no. 7 on the corner of Stolyarniy pereulok, from August 1864 till January 1867. It was at this flat that he met Anna Snitkina, a stenographer to whom he dictated the final instalment of *Crime and Punishment* (parts had already been serialized) and the whole of *The Gambler*. Four months later they were married. His brother, too, lived on the street; together they published *The Times* and *Epoch* reviews, neither of which prospered.

Although Dostoevsky referred to streets by their initials, his descriptions are precise enough to locate the fictional abodes of his characters. **Raskolnikov's lodgings** were on Stolyarniy pereulok ("S—Lane"). The building could be no. 5 on the corner of Grazhdanskaya ulitsa – whose stairwell has the requisite thirteen steps that he descended "like a cat" from his attic – or no. 9, with its yardkeeper's lodge, where he espied the axe that he stole for a murder weapon. The stairwells of both bear graffiti such as "Don't kill, Rodya" (the diminutive of Raskolnikov's forename, Rodyon), and are usually locked, but tour guides should know the current door-code, or you could hang around until someone opens the door. Similarly, there are two possibilities for the saintly streetwalker **Sonya Marmeladov's lodgings**, namely no. 63 or no. 73 on the Griboedov embankment, which she patrolled for clients in the novel.

You can trace the circuitous **murder route**, from Stolyarniy pereulok across Kokushinskiy most ("K—Bridge"), down Sadovaya ("S—Street") and along what is now prospekt Rimskovo-Korsakova, to the **moneylender's flat** on the Griboedov Canal. House no. 104 fits the bill perfectly, with its dank inner yard reached by a potholed tunnel. If entrance #2 isn't locked you can climb the stairs to flat #74, fingered as the place where Raskolnikov struck at her "thin, fair, graying hair" until "blood gushed out as from an overturned tumbler". He fled through the rear tunnel exiting on Srednaya Podyacheskaya ulitsa.

Other itineraries can give a fuller picture of Dostoyevsky's life. An obvious next stop is the **Dostoyevsky Museum** in the Vladimirskaya district (p.217), only one stop by metro from Sadovaya station on Sennaya ploshchad. On the square itself, the building with a four-columned portico on the western side (no. 65) is the **police station** to which Raskolnikov was summoned and where Dostoyevsky himself later spent two nights in 1874, for quoting the tsar's words without permission in his journal *The Citizen*. He enjoyed the seclusion of his cell, rereading Hugo's *Les Misérables* and reflecting on the turns his life had taken within a mile or so of the Haymarket. At 28, he belonged to the **Petrashevsky Circle** of utopian socialists who met in the house of Mikhail Butashevich-Petrashevsky, on **ploshchad Turgeneva**, until their arrest in 1849. Though Dostoyevsky hid his role in setting up an illegal printing press, he and twenty others were sentenced to death for treason. Their mock execution on **Semyonovskiy plats**, across the river, presaged years of hard labour in Siberia, where his beliefs changed utterly. And his marriage to Anna – which set him on the path to fatherhood and financial security – was consecrated at the **Trinity Cathedral**, not far from the execution ground. The last two are shown on the accompanying map but described in Chapter 6.

The Railway Museum and Yusupov Garden

Besides the Dostoyevsky trail there are a couple of minor sights 100m or so beyond Sennaya ploshchad. At Sadovaya ul. 50, the **Railway Museum** (Muzey Zheleznodorozhnovo Transporta; Mon–Thurs & Sun 11am–5pm; closed the last Thurs of each month; $1.25) retains a statue of Lenin hailing the railway workers and a model of an armoured train used in the Civil War. The rooms also contain intricate scale models of bridges and locomotives (including some futuristic bullet trains that were never built), and a walk-through section of an old "soft class" sleeping carriage, with velvet upholstery and Art Nouveau fixtures, including a bath tub. If you take the trouble to arrange a tour in Russian (☎315 14 76), they'll switch on the model railways. But for real-life trains, you can't beat the Outdoor Railway Museum near the Obvodniy Canal (see p.228).

In summer, the adjacent **Yusupov Garden** is perfumed with the smell of lilac trees and thronged with sunbathers. It was originally the grounds of a **Yusupov Palace** on the Fontanka that later became an engineering institute; the Yusupovs bought another palace beside the Moyka, where the last of the dynasty murdered Rasputin (see p.111). He might be pleased that the Tea

Pavilion of their old pile on the Fontanka now houses one of St Petersburg's top restaurants, *Dvoryanskoe Gnezdo* (The Noble Nest; see p.361). See pp.114–117 for details of the St Nicholas Cathedral and other sights beyond the Griboedov Canal.

West of St Isaac's

The area **west of St Isaac's** has fewer obvious sights than the quarter between the Moyka and the Fontanka, so it pays to be selective. Apart from the mansions on Bolshaya Morskaya ulitsa and the Main Post Office on Pochtamtskaya ulitsa, there's not much to see until you hit ploshchad Truda and New Holland, or the further reaches of the Neva embankment, roughly 800m beyond Isaakievskaya ploshchad. However, there is a nice feel to the locality, whose leafy embankments and residential character give it a genteel atmosphere and make for pleasant evening walks during the summer. The area is shown in detail on the map on p.98.

Along Bolshaya Morskaya ulitsa

Such attractions as there are in the immediate vicinity present a discreet face to the world, particularly along **Bolshaya Morskaya ulitsa**. Several big names in pre-revolutionary Petersburg lived on the northern side of the road, where Montferrand built mansions for the industrialist Pyotr Demidov (no. 43) and the socialite Princess Gagarina (no. 45). The latter is now the **House of Composers** (Dom kompozitorov), whose picturesque coffered hall can be admired under the pretext of visiting the restaurant in the building.

Next door to the House of Composers, at no. 47, the **Nabokov Museum** (Mon–Fri 11am–5pm, Sat & Sun noon–5pm; $0.75; Ⓦwww.nabokovhouse .spb.ru) occupies the birthplace and childhood home of the great Russian writer, unfairly best known abroad for his novel *Lolita*. Opened in 1997, it is the foremost centre for Nabokov studies in Russia, hosting events ranging from jazz concerts and exhibitions of contemporary art to an annual Bloomsday (June 16) honouring Joyce's *Ulysses* (the two writers admired each other's work). Besides some of Nabokov's personal effects and first editions, visitors can see the oak-panelled library and walnut-ceilinged dining room that he lovingly described in *Speak, Memory*. The Nabokov family was immensely wealthy and epitomized the cosmopolitan St Petersburg intelligentsia: the children all spoke three languages and their father helped draft the constitution of the Provisional Government, only to be killed in Berlin in 1922 in the act of shielding the Kadet leader, Milyukov, from an assassin. Guided tours in English can be booked on ☏315 47 13.

On the anniversary of Nabokov's birth (April 23 by the New Calendar), the museum organizes an excursion to the family's **country estate at Rozhdestveno**, 70km from St Petersburg, whose mansion is being reconstructed following a fire in 1995 – see the museum's website for details.

The House of Architects and around

Across the road at no. 52, the **House of Architects** (Dom arkhitektorov) boasts a splendid interior – its original owner entertained the tsar in the Bronze Hall, whose malachite panels and gilded stucco work make the panelled dining room downstairs seem drab by comparison. This is now the *Nikolay* restaurant (see p.361), whose management will give guests a twenty-minute tour ($2) of the upstairs rooms if they're not too busy.

A bit further on, beside the River Moyka, the asymmetrical **Communications Workers' Palace of Culture** is a local landmark dating from the 1930s, when the existing Constructivist building was grafted onto a German church that existed before the Revolution. From here you can walk across **Fonarniy most** (Lamp Bridge) – whose lampposts are shaped like treble clefs – to visit the Yusupov Palace (p.110) on the Moyka or the Haymarket district (p.104), or head up towards the post office and Konnogvardeyskiy bulvar.

Along Pochtamtskiy pereulok

Heading north along Pochtamtskiy pereulok you'll pass the **Museum of Religion** (11am–6pm; closed Wed & the last Fri of each month; $3) on the corner on Pochtamtskaya ulitsa. Ironically, many of the curators of the notorious Museum of Atheism (see p.70) were devoutly religious and safeguarded holy relics until atheism ceased to be state policy. The religions of ancient Egypt, Greece and Rome, Judaism, Buddhism and Islam are all represented by artefacts, but most of the exhibits relate to Russian Orthodox Christianity – jewelled icons, chalices, vestments and suchlike.

Around the corner you'll sight the **Main Post Office** (Glavniy pochtamt; Mon–Sat 9am–7.45pm, Sun 10am–5.45pm), with its distinctive overhead gallery spanning Pochtamtskaya ulitsa. Designed by Nikolai Lvov in the 1780s, the post office originally centred on a stable yard whence coaches departed to towns across Russia, measuring their distance from the capital from this spot; the gallery leading to the Postmaster General's house across the street was added in 1859. It's worth popping inside to see the Style Moderne hall, with its ornate ironwork and glass ceiling, created by the conversion of the original courtyard early last century.

Outside, the gallery displays a **Clock of the World**, whose square outer face shows Moscow time, the standard against which all Russian time-zones are measured, while the round, inner face gives the hour in major cities across the world – a replica got trashed during the high-speed tank and car chase in the Bond film *Goldeneye*.

One block north, the **Popov Museum of Communications** (pre-arranged **tours** in Russian only on ☎315 48 73) on the corner of ultisa Yakubovicha was founded in 1876 as the Telegraph Museum to enlighten Russians about this foreign technology – but it wasn't long before Russia could boast of its own revolutionary invention. Russians regard **Alexander Popov** (1859–1906) rather than Marconi as the inventor of the radio, since Popov transmitted a signal in the laboratories of St Petersburg University on March 24, 1896, almost a year before Marconi – but news of his achievement was slow to leave Russia, whereas Marconi was a skilled self-publicist. The museum covers communication through the ages, with a vast collection of Tsarist and Soviet stamps, and instruments from switchboards to televisions. Popov himself lived at Pochtamtskaya ul. 18.

From Konnogvardeyskiy bulvar to the Nikolaevskiy Palace

Just around the corner from the Popov Museum, the broad, tree-lined **Konnogvardeyskiy bulvar** runs from the Triumphal Columns near the

Horseguards' Manège to ploshchad Truda, 650m southwest. Laid out in 1842 along the course of an old canal, Konnogvardeyskiy bulvar (Horseguards' Boulevard) got its name from the regimental barracks that stood at no. 4. The **Museum of Russian Vodka** (daily 11am–10pm; $1) at no. 5 contains a few historical exhibits, but is basically a retail outlet for flavoured vodkas, which can be sampled on the spot ($15 for a tasting session). At the far end of the boulevard on ploshchad Truda (Labour Square) stands the huge Italianate **Nikolaevskiy Palace**, built by Stakenschneider for Grand Duke Nicholas, but used as a boarding school for young noblewomen until after the Revolution, when it was allocated to the city's Trade Union Council as a Palace of Labour. Nowadays, its grand **ballroom** is used for nightly "folklore" concerts (p.374), and you should at least nip inside the lobby to see the vast double staircase, while a visit to room 44 on the first floor will reward you with the sight of the ornately panelled **Moorish Smoking Room**. From ploshchad Truda you can head south to New Holland, or north to the Neva embankment.

From New Holland to the Neva

Early in the eighteenth century, a canal was dug between the Moyka and the Neva, creating a triangular islet later known as **New Holland** (Novaya Gollandiya). Surrounded by water, it offered an ideal storage place for inflammable materials, such as timber, which could then be transported by barge to the shipyards. In 1763, the wooden sheds were replaced by red-brick structures of different heights, for storing the timber vertically. The most distinctive feature is the great **arch** facing the Moyka, which spans a canal leading to the centre of New Holland, where a large basin saw the first trials of the scientist Krylov's design for a non-capsizeable boat. Although you can't enter New Holland – it still belongs to the navy – the complex looks bleakly romantic, with a row of Dutch-looking houses to the east.

Several decrepit former palaces in the vicinity confirm that this was once a fashionable quarter of the city. On the Moyka embankment to the south, Nicholas I's sister, Grand Duchess Kseniya, lived at no. 108, while Grand Duke Alexei occupied a palace (no. 122) near the naval shipyard on Novoadmiralteyskiy Island. As Admiral-General, he bore much of the blame for the navy's unpreparedness in the Russo–Japanese war. The most evocative is the golden-yellow **Bobrinskiy Palace**, between the Admiralty Canal and Galernaya ulitsa. It was built for the illegitimate son of Catherine the Great and Grigory Orlov, who was smuggled out of the Winter Palace at birth, wrapped in the fur of a beaver (*bobyor* in Russian) – hence the surname under which he was raised by foster-parents until Catherine seized power and brought him to court as Count Bobrinskiy.

Along the Neva embankment

Further north, the Neva embankment is lined with mansions from the eighteenth century, when it was first called the **Angliyskaya naberezhnaya** (English Quay), as it is again now. This fashionable promenade was the centre of St Petersburg's flourishing British community in the nineteenth century (see box on p.115). Its Soviet-era name – Red Fleet Embankment – alluded to the bombardment of the Winter Palace by the cruiser *Aurora* at the outset of the Bolshevik Revolution. On the night of October 25, 1917, the *Aurora* steamed into the Neva and dropped anchor near the middle span of what is now most Leytenanta Shmidta (Lieutenant Schmidt Bridge), trained its guns over the roof of the Winter Palace and at 9.40pm fired the (blank) shots that "reverberated around the world". The event is commemorated by a granite **stela** inscribed with a hammer and sickle, near the bridge. During summer, giant cruise liners are often moored beyond the bridge.

The main point of interest is **Rumyantsev Mansion** (Osobnyak Rumyantseva; 11am–5pm, Tues till 4pm; closed Wed & the last Thurs of each month; $1.25) at Angliyskaya nab. 44, housing a museum on the history of the city. While a few rooms have been restored to their pre-revolutionary opulence, it's a grim exhibition of **life during the Blockade** that makes this museum compelling. A model anti-aircraft position and a life-sized bomb shelter represent the defence of the city; dioramas portray the effort to survive during winter, when water had to be drawn through holes in the ice and firewood scavenged from snowdrifts to feed the tiny makeshift stoves known as *burzhuiki*. Supplies arrived by the "Road of Life" across Lake Ladoga, enabling Leningrad to maintain a basic existence until the Blockade was broken in January 1944 and the Red Army went onto the offensive. A copy of the diary of 11-year-old Tanya Savicheva, recording the deaths of members of her family, is also on display. To get the most from the exhibition you can arrange a **tour** in English (☏311 75 44; $13 group rate).

Between the Yusupov Palace and the Blok Museum

The area between the Yusupov Palace and the Blok Museum knits together several strands in the city's cultural history, being the site of the **Conservatory** and the **Mariinskiy Theatre** (home of the Kirov Ballet); the **synagogue** and the much-loved **St Nicholas Cathedral**; the fabulous **Yusupov Palace**, where Rasputin was murdered; and the former **residence of the poet Blok**. It's a ten- to fifteen-minute walk from St Isaac's to the Yusupov Palace, and not much further to the Mariinskiy, from where it's just a few blocks to the cathedral or the synagogue. From here, a further fifteen-minute walk or a short tram ride takes you to the Blok Museum, set somewhat apart on the western edge of the Kolomna district. The Mariinskiy and St Nicholas Cathedral can also be reached by following the Griboedov Canal as it bends around beyond Voznesenskiy prospekt. This route takes you past the beautiful **Lviniy most**, or Lion Bridge, whose suspension cables emerge from the jaws of four stone lions with wavy manes.

The Yusupov Palace on the Moyka

The **Yusupov Palace** (Yusupovskiy dvorets) on the Moyka embankment (not to be confused with the palace of the same name on the Fontanka – see p.106) is famed as the scene of Rasputin's murder by Prince Yusupov, but really deserves a visit in its own right as the finest palace in St Petersburg, embodying the tastes of four generations of nobles and rivalling the residences of the tsars, but on a more intimate scale. Situated at nab. reki Moyki 94, between the Pochtamtskiy and Potseluev bridges, the building still belongs to the Union of Educational Workers, which used it as a headquarters and clubhouse during Soviet times, but now functions as a museum and may even be rented for private parties, with ballet dancers, musicians and liveried servants – if you have $10,000 to spare.

The museum offers two kinds of **guided tours** every day. If you're not able to do both, opt for the general tour of the ceremonial rooms and theatre that runs every hour on the hour (11am–5pm; $8.30); it's in Russian but the price includes an audio guide in English. The cellar where Rasputin was murdered is covered by a separate tour (11.15am, 3pm & 5.15pm; $3.30), also in Russian – an English-speaking guide can be arranged for an additional $3. From October to June you can also book a tour of the private apartments of Princess Zinaida and Irina (☎314 88 93; cost varies with the size of the group). Photography ($2) is allowed, but flashes and video cameras aren't.

The ceremonial rooms

The magnificent **ceremonial rooms** were created or reworked by each successive Yusupov as they came into their inheritance, so the diversity of styles is matched by the personalities behind them, from Boris – who started the ball rolling in the 1830s – down to his great-grandson Felix in the 1900s. Tours begin with a suite of rooms designed in the 1860s by the Italian Ippolito Monighetti for Boris's son Nikolai, featuring a *faux marbre* billiard hall, an embossed **Turkish study** and an extravagant **Moorish dining hall** with gold filigree arabesques and "blackamoor" figures holding incense vases. After his wife died, Nikolai slept in a small study-bedroom linked by a private staircase to the apartments of his daughter, Zinaida, whose portrait by Serov hangs downstairs. There is also a **buffet room** with embossed leather walls and ceramics standing in for the pilfered family silver; notice the crane-headed walking sticks in the corner.

Ascending the voluptuous marble **State Staircase**, flanked by allegorical statues of Asia, Africa, Europe and the Americas symbolizing hospitality beneath a chandelier holding 130 candles, you reach the classical rooms designed by Andrei Mikhailov for Prince Boris in the 1830s, with green, blue and red **drawing rooms** preceding a **large rotunda**, a white colonnaded **concert hall** and a **ballroom** with a barrel-vaulted ceiling that's really a *trompe l'oeil* canvas hung from chains. After these were completed, Boris had an entire wing built to house the **art collection** amassed by his own father, Nikolai, at Arkhangelskoe outside Moscow, including the **Canova Rotunda** – which contains the celebrated *Cupid and Psyche* and *Cupid with a Bow and Quiver* by the sculptor after whom it is named – and a lovely private **theatre** where Glinka's opera *Ivan Susanin* was premiered in 1836 by the Yusopov troupe of freed-serf actors, who also served as oarsmen on the Moyka and the Neva. The Renaissance-style **Tapestry Hall** that Boris added in the 1840s and the coffered **Oak Dining Room**, commissioned by Zinaida in the 1890s, fit harmoniously into the ensemble.

The cellar

Although small and plain compared to the rest of the palace, few visitors can resist visiting the site of **Rasputin's murder**, where a waxworks tableau portrays the events of December 16, 1916. The deed was planned by Prince Felix Yusupov, the ultra-monarchist Vladimir Purishkevich, the tsar's cousin, Grand Duke Dmitri, Dr Lazovert (who obtained the cyanide) and Guards' Captain Sukhotin. The last four waited in Yusupov's apartments while the Prince led Rasputin – who had been lured to the palace on the pretext of an assignation with Yusupov's wife Irina – to the cellar, where two rooms had been furnished and a table laid with cakes and bottles of sweet wine, laced with cyanide. The poison, however, failed to have any effect, and so Yusupov hurried

Rasputin

Born in the Siberian village of Povroskoe in 1869, **Grigori Novyk** supposedly acquired the nickname "Rasputin" (meaning "dissolute") by virtue of his sexual vitality: his wife (by whom he had four children) said of his philandering, "it makes no difference, he has enough for all". Wanted for horse-rustling, Rasputin sought refuge in a monastery, emerging as a wandering holy man (*starets*). After a two-year pilgrimage to Mount Athos in Greece he returned home to preach, attracting a wide following. An entrée into provincial Kazan society led to the salons of St Petersburg via a chain of female admirers, who introduced Rasputin to the tsar and tsaritsa in November 1905. He proved a godsend to the royal family owing to his unique power to alleviate the internal bleeding of their haemophiliac son, Alexei, whom conventional physicians were unable to help. In 1907, Alexei had a severe attack while Rasputin was in Siberia. Alerted by telegram, he replied, "the illness is not as serious as it seems. Don't let the doctors worry him" – and from that moment on Alexei began to recover.

As Rasputin's influence at court increased, his enemies multiplied. Although he was against Russia entering World War I (and crucially absent when the decision was taken), he was blamed for the mistakes of the corrupt ministers appointed on his recommendation. His orgies in Moscow and Petersburg were a public scandal; worse still, it was whispered that he kept the tsar doped and slept with the empress (or her daughters). Aristocratic and bourgeois society rejoiced at his murder, but the peasants were bitter, believing that Rasputin was killed because he let the tsar hear the voice of the people. Rasputin himself prophesized that should he be killed by the nobility, the monarchy would not survive – true to his words, the February Revolution occurred less than three months after his death.

upstairs, fetched his revolver and shot Rasputin from behind. Yusupov relates how he left Rasputin for dead, but when he returned later, Rasputin leapt up and tried to strangle him, before escaping into the courtyard, where Purishkevich finished him off with four shots. When the coast was clear, the body was driven across the city and dumped, bound but unweighted, into the Malaya Nevka – but instead of being carried out to sea, the corpse was washed ashore downstream and found on January 1, 1917.

The results of the autopsy remained unknown until the publication of Edvard Radzinsky's *Rasputin: The Last Word*, which used hitherto secret documents to argue that Yusupov invented the tale of Rasputin's supernatural vitality to make his own role seem more heroic, and conceal the fact that he bungled by over-diluting the poisoned wine – though another theory states that Dr Lazovert substituted a harmless chemical for the cyanide (as he swore on his deathbed) or that Rasputin's alcoholic gastritis made him immune. Whatever the truth, the conspirators escaped remarkably lightly, the Grand Duke being exiled to Persia and Yusupov to his estates in the Crimea, while the others weren't punished at all.

The private apartments

By prior arrangement (see p.111) you can also tour the **private apartments**, which are as grand as the ceremonial rooms, but smaller. **Princess Zinaida's suite** was designed by Monighetti and redone by Alexander Stepanov after she inherited the palace in 1890. Her Rococo **Porcelain Boudoir** and **White Drawing Room** are perhaps the finest rooms in the palace, with an intimacy also characteristic of the **Henri II Drawing Room** – none of which bears any trace of her estranged husband, but bespeak an enjoyable widowhood. She eventually moved out after her son, Felix, married the tsar's niece, Princess Irina, and the couple commissioned their own apartments, designed in the Neoclassical style by Andrei Vaitens and Andrei Beloborodov, and finished only a year before the Revolution. **Irina's suite** is notable for its **Silver Bathroom**, while **Felix's suite** contains an exhibition on the history of the Yusupov family, which was of Tatar origin. Before fleeing Russia they hid much of their jewellery in the palace cellars, to be discovered by the Communists; to sustain Felix's spendthrift habits in exile, Irina opened a fashion house catering to Russian émigrés, and later won the vast sum of £25,000 in damages from MGM, for defaming her character in the film *Rasputin the Mad Monk*. A **ballroom** and a delightful **winter garden** complete the tour.

The Mariinskiy Theatre and Conservatory

Teatralnaya ploshchad (Theatre Square), southwest of the Yusupov Palace, is home to two of St Petersburg's most revered cultural institutions: the Mariinskiy Theatre and the Conservatory. The **Mariinskiy Theatre**'s exterior is as graceless as its interior is lovely, a sea-green chest enclosing an auditorium upholstered in blue velvet and silver brocade, ablaze with lamps and chanderliers. Yet backstage is so cramped that the 1590 staff have only forty percent of the space required by law; recently, the outmoded technical systems were cruelly exposed by a fire that destroyed its entire collection of historic stage sets. To resolve these problems, a **new theatre** building is to be constructed across the canal behind the old one, with a bridge linking the two. The first design chosen was pretty radical and caused a furore, resulting in a second competition in 2003, won by Dominique Perrault (designer of the National Library in Paris). His design for a 2000-seat theatre covered by a carapace or "veil" of glass threaded with gold-coloured anodized aluminium strips, is almost as controversial, and has been criticized for being unsuited to St Petersburg's climate (a glass-roofed aqua park in Moscow collapsed under the weight of snow in 2004). Work is set to begin soon and scheduled for completion in 2008 – you can follow progress on the Mariinskiy's **website** (Ⓦ www.mariinsky.spb.ru).

The Mariinskiy was established in 1860 (though ballet performances didn't start until twenty years later); its **golden era** was at the turn of the last century, when audiences watched Anna Pavlova, Mathilde Kshesinkaya and Vaclav Nijinsky dance, and heard Fyodor Chaliapin sing. Most of the company's stars left shortly before or after the Revolution, but following a lean period, it gained new popularity in the Soviet era thanks to composers Prokofiev and Khachaturian, and dancers such as Galina Ulanova. Having suffered in the 1980s, today it flourishes under the direction of Valery Gergiev, far eclipsing its old rival the Bolshoi Theatre in Moscow. The company remains best known abroad as the **Kirov**, a title bestowed on it in 1935, when numerous institutions were renamed in honour of this Bolshevik "martyr"; but natives of the city have always called it by its affectionate diminutive, "Mariinka". For information on dancers, performances and tickets, see p.376.

Opposite the Mariinsky stands the **Conservatory**, the premier institution of higher musical education in Russia, founded in 1862 by the pianist and composer Anton Rubinstein – though the building wasn't completed until the 1880s. Rubinstein hated Russian music and ran the institution on conservative, European lines, though his regime relaxed sufficiently to allow the premieres here of Mussorgsky's *Boris Godunov* (1874), Borodin's *Prince Igor* (1890) and Tchaikovsky's *The Sleeping Beauty* (1890). Tchaikovsky was one of the Conservatory's first graduates, while another, Shostakovich, taught here in the

1930s. Since 1944 it has been named after the composer Rimsky-Korsakov, whose **statue** stands near the building (as does one of Glinka, after whom the street crossing the square is named).

Leading figures in the world of music and drama once lived close to the Conservatory. The choreographer **Michel Fokine** (1880–1942) had an apartment at nab. kanala Griboedova 109, to the southeast; ballerina **Tamara Karsavina** owned a house (no. 8) on the Kryukov Canal, northwest of the Mariinskiy; while ul. Glinki 3–5 was the family home of **Igor Stravinsky** (1882–1971), until he married his first cousin – contrary to Orthodox custom – and had to leave home to spare his family the shame.

The St Nicholas Cathedral

Looking down ulitsa Glinki you'll see one of the loveliest **views** in the city: the golden onion domes of the St Nicholas Cathedral, superimposed against the massive blue cupolas of the Trinity Cathedral beyond the Fontanka (see p.221). Traditionally known as the "Sailors' Church" after the naval officers who prayed here, the **St Nicholas Cathedral** (Nikolskiy sobor) is a superb example of eighteenth-century Russian Baroque, by Savva Chevakinsky. The exterior is painted sky blue, with white Corinthian pilasters and aedicules (window surrounds), crowned by five gilded cupolas and onion domes. Its low, vaulted interior is festooned with icons and – as at other working cathedrals – you might find a funeral in one part of the nave and a baptism in another going on simultaneously. During **services** the cathedral resounds with the sonorous Orthodox liturgy, chanted and sung amid clouds of incense. In Tsarist times, the lofty freestanding **bell tower** used to harbour a flock of pigeons, fed "with the rice which the pious place there for the dead". Legend has it that the bells of St Petersburg ring whenever someone makes an offering pleasing to God. A fairytale relates how two waifs intended to donate a crust of bread and a one-kopek coin, but the boy gave the bread to a sick beggar and stayed to nurse him, telling his sister to go on alone. When she arrived at St Nicholas just before closing time, the offering tables were laden with gold coins and gifts, but – as she put her kopek down – the bells tolled across the city.

It's worth carrying on to the junction of the River Moyka and the Kryukov Canal, behind the cathedral, where you can see at least **seven bridges** at once, more than from any other spot in St Petersburg. They frequently appear in *White Nights*, Dostoyevsky's most romantic novel.

West to the Synagogue and Blok Museum

The **Kolomna district** beyond the Kryukov Canal was once full of wooden houses, inhabited by tradespeople, clerks and workers at the iron foundry on Matisov Island – the setting for Pushkin's *Little House in Kolomna* and Gogol's *Portrait*. This humble social profile might explain why St Petersburg's synagogue was sited here, though by that time the district was becoming gentrified thanks to its proximity to the Mariinskiy and the Conservatory – until the Revolution threw the process into reverse. Today, grim 1930s blocks line the way to the docks along **ulitsa Dekabristov**, so there isn't any point in **walking** beyond the synagogue, past the due-to-be-demolished First Five-Year Plan Palace of Culture. To reach the Blok Museum, ride **tram** #31 or #90 from Teatralnaya ploshchad down ulitsa Dekabristov, alighting when the tram turns off at Angliyskiy prospekt.

The Synagogue

St Petersburg's synagogue stands discreetly off ulitsa Dekabristov, its corkscrew-ribbed cupola poking above the rooftops on the corner of Lermontovskiy prospekt. Jews were the most oppressed minority within the Tsarist Empire, where they were largely confined to the Pale of Settlement and barely tolerated in the capital prior to the reforms of Alexander II. Not until 1893 was the community secure enough to build a synagogue and cultural centre, in the Moorish style of synagogues in Eastern Europe. Unlike there, the city's Jewish community escaped the Nazi genocide, but its religious and cultural life was severely restricted for most of the Soviet era. Perestroika both strengthened and diminished it, inaugurating freedoms and opening the floodgates of emigration to Israel. Although far-right parties still foment anti-Semitism, the pogroms that were feared in the early 1990s never materialized and Israel no longer seems a desirable alternative to life in St Petersburg, where Jewish organizations are flourishing as never before. There's an informative exhibition on Jewish history in the foyer of the **Great Synagogue** (Bolshaya sinagoga), whose magnificent prayer hall, with its stucco squinches and stalactite mouldings, has been restored with donations from the Saffra family and others from the diaspora. Besides the celebration of Jewish holy days, it hosts occasional **Klezmer music festivals**, while the enclave includes a **Small Synagogue** used for everyday worship and a *Yeshiva* that dispenses cheap meals to Jewish pensioners. To enter either synagogue men must wear a skullcap.

The Blok Museum

The Symbolist poet **Alexander Blok** (1880–1921) belonged to the so-called "Silver Age" of Russian poetry, which lasted from the beginning of the last century to the mid-1920s, by which time many of its greatest talents had died, killed themselves, or been forced into internal exile by official hostility. Blok's

St Petersburg's Brit Pack

While the contributions of French, Italian and German architects and sculptors are writ large in the city's buildings and monuments, the Britons involved in its development are barely known today. The first to make a splash was **Samuel Greig**, who came to Russia as a 29-year-old naval lieutenant, and won the rank of admiral by burning the Turkish fleet at Chesma Bay and defeating the Swedish navy in the Baltic. His son, **Alexis Greig** also became an admiral, leading the defence of Sevastopol against the British in the Crimean War. Of more significance to the city were engineers like **Charles Baird**, who turned a small workshop on Matisov Island into a foundry that cornered the market in riverboat manufacturing and forged the spans of all the suspension bridges in the city; he also inaugurated a steamboat service between St Petersburg and Kronstadt. Fellow Scotsman **Carl Gascoigne** set up a cannon foundry that made some of the pillars of Kazan Cathedral, and was the first director of what would later become the Putilov Works (now Kirovskiy zavod). Catherine the Great invited **Thomas Dimsdale** to vaccinate her against smallpox and inoculate thousands of others at his "Smallpox House" on Kamennoostrovskiy prospekt, and hired **Charles Cameron** and English landscape designers to work at Tsarskoe Selo. Alexander I invited **George Dawe** to depict the marshals in the 1812 Gallery in the Winter Palace, while Nicholas I's favourite portraitist, **Christine Robertson**, actually had a studio in the palace. But the largest contingent consisted of nannies and governesses, who went home in penury after the Revolution. The graves of Britons who were buried in Russia are mostly in the Smolensk Lutheran Cemetery on Vasilevskiy Island (see p.172).

Within the Fontanka

Streets and squares

Admiralteyskaya naberezhnaya	Адмиралтейская набережная
Angliyskaya naberezhnaya	Английская набережная
Angliyskiy prospekt	Английский проспект
ploshchad Belinskovo	площадь Белинского
Bolshaya Konyushennaya ulitsa	Большая Конюшенная улица
Bolshaya Morskaya ulitsa	Большая Морская улица
ploshchad Dekabristov	площадь Декабристов
Dvortsovaya naberezhnaya	Дворцовая набережная
Dvortsovaya ploshchad	Дворцовая площадь
Gorokhovaya ulitsa	Гороховая улица
kanal Griboedova	канал Грибоедова
Italyanskaya ulitsa	Итальянская улица
Isaakievskaya ploshchad	Исаакиевская площадь
ploshchad Iskusstv	площадь Искусств
Kaznacheyskaya ulitsa	Казначейская улица
Konnogvardeyskiy bulvar	Конногвардейский бульвар
Konyushennaya ploshchad	Конюшенная площадь
Lermontovskiy prospekt	Лермонтовский проспект
Malaya Konyushennaya ulitsa	Малая Конюшенная улица
Malaya Morskaya ulitsa	Малая Морская улица
Marsovo pole	Марсово поле
Mikhailovskaya ulitsa	Михайловская улица
Millionnaya ulitsa	Миллионная улица
naberezhnaya reki Fontanki	набережная реки Фонтанки
naberezhnaya reki Moyki	набережная реки Мойки
Nevskiy prospekt	Невский проспект
ploshchad Ostrovskovo	площадь Островского
Sadovaya ulitsa	Садовая улица
Sennaya ploshchad	Сенная площадь
Stolyarniy pereulok	Столярний переулок
Suvorovskaya ploshchad	Суворовская площадь
Teatralnaya ploshchad	Театральная площадь
ploshchad Truda	площадь Труда
Voznesenskiy prospekt	Вознесенский проспект

Metro stations

Gostiniy Dvor	Гостиный двор
Nevskiy Prospekt	Невский проспект
Sadovaya	Садовая
Sennaya Ploshchad	Сенная площадь

Museums

Blok Museum	музей-квартира А.А. Блока
Russian Ethnographic Museum	Русский Этнографический музей
Hermitage	Эрмитаж
Museum of Religion	музей Религии
Museum of Russian Political History	музей политической истории России
Museum of Russian Vodka	музей Русской водки
Nabokov Museum	музей Набокова
Popov Museum of Communications	музей Связи им. А.С. Попова
Pushkin Museum	музей-квартира А.С. Пушкина
Railway Museum	музей Железнодорожного транспорта
Rumyantsev Mansion	особняк Румянцева
Russian Museum	Русский музей
Theatre Museum	Театральный музей
Zoshchenko Museum	музей М.М. Зощенко

first poems expressed his passion for Lyubov Mendeleyeva, the actress daughter of the scientist Mendeleyev, whom he married in 1903. Later, Blok told Stanislavsky, "Russia is the theme of my life", a theme that reached its apotheosis in the winter of 1918 with *The Twelve* (*Dvenadtsat*), Blok's fusion of religious imagery, slang, revolutionary slogans and songs. Watched over by Jesus Christ, a dozen Red Guards march through a blizzard and the maelstrom of the Revolution, whose imperative Blok voiced as:

**Comrades, take aim and don't be scared,
Let's blast away at Holy Russia.**

The Twelve caused a sensation amongst his fellow poets, yet the Bolsheviks barely acknowledged it, perhaps because, as Kamenev admitted, "it celebrates what we, old Socialists, fear most of all". For the last two years of his life, Blok suffered from scurvy, asthma, delirium and depression. Sensing his end, he wrote bitterly, "Dirty rotten Mother Russia has devoured me as a sow gobbles up her sucking pig." Gorky tried to get him into a Finnish sanatorium, but he died on August 20, 1921.

In 1980, his former apartment at ul. Dekabristov 57, overlooking the Pryazhka Canal, was turned into the **Blok Museum** (11am–8pm, Tues till 5pm; closed Wed & the last Tues of each month; $1.50). Having collected a pair of slippers from the downstairs lobby, you can visit an exhibition of Blok's childhood drawings, photos of the poet and first editions of his work on the floor above. Two floors up, Blok and Lyubov's **apartment** is preserved much as it was when they lived there, with their brass nameplate on the door, and an antique telephone and hat stand in the hall. The *babushka* keeps the houseplants and flowers (which Blok loved) well watered, and can point out the display of first drafts of *The Twelve*. Finally, after going back down to the first floor, you'll be admitted to a room containing Blok's stubbled **death mask** and a sketch of Blok on his deathbed, drawn on the last page of his writing pad. The apartment hosts **concerts** of chamber music (☎113 86 31 for details) and commands a lovely **view** over the Pryazhka.

Across the road, the ballerina **Anna Pavlova** (1881–1931) lived in the apartment building on the southwestern corner of ulitsa Dekabristov and **Angliyskiy prospekt** (formerly named prospekt Maklina after John Maclean, one of the leaders of Scotland's "Red Clydeside", as a mark of international solidarity in 1918). The restoration of its traditional name pays tribute to the Britons who contributed to the city's development in olden days (see box on p.115).

The Hermitage

Many tourists come to St Petersburg simply to visit the **Hermitage** (Ermitazh; эрмитаж), one of the world's great museums. To visit all 350 exhibition rooms would entail walking a distance of about 10km and, at the last count, the collection contained over three million items – it was calculated that merely to glance at each one would take nine years. The museum owns more than 12,000 sculptures, 16,000 paintings, 600,000 drawings and prints, and 250,000 works of applied art, plus 700,000 archeological exhibits and a million coins and medals, and although only a small percentage of these is on show, it's still more than enough to keep you captivated.

The Hermitage has excellent examples of Italian High Renaissance art, as well as unparalleled groups of paintings by Rembrandt, the French Impressionists, Picasso and Matisse – not to mention fabulous treasures from Siberia and Central Asia, Egyptian and Classical antiquities, and Persian and Chinese artworks, among others. Last but certainly not least, there is the interior of the **Winter Palace** itself, with its magnificent **state rooms**, where the tsars once held court and the Provisional Government was arrested by the Bolsheviks (the history of the Winter Palace is related on p.76).

The history of the Hermitage

Although Peter the Great purchased maritime scenes during his visit to Holland, and his immediate successors commissioned portraits by foreign and Russian artists, the Hermitage collection really began with **Catherine the Great**, who saw how other monarchs set store by their art collections and began accumulating one to enhance her own prestige. A shrewd and lucky buyer, she bought 225 Old Masters in 1794 from the Prussian merchant Gotzkowski, after her rival Frederick the Great had turned them down for lack of cash; 600 paintings from Count Brühl of Saxony (1769); 400 first-rate pictures from the Crozat collection (1772); 198 Flemish and Italian master-pieces formerly owned by the British Prime Minister Walpole (1779); 119 canvases (including nine Rembrandts and six Van Dycks) from the collection of Count Baudouin (1781); 250 Roman busts and bas-reliefs from a director of the Bank of England; and 1200 architectural drawings coveted by Emperor Joseph. She also commissioned Wedgwood and Sèvres dinner services, furniture, portraits and some 32,000 copies of antique cut gems – making her one of the greatest art collectors of all time.

Catherine invited select guests to **parties** in the Small Hermitage that she built to display her art collection, and composed "Ten Commandments" for their behaviour, ranging from "All ranks shall be left outside the doors, similarly hats, and particularly swords", to "Eat well of all things, but drink with moderation so that each should be able always to find his legs on leaving the doors". Anyone who violated the rules had to drink a glass of water and read aloud from the poem *Telemachiad* – a far cry from draining a chalice of port, as Peter the Great had punished breaches of etiquette. Though restricted to a small circle, these parties set a precedent for her successors to display the Imperial art collection – on which they, too, spent lavishly.

Catherine's grandson, Alexander I, cannily acquired 98 pictures from Napoleon's wife Josephine – many stolen from other collections – right under the noses of fellow sovereigns attending the Congress of Versailles in 1815. With Nicholas I's purchase of the collection of Napoleon's stepdaughter, the Russian monarchy could at last boast of owning the finest art collection in Europe. Moreover, in 1852, Nicholas decided to open the Hermitage to "decent citizens" on certain days, and appoint professional curators, making it more like an institution than a private hobby.

After the October Revolution, the Winter Palace and Hermitage became a state **museum**, which both benefited and suffered from Bolshevik policies. Its collection grew three-fold as a result of artworks **expropriated** from the Yusupov, Shuvalov, Stroganov, Rumyantsev and Steiglitz collections, plus Impressionist paintings and works by Picasso and Matisse, owned by the Moscow millionaires Shchukin and Morozov. Yet the Hermitage had to surrender many outstanding pictures to Moscow's Pushkin Museum of Fine Arts, and allow the foreign **sale** of major works by Rembrandt, Rubens and Van Eycks in the 1920s and 1930s, when the regime needed hard currency to buy imported machinery – though staff did manage to prevent the sarcophagus of St Alexander Nevsky from being melted down for its silver.

In 1941, staff evacuated 45 carriage-loads of items to Sverdlovsk before the **Blockade** of Leningrad began. As the able-bodied were drafted to fight or dig trenches, invalid or aged curators and attendants strove to protect the thousands of remaining treasures and the building itself from incendiary bombs, shells, ice and damp, during months without electricity or heating. Some two thousand people lived in the palace's cellars, which served as a bomb shelter. While scholars continued their research and gave lectures by candlelight, guides described the works that normally hung in the rooms for the benefit of troops on leave from the front, affirming the values of scholarship and civilization in the face of hardship and Nazi aggression.

Although the Hermitage was patched up and secretly acquired priceless "**trophy art**" seized by the Red Army in Europe (see p.131), Party ideology and xenophobia cramped its style and limited contacts with foreign museums and scholars for much of the postwar era. In Brezhnev's time, pictures from its collection were often presented to "friends" of the Soviet Union – leading to the widely believed (but false) rumour that the local Party boss, Grigori Romanov, borrowed an Imperial dinner service for his daughter's wedding party, and that several pieces were broken.

Belated repairs to the buildings began in 1985, but shrinking state budgets and spiralling inflation stymied progress, obliging the Hermitage to rely on funding from UNESCO, the Dutch government and French sponsors. While its first joint ventures were poorly conceived, the Hermitage's current director, **Mikhail Piotrovsky** has signed **agreements** with several top museums abroad to exhibit treasures from the Hermitage in return for income and art loans. The Hermitage Rooms at Somerset House in London and the Hermitage-Guggenheim Museum in a Las Vegas casino have been followed by a partnership with Vienna's Kunsthistorisches Museum, and other deals are in the pipeline.

Under Piotrovsky's **modernization** strategy, new heating, humidity-control and fire-detection systems, and UV-filtering on the windows, have been installed in most of the rooms; the first full, digitalized inventory of its vast collection is under way; and new exhibition space in the General Staff building is set to grow. Yet while facilities for visitors in the Hermitage have greatly improved, the sheer number of people (three million every year, mostly in the summer) continues to put a strain on the fabric of the buildings. Geraldine Norman's *The Hermitage: The Biography of a Great Museum* is an engrossing account of its history.

Visiting the Hermitage

Although the Hermitage's **opening hours** (10.30am–6pm, Sun till 5pm; closed Mon) are similar to other museums in St Petersburg, the **queues** during the summer months are in a league of their own, stretching as far as the Alexander Column. If you're around then, it's worth signing up for the **tours** offered by various local tourist agencies or the Hermitage's own **excursions bureau** (☎311 84 46 or 213 11 12 11.30am–1pm & 2–4pm; closed Mon), whose clients use the group entrance on the Neva embankment. The bureau offers diverse thematic tours in various languages, at different rates for groups and individuals – book as far ahead as possible. It's easy to "lose" a group and stay on till closing time if you wish. Otherwise, turn up at the main **entrance** on Dvortsovaya ploshchad an hour before the museum opens and hope that you won't have to wait too long. Alternatively, you could order a ticket through the **online booking** service and receive an email voucher that lets you jump the queue and go straight to a *kassa* to collect your ticket. Or you might find enterprising Russians who will "sell" you their place in the queue on Dvortsovaya ploshchad – you may get some dirty looks but there's nothing illegal about it.

The **time** of year also counts, as some parts of the museum are closed when all the room attendants take their summer holidays (though this isn't likely to happen to the Rembrandt room or the French Impressionists). The Hermitage also tends to be less crowded after 2pm, when many groups have come and gone. **Disabled access** isn't as good as at the Tretyakov Gallery in Moscow, but there's a special entrance on the square with a lift; wheelchairs are available; and museum porters will carry people up stairs where no lifts or ramps exist. It's wise to contact the information desk in the lobby ahead of the visit, so that someone will be there to open the gate, and explain which areas of the museum you want to visit.

Tickets sold at *kassas* #1, #2 and #3 in the Winter Palace lobby come in two forms: a regular one covering the Winter Palace and Hermitage ($10.60), and a combined ticket ($19) that includes the nearby General Staff annexe and Peter's Winter Palace (see p.77), plus the Menshikov Palace on Vasilevskiy Island (p.165) – though since this is valid for only one day, you'll have to rush to make full use of it. **Under-17s** and card-carrying **students** are admitted free of charge to all these museums, but not exempted from buying a permit for camera ($3) or video ($8.60) **photography** (from *kassas* in the lobby or room 99 near the disabled entrance). Online bookers pay more for regular ($16) or combined ($24) tickets, but photo permits are included in the price.

You can get a free **floor plan** from the **information desk** in the centre of the lobby. English-language plans adhere to the British convention for numbering floors (ie ground floor, then first floor) rather than the usual Russian and US system, whereby the ground floor is called the first floor; they also display the buildings the other way up from the plans in this book. In the enfilade beside the Jordan Staircase are rows of **shops** selling Hermitage souvenirs, art reproductions and **books**, ranging from a paperback guide ($15) to a one- or two-volume hardback catalogue ($26–40) or a triple **CD-ROM** of the collection ($50), plus lavishly illustrated tomes on specific subjects. Across the way is an **Internet café** ($2 per hour) that allows free access to the Hermitage **website** (Ⓦwww.hermitagemuseum.org). This features highlights of the collection and such useful information as which sections are closed at present (under "Collection Status"), forthcoming temporary exhibitions (also advertised at *kassa* #3), lectures and other events.

Audio guides in English, French, Spanish and other languages are available at the top of the Jordan Staircase near the entrance to the State Rooms. The five versions on offer cover the State Rooms; a general tour of the Hermitage collection; Flemish and Dutch art; from Impressionism to Picasso; and the "trophy art" exhibition known as "Hidden Treasures Revealed" or "French paintings of the nineteenth and twentieth centuries" (see p.131) – each of which costs $4.60. Like the bookshop, they take **credit cards** (Visa, MasterCard or Maestro) or rubles from the **ATM** by *kassas* #1–#2 or the **exchange** office beside the excursions bureau.

Frequent visitors might consider joining the **Friends of the Hermitage**; $100 gets you free entry to the Hermitage and the Menshikov Palace for a year, plus a twenty-percent discount at their shops; for $200 you can bring a friend for free and get invitations to opening parties; for $500 two people, with other privileges. Details are on the website.

Less glamorously, **toilets** (only on the first floor, near the café, a cloakroom and the Jordan and Council staircases) are quite grungy and often lack toilet paper. Also beware of ending up far away from the **cloakroom** where your coat or bag is stashed near closing time, as they start barring access to some wings half an hour beforehand.

Touring the collections

It's impossible to see all the finest works in the Hermitage during a single visit, so concentrate on what interests you most rather than wandering aimlessly from room to room. To help you plan your visit and for ease of reference, the main **collections** are listed in the box on p.122 and the rest of this chapter is arranged along similar lines.

The State Rooms are a must and few would miss the Impressionists, Post-Impressionists, Rembrandt or Leonardo – but beyond that everyone has their own preferences, so it's tricky to suggest an **itinerary**. If you're planning a **whole day** at the Hermitage, it makes sense to visit far-flung "specialist" sections like the Siberian artefacts first (they're likelier to close early), and devote the afternoon to the State Rooms and artworks that tour groups focus on (which are most crowded in the morning). If you have only a **few hours**, a minimalist itinerary might go as follows. Visit the State Rooms on the second floor of the Winter Palace first; pass through the Pavilion Hall of the Small Hermitage and whiz around the Italian, Flemish, Dutch and Spanish art on the second floor of the Large Hermitage, before nipping upstairs to the Impressionists. Finally, head downstairs to the first floor to see the Hall of Twenty Columns, the Kolyvan Vase and the Classical antiquities on your way out of the museum.

Bear in mind that some rooms may be closed for restoration, or open erratically owing to lack of staff, so if you want to see a particular section it's worth checking in advance at the excursion bureau. Once you're inside the Winter Palace, it's hard to know where one building ends and another begins,

Where to find what in the Hermitage

This checklist gives the floor and room numbers of the **main permanent exhibitions**. Those marked by asterisks may be open at irregular times as staff numbers allow; the ones in bold type are especially recommended.

Archeology and Siberian artefacts	Winter Palace first floor 11–27
Central Asian artefacts	Winter Palace first floor 55–66*
Classical antiquities	Small & Large Hermitages first floor 101–131
Dutch, Flemish and Netherlandish art: 15th–18th century	Large Hermitage second floor 245–254, 258, 261 & 262
Egyptian antiquities	Winter Palace first floor 100
English art: 17th–19th century	Winter Palace second floor 298–300
Fabergé jewellery	Winter Palace second floor 307
French art: 15th–18th century	Winter Palace second floor 272–289
French art 19th & 20th century (trophy art)	Winter Palace second floor 143 –146
German art: 15th–18th century	Winter Palace second floor 263–268*
Italian art: 13th–16th century	Large Hermitage second floor 207–230
Italian art: 16th–18th century	Large Hermitage second floor 231–238
Modern European art	Large Hermitage third floor 314–350
Numismatic collection	Large Hermitage third floor 398–400*
Oriental art and culture	Large Hermitage third floor 351–397*
Russian art and culture	Winter Palace second floor 151–173
Russian palace interiors	Winter Palace second floor 175–187
Spanish art: 16th–18th century	Large Hermitage second floor 239 & 240
State Rooms	Winter Palace second floor 155, 156, 188–198, 204, 271, 282, 289 & 304–307
Treasure Galleries	Winter Palace first floor 42 & Large Hermitage first floor off room 121

and direction signs are often misleading. However, almost all rooms are numbered, usually on a plaque above the inside of the doorway. While most paintings are now captioned in English as well as Russian, the ongoing process of relabelling has yet to reach less-visited sections, which are also unlikely to be covered by the museum's audio guides.

Archeology and Siberian artefacts

The Hermitage's collection of **Archeology and Siberian artefacts** is undeservedly one of the least visited sections of the museum (rooms 11–27 & 55–66). It requires a detour into the dingy west wing of the Winter Palace, but in return you'll be rewarded with some weird and wonderful artefacts, the most exciting of which are provided by the nomadic tribes of the fifth and fourth centuries BC, who buried their chiefs deep under the earth with all the paraphernalia required for the afterlife. Between 1929 and 1949, archeologists excavated five burial mounds at **Pazyryk** in the Altay highlands, uncovering a huge log chamber and sarcophagus containing the body of a chief, a felt rug as large as half a tennis court, draped over poles to form a tent, and a funerary chariot and the carcass of a horse (all in **room 26**). Other objects uncovered included a human head and a tatooed shoulder (due to be returned to the Altay Republic in 2004), appliqué saddles and reindeer horns that were affixed to

Room currently closed

▶ General Staff (Hermitage Annexe)

HERMITAGE: First Floor

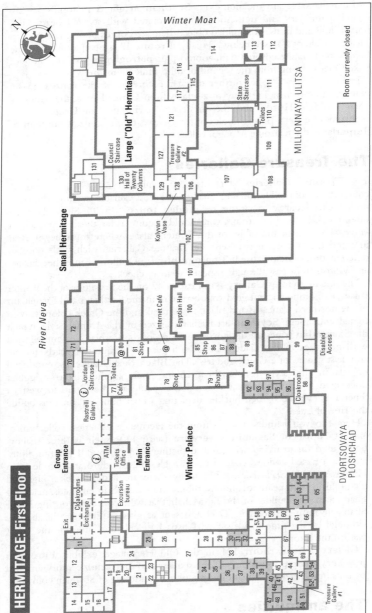

Winter Moat

River Neva

Small Hermitage

Large ("Old") Hermitage

MILLIONNAYA ULITSA

Council Staircase

Hall of Twenty Columns

Treasure Gallery #2

State Staircase

Toilets

Kolyvan Vase

Internet Café

Egyptian Hall

Rastrelli Gallery

Jordan Staircase

Toilets

Café

Shop

Shop

Shop

Shop

Cloakroom

Disabled Access

Group Entrance

Exit

Exchange

Cloakrooms

ATM

Tickets Office

Excursion bureau

Main Entrance

Winter Palace

Treasure Gallery #1

DVORTSOVAYA PLOSHCHAD

horses' heads for ceremonial burials, and a brazier and tent used for smoking marijuana (**room 22**), all of them preserved by the permafrost.

Also remarkable are the numerous **Scythian artefacts** in rooms 16–20, including military and domestic items decorated with stylized bears, elks, horses, lions and birds – the gilded objects here are **copies** of originals now in Treasure Gallery #1 (see below). Finally, if **room 12** is open, don't miss the huge slab of granite covered with zoomorphic **petroglyphs** from the shore of Lake Onega, dating from the second or third millennium BC.

Treasure Gallery #1 lies further down the corridor, while **rooms 55–66** exhibit an ever-changing array of artefacts from **Central Asia**, the Mongol-Tatar **Golden Horde** and the mysterious civilization of **Uratu**, in the highlands of eastern Turkey. Look out for the two-tonne bronze **Cauldron of Tamerlane**, the fearsome Mongol ruler.

The Treasure Galleries

The **Treasure Galleries** (Dragotsenosti Galleryii) or "Golden Rooms" contain some of the Hermitage's smallest and most valuable treasures, displayed under strict security to visitors on **guided tours** ($15.70). Since these are often block-booked by groups, you should enquire as far ahead as possible in *kassa* #1 or #2 in the lobby of the Winter Palace, where tours begin. Bear in mind that there are two separate Treasure Galleries, each with tours at different times (as advertised). **Photography** is not allowed in either gallery, and visitors must pass through a special security check.

The one to go for is **Gallery #1** in **room 42** on the first floor of the Winter Palace, exhibiting ancient goldwork by the nomadic Scythians and Sarmatians of the northern Caucasus and Black Sea littoral, and the Greek colonists who traded with them. **Scythian** art is characterized by the Animal Style, which the **Sarmatian** tribes on the northern shores of the Caspian Sea embellished with gems (as in the diadem inset with garnets, turquoises, pearls and an amethyst cameo of a Greek goddess). The **Black Sea Greeks** also produced objects in this style for Scythian clients, such as the electrum goblet discovered in a tumulus near Kerch – that could also be found in western Siberia, as evinced by belt buckles depicting a boar hunt and dragons beside the Tree of Life.

Here, too, you'll find star items from the Hermitage's peerless collection of ancient Persian or **Sassanid silverware** (see p.140), such as three shallow bowls used for drinking wine, one depicting King Shapur II hunting lions, another a naked goddess clasped by an eagle, and the third an episode from Firdousi's poem *Shahnameh*. Additionally, there are **Mogul** tables, jugs and plates inlaid with pearls, diamonds, rubies and Colombian emeralds, made for Shah Jehan (the builder of the Taj Mahal), that were plundered during Nadir Shah's invasion of Delhi in 1739 and sent as gifts to Empress Elizabeth – although by the time they reached Russia by elephant, Catherine the Great was on the throne.

Gallery #2, off **room 121** in the Old Hermitage, exhibits **European jewellery** and precious stones of the sixteenth to nineteenth century, amassed by tsars from Peter the Great onwards, plus a smattering of Scythian goldwork.

The antiquities

Even if your interest in this collection is limited, a stroll through the first-floor **antiquities** rooms (100–131) is highly recommended. One of the least crowded parts of the Hermitage, the rooms are perfectly in keeping with their contents, marvellously decorated with a variety of Antique features and motifs, one of the best examples being the Hall of Twenty Columns.

Recently reopened after many years, the **Assyrian and Mesopotamian antiquities** in **room 89** were acquired by the Hermitage between 1860 and 1914. Stone reliefs from the palaces of Sargon II and Assurnasirpal II, and a huge inscribed slab from the main square of Palmyra, are juxtaposed with delightful Sumerian charm seals engraved with episodes from the Epic of Gilgamesh. However, most visitors head for the Egyptian Hall (**room 100**) and its **Egyptian antiquities**, consisting mainly of funerary artefacts taken from the Middle Kingdom tombs of four Pharaonic officials, whose painted sarcophagi and shrivelled mummies occupy centre stage. In the hall's display cases are amulets and heart scarabs intended to ensure the officials' safe passage into the afterlife, *shabti* (funerary) figures to perform menial tasks on their behalf, and texts from the *Book of the Dead* showing the judgement of Osiris. Sadly, there are no captions in English here.

Classical antiquities

The more extensive **Classical antiquities** (Greek and Roman) section begins with displays of Roman bas-reliefs in the corridor (**room 102**). From room 106 in the Large Hermitage you can go either left or right, but you'll have to retrace your steps at some point if you want to see the whole section.

Heading left, into **room 128**, you're confronted by the colossal **Kolyvan Vase**, whose elliptical bowl is over 5m long and 3m wide. Carved from Altay jasper over eleven years, the nineteen-tonne vase required 154 horses to drag it to Barnaul, whence it was hauled across frozen rivers to St Petersburg, to be kept in a shed while the walls of the New Hermitage were built around it. In **room 129** you'll find a gold funerary wreath inset with carnelian and some amusing little bronze mice nibbling nuts. Next door is the **Hall of Twenty Columns** (**room 130**), painted with Greco-Egyptian motifs and filled with Apulian amphorae and breastplates, Campanian vases and Etruscan bronzes from the third or fourth century BC. **Room 131** displays busts of the emperors Titus and Vespasian, and exits near the **Council Staircase**, whose orange and pink marble walls and wine-red pillars presage the European art on the floor above (see p.132).

Alternatively, head right from room 106 into the green marble **Jupiter Hall** (**room 107**), devoted to Classical statues, of which Venus disrobing, a vast seated Jupiter, and a club-wielding Muse of Tragedy are the most eye-catching. There are more fine statues in the rooms beyond, particularly **room 109**, where you'll find the lovely **Tauride Venus** acquired by Peter the Great from Pope Clement XI. From room 110, overlooking the muscular atlantes supporting the facade on Millionnaya ulitsa, you can reach the second floor via the **State Staircase**, its three flights flanked by tawny marble walls and grey columns.

Staying on the first floor, in **rooms 111–114** you can see superb Attic vases decorated with fine red-and-black figurative designs, and some rather dry Roman copies of Greek sculptures. However, the real incentive to carry on is to view Catherine the Great's collection of antique cameos and intaglios (**room 121**). The lapidary **Gonzaga Cameo** is one of the largest in the world – a triple-layered sardonyx bearing the profiles of Ptolemy Philadelphus and Queen Arsinoe, carved in Alexandria during the third century BC. Another superb example of Alexandrian craftsmanship is the head of Zeus, from the same era.

△ An atlante on the facade of the Large Hermitage

The State Rooms

The second-floor **State Rooms** of the Winter Palace are as memorable as anything on display in the Hermitage, and best seen while you've still got plenty of energy. Glittering with gold leaf and crystal chandeliers, and boasting acres of marble (mostly artificial), parquet, frescoes and mouldings, they attest to the opulence of the Imperial court. Having witnessed gala balls and thanksgiving services, investitures and declarations of war, the State Rooms then provided a stage for the posturings of the Provisional Government. For reasons that will make sense once you're embarked on the tour, certain rooms (nos. 155, 156, 188–198, 271 & 282) are covered below and the rest (nos. 204, 289 & 304–307) on p.130.

The most direct route from the Hermitage's lobby is by the **Jordan Staircase**, whose twin flights are overlooked by caryatids, *trompe l'oeil* atlantes and a fresco of the gods on Mount Olympus by Gaspar Diziani. The walls and balustrades drip with decoration – a typically effusive design by Bartolomeo Rastrelli, who created similar stairways for the Imperial summer palaces at Peterhof and Tsarskoe Selo. What you see, however, owes as much to Vasily Stasov, who restored the State Rooms after a devastating fire in 1837 and toned down some of the wilder excesses of his predecessors.

From the top of the staircase, you can strike out on two separate excursions into the State Rooms, one culminating in the Alexander Hall, the other leading to the Malachite Room. We've described the former route first – the amount of backtracking involved to cover both is about the same.

To the Alexander Hall

This series of rooms in the east wing of the palace is known as the **Great Enfilade**. Passing through the door on the left of the landing, you enter the **Field Marshals' Hall** (**room 193**), so called because of the portraits of Russian military leaders that hung here before the Revolution; one has now been returned and others may follow. The hall was originally designed by Montferrand, whose careless juxtaposition of heating flues and flammable materials may have caused the great fire of 1837, which started in this room. Its current form reflects Stasov's Neoclassicism: pearly white, festooned with outsized vases and statuary, and dominated by a massive bronze chandelier. In the corner stands a **coronation carriage**, ordered by Peter the Great while he was in Paris.

The next stop is **Peter's Throne Room** (**room 194**). Its title is purely honorific, since Peter the Great died over a century before Montferrand designed the room, but the atmosphere is palpably reverential. The walls are covered with burgundy velvet embroidered with Romanov eagles, while an oak and silver throne commissioned by Empress Anna from London occupies a dais below scores of gilded birds converging on the chamber's vault. A photograph shows the damage caused to the room by a Nazi shell.

Stasov's Neoclassical decoration ran riot in the adjacent **Armorial Hall** (**room 195**). Stucco warriors and battle standards flank the doors at either end, while gilded columns, giant lampstands and cases full of silverware vie for your attention. Also in this room is a restored late eighteenth-century Imperial carriage, of which Fabergé made a tiny copy only 6cm long to go inside one of the eggs commissioned by the Imperial family. The **1812 Gallery** (**room 197**) was modelled by Rossi on the Waterloo Chamber at Windsor Castle (also built to commemorate the victory over Napoleon). An Englishman, George Dawe, was commissioned to paint the portraits of Russian military leaders that line the barrel-vaulted gallery (some died before the portraits were completed

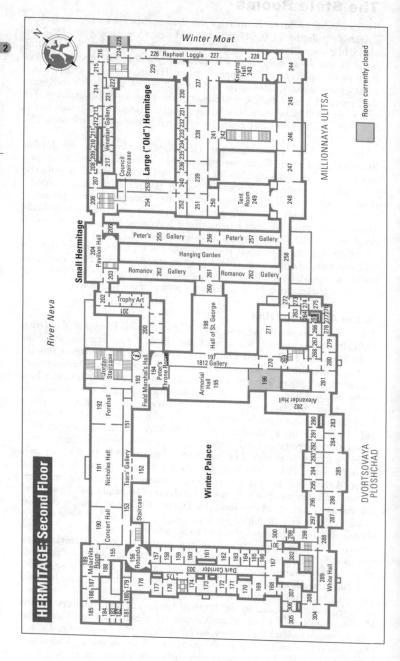

HERMITAGE: Second Floor

Room currently closed

Winter Moat

River Neva

MILLIONNAYA ULITSA

DVORTSOVAYA PLOSHCHAD

N

Large ("Old") Hermitage

Small Hermitage

Winter Palace

226 Raphael Loggia 227

228

216 215 214 224 225

229

237

Knights Hall 243

244

245

246

247

248

222 221

Venetian Gallery

217

Council Staircase

207

230 231 232 233 234 235 236

238

241 242

240 239

253 254 252 251 250

Tent Room 249

206

205

Peter's Gallery 255

256

Peter's Gallery 257

258

204 Pavilion Hall

Hanging Garden

203

Romanov Gallery 262

261

Romanov Gallery 262

260

202

Trophy Art 201

200

198 Hall of St. George

271

272 273 274 275

263 264 265 266 276 277 278

193 Field Marshal's Hall

197 1812 Gallery

270 269

267 268 279 280

i

Jordan Staircase

194 Peter's Throne Room

195 Armorial Hall

196

281

192 Forehall

191 Nicholas Hall

151

152 Tsars' Gallery

282 Alexander Hall

290

283

284

285

153 Staircase

190 Concert Hall

189 Malachite Room

188

187 186 185 184 183 182 181 180 179

178

177 176

156 Rotunda

175 174 173 172 171 170 169 168

157 158 159 160 161 162 163 164 165 166 167

303 Dark Corridor

291 292 293 294 295 296 297

286

287

288

298 299 300 301 302

289 White Hall

307 308 306 305 304

and the gaps remain unfilled). Alexander I and his ally, Frederick Wilhelm III of Prussia, merit life-sized equestrian portraits at the northern end.

Alongside the 1812 Gallery lies the eight-hundred-square-metre **Hall of St George** (**room 198**) – the main throne room. Built by Quarenghi, with lavish use of Carrara marble, the hall was inaugurated on St George's day in 1795 and became associated with solemn acts of state. Here, Alexander I swore that he would never make peace until Napoleon had been driven from Russia, and Nicholas II similarly vowed to defeat Germany at the outbreak of World War I. The emperor's throne is the only piece of furniture in the hall, its parquet floor consisting of sixteen kinds of wood.

To the left of room 270 is the **Cathedral** (**room 271**), used originally as the private court chapel and not as large as its name suggests. Rastrelli's gilded Baroque interior was hardly touched by the fire of 1837, and the proportions are such that the ceiling seems to soar into the heavens, despite the small scale. Walk back through room 270, left into 280 and then turn right through 281 to emerge in the magnificent **Alexander Hall** (**room 282**), designed by Alexander Bryullov in 1837 to commemorate the Napoleonic Wars. The military theme is reflected in the sky-blue and white bas-reliefs that cover the walls. Also notable are the stucco palm "umbrellas" that sprout from the vaulting and the intricate parquet floor. The hall is used for temporary exhibitions and interrupts a series of rooms devoted to French art (see p.135). At this point, you'll need to retrace your steps to the Jordan Staircase to see the rest of the state rooms.

To the Malachite Drawing Room and beyond

The river-facing **Neva Enfilade** contains some of the most famous rooms in the Winter Palace, chiefly associated with Nicholas II and the Provisional Government. Immediately ahead of the Jordan Staircase is a **Forehall** (**room 192**), centred on a malachite and bronze pavilion that was used for champagne buffets whenever balls took place in the adjacent **Nicholas Hall** (**room 191**). Named after the portrait of Nicholas I installed here in 1856, the hall can accommodate five thousand people and is used, along with the Forehall and the Concert Hall, to stage prestigious temporary exhibitions.

At this point, it's worth a detour into the corridor (**rooms 151 & 153**), designated the **Gallery of Russian Tsars**, hung with portraits of the same. Of particular interest are two of Catherine the Great, painted fourteen years apart; her luckless son Paul, his snub nose flatteringly filled out; and Nicholas II, in a humble pose suited to his posthumous canonization as an Orthodox martyr. The nearby **Concert Hall** (**room 190**) affords a fine view of the Rostral Columns, across the Neva. By the far wall stands the enormous Baroque **sarcophagus** of St Alexander Nevsky, resembling a giant pen-and-ink stand and consisting of 1.5 tonnes of silver covering a wooden armature.

The **Malachite Drawing Room** (**room 189**), beyond the Concert Hall, was created by Bryullov in 1839 for Nicholas I's wife, Alexandra Fyodorovna, its pilasters, fireplace, tables and knick-knacks fashioned from over two tonnes of the lustrous green stone (from the Urals) that gives the room its name. Kerensky's Provisional Government met here from July 1917 until their arrest by the Bolsheviks three months later, and it's easy to imagine the despondent ministers slumping on the divan before adjourning to the adjacent **White Dining Room** (**room 188**), hung with allegorical tapestries of Africa, Asia and America. Here they were arrested (Kerensky had already fled) and obliged to sign a protocol dissolving the Provisional Government – the mantelpiece clock was stopped at that moment (2.10am).

From here you enter the barrel-vaulted **Moorish Dining Room** (**room 155**), named after the black ceremonial guards costumed as Moors, who stood outside in Tsarist times. Beyond lies the **Rotunda** (**room 156**), a lofty circular room with a coffered dome encircled by a balcony. In the centre stands a model of a triumphal column topped with a statue of Peter, which he planned to erect outside the palace, but which was never built. From the Rotunda, you can continue southwards into the section on Russian art and culture (see below), or go back through the Malachite Drawing Room to visit the exhibition of Russian palace interiors.

Russian palace interiors

Opened in the 1980s as a temporary exhibition, the **nineteenth-century Russian palace interiors** proved so popular that they have remained in place ever since. The exhibition (closed for lunch 12.30–1.30pm) consists of a series of rooms (**175–187**), each arranged with furniture and objects of applied art re-creating the interior styles of each decade from the early 1800s to the Revolution. From the Empire-style Music Room, with its exquisite instruments by Hambs, you progress to the late nineteenth-century Oriental Smoking Room, Nicholas II's Gothic Library, the Style Moderne nursery with its luxurious child-sized furniture (used by Nicholas and Alexandra's children), and finally a neo-Russian room by Malyutin. Much of the furniture was designed by the architects who were working on the building at the time; in the Gothic Study, which represents the 1890s, even the waste bin forms an integral part of the ensemble.

Russian art and culture

The section on **Russian art and culture** nominally starts with the Gallery of Russian Tsars (see p.129) and the adjacent room 152, containing a copy of Kneller's famous portrait of the young Peter the Great. It then resumes in room 157, beyond the Rotunda, and includes rooms on both sides of the Dark Corridor (though not all of them are open) containing a miscellany of objects including sundials, a universal clock, equipment for extracting teeth and engravings showing the rapid growth of St Petersburg. You'll also find busts of Peter and Menshikov and some of the many objects that Peter created in his private turnery, including an impressive multi-tiered ivory chandelier. In 1880, Alexander II narrowly escaped death when a bomb exploded below room 161, killing eleven soldiers at lunchtime.

Rooms 168–173 exhibit an array of more familiar items, the result of Peter's bringing in foreign craftsmen and the subsequent boom in painting and the applied arts during Catherine the Great's reign. Look out for the lizard-armed chair designed by Catherine's favourite architect, the Scotsman Charles Cameron, in room 171. Paul's throne as Grand Master of the Knights of Malta (see p.283) is in room 172, followed by incredible filigree ivory vases and the uniquely Russian steel dressing-table and desk sets in room 173 – a specialty of Tula craftsmen. From here you can continue on to the White Hall and Gold Drawing Room (see below) or return to the Field Marshals' Hall (see p.127) and head for the Western European art section in the Large Hermitage (see p.131).

The White Hall and Gold Drawing Room

Running round the southwest corner of the Winter Palace are several further state rooms that were revamped after the fire of 1837 for the wedding of the future Alexander II and Maria of Hessen-Darmstadt. The only significant interior to survive in its original restored state, however, is Bryullov's **White Hall** (room 289), its lightness and airiness in contrast to the surrounding apartments. It now houses some skilfully made furniture along with eight large landscapes and many smaller works by **Hubert Robert**, a French artist who found fame in Russia while remaining largely unknown in Western Europe.

From here you emerge into one of the palace's most vulgar state rooms, the **Gold Drawing Room** (room 304), redecorated by Bryullov in the 1850s. Inspired by the interiors of Moscow's Kremlin, its patterned walls and vaulted ceiling are gilded all over. The room contains French and Italian cameos displayed in hexagonal cases.

The next room along, the **State-Corner Study** (room 305), contains Sèvres porcelain and pieces from the Josiah Wedgwood "**Green Frog Service**" made for Catherine the Great – the frog being the whimsical coat of arms that she chose for her Chesma Palace. Beyond lies the 1850s **Raspberry Boudoir** (room 306) – the former private room of Alexander II's wife, Maria Alexandrovna – decorated in "Second Baroque" style, with rich crimson brocatelle hangings by Cartier, plus gold and mirrors galore – a decor designed by Gerald Bosset.

Bringing this sequence of rooms to an end with a flourish, **room 307** displays **Fabergé jewellery** from the collections of the Hermitage, other museums in St Petersburg and the Imperial palaces. Among the array of tiaras, bracelets and cigarette cases, look out for the exquisitely delicate *Cornflower* and *Daisy*, carved from rock crystal.

French paintings from the nineteenth and twentieth centuries

In 1993, the Hermitage became the first museum in Russia to admit possession of stores of "**trophy art**", appropriated from Germany at the end of World War II – some of it had previously been stolen by the Nazis in occupied Europe. As Russian legislators are at one with public opinion in opposing the return of any artworks until Russian claims for treasures despoiled by the Nazis are settled, the exhibition **in rooms 143–146** (which closes at 5pm, 4pm on Sun) is likely to remain for the foreseeable future – although mindful of its sensitive status, the Hermitage has scrapped its previous title "Hidden Treasures Revealed", and coyly omits all of the artworks therein from its website.

The exhibition includes ten **Renoirs**, ranging from *Woman Brushing her Hair* to the light-filled *Low Tide at Yport*; four **Van Goghs**, notably the *White House at Night*; **Monet's** lush *Garden in Bordighera*; **Gauguin's** *Late Afternoon* and *Two Sisters* from his Tahitian period; and six **Cézannes**, including a *Mont Sainte-Victoire* and *Bathers*. Also look out for the *Road to Castel Gondolfo*, by **Derain**, the *Place de la Concorde* by **Degas**, and **Manet's** *Portrait of Mme Isabelle Lemonnier*. **Daumier's** *The Burden*, with its toiling laundress and child, is a rare exception to the prevailing mood of sunny optimism.

Italian art: thirteenth to eighteenth century

Spread through a score of small rooms (207–238) in the Large Hermitage, **Italian art** is well represented, with works by Leonardo, Botticelli,

Michelangelo, Raphael and Titian, although there is a poor showing of works by the stars of the early Renaissance.

The most direct approach is via the Council Staircase (from Antiquities on the first floor), which emerges at the start of the section. Alternatively, if you are coming from the Field Marshals' Hall (room 193), head along the corridor (rooms 200 & 201) and over the covered bridge into another state room, the **Pavilion Hall** (room 204). Built by Stackenschneider in 1856, this dazzlingly light room combines elements of Classical, Islamic and Renaissance architecture, with a gilded balcony overlooking a mosaic based on one discovered in a Roman bathhouse. Taking centre stage is the **Peacock Clock**, a miracle of craftsmanship by the English jeweller James Coxe, which once belonged to Catherine's lover Potemkin. Check with the general information office as to which days the peacock "performs" – spreading its tail as the cockerel crows on the hour, while a mushroom rotates in surreal accompaniment.

Simone Martini to Leonardo da Vinci

Room 207 boasts a typically graceful, colourful *Madonna* by the thirteenth-century Sienese painter **Simone Martini**, and an equally opulent *Five Apostles* by **Gentile da Fabriano** (one of his relatively few surviving compositions). A tiny polygonal chamber leads to room 209, containing the radiant *St Augustus's Vision* by **Fra Filippo Lippi**, and work by the Dominican **Fra Angelico**, whose fresco *Madonna and Child, St Dominic and St Thomas Aquinas* is the largest painting in the room. Della Robbia terracottas and superb bas-reliefs by Rossellino fill the next few rooms. Room 213 holds two small paintings by the distinctive hand of **Botticelli**, two serene canvases by **Pietro Perugino**, an Umbrian painter who worked on the Sistine Chapel and is best known as Raphael's teacher, and some gentle works by **Filippino Lippi**.

The high coffered ceiling and ornate decor of **room 214** rather upstage the only two works by **Leonardo da Vinci** in Russia. The earlier one – a lively piece with a youthful Mary dandling Jesus on her knee – is known as the *Benois Madonna*, after the family who sold it to Nicholas II in 1914. The other is the *Madonna Litta*, a later and more accomplished work, depicting the Virgin suckling the infant Jesus.

The following room focuses on Leonardo's immediate successors: *Portrait of a Woman* (also known as *Colombine* or *Flora*) is by his most faithful pupil, **Francesco Melzi**, in whose arms he died.

The Raphael Loggia, Michelangelo and Caravaggio

Continue through room 216 with its few examples of Mannerist works into the **Raphael Loggia** (**rooms 226 & 227**), a long, lofty gallery lit by large windows overlooking the Winter Moat and the Hermitage Theatre. Commissioned by Catherine the Great, it was created between 1783 and 1792 by Quarenghi as a copy of Raphael's famous gallery in the Vatican Palace. Every surface, wall and vault is covered with copies on canvas of Raphael's frescoes, made by a team of artists under Christopher Unterberger. Notice how the Romanov double-headed eagle has been substituted for the papal coat-of-arms.

To the right as you enter the loggia is **room 229**, whose highlights include Raphael's *Madonna Conestabile*, completed at the age of 17. His slightly later *Holy Family* depicts a beardless, though still fairly aged, Joseph, and an uncertain Madonna and Child. Straight ahead in the Small Skylight Room

(**room 237**) are vast canvases by **Tintoretto**, **Veronese** and other High Renaissance luminaries, while to the right in **room 230** you'll find frescoes by the School of Raphael and a sculpture by **Michelangelo** – the spiritually anguished *Crouching Youth* – whose taut musculature bears the sculptor's chisel marks. The famous *Lute Player* by **Caravaggio** can be found in room 232 and **Alessandro Magnasco's** *Banditti at Rest* in **room 233**.

To view the rest of the Italian art collection you'll need to retrace your steps to room 216. On the way back, if you have time for a small detour, turn right through room 237 (instead of left into room 229) into the **Gallery of Ancient Painting** (**room 241**), which, despite its name, displays eighteenth-century European sculpture, including Canova's *Three Graces* and *Repentant Magdalene*. The **Knights' Hall** (**room 243**) beyond has exhibitions from the vast stores of highly decorated European weapons and armour in the Imperial arsenal; the four cavalry horses were stuffed by Klodt, who sculpted the ones on Anichkov most. In the adjacent **Twelve-Column Hall** (**room 244**) are temporary exhibitions of delicate artworks such as textiles, icons or watercolours.

Veronese, Titian and Giorgione

Once back in room 216, turn left along a corridor to **room 222**, which contains a few paintings by **Veronese**, including a confident *Self-portrait* and a superb *Pietà*. This leads into the **Venetian Gallery**, where **room 221** displays paintings by **Titian**, the most famous being the *Danae* – one of five versions of the same subject which Titian made (the best known is in the Prado) – in which a Michelangelesque nude languishes on a bed while Zeus appears as a shower of golden coins, though some regard the powerful *Saint Sebastian* and sensuous *Penitent Magdalene* of his final years as finer works. His *Portrait of a Young Woman* wearing a man's cloak, with one arm drawn across her breast, hangs in room 219. In between, you can admire the **Embriachi ivories** in room 218 – pieces of carved walrus tusk used to make altars in the sixteenth century – and **Giorgione's** *Judith*, one of the few paintings in the world that is firmly attributed to him (in **room 217**).

Spanish art: fifteenth to eighteenth century

The Hermitage's collection of **Spanish art** is the largest in the world outside Spain. Among the earlier works in room 240 are a superb late fifteenth-century Gothic *Entombment of Christ* by an unknown master, and **El Greco's** painterly depiction of *SS Peter and Paul* – according to legend, it was St Paul who converted the painter's native Greek island of Crete to Christianity.

Room 239, the Large Skylight Room, displays examples of the flowering of Spanish art during the seventeenth century – large religious works created for churches and monasteries, as well as more intimate pieces. Among the monumental compositions are *St Jerome Listening to the Sound of the Trumpet* by **Ribera**, and **Zurbarán's** *St Laurentio* altarpiece, painted for the Monastery of St Joseph in Seville, which shows the grid on which the saint was roasted to death. **Murillo's** *Immaculate Conception* differs from the usual presentation of the Virgin with her feet on the moon and stars overhead by taking the Assumption as its leitmotif – hence the picture's other title, *The Assumption of the Madonna*. His sugary *Adoration of Christ* is accompanied by the cheeky *Boy with a Dog*, equally typical of his sentimental style.

While religious themes were esteemed, **Velázquez** was equally willing to paint what were scornfully called *bodegón* (tavern) scenes, such as *Luncheon* – the figure on the right is supposedly Velázquez himself, who was only 18 at the time. In later life he concentrated largely on portrayals of the Spanish royal family: his *Portrait of Count Olivarez* depicts the *éminence grise* and power behind the throne, who was also a friend of the artist. Another penetrating work is **Goya**'s portrait of the actress Antonia Zaráte, who died of consumption shortly after the completion of this picture, which betrays her inner anxiety.

Dutch, Flemish and Netherlandish art: fifteenth to eighteenth century

One of the Hermitage's great glories is its **Dutch, Flemish and Netherlandish art** collection. As well as one of the largest gatherings of works by Rembrandt outside the Netherlands, you'll also find one of the world's finest collections of paintings by Rubens and Van Dyck, many of which came from the Walpole Collection of Houghton Hall in Norfolk, bought by Catherine the Great in 1779 (see "English art", p.137). If you've come from the Italian art section, you'll start with the Rembrandts in room 254. Be warned that these are amongst the most crowded rooms in the Hermitage.

Rembrandt

In **room 254**, the twenty or so paintings by **Rembrandt** include some of the finest works from his early period of success in the 1630s, including light, optimistic canvases such as *Flora*, a portrait of his wife Saskia, completed shortly after their marriage. *The Sacrifice of Isaac* is from the same period, though more serious in content, while the *Descent from the Cross* is set at night to allow a dramatic use of light which focuses attention on the body of Christ and the grief-stricken Mary, prematurely aged and on the verge of collapse.

Rembrandt's *Danae*, slashed by a deranged visitor in 1985, is back on show after years of restoration, accompanied by an exhibition on the dilemmas and technicalities of restoring such damaged canvases. The picture was one of Rembrandt's personal favourites, and he parted with it only when he was forced to declare himself bankrupt in 1656.

Bankruptcy was not the only misfortune that Rembrandt suffered in later life: Saskia had died in 1642, shortly after giving birth to their fourth child, but Rembrandt married again in 1645, the same year he painted the calm domestic scene in *The Holy Family*, set in a Dutch carpenter's shop. The heavenly reward of the penitent is the theme of *The Return of the Prodigal Son*, bathed in scarlet and gold, one of Rembrandt's last canvases.

To the Tent Room and beyond

The vast **Tent Room** (**room 249**), so called because of its unusual pitched roof and beautiful coffered ceiling painted in pastel shades, is stuffed with seventeenth-century Dutch genre paintings by **Frans Hals**, Jan Steen, Salomon van Ruisdael, and others. Beyond, **room 248** is also lavishly decorated, with artificial marble columns supporting a finely patterned ceiling, hung with an octagonal chandelier resembling miniature organ pipes. Among the many paintings here are several small canvases by **Jan Brueghel**, son of the great Pieter Brueghel the Elder (none of whose works appears in the Hermitage). Jan was an accomplished artist in his own right, a specialist in landscapes and still lifes, which are hung by the window.

Rubens and Van Dyck

Works by **Rubens** at the height of his career (1610–20) fill **room 247**, including *Descent from the Cross*, a famous altarpiece painted for the Capuchin monastery at Lierre, near Antwerp. In Rembrandt's version, the reality of human suffering and the use of light were paramount, whereas Rubens stressed the contrast between the clothes of the figures and the pallid body of Christ. One late work, painted in the last year of his life, rejects the traditional portrayal of *Bacchus* as a youthful partygoer and depicts him instead as a jovial slob, enveloped in folds of fat.

As was usual when commissions poured in, students in Rubens' studio worked on the master's paintings, amongst them the young **Van Dyck**, who contributed to the *Feast at the House of Simon the Pharisee*, a resolutely secular treatment of a biblical theme. Later, he was court painter to (and knighted by) Charles I of England, producing some of his finest portraits, including those of the architect Inigo Jones, Thomas Wharton, Charles I and Queen Henrietta Maria, all of which are on display in **room 246**, together with earlier works, such as a wonderful self-portrait.

Retracing your steps through room 248 brings you to a corridor (room 258) lined with Flemish landscapes and winter scenes by Leytens and Savery. Off this are two enfilades overlooking Catherine's **Hanging Garden**, called **Peter's Gallery** (rooms 255–257) and the **Romanov Gallery** (rooms 261–263). The former may soon exhibit seventeenth-century Dutch paintings, while the latter is hung with medieval and early Flemish art. Look out for **Roger van der Weyden**'s *St Luke and the Virgin*, the two halves of which were purchased separately by the Hermitage before it was realized that they belonged together. Other gems are Robert Campin's diptych *Trinity, Virgin and Child*, Lucas van Leyden's *Healing of the Blind Man*, and Dirk Jacobsz's brilliant group portraits of the Amsterdam Shooting Corporation. At the end of Peter's Gallery is a **Study** (room 205) designed by Quarenghi – the only room in the Winter Palace to retain its original eighteenth-century decor: strawberry-coloured walls, a gold and white ceiling and yellow *faux marbre* columns.

German art: fifteenth to eighteenth century

The Hermitage's collection of **German art** from the fifteenth to eighteenth century is conveniently approached from the Dutch, Flemish and Netherlandish art section by continuing along the corridor (room 258) through to **room 263**. Unfortunately, this section is usually closed in summer, but if you are here at other times, you'll be able to see a few paintings by well-known names, including Lucas **Cranach the Elder**'s *Portrait of a Woman* and the first of his series of *Venus and Cupid* paintings, which dates from 1509. Ambrosius **Holbein**, older brother of Hans, lived a short life – his *Portrait of a Young Man* was completed at the age of 23, shortly before he died.

French art: fifteenth to eighteenth century

Thanks to an obsession with all things French during Catherine's reign, the Hermitage features an impressive collection of **French art**, particularly from the seventeenth and eighteenth centuries. The Romanovs employed many French artists, starting with Caravaque, who was engaged by Peter the Great and remained in Russia until his death. Nevertheless, this art has lost its appeal for many, bound up as it is with the cloyingly frivolous tastes of the French and Russian aristocracy, and these rooms (272–281 & 283–288) are among the least visited in the Hermitage.

The collection begins in room 272 with French fifteenth- and sixteenth-century metalwork, blue Limoges enamel tiles and carved furniture. The earliest French paintings, from the fifteenth and sixteenth centuries, are in room 274, while room 275 displays **Simon Vouet**'s allegorical portraits. The next two rooms contain fairly minor works, but for those not enamoured of cherubs, there's the happy sight of them being slaughtered en masse by Roman soldiers in Bourdon's *Massacre of the Innocents*.

From Poussin to Greuze

The Hermitage is particularly renowned for its collection of paintings by **Nicolas Poussin**, the founder of French Neoclassicism, whose artistic philosophy of order, reason and design was the antithesis of Rubens' more painterly style – the few drops of blood visible on Poussin's frenetic *Battle of the Israelites with the Amalekites* are purely symbolic. Also in **room 279** is his best-known work in the Hermitage, the colourful *Landscape with Polyphemus*, whose orderly symbolism encapsulates Poussin's rational philosophy of painting.

The other great French artist of the day was **Claude Lorrain** (real name, Claude Gellée), who began his career as a pastry cook to an Italian painter. **Room 280** exhibits tranquil pastoral scenes of the lost Golden Age of Antiquity, and his use of light – as in *The Four Times of Day* cycle – greatly influenced English artists such as Turner. But the primary role of art during the Golden Age of the "Sun King" was the glorification of absolute monarchy, as depicted in Pierre Mignard's gigantic *Magnanimity of Alexander the Great* in **room 281**.

Passing through the Alexander Hall, one of the Winter Palace's state rooms (see p.129), you soon come to **room 284**, with its works by **Antoine Watteau**. Best known for his cameos of socialites frozen in attitudes of pleasure – *The Embarrassing Proposal* is a good example – Watteau's paintings seem frivolous and insincere to contemporary eyes, but his technique of "divisionism" (juxtaposing pure colours on the canvas, rather than mixing them on the palette) was a major influence on Seurat and the Pointillist school.

Room 285 has a few works by Watteau's followers **Nicolas Lancret** and **Jean-Baptiste Pater**, but the most powerful piece is **François Lemoyne**'s voluptuous and wicked *Jupiter and Io* – thought to be a copy of a lost painting by Correggio – in which Jupiter disguises himself as a cloud in order to seduce the young maid. The room also contains paintings by **François Boucher**, whose talents were considered by many to be wasted on the production of profitable pictures of frolicking goddesses and cherubs.

The intellectual atmosphere of Enlightenment France implicit in the paintings in **room 287** contrasts with the more corporeal works in previous rooms. **Chardin**'s marvellous *Still Life with the Attributes of the Arts*, commissioned by the St Petersburg Academy of Art, was sold by the Hermitage in 1849 under orders from Nicholas I, and only re-acquired by the museum during the Soviet period. The statue of the aged philosopher Voltaire by **Houdon** escaped a similar fate when, instead of following Nicholas's order to "get rid of this old monkey", a far-sighted curator locked it out of sight in the Hermitage library.

Critics have accused **Jean–Baptiste Greuze**, whom Catherine the Great greatly admired, of "insincerity, artificiality and misplaced voluptuousness".

Judging by the works in **room 288**, it's difficult to disagree, yet he was originally popular precisely because "morality paintings" such as *Spoilt Child* and *Paralytic Helped By His Children* represented a move away from the frivolity of the Rococo.

English art: seventeenth to nineteenth century

When the Hermitage opened to the public in 1852, it was the only gallery in Europe with a collection of **English art** (**rooms 298–300**). Its core consists of the famous **Houghton Hall Collection** of Sir Robert Walpole, which Catherine the Great purchased from his dissolute grandson for a paltry £40,000 – thereby achieving posthumous revenge on Walpole, who had called her the "philosophizing tyrant". To rub it in, her buyer left a portrait of the empress on the bare walls of Houghton Hall. The majority of the works were Italian or Flemish, but there were enough English paintings from the sixteenth to the eighteenth century to kick-start a collection.

In 1790, the Hermitage acquired three large canvases by **Joshua Reynolds**, including *The Infant Hercules Strangling Serpents*, one of the last paintings he completed before he went blind. Commissioned by Catherine, it is meant to symbolize Russia besting her foes, but also features several of Reynolds' English contemporaries (including Dr Johnson as Tiresias). Two other masterpieces are **Thomas Gainsborough**'s *Portrait of a Lady in Blue*, and *The Forge* by **Joseph Wright** of Derby. Also in the collection is part of the unique 944-piece "Green Frog Service" made by **Josiah Wedgwood** for Catherine's Chesma Palace (another part of which is on display in room 305; see p.131).

Modern European art

After the State Rooms, the **third floor** of the Winter Palace is the most popular section of the Hermitage, covering **modern European art** in the nineteenth and twentieth centuries (**rooms 314–350**). To get there, take the staircase leading off from room 269 on the second floor, which brings you out at the beginning of the collection. Its breadth is impressively wide, but the highlight is undoubtedly the unique collection of works by **Matisse** and **Picasso**, which was assembled largely by two Moscow philanthropists, Sergei Shchukin and Ivan Morozov. Between them, they bought nearly fifty paintings by each artist in the five years before World War I, and they were largely responsible for collecting the fine spread of Impressionist paintings also on display in this section.

In few other places in the world did such brilliant collections exist, and the works influenced a whole generation of Russian artists. Following the October Revolution, both collections were confiscated by the state, and in 1948 were divided between the Pushkin Museum of Fine Arts and the Hermitage. However, whereas Morozov was coerced into assigning his pictures to the state, Shchukin never did, and when one of the Matisses was sent to Italy in 2000, his grandson filed a lawsuit for its recovery, obliging the Hermitage to order its immediate return to Russia.

As it's intended eventually to move the Hermitage's Impressionist and Post-Impressionist art into the General Staff building, you should expect to find major changes in this section from 2005 onwards, as pictures are taken down to be crated for the short journey across the square to their new home.

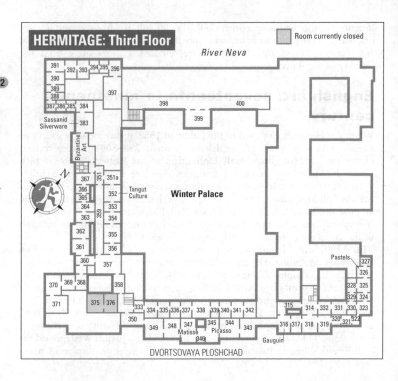

HERMITAGE: Third Floor

Room currently closed

River Neva

Sassanid Silverware

Byzantine Art

Tangut Culture

Winter Palace

Pastels

Matisse

Picasso

Gauguin

DVORTSOVAYA PLOSHCHAD

From Gros to Gauguin

The earliest works currently on show in this section are in **room 314**, which features early nineteenth-century portraits by **Roland Lefevre** and a swash-buckling picture of Napoleon by **Antoine-Jean Gros**, a pupil of David, but one whose fiery palette displays his admiration for Rubens. Next door in **room 332** you'll find some early nineteenth-century paintings by **Prud'hon** and **Guerin**; beyond here, in **room 331**, **Ingres'** portrait of *N.D. Guryev* provides a marvellous contrast to the Romanticism epitomized by two small canvases by **Eugene Delacroix**, *Moroccan Arab Saddling a Horse* and *Lion Hunt in Morocco*, both inspired by his visit to that country in 1832.

At the far end of this section, it's worth a detour to see the **pastels** by **Degas**, **Picasso** and others in **room 326**, before retracing your steps and turning the corner into **rooms 321–322**, which are devoted to the forerunners of Impressionism: the artists of the Barbizon School. Small and shimmering pearly landscapes by **Camille Corot** and gentle works by **Charles-François Daubigny** contrast with **Constant Troyon**'s large *On the Way to the Market*, filled with early morning light.

From here, the adjacent **room 320** takes you straight into the world of the Impressionists with **Renoir**'s full-length, richly clothed *Portrait of Jeanne Samary*. Aside from a couple of simple landscapes by **Alfred Sisley**, room 319 is dominated by **Monet**, ranging from early works such as the bright, direct *Woman in a Garden* (1867) to the atmospheric, fog-bound *Waterloo Bridge* (1903). **Room 318** contains a good sample of **Cézanne**'s work, including a typically contemplative portrait, *The Smoker*, and one of the *Mont Sainte-*

Victoire series, whose chromatic blocks provided a point of departure for Cubism. The only one of the older generation of Impressionists to appreciate Cézanne in his lifetime was **Pissarro**, represented here by *Boulevard Montmartre* and *French Theatre Square.*

Arles Women, an unusual canvas painted by **Van Gogh** whilst under Gauguin's influence, dominates **room 317**, which also contains a couple of Van Gogh landscapes and the little-known *Arena at Arles.* Alongside these are a couple of small canvases by the self-taught **Henri Rousseau** and Pointillist works by **Paul Signac** and **Henri-Edmond Cross**.

Room 316 is entirely devoted to paintings by **Gauguin** inspired by his sojourn in Tahiti, including *Sacred Spring: Sweet Dreams* (painted in Paris) and *Woman Holding a Fruit*, thought to depict his Tahitian wife Tehura.

For the rest of the collection, head across the balcony above the Alexander Hall to **room 343**, which marks the beginning of the later, mostly twentieth-century collection, with its landscapes, interiors and Parisian street scenes by **Jean Édouard Vuillard** – works by his contemporaries Bonnard and Denis have already been transferred to the General Staff building (see p.75).

The Picasso and Matisse collections

Don't be surprised if some works by these artists are on loan to other museums. The **Picasso** collection begins in **room 344** and covers his best-loved early periods. The earliest picture is *The Absinthe Drinker* of 1901, and there are also two paintings from his Blue Period (1901–04) – the larger, *Sisters*, features gaunt, emaciated figures typical of his style at the time. There are several early Cubist works, such as the discernibly figurative *Woman with a Fan* (1908), while **room 345** concentrates on later Cubist pieces, such as his *Still Life* of 1913, along with some of his ceramics from Antibes.

A number of **Matisse**'s most important works were commissioned by his patron, Shchukin, whom he visited in St Petersburg several times between 1908 and 1913, though the earliest paintings on display are a series of neo-Impressionist still lifes (**room 346**) dating from 1898–1901. Later works include the heavily outlined, Fauvist *Nude, Black and Gold* (1908), while colour and decoration are more important than subject matter and perspective in the profusely ornate *The Red Room* of 1908 (**room 347**), which was designed for Shchukin's dining room, thus fulfilling Matisse's stated objective to create art "as relaxing as a comfortable armchair".

The focal points of room 347, however, are two paintings commissioned by Shchukin for his staircase – *Music* and *The Dance* – which marked a turning point in Matisse's career, the pink flesh of his earlier versions being replaced with red-hot primitive figures on a deep green-and-blue background. When first exhibited in October 1910 at the Salon d'Automne in Paris, they were panned by French and Russian critics. Shchukin took fright at their reaction and cancelled the commission, but changed his mind on the train back to Russia. After the pictures were hung in his mansion, Shchukin feared that the nude flautist would disturb his female guests, and personally painted out the musician's genitals.

One of Matisse's portraits of his mistress and model Lydia Delektorskaya can be seen next door in **room 348**. The other works in this room, such as *Arab Coffee House* and *Sur La Terrasse*, are on Spanish and Moroccan themes, but display many of the pictorial qualities associated with Russian folk art and icons, reflecting the lasting impact on Matisse of his visits to Russia.

Vlaminck to Kandinsky

Fauvism – characterized by the use of bright colours and simplified forms – links the painters whose works are exhibited in **room 349**, though few of the paintings here are representative of that style. The startling and deliberately provocative portraits of fashionable Parisians are by the Dutch artist **Kees van Dongen**, who hovered on the edge of Berlin's *Die Brücke* group and the Fauvist circle. **Maurice de Vlaminck**, a racing cyclist and violinist who boasted he had never set foot inside the Louvre, is represented by several atypical early Cézanne-type landscapes. **Albert Marquet**, though associated with the Fauvists, is actually better known for his rather dour port scenes, some of which are on display here. The childlike paintings by **André Derain** in **room 350** are better examples of Fauvism, though here too you'll find some unusually dark early landscapes and a thoroughly Cubist *Unknown Man Reading Newspaper*. There are also several figurative works by the card-carrying Communist **Fernand Léger**, dating from 1932 to 1948.

Room 334 is the only one in the Hermitage to feature modern Russian artists, with four paintings by **Vasily Kandinsky** (who spent much of his life abroad) and an iconic *Black Square* by **Kazimir Malevich**. Rooms 334–336 are used to display a bequest of modern Italian sculpture, while **room 338** retains a few landscapes by the American artist **Rockwell Kent**, whose ideal of manliness in the face of nature is exemplified by his *Seal Hunt in North Greenland*. **Rooms 339–341** have a higgledy-piggledy selection of late nineteenth- and early twentieth-century Spanish, Dutch and German works, plus several paintings by **Caspar David Friedrich**.

Oriental art and culture and the Numismatic Collection

The western wing of the third floor is devoted to **Oriental art and culture**, from Mameluke glassware to Japanese woodcuts – but it's hard to give specific directions, as many sections are being reorganized. One fixed point is the **Byzantine collection** (**rooms 381, 381a & 382**), with its magnificent silverware and carved ivory, including a superb diptych depicting gladiatorial battles between men and beasts. Another is the collection of **Sassanid silverware** (**room 383**), made in Iran between the third and seventh centuries and used as trade goods by merchants buying furs in Siberia, where the indigenous peoples venerated them as sacred totems. Also look out for artefacts from the **Tangut culture** of Mongolia that was laid waste by Genghis Khan in 1227, leaving only the city of Khara-Khoto to be excavated by Kozlov in 1907–9, whence came the two-headed Buddha statue in **room 352**. If the section on **Indian art** (**rooms 368–371**) is open, don't miss the heads of a Bodhisattva and a monk from the Cave of a Thousand Buddhas monastery.

The **northern wing** of the third floor is accessible via a staircase from the Rotunda (room 156) on the second floor and harbours a **Numismatic Collection** (**rooms 398–400**), including Russian medals and Classical intaglios in gold mounts; only a selection is on view at any one time in temporary exhibitions (open Tues & Thurs).

The Russian Museum

The origins of the **Russian Museum** (Russkiy muzey; Русский музей) date back to the reign of Alexander III, who began to buy Russian art at the end of the nineteenth century with a view to establishing a national museum. His plans were realized by his son Nicholas II, who purchased the Mikhailovskiy Palace and opened it in 1898 as the nation's first public museum of Russian art, named after Alexander III. After the Revolution it was renamed the Russian Museum and acquired thousands of artworks confiscated from private collections. During the 1930s, the museum expanded into the palace's Rossi Wing and, later, into the Benois Wing beside the Griboedov Canal, named after its architect, Leonti Benois.

Along with the Tretyakov Gallery in Moscow, the museum contains the finest collection of **Russian art** in the world – some 400,000 works in total – ranging from medieval icons to the latest in conceptual art. The works neatly mirror Russia's history, tracing the development of the nation's art from Peter the Great's insistence on a break with old Muscovite traditions to the officially approved style of the latter-day Romanovs; from the soul-searching of the Wanderers and the explosion of Symbolism and Futurism to the Stalinist art form known as Socialist Realism and, most recently, Western-inspired multimedia.

Although nearly everything kept locked away during the Soviet years has long since been opened up, the cash-strapped museum earns money by sending many of its most popular works (from the Russian avant-garde collection) for exhibition abroad, so Russians are still unable to see a major part of their heritage. However, some avant-garde works are on show and others are included in **temporary exhibitions** in the Benois Wing.

On a more positive note, in recent years the Russian Museum has acquired three new buildings: the **Marble Palace** (see p.84), the **Engineers' Castle** (see p.89) and the **Stroganov Palace** (see p.71), enabling it to show more of its eighteenth-century art collection and some of the thousands of works of Russian applied art formerly relegated to the stores for lack of space.

Visiting the Russian Museum

The museum is located on ploshchad Iskusstv, off Nevskiy prospekt, less than ten minutes' walk from Gostiniy Dvor or Nevskiy Prospekt metro stations. Though there's rarely much of a queue during **opening hours** (10am–6pm, Mon till 5pm, closed Tues), you may have to wait outside for a while if the building gets too crowded. Once through the main gates, head right across the courtyard to the eastern side of the main portico and go downstairs into the basement, where **tickets** ($8; students/children $4) and **photo permits** ($1.60) are sold. Be sure to pick up a **floor plan** of the museum here, as none is available at the shops or information points upstairs. Cloakrooms, **toilets** and a reasonably priced **café** are also situated in the basement.

Upstairs in the main entrance hall of the Mikhailovsky Palace you'll find two **information** points that usually have someone who speaks English on duty, though they're not particularly helpful. **Guided tours** in English can be arranged in advance (☎314 34 48) for $10 per person up to a maximum of ten people, and it's not difficult to tag along behind a tour group for some free commentary, but most visitors are content to rent an **audio guide** from the desk in the lobby ($8; ID required as deposit), or do without. The museum **shop** sells reproductions, souvenirs and all kinds of glossy books, videos and CD-ROMs (featuring icons and the avant-garde, Malevich and Aivazovsky), but its standard **guidebook** gives almost no information about the artists or where to find specific works in the museum.

For a minimum annual donation of $100 anyone can become a **Friend** of the Russian Museum and qualify for free entry and other privileges depending on the size of the donation; gold card donors get invited to events attended by VIPs such as Rostropovich, Brian Eno or even Putin. Phone (☎315 15 85) or email (✉friends@rusmuseum.ru) for details. The Russian Museum's **website** (🅦www.rusmuseum.ru) is less user-friendly than the Hermitage's, with only a smattering of art online. It gives details of current and future **temporary exhibitions**, usually hosted in the **Benois Wing**; these are widely advertised in the local media and require a **separate ticket** ($8), sold at the Benois Wing's entrance on the Griboedov Canal.

This chapter covers the permanent exhibition, whose art **collection** is arranged more or less chronologically, from top to bottom, starting on the second floor of the palace, continuing downstairs, then in the Rossi Wing and finally upstairs on the second floor of the Benois Wing. If that sounds confusing, well, it is. Some visitors don't bother with that order, and instead begin with the Vasnetsov and Repin rooms on the first floor of the palace and carry on through the Rossi and Benois wings, leaving the earlier Russian art on the second floor of the palace till last – if at all.

Since works from the collection are often on loan to other museums and rooms are gradually being modernized, there are bound to be some differences between our account and what's on view at the time of your visit. Almost all exhibits are titled in both Russian and English, so you can easily identify them – but room numbering leaves much to be desired.

Mikhailovskiy Palace (second floor)

To view the works on the **second floor** chronologically, start in room 1 and walk anticlockwise round the building – an approach that emphasizes the giant leap from early icon painting to the art of the eighteenth and nineteenth centuries. If you're here solely for the modern stuff, you could skip this floor of the palace entirely, but it would be a shame to miss out on the icons in rooms 1–4, or such extravaganzas as *The Last Day of Pompeii* or *The Ninth Wave*, in room 14.

Russian icons

For many centuries Russian art was exclusively religious in theme, and limited to mosaics, frescoes and **icons**, the holy images venerated in Orthodox

Room currently closed

14

12

11
White Hall

10

9

8

7

6

5

13

15

16

17

1

2

3

4

Mikhailovskiy Palace

Rossi Wing

N

RUSSIAN MUSEUM: Second Floor

▼ *ploshchad Iskusstv*

churches and households. The early icon painters were medieval monks for whom painting was a spiritual devotion, to be accompanied by fasting and prayer. Icons were repainted when their colours dulled and were often overlaid with golden, gem-encrusted frames. Their style and content were dictated by the canons of Byzantine art, faithfully preserved by the schools of Vladimir and Suzdal. However, a bolder and brighter Russian style emerged at Novgorod from the twelfth century onwards, which was to influence strongly the development of Russian art as a whole, and even the work of such "foreign" artists as Theophanes the Greek.

Icon painting reached a crossroads in the seventeenth century, when Russia's Orthodox Church was split between supporters of the reformist Patriarch Nikon and the arch-conservative Avvakum, both of whom opposed any innovations in painting. Nikon poked out the eyes of icons that offended him, while Avvakum fulminated against those who depicted Immanuel the Saviour "like a German, fat-bellied and corpulent". Ironically, the result was a gradual secularization of art, as Tsar Mikhail Romanov encouraged a new form known as the *parsuna*, or the representation of an ordinary human being – in fact, somewhere between an icon and realistic portraiture. Artists also began to paint on canvas as well as the traditional wooden panel, and although icon painting continued right up to the 1917 Revolution, its glory days had long passed, as Russia's leading painters concentrated on secular art.

One of the oldest works in **room 1** is the small, early twelfth-century icon, *The Archangel with the Golden Hair*, originally part of a deesis – the third and most important tier of an iconostasis, with Christ in Majesty occupying the central position. In **room 2** you'll find the fourteenth-century icon *Boris and Gleb*, depicting the young princes of Kiev who were murdered by their elder brother Svyatopolk, and *The Anastasis*, a dramatic black and red composition from the Pskov school of the fourteenth to sixteenth century.

Room 3 showcases panels by known masters. The monk **Andrey Rublev** (c.1360–1430) and his "fellow faster" **Daniil Cherny** collaborated on the two-metre-high *Apostle Peter and Apostle Paul*, which originally formed part of the iconostasis of the Assumption Cathedral in Vladimir. Their spiritual successor in the second half of the fifteenth century was a Muscovite, **Dionysius**, whose *Archangel Gabriel, St John Chrystostomos* and *Grigory the Theologian* hang here. Most of the icons in **room 4** are from monasteries in northern Russia such as the Church of the Transfiguration at Tver – whence came *The Descent into Hell* and the *Hodegetria Mother of God* – but you'll also see examples of the seventeenth-century Moscow style, minutely detailed and heavily shaded with lots of red and gold.

Petrine art

Since many of the paintings of eighteenth-century Russia compare poorly with those of the West, the reasons for viewing them are as much historical as artistic. The reign of **Peter the Great** marked a turning point in Russian art. On his famous grand tour of Europe in 1697, the tsar began avidly buying pictures, initiating an activity that was to become an obsession with the later Romanovs. Then, in his determination to establish St Petersburg as the new artistic centre of Russia, Peter transferred the state icon workshop here from the Kremlin Armoury in Moscow, although he had no intention of building on that tradition, being intent instead on introducing Western art forms to Russia.

Encouraged by Peter, many foreign artists settled permanently in St Petersburg, among them Gottfried Tannhauer, who may have painted the scene of Peter on his deathbed and the portrait of the young Elizabeth Petrovna in **room 5** – although the Russian Museum attributes both pictures to **Ivan Nikitin** (c.1680–1742), whose mastery of Western techniques is also manifest in his portraits of a Hetman (Cossack leader) and Tsarevna Praskovia Ivanova. Nikitin was one of several young Russian artists whom Peter sent abroad to be trained – a policy that had a great impact in the long term, though Nikitin himself fell victim to intrigues and was exiled to Tobolsk. Another promising artist trained abroad was **Andrey Matveev** (1701–39), whose unfinished *Self-portrait of the Artist and his Wife* is one of only a few of his canvases to have survived (in room 6).

Art under Elizabeth and Catherine

It wasn't until Elizabeth ascended the throne that Peter's plans to found a Russian **Academy of Arts** came to fruition. In 1757, an edict by the Senate established an academy in St Petersburg, although in its early years it remained an administrative department of Moscow University. **Room 6** features a medley of portraits by Elizabeth's court painter **Ivan Vishnyakov** (1699–1761), the Sheremetev family's serf-artist **Ivan Argunov** (1729–1802), and **Alexei Antropov** (1716–95), who served Catherine the Great. Antropov's best-known work is a *Portrait of Peter III*, Catherine's detested husband, whose elongated body and minuscule head are overwhelmed by an excess of background detail. Room 6 also contains mosaic portraits of Peter and Catherine produced by the Imperial Glass Factory, and a bewigged bust of Prince Menshikov by Ivan Vitali.

The main reason to pause in **room 7** is to admire its gilded ceiling and a matronly bronze statue of Empress Anna, known as *Anna Ivanovna and an Arab Boy*, by the Italian sculptor Bartolomeo Rastrelli, father of the famous architect. **Room 8** is largely given over to the talented **Fyodor Rokotov** (1736–1808), whose lively bust-length portraits put the emphasis firmly on the characters of the sitters. Also note the portrait by an unknown artist of the future tsar Peter III, wearing a red coat with a green sash.

Room 9 concentrates on the work of the Ukrainian **Anton Losenko** (1737–73), whose rather awkward *St Vladimir and Rogneda* was the first attempt by a native painter to depict a national historical subject on a large scale. His other canvases are concerned with more traditional biblical subjects, such as the (comically translated) *Wonderful Catch,* depicting Jesus doing a bit of proxy fishing, and a typically academic portrait of *Cain.* There's also a bronze *Prometheus* having his liver picked out, by Fyodor Gordeev.

The centrepiece of **room 10** is the life-sized statue, *Catherine, the Legislator,* by **Fyodor Shubin** (1740–1805), Russia's first great sculptor – Catherine and Potemkin were virtually the only enthusiastic patrons of his flowing Rococo style. On the walls hang paintings by **Dmitri Levitsky** (1735–1822), a Ukrainian Pole who, having never travelled abroad, could justifiably claim to be Russia's first truly homegrown talent. In 1770 he took the Academy by storm, exhibiting over twenty canvases including a portrait of the institution's director, Kokorinov. His best-known works, however, are the series of light-hearted portraits of Catherine's favourite pupils from the Smolniy Institute for Young Noblewomen.

Apart from the main staircase, **room 11**, known as the **White Hall** (Beliy zal), is the finest example of the original white, gold and mauve-grey Neoclassical decor, designed – right down to the furniture – by the palace's architect, Carlo Rossi. Working with him on the grisaille decor was **Vladimir Borovikovsky** (1757–1825), the most sought-after portraitist of the late eighteenth century. **Room 12** displays his *Catherine the Great in the Park at Tsarskoe Selo* – a remark-ably frank portrayal of the elderly empress, exercising one of her dogs – and one of Tsar Paul, dwarfed by sumptuous robes and drapery.

Romanticism and the Academy style

Romanticism in the pictorial arts was personified by **Orest Kiprensky** (1782–1836), the illegitimate child of a noble and a serf, who had tragic affairs, drank recklessly and died of tuberculosis in Rome. The finest of his early portraits in **room 13** is of Evgrav Davidov, a beefy young Hussar officer who lost an arm and a leg in battle shortly after the picture was completed. Napoleon's invasion of Russia in 1812 and the eventual triumphal entry of Russian forces into Paris were reflected in a marked shift towards Neoclassicism and patriotic themes, which became the hallmark of the **Academy style** for decades afterwards.

Room 14 is hung with monumental canvases, including two commissioned for the Mikhailovskiy Palace, *The Siege of Kazan* and *Coronation of Mikhail Fyodorovich* by **Grigori Ugryumov** (1764–1823). None can match the sheer theatricality of *The Last Day of Pompeii,* painted by **Karl Bryullov** (1799–1852) while he was living in Rome. With this work, he became the first Academy painter to enjoy an international reputation: it was hailed as a masterpiece by Italian critics and won the Grand Prix at the Paris Salon in 1834. Sir Walter Scott reportedly sat for an hour in front of it before pronouncing that it was "not a painting but an epic" (though unkind commentators claim Scott's apparent devotion was due more to his great age and immobility).

While many Russians read *The Last Day* as an allegory of St Petersburg's fate (the city had been flooded some years earlier), another famous painting – *The Ninth Wave,* depicting a battered ship about to be sunk by a huge wave in a stormy sea – was said to prophesy the downfall of the Romanovs Its creator, **Ivan Aivazovsky** (1817–1900), specialized in large seascapes and views of Constantinople and the Crimea. The seascapes were painted from memory in the studio rather than from life, as Aivazovsky believed that "the movements of the living elements elude the brush". He produced a staggering four to five thousand pictures and enjoyed an international reputation.

A third graduate to win renown abroad was **Alexander Ivanov** (1806–58), whose superb draughtsmanship won him a Gold Medal and a grant to study in Italy, where he spent most of his life. After being made an academician for *The Appearance of Christ before Mary Magdalene,* he wrote to his father, "You think that a lifelong salary of 6000–8000 rubles and a safe place in the Academy is a great blessing for an artist . . . but I think it is a curse." You can see this picture and his *Joseph Interprets Dreams* in **room 15**, but the vast final study for Ivanov's best-known work, *Christ's Appearance before the People*, was away on loan when last heard.

As a reaction to the repressive policies of Alexander I and Nicholas I, many artists chose to live abroad, mostly in Italy, where they could paint more freely. Rome was the favoured destination and from 1820 onwards there was a semi-permanent Russian colony which included the likes of Ivanov, Bryullov and **Silvestr Shchedrin** (1791–1830), whose Italian landscapes line the small corridor designated **room 16**. Room 17, just before the landing, is covered under "Genre and landscape painting", below.

Mikhailovskiy Palace (first floor)

On the **first floor** you can see how Russian art gradually escaped from its academic confines and came of age in the late nineteenth century. Rooms in the Mikahailovskiy Palace trace this development as far as the works of Repin and Vasnetsov, beyond which the story continues in the Rossi Wing (see p.149). If you wish to skip the lead up to Repin, you can go straight into room 38 at the bottom of the stairs instead of turning left into room 18, where the first-floor exhibition begins – though it would be a shame to miss the academic blockbusters in room 21.

Genre and landscape painting

While state commissions usually went to artists who produced safe, monumental academic works, the late eighteenth- and nineteenth-century

nobility and merchant class developed a taste for **genre painting** – scenes of rural or small-town life in particular. Its earliest practitioners were **Alexei Venetsianov** (1780–1847) and his pupil, **Grigori Soroka** (1823–64), whose work hangs in **room 17** upstairs. Venetsianov's *Cleaning the Sugar-beet* strikes an authentic note of misery, but *In The Threshing Barn* resembles a stage-set for figures in dreamlike poses; Soroka's river scenes carry more conviction. Genre painting continues downstairs in **room 18**, with scenes of artisans and bourgeois life by **Pavel Fedotov** (1815–52), whose *The Major's Courtship* – in which a self-satisfied officer comes to inspect his unwilling young bride – is infused with social criticism. Also in this room is the model for Klodt's statue of Nicholas I near St Isaac's Cathedral. **Room 19** exhibits portraits by **Vasily Tropinin** (1770–1857), whose sitters are depicted in a sketchy but precise style vaguely reminiscent of Ingres.

Antiquity continued to be the subject of major commissions – views of Rome (**room 20**) or historic events (**room 21**). Vast canvases such as *Christian Martyrs in the Colosseum* by **Konstantin Flavitsky** (1830–66), and *Nero's Death* by **Vasily Smirnov** (1858–90), titillated patrons with the thrill of blood, while **Genrikh Semiradsky** (1843–1902) specialized in erotic pagan scenes with titles like *Purina at the Posiedon Celebration in Elusium*.

Genre painting resumes in **room 23** with such works as Solomatkin's sentimental *Policemen Singing Praises*, Gribokov's comic *Quarrel of Ivan Ivanovich and Ivan Nikitforovich*, and a portrait of the writer Turgenev by **Vasily Perov** (1834–82). The son of a baron exiled to Siberia, Perov began his career with satires against corrupt officialdom and had several works banned by the authorities, but later made his peace with the establishment. The museum sometimes exhibits his *Monastery Refectory*, which shows monks boozing and guzzling while the poor get short shrift.

Room 24 is largely devoted to **landscapes** by **Alexei Savrasov** (1830–97), generally reckoned to be the "father of Russian landscape painting" and renowned as the teacher of Levitan (see p.150), who was to surpass his achievements. Though best known for *The Rooks Have Returned* in the Tretyakov Gallery, Savrasov is well represented here by *The Flood of the Volga at Yaroslavl*, *Steppe in Daytime* and *Sunset over the Marshes*.

The Wanderers

In 1863, fourteen of the Academy's most talented pupils refused to paint the mythological subject set by their examiners, and left to set up an artists' co-operative that was the genesis of the Society for Travelling Art Exhibitions – known as the **Wanderers** (*peredvizhniki*) – which evaded censorship by showing their paintings at "wandering" exhibitions in the provinces. Most of these artists were in sympathy with the Populist movement and abided by Chernyshevsky's dictum that "Only content is able to refute the accusation that art is an empty diversion".

The Wanderers' leader, **Ivan Kramskoy** (1837–87), vowed to create a truly Russian school of art, and is best known for his Slavic *Christ in the Wilderness* (in the Tretyakov Gallery). His portraits in **room 25** are little different in style from those of his contemporaries in the West, but notable for their challenging stares, as in *Insulted Jewish Boy* and *Inconsolable Grief*. There's also a cute life-size statue of a child taking its first steps, by Fyodor Kamonssky.

Room 26 is devoted to the work of **Nicholas Ge** (1831–94), whose name is pronounced – and often spelled – "Gay". The grandson of a French émigré, Ge was torn between mathematics and painting until the award of the Academy's Gold Medal and a travel bursary decided the issue. One of the founder members of the Wanderers, he soon turned from landscapes to religious themes under the influence of Ivanov. Two of Ge's most striking works are *Christ and His Disciples Come into the Garden of Gethsemane* and *The Last Supper* – the latter's departure from traditional iconography horrified the critics. But the painting for which he is best known to Russians is *Peter I Interrogating Tsarevich Alexei at Peterhof* – Peter later had his son killed.

During the Wanderers' meanderings, landscape painters were forging ahead on the path beaten by Savrasov. In **room 27** hang *Oak Trees*, *In the Thicket* and *Mast Pine Grove* by **Ivan Shishkin** (1832–98), lauded for their meticulous detail, but said by some critics to lack a sense of place – a charge that can't be levelled at the wintry Russian landscapes of **Fyodor Vasiliev** (1850–73) in **room 28**. His desolate *The Thaw* was painted in the year that he became seriously ill with tuberculosis, but *View of the Volga with Barques*, from the year before, exudes freshness.

Room 29 behind the main staircase contains two **computers** for accessing the museum's website, and leads into **room 30**, featuring Populist art, characterized by its strong social commentary. Titles like *Dividing the Family Property* by **Vasily Maximov** (1844–1911) and *The Convicted Person* and *Doss House*, both by **Vladimir Makovsky** (1846–1920), tell their own tale. Also notice *Before the Wedding*, by **Firs Zhuravlyev** (1836–1901), whose weeping bride and baffled parents invite speculation about a loveless match or shameful secret.

Other concerns are evident in **room 31**, which is dominated by *To the War* by **Karl Savitsky**, where conscripts are bid a tearful farewell at the station. While *Harvesting* by **Grigori Myasoyedov** (1834–1911), the so-called "father" of the Wanderers, exudes the bucolic optimism later associated with Socialist Realism, Chizkov's statue of an *Unfortunate Peasant* bespeaks poverty and desperation on the land.

A vulpine, white-marble Mephistopheles and statues of Spinoza and Nestor the Annalist by **Mikhail Antokolsky** (1842–1902) lead to a vast canvas by **Vasily Polenov** (1844–1927) that dominates **room 32**. In *Christ and the Adulteress*, Christ's humility is contrasted with the vicious piety of the priests, who incite the mob to stone a woman to death – an expression of sympathy for the sinner and contempt for the smug that resonated with Dostoyevsky's conception of Christianity.

The Repin rooms

Ilya Repin (1844–1930) was a late recruit to the Wanderers and subsequently became the foremost realist painter of his generation. Apprenticed at an early age to an icon workshop, he was later trained at the Academy, where he produced prize-winning student works such as *Christ Raising the Daughter of Jairus* and *A Negro Woman*. These hang in **room 33**, together with an underwater scene from the fairytale *Sadko* and the painting that made him famous – *Barge-haulers on the Volga*, a study in human drudgery and degradation that became an icon for the Populist movement and was later praised by Lenin as brilliant propaganda. In **room 34** you'll find Repin's portraits of the composers Rubenstein and Glazunov, and his lively historical work, *The Zaporozhe Cossacks Writing a Mocking Letter to the Sultan*, in which swarthy warriors compose a reply to Sultan Mohammed IV's ultimatum – a lavishly detailed painting that took over twelve years to complete at Repin's studio-house in Karelia (see p.297).

In **room 35**, his portrait of Tolstoy, bare-footed and dressed like a peasant, is juxtaposed with three large pictures on very different subjects. *Leave-Taking of a Recruit* is in the sombre tradition of Savitsky's *To the War* (see above); *October*

17, 1905 shows a crowd rejoicing at Nicholas II's assent to a constitution and parliament; while the oddly named *What a Scope* depicts a bourgeois couple frolicking on a beach without a care in the world.

Lastly, in **room 54** (off the Surikov section – see below) hangs Repin's *Ceremonial Meeting of the State Council, 7 May 1901*, a vast work that required scores of preliminary studies (some of which are on display). The councillors are painted like a still life, while Nicholas II is reduced to insignificance in the Grand Hall of the Mariinskiy Palace.

Surikov and Vasnetsov

During the 1880s, Russian historical painting adopted a form of Slavic mysticism, the leading exponent of which was Siberian-born **Vasily Surikov** (1846–1916), who studied at the Academy and was influenced by Ivanov. After his *Morning of the Execution of the Streltsy* (in Moscow), Surikov is best known for the huge canvases in **room 36**, particularly *Yermak's Conquest of Siberia*, which depicts the Cossacks storming across the River Irtysh to smash the Tatar hordes in 1595. After the death of his wife, Surikov retreated to Siberia, but in 1891 resumed his career with the festive *Taking the Snow Fortress by Storm*. Even cheerier is *Suvorov Crossing the Alps*, in which the army seems to be tobogganing down the mountain like a group of excited schoolboys. In **room 37** hangs Surikov's colossal painting of the Cossack rebel leader Stepan Razin, brooding in a boat on the River Volga.

Viktor Vasnetsov (1846–1926) was a priest's son who quit the seminary to apprentice himself to a lithographer and later won a place at the Academy. His penchant was for ancient Russian prehistory, myths and legends, which inspired such big dramatic compositions as *Scythians and Slavs Fighting* and *A Russian Knight at the Crossway* – though Vasnetsov also tackled contemporary subjects such as *A Festival on the Outskirts of Paris*, which likewise hangs in **room 38**.

The Rossi Wing

The exhibition continues on the first floor of the **Rossi Wing** (fligel Rossi), beyond the Surikov section and Repin's *Meeting of the State Council*. **Temporary exhibitions** of prints or textiles in the corridor (room 49) parallel to the enfilade and an array of **busts, casts** and **models** for statues in rooms 56–58 might tempt you off the trail, but it's worth sticking with the permanent exhibition of paintings.

Room 39 attests to the fashion for Orientalism, which for Russian artists encompassed not just the Holy Land, but also Central Asia, the Caucasus and the Balkans. The genre's leading exponent, **Vasily Vereshchagin**, was renowned for scenes such as *At the Entrance to the Mosque* and *In Jerusalem, The Royal Tombs*, and also for his anti-war pictures, typified by *Skobelov at Shipka*, where a vainglorious Russian general taking the salute is mocked by piles of dead soldiers in the foreground.

Rooms 40 and **41** focus on the work of **Arkhip Kuindzhi** (1841–1910), who grew apart from the Wanderers as he made ever greater use of colour as a symbolic element in stunning Caucasian landscapes – a tendency taken to its extreme by his pupil Roerich (see p.152). Another exotic Orientalist work, Konstantin Makovsky's *The Removal of the Sacred Carpet in Cairo*, hangs in **room 42**.

Exotic scenes of seventeenth-century Moscow by **Apollinary Vasnetsov** (brother of Viktor), Clavdy Lebeedeev and other artists fascinated by Old Russia – before the westernizing and, as they saw it, corrupting influence of

Peter the Great – are the leitmotif of **rooms 43** and **45**. The latter focuses on **Andrey Ryabushkin** (1861–1904), whose famous painting *They Are Coming* shows Muscovites nervously awaiting the arrival of the first Europeans. His *Moscow on a Festival Day* revels in the mud of the wooden city and its Kremlin, while his *Seventeenth-century Merchant Family* has characteristics of the archaic *parsuna* form (see p.143).

Sandwiched between Slav historicists, **room 44** is devoted to **Isaak Levitan** (1860–1900), widely regarded as the greatest Russian landscapist of the nineteenth century. His *Silence, The Lake* and *Moonlit Night* are characterized by their limpid rivers and soft light, and devoid of any hint of social criticism. For this you need to visit **room 46**, where the hardships of the poor are depicted in *Gleaning Coal in an Abandoned Pit* and *A Woman Spinner*, by **Nikolai Kasatkin** (1850–1930).

The final artist covered in the Rossi Wing is **Filip Malyavin** (1869–1940), a lay brother at the Russian monastery on Mount Athos in Greece before he took up painting. Most of the pictures in **room 47** are impressionistic portraits of actors, singers and critics, but his brilliant later, freer compositions of peasant women with billowing scarves and skirts, suggestive of Gauguin or Klimt, are represented by *Two Girls* on the far wall.

Room 48 contains a small **shop** and marks a divergence of ways. At this point you either turn right along a corridor past a larger-than-life **statue of Yermak** with a battleaxe, and **upstairs into the Benois Wing** to continue the tour of the art collection – or investigate the folk art section in the Rossi Wing, straight ahead.

Folk art

Though not all ten rooms may be open, this section offers an overview of traditional **Russian folk art** and handicrafts. Most of the exhibits were part of everyday life in Russian villages and many had a mystical significance. The first room displays *naboyki*, or block-printed indigo textiles and glazed tiles of the type often used to decorate seventeenth- and eighteenth-century buildings. Wood was used for making dwellings and all kinds of tools and objects from washboards to butter churns, often carved with geometric patterns and pagan symbols – especially the pediments of cottages. The rooms that follow are filled with the sort of things still produced by contemporary craftsmen, such as toys, lace, ceramics and lacquerware, plus a huge display of painted wooden cups and plates from Khokloma.

The Benois Wing

The **Benois Wing** (korpus Benoua) holds the museum's collection of late nineteenth- and twentieth-century Russian art – the permanent collection is housed on the second floor, while the first floor is given over entirely to **temporary exhibitions** of contemporary Russian and world art. Bear in mind that some of the better-known avant-garde works in the permanent collection are often out on loan to museums around the world and may not be on show when you visit.

To reach the second floor from the main building, head along the corridor from room 48 on the first floor of the Rossi Wing and upstairs to room 66; the first floor is accessible only via the Benois Wing's own entrance on the Griboedov embankment, where separate tickets for temporary exhibitions are sold – opening hours are the same as for the main exhibition in the Russian Museum (tickets for which are also sold there).

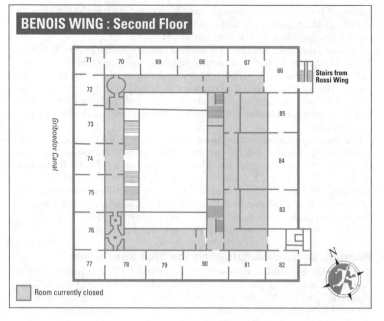

BENOIS WING : Second Floor

71 70 69 68 67 66 Stairs from Rossi Wing

72

85

73

74 84

75

83

76

77 78 79 80 81 82

Griboedov Canal

N

Room currently closed

Abramtsevo artists, the World of Art and Symbolism

Room 66 pitches you into the fantastic world of **Mikhail Vrubel** (1856–1910), one of the leading lights of the **Abramtsevo artists' colony** at the country estate of the Moscow millionaire Mamontov. Vrubel's febrile, lushly textured paintings had a huge impact in Russia, and while his beefy *Russian Hero* now looks comic, time hasn't diminished the force of *Demon in Flight* – a panel from the cabalistic "Demon" series that precipitated his mental breakdown. The pagan intensity of these works in **room 67** is contrasted with the quiet mysticism of **Mikhail Nesterov** (1862–1942), whose religious paintings fell from favour in Soviet times, obliging him to concentrate on portraiture.

While they shared the Abramtsevo artists' love of Russian folk art and myths, the **World of Art** (Mir Iskusstva) movement in St Petersburg (see p.203) was equally inspired by French Mannerism and eighteenth-century court life – typified by works in **room 68** such as *Harlequin and Lady* by **Konstantin Somov** (1869–1939), and the *Commedia dell'arte* by **Alexander Benois** (1870–1960). Benois and **Léon Bakst** (1866–1924) designed costumes and stage sets for Diaghilev's Ballets Russes, and Bakst's dramatic tastes are given full rein in an apocalyptic vision of flooded temples and mega lightning-bolts, called *Terror Antiques*. **Room 69** displays gouache designs for Diaghilev's productions of *Carmen* and *The Rite of Spring*, by the theatrical designer **Alexander Golovin** (1863–1930) and the artist Roerich (see overleaf), together with paintings of ballet dancers and *The Bathhouse* by **Zinaida Serebryakova** (1884–1967), whose proto-feminist work was to influence Soviet art through to the 1970s.

Valentin Serov (1865–1911) was largely brought up at Abramtsevo and was one of the most technically accomplished artists of his time. While most of his work here consists of society portraits (Count Felix and Princess Yusupov, the parents of Rasputin's assassin, among them), his versatility is evident in his stark depictions of a rural hovel in winter, troops charging demonstrators (**room 70**) and set designs for the opera *Judith* (**room 71**).

Another member of the Abramstevo circle, **Konstantin Korovin** (1861–1939), was the first Russian artist to turn to Impressionism in the 1880s, and was later invited by Diaghilev to design the cover of the first issue of the journal *World of Art*. **Room 72** juxtaposes his artistic journey from boulevard scenes of Paris and Yalta to decorative still lifes with pictures by his fellow Impressionist **Igor Grabar** (1871–1960) and some early works by Larionov (see opposite).

The landscapist **Konstantin Yuon** (1875–1958) didn't belong to either artistic circle, but his bright, panoramic folk scenes likewise emphasized decorative elements, a tendency taken even further by **Boris Kustodiev** (1878–1927). **Room 73** exhibits three of his best-known works: a fleshy *Merchant's Wife at Tea*; a snowy landscape with troikas, *At Shrovetide*; and a copy of his portrait of Chaliapin in the singer's former home (see p.190). After the Revolution, both artists found favour with the new regime by producing panoramic views of proletarian festivals and Communist utopias.

Roerich, Borisov-Musatov and the Blue Rose group

The Russian **Symbolist movement** inaugurated by Vrubel involved artists both inside and outside the Abramtsevo colony and the World of Art. **Nikolai Roerich** (1874–1947) was passionately interested in archeology and the Orient. His Symbolist use of saturated colour was first applied to subjects from Russian history, such as *Prince Igor's Campaign* and later to Oriental mysticism, particularly after he went to live in India and Tibet. Also exhibited in **room 74** are paintings by **Viktor Borisov-Musatov** (1870–1905), whose *Self-portrait with His Sister* hints at the sexual tension between them, veiled with symbolism in the pictures of young women espied in gardens, which made up most of his oeuvre.

Musatov's followers at the Moscow School of Painting, Sculpture and Architecture became known as the **Blue Rose** group after the name of their first exhibition in 1907. Sharing a love of blue (symbolizing spirituality), dreams, and simplification of forms, they each sought a world of their own. **Pavel Kuznetsov** (1878–1968) found his ideal life with the Kirghiz nomads, portrayed in *Evening in the Steppes* and other works where soft blues and yellows predominate, whereas **Martiros Sariyan** (1880–1968) rendered the Near East in hues of red, yellow and indigo. Both artists are well represented in **room 75**, along with others in the group.

Petrov-Vodkin and the Jack of Diamonds

Kuzma Petrov-Vodkin (1878–1939) was initially a Symbolist but remained independent of many of the groups that came and went in the 1900s. His theories on composition and spatial construction of the picture surface were highly influential on Soviet painters well into the 1970s, while his pre-revolutionary paintings made him popular with the authorities, at least until the rise of Socialist Realism. **Room 76** highlights his early works, such as *Boys*, *Dream*, *On the Firing Line*, an intense self-portrait and an iconic *Mother*; his art after the Revolution appears in room 83 (see p.154).

The next two rooms feature artists from the **Jack of Diamonds** society that existed from 1910 to 1916. Cézanne was the main influence on **Aristarkh Lentulov** (1882–1943) and **Robert Falk** (1886–1958), whose *Landscape with*

Lavra, still lifes and portraits hang in **room 77**, together with the bizarre *Lady with Pheasants* by **Ilya Mashkov** (1881–1944) and a famous portrait of the poetess Akhmatova by **Nathan Altman** (1889–1970), whose semi-Cubist *Sunflowers* is also on display.

Kandinsky, Goncharova and Larionov

Room 79 features a changing array of works by three major artists. **Vasily Kandinsky** (1866–1944) spent much of his career in Munich, where with Franz Marc he launched the *Blaue Reiter* (Blue Rider) group, which dealt a deathblow to European naturalism. Kandinsky believed in abstraction from nature and the spiritualization of art; each colour was thought to have a "corresponding vibration of the human soul". Although his theories greatly influenced many artists, in 1920 the Institute of Artistic Culture rejected them as too "subjective" and Kandinsky left Russia to take up a post at the Weimar Bauhaus. However, the Russian Museum retains many works from three series designated *Impressions, Improvisations* and *Compositions,* plus individually titled paintings such as *Dusk* and *Picture with Edges.*

In the years before the outbreak of war in 1914, Russian art was in ferment with movements akin to the *Blaue Reiter* and Cubism. The leading exponents of what became known as **Primitivism** were **Natalya Goncharova** (1881–1962) and **Mikhail Larionov** (1881–1964), both of whom quit the Jack of Diamonds in 1911 to form a new group, the Donkey's Tail. Goncharova asserted that all art was dead or decadent, except in Russia; that Picasso was a fraud and Cubism was old hat. Works such as *Four Evangelists, Whitening Linen* and *Sunflowers and Peasants* drew on folk art and icons for inspiration, while Larionov depicted drunks and whores and daubed his canvases with obscenities. Later, he launched a new style called **Rayonism**, whose manifesto declared that the genius of the age consisted of "trousers, jackets, shoes, tramways, buses, aeroplanes, railways, magnificent ships ..." In Rayonist pictures rays of light break the object up, scatter it across the picture surface, creating a sense of movement, progression and disintegration. You'll also find a single picture by the Georgian artist **Niko Pirosmanashvili** (1863–1918), who pursued his own style of Primitivism and was so poor that he often painted on scraps of wood or tarpaulin.

Futurism

Some people visit the museum simply to see the art in **rooms 80–82**. As with room 79, paintings get rotated or sent abroad, but you can be sure of finding something by all of the big names in Russian **Futurism** – a catch-all term for the explosion of artistic styles and theories between 1910 and 1920. Early Futurists, such as the Burlyuk brothers and Mayakovsky, were out to shock – the Futurist manifesto was entitled *A Slap in the Face of Public Taste.* More cerebral was **Kazimir Malevich** (1878–1935), whose Cubo-Futurism – influenced by the bold lines of icons and peasant woodcuts – evolved into what he termed **Suprematism**, the "art of pure sensation". The Russian Museum has 136 works by Malevich, ranging from geometric canvases like *Black Circle* and *Suprematism: Yellow and Black* to the figurative *Red Cavalry.* Also look out for *Abstract Compositions* by **Olga Rozanova** (1886–1918), whose minimalism was later applied to ceramics and fabrics for the masses (now collector's items).

Malevich's rival for ascendancy over the avant-garde movement was **Vladimir Tatlin** (1885–1953), whose early paintings, such as *The Sailor* (a self-portrait), gave little hint of what was to come. Having anticipated Dadaism with his junk collages, Tatlin experimented with theatre design and the "Culture of Materials". What came to be called **Constructivism** owed much to his collaboration with the theatre director Meyerhold and the painters **Lyubov Popova** (1889–1924) and **Nadezhda Udaltsova** (1885–1961). Much of their conceptual work was never realized: Tatlin's glider, *Letatlin*, never left the ground, while his *Monument to the Third International* – intended to be over 396m high and revolve on its axis, near the Peter and Paul Fortress – got a dusty response from Lenin.

Pavel Filonov (1883–1943) developed a system of "analytical art" to reflect the atomic nature of reality, layering detail upon detail to create such kaleidoscopic masterpieces as *Live Head*, *The Regeneration of Man*, *King's Feast* and *Formula of the Petrograd Proletariat*. Also look out for the vibrant red *Colour Composition* by **Boris Ender** (1893–1960) – an early pioneer of what would later be termed Abstract Expressionism – and work by **Alexander Rodchenko** (1891–1956), best known for his designs for ceramics, clothing and furniture, and for his photomontages, an art form that he invented.

Agitprop and Socialist Realism

Many of these artists threw themselves into the Revolution and produced what became known as **agitprop**, or "agitational propaganda". Posters became the new medium, brilliantly exploited by Mayakovsky (see p.217), Rodchenko and Vladimir Lebedev, and often aimed at promoting public health, literacy and recruitment for the Red Army. Although many Futurists derided easel painting, it too served for agitprop, from Malevich's *Red Cavalry* (see p.153) to Petrov-Vodkin's *Death of a Commissar* or the horrific *Disabled Veterans* by **Yuri Pimenov** (1903–77), in **room 83**.

By the late 1920s the avant-garde movement was divided between those who saw art as a spiritual activity, which, by becoming useful, ceased to exist, and those who insisted that artists must become technicians to bring "art into life" for the benefit of the masses. **Room 84** showcases work on themes such as sport, labour and collectivization, treated with freshness and vigour by artists who came of age at this time. **Alexander Deineka** (1899–1969) depicted steel- and textile-workers in stark tones and dramatic compositions, and later produced World War II masterpieces such as *Downed Flier*. Also full of energy are *Militarized Komsomol* and a tough, sexy *Metro Worker* with her steam-drill, by **Alexander Samokhvalov** (1894–1971).

The debate raged on until Stalin put an end to it all by making **Socialist Realism** obligatory in 1932. Its principles, as articulated by his mouthpiece Zhdanov, were *partiinost*, *ideinost* and *narodnost* (Party character, socialist content and national roots). While this still allowed some room for stylistic variation – as in Pimenov's bleak *Front Line Road* or Konchalovsky's folksy portrait of the writer Andrey Tolstoy in **room 85** – the prevailing style was a Stalinist take on nineteenth-century academicism. Works in this genre are legion, but rarely on display in the Russian Museum, except for major thematic exhibitions on the first floor of the Benois Wing. Its chief exponents were **Isaak Brodsky** (1884–1939), responsible for such works as *Lenin in the Smolniy*, and **Alexander Gerasimov** (1881–1963), to whom the world is indebted for *Stalin at the XVIth Congress of the Communist Party*.

Vasilevskiy Island

Buffeted by storms from the Gulf of Finland, **Vasilevskiy Island** (Vasilevskiy ostrov) cleaves the River Neva into its Bolshaya and Malaya branches, forming a strategic wedge whose eastern tip – or **Strelka** – is as much a part of St Petersburg's waterfront as the Winter Palace or Admiralty. The Strelka's **Rostral Columns** and former Stock Exchange (now the **Naval Museum**) are vivid reminders that the city's port and commercial centre were once located here, while another, more enduring aspect of Vasilevskiy's erstwhile importance is the intellectual heritage bequeathed by St Petersburg's **University**, bolstered by a clutch of museums, including Peter the Great's infamous **Kunstkammer**, or "chamber of curiosities".

Originally, Peter envisaged making the island the centre of his capital. The first governor of St Petersburg, Alexander Menshikov, was an early resident (his **Menshikov Palace** is now the oldest building on the island) and Peter compelled other rich landowners and merchants to settle here. By 1726 the island had ten streets and over a thousand inhabitants, but wilderness still predominated and wolves remained a menace for decades to come. Living on the island also entailed hazardous crossings by sailing boat, as Peter had banned the use of rowing boats in order to instil a love of sailing, but unfortunately the ex-ferrymen made poor sailors. Moreover, Vasilevskiy Island became isolated from the mainland whenever a storm blew up or the Neva was choked with ice, dooming any hope of the island becoming the centre of St Petersburg.

Although Peter's plan for a network of canals was thwarted by Menshikov, who had them built so narrow as to be useless, their layout determined the grid of **avenues** and **lines** (see box below) within which subsequent development occurred. Politically, the proximity of factories and workers' slums to the university's student quarter fostered local militancy during the revolutions of 1905 and 1917. In Soviet times, the western side of the island was extensively

The linii

The island's three main avenues – Bolshoy, Sredniy and Maliy prospekts – are crossed at right angles by thirteen streets designated as pairs of **linii** (lines) and numbered as such, for example, 1-ya & 2-ya liniya, abbreviations respectively of pervaya liniya and vtoraya liniya, meaning "first" and "second lines".

Odd-numbered liniya refer to the western side of the street (where the buildings have even numbers); even-numbered liniya to the eastern side (where buildings have odd numbers). House numbers ascend as you move away from the River Bolshaya Neva, hitting 14–17 around Bolshoy prospekt and the low 30s at Sredniy. When writing addresses, people usually add "V.O." ("B.O." in Cyrillic) for Vasilevskiy ostrov, to avoid any confusion with Bolshoy or Maliy prospekt on the Petrograd Side.

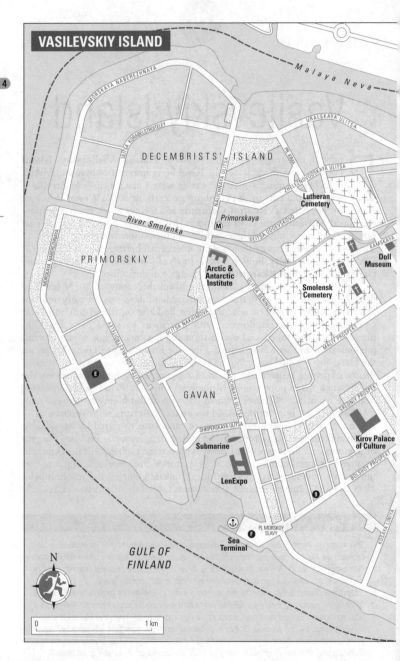

VASILEVSKIY ISLAND

Malaya Neva

URALSKAYA ULITSA

DECEMBRISTS' ISLAND

ULITSA KORABELSTROITELEY

NAUCHNAYA ULITSA

PR. KIMA

ZHELEZNOVODSKAYA ULITSA

Lutheran Cemetery

River Smolenka

Primorskaya Ⓜ

ULITSA ODOEVSKOVO

KAMSKAYA

MORSKAYA NABEREZHNAYA

PRIMORSKIY

Arctic & Antarctic Institute

ULITSA BERINGA

Smolensk Cemetery

Doll Museum

ULITSA NAKHIMOVA

MALIY PROSPEKT

ULITSA KORABELSTROITELEY

Ⓔ

GAVAN

NALICHNAYA ULITSA

SREDNIY PROSPEKT

SHKIPERSKAYA ULITSA

Submarine

Kirov Palace of Culture

LenExpo

BOLSHOY PROSPEKT

Ⓐ

Ⓕ PL MORSKOY SLAVY

Ⓐ

Sea Terminal

KOSAYA LINIYA

GULF OF FINLAND

N

0 _____ 1 km

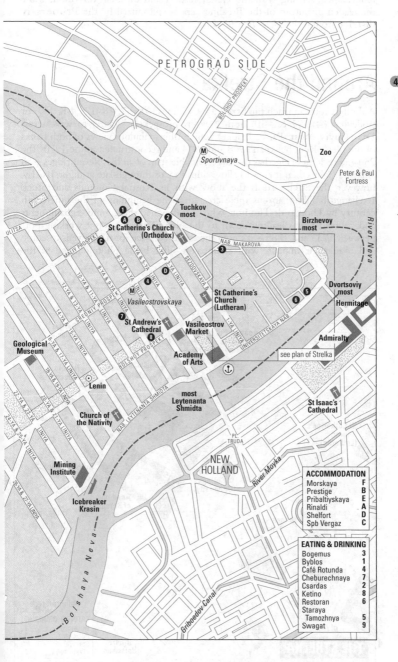

PETROGRAD SIDE

VASILEVSKIY ISLAND

4

Sportivnaya

Zoo

Peter & Paul Fortress

River Neva

Tuchkov most

Birzhevoy most

St Catherine's Church (Orthodox)

NAB. MAKAROVA

Dvortsoviy most

St Catherine's Church (Lutheran)

Hermitage

Vasileostrovskaya

St Andrew's Cathedral

Vasileostrov Market

Admiralty

see plan of Strelka

Geological Museum

Academy of Arts

St Isaac's Cathedral

Lenin

most Leytenanta Shmidta

Church of the Nativity

PL. TRUDA

NEW HOLLAND

River Moyka

Mining Institute

Icebreaker Krasin

Bolshaya Neva

Griboedov Canal

ACCOMMODATION
Morskaya	F
Prestige	B
Pribaltiyskaya	E
Rinaldi	A
Shelfort	D
Spb Vergaz	C

EATING & DRINKING
Bogemus	3
Byblos	1
Café Rotunda	4
Cheburechnaya	7
Csardas	2
Ketino	8
Restoran Staraya Tamozhnya	5
Swagat	9

157

redeveloped, starting with the Gavan district and the **Sea Terminal**, while the leaden gigantism of the Brezhnev era is epitomized by the **Primorskiy district** around the *Hotel Pribaltiyskaya*.

Around the Strelka

Although you can reach the **Strelka** by minibus (#K-47, #K-129, #K-147) or trolleybus (#1, #7 & #10) from Nevskiy prospekt, it's better to walk across **Dvortsoviy most** (Palace Bridge), which offers fabulous views of both banks of the Neva. Built between 1908 and 1914 and reconstructed in the 1970s, the 250-metre-long bridge has the largest liftable span of all the Neva bridges – an amazing sight when it rises to allow ships to pass through late at night. By day, however, the Strelka steals the show with its Rostral Columns and Stock Exchange building, an ensemble created at the beginning of the nineteenth century by Thomas de Thomon, who also designed the granite embankments and cobbled ramps leading down to the Neva. This area was a working port between 1733 and 1885 – it's now the favoured place for newlyweds to come and toast their nuptials with champagne after being photographed at the

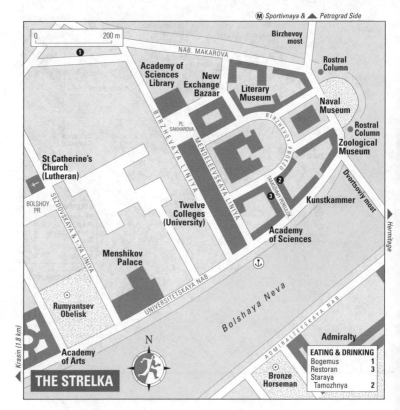

△ A Rostral Column on the Strelka

Bronze Horseman. Many make further stops at Peter's Cabin and the cruiser *Aurora* on the Petrograd Side.

The Rostral Columns

Designed as navigational beacons, the twin brick-and-stucco **Rostral Columns** (Rostralnye kolonny) stand 32m high and once blazed with burning hemp oil at night; now gas-fired, the torches are lit only during festivals, such as Navy Day on the last Sunday in July (see box opposite). Their form derives from the Imperial Roman custom of erecting columns decorated with the sawn-off prows, or *rostrae* (beaks), of Carthaginian galleys captured in battle – although it is of course Russian naval victories that are honoured by these Rostral Columns. Figures at the base of each column personify Russia's great trade rivers: the Dnieper and Volga (on the column nearest Dvortsoviy most), and the Volkhov and Neva.

The Naval Museum

A sculptural tableau of Neptune harnessing the Baltic's tributaries surmounts the columned facade of St Petersburg's old Stock Exchange (Birzha), a monumental pile modelled on the temple of Paestum in southern Italy. Made redundant by the Bolshevik Revolution, the building was later turned into the **Naval Museum** (Voenno-Morskoy muzey; 11am–6pm, closed Wed & the last Thurs of each month; $3.20). From the entrance around the left side of its broad stairway, head upstairs, past a ballistic missile and statues of Red sailors, to see the host of model ships in the former exchange hall. The prize exhibits here are the *botik* (boat) in which Peter learned to sail – a vessel dubbed the "Grandfather of the Russian Navy" – and Russia's oldest surviving submarine, designed by Dzhevetsky 1881. Exhibits recounting the disaster at Tsushima Bay (see box opposite) are relegated to the back of the hall, while the surrounding rooms chart events during the Revolution and World War II (with mug shots of the *Potemkin* mutineers and Kronstadt sailors) and conclude with the navy's postwar expansion. A collection of carved figureheads from eighteenth-century vessels fills the staircase up to the top floor, which is used for temporary exhibitions. Additionally, the Naval Museum runs two historic vessels as museums – the cruiser *Aurora* (p.186) and the submarine *Narodovolets* (p.169).

The Literary Museum

Early last century the Strelka's warehouses and customs building were all converted to academic use, with the Northern Warehouse becoming an institute for soil sciences, while the Customs House on naberezhnaya Makarova was taken over by the Institute of Russian Literature. Familiarly known as the "**Pushkin House**" (Pushkinskiy dom), it's home to a fusty **Literary Museum** (Mon–Fri 11am–5pm; $3) with four rooms of furniture such as Gogol's armchair and Tolstoy's desk, portraits and personal effects, including the poet Lermontov's cavalry sabre and Tolstoy's shirt and boots. Bibliophiles can book a guided **tour** in English (☎328 05 02; $3) to make sense of the exhibits, but are likely to be disappointed by the lack of manuscripts on display. A few years ago, the director of the institute ordered them to be stashed away in a state-of-the-art **archive** in the inner courtyard. A computer glitch caused the doors to lock (nearly trapping two archivists) and fire-suppressant gas to flood the interior. Two cylinders

The Russian navy

Before Peter the Great founded the **Russian navy** in 1696, the country had no seafaring tradition. Initially composed of one ship and three admirals, the navy developed by trial and error using techniques imported from Holland and England, where the tsar had studied shipbuilding. At first, the emphasis was on building galleys rather than heavier men o' war – a strategy that paid off when the lighter Russian boats outmanoeuvred the Swedish fleet in the shallow waters off **Hangö** in 1714. But substandard ships and seamanship remained a problem until the reign of Catherine the Great, when in 1770 Russia won its first major sea battle at **Chesma Bay** in the Aegean.

Like its contemporary British counterpart, the Tsarist navy relied on the press gang and savage discipline, and by the end of the nineteenth century its vessels had become outmoded and its leadership incompetent. In 1904, the Pacific Fleet was decimated by a surprise Japanese attack on **Port Arthur**, on Russia's Pacific coast. Ordered to sail halfway around the world to avenge this, the Baltic Fleet almost caused a war with Britain by firing on an English fishing fleet in dense fog, believing it to be the Japanese navy. When the Russian fleet finally arrived in Japanese waters seven months later, it was annihilated in two days of fighting at **Tsushima Bay**.

Henceforth, the navy was more noted for its **mutinies**, starting with that of the crew of the battleship *Potemkin* of the Black Sea Fleet in 1905. Sailors of the Baltic Fleet played a major role in the revolutions of 1917, and in 1921 they came out against the Bolsheviks, who crushed the **Kronstadt revolt** with characteristic ruthlessness. Essentially limited to an ancillary role during **World War II**, the navy remained a poor relation of the other services until the 1970s, when it underwent a massive, hubristic expansion under **Admiral Gorshkov**, who dreamt of projecting Soviet naval power across the globe.

The demise of the USSR saw the Soviet navy carved up among Russia, Ukraine and Azerbaijan – the Russian navy's bitter wrangles with Ukraine over the Crimean Fleet were followed by the galling sight of Ukrainian and NATO warships on joint exercises in the Black Sea. This gave Russia's naval chiefs an ironclad excuse not to scale down their operations, something they achieved – despite the naval budget being slashed during the Yeltsin years – by not paying or feeding sailors and skimping on maintenance and technical support. The resulting decline in safety standards and morale made a tragedy inevitable.

In August 2000, the nuclear submarine *Kursk* **sank** 100m onto the Arctic seabed after an explosion in its torpedo room. The Russian navy's own undersea rescue unit had been run down to save money, but the high command refused foreign offers of help for nearly a week, by which time any hope of saving the men still alive in the aft compartments had gone – to the fury of the public. While the dead were eventually recovered and given state funerals (in St Petersburg at the Serafimov Cemetery, where a monument has been erected), the larger question of safety remained – for another sub went down with all hands in September 2003.

Meanwhile, the **Baltic Fleet** remains based in St Petersburg, a city with three naval colleges and shipyards galore. In the run-up to **Navy Day** (last Sun in July), battleships and submarines are anchored mid-river in the heart of the city, before the festival starts with a regatta and ends with fireworks and drunken sailors roaming Nevskiy prospekt, while the Rostral Columns blaze after dark.

exploded, vaporizing some manuscripts and plastering Lermontov's on the ceiling; Pushkin's papers were saved only by a fluke. The debacle was kept secret until the director had been confirmed as an Academician.

Behind the Literary and Naval museums is a crescent-shaped plaza that was once the commercial hub of the island. Here you'll see the **New Exchange**

Bazaar, a scaled-down version of Gostiniy dvor, built by Quarenghi in the early nineteenth century. Once a bustling market, it's now a service depot for the Academy of Sciences Library over the road. The library itself contains around nine million volumes, including *The Apostle*, Russia's first printed book, dating from 1564, as well as Peter the Great's own library and schoolbooks belonging to the poet and scientist Lomonosov.

The Zoological Museum

Of more popular appeal is the **Zoological Museum** (Zoologicheskiy muzey; 11am–6pm, closed Fri; $1), located in the Southern Warehouse on Universitetskaya naberezhnaya (University Embankment) facing Dvortsoviy most. Founded in 1832, the museum has one of the finest collections of its kind in the world, with over one hundred thousand specimens, including a set of stuffed animals that once belonged to Peter the Great (among them his dog Titan and his warhorse Lizetta). Upstairs, you're confronted by the skeleton of a blue whale, along with models of polar bears and other Arctic life. The side hall traces the evolution of vertebrates and invertebrates (note the giant Kamchatka crab), as well as mammals, with realistic tableaux of stuffed animals showing each species in its habitat.

The museum's beloved prehistoric **mammoths** are accompanied by models and photographs detailing their excavation – the most evocative display shows the discovery of a 44,000-year-old mammoth in the permafrost of Yakutsia in 1903. Other finds in 1961 and 1977 (the latter a baby mammoth) are recalled with photographs, as the actual animals themselves are in museums elsewhere. The top floor of the museum is devoted to **insects**, including a selection of live ones.

The Kunstkammer

The **Kunstkammer** (11am–6pm, closed Mon & the last Tues of each month; $3), next door, is even more alluring to visitors; there's usually a queue at the entrance around the side of the sea-green building with its distinctive poly-gonal tower. Founded by Peter in 1714, its name (meaning "art chamber" in German) was an attempt to dignify his fascination for curiosities and freaks. Forming the centrepiece of the collection were two thousand preparations by the Dutch embalmer Frederik Ruysch and an ethnographic "chamber of wonders", also purchased in Holland. In Russia, Peter offered rewards for "human monsters" and unknown birds and animals, with a premium for especially odd ones. Dead specimens had to be preserved in vinegar or vodka (for which their original owners were reimbursed by the Imperial pharmacy), while, to attract visitors, each received a glass of vodka. Originally, the Kunstkammer even had live exhibits, such as a man with only two digits on each limb, and a hermaphrodite (who escaped). After the Revolution, it's said, an impoverished aristocrat found work there, and secretly drained off the spirit in which the curios were preserved to sell to unsuspecting drinkers.

At the time of writing, the **curios** are divided between two floors and amount to little more than a freak show, but they should eventually all be displayed on the first floor in a more scholarly fashion. While modern science can account for the Siamese twins, dwarves and a two-headed calf, it's almost impossible for us to share the eighteenth-century taste for adorning dead babies' limbs with ruffles or baubles to emphasize their pathos and beauty – nor for having giants as domestic pets. Although the outsized penis of Peter's favourite giant, "Bourgeois", is no longer exhibited, you can still see his skeleton, plus surgical and dental instruments and teeth pulled by the tsar himself, a keen amateur dentist who kept records of his victims, among them "a person who made tablecloths" and "a fast-walking messenger".

The rest of both floors is taken up by the **Museum of Anthropology and Ethnography** (Muzey Antropologii i Etnografii), displaying everything from Balinese puppets to Inuit kayaks and including some lovely dioramas of native village life. Africa and the Americas are dealt with on the first floor and the section upstairs covers Southeast Asia, the Antipodes and Melanesia. Many of the exhibits are beautifully crafted, and their sheer diversity makes this a fascinating museum, despite the fact that the captions are in Russian only. Guided **tours** ($8 group rate) in English can be booked in advance (☎328 14 12), including specialized ones on subjects such as tribal initiation ceremonies. The museum also hosts contemporary art **exhibitions** and **events**; its **website** (🌐www.kunstkamera.ru) has lots of historical facts but little up-to-date information.

Hopefully you'll also be able to see the **Great Academic Globe** in the tower, which has just emerged from decades of restoration. A kind of eighteenth-century planetarium, it was stolen from Tsarskoe Selo during the Nazi occupation and recovered in Lübeck in 1947. Spectators sit inside the globe, which rotates on its axis, causing the planets and stars painted on the inner surface to revolve. It was partly designed by the "Russian Leonardo", **Mikhail Lomonosov** (1711–65), a fisherman's son from Archangel who codified Russian grammar, studied minerals and the heavens, and anticipated Dalton's theory of the atomic structure of matter in his *Elementa Chymiae Mathematica* (1741). A **museum** recreating his study-laboratory – reached by a staircase off the Bali and Micronesia gallery on the second floor – will reopen at some point in the future (☎328 10 11 for information).

The Academy of Sciences

The next building along Universitetskaya naberezhnaya houses the **Academy of Sciences** (Akademiya nauk), the idea for which, like so many Russian institutions, was first mooted by Peter (who asked the German scientist and philosopher Leibnitz to devise a constitution), but only formally established after his death. In 1934, the academy's administrative functions were transferred to Moscow, leaving the Leningrad branch in charge of various institutes, the Zoological Museum and the library. Its austerely Neoclassical headquarters – built by Quarenghi between 1784 and 1787 – feature a **mosaic** of the Battle of Poltava by Lomonosov on the upper landing of the grand staircase, which can be glimpsed from the lobby (you probably won't be allowed any further). A **statue of Lomonosov** stands on Mendeleevskaya liniya, just beyond the academy.

The Twelve Colleges and the University

The western side of Mendeleevskaya liniya is flanked by the second-oldest building on the island, the **Twelve Colleges** (Dvenadtsat kollegii), its 400-metre-long facade painted sienna red with white facings, as in Petrine times. Executed by Trezzini, the building was designed to epitomize Peter's idea of a modern, efficient bureaucracy: the separate doors to the dozen different departments signified their autonomy and the uniform facade their common purpose. He was later enraged to discover that Menshikov had tampered with the plans, reducing the size of the buildings so as not to intrude on his own estates.

The *kollegii* were eventually replaced by ministries across the river, and in 1819 the building was given to **St Petersburg University** (Universitet Sankt-Peterburga). A bastion of freethinking and radicalism in Tsarist times, it educated many famous names in science, literature and politics. It was here that **Dmitri Mendeleyev** (1834–1907) worked out the Periodic Table of Elements having dreamt of the solution that had eluded him for months in 1869; his study at Mendeleevskaya liniya 2-ya has become a small **museum** (Mon–Fri 11am–4pm; $2) preserving his laboratory equipment and personal effects. The rector's house was the childhood home of the Symbolist poet Alexander Blok (who married Mendeleyev's daughter), while Alexander Popov sent what was arguably the world's first radio signal from the university labs (see p.108). Other alumni include Nikolai Chernyshevsky, author of the Utopian revolutionary novel *What is to be Done?*; Alexander Ulyanov, hanged for plotting to kill Alexander III; his brother Vladimir Ilyich – better known as Lenin – who graduated with honours in law in 1891; and Russia's president, Vladimir Putin, who joined the KGB after completing his law degree in 1975.

The university's students were at the forefront of nineteenth-century protests, and during the 1905 Revolution thousands of workers gathered here every evening to seek news and leadership. In Stalinist times, scores of students and staff were sent to the camps and, adding insult to injury, the university was later named after Andrei Zhdanov, former Leningrad Party boss and scourge of the intelligentsia. Having dropped Zhdanov's name in the Gorbachev era, the university considered for a while whether to adopt Peter the Great or academician and dissident Andrei Sakharov as its namesake, but decided to stay simply with "St Petersburg" – though Sakharov's name was bestowed on the square at the far end.

To the Menshikov Palace

Continuing westwards along the riverfront down Universitetskaya naberezhnaya, you'll come to the pale-yellow former barracks of the **First Cadet Corps**, which trained the sons of the aristocracy for a military career. Cadets usually joined between the ages of 10 and 14 – a contemporary report states that "on one occasion, when formed in square and charged by cavalry, their little hearts failed them and they took to their heels in all directions". Their summer manoeuvres were observed by the tsar, who took a great interest in his "Lilliputian regiments".

In July 1917 the barracks hosted the First Congress of Workers' and Soldiers' Deputies, in which only ten percent of the deputies were Bolsheviks. When a speaker claimed that there wasn't a party willing to take control, Lenin shouted from the floor, "There is! No party has the right to refuse power and our party does not refuse it. It is ready to assume power at any time." In honour of his chutzpah, a nearby street is named Sezdovskaya (Congress) liniya. Another figure associated with the street was **Heinrich Schliemann**, who lived at no. 28 while he was trading in indigo, earning the fortune that enabled him to discover the gold of Troy. Schliemann initially offered the treasure to the Hermitage but the tsar refused because the German was a bigamist, so it ended up in a museum in Berlin – an error that the Soviets rectified by seizing it as "trophy art" in 1945; it now reposes in the Pushkin Museum of Fine Arts in Moscow. On the embankment is a **monument** like a giant open book, inscribed with an ode by Pushkin, which was erected for the city's three hundredth anniversary.

The Menshikov Palace

The chief reason to walk this far is to visit the **Menshikov Palace** (Menshikovskiy dvorets), a gabled golden-yellow building beside the old First Cadet Corps. Built in the early eighteenth century, it was the first residential structure on Vasilevskiy Island and the finest one in the city, surpassing even Peter's Summer Palace – the tsar had no objections, however, preferring to entertain at the Menshikov Palace, which was furnished to suit his tastes. Though not as sumptuous as the later Imperial palaces, it sports fine Petrine-era decor and comes under the auspices of the Hermitage. The entrance is below street level, past the main portico. During **visiting** hours (10.30am–4.30pm, closed Mon; $7) you must join a guided tour in Russian (every half hour), but you can slip away from the group once the tour is under way.

On the first floor is the **kitchen** and a **dining room** furnished with tapestries. Objects on display include period costumes, plus a lathe and tools belonging to Peter. The statues in the Italianate hallway were imported from Europe by Menshikov in his desire to emulate Peter, and the stairway bears their entwined monograms. The rooms upstairs commence with the **secretary's quarters**, featuring plans of Kraków, Leyden and Utrecht, followed by two rooms faced with white and blue Dutch tiles. Family portraits and seascapes hang on silk ribbons, as was the fashion at that time.

The room containing the German four-poster bed and brass foot-warmer served as a bedroom for the sister of Menshikov's wife, while Menshikov's sumptuous **Walnut Study** is decorated with gilded pilasters and a portrait of Peter. Still more alien to Russian traditions was the **Grand Hall**, with its full-length mirrors that reflected couples dancing together (prior to Peter's time,

Prince Menshikov

Of all the adventurers that staked their fortunes on Peter the Great, none was closer to the tsar than **Alexander Menshikov** (1673–1729). Humbly born (it was rumoured that he sold pies on the streets of Moscow as a child), Menshikov accompanied Peter on his Grand Tour of Europe in 1697. The tsar liked his enthusiasm for shipbuilding and carousing, and his artful blend of "servility, familiarity and impertinence": soon they were inseparable.

After helping to crush the *streltsy* mutiny, Menshikov was showered with favours and responsibilities, becoming commandant of Shlisselburg and the first governor of St Petersburg. In 1703 he acquired a mistress whom Peter subsequently took a fancy to, married in secret and later crowned as Catherine I. The tsar addressed Menshikov as *Mein Herz* (My Heart), causing speculation that their relationship went "beyond honourable affection". In any event, Peter tolerated Menshikov's vanity (exemplified by the latter's palace at Oranienbaum, which was grander than the tsar's) and persistent corruption, forgiving peculations that others would have paid for with their lives.

As Peter lay dying, Menshikov engineered Catherine's succession as empress, then had all charges pending against himself annulled. He continued to flourish until Catherine's demise in 1727 when – accused of treason and fined 500,000 rubles – he was exiled to his Ukrainian estates by the boy-tsar Peter II, but allowed to depart with sixty wagon-loads of valuables. Less than a year later, however, Menshikov and his family were stripped of all their possessions and exiled to the remote Siberian village of Berezovka, where they died in poverty. A famous painting by Repin (in the Russian Museum) depicts Menshikov brooding over his fate in a hut, with his family huddled together for warmth.

mirrors were anathematized by the Orthodox Church and men and women rarely socialized together at all). Notice the cherubs holding the candelabras and the unique organ-clock, made in England. In Menshikov's day, the hall once hosted a "Dwarves' Wedding" for Peter's entertainment, with little tables in the centre set with miniature cutlery. Though the dwarves' drunken cavorting provoked hilarity, Menshikov regretted that they couldn't fire a tiny cannon specially cast for the occasion, for fear of disturbing his only son, lying ill elsewhere in the palace. The boy expired that night (which didn't stop Menshikov from celebrating his own name day soon afterwards) and the dwarf bride later died in childbirth – marriages between dwarves were subsequently forbidden.

Across the landing are the re-created rooms of his wife Dariya, filled with statues and Oriental porcelain – a prelude to the magnificent dining room and **master bedroom** decorated with Chinese silk wall hangings (not original to the palace), and Menshikov's **Blue Study**, with its ceiling fresco of Peter as Mars.

On the **embankment** outside the palace you can see the granite abutments of the old St Isaac's Bridge of 1729 – the first bridge across the Neva. The abutments supported a wooden pontoon bridge that had to be dismantled annually before the river froze and rebuilt after it thawed; it finally burned down in 1916.

On to the Krasin

Beyond the Menshikov Palace the sights are fewer and further apart, and as all public transport turns inland at 8–9-ya liniya, one has to walk the rest of the way from there to the *Krasin* and the Mining Museum (1.2km). But it's tempting to walk the initial stretch anyway, as there are several sights within a few blocks. Beyond Sezdovskaya and 1-ya liniya you come first to a shady park centred on the **Rumyantsev Obelisk**, commemorating the victories of Marshal Rumyantsev in the Russo-Turkish wars of 1768–74. Hewn from black granite and surmounted by a gilded orb and eagle, it was erected on Marsovo pole in 1799 and transferred to its present site in 1818.

The Academy of Arts and Pavlov Museum

On the western side of the park is the **Academy of Arts** (Akademiya khudozhestv), a huge mustard-coloured edifice built between 1764 and 1788 by Vallin de la Mothe and Alexander Kokoroniv. Set up by Empress Elizabeth and Catherine the Great, the academy trained artists, commissioned art that extolled the state and censored work deemed to be subversive. Students joined at the age of 6 and graduated at 21. Its roll call of graduates includes the architects Zakharov and Voronikhin; Pyotr Klodt, sculptor of the horses on Anichkov most; and the painters Karl Bryullov and Ilya Repin. Most of the building is now occupied by the Repin Institute of Painting, Sculpture and Architecture, but the Russian Academy of Arts maintains a **museum** (Wed–Sun noon–6pm; $2) on the second and third floors. This is known as the "**Academic Circle**" because it rings a circular inner courtyard, and its art collection includes student works by Repin and Polonev. Diploma work by today's students is exhibited each September in the grandiose Parade Hall, and there are temporary exhibitions of stuff from the storerooms, such as Sir

Charles Barry's original designs for the Houses of Parliament in London. It's possible to book a **tour** in Russian (☎323 64 96; $10 group rate).

Two serene-faced Egyptian **sphinxes** ennoble the embankment outside. Carved from Aswan granite and weighing 32 tonnes apiece, they were found at Luxor in the 1820s and brought to Russia in 1832. A hieroglyphic inscription identifies them with Pharaoh Amunhotep III (1417–1379 BC), "Son of Ra, ruler of Thebes, the builder of monuments rising to the sky like four pillars holding up the vault of the heavens".

It was just around the corner from the academy, on 4–5-ya liniya, that the six-thousand-strong Vasilevskiy Island contingent of the workers' march on "Bloody Sunday" (see p.73) was confronted by soldiers and mounted police, who then charged the crowd. Students and workers began to arm themselves and erect barricades, which the authorities smashed with volleys of rifle and cannon fire, killing and wounding hundreds.

Further along the embankment, the **Academicians' House** (Dom akademikov), on the corner with 6–7-ya liniya, has provided permanent accommodation for more than eighty scientists and linguists over the 250 years since it was built – hence the plaques on its facade. The Nobel Prize-winning physiologist Ivan Pavlov lived from 1918 until his death in 1936 in apartment #18. Now the **Pavlov Memorial Museum** (Mon–Fri 11am–1pm & 2–4pm; free), it features a laboratory where the aged scientist could work without going to the Institute of Experimental Medicine (p.191), and a study filled with personal effects (under renovation). To learn about Pavlov's life and work, come on Tuesday, when English-speaking Mr Lapovok can conduct a **tour** (☎234 59 00; free, but donations welcome; best to ring in advance).

Along naberezhnaya Leytenanta Shmidta

Between 1842 and 1850, the first permanent stone bridge across the Neva was erected near the Academicians' House and named after St Nicholas. It was rebuilt and widened in the 1930s, and its present name, **most Leytenanta Shmidta**, honours Lieutenant Pyotr Schmidt, who led a mutiny aboard the cruiser *Ochakov* during the 1905 Revolution and signalled to the tsar, "I assume command of the Southern Fleet. Schmidt."

In 1918, his name was also bestowed upon the embankment beyond – naberezhnaya Leytenanta Shmidta – where he attended the **Higher Naval College** at no. 17. The oldest in Russia, the college boasts of having trained Rimsky-Korsakov (before he decided to study music) and several admirals. Whereas tributes are also paid to Nakhimov (the defender of Sebastopol), Lazarev (co-leader of the 1820 Antarctic expedition) and Krusenstern (who circumnavigated the globe in 1803–6), a veil is drawn over Rozhestvensky (who led the Baltic Fleet to disaster at Tsushima Bay) and Kolchak (a White Army leader during the Civil War). A plaque recalls that Lenin delivered a lecture here in May 1917 entitled "War and Revolution". Two hundred metres further west is the Byzantine-style **Church of the Nativity**, whose gilded tracery and swirly green domes lend a dash of glamour to the drab waterfront. From there it's another 500m to the Mining Institute and the icebreaker *Krasin*, at 21-ya liniya.

The **Mining Institute** was founded by Peter the Great to locate new sources of minerals throughout the empire – particularly in the Urals – and train mining engineers and industrialists; graduates were ranked alongside officers and civil servants in the Petrine table of ranks. Even today, students and staff wear a black uniform with badges of rank, like the military and naval colleges. Statues of Pluto abducting Proserpine and Hercules struggling with Antaeus flank the institute's Classical portico, while Peter's boast that "Our Russian state abounds in riches more than many other lands and is blessed with metals and minerals" is borne out by the Geological Museum on Sredniy prospekt (see p.170).

The Krasin

Moored across the road from the Mining Institute is the **icebreaker Krasin**, a veteran of the Soviet "Conquest of the North" granted honourable retirement as a floating **museum** (10am–6pm, closed Mon; $4; camera/video $3/$5). A tour is mandatory but you don't have to book ahead, and the exhibition charting its history is labelled in English. The ship was in fact built for the tsar's navy at Newcastle-upon-Tyne in England, but impounded after the Revolution until Trade Commissar Krasin ransomed it back in 1921. Renamed in his honour, the icebreaker was at the forefront of the international mission to rescue Nobile's trans-polar airship expedition of 1928, and saved a passenger steamer on its way back to Norway. In World War II, it was the only Soviet ship in the historic convoy to Murmansk, code-named PQ-15, which ran the gauntlet of Nazi U-boats in order to deliver vital war materials to the USSR. Picking up Gagarin on his splashdown from orbit was another highpoint before the *Krasin* was relegated to other duties by the advent of nuclear-powered icebreakers in the 1960s.

The ship's spacious bridge contains both antique and modern instruments, and the lifeboats and machinery on deck are likewise a mix of old and new. The extreme environment in which it operated obliged the *Krasin* to carry a tow-rope measuring 68mm in diameter and two giant spanners weighing 300 kilos, for replacing the propeller shaft. The tour guide is keen to learn the foreign equivalents of nautical terms such as "Crow's Nest" (which Russians call a "Kennel").

Bolshoy prospekt and the Sea Terminal

Vasilevskiy Island's main axis is the wide and shady **Bolshoy prospekt**, running 3.5km from Sezdovskaya liniya southwest to the Sea Terminal. Lined with a mixture of Art Nouveau town houses and 1960s apartment buildings, the nicest stretch is around the Vasileostrov Market, within walking distance of Vasileostrovskaya metro station or Universitetskaya naberezhnaya – or you can get there by #10 trolleybus from Nevskiy prospekt. **Minibuses** #K-47 and #K-129 run the length of Bolshoy prospekt to the Sea Terminal.

From Sezdovskaya to 6–7-ya liniya

The Sezdovskaya end of the prospekt is distinguished by the former Lutheran **Church of St Catherine** (Tserkov Svyatoy Yekateriny), a porticoed Neoclassical edifice that once catered to the island's German community and is now a recording studio, although the recording company that uses it, Melodiya, sponsors services and concerts in the church on Sundays. The apartment building at Bolshoy pr. 6 was the scene of a well-known tragedy of the Blockade. Between December 1941 and May 1942, 11-year-old **Tanya Savicheva** recorded in her diary the deaths of her sister, grandmother, brother, uncles and mother – all from starvation. Tanya herself was evacuated, but died the following year. Her diary is now in the Rumyantsev Mansion (see p.110).

Three blocks west of the church, scaffolding shrouds the **Vasileostrovskiy Market** and its eighteenth-century forerunner, the Andreevskiy bazaar. Around the corner on 6–7-ya liniya the turreted building at no. 16 is the **oldest pharmacy** in St Petersburg, established by Professor de Pohl and sons over 120 years ago – it's worth popping inside to see the elegant teak cabinets and engraved glass cash desk (Mon–Fri 8am–8pm, Sat 10am–6pm). A doctor of philosophy, chemistry and pharmacology, Pohl invented several medical compounds still used today.

Opposite the market, the elegant pink-and-white **Cathedral of St Andrew** (Andreevskiy sobor) – containing a superb Baroque iconostasis – graces a recently pedestrianized stretch of **6–7-ya liniya**, between Bolshoy and Maliy prospekt, where rollerbladers glide past street furniture and shrubbery. This and other modest civic improvements are popularly credited to the fact that Putin's mother lives on Vasilevskiy Island (on 2-ya liniya), previously feeling itself neglected by comparison with other parts of the inner city. Beyond 6–7-ya liniya the only sights are a fairly modest **Lenin statue** in the park between 14–15-ya and 16–17-ya liniya, and a nineteenth-century **fire station** three blocks on. Its tower was used for fire spotting before the advent of telephones.

The Sea Terminal and the submarine

Beyond the fire station, the avenue is flanked by decaying factories and depots, culminating in the **Sea Terminal** on ploshchad Morskoy slavy (Marine Glory Square). Moribund for nearly a decade since passenger services to Finland were liquidated and foreign hotel ships left, the terminal is hoping that the resumption of Silja Line cruises from Helsinki and Tallinn will revive its fortunes and bring guests to the refurbished **Hotel Morskaya**. Otherwise, the area is only busy during trade fairs at **LenExpo**, 500m north of the hotel.

Beyond LenExpo a mothballed **submarine**, the *D-2 Narodovolets* (11am–5pm; closed Mon, Tues & the last Thurs of each month; $3), is surreally perched above an inlet used by yachts. The only survivor of six "Dekabrist" class diesel submarines constructed at the Leningrad Baltic shipyards in the late 1920s, it saw active service with the Northern Fleet in the Bering and White seas and with the Baltic Fleet during World War II, before its retirement in 1956. It was rescued from the scrapyard and in 1994 opened as a branch of the Naval Museum dedicated to the submarine service. The mandatory guided **tour** in Russian is conducted by an affable ex-nuclear submariner who – if the Cold War had turned hot – might have been instrumental in wiping your hometown off the map.

The sub is divided into seven sections by watertight doors, each with a brass plaque showing the alphabet in Morse code, so that crewmen could communicate by knocking if the internal system failed. The **interior** is cramped, but much less than it would have been for the 53-man crew, as many of the bunk beds have been removed. You can't help marvelling at the minuscule size of the captain's cabin, the cook's galley, and the toilet cubicle – not to mention the torpedo room, where crewmen slept alongside the torpedoes. One's reluctant respect for the crew (six of whom are still alive) is enhanced when you learn that, in the event of an emergency, they were obliged to escape by swimming out through the torpedo tubes, and that their diving suits were strong enough to protect them from the pressure only at one-third of the depth at which the sub might be in operation.

Sredniy prospekt

The island's "Middle Avenue", **Sredniy prospekt**, runs parallel to Bolshoy prospekt, 500m to the north. Starting from Vasileostrovskaya metro station on the corner of 6–7-ya liniya, you can catch tram #11 or #40 along the length of the prospekt, past a few places worth a mention. Head northeast to the corner of 2–3-ya liniya, where you'll find the Gothic **Lutheran Church of St Michael**, which until a few years ago housed a toy factory but now belongs to various Lutheran missionary organizations and holds regular services (Sun 9.30am in English, 11.30am in Russian). On Sezdovskaya liniya stands the Orthodox **Church of St Catherine**, whose lofty dome and belfry are a local landmark.

Travelling the other way, out towards Gavan, you'll pass a handsome pair of Art Nouveau apartment buildings on the corner of 10–11-ya liniya. Across the road from the second one is a shabbier building (no. 64) where **Stalin** lived after returning from his Siberian exile in March 1917. Though other comrades cold-shouldered him, Stalin was welcomed by Sergei Alliluev, an old friend from the Caucasus who offered him lodgings. Here, Stalin met the Alliluevs' youngest daughter, Nadezhda, whom he later married. Her death in 1932 is ascribed either to suicide (motivated by grief and shame at the purges), or a fatal beating by her husband. Their daughter said that any trace of love or pity in Stalin's character died with her, which might explain his well-known dislike of Leningrad – though the city's cosmopolitan sophistication and Tsarist past obviously rankled too.

Sredniy prospekt's chief attraction is the fabulous **Geological Museum** (Mon–Fri 10am–5pm; free) at no. 74. With over a million exhibits, including dinosaur fossils and mammoths' tusks, you'll be dazed by their variety. Among the star items are a 1.5-metre-long crystal from the Altay Mountains, a chunk of Urals malachite weighing 1054kg, a copper nugget from Kazakhstan weighing 842kg, and an iron meteorite that landed in Siberia. But the show is stolen by a vast **mosaic map** of the Soviet Union studded with diamonds, rubies and other gems from 500 sites, which required the work of over 700 people and won a prize at the Paris Exposition in 1937; it later stood in the St George's Hall of the Hermitage for 34 years. A Soviet hammer and sickle made of gems glitters nearby.

Four blocks further on rears the vast **Kirov Palace of Culture**. Intended to be the largest institution of its kind in the USSR when it was built in the 1930s, this prefabricated shed epitomizes the ugly side of Soviet Constructivism. It was designed by Noy Trotsky, who also built the Bolshoy dom HQ of the secret police and the postwar House of Soviets. If the architect had been related to his famous namesake, he might have ended up inside the Bolshoy dom instead of building it. The crumbling palace now hosts numerous small firms, the local Jewish society and discos.

The Primorskiy district

Beyond the factories north of Sredniy is **Maliy prospekt**, or "Small Avenue" – in fact it's just as long, but grimmer in parts, and the only real reason to visit is the Doll Museum and the Smolensk cemeteries on the banks of the River

Streets and squares

Birzhevaya liniya	Биржевая линия
Bolshoy prospekt	Большой проспект
Kamskaya ul.	Камская ул.
ul. Korablestroiteley	ул. Кораблестроителей
nab. Leytenanta Shmidta	наб. Лейтенанта Шмидта
nab. Makarova	наб. Макарова
Maliy prospekt	Малый проспект
Mendeleevskaya liniya	Менделеевская линия
Nalichnaya ul.	Наличная ул.
Sezdovskaya liniya	Съездовская линия
Sredniy prospekt	Средний проспект
Universitetskaya nab.	Университетская наб.

Metro stations

Primorskaya	Приморская
Vasileostrovskaya	Василеостровская

Buildings and museums

Academy of Arts	Академия художеств
Academy of Sciences	Академия наук
Doll Museum	музей Кукол
Geological Museum	Геологический музей
Literary Museum	Литературный музей
Menshikov Palace	Меншиковский дворец
Museum of Anthropology and Ethnography	музей Антропологии и этнографии
Naval Museum	Военно-Морской музей
St Petersburg University	Университет Санкт-Петербурга
Submarine *D-2 Narodovolets*	Подводная лодка Д-2 Народоволец
Zoological Museum	Зоологический музей

Smolenka. Beyond them, the vast "New Maritime" – or **Primorskiy** – district sprawls as far as **Decembrists' Island** (ostrov Dekabristov), the burial place of the executed participants of the Decembrist uprising. Gigantic blocks of high-rises and avenues that become gale-strength wind tunnels in winter make this area a shock for guests at the Swedish-built *Pribaltiyskaya Hotel*, but residents cherish their view over the Gulf of Finland, and the sea wall is an impressive sight, especially when it catches the sun around dusk. Decaying shipyards, streets named after shipbuilders (Korablestroiteley), skippers (Shkiperskiy), bosuns (Botsmanskaya) and midshipmen (Michmanskaya), and the presence of the Arctic and Antarctic Institute, are all reminders of the district's maritime heritage.

The Doll Museum and Smolensk cemeteries

The **Doll Museum** (muzey Kukol; Tues–Sun 11am–6pm; $3) at Kamskaya ul. 8 isn't always as cute as you'd imagine, since the Russian word for doll, *kukol*, also means "puppet" and can cover erotic manikins as well – so it's best to phone (☎327 72 24) to check they're not staging an adults-only exhibition before taking your kids. However, the 1500-odd specimens usually on display are mostly antiques and quite innocuous, aimed at putting visitors in the mood to buy something by contemporary doll-makers, for whom the museum is a retail outlet. On Sundays visitors have a chance to make a doll for themselves. Young girls will love it, but parents could end up reaching for their credit cards.

Kamskaya ulitsa ends at the gates of the **Smolensk Orthodox Cemetery** (Smolenskoe pravoslavnoe kladbishche), named after the Smolensk Field, where the revolutionary Karakizov was hanged in 1866 for his attempt on the life of Alexander II, and another unsuccessful assassin, Solovyov, was executed in 1879. Many of the graves are smothered with vegetation, but the church inside the walls, and the **Chapel of Kseniya Peterburgskaya** (the city's favourite saint) – where believers kiss the walls – are both carefully tended. Since the cemetery was reserved for Orthodox believers, the dead of other denominations (mainly foreigners) were relegated to the smaller **Smolensk Lutheran Cemetery** (Smolenskoe lyuteranskoe kladbishche), north of the River Smolenka. The graves of a few British families are here, including those of the Scot Charles Baird, owner of a St Petersburg iron foundry, which made the neo-Gothic memorials on his family graves. Admiral Samuel Greig, the hero of Chesma, and his son, Admiral Alexis Greig, who led the defence of Sebastopol against the British during the Crimean War, are both buried in a family plot beside the central alley. To **get there** from Vasileostrovskaya metro, catch minibus #K-249 or tram #1, which terminate almost opposite the Doll Museum. Further on, a bridge to the right leads to the Lutheran cemetery.

5

The Peter and Paul Fortress, Petrograd Side and the Kirov Islands

Across the Neva from the Winter Palace, on the small Zayachiy (Hare) Island, lies the **Peter and Paul Fortress** – the historic kernel of St Petersburg, dating from 1703. This doughty fortress-cum-prison has had many of its buildings converted into museums and features a splendid cathedral containing the tombs of the Romanov monarchs. From the fortress, you can walk across to the urban mass of the **Petrograd Side** (Petrogradskaya storona), a mainly residential area crammed with Style Moderne buildings, which owes its character to a housing boom that started in the 1890s: by 1913 its population had risen from 75,000 to 250,000, after the newly completed Troitskiy most (Trinity Bridge) made the Petrograd Side accessible from the city centre. Aside from the **Alexander Park** – with its all-night beer dens and pubs – most visitors make a beeline for the landmark **Mosque** and the **Museum of Russian Political History**, before heading east along the embankment to the legendary cruiser **Aurora**, which fired the opening shots of the Bolshevik Revolution. Inland, statues and **memorial apartments** commemorate famous people who lived or worked on the Petrograd Side, such as the opera singer Chaliapin and the Party leader Kirov. Alternatively, you can enjoy a bird's-eye view of the city from the **Television Tower** or check out exotic flora at the **Botanical Gardens** on the adjacent Aptekarskiy Island.

More appealing still are the wooded **Kirov Islands**, northwest of the Petrograd Side, bounded by the Malaya, Srednaya and Bolshaya Nevka rivers. Long favoured as recreational areas, **Kamenniy** and **Yelagin** islands feature a host of picturesque *dachas* and official residences, as well as two summer **palaces**, while **Krestovskiy** island sports the mega-sized Kirov Stadium, an amusement park and other amenities.

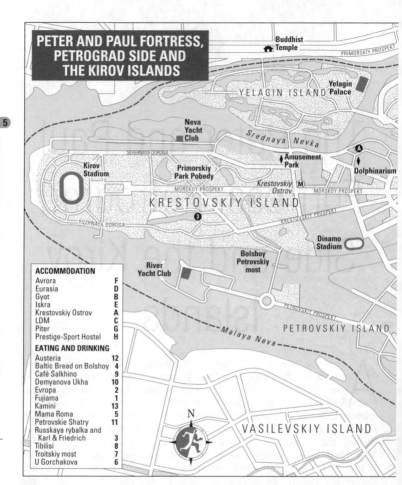

PETER AND PAUL FORTRESS,
PETROGRAD SIDE AND
THE KIROV ISLANDS

ACCOMMODATION
Avrora   F
Eurasia   D
Gyot   B
Iskra   E
Krestovskiy Ostrov   A
LDM   C
Piter   G
Prestige-Sport Hostel   H

EATING AND DRINKING
Austeria   12
Baltic Bread on Bolshoy   4
Café Salkhino   9
Demyanova Ukha   10
Evropa   2
Fujiama   1
Kamini   13
Mama Roma   5
Petrovskie Shatry   11
Russkaya rybalka and
  Karl & Friedrich   3
Tibilisi   8
Troitskiy most   7
U Gorchakova   6

Approaches

Many of the prime sights – including the fortress – are within five to ten minutes' walk of **Gorkovskaya metro** station (on the Moskovsko–Petrogradskaya
line). A slower but more scenic way of getting to the fortress from the city
centre is **by tram** across Troitskiy most; take number #2, #34 or #54 from the
northeast corner of Marsovo pole. Coming **on foot** from Vasilevskiy Island
takes fifteen minutes – en route you'll cross **Birzhevoy most** (Exchange
Bridge), from where there are fine views of the fortress and of the floating
bars around the Kronverk Moat. Walking across the handsome, but busy, 526-
metre-long **Troitskiy most** isn't especially enjoyable on account of the traffic
and (in summer) the heat, although it does provide a superb view of the
Strelka. For a week or so each spring, when the fish are rising, the bridge is
packed with fishermen day and night.

The Peter and Paul Fortress

Built to secure Russia's hold on the Neva delta, the **Peter and Paul Fortress** (Petropavlovskaya krepost) anticipated the foundation of St Petersburg by a year – and may even have suggested to Peter the Great the idea of building a city here. During 1703, forced labourers (who perished in their thousands) toiled from dawn to dusk on Zayachiy Island, constructing the fortress in just seven months. The crude earthworks were subsequently replaced by brick walls under the direction of Trezzini and later faced with granite slabs. Work proceeded on a section-by-section basis so as not to weaken the defences, whose cannons and four-metre-thick walls were never actually tested by an invader – though contemporary observers reckoned that the hexahedral layout

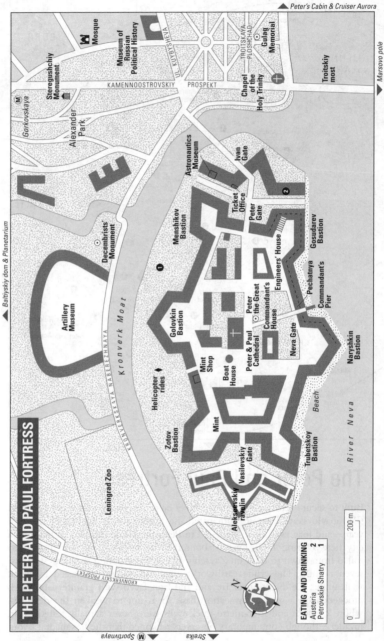

THE PETER AND PAUL FORTRESS

Peter's Cabin & Cruiser Aurora ▲

Mosque

Museum of Russian Political History

Steregushchiy Monument

Gulag Memorial

TROITSKAYA PLOSHCHAD

UL KUYBYSHEVA

KAMENNOOSTROVSKIY PROSPEKT

Chapel of the Holy Trinity

Troitskiy most

Marsovo pole ▶

Gorkovskaya Ⓜ

Alexander Park

Astronautics Museum

Ivan Gate

Ticket Office

Peter Gate

②

Menshikov Bastion

Decembrists' Monument

Kronverk Moat

①

Gosudarev Bastion

Bathyskiy dom & Planetarium ▲

KRONVERKSKAYA NABEREZHNAYA

Artillery Museum

Golovkin Bastion

Peter the Great

Engineers' House

Pechatnya

Commandant's House

Commandant's Pier

Mint Shop

Peter & Paul Cathedral

Neva Gate

Helicopter rides

Boat House

Beach

Naryshkin Bastion

Leningrad Zoo

Mint

Zotov Bastion

River Neva

KRONVERKSKIY PROSPEKT

Vasilevskiy Gate

Alekseevskiy ravelin

Trubetskoy Bastion

N

200 m

EATING AND DRINKING
Austeria 2
Petrovskie Shatry 1

0

Strelka ▶   Sportivnaya Ⓜ ▶

would have precluded concentrated defensive fire, making the fortress a pushover for any determined assailant.

The fortress's role as a **prison** dates back to 1718, when Peter the Great's son, Alexei, was tortured to death within its walls. The "Secret House", built to contain Empress Anna's opponents, was subsequently used by Nicholas I to hold the Decembrists; later generations of revolutionaries were incarcerated in the Trubetskoy Bastion. The fortress was known as the "Russian Bastille", its grim reputation surpassed only by that of the Shlisselburg fortress on Lake Ladoga (see p.304), until the Soviet era made other prisons synonymous with even greater terror.

Today the fortress is cherished as a historic monument – especially its cathedral, which is revered by monarchists as the burial place of the Romanovs. Incongruously, the island on which the fortress is sited is a magnet for sunbathers, who pack its grassy spaces and pebbly **beaches** in summer, and for the hardy folk known as *morzhi* (walruses), who break holes in the ice in winter to swim in temperatures of -20°C. You can even take a **helicopter** ride over the fortress and the Neva basin; it takes off and lands on the grass near the Golovkin Bastion (see p.41 for details).

While the island is permanently accessible, the Peter and Vasilevskiy gates of the fortress are closed at midnight. The museums within its precincts keep regular **opening hours** (Mon & Thurs–Sun 11am–6pm, Tues 11am–5pm; closed Wed & the last Tues of each month), the exceptions to this rule being the cathedral and the Prison Museum (daily from May 9 to mid-September; rest of year same hours as above), the Pechatnya and the Neva panorama walkway (both daily till 7pm year round). A single **ticket** ($4) valid for all the museums (including photography) is sold at the *kassa* in the Ioannovskiy ravelin, near the Ivan Gate, and at the Boat House outside the cathedral. There are extra entry fees for the Neva panorama and various short-term exhibitions of wax figures, payable on the spot. As it's easy to find your way around the fortress and there are information boards in different languages, there's no real need to book a **tour** in English (☎378 70 76 or mobile ☎9056273).

The gates, ramparts and bastions

Approached by a wrought-iron footbridge on the east side of the fortress, the yellow-and-white **Ivan Gate** (Ioannovskie vorota) penetrates an outlying rampart, the **Ioannovskiy ravelin**, which was added to the fortress in 1740. It's the last place you'd associate with space travel, but it once accommodated the research laboratory where the first Soviet liquid-fuelled rocket was developed in 1932–33. Today, the **Astronautics Museum** – off to the right as you come through the Ivan Gate – traces the history of the Soviet space programme from *Sputnik* to the *Mir* orbital station, paying homage to the visionary scientist Konstantin Tsiolkovsky. Decades before the first satellite was put into orbit, he suggested multistage rockets to overcome the adverse mass/fuel ratio, concluding that "Our planet is the cradle of reason, but we cannot live in a cradle for ever". For a small fee, visitors may photograph each other sitting inside a cramped re-entry capsule of the kind that Soviet cosmonauts returned to Earth in.

Straight ahead is the main entrance to the fortress proper, where balalaika players lurk in the shadows of the **Peter Gate** (Petrovskie vorota). Designed by Trezzini as a triumphal arch, the gate sports the double-headed eagle of the Romanovs and a wooden bas-relief depicting St Peter casting down the evil magus Simon. Lest anyone should miss the allegory of his defeat of Charles XII

The death of Tsarevich Alexei

The life and death of **Tsarevich Alexei** (1690–1718) is a shameful indictment of his father, Peter the Great. Since childhood, the timid Alexei took after his mother, Evdokiya, whom Peter confined to a convent when Alexei was eight. His pious temperament was the antithesis of Peter's; his hostility to foreign innovations another cause of paternal contempt and filial bitterness. Ordered to live abroad, he communicated with clerics opposed to Peter's policies, promising to repeal them once he became tsar. When Peter told him to mend his ways or be "cut off like a gangrenous growth", Alexei offered to renounce the succession and become a monk, but then claimed sanctuary in Austria. Inveigled back home, he foolishly disclosed accomplice "conspirators" who, under torture, identified others. The tsar then confined Alexei in the Gosudarev Bastion and ordered his **interrogation** to begin with 25 lashes.

Although subsequent "confessions" convinced Peter that Alexei's death was essential to preserve his own security, he tried to shift the decision on to the clergy (who equivocated) and a secular court (which endorsed the verdict). Two days later the tsarevich was dead – officially from apoplexy, though rumour suggested that Peter himself beat Alexei to death. Ironically, the demise of the tsar's younger son, Peter Petrovich, a year later left Alexei's infant (also called Peter) the only surviving male of the Romanov line.

of Sweden, Tsar Peter appears among the onlookers, wearing a laurel wreath, while his martial and legislative virtues are personified by statues of Minerva (left) and Bellona (right), in niches flanking the gate.

Each of the six fortress bastions is named after the individual responsible for its construction, namely the *Gosudar* (Sovereign) and his cohorts Menshikov, Naryshkin, Zotov, Golovkin and Trubetskoy. The **Gosudarev Bastion** was the site of Tsarevich Alexei's death (see box above) and, on a lighter note, a blue walrus painted on its outer wall signifies that the *morzhi* swim nearby. A ramp within the fortress leads to a walkway affording a **panoramic view of the Neva basin** ($1.60), which runs from the Gosudarev to the **Naryshkin Bastion**. Beside the latter are two **cannons** which fire a single shot every day at noon (a custom originating in the eighteenth century, when few people had clocks), and a 24-gun salute at 8pm on January 27 to mark the anniversary of the breaking of the siege of Leningrad; a shot fired at any other time signifies a flood warning. In 1917, the Bolsheviks agreed that a red lamp hung on the bastion's flagpole would be the signal for the *Aurora* to open fire on the Winter Palace, but when the moment arrived, the only lantern available wasn't red and couldn't be attached to the flagpole – so they had to wave it instead.

Between these two bastions is the **Neva Gate**, whose Neoclassical arch lists the "catastrophic" floods that have befallen St Petersburg (less serious ones being too numerous to count). The glorious view of Palace Embankment across the Neva from here would have afforded little consolation to prisoners leaving from the **Commandant's Pier**, bound for the gallows at Shlisselburg. In the passageway leading through to the fortress from the pier, you'll find the entrance to the **Pechatnya**, a museum demonstrating the art of printing with the help of half-a-dozen working vintage presses. It also exhibits finds from excavations within the fortress, including the remains of an original cell. The **beach** between the Naryshkin and Trubetskoy bastions hosts an annual **festival of sand sculptures** in July (daily 10am–10pm; $1.60).

The Engineers' House and the Commandant's House

The tree-lined path from the Neva Gate to the centre of the fortress is flanked to the southeast by the **Engineers' House** (Inzhenerniy dom). Originally occupied by military engineers, this now houses a Museum of Old Petersburg, starting with eighteenth- and nineteenth-century cityscapes and progressing through to Art Nouveau crafts, via re-created period domestic interiors and imaginative pictorial store-front signs aimed at the illiterate.

Just along from the Engineers' House is a controversial **statue of Peter the Great**, unveiled in 1990. While some regard it as a slur on the city's founder, more people are intrigued by its (slightly) exaggerated portrayal of Peter's extraordinary physique. His spidery legs and fingers, massive torso and rounded shoulders are offset by a tiny head that uncannily resembles that of Marlon Brando as Don Corleone in *The Godfather*. Its sculptor, Mikhail Shemiakin, has lived in America since the early 1970s, and the statue was a gift to the country of his birth.

Further along stands the **Commandant's House** (Ober-Komendantskiy dom), built in the 1740s and used for major political trials throughout the following century. Closed for renovation at the time of writing, it previously featured an exhibition on the history of the fortress that included a mock-up of the room where the Decembrists and the Petrashevsky Circle were interrogated in the presence of Nicholas I (who personally dictated their sentences). Besides the fortress and its prisoners, the commandant was responsible for informing the tsar when the Neva became navigable, by bringing him a goblet of river water.

The Peter and Paul Cathedral

The golden spire of the **Peter and Paul Cathedral** (Petropavlovskiy sobor) signals defiance from the heart of the fortress. "A hundred cannon, impregnable bastions and a garrison of 3000 men defend the place, which can be desecrated only when all St Petersburg lies in ruins," asserted *Murray's Handbook* in 1849. As a token of Peter's intent, a wooden church was erected on this site as soon as the fortress had been founded, replaced by a stone cathedral once the defences were upgraded. Looking far more Protestant than Orthodox, the cathedral's soaring spire was a visible assertion of Peter's wish that the skyline of St Petersburg be the antithesis of Moscow's.

The **belfry** was erected first and the ground was allowed time to settle beneath its weight before work commenced on the remainder of the cathedral, which was completed by Trezzini in 1733, long after Peter had died. The facade of the cathedral looks Dutch, while the gilded **spire** was deliberately made higher than the Ivan the Great Bell Tower in the Kremlin – at a height of 122m it remained the tallest structure in the city until the construction of the television tower in 1962. When the angel on top of the spire was blown askew in 1830, a roofer – Pyotr Telushkin – volunteered to climb up and fix it, using only a rope and hook, a feat later repeated by professional alpinists who camouflaged the spire to save it from the Luftwaffe in World War II and have restored it twice since then. During the 1997 **restoration**, the alpinists found a note in a bottle left by those who restored it forty years earlier. Addressed to "future climbers", the note complained of low pay and time pressures. Continuing the tradition, the restorers of 1997 left their own message in a bottle for the next team to scale the spire.

The **interior** is painted in tutti-frutti colours, with marbled columns ascending to a canopy of gilded acanthus leaves. Sited around the nave are the **tombs** of the Romanov monarchs from Peter the Great onwards (excluding Peter II and Ivan VI), whose coffins repose in vaults beneath the sarcophagi. All have marble slabs (designed in 1865, when the cathedral underwent major restoration) except for those of Alexander II and his wife, whose sarcophagi of Altay jasper and Urals rhodonite took seventeen years to carve and polish. The tombs of Peter (the only one sporting a bust of its occupant) and Catherine the Great are situated to the right of the iconostasis. Alexei is said to have been interred under the aisle, where "he would always be trampled on", but was actually buried in the family vault below Peter's sarcophagus.

On July 17, 1998, the remains of Russia's last royal family were finally laid to rest here, exactly eighty years after they were executed by the Bolsheviks in Yekaterinburg. Located in a separate chapel, off to the right as you enter the cathedral, the tomb officially contains the remains of Nicholas II, Alexandra and three of their five children, plus four servants who were shot with the family – although the Church remains sufficiently doubtful of their authenticity that, despite canonizing them as Orthodox martyrs, it has not declared the remains to be holy relics.

As a devout Slavophile, Nicholas would have probably preferred to end up in Moscow's Cathedral of the Archangel (where rulers before Peter the Great were buried) rather than in St Petersburg – which he detested – in a cathedral that looks more Protestant than Orthodox. The only icons to be found are on the **iconostasis**, dominated by the archangels Gabriel and Michael and framed by what look like stage curtains, with tassels and cords, all in wood. This lovely piece of work was designed by Ivan Zarudny and carved by Moscow craftsmen in the early eighteenth century. Nearby stand a pulpit (unusual in an Orthodox church) and a dais where the tsar's throne once stood.

The Male Choir of St Petersburg sings in the cathedral twice a week (Mon & Fri at 7pm) during the summer months and occasionally in other seasons (℡230 03 29 for details), and other **concerts** are staged during the period of the White Nights. Tickets are sold on the spot.

The Grand Ducal Mausoleum

A side door leads from the nave into a corridor on the left lined with plans of the fortress and photos showing how it was protected in wartime and restored afterwards. In a room off the corridor is an exhibition on the **history of the Mint**, containing Tsarist and Soviet coins and medals. Look out for the medallion bearing Stalin's head and the replicas of the plaques that were sent to the Moon, Mars and Venus by Soviet spacecraft, all of which were manufactured in the fortress mint. You may also encounter a man dressed as Peter the Great, operating the hand-turned lathe with which he crafted many objects now exhibited in the Hermitage.

At the end of the corridor is the lofty **Grand Ducal Mausoleum** (Usypalnitsa), built for Nicholas II's cousins in the early twentieth century as the cathedral itself became too crowded for the burial of any but the closest relatives. The principal tomb belongs to Archduke Vladimir, the heir to the Romanov dynasty, who was born in Belgium after the Revolution and died in Miami – his remains were returned to Russia in 1992.

The Boat House and Mint

Opposite the cathedral exit stands a **Boat House** (Botniy dom) topped by a nymph with an oar, symbolizing navigation. The Neoclassical pavilion was erected in the 1760s to preserve the small boat in which Peter made his first sailing trips on the River Yauza, outside Moscow. That original boat now reposes in the Naval Museum (see p.160), while the Boat House contains an exact replica.

In the surrounding courtyard on January 27, 1919, the Bolsheviks shot four grand dukes and other hostages taken at the start of the Red Terror the previous year, and whom they had sentenced to death in retaliation for the murders of Rosa Luxemburg and Karl Liebknicht in Berlin. When Maxim Gorky pleaded for the life of Grand Duke – and liberal historian – Nikolai Mikhailovich, Lenin replied: "The Revolution does not need historians." As yet, there is no memorial to the dozens shot here during the Civil War.

Across the courtyard looms the **Mint** (Monetniy dvor), a yellow-and-white edifice dating from the 1790s, before which time coins were minted in the Naryshkin and Trubetskoy bastions. The world's first lever press for coining money was devised here in 1811 and the Mint continued to produce coins till the end of the Soviet era; its output is now limited to military medals and commemorative medallions, copies of which are sold in a **shop** (daily 10am–6pm) across the yard. The Mint itself is closed to the public.

The Trubetskoy Bastion

The **Trubetskoy Bastion** at the southwestern corner of the fortress was converted into a jail under the supposedly liberal Alexander II, and soon became the regime's main interrogation centre and a prison for generations of revolutionaries. First to be confined here were members of the Zemlya i Volya (Land and Liberty) and Narodnaya Volya (People's Will) organizations – the latter group responsible for killing Alexander himself. Next came would-be assassins such as Lenin's brother, Alexander Ulyanov; Socialist Revolutionary bombers such as Vera Figner; and Gorky and Trotsky in 1905. After the February Revolution, Tsarist ministers were imprisoned here, to be followed by members of the Provisional Government once the Bolsheviks took over. In a final turn of the wheel of repression, radical Kronstadt sailors were kept here before being shot or sent to the Gulag in 1921. The following year the prison became a museum to the infamies of Tsarism, omitting any mention of its role after the Revolution, a period that is still glossed over by tour guides.

The Prison Museum

Selective coverage aside, the **Prison Museum** fails to convey the full horror of conditions in Tsarist times. The accessible **cells** are stark and gloomy, but far worse ones existed within the ramparts, where the perpetual damp and cold made tuberculosis inevitable. Prisoners were never allowed to see each other and rarely glimpsed their jailers. Some were denied visitors and reading material for decades; many went mad after a few years and several committed suicide. The **corridors** were carpeted to deaden sound, enabling the "Specials" to creep up and spy through the door slits without warning. This green-cloaked elite were the only guards allowed to see the prisoners' faces or give them orders (conversations were forbidden), but they were never told the prisoners' names in order to prevent word of their identity reaching the outside world. Inmates managed to communicate amongst themselves by knocking out messages in the "prisoners' alphabet" – a kind of Morse code – but anyone caught doing so risked being confined to an unlit punishment cell (*kartser*) and fed on bread and water. Once a fortnight, each inmate was escorted to the **bathhouse** in the courtyard for a solitary scrub and exercise, but the corridor windows were painted over so that none might see who was exercising. A monument and a quotation from the anarchist Prince Kropotkin (a former prisoner) commemorate the prisoners' sufferings.

Another entrance beside the museum leads to a separate exhibition of wax figures, entitled **Mysteries of History** (daily 11am–7pm; $1.25) – basically a romp through the demises of Tsar Paul, Tsarevich Alexei, Empress Anna and Princess Tarakanova. Tarakanova was the illegitimate child of Empress Elizabeth and Count Razumovsky, and was lured back to Russia by Catherine the Great's lover Orlov. Legend has it that she perished when the Neva flooded her cell in the fortress (as in a famous painting by Flavitsky), but in fact she was confined to a convent for 25 years until Catherine died – by which time she had come to accept her fate and chose to remain a nun.

The Alekseevskiy ravelin

Leaving the fortress by its western **Vasilevskiy Gate**, you'll notice a U-shaped outbuilding marking the site of the now-demolished **Alekseevskiy ravelin**. Built by Empress Anna in the 1730s, this bastion contained the first long-term prison in the fortress, its maximum security "**Secret House**" reserved for those who fell foul of the intrigues of Anna's favourite, Count Biron. Here, too, Catherine the Great confined Alexander Radishchev for criticizing Russia's backwardness in his *Journey from St Petersburg to Moscow* (1780); and Alexander I imprisoned Ivan Pososhkov, author of *On Poverty and On Wealth*, who died in captivity in 1826. Under Nicholas I, the prison held many of the Decembrists and the Petrashevsky Circle (including Dostoyevsky); Bakunin (whose grovelling *Confessions* saved him from the gallows); and Chernyshevsky (who wrote *What is to be Done?* whilst in prison). The fortress commandant used to approach the critic Belinsky on the street and ask, "What's taking you so long? We've got a nice warm cell waiting for you."

Around the Kronverk

Apart from its own ramparts and bastions, the Peter and Paul Fortress was further protected by a system of outlying ramparts called the **Kronverk** – a name later given both to the moat separating Zayachiy Island from the "mainland" Petrograd Side and to the avenue encircling a park containing the zoo and the Artillery Museum. Over summer the waterway is busy with **motorboats** doing a half-hour tour of the Neva basin (leaving from the island side of Ioannovskiy most; $5) and sometimes even powerboat races.

The zoo

Northwest of the fortress across the moat and entered from Kronverkskiy prospekt, the **Leningrad Zoo** (May–Oct daily 10am–7pm; Nov–April Tues–Sun 10am–5pm; $2.60; Ⓦ www.lenzoopark.spb.ru), as it is still named, dates back to 1865 – and looks its age. Long starved of funds, it has had to send its elephants and hippopotamuses to other zoos, and the modernization of its enclosures has been endlessly delayed. The zoo is proud, though, of having bred polar bears and giraffes since the 1930s, and of the fact that none of the animals was eaten during the Blockade. It currently holds nearly 2000 animals and birds; those from warm climes spend the winter in heated quarters and can be seen only when they move into summer enclosures. Winter is the time to see polar foxes, sables, martens, elk and deer with their fur at its thickest.

The Artillery Museum

Across the Kronverk Moat from the fortress's Golovkin Bastion stands a vast horseshoe-shaped arsenal, fronted by tanks and missile launchers. Inside, the **Artillery Museum** (Voenno-Istoricheskiy muzey Artillerii; 11am–6pm; closed Sun & Mon & last Thurs of each month; $4) has displays of artillery from medieval times until 1812, along with the pike that Peter carried as a foot soldier, an ornate coach from which Kutuzov harangued his troops at Borodino, and regimental banners (one depicting the Last Judgement, with foreigners writhing in hell).

Amongst the World War II exhibits upstairs are a "Katyusha" multiple-rocket launcher, a huge mural of trench warfare at Stalingrad and a diorama of Kursk, where the biggest tank battle in history took place. Next comes a corridor devoted to Signals, climaxing with a model of the ruined Reichstag and a gleeful painting of Hitler committing suicide.

Back downstairs in Hall 10 you'll find **Lenin's armoured car**, *Enemy of Capital*, on which he rode in triumph from Finland Station on April 3, 1917, making speeches from its gun turret. Nearby is a model of a dog with a mine strapped to its back; the Soviets trained them to run underneath Nazi tanks. Also notice the snazzy Red Army **uniforms** of the Civil War era, designed by a Futurist artist later killed in the purges. Guided tours in Russian can be arranged in room 115 or by phone (☏233 03 82).

The Decembrists' Monument

On a grassy knoll just to the east of the arsenal, the **Decembrists' Monument** marks the spot where five leaders of the revolt were executed in July 1826. The gallows were erected in front of the condemned officers, who were ritually degraded by having their epaulettes torn off and their swords broken before the hoods and nooses were slipped over their heads. The ropes broke for three of the men, but rather than being reprieved (as was customary in such cases), fresh ropes were brought and the hangings were repeated. The obelisk is inscribed with a poem by Pushkin, dedicated to a friend sentenced to a term of hard labour in Siberia for his part in the revolt:

> Dear friend, have faith;
> The wakeful skies presage a dawn of wonder,
> Russia shall from her age-old sleep arise,
> And despotism shall be crushed;
> Upon its ruins our names incise.

The Alexander Park and Kronverkskiy prospekt

The **Alexander Park** (Aleksandrovskiy park) is a playground for Petersburgers of all ages. Laid out in 1845, it starts near the fortress as a shady Romantic meander past a grotto and the **Steregushchiy Monument**, which commemorates the sailors who scuttled their torpedo boat rather than let it be captured at Tsushima Bay in 1904. Gorkovskaya metro station and dozens of kiosks mark an abrupt change of mood, with teenagers hanging out drinking and playing

Orphaned and sent out to work as a young boy, Alexei Maximovich Peshkov (1868–1936) achieved success in his thirties under the *nom de plume* **Maxim Gorky**. A natural radical, he took a leading role in the 1905 Revolution, for which he was sentenced to prison. After protests from Western writers, his prison sentence was commuted to exile abroad, where he raised funds for the Bolsheviks from his hide-away on Capri (taking time out to play Lenin at chess). Returning home in 1913, Gorky continued to support the Bolsheviks until after the Revolution, when he began to attack Lenin for seizing power and relying on terror.

Having left Russia in 1921 – ostensibly on the grounds of ill health – Gorky was wooed back home in 1928 to become chairman of the new Union of Soviet Writers. His own novel *Mother* was advanced as a model of Socialist Realism, the literary genre promulgated by the Union in 1932. He also collaborated on a paean to the White Sea Canal (see p.312) – "the first book in Russian literature to glorify slave labour", according to Solzhenitsyn. As a murky finale, Gorky's mysterious death in 1936 was used by Stalin as a pretext for the arrest of Yagoda, head of the NKVD secret police. Decades of official acclaim have tarnished his reputation and nowa-days Gorky's work is often scorned as trite agitprop, lacking depth and subtlety.

guitars, and families heading for the **funfair** deeper into the park (see p.394). Behind this rises an enfilade of Stalinist edifices, composed of the **Baltiyskiy dom** venue for arts festivals (p.377), a **Planetarium** (p.393), **Music Hall** (p.379) and a casino with a courtesy limo outside. Nearby are **all-night bars** where you can eat *shashlyk*, drink and people-watch – although the *Red Lion Pub* looks the most inviting option, it's actually poor value compared to its nameless neighbours. If it's **clubbing** you want, *Par.spb* (see p.368) is close by the Baltiyskiy dom and *Tunnel* (see p.369) a few blocks beyond the park.

Its perimeter is marked by **Kronverkskiy prospekt**, an arc that intersects with Kamennoostrovskiy prospekt near Gorkovskaya metro and ends at Troitskaya ploshchad (see the following sections). **Trams** #6 and #63 run along it en route to and from Vasilevskiy Island. Until 1993 Kronverkskiy prospekt bore the name of the writer **Maxim Gorky**, who lived at no. 23 from 1914 to 1921. The dropping of his name reflects Gorky's diminished status in the post-Communist era, although Gorkovskaya metro station isn't likely to change its name.

Around Troitskaya ploshchad

A leafy expanse framed by main roads, **Troitskaya ploshchad** is named after the Trinity Cathedral (Troitskiy sobor) that once formed the nucleus of the Petrograd Side's merchants' quarter. In 1905, the square was the scene of one of the worst massacres of "Bloody Sunday", when 48 people were killed and scores wounded after soldiers opened fire on demonstrators approaching Troitskiy most to the south. In 1917, Trotsky harangued crowds here before the October Revolution, and in Soviet times it was called Revolution Square. Its present appearance dates from the mid-1930s, when the cathedral was demol-ished to make way for a gigantic Stalinist administrative building and the square was turned into a park. In recent years it has been solemnized by a bell-shaped **Chapel of the Holy Trinity**, faced with red and brown granite, and a **memorial to victims of the Gulag** made of a boulder from the Solovetskiy penal colony. Hundreds gather here to remember the dead on the Day of Victims of the Repression (October 30).

The Museum of Russian Political History

Behind the park on ulitsa Kuybysheva stands the former **house of Mathilda Kshesinskaya** (1872–1971), Russia's prima ballerina before the Revolution, whose affair with Crown Prince Nicholas (later Nicholas II) was once the talk of St Petersburg. Gorky sniffed that she earned it "with leg-shaking and arm-swinging", but it was probably a gift from Nicholas. The house is the epitome of Style Moderne elegance, trimmed with tiles and floral tracery. In March 1917 the Bolsheviks commandeered it as their headquarters: Lenin came here straight from the Finland Station, addressed crowds from its balcony and mapped out Party strategy here until July 1917, when a Provisional Government clampdown sent the Bolsheviks into hiding and the house was wrecked by loyalist troops.

After restoration, it was an obvious home for the Museum of the Great October Socialist Revolution, which moved here from the Winter Palace in 1957. In 1991 this was recast as the **Museum of Russian Political History** (10am–6pm; closed Thurs; $2.60). Initially stridently anti-Communist in tone, it now strives for a non-partisan look at political movements in Russia over the last century or so. If you're interested in the subject or in Kshesinskaya (to whom a section is devoted), it's worth booking a **tour** in English (☎233 03 82; $6.60). You don't need any knowledge of Russian though to enjoy the snazzy Soviet porcelain decorated with slogans, and caricatures of Lenin from newspapers that would be shut down once the Bolsheviks seized power – nor to feel a frisson in the second-floor quarters used by the Central Committee in July 1917, including the room occupied by Lenin.

The Mosque

Further north looms St Peterburg's **Mosque** (Mechet; daily 10am–7pm), an exotic feature of the skyline. Its ovoid cupola (copied from the Gur Emir Mausoleum of Tamerlane in Samarkand) and the fluted finials of its twin minarets are faced with brilliant azure tiles, greatly enlivening the severe facade, whose Islamic identity is otherwise apparent only from the arabesques around its portals. Constructed between 1910 and 1914 at the behest of the last emir of Bukhara to serve the city's Sunni Muslim community, the mosque has finally emerged from over a decade's restoration, and its interior looks stunning. However, the *jamat* (congregation) is wary of strangers – understandably, given racist attacks and FSB surveillance – so admission is by no means certain. Women must wear a headscarf and long, baggy clothing; men long trousers and a collared shirt; removing shoes (and having clean feet) are mandatory.

East along the embankment

Walking east from Troitskaya ploshchad along the Neva embankment, you cannot imagine this area as the bustling port it was in Petersburg's infancy until you encounter **Peter's Cabin** (Domik Petra; 10am–5pm; closed Tues & the last

Mon of each month; $2) in a park halfway along. Encased in a brick structure and preserved as a museum, it was built by army carpenters in May 1703 to enable the tsar to keep a close eye on the construction of the Peter and Paul Fortress over that summer. Its rough-hewn pine logs are painted to resemble bricks and there are only three rooms. Peter slept on a cot in what doubles as the hallway; the dining room and study look ready for his return. The museum includes his frock coat and pipe and a rowing boat that he made himself, as well as engravings of St Petersburg, Kronstadt and the battles of Hangö and Poltava.

On the embankment opposite the cabin are two **Shih Tza** (lion) statues of the kind that flank temples in China and Mongolia, brought here in 1907 from Kirin in Manchuria, where the Tsarist Empire was contending with Japan for control of the region's mineral resources.

Further along stands the imposing **residential block** of the Nakhimov Academy, a mustard-coloured building topped by Red Guard and Sailor statues (now accompanied by neon advertising) and decorated with Futurist stucco panels featuring tractors, banners and ships' prows. At the far end of the embankment, the large fountain outside the peacock-blue, Baroque-style **Nakhimov Naval Academy** is yet another popular spot for newly-weds to be photographed. As a college for aspiring naval officers, the academy's title and setting could hardly be more inspirational: named after the "hero of Sebastopol" in the Crimean War, the academy is bang opposite the warship whose cannon heralded the October Revolution.

The Aurora

The cruiser **Aurora** (kreyser *Avrora;* 10.30am–4pm; closed Mon & Fri; free) looks comically miscast for its dramatic role in history, resembling an outsized model battleship complete with smart paint job and gleaming brasswork. Having long been an icon of the Revolution, it is now mocked by some as "the world's deadliest weapon – with one shot, it ruined the country for 75 years". Yet few would wish to see the *Aurora* removed, or credit the rumour that the original was secretly replaced by a less decrepit sister ship when it went for a refit in the 1970s. As a historical relic, it inspires affection across the political spectrum.

The 6731-tonne cruiser experienced a baptism of fire at Tsushima Bay, when it was one of the few ships in the Baltic Fleet that avoided being sunk by the Japanese. Docked in Petrograd for an overhaul just before the February Revolution, the *Aurora* was the first ship in the fleet to side with the Bolsheviks. On the night of October 25 it moved down-river and dropped anchor by what is now most Leytenanta Shmidta. At 9.40pm its forward cannon fired the historic blank shot at the Winter Palace – the first in a sporadic barrage that accompanied the "storming" of the building (see p.73). After the palace had fallen, the ship's radio was used to broadcast Lenin's address, "To the Citizens of Russia!", proclaiming the victory of the proletarian revolution.

In the early 1920s the *Aurora* was converted into a training ship. With the advent of war in 1941, its heavy guns were removed for use on the Leningrad front, and the outmoded vessel was holed by the Luftwaffe and scuttled near Oranienbaum. Raised in peacetime, it was moored in its present location and declared a national monument in 1948, later opening as a museum – though it still belongs to the Russian navy and has a crew of eighty, fifty of whom live aboard the ship.

During **visiting** hours you can wander round on deck and tour a historical exhibition in four wardrooms below. One preserves hammocks, tables and ration lists for the crew in Tsarist times (though the room would have been far more crowded then). Elsewhere, note the portrait of the ship's captain framed by armoured plate with a hole left by the shell that killed him at Tsushima; and a model of the schooner *Granma* (dubbed "the little sister of the *Aurora*"), which landed Fidel Castro and his *compañeros* in Cuba, in the room full of "fraternal gifts" from the days when international socialism meant something.

To see more, book an English-language **tour** (☎230 84 40; $3) of the engine rooms and ammunition magazines on the lower armoured deck. Before the Revolution sailors held subversive meetings in the engine room since officers seldom went there, as it was noisy and dirty. Its three steam engines still work. Disappointingly, you barely glimpse the officers' wardroom where the whole crew now eats, never mind the captain's cabin, containing a piano from the Imperial yacht *Shtandart*.

Kamennoostrovskiy prospekt

Architecturally and socially, Petrograd Side takes its tone from **Kamennoostrovskiy prospekt** (Stone Island Avenue), an urban canyon that peters out as it approaches its namesake island. Many Petersburgers feel this avenue is at least as elegant as Nevskiy prospekt, with as much to offer in the way of shops, cinemas, restaurants and fine architecture – especially around Avstriyskaya ploshchad (Austrian Square), at the intersection with ulitsa Mira. The initial stretch from the Neva to the intersection is flanked by imposing villas and apartment buildings, built early last century when the avenue suddenly became a fashionable place to live. The area beyond Petrogradskaya metro station is less notable from an architectural viewpoint, but Aptekarskiy Island, at the prospekt's northern end, has several attractions. As the avenue is 2.5km long and it's 1km between metro stations, a **minibus** (#K-46 or #K-76) can save you a lot of footslogging between sights.

Around Gorkovskaya metro

Across the road from the Gorky statue at the lower end of the avenue stands a U-shaped **Style Moderne apartment building** (nos. 1–3) designed by Fyodor Lidval in 1902. The upper storeys are decorated with stucco shingles and fairytale beasts, while bizarre fish flank the main entrance, whose lobby contains stained-glass panels. At no. 5 is the beige-and-white former **villa of Count Sergei Witte**, the great industrialist of Tsarist Russia, who started as a railway clerk and rose through the civil service to become Finance Minister. Though he was highly successful in unleashing capitalist energies within Russia, his hopes for political liberalization were consistently dashed by Nicholas II, who also ignored his advice on foreign affairs: after Witte was assassinated by an ultra-right fanatic in 1915, Nicholas remarked that his death was "a great relief" and "a sign from God".

Lenfilm Studios

Another token of talent spurned lies 100m up the avenue, in a Doric-porticoed, yellow building (nos. 10–12), set back behind a garden on the left. Founded in 1918 on the site of the Akvarium Summer Theatre (where the

Lumière brothers had presented the first motion picture in Russia on May 4, 1896), the **Lenfilm Studios** were once the glory of the Soviet cinema industry, producing up to fifteen movies a year. During its golden era, between the wars, most of the films, such as the Vasilev brothers' *Chapaev*, focused on ordinary people making history. In the postwar period, Lenfilm gained international kudos with Kozintsev's adaptations of the works of Shakespeare, but many directors had their best work suppressed for years, until perestroika changed everything. The subsequent release of over two hundred banned films, followed by a new wave of *chernukha*, or "black" movies, dealing with Stalin and the camps, rapidly sated the public who had discovered the delights of home videos and Hollywood in the meantime.

The loss of its audience and state subsidies caused a crisis of confidence within Lenfilm, which was eventually broken up into smaller studios. These continue to produce highly acclaimed films – Aranovich's *Year of the Dog* and Andrei Balabanov's *The Castle*, *Brother*, and *Of Freaks and Men* – but more income is now generated by Lenfilm studio crews working on foreign productions such as the Bond film *Goldeneye*, the spy thriller *Midnight in St Petersburg* and the romantic drama *Onegin*, or producing TV soaps and cop shows for the home market. Lenfilm's **website** (Ⓦwww.lenfilm.ru) features news of ongoing projects, press releases and a cine-bibliography of all the films ever made there. It's in Russian only at present, but an English-language version is under construction.

The Kirov Museum

Of more tangible historic interest is the hulking building at nos. 26–28, built shortly before World War I by the fashionable architect Leonty Benois. After the Revolution its luxury apartments were assigned to Bolshevik officials, including the head of the Leningrad Party organization, **Sergei Kirov**, who lived in apartment no. 20 until his murder in 1934. The **Kirov Museum** (muzey S.M. Kirova; 11am–6pm; closed Wed & the last Tues of each month; $1) presents him as an intellectual with a library of over 20,000 volumes; a man of the people who went hunting and fishing (his rods and shotgun are displayed); and a leader whose study had a hotline to the Kremlin and a polar bearskin rug. Behind the desk hangs a picture of Stalin, who almost certainly organized Kirov's assassination as a pretext for unleashing the Great Terror (see p.424). In the hall you can see the uniform Kirov was wearing when he was shot at the Smolniy; the cap has a bloodstained hole at the back and the tunic is torn where medics tried to re-start his heart.

Kirov was posthumously lauded as a Bolshevik martyr, and his name bestowed on streets across the USSR – including the avenue outside the apartment, which became Kirovskiy prospekt. While the museum ignores the big questions about Kirov's demise (and his own readiness to "make short work of enemies"), it mounts interesting temporary **exhibitions** of Socialist Realist posters and Stalin-era artefacts on themes such as "Our Happy Childhood".

From ploshchad Tolstovo to the River Karpovka

A couple of blocks further north, the avenue meets Bolshoy prospekt at **ploshchad Tolstovo** (Tolstoy Square), flanked by a building known as the **Tower House**, encrusted with balconies and crenellations copied from English, Scottish and Andalusian castles. Shortly afterwards you'll see the

Soviet-era **Dom Mod** (Fashion House) beside **Petrogradskaya** metro station, opposite the **Lensoviet Palace of Culture**, which is now home to an array of slot machines, along with film screenings and jazz and pop gigs (see "Clubs and live venues", p.369). Further on is a large house (nos. 44–46), with central arches, built just before World War I for the last emir of Bukhara who, in 1920, fled from the Red Army to Afghanistan, "dropping favourite dancing boy after favourite dancing boy" to impede his pursuers.

Beyond the house, the **River Karpovka** flows westwards from the Bolshaya to the Malaya Nevka, separating "mainland" Petrograd Side from Aptekarskiy Island, which is reached by the Pioneers' Bridge. Before crossing over, consider a detour along the shabby "mainland" side to see the Convent of St John or visit the Toy Museum on ulitsa Vsevoloda.

The six-room **Toy Museum** (muzey Igrushky; 11am–6pm; closed Mon & the last Tues of each month; $3.30) is a private venture, aimed at aficionados and collectors rather than kids seeking a hands-on experience. Their contemporary art-toys made of papier-mâché, logs or ceramics, wouldn't survive a day in a playroom. Vintage items include a Wilhelmine doll's house and a Bauhaus model from the 1950s made in Germany; an Edwardian tea service; and Russian, Asian and African rag dolls in folk costumes. Some wonderful Nigerian toys made from recycled tin cans, and work by contemporary local toy-makers such as Olga Gepp and Irina Sulmeneva, bring the exhibition up to date.

Round the corner, a red-granite plaque on the wall of nab. reki Karpovki 32 commemorates a crucial **meeting of the Central Committee**, on October 10, 1917. Held in the apartment of a Menshevik whose Bolshevik wife knew that he would be out for the night, its members arrived in disguise (Lenin shaved off his beard and wore a wig which kept slipping off his head), and only twelve out of twenty-one came. Lenin persuaded everyone but Zinoviev and Kamenev to endorse his proposal that preparations for a coup should begin (though no firm date was set). Thus the most momentous decision in the history of the Party was reached by a minority of the Central Committee, and recorded by Lenin in pencil on sheets torn from a child's notebook.

From here you can cross a bridge to the **Convent of St John** (Ioannovskiy monastir) on Aptekarskiy Island. This brown-and-white complex crowned by Byzantine domes and gilded crosses, was built to house the tomb of Father John of Kronstadt, a famous late nineteenth-century preacher, anti-Semite and friend of the Imperial family. The convent was an early target in the anti-religious campaigns of the 1920s, when its nuns were deported to the Solovetskiy Islands for refusing to support a quisling church movement. It was re-established in the early 1990s and its church is open for public services. Conversely, further on towards Kamennoostrovskiy prospekt, the flags of many nations flap outside a vast hotel still unfinished fifteen years on, after its Yugoslav investors pulled out.

Aptekarskiy Island

A leafier extension of the Petrograd Side, the Apothecary's or **Aptekarskiy Island** takes its name from the medicinal kitchen gardens established beside the Karpovka in 1713. A little over a century later, these became the Imperial **Botanical Gardens** (Botanicheskiy sad; daily 10am–9pm; $0.30), an institution that was so deeply Sovietized in Communist times that it remains mired in the Era of Stagnation even today. It's a shame, for the **greenhouses** (11am–5pm; closed Fri) contain over 6500 species and cultivated varieties, from as far away as Brazil and Ethiopia – but rather than being able to wander freely you must join a forty-minute **tour** ($1.25) of either the tropical (open year-round), subtropical (mid-Sept to June) or water plants (mid-May to Sept) sections – buy a ticket at the main entrance. The tropical bit is notable for its huge banana plant – one of several specimens sporting a medal ribbon for having survived the Blockade – and a torch-thistle cactus dubbed the "Queen of the Night", which flowers for one night in June (the place stays open till 4am for the event). While the greenhouses are falling apart, the rest of the gardens are a mess of bulldozer tracks and prefab shacks, as a refurbishment plan that nobody seems to understand limps on year after year.

The main entrance to the gardens lies 600m east of Kamennoostrovskiy prospekt along ulitsa Professora Popova, named after the scientist Alexander Popov whom Russians credit with inventing the radio (see p.108). Across the road from the gardens, with its main building constructed in an odd mixture of English Gothic and Style Moderne, the **Electro-Technical Institute** is where Popov spent his final years refining his invention and exploring the electromagnetic spectrum. His abode-cum-laboratory is preserved as the **Popov Museum** (Mon–Fri 11am–4.30pm; free) at ul. Professora Popova 5. Dr Who would feel at home amongst its Edwardian jumble, but the scienti-fic import of its contents and Popov's work will be lost on visitors who can't speak Russian.

In Popov's time, the street would have been heavily guarded owing to the presence at its far end of the *dacha* of Count **Pyotr Stolypin**. Stolypin was Nicholas II's ablest minister after Witte (and Witte's bitter rival), and oversaw the suppression of the 1905 Revolution (prison trains were dubbed "Stolypin wagons"), whilst banking his hopes for future stability on the growing class of wealthy peasants. In 1906, a Socialist Revolutionary suicide squad blew up the *dacha*, killing 32 people, but not their intended target, Stolypin – he was shot dead five years later by a lone assassin at the Kiev Opera House.

A few blocks up Aptekarskiy prospekt, St Petersburg's red-and-white **Television Tower** (Telebashnya; 10am–6pm; closed Mon) was the first in the Soviet Union – built by an all-female construction crew in 1962 – and is the city's tallest structure, surpassing the spire of the Peter and Paul Cathedral. Originally 316m in height, it stood one metre higher than the Eiffel Tower until 1985, when a new, shorter antenna was installed, reducing its height by six metres. On windy days the tower sways almost two metres. Unless access is suspended for security reasons, you can enjoy a fabulous **view of the city** from its observation platform, 191m up. Individual or group tours can be arranged at any time (☏234 78 87), or you can just turn up for the tour at 2pm on Saturday. Tours cost $4 per person if you're in a group of ten or more; $30 for a group of under six persons. To **get there** from Petrogradskaya metro, ride two stops on trolleybus #31 or bus #10 or #128, walk down to the Kantemirovskiy most, turn right and walk down to the gates facing the river.

Chaliapin's apartment

The penultimate side street off Kamennoostrovskiy prospekt once resounded to the legendary bass-baritone of opera singer **Fyodor Chaliapin** (1873–1938), who settled at ul. Graftio 2b in 1914, having made his fortune in classic rags-to-riches fashion. Born in Kazan, he worked as a porter and steve-dore before joining a dance troupe at the age of 17. He made his operatic debut in the provinces and eventually landed a job at the Mariinskiy Theatre, but won renown in Moscow, first at the Private Opera and then as a soloist at the Bolshoy, notably in the title roles of *Boris Godunov* and *Ivan the Terrible*. Together with Nijinsky, he was the star of Diaghilev's Ballets Russes, which took Paris by storm in 1909. Initially enthused by the Revolution, Chaliapin was later branded an "enemy of the people" after he refused to return from a tour and settled in Paris (where Diaghilev and Benois already lived). It was over fifty years before his old apartment (by then a communal flat shared by thirteen families) became a museum, and even then it was coyly called the "Opera Section" of the Theatre Museum until Raisa Gorbacheva had Chaliapin's Soviet citizenship posthumously restored.

The **memorial apartment** (noon–6pm; closed Mon & Tues & the last Fri of each month; $3) is stuffed with antique furniture safeguarded by Chaliapin's chef (to whom he left the flat), and possessions donated by his daughters. A famous life-size portrait by Kustodiev portrays Chaliapin as the sublime personification of Russian folk culture (represented by a winter fair), while another full-length picture of him as an ancient demigod cracked two hours before his daughter Martha heard of his death in Paris. As befits a sybarite, his dining room is vast, with a table that could expand to seat thirty, and a divan to match; the antique weapons on the walls were used by Chaliapin during stage performances, while the amazing dragon-chair was a gift from Gorky. You can hear extracts from his most popular songs in what used to be the kitchen; chamber music **concerts** are held there from October to mid-April (Sat & Sun 4pm; ☎234 10 56 for details and bookings).

Pavlov and the Institute of Experimental Medicine

The name of the last street on the right – Akademika Pavlova – honours the scientist **Ivan Pavlov** (1849–1936), who worked for almost five decades at the **Institute of Experimental Medicine**. The son of a village priest, Pavlov was educated at a seminary, then studied science at St Petersburg University and medicine at the Military Academy, before becoming director of the institute in 1891. From investigating blood circulation he turned to digestion, developing the theory of conditioned reflexes through his experiments on **dogs**. Awarded the Nobel Prize for medicine in 1904, he continued his research after the Revolution with the support of Lenin, who considered Pavlov's work a major contribution to materialist philosophy. Ironically, Pavlov was a devout Christian, but the regime turned a blind eye to his role as a church elder, awarding him a pension of twenty thousand rubles on his 85th birthday, when Pavlov had a statue of a dog erected in the institute's forecourt.

Bolshoy prospekt

The Petrograd Side's other main axis is **Bolshoy prospekt**, an apartment-lined thoroughfare that meets Kamennoostrovskiy prospekt at ploshchad Tolstovo. Public **transport** follows a one-way system – down Bolshoy prospekt towards Vasilevskiy Island, and up Bolshaya Pushkarskaya ulitsa to Kamennoostrovskiy prospekt. As Bolshoy prospekt's sights unfold more dramatically when approached from the direction of Vasilevskiy Island, you might prefer to take a minibus (#K-10, #K-120, #K-690) from Vasileostrovskaya metro station, getting off the other side of Tuchkov most. Alternatively, take the metro directly to Sportivnaya station, near the northern end of the bridge.

Reached via **Tuchkov most** from Vasilevskiy Island, the warehouses, wharves and islets along the waterfront lend grandeur to the moated

Zenit

The "City of Lenin" may have reverted to St Petersburg, but its premier soccer team certainly won't be returning to its original title. When founded in 1931, it was called "Stalinets", but the team's lack of success reflected badly on the Great Leader, so in 1940 it assumed the name of its sponsor – the Zenit optical company (had this not occurred, and had Stalin's vision of a 200,000-seater stadium in Moscow been realized, the Soviet Cup Final might conceivably have been billed as "Stalin Leningrad v. Stalingrad, at the Stalin Stadium").

During Soviet times, the team's poor performance was ascribed to the fact that Zenit had to play its first matches of the season in southern resort towns and train indoors (disparaged as "drawing-room football") while its own pitch at the Kirov Stadium thawed and dried out – though this didn't seem to hamper the city's traditional "second" team, Lokomotiv St Petersburg, to whom many fans transferred their allegiance during the early 1990s, when Zenit languished in the second division. However, since moving to the Petrovskiy Stadium (which has undersoil heating), Zenit has not only muscled its way back into the first division but even won the cup from its hated rivals, Spartak Moscow, in 1999, and its fans are now legion in the city. The club's blue-and-white colours can be seen flying from cars whenever there's a match at their home ground.

Petrovskiy Stadium (formerly the Lenin Stadium) that's home to St Petersburg's premier football club, **Zenit** (see box above), and the circular **Yubileyniy Sports Palace** across the avenue, which hosts ice hockey and volleyball matches, and pop concerts. An iconic plaque on the wall facing the stadium recalls the 1991 killing of pop singer **Igor Talkov** by the bodyguard of another performer after a row over who should play first – Talkov's fans blamed a "Jewish conspiracy" and the far right adopted him as a martyr to their cause.

Further inland rise the proud belfry and onion domes of the **Prince Vladimir Cathedral** (Knyaz Vladimirskiy sobor; open for services only), an eighteenth-century fusion of Baroque and Classical styles by Trezzini and Rinaldi. Since it reopened in the mid-1990s, one of the icons in its possession has been identified as the miraculous *Our Lady of Kazan* that disappeared from the Kazan Cathedral ninety years earlier (see p.71). In pre-revolutionary times, the cathedral lent its name to the Vladimir Military Academy, whose cadets resisted the Bolshevik takeover until the building was bombarded. It subsequently became an academy for "Red Cadets", after whom the street on which it stood was renamed ulitsa Krasnovo Kursanty.

Freud's Dream Museum

In the Institute of Psychoanalysis at Bolshoy pr. 18a, **Freud's Dream Museum** (Tues & Sat noon–5pm; $0.25; ☎235 28 57; ⓦwww.freud.ru) is a brave attempt to represent ten of the dreams on which Freud based his theory of the unconscious mind, using spectrally lit images and objects such as suitcases or antique figurines. This voyage into Freud's psyche is the brainchild of Viktor Mazin, who has forged links with Freud museums and psychoanalytical circles in Vienna, London, Helsinki and Los Angeles, and collaborated on exhibitions with local artists such as Olga Torebluts and Andrei Khlobistyn. Mazin is keen to stress the contribution made to psychoanalysis by Russian émigrés, and that – contrary to Western belief – the subject was never banned in the Soviet Union, but merely pushed to the margins of psychiatry. If Lenin had been succeeded by Trotsky rather than Stalin, psychoanalysis might have become an aspect of Soviet ideology, for Trotsky saw it as a new dimension of dialectical materialism – unlike the paranoid Georgian, who would surely have liquidated anyone who tried to get him on the couch.

The Kirov Islands

The verdant archipelago lying off the northern flank of Petrograd Side is officially known as the **Kirov Islands** (Kirovskie ostrova), but everyone in St Petersburg uses the islands' traditional individual names: **Kamenniy**, **Yelagin** and **Krestovskiy**. Originally bestowed upon Imperial favourites, the islands soon became a summer residence for the wealthy and a place of enjoyment for all. This is still the case, except that most of the villas now belong to either institutions or foreigners, with telltale Mercedes parked along the quiet avenues and birch groves. Kamenniy and Yelagin islands harbour elegant palaces – one of which you can go inside – while Krestovskiy Island sports a gigantic stadium.

The only drawback is the size of the archipelago: seeing it all entails more walking around than is pleasant unless you use what limited **public transport** is available.

Approaches

The eastern end of **Kamenniy Island** is accessible by minibus from Kamennoostrovskiy prospekt (#K-46) or the Kronverk (#K-134) or a ten-minute walk from Chernaya Rechka metro on the Vyborg Side. To reach Krestovskiy Island, take minibus #K-222 from Petrogradskaya metro, or ride the metro to Krestovskiy Ostrov station. **Yelagin Island** can be reached on foot from Primorskiy prospekt, 2.5km west of Chernaya Rechka metro (tram #2 via ulitsa Savushkina, or bus #411 along the embankment), taking in the Buddhist Temple en route (see p.238).

Kamenniy Island

Reached from Aptekarskiy Island by the handsome Kamennoostrovskiy most, adorned with bronze reliefs and granite obelisks, Stone or **Kamenniy Island** lends its name to the Petrograd Side's main avenue, as well as the palace on the island's eastern tip. Built in 1776 by Catherine the Great for her son Paul, the **Stone Island Palace** (Kamennoostrovskiy dvorets) was inherited by Alexander I, who oversaw the war against Napoleon from here. Appropriately, it is now a military sanatorium, so you'll have to peer through the fence to see the columned portico with steps leading down to the water, or the English-style garden, but you can get a good view of the ornate frontage from the north. Nearer the main road stands the **Church of St John the Baptist**, a Gothic edifice by Yuri Felten, who probably also supervised the construction of the palace. Turned into a sports hall after World War II, it was re-established as a church in 1990 and recently restored as an exhibition hall.

Kamenniy Island was originally owned by Peter the Great's chancellor, Gavril Golovkin, and later passed into the hands of Alexei Bestuzhev-Ryumin, who brought thousands of serfs from Ukraine to drain the land and build embankments. By the end of the eighteenth century several aristocrats had built summer homes here, and in 1832 Russia's oldest noble family commissioned the architect Shustov to build the **Dolgorukov mansion** at nab. Maloy Nevki 11,

200m west of Kamennoostrovskiy most. A little further along the embankment are two green-and-gold Grecian **sphinxes** – the leafy area around them makes a nice spot to sit and rest a while. For a longer walk, carry on to **Peter's tree** at the crossroads near the bridge to Krestovskiy Island – reputedly planted by Peter the Great, and now a stump protected by bollards – and follow the road on towards Yelagin Island to see the wooden **Kamenniy Island Theatre**, dating back to the 1820s. Further inland, BMWs prowl between high-walled **villas** belonging to the government, mafiosi, and the diplomatic community.

Yelagin Island

Known before the Revolution as the "Garden of Joy", on account of the orgiastic revels which took place here during the White Nights, **Yelagin Island** (daily: summer 6am–11pm; winter 10am–8pm) is nowadays designated a "Central Park of Culture and Rest", with traffic banned from its roads, and access from the archipelago and the mainland limited to wooden footbridges. Though largely deserted on working days, its serpentine lakes and shady clearings attract families at weekends and hordes of revellers on public holidays. During summer, people go **swimming** in the sedge-lake beside the main path, rent **rowing boats** ($5 an hour) or take a **cruise on the Gulf of Finland** from the landing stage on the southern side of the island (daily: hourly 1–8.30pm; $3). If a two-kilometre walk doesn't faze you, there's the lure of watching the sun set over the Gulf of Finland from a spit of land at the extreme west of the island dignified by granite lions. Alternatively, you can visit the Yelagin Palace, stroll across the island and cross a bridge to reach the Buddhist Temple on the Vyborg Side (see p.238).

The Yelagin Palace

The island's chief attraction is the **Yelagin Palace** (Yelaginskiy dvorets; 10am–5pm; closed Mon & Tues; $2), commissioned by Alexander I for his

---

Alexander I

Alexander I embraced his destiny with reluctance, being fated to spend his reign (1801–25) dealing with Napoleon when all he really wanted to do was live quietly in Switzerland as a private citizen. Though his armies would make Russia a major European power, Alexander learned to detest the military during childhood, when he was made to drill in all weathers by his father, Paul – accounting for his morbid horror of rain. Shy, short-sighted, and partially lame and deaf, he felt happier in the company of his grandmother, Catherine the Great, who shared his interest in free thinking.

When Alexander consented to a coup against his father, he didn't anticipate that Paul would be murdered (p.90). Upon hearing the news, Alexander burst into tears, until one of the conspirators snapped, "Stop playing the child and go rule!" As tsar, his sense of guilt possibly inclined him to propose a utopian European confederation at the Congress of Vienna, whose failure turned him towards religion. In the winter of 1825, he reportedly died whilst on holiday in the Crimea, but wild rumours of trickery impelled his mother to travel to Moscow and privately view the body in its coffin (which, against normal practice, had already been sealed). Despite a positive identification, tales persisted that she had lied and Alexander had faked his own death to become a hermit and atone for Paul's murder. Many legends identified him with a holy man called Dmitri of Siberia, and it is also said that a curious descendant opened Alexander's coffin, to find only sand and medals inside.

mother, Maria Fyodorovna, in 1817. Eyebrows must have been raised when the job was given to Carlo Rossi, as rumour had it that he was fathered by Tsar Paul, Maria Fyodorovna's late husband, and thus was Alexander's half-brother. Whatever the truth, Rossi proved equal to his first major commission, creating an ensemble of graceful Neoclassical buildings, decorated with the utmost refinement.

The palace has half-a-dozen exquisite **state rooms** linked by bronze-inlaid mahogany doors. Their superb parquet floors and moulded friezes are offset by motifs in *grisaille* – a technique using different shades of one or two colours to suggest bas-relief – while the **Grand Hall** boasts a plethora of statuary and *trompe l'oeil*. A sumptuous walnut study-ensemble on loan from the *Grand Hotel Europe* is the highlight of the palace's collection of antique furniture, besides which there are permanent exhibitions of Style Moderne **samovars** and **artistic glass** from the Soviet era. Temporary exhibitions are held on the upper floor and require a separate ticket (although they're not usually worth the extra expense).

Krestovskiy Island

The 420-hectare **Krestovskiy Island** was the last of the Kirov Islands to be developed, since its swampy terrain and proximity to the slums of the Petrograd Side deterred the wealthy from building here. Before the Imperial Yacht Club based itself on the island, Krestovskiy was "peculiarly the resort of the lower classes", to where, *Murray's Handbook* observed, "flock the Muzhik and the Kupez in gay gondolas, to enjoy, in the woods, their national amusements of swings and Russian mountains". Following the Revolution, entertainments became organized and sports facilities were developed, starting in 1925 with the **Dinamo Stadium** beside the Malaya Nevka and culminating in the building of the extraordinary Kirov Stadium at the western end of the island. The latest addition is the **Wonder Island Amusement Park** (Mon 3–10pm, Tues–Fri noon–10pm, Sat & Sun 11am–10pm), the largest and best equipped in the city. It's near Krestovskiy Ostrov metro, on the way to the bridge that leads to Yelagin Island.

Primorskiy Park Pobedy and the Kirov Stadium

The avenue leading to the Kirov Stadium bisects the **Primorskiy Park Pobedy** (Seaside Park of Victory). The park poignantly recalls the autumn of 1945 when one hundred thousand malnourished citizens honoured the dead of the Blockade and celebrated their own survival by creating two large Victory Parks – one in the south of the city, the other on Krestovskiy Island:

> Early in the morning, the people
> of Leningrad went out
> In huge crowds to the seashore,
> And each of them planted a tree
> Upon that strip of land, marshy, deserted
> In memory of that great Victory Day,
> Look at it now – it is a comely orchard . . .
>
> Anna Akhmatova

Construction of the **Kirov Stadium** (Stadion imeni S.M. Kirova), the largest stadium in Russia after the Lenin Stadium in Moscow, began in 1932, but it wasn't completed until 1950 owing to the war. Its design was simple and its

The Peter and Paul Fortress, Petrograd side and the Kirov Islands

Streets and squares

ul. Akademika Pavlova	ул. Академика Павлова
Avstriyskaya ploshchad	Австрийская площадь
Bolshoy prospekt	Большой проспект
ul. Graftio	ул. Графтио
Kamennoostrovskiy prospekt	Каменноостровский проспект
Kronverkskiy prospekt	Кронверкский проспект
ul. Kuybysheva	ул. Куйбышева
Maliy prospekt	Малый проспект
ul. Professora Popova	ул. профессора Попова
nab. reki Karpovki	наб. реки Карповки
ploshchad Tolstovo	площадь Толстого
Troitskaya ploshchad	Троицкая площадь

Metro stations

Chkalovskaya	Чкаловская
Gorkovskaya	Горьковская
Krestovskiy Ostrov	Крестовский Остров
Petrogradskaya	Петроградская
Sportivnaya	Спортивная

Museums

Artillery Museum	Военно-Исторический музей Артиллерии
Chaliapin memorial apartment	мемориальная квартира Ф.И. Шаляпина
Freud's Dream Museum	музей Сновидений Зигмунда Фрейда
Kirov Museum	музей С.М. Кирова
Museum of Russian Political History	музей политической истории России
Peter's Cabin	домик Петра
Popov Museum	музей Попова
Toy Museum	музей Игрушки
Yelagin Palace	Елагинский дворец

execution revolutionary – for the stadium was fashioned from mud. More than one million cubic metres were scooped from the Gulf bed and piped inland to build a ring-shaped mound. The "crater" bottom became the sports arena, its inner walls terraced to provide seating for 75,000 spectators, and the exterior was embellished with grand colonnades. Alas, the architects didn't take account of the weather on the Gulf, which makes the stadium the most bracing of all the great Socialist Super Bowls and renders the pitch unusable for six months of the year. Nowadays it's rarely used, since the smaller Petrovskiy Stadium has better facilities, including under-field heating. At the start of the avenue that leads to the stadium's gigantic stairway, you'll see V.B. Pinchuk's **statue of Kirov** in ticket-collecting mode. The motor circuit near the stadium hosts **Formula 1600 Races** on the first Sunday in July, as well as amateur **Go-Karting**. The stadium can be reached from the Petrograd Side by taking **minibus** #K-222 from Petrogradskaya to Krestovskiy Ostrov metro station and then walking (around 15min).

Across the Malaya Nevka

On the south side of Krestovskiy Island, the Malaya Nevka is spanned by several bridges including **Bolshoy Petrovskiy most**, from which **Rasputin's**

body was dumped after he was shot at the Yusupov Palace. As an autopsy revealed, Rasputin was still alive, and the freezing water shocked him out of unconsciousness, for he apparently managed to free one hand and cross himself before drowning. The body was found washed up down-river after someone spotted one of his boots lying on the ice. The bridge connects with a detached sliver of the Petrograd Side known as **Petrovskiy Island**. Until the beginning of the last century, it was the weekend haunt of the city's German community, and though it's mostly been built over since, several small parks remain. Its western tip – Petrovskaya Kosa – harbours the **River Yacht Club**, which offers sailing trips around the Gulf; to get there, take trolleybus #7 from Sportivnaya metro to the end of the line, then walk the remaining 600m.

Liteyniy, Smolniy and Vladimirskaya

The areas of **Liteyniy, Smolniy** and **Vladimirskaya** make up the remainder of central "mainland" St Petersburg and provide the chief points of interest between the River Fontanka and the Obvodniy Canal. Predominantly residential, the districts largely developed in the latter half of the nineteenth century, and to natives of the city each has a specific resonance. **Liteyniy prospekt** has been a centre of the arts, shopping and – with the secret police headquarters at its northern end – repression since the late nineteenth century. A couple of kilometres to the east lies the **Smolniy** district, whose focal point, Rastrelli's rocket-like **Smolniy Convent**, is a must on anyone's itinerary, as is the **Smolniy Institute**, from where the Bolsheviks launched the October Revolution.

Further south, the cemeteries at the **Alexander Nevsky Monastery** are the resting place for some of the city's most notable personalities, while back nearer the city centre is the bustling market quarter of **Vladimirskaya**, with its cluster of museums, including Dostoyevsky's apartment. Running southwest from Vladimirskaya is **Zagorodniy prospekt**, home of a musical tradition particularly associated with the Rimsky-Korsakov Museum, while further south is the blue-domed **Trinity Cathedral**.

Liteyniy prospekt

Liteyniy prospekt – running due north from Nevskiy prospekt to the Neva – is one of the oldest streets in the city, taking its name from the Liteyniy dvor, or "Smelting House", a cannon foundry established on the left bank of the Neva in 1711. It quickly became a major shopping street and the next most important avenue on the south bank after Nevskiy. While Liteyniy has fewer grand edifices, several eye-catching churches and museums can be seen on the side streets, and window-shopping and street-life are diverting. The following account meanders back and forth, on and off the prospekt, more than you're likely to. If you wish to visit the Sheremetev Palace on the Fontanka, it makes sense to do so before joining Litneyniy by way of ulitsa Belinskovo. If you have only got limited time you can see Liteyniy's sights from tram #90 or minibus #K-258, which go as far as the Bolshoy dom. Note that buildings are numbered starting from the Neva, rather than Nevskiy prospekt, as you might expect.

The Sheremetev Palace on the Fontanka

Along the Fontana embankment, to the north of Anichkov most, stands an array of ex-palaces founded in the eighteenth century and rebuilt a century later, many becoming institutes or hospitals even before the Revolution. Among them is the **Sheremetev Palace** at no. 34, whose golden-yellow facade set back behind majestic wrought-iron gates is one of the glories of the embankment. Named after one of Peter the Great's marshals, who built a palace here in 1712, the existing building was erected in the mid-eighteenth century, and was known as the Fontanniy dom (Fountain House) because of the many fountains, fed by the river, which once played in its grounds – a nickname that's still used today. After the Revolution, it was converted into communal flats for writers, artists and scholars.

One of the greatest poets of Russia's "Silver Age", Anna Akhmatova, lived in a series of rooms on the third floor of the southern wing between 1933 and 1941 and again from 1944 to 1952 – some of the worst years of her life (see box). The palace's **Akhmatova Museum** (10am–5.30pm; closed Mon & the last Wed of each month; $1.70) consists of six rooms containing exhibits relating to her life; she lived, worked and slept in three of them, one of which she exchanged with the ex-wife of her third husband, Punin, after she left him in 1938. Here you'll find her desk, above which hangs a pen-portrait by Modigliani, the only surviving one of a series executed during a trip to Paris in 1911. You can also see the secret police file on the poet Osip Mandelstam, who was murdered in the Great Terror, and many letters from Boris Pasternak.

Anna Akhmatova

Born in Odessa in 1889 and brought up in Tsarskoe Selo, **Anna Akhmatova** lived most of her life in St Petersburg, where she married Nikolai Gumilyov, an Assyriologist and founder of the Poets' Guild. Together with Osip Mandelstam, they made the guild the centre of the movement known as **Acmeism**, whose avowed principles were clarity and freshness. Akhmatova's marriage to Gumilyov was an unhappy one (they divorced in 1918), and after he was executed by the state in 1921 for treason, the stigma attached to Akhmatova kept her silent for the next decade.

The mass purges of the mid-1930s impelled her to write again – not least because Mandelstam, her son Lev and her third husband, Nikolai Punin, were all arrested. Her *Requiem* cycle is the finest poetry to have emerged from that terrible era. With the outbreak of war, Akhmatova threw herself into the patriotic cause, writing one of the great Russian war poems, *Courage*. Having experienced the first winter of the Blockade before being evacuated to Tashkent, she gradually re-established her career and had several works published.

In 1946, shortly after returning to Leningrad, Akhmatova was vilified once more in the infamous "cultural report" by Party Secretary Zhdanov, which described her as "a nun and a whore, who combines harlotry with prayer". She was put under 24-hour surveillance and Lev was arrested for the third time, until, in 1950 – like so many before her – she gave in and wrote a series of poems glorifying Stalin. Finally, following Khrushchev's denunciation of Stalinism, Lev was freed and Akhmatova herself began to benefit from the "thaw". Her works were published again, she was allowed to travel abroad for the first time in fifty years and, until her death in 1966, enjoyed the acclaim so long denied her.

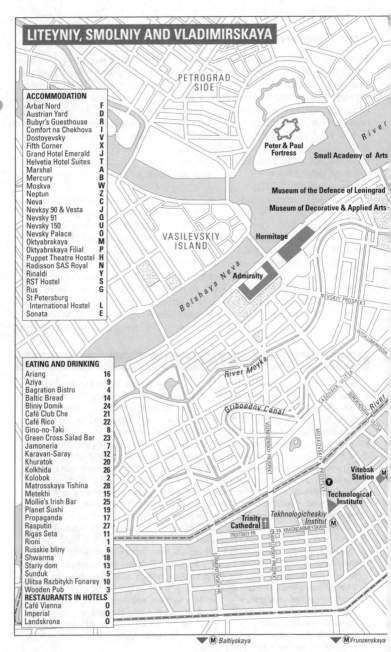

LITEYNIY, SMOLNIY AND VLADIMIRSKAYA

ACCOMMODATION

Arbat Nord	F
Austrian Yard	D
Bubyr's Guesthouse	R
Comfort na Chekhova	I
Dostoyevsky	V
Fifth Corner	X
Grand Hotel Emerald	J
Helvetia Hotel Suites	T
Marshal	A
Mercury	B
Moskva	W
Neptun	Z
Neva	C
Nevksy 90 & Vesta	J
Nevsky 91	Q
Nevsky 150	U
Nevsky Palace	O
Oktyabrskaya	M
Oktyabrskaya Filial	P
Puppet Theatre Hostel	H
Radisson SAS Royal	N
Rinaldi	Y
RST Hostel	S
Rus	G
St Petersburg International Hostel	L
Sonata	E

EATING AND DRINKING

Ariang	16
Aziya	9
Bagration Bistro	4
Baltic Bread	14
Bliniy Domik	24
Café Club Che	21
Café Rico	22
Gino-no-Taki	8
Green Cross Salad Bar	23
Jamoneria	7
Karavan-Saray	12
Khuratok	20
Kolkhida	26
Kolobok	2
Matrosskaya Tishina	28
Metekhi	15
Mollie's Irish Bar	25
Planet Sushi	19
Propaganda	17
Rasputin	27
Rigas Seta	11
Rioni	1
Russkie bliny	6
Shwarma	18
Stariy dom	13
Sunduk	5
Ulitsa Razbitykh Fonarey	10
Wooden Pub	3
RESTAURANTS IN HOTELS	
Café Vienna	0
Imperial	0
Landskrona	0

PETROGRAD SIDE

Peter & Paul Fortress

Small Academy of Arts

Museum of the Defence of Leningrad

Museum of Decorative & Applied Arts

VASILEVSKIY ISLAND

Hermitage

Admiralty

Bolshaya Neva

NEVSKIY PROSPEKT

ULITSA LOMONOSOVA

River Moyka

Griboedov Canal

SADOVAYA ULITSA

GOROKHOVAYA ULITSA

River

VOZNESENSKIY PROSPEKT

MOSKOVSKIY PROSPEKT

Vitebsk Station Ⓜ

Technological Institute

Ⓨ

Tekhnologicheskiy Institut

Trinity Cathedral †

Technological Institute Ⓜ

TROITSKIY PR.

IZMAILOVSKIY PROSPEKT

1-YA KRASNOARMEYSKAYA

LERMONTOVSKIY PR.

▼ Ⓜ Baltiyskaya   ▼ Ⓜ Frunzenskaya

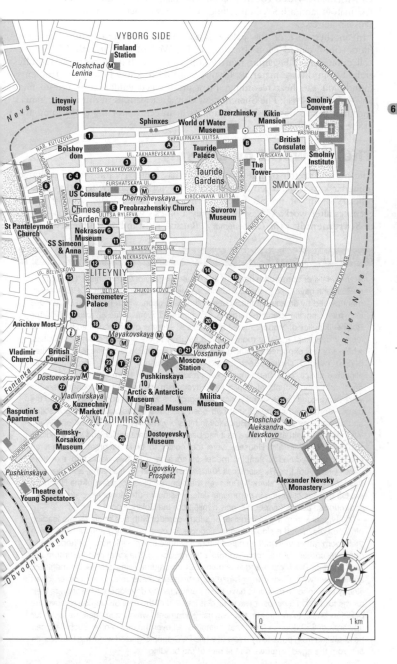

VYBORG SIDE

Finland
Station

*Ploshchad
Lenina*

Liteyniy
most

Neva

Sphinxes
World of Water
Museum

Dzerzhinsky Kikin
Mansion

Smolniy
Convent

Bolshoy
dom

SHPALERNAYA ULITSA

Tauride
Palace

British
Consulate

Smolniy
Institute

UL. ZAKHAREVSKAYA

TVERSKAYA UL.

Tauride
Gardens

The
Tower

SMOLNIY

ULITSA CHAYKOVSKOVO

FURSHATSKAYA UL.

US Consulate

Chernyshevskaya

KIROCHNAYA ULITSA

Chinese
Garden

Preobrazhenskiy Church

Suvorov
Museum

ULITSA RYLEEVA

St Panteleymon
Church

Nekrasov
Museum

SS Simeon
& Anna

BASKOV PEREULOK

ULITSA NEKRASOVA

UL. BELINSKOVO

LITEYNIY

ULITSA ZHUKOVSKOVO

River Neva

ULITSA MOISENKO

Sheremetev
Palace

Anichkov Most

Mayakovskaya

*Ploshchad
Vosstaniya*

PR BAKUNINA

Vladimir
Church

British
Council

Dostoevskaya

Moscow
Station

NEVSKY PROSPEKT

Vladimirskaya

Pushkinskaya
10
Arctic & Antarctic
Museum

Bread Museum

Militia
Museum

Rasputin's
Apartment

Kuznechniy
Market

VLADIMIRSKAYA

Rimsky-
Korsakov
Museum

Dostoyevsky
Museum

*Ploshchad
Aleksandra
Nevskovo*

Pushkinskaya

*Ligovskiy
Prospekt*

Theatre of
Young Spectators

Alexander Nevsky
Monastery

Obvodniy Canal

N

0   1 km

Downstairs is a **video room** screening Russian-language documentaries about Akhmatova, and a bookshop selling audiotapes of her poems read by famous Russian actresses.

In another part of the palace is the **Musical Instruments Museum** (noon–5pm; closed Mon, Tues & the last Wed of each month; $5), whose collection runs the gamut from Polish violins to Buryat horns, beautifully crafted from diverse materials. If you're curious to know how the instruments sound, you can hear recordings on a pre-booked guided **tour** (group rate $6.70; ☎272 44 41). The Sheremetevs were great patrons of music and drama, and their palace was one of the capital's main centres for the performing arts in the eighteenth century.

The art world on Liteyniy

The middle stretch of Liteyniy prospekt has a literary and artistic pedigree going back to 1837, when the would-be novelist Goncharov rented a "modest official's room" at no. 52, where he lived for sixteen years, writing in the evenings after work. At least it was only a block's walk to the editorial offices of **Sovremennik** (*The Contemporary*), Russia's most influential literary journal

Kommunalki

Kommunalki or **communal flats** are an enduring legacy of Communism. Generations of Russians have lived in them, and millions still do. A communal flat is a large apartment owned by an affluent family before the Revolution, which has been subdivided into many smaller, tenanted rooms. *Kommunalki* were a literal example of the Bolshevik policy of "squeezing the bourgeoisie" – former owners counted themselves lucky if they kept a single room – and a solution to the housing crisis in the cities, where workers expected something better than a flophouse and millions of displaced people needed shelter. Each block had a Party-run housing committee that allocated space, regulated tenants' lives and "mobilized" them for *subbotniki* (work days) and other rituals of public life. Favouritism and bribery flourished; tenants were denounced to the secret police by neighbours who coveted their space; and the carpeted, mirrored stairways that had been the pride of the bourgeoisie got soiled and broken – as satirized by Bulgakov in his story *The Heart of a Dog*. World War II left the housing situation as dire as it had been twenty years earlier, and the grandiose *Staliniskiy domi* (Stalin Houses) were too costly to build in great numbers, so Khrushchev decreed a simpler model of housing with five floors (so elevators weren't required) that Russians call *Khrushchoby* (a pun on his name, and the word *trushchoby*, meaning "slums"). But even the high-rise block-building of the Brezhnev era left millions still living in communal flats; President Putin spent his childhood in a *kommunalka* at Baskov per. 12, only a mile from the Bolshoy dom.

The typical *kommunalka* consists of a long corridor with five or six rooms leading off. Each may sleep a single tenant, a couple, or even a family. Each has a fridge in their room rather than in the shared kitchen (whose stove, sink and worktops are at opposite corners of the room, to make things worse); the toilet and bathroom are also shared. The friction and frustrations of communal living are easily imagined, and explain why a flat in a high-rise suburb seems preferable. Many poorer (often elderly or alcoholic) residents have been persuaded by developers to exchange their rooms for flats in a *novostroyke* (new district) so that the new owner can remove the partition walls to re-create the original apartment, which can then be sold for upwards of $50,000 – a trend that's manifest all over the city centre. Such flats can be identified from outside by a row of white PVC double-glazed windows that stands out from the aged windows on the rest of the building.

from the 1840s till the 1870s. This was co-edited by **Nikolai Nekrasov** and **Ivan Panaev**, who lived in adjacent apartments at no. 36 and both enjoyed a cosy *ménage à trois* with Ivan's wife, Avdotya Panaeva – herself a writer. All three campaigned for the emancipation of women – but it was for highlighting the plight of the peasants before and after the Emancipation Act in 1861 that Nekrasov fell foul of the censors, thus earning posthumous approval in Soviet times, when his apartment was turned into the **Nekrasov Museum** (11am–5pm, Thurs till 8pm; closed Tues & the last Fri of each month; $3). It was an unlikely editorial office: the comfortably furnished suite even includes a ballroom. Nekrasov's bedroom is laid out as it was in the last year of his life, reconstructed from the sickbed scene which hangs *in situ*.

In the decades before the Revolution, the standard-bearer was the **World of Art** (Mir iskusstva) movement and magazine, whose influence long outlasted its relatively short life (1898–1904). Partly in reaction to the didactic artistic movements of the nineteenth century, the movement's philosophy was "Art for Art's sake". The magazine was produced in full colour, with elaborate wood-cuts and typography and promoted Style Moderne (the native version of Art Nouveau), as well as hitherto neglected aspects of Russian culture. Artists Alexandre Benois, Léon Bakst and Nikolai Roerich provided most of its material, but the magazine owed much to **Sergei Diaghilev**, the impresario known for his Russian ballet seasons in Paris, and he edited it from his apartment at no. 45, near the corner of ulitsa Belinskovo (named after the critic Vissarion Belinsky).

Diaghilev lived conveniently near the literary salon run by the "decadent Madonna" **Zinaida Gippius** and her husband **Dmitri Merezhkovsky**, whose Symbolist soirees were only eclipsed by the advent of "Wednesdays" at The Tower (p.207). Gossip columns drooled over Gippius's pagan sensuality in an era when "Destruction was considered good taste, neurasthenia a sign of sophistication ... People made up vices and perversions for themselves so as not to seem insipid". After they emigrated in 1919, the grand apartments in the **Muruzi House** (no. 24) were divided into communal flats (see box on p.202). Nobel Prize-winning poet **Joseph Brodsky** spent his childhood in a "room and a half" of flat #28, shared with three other families. The Muruzi House is on the corner of ulitsa Pestelya, and its Moorish facade was renowned as the grandest of any apartment building in St Petersburg when it opened in 1874.

The Preobrazhenskiy Church

A short way down ulitsa Pestelya, off Liteyniy, an oval wrought-iron grille enclosing captured Turkish cannon surrounds the Cathedral of the Transfiguration, better known as the **Preobrazhenskiy Church**. The original regimental church, which burnt down in 1825, was erected by **Empress Elizabeth**, the daughter of Peter the Great, as a token of gratitude to the Preobrazhenskiy Guards, whom she won over in her bid for power in 1741 with the immortal rallying cry: "Lads! You know whose daughter I am. Follow me." The present five-domed, Neoclassical structure was designed by Stasov in the late 1820s and served as an ad hoc military museum during the nineteenth century. It is now a working church again, and its **choir** is one of the best in the city (most of its members also sing in the Kapella Choir) and can be heard at daily services at 10am and 6pm.

Returning to Liteyniy and continuing north towards the Bolshoy dom, you'll see the pagoda roofs and gateways of a small **Chinese Garden**, that provides a much needed splash of colour on the prospekt. This is probably the nicest of the monuments and other gifts that St Petersburg received for its three hundredth birthday from foreign countries and cities – so hats off to the People's Republic of China.

Solyanoy pereulok

To the west of Liteyniy prospekt is a quiet residential enclave with many *kommunalki* formerly assigned to street cleaners or artists (for whom the upper-storey flats made great studios), giving it a bohemian air. Apart from being a pleasant area to stroll through, there are several sights on **Solyanoy pereulok** (Salt Lane), which runs parallel to the Fontanka embankment, starting with the early Baroque terracotta-and-white **Church of St Panteleymon** on the corner of ulitsa Pestelya – it's now a working church again after many years of service as the Museum of the History of Leningrad.

The Mukhina College, next door, has been Russia's leading school of applied arts since it was founded by the philanthropist banker Baron Steiglitz in 1876. Steiglitz believed in inspiring students by surrounding them with fine art and design, and donated his own collection of tapestries, glassware, furniture and paintings, as did his son. After the Revolution, the best was taken for the Hermitage and the Steiglitzes were cast as "feudal exploiters", while the magnificent interior – designed by its first director, Max Messmacher, after St Mark's Library in Venice – was crudely painted over. Further damage was sustained in World War II, when a German shell holed the gigantic glass roof of the Medici Hall, only recently repaired. Students had a hand in the original decor and have been helping to restore the decorations since the war, without any funding from the Ministry of Education that owns the building. Its **Museum of Decorative and Applied Arts** (daily 11am–4.30pm; closed Aug; $2) has a fab collection of tiled stoves (*pechki*), Russian dolls, porcelain and furniture, while each hall is in a different style – Renaissance, Baroque, Flemish and medieval Russian. Student diploma exhibitions are held in the Medici Hall in July. The museum is entered via the *Sol-Art Gallery*; on your way in, note the lampstand in front of the building whose base features four cherubs practising the decorative arts.

Further up the street, twin anti-aircraft cannons flank the entrance to the **Museum of the Defence of Leningrad** (10am–5pm, Tues till 4pm; closed Wed & the last Thurs of each month; $1.65), devoted to "the Blockade" – the three-year siege of the city during World War II. The museum consists of one large exhibition hall on the second floor, with a fine array of wartime posters, including Todize's famous *Rodina-Mat zovyot!* (The Motherland calls!). The centrepiece is a reconstruction of a typical apartment during the Blockade, complete with boarded-up windows, smoke-blackened walls and a few pieces of furniture – the rest having been used as fuel on the tiny stove. Around the edges of the hall are exhibits on artistic life during the siege. It's a measure of the importance of the arts in the city that, despite the desperate lack of resources, several theatres and concert halls functioned throughout the Blockade, and even during the dreadful winter of 1941–42, Leningrad's starving citizens continued to attend exhibitions and concerts. The museum opened just three months after the Blockade was lifted and citizens donated many of its 37,000 exhibits – a sign of the collective pride and solidarity which Stalin so feared that he purged Leningrad's Party cadres and intelligentsia yet again in 1948, when the museum's director was shot.

For light relief, stroll on to the embankment facing the Summer Garden, to find the **Small Academy of Arts** at nab. reki Fontanki 2. Established by

Academician Gubenko, this offers children over 5 years old free master classes by restorers from the Hermitage and Russian Museum, in painting, sculpture, ceramics and other arts. Over the years, they've transformed the **courtyard** where the academy is located into a riot of mosaics and creatures, like a scaled-down version of one of Gaudí's parks in Barcelona.

The Bolshoy dom

The city's record of heroism is even more poignant given that it owed so much of its suffering not to Russia's enemies, but to its own government – above all, to the Stalinist purges following the assassination of the Leningrad Party secretary, Sergei Kirov, in 1934. This purge was implemented from the headquarters of the secret police, universally known as the **Bolshoy dom** (Big House), from whose roof – it was said – "you can see Kolyma" (a labour camp in the Arctic Circle).

With chilling consistency, the Bolshoy dom – at Liteyniy pr. 4 – stands on the site of the old St Petersburg Regional Court, the scene of some of the most famous political trials in Tsarist times. By the late 1870s, public opinion had begun to turn in favour of the radicals who were arraigned in the mass trials of "the 50" and "the 193"; when Vera Zasulich shot a police chief who had ordered an imprisoned student to be flogged, she too was tried here, but was acquitted to popular acclaim. The Nihilist assassins of Alexander II were condemned to death here, as was Lenin's brother for his attempt on the life of Alexander III; and Trotsky and other leaders of the 1905 Revolution wound up in the court after the December clampdown.

After the court was torched in the 1917 February Revolution, a new building was custom-built for the OGPU – as the secret police were then known. Designed in 1931–32 by a trio of architects led by Noy Trotsky (no relation), it was one of the few large buildings erected in the city centre between the wars, and featured three subterranean levels plus the seven floors above ground. Ironically, during the Blockade it was one of the most comfortable places in Leningrad: heated (for the benefit of the jailers), shellproof and with a reliable supply of food – although political prisoners had to share cells with cannibals arrested for eating or selling human flesh.

The present occupants of the Bolshoy dom style themselves the **Federal Security Service** (**FSB**), the post-Soviet name for the old KGB. Though ostensibly reformed under Yeltsin, the FSB still saw fit to persecute a Russian naval officer who revealed details of radioactive pollution in the Baltic and Bering seas to Norwegian ecologists, and is believed to have smeared the procurator general after he began investigating corruption in the Kremlin. Yet its reputation (like that of its former boss, Vladimir Putin) has risen as fear of crime and terrorism has eclipsed the anxiety that the KGB once inspired.

In a similar vein, around the corner at Shpalernaya ul. 25, is the old Tsarist **House of Detention**, rebuilt after it was burnt down by demonstrators in the February Revolution. Almost every notable revolutionary was interned here at some point, including Lenin, who spent fourteen months in the House of Detention before being exiled to Siberia in 1897. According to veteran revolutionaries who experienced both Tsarist and Soviet prisons, conditions were far better in the former, which tolerated visits by prisoners' wives, gifts of food at Easter and Christmas and inspections by the Political Red Cross (a charity whose Petrograd branch was shut down by the Bolsheviks in 1926).

As a sombre finale to this side of the city's history, you can walk to the riverside and east along the embankment to see Mikhail Shemiakin's 1996 memorial to the victims of political repression. It consists of two **sphinxes**, whose serene countenances are half eaten away to reveal their skulls beneath, and a miniature cell window mounted on the embankment wall, through which you can peer across the river towards Kresty Prison, where so many victims of the purges were incarcerated (see p.235). Appositely, this stretch of the embankment is named after Robespierre, the instigator of the Terror during the French Revolution.

The Smolniy district

Tucked into a bend in the River Neva, the **Smolniy district** is a quiet, slightly remote quarter. Most tourists are drawn here by the **Smolniy Convent**, while Petersburgers come to visit the **Tauride Gardens**. In Tsarist times the district was called Rozhdestvenskiy, after the regiment which had its barracks in the area, but with the establishment of the State Duma and, later, the Petrograd Soviet in the Tauride Palace, the district evolved into the country's main centre of power. The Smolniy Institute was the Bolsheviks' principal base during and after the October Revolution; it subsequently became the Leningrad Party headquarters, and now houses the Governor's office.

Although it's possible to walk two kilometres from Chernyshevskaya metro, through the Tauride Gardens and on to the Smolniy, it's wise to save your energy by riding some of the way. **Minibuses** to the Smolniy can be boarded anywhere along Nevskiy prospekt between Nevskiy Prospekt and Ploshchad Vosstaniya metro stations (#K-129 and #K-147 run the length of Suvorovskiy prospekt); at Chernyshevskaya metro (#K-46 via Shpalernaya ulitsa, #K-136 via Kirochnaya ulitsa); Marsovo pole in the centre or Gorkovskaya and Petrogradskaya metro stations on the Petrograd Side (#K-46).

Along Furshtadtskaya ulitsa

If you're intent on walking, head east down **Furshtadtskaya ulitsa** from Chernyshevskaya metro. This leafy avenue is lined with imposing mansions and was one of the most fashionable streets in pre-revolutionary St Petersburg. The leading Duma politicians Rodzyanko and Guchkov lived at nos. 20 and 36 respectively; at the other end of the political spectrum, Pyotr Lavrov, the nineteenth-century agrarian populist, lived at no. 12; while Dmitri Stasov, a lawyer who defended revolutionaries and hid Lenin for a time in 1917, lived in the same building as Rodzyanko. Nowadays the US, Austrian and German **consulates** are located here; anyone trying to photograph the American consulate risks having their film confiscated. The street culminates in the pink, neo-Baroque **Palace of Weddings**, or registry office, which sports a fancy covered bridge.

The Tauride Gardens and around

At the end of Furshtadtskaya are the **Tauride Gardens** (Tavricheskiy sad), which back onto the Tauride Palace. The gardens are now primarily a children's park, boasting an antiquated **fairground** on the western side, though there's the usual panoply of ponds, sunbathers, drinkers and courting couples. Approaching via Shpalernaya ulitsa, you'll pass the **House of Flowers** (Tues,

Wed & Fri–Sun 11am–7pm), a series of heated greenhouses for raising tropical flowers and shrubs, which doubles as a garden centre. It's a good place to warm up if you're passing by during wintertime.

Near the southeastern corner of the park, at the busy junction of Kirochnaya and Tavricheskaya ulitsa, stands the **Suvorov Museum** (10am–6pm; closed Tues, Wed & the first Mon of each month), a quasi-fortified building erected in 1902 to commemorate the eighteenth-century generalissimo Alexander Suvorov. The museum displays Suvorov's personal effects, period militaria and antique toy soldiers, while its exterior is distinguished by colourful mosaics depicting his departure for the Italian campaign of 1799, and Russian troops crossing the Alps. The former features a small fir-tree made by the writer Zoshchenko as a child; his artist father designed the mosaics. "The harder the training, the easier the battle," was one of Suvorov's favourite maxims, many of which were taught to schoolchildren in Soviet times, although Suvorov himself was so sickly as a child that he wasn't signed up for the Guards until the age of 12, unlike his contemporaries, who were "put down" for their regiments at birth.

Tavricheskaya ulitsa, on the eastern side of the park, contains some impressive early twentieth-century buildings along its southern section, many of them now largely owned by mafiosi from the Tambov and Solnechnoe gangs, to the despair of law-abiding residents. Overlooking the gardens, the top floor of the circular tower on the corner of Tverskaya ulitsa once hosted the salon known as "**The Tower**" (Bashnya), frequented by Akhmatova, Blok, Mandelstam, Roerich and others. The sprawling open-plan apartment belonged to the mystic and poet Vyacheslav Ivanov, who presided like a high priest over his famous "Wednesdays" – intellectual free-for-alls that often lasted for days. The salon died out after Ivanov emigrated in 1912, but urban legend has it that a cabal of tower-dwelling mystics still watches over the city.

The Tauride Palace

Situated in the northeastern corner of the park, the **Tauride Palace** (Tavricheskiy dvorets) was built by Catherine the Great for her lover, Prince Potemkin, the brains behind the annexation of the Crimea (then known as Tauris or Tavriya, hence the palace's name). Completed by Stasov in 1789, the palace is one of the city's earliest examples of austere Neoclassicism. From

Prince Potemkin

Born into poverty in the Smolensk region, **Grigori Potemkin** (1739–91) – pronounced "Pot*yom*kin" – joined the army and quickly rose through the ranks, largely owing to his bottomless reserves of energy and courage. Physically imposing, but far from beautiful (he got rid of an infected eye by deliberately lancing it in a fit of impatience), Potemkin was soon noticed by Catherine the Great and became her lover. Between campaigns he would arrive unannounced at the Winter Palace, unshaven and clad only in his dressing gown and slippers. Even after she took other lovers – some of whom he selected – Potemkin remained her foremost friend and courtier, demonstrating his mastery of diplomacy during her inspection tour of the Crimea in 1787. As governor general of the newly conquered region, he was at pains to portray it as more prosperous than it was: fake villages were erected along Catherine's route, while local peasants were given a fresh set of clothes and ordered to look cheerful – a trick perfected in the Soviet era, when "Potemkin tours" of factories and towns were *de rigueur* for VIPs and foreign tourists.

Shpalernaya ulitsa, you can still admire the yellow main facade, whose six-columned portico is almost entirely devoid of decorative detail, but the original view north across the Neva is now obscured by factories, and the fabulous interior was deliberately ruined by Catherine's son, Paul, who turned it into a stables and barracks for the Horseguards. Potemkin occupied the palace for just over a year before his death in 1791, and threw the greatest New Year's Eve Ball the city had ever witnessed in a final effort to revive Catherine's love for him. Over three thousand guests filled the rooms, which were lit by fourteen thousand multicoloured oil lamps and twenty thousand candles. At the entrance, the guests were met by an elephant covered in gems and ridden by a Persian; beyond, a curtain lifted to reveal a stage on which ballets and choral works were performed.

The palace is now in the hands of local authorities and closed to the public, but it retains a vital place in the city's history. In 1905, it was chosen as the venue for the **State Duma**, which – following the first parliamentary elections in Russian history – was inaugurated in May 1906. On February 27, 1917, in the final throes of the Tsarist autocracy, over thirty thousand mutinous troops and countless demonstrators converged on the palace; inside a Provisional Committee was formed, which later became the Provisional Government, while in another wing of the palace, the Petrograd Soviet was re-established, thus creating a state of "dual power" that persisted until the October Revolution.

On January 5, 1918, the long-awaited **Constituent Assembly** met for the first and last time in the Tauride Palace. As the first Russian parliament elected by universal suffrage, this was meant to be "the crowning jewel in Russian democratic life", but Lenin already privately regarded it as "an old fairytale which there is no reason to carry on further". Having received only a quarter of the vote, the Bolsheviks surrounded the palace the following day, preventing many delegates from entering; Red Guards eventually dismissed those inside the building with the words: "Push off. We want to go home."

In the 1930s the palace was home to the All-Union Communist University and, following the war, housed the Leningrad Higher Party School up until 1990. It is now used for prestigious conferences and meetings.

Along Shpalernaya ulitsa

Shpalernaya ulitsa is a ley-line of past and present centres of power, linking the Bolshoy dom and the Smolniy, the Tauride Palace and a slew of barracks. When planning their seizure of power, the Bolsheviks included an objective on their doorstep – the eight-storey **Water Tower** near the Neva, which was the nerve centre of the city's water and sewage system, and an ideal observation point. The tower was built in 1861, in an attempt to end cholera epidemics by delivering filtered river water. After the 1908 epidemic the City Duma commissioned a larger plant from Siemens, completed just before the war; but the tower remained the water company's headquarters, with its own laboratory – and is still in the hands of Vodakanal. As the city's tap water is notoriously contaminated with giardia and heavy metals, it seems cheeky of Vodakanal to brag of its achievements, but the **World of Water Museum** (muzey "Mir Vody"; 10am–5pm; closed Mon, Tues & the last Fri of each month; free) is a slick effort, abetted by the British Council. Children will like the cascade of lights in the atrium and the antique toilets among the exhibits upstairs. These include a wooden water pipe from Petrine times; early fire engines; photos of luxurious *banyas* like Yegorov's – with doormen, ferns and a bridge above its pool; and a re-creation of a room during the Blockade, with its life-giving stove and mandatory portrait of Stalin. Sadly, the captions are in Russian only, so most foreigners will emerge unaware of Vodakanal's pledge to ensure proper drinking water and that only treated sewage will be pumped into the Gulf of Finland, by – wait for it – 2015. However, the **view** from the tower's observation deck is great, and the garden and the statue of an old water carrier and his dog in the grounds are delightful.

A block or so beyond, you'll find a **statue of Felix Dzerzhinsky**, the "steel-eyed, spade-bearded" Polish-Lithuanian founder of the Soviet secret police, the Cheka. Erected in 1981, the statue was described by one Soviet guidebook as expressing his "decisiveness and iron will", though when slick with rain it looks more like a rubber-fetishist's dream, clad in glistening jackboots, greatcoat and peaked cap.

Just past Dzerzhinsky, set back from the corner of Stavropolskaya ulitsa, is the orange **Kikin Mansion**, a modest Baroque country house. One of the oldest surviving buildings in the city, it was erected in 1714 for Alexander Kikin, the head of the Admiralty and one of Peter the Great's companions on his Grand Tour of Europe. Later, however, Kikin was a prime mover in the conspiracy against Peter, which involved the tsar's son, Alexei – both he and Kikin were tortured to death as a result. Peter used the mansion to house his Kunstkammer collection. Damaged by shellfire in World War II, the house has since been restored to something akin to its former glory and now serves as a children's music school.

The Smolniy Complex

From the Kikin Mansion, it's impossible to miss the glorious ice-blue cathedral towering on the eastern horizon, which is the focal point and architectural masterpiece of the **Smolniy Complex**. Prosaically, its name derives from the Smolyanoy dvor, or "tar yard", sited here in the eighteenth century to caulk Peter the Great's warships. Later, Empress Elizabeth founded a convent on the site and Catherine the Great also started a boarding school for the daughters of the nobility – the Smolniy Institute for Young Noblewomen – which later became the headquarters of the Bolsheviks during the October Revolution.

The Smolniy Convent

Rastrelli's grandiose plans for the **Smolniy Convent** (Smolniy monastyr; 11am–4pm; closed Thurs; $3.50) were never completed, not least because Empress Elizabeth's personal extravagance almost bankrupted the Imperial coffers. Had the original plans been realized, the building would be entirely different in character. Apart from the proposed Rococo detailing, the major omission is a 140-metre-high bell tower, which would have been the tallest structure in the city. As it turned out, the empress ran out of money and the building was finished by Stasov only in 1835, in a more restrained Neoclassical fashion and with a bell tower less than half of the proposed height.

Nevertheless, the view of the **exterior** from ploshchad Rastrelli is superb: the central five-domed cathedral offset by four large matching domes which rise in perfect symmetry from the surrounding outbuildings. The cathedral's austere white **interior** is disappointingly severe and suffered from neglect during the Soviet era, so it's not worth paying to go inside unless you're interested in seeing whatever temporary exhibition is showing on the first floor, or feeling energetic enough to climb up the 63-metre-high bell tower for a stupendous **view** of the Smolniy district. In addition to services held here on weekends

△ The cathedral of Smolniy Convent

and religious holidays, the cathedral also hosts **concerts** from early September until late June (☎271 91 82 for details and bookings).

The Smolniy Institute

The **Smolniy Institute** – now the Governor's office – was built in 1806–8 to house the Institute for Young Noblewomen, but gained its notoriety after the Bolshevik-dominated Petrograd Soviet moved here from the Tauride Palace in August 1917. Soon, the Smolniy was "deep in autumn mud chomped from thousands of pairs of boots", with Red Guards sleeping in its dormitories and armoured cars parked in the courtyard. Here, too, the powerful **Military Revolutionary Committee** was established, which the Bolsheviks used as a legal means of arming their supporters in preparation for a coup. On the evening of October 25, the second **All-Russian Congress of Soviets** met at the Smolniy to the sound of shellfire. The Bolsheviks, who had a sizeable majority, tried to present the coup as a *fait accompli*, though fighting was still going on and the Provisional Government had yet to be arrested in the Winter Palace. When the Menshevik opposition called for an immediate ceasefire, Trotsky retorted: "You are miserable bankrupts, your role is played out. Go where you ought to be: into the dustbin of history." The next day, Kamenev announced the abolition of the death penalty and the release of all political prisoners (except those whom the Bolsheviks were rounding up), while Lenin read out the first two decrees of the Soviet government – calling for an end to the war and for the handing over of all private land to Peasant Committees and Soviets. The Smolniy served as the seat of Soviet power until March 1918, when the city's vulnerability to the Germans impelled the government to move to Moscow.

Later, as the headquarters of the Leningrad Party organization, the Smolniy Institute witnessed the **assassination of Kirov**, the local Party boss, by Leonid Nikolaev on December 1, 1934. Stalin (who is thought to have masterminded the plot) immediately rushed to Leningrad and personally interrogated Nikolaev, before passing an illegal decree enabling capital sentences to be carried out immediately – whereupon Nikolaev and 37 others were promptly executed. This marked the beginning of a mass purge of Leningrad during which as many as one-quarter of the city's population may have been arrested, the majority of them destined for the Gulag.

Nowadays, the Smolniy isn't open to visitors, though nobody minds if you stroll around the **monuments** in the gardens out front. In 1923–24 two simple commemorative propylaea were built, with the inscriptions "Workers of All Countries Unite!" and "The First Soviet of the Proletarian Dictatorship". The busts of Marx and Engels still face each other across the gravel paths, while Lenin himself stands before the porticoed entrance. The square in front of the propylaea is also the site of the **British Consulate**, which rejoices in the address 5 ploshchad Proletarskoy dikatatury (Dictatorship of the Proletariat Square).

To Stariy Nevskiy and back

More than half of **Nevskiy prospekt** – some 2.5km – lies to the east of the River Fontanka, but for much of its length holds little of interest. Its chief attraction is the **Alexander Nevsky Monastery**, in the grounds of which are buried the city's most illustrious writers, artists and politicians. At some point you may also find yourself in **ploshchad Vosstaniya**, halfway along the prospekt, a major road and metro junction and home to Moscow Station. Beyond the station, the avenue is traditionally known as **Stariy Nevskiy** – or "Old Nevskiy" – though it's not marked on maps as such. Now designer shops and restaurants are bringing some chic to this previously drab section of the prospekt, but it still doesn't reward strolling in the way that downtown Nevskiy does. This account starts at the monastery and works back towards the centre. It's best to use the metro to reach the monastery, and then Ploshchad Vosstaniya/Mayakovskaya stations, within walking distance of everything else; or travel back above ground to name-check the shops, on tram #44, trolleybus #1 or minibus #K-39 – though not if you're in a hurry, as the traffic can be awful.

Alexander Nevsky Monastery

Nevskiy prospekt ends as it begins, beside the Neva – at a spot where an ancient Russian hero is honoured by the **Alexander Nevsky Monastery** (Aleksandro-Nevskaya lavra; daily from dawn till dusk; free) and a lance-wielding equestrian statue. This was once believed to be the site of the thirteenth-century battle in which Prince Alexander of Novgorod defeated the Swedes, thus earning himself the sobriquet "Alexander Nevsky" (the name

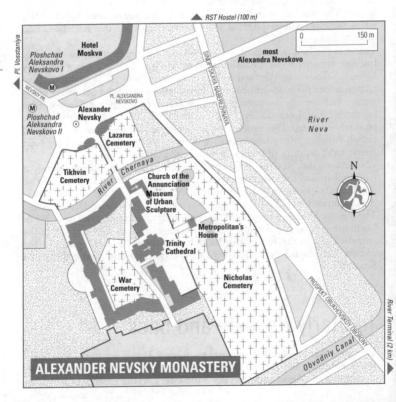

ALEXANDER NEVSKY MONASTERY

"Nevsky" being derived from the River Neva). Having thrashed the Swedes himself, at Poltava, Peter the Great felt secure enough to found a monastery in St Petersburg, ten years after he began the city, and in 1724 he ensured its holiness by having the remains of the canonized prince transferred from Vladimir to the monastery. In 1797 it became one of only four in the Russian Empire to be given the title of *lavra*, the highest rank in Orthodox monasticism. As at all Orthodox monasteries, you won't be allowed inside wearing shorts or skimpy clothing, but they don't insist that women wear long skirts and headscarves, as at Valaam.

The Tikhvin and Lazarus cemeteries

Many tourists visit the monastery with the main aim of looking around the two cemeteries, separated by the walled path by which you enter its precincts. Both are covered by one ticket, sold at the entrance to the **Tikhvin Cemetery** (Tikhvinskoe kladbishche; daily: April–Oct 9.30am–8pm; Nov–March 9.30am–4pm; $2). Established in 1823, it boasts many of the big names in Russian culture. The *babushka* at the gate will point you towards **Dostoyevsky**'s grave, which is just as well since his name is difficult to decipher from the ornate Cyrillic. Moving along the right-hand wall towards the chapel, you'll reach a cluster of graves belonging to some of Russia's greatest composers. The first belongs to **Rimsky-Korsakov** and is adorned with a medieval Russian cross inset with icons; **Mussorgsky** is buried next to him, the grave decorated with a phrase from one of his works; while **Borodin**'s snippet from *Prince Igor* is set in a gilded mosaic behind his bust. **Tchaikovsky** has a grander, monumental tomb set in its own flowerbed. Other figures buried here include the composers **Rubinstein** and **Glinka**, the painters **Kustodiev** and **Serov**, the fabulist **Krylov**, the critic **Stasov** and the actor **Nikolai Cherkassov**, who played *Ivan the Terrible* in Eisenstein's trilogy of films. A map in Cyrillic in the southeastern corner of the graveyard shows the location of all the graves.

The smaller **Lazarus Cemetery** (Lazarovskoe kladbishche; April–Oct 9.30am–6.30pm; Nov–March 9.30am–4pm; closed Thurs) is the oldest in the city, established by Peter the Great, whose sister Natalya was buried here in 1716. There are fewer celebrities, but it's just as interesting in terms of funereal art: the tombs are strewn with death masks, skulls and crossbones and other sculptures. By consulting the map to the left of the entrance, you should be able to locate the tombs of the polymath **Lomonosov**, the architects **Rossi**, **Quarenghi**, **Voronikhin** and **Starov** (who built the Trinity Cathedral, see below), and Pushkin's wife, **Natalya Goncharova**, who is buried under the name of her second husband, Lanskaya. Other famous Russians are buried in the Literatorskie mostki graveyard, described on p.230.

The monastery and Trinity Cathedral

Beyond the narrow River Chernaya, the monastery proper forms a raspberry-red, two-storey enclosure around a tree-filled quadrant, which serves as a cemetery for Communist activists and heroes of World War II. Trotsky's driver is buried in the grave beneath the curious ensemble of iron chains and wheels, facing the cathedral. On the way you'll pass Trezzini's **Church of the Annunciation**, completed in 1722. This was the original burial place of Peter III, Catherine the Great's deposed husband, but on her death their son Paul had his father reburied in the traditional resting place of the Romanov rulers, the Peter and Paul Cathedral. With a ticket from the kiosk outside, you can enter to see the **tombs** of Princess Regent Anna Leopoldovna; Empress Elizabeth's lover, Razumovsky, and her adviser Count Shuvalov; Catherine's statesman, Prince Golitsyn, and her illegitimate grandson, Prince Bobrinsky; Paul's tutor and minister, Panin; Count Miloradovich, who was shot for leading the Decembrists' revolt; several Georgian crown princesses; and generalissimo Suvorov. The Soviets got round its tsarist antecedents by renaming the church the **Museum of Urban Sculpture** (11am–5pm; closed Mon & the last Thurs of each month; $2; ⓦwww.necropolis.spb.ru) – a status it retains, though services are once again held there. Upstairs is a large collection of models and designs for the city's monuments and sculptures.

Trezzini also drew up an ambitious design for the monastery's **Trinity Cathedral** (not be confused with the Trinity Cathedral beyond Zagorodniy prospekt), but failed to orient it towards the east, as Orthodox custom required, so the plans were scrapped. The job was left to Ivan Starov to finish, who completed a rather more modest building in a Neoclassical style that sits awkwardly with the rest of the complex. The **interior**, however, is worth seeing, but bear in mind that this is a working church, not a museum, and usually closed for cleaning between 2 and 5pm. On Sundays it is pungent with incense and packed with worshippers genuflecting, kissing icons and lighting candles, while its choir is one of St Petersburg's best. The red agate and white marble **iconostasis** contains copies of works by Van Dyck and Rubens (among others), and the relics of St Alexander Nevsky are enshrined in a silver **sarcophagus** (a modest copy of the original, in the Hermitage), that draws hundreds of worshippers on his name day (September 12).

To escape the crowds, head round the back of the cathedral to the **Nicholas Cemetery** (daily: summer 9am–9pm; winter 9am–6pm; free), an overgrown graveyard where the monastery's scholars and priests are buried, as well as ordinary folk. Here you'll also see the eighteenth-century **Metropolitan's House**, the residence of the spiritual leader of St Petersburg's Orthodox community.

The Militia Museum

The intriguing **Militia Museum** is known to few tourists or ordinary Petersburgers, being primarily intended for the Militia (police) themselves. Its discretion is matched by its location, on the right-hand side of the courtyard of Poltavskaya ul. 12, running south off Nevskiy prospekt midway between the Alexander Nevsky Monastery and ploshchad Vosstaniya. There's no sign as such, but Militia notices and roster-boards give the game away. You can **visit** only by arrangement (Mon–Fri 10am–6pm; $20 group rate, individual price negotiable; ⓣ279 42 33) and must take a guided tour in Russian, which is interesting if you're able to understand the language or can bring an interpreter along.

Five halls trace the **history of the Militia**, since its establishment in 1917 until the 1970s, starting with their activities during the Civil War and the NEP era, when gangsterism and fraud in Russia were as rife as they are today – look out for the mug shots of notorious 1920s criminals such as "Belka" (Squirrel) and the Alexandrov safe-cracking gang. During World War II, the Militia were responsible for civil defence in Leningrad and active as partisans behind enemy lines; there is also material documenting the Militia's social work amongst gangs of orphans. Further exhibits relate to some of the more macabre cases that the Militia were called upon to solve, including gruesome photos of dismembered bodies from the Rosenblat and "Head in a Bucket" **murder cases** of the 1940s. Dioramas of muggings and the stuffed police tracker dog

Sultan provide a light interlude. The main hall with its crimson banners is used for swearing in new recruits and another room (not open to visitors) contains mocked-up crime scenes on which trainee officers get to practise their forensic techniques.

Coincidentally, one of the most notorious crimes in the city's recent history happened only five minutes' drive from the museum, in 1997, when St Petersburg's Vice-Governor, Mikhail Manevich, was killed by a rooftop sniper as his car turned off Nevskiy prospekt on to ulitsa Marata. Nobody has ever been arrested for the crime, and even the police admit that it will probably never be solved – though it's thought that the motive was to halt his investigation of fraudulent city property deals.

Around ploshchad Vosstaniya

At the only bend in Nevskiy prospekt, the traffic-clogged intersection of **ploshchad Vosstaniya** (Uprising Square) is dominated by **Moscow Station** (Moskovskiy vokzal), whose grand peach-and-white facade looks more like a palace than a rail terminal; the architect built an identical one at the other end of the line in Moscow. Today, the facade is all that remains of the original station, which has been totally modernized inside. While Communists and war veterans protested when the bust of Lenin in the hall was replaced by one of Peter the Great, there were only shrugs when European Union funds to build a business centre behind the station were embezzled, leaving a vast **pit** that's set to become the most expensive parking lot in Europe.

The square itself was previously called Znamenskaya ploshchad, after a church that was demolished in 1940 and replaced by the spired rotunda of Ploshchad Vosstaniya metro station (linked by a pedestrian subway to Mayakovskaya metro, further up Nevskiy). The square witnessed some of the bloodiest exchanges between police and demonstrators during the February Revolution, hence its current name: it was at a mass gathering on February 25 that Cossacks first turned on the police, shooting the leader of a mounted detachment. The battle for control of the square raged until the following day, when forty demonstrators were killed. The central **obelisk** was erected in 1985, on the site of a much ridiculed statue of Alexander III, that was removed in 1937 and can now be seen in the courtyard of the Marble Palace (p.84). The *Oktyabrskaya Hotel*, across the square from the station, has a **rooftop sign** that proclaims in Russian: "Leningrad – Hero City". Almost a dozen towns and cities were so designated, to honour their heroism during World War II.

Pushkinskaya 10

From ploshchad Vosstaniya, turn left down Ligovskiy prospekt and pass through the arch of no. 53 to reach the famous artists' colony known as **Pushkinskaya 10** (Pushkinskaya desyat). One of the first buildings in the city to be occupied by artists and dropouts, Pushkinskaya 10 remains a vital force on St Petersburg's cultural scene, even though the building itself has largely been refurbished and sold off to wealthy buyers – this is why visitors can no longer use the gated entrance on Pushkinskaya ulitsa, but must enter from Ligovskiy prospekt, even though the galleries and studios remain in the middle wings. Most are open to visitors from mid-afternoon onwards, maybe just one or two days a week; admission charges are levied only for concerts and other special events.

Entering the yard you'll find the **Fish Fabrique Café** – a low-key meeting place for musicians and artists – and a plan of the four blocks that comprise the colony. Photos of artists, parties and happenings line the stairs from the information bureau on the first floor of block B to the **Museum of the New Academy of Fine Arts** (Sat 3–7pm) on the fourth floor, celebrating two decades of work by diverse artists sharing an aesthetic known as Neo-Academism, whose "cruel naiveté" subverts both classicism and postmodernism; and the **KINO-FOT** film gallery on the seventh (Wed–Sun 3-7pm). In block C, above the **John Lennon Temple** of Love, Peace and Music (where the anniversary of his birth is commemorated) and the **FOTOimage** gallery (Sat 4–7pm) on the second floor, the work of the New Academy's founder – the late Timur Novikov – and colleagues are showcased in the **Museum of Nonconformist Art** (Wed–Sun 3–7pm) on the fourth floor. Check out what's on at the **Techno-Art Centre** (Tues–Sat 3–8pm) on the first floor of block D, and the **Gallery of Experimental Sound** on the third floor, hosting concerts (Mon & Tues from 8pm). The adjacent **café** is the nexus of St Petersburg's "cyber feminist" scene (see p.404).

Around Mayakovskaya metro

Bohemian traditions run deep in the neighbourhood around Pushkinskaya 10. The poet Mayakovsky (see box on p.217) lends his name to the nearby **Mayakovskaya** metro station – whose crimson mosaic platform walls are adorned with his visage – and to **ulitsa Mayakovskovo** on the other side of the prospekt, where he lived at no. 52 during 1915–17 to be close to Lili Brik, who lived nearby with her husband. On the same street, the absurdist writer **Daniil Kharms** resided for much of his life at no. 11, being known for his affected English plus fours and pipe, and for bowing to antique lampposts. His fate was even crueller than Mayakovsky's: arrested by the Soviet secret police and declared insane, he died in prison. In a Kharms-like twist, his wife – who was long thought to have died in the Blockade – was found to be living in Brazil in 1999. She hardly remembered him and wondered what all the fuss was about.

Vladimirskaya

Vladimirskaya metro station, south of Nevskiy prospekt, forms the nucleus of the vibrant, slightly seedy **Vladimirskaya** area, whose sights include Kuznechniy Market, Dostoyevsky's apartment, the Arctic and Antarctic Museum, and the Bread Museum. Further southwest, **Zagorodniy prospekt** cuts through a tract of the inner suburbs associated with Dostoyevsky and Rasputin, to the Technological Institute – the birthplace of the Petrograd Soviet – and the Trinity Cathedral (not to be confused with the cathedral at the Alexander Nevsky Monastery).

Around Kuznechniy pereulok

Coming by metro, you'll either arrive at Dostoevskaya metro, with its elegantly simple marble platforms, or at the older Vladimirskaya metro (to which Dostoevskaya is linked by an underground passage), with ornate lamps and a mosaic of prosperous peasants – before emerging near Kuznechniy Market, on the southern side of **Kuznechniy pereulok**. Just around the corner to the left from Vladimirskaya, a bronze **statue of Dostoyevsky** sits pensively, while peddlers and beggars vie for custom by the **Vladimir Church** on the corner

Vladimir Mayakovsky

Futurist poet **Vladimir Mayakovsky** was born in Georgia in 1893. An enthusiastic supporter of the Bolshevik cause from an early age (he was elected to the Moscow committee when only 14 years old), Mayakovsky was arrested several times and given a six-month prison sentence in 1909. On his release, he enrolled at the Moscow Institute of Painting, Sculpture and Architecture and became friends with the Futurist painter, David Burlyuk. Together with other **Futurists**, they published a manifesto entitled *A Slap in the Face of Public Taste* and embarked on a publicity tour across Russia. Mayakovsky wore earrings and a yellow waistcoat with radishes in the buttonholes, scrawled obscenities on his face in greasepaint and recited avant-garde verses – the original punk, no less.

He threw himself into the October Revolution, becoming its keenest celebrant and propagandist: as a friend remarked, "Mayakovsky entered the Revolution as he would his own home. He went right in and began opening windows." Though his reputation as a poet rests on his romantic, pre-revolutionary work, he is best known for his later propagandist writing, such as the poem "150,000,000", which pits Ivan against world capitalism. One of the founders of the **Left Front of Art (LEF)**, an agitprop group whose members included Osip Brik and Alexander Rodchenko, Mayakovsky also produced graphic art during the 1920s, including over six hundred giant cartoon advertisements with captions for the Russian Telegraph Agency, ROSTA.

In 1930, five years after condemning the poet Yesenin for his "unrevolutionary" **suicide**, Mayakovsky killed himself in Moscow at the age of 37, with a revolver which he had used twelve years before as a prop in a film called *Not for Money Born*. His last unfinished poem lay beside him. Various motives have been advanced, ranging from despair over his love for Lili Brik to disillusionment with Soviet life, the philistinism of its censors, and hostile reviews of his most recent work. Whatever the truth, thousands filed past his open coffin at the Writers' Union, while a few years later Stalin decreed that "Mayakovsky was and remains the most talented poet of our Soviet epoch. Indifference to his memory and to his work is a crime." From then on, in the words of Pasternak, "Mayakovsky was sold to the people much as Catherine the Great had sold potatoes to the peasants."

of Kuznechniy pereulok, as in his time. A yellow Baroque beauty with five bronze onion domes and a Neoclassical bell tower, the church has now been restored, having served as an ambulance station until 1989. Its upstairs nave has a beguiling raspberry, pistachio and vanilla colour scheme.

The indoor **Kuznechniy Market** (Kuznechniy rynok; Mon–Sat 11am–8pm) is the best-stocked and most expensive market in the city. Also known as the Vladimirskiy Market, it offers fresh produce from all over the former Soviet Union: melons from Kazakhstan, tomatoes from Georgia, farmhouse honey, sour cream, hams and gherkins, not to mention imports such as kiwi fruit. Most vendors offer the chance to taste a sliver before buying – poor pensioners obtain breakfast by visiting a score of stalls. Outside the market are unlicensed sellers of herbs, mushrooms or berries that they've grown at their *dacha* or gathered in the woods; they flee when the police appear, only to return once they've gone.

The Dostoyevsky Museum

At Kuznechniy per. 5, beyond the market, the **Dostoyevsky Museum** (11am–6pm; closed Mon & the last Wed of each month; $2; ☎311 40 31, Ⓦwww.md.spb.ru) occupies the apartment into which Dostoyevsky and his

Dostoyevsky

Born in Moscow in 1821, one of seven children fathered by a depressive, alcoholic physician, **Fyodor Dostoyevsky** lost his mother when he was 16 and his father (who was probably murdered by the family's serfs) two years later. A brief flirtation with socialist politics ended in Dostoyevsky's arrest and a death sentence, commuted at the last moment to four years' hard labour, plus further service as an ordinary soldier. In prison, he recanted socialism and liberalism and became an ardent supporter of autocracy and Orthodoxy, but was regarded by the police as a subversive for many years afterwards. "How many lawbreakers they close their eyes to, while me they watch with suspicion and an eagle eye, a man who is devoted to the Tsar and the fatherland with all his heart and soul. It is an insult!" he raged. His first marriage and subsequent affairs were all dismal failures; gambling drained his meagre resources and he suffered from epilepsy. In 1866, to meet a tough deadline, he hired a 20-year-old stenographer, **Anna Snitkina**, to whom he dictated *The Gambler* in less than a month. Soon afterwards they married and she became his permanent secretary, gradually cured him of gambling, and made him a solid family man for the last quarter of his life.

While Dostoyevsky is posthumously renowned in the West as one of the greatest writers of the nineteenth century, his **reputation** inside Russia was long denigrated by the Left, which condemned him for engaging in polemics against the Nihilists. Between the 1930s and 1950s he wasn't even mentioned in Soviet textbooks, although he was eventually rehabilitated as a realist whose flaws embodied the contradictions of his era. None of his descendants dared reveal their identities until the early 1990s, when his great-grandson Andrei emerged from obscurity and undertook a tour of foreign literary societies, whom he disconcerted by his obsession with acquiring a Mercedes – with this, he now scrapes a living as an unregistered taxi driver. A decade later, his sister Tatyana appealed for help in an open letter to a weekly newspaper, bitterly comparing her life as a pensioner struggling to survive on $33 a month to the poor of *Crime and Punishment*. None of the six direct descendants of Dostoyevsky still alive in St Petersburg receives any royalties from the millions of his books sold over the years.

wife moved in 1878, to escape the memory of their previous flat, where their son Alexei died. Like many of the twenty or so places where Dostoyevsky lived in St Petersburg, it is on a corner. Reconstructed on the centenary of the writer's demise, using photos and drawings, the flat is surprisingly bright and cheerful: thanks to Anna, he enjoyed a cosy domestic life while creating his brooding masterpieces – the children would push notes under his door, reading "Papa, we love you". Dostoyevsky died of a throat haemorrhage while writing his diary; the clock in the study where he wrote *The Brothers Karamazov* is stopped at the exact time of his death: 8.38pm, on January 28, 1881. Also on display is a printed announcement of Dostoyevsky's exile and a set of prison leg-irons, such as he wore en route to Siberia. All the rooms are captioned in English, so you don't really need an audio guide ($2.30). At noon on Sundays, Russian **films** of the writer's novels are screened downstairs; videos of the same, Dostoyevsky T-shirts and mugs are sold in the lobby.

The Arctic and Antarctic Museum

Across the intersection of Kuznechniy pereulok with ulitsa Marata is the former Old Believers' Church of St Nicholas, which was closed down by the Bolsheviks and reopened in 1937 as the **Arctic and Antarctic Museum** (10am–6pm; closed Mon, Tues & the last Fri of each month; $2.50;

@www.polarmuseum.sp.ru). The Old Believers, of whom there are about a hundred in St Petersburg, are trying to get the church back, but the museum isn't budging. Its history is entwined with the "Conquest of the North", an era when Polar exploration and aviation were as prestigious as space travel thirty years later. Not only did the Soviet Union create oil towns, research bases and fishing stations, supplied over thousands of miles; it boasted towns beyond the Arctic circle that grew vegetables, enjoyed symphony orchestras and had sunlamps in their kindergartens. Since the end of Communism these have literally fallen apart; anyone able to has fled, and the remaining inhabitants are being relocated with European Union funding.

The museum reflects the glory days. Its marble-columned hall is filled with stuffed polar wildlife, a mammoth's skull and tusk and the skiplane in which V.B. Shabrov flew from Leningrad to the Arctic in 1930. Off to the sides, at the back, are the leather tent used in the 1937–38 Soviet North Pole expedition and a model of a roomier hut with bunk beds and a portrait of Lenin, used by another group in 1954 – look out for the surgical tools that one explorer used to operate on himself. The dioramas of base camps and logistics are self-explanatory and uncontentious, unlike the exhibits upstairs, which purport to show how Soviet rule improved the lives of the Arctic peoples – a reindeer-skin jacket embroidered with a Proletarian breaking the shackles of Exploitation sums up the desired impression, while the havoc wrought by the oil and gas industries and the nuclear contamination of Novaya Zemlya and the Kola Peninsula are barely mentioned. The museum's website has some excellent polar links and details of Vicaar, an Arctic expedition and tourism agency, set up to earn money for the museum.

The Bread Museum

If your appetite for museums is unsated, carry on to the end of Kuznechniy pereulok and turn right onto Ligovskiy prospekt, to find the **Bread Museum** (Tues–Sat 10am–5pm; $1.50) at no. 73. Located on the fourth floor of a store (take a lift from the foyer), the museum traces the history of a commodity dear to Russian hearts. Traditionally, weddings, funerals, births and holy days each had their own special loaves, some as large as pillows. Peter the Great brought Germans over to run the city's first bakeries and then outraged the populace by imposing a bread tax. Baking remained a male profession until World War I, when women were employed to alleviate the labour shortage and bread queues that were a major cause of the February Revolution. There are horrific photos from the famine of the early 1920s, and a moving section on the Blockade, when the daily bread ration was little larger than a pack of cigarettes and contained ingredients such as sunflower husks and oak bark.

Along Zagorodniy prospekt

The area around present-day **Zagorodniy prospekt** ("avenue beyond the city") was virgin forest until the middle of the eighteenth century when, in an effort to develop the area, Empress Anna divided it between two regiments of the Imperial Guard: the Semyonovskiy and the Izmailovskiy. Their paths through the woods paved the way for future streets and their massive parade ground (twice the size of Marsovo pole) became the site of St Petersburg's Hippodrome and the Vitebsk Station.

By the latter half of the nineteenth century, Zagorodniy prospekt had developed into a fashionable residential area associated with the city's musical elite. The director of the Conservatory, Rubinstein, lived for a while at no. 9 and

Tchaikovsky spent a couple of years at no. 14. Just south of the intersection of streets known as the **Five Corners**, which witnessed violent clashes during three revolutions, is the **Rimsky-Korsakov Museum** (11am–6pm; closed Mon, Tues & the last Fri of each month; $1.50), located in the composer's former apartment on the third floor of the building in no. 28's courtyard. It contains over 250 items kept by his widow and descendants after his death in 1908, in anticipation of the opening of just such a museum: among them are two of his conductor's batons and a costume from his opera *The Snow Maiden*, designed by the artist Vrubel. The walls of the study are hung with portraits of composers Rimsky-Korsakov admired, including one of Glinka, the father of Russian musical nationalism. At weekly soirees in the sitting room, Chaliapin sang and Rachmaninov, Scriabin and Stravinsky played the piano – **concerts** still take place in the apartment every Wednesday from October onwards (℡113 32 08 for details and bookings). Another music-lovers' mecca is the **Jazz Philharmonic Hall** (see p.371) at no. 27, further along and across the road.

Pionerskaya ploshchad

Southwest of the Rimsky-Korsakov Museum, just to the east of Pushkinskaya metro, is the former stamping ground of the **Semyonovskiy Guards**, the second of the elite regiments founded by Peter before he became tsar. Their regimental parade ground – then known as Semyonovskiy plats – was the scene of the **mock execution of Dostoyevsky** and other members of the Petrashevsky Circle, a sadistic drama devised by Nicholas I. On December 22, 1849, after eight months in the Peter and Paul Fortress, the 21 men were brought here to face a firing squad. The first three were tied to a post (Dostoyevsky was in the next batch), hoods were pulled over their faces and the guards took aim, when an aide rode up with a proclamation and the general in charge read out the commutation of their sentences to *katorga* (hard labour). Two days later, fettered at the ankles, they began their 3000-kilometre trek to Omsk prison in Siberia. It was here, too, that the assassins of Alexander II were hanged in 1881. One of the Nihilists was so heavy that the rope broke twice, whereupon the crowd began calling for a reprieve, but to no avail. Public executions were subsequently discontinued for fear of civil disorder.

In Soviet times the parade ground became a park and was renamed Pionerskaya ploshchad after the Communist youth organization, the Pioneers, and became the site of the **Theatre of Young Spectators** (TYuZ). At the park entrance stands a larger-than-life statue of **Alexander Griboedov** (1795–1829), a soldier and diplomat turned playwright who got into trouble with the censors for his *Woe from Wit* and was arrested for his Decembrist connections, but later rehabilitated and made an envoy to Persia. Alas, on their arrival in Tehran, he and his party were murdered by a mob which sacked the Russian Embassy after an Armenian eunuch had taken refuge there. During Soviet times, his name was bestowed upon the city's loveliest canal, which had previously been named after Catherine the Great.

Rasputin on Gorokhovaya ulitsa

Heading from Zagorodniy prospekt northwest up Gorokhovaya ulitsa (Street of Peas) for 100m brings you to the gloomy residential building at no. 64 that once housed **Rasputin's apartment** – on the third floor at the rear of the courtyard (now a *kommunalka* and not open to visitors). The apartment was kept under permanent surveillance by the Tsarist Okhrana and, as noted by their agents, was visited regularly by Rasputin's aristocratic devotees and a host of other women hoping to win favours at court. Rumours abounded of orgies in which the participants formed a crucifix with their naked bodies; though the reality was much cruder: Rasputin swiftly serviced the ladies in a room containing only an icon and an iron bed, before he arose muttering, "Now, now, Mother. Everything is in order."

The street is also mentioned in Russian literature. The denouement of Dostoyevsky's *The Idiot* takes place in Rogozhin's house on Gorokhovaya ulitsa, "not far from Sadovaya ulitsa", while the Rasputin-like Stavrogin in *The Possessed* commits his crime on the street. Another fictional resident was the famously indolent Oblomov, in Goncharov's novel of the same name.

Vitebsk Station and Tekhnologicheskiy Institut

It's worth taking the metro to Pushkinskaya purely to see **Vitebsk Station** (Vitebskiy vokzal), which was the first train terminal in Russia when it opened in 1837, connecting St Petersburg with the palaces at Tsarskoe Selo and Pavlovsk. The existing station, built in 1904, is the finest **Style Moderne** edifice in St Petersburg, restored for the city's tercentenary. Its facade, halls and waiting rooms are a feast of Art Nouveau ironwork and stucco, tiles and stained-glass windows, with a grand stairway to the ex-Imperial Waiting Room, decorated with murals of the palatial destinations. Near the platforms serving the palaces stands a replica of a nineteenth-century steam train that once operated on the route. An early passenger wrote that "the train made almost one *verst* (kilometre) a minute . . . sixty *versts* an hour, a horrible thought!" Besides trains to the palaces, Vitebsk Station is the terminus for Ecolines coaches to Rīga, which leave from the square outside; the Ecolines ticket office is in the station (see p.20).

One stop further by metro, the interchange station and the square called **Tekhnologicheskiy Institut** take their name from the Technological Institute, whose lecture theatre hosted the first meeting of the short-lived St Petersburg Soviet of Workers' and Soldiers' Deputies, created during the 1905 Revolution. Under the leadership of Trotsky, Gorky and others, its executive committee assumed the responsibilities of government, issuing a spate of decrees from the Free Economic Society building across the square (no. 33), now called the **Plekhanov House**.

The Trinity Cathedral

Last but not least, west along 1-ya Krasnoarmeyskaya ulitsa (one stop on tram #28 or #34 from Tekhnologicheskiy Institut, or bus #10 down Voznesenskiy prospekt) stands the huge **Trinity Cathedral** (Troitskiy sobor), whose ink-blue **domes** – visible from all over this part of town – were once spangled with golden stars, like the nearby chapel on the corner of Izmailovskiy prospekt. The Orthodox config-uration of four domes surrounding a larger one dates back to the seventeenth century, when Patriarch Nikon banned tent-roofed churches in favour of a new style, theologically justified as a symbol of the four evangelists and "the seat of the Lord Himself". The cathedral, however, is purely Neoclassical: designed in 1828–35 by Stasov, its only **exterior** decoration consists of a frieze of seraphim beneath the cornice and a bas-relief above the portico.

In Tsarist times it was the garrison church of the Izmailovskiy Guards, front-ed by an enormous column made of captured Turkish cannons. It was here that Dostoyevsky married Anna Snitkina in 1867, four months after he hired her as a secretary (see p.218). The cathedral was closed down in 1938 and only reopened in 1990; its **interior** is devoid of any adornment, except icons.

Streets and squares

ploshchad Aleksandra Nevskovo	площадь Александра Невского
Bolshoy Kazechniy pereulok	Большой Казечный переулок
Furshtadtskaya ul.	Фурштадская ул.
Kirochnaya ul.	Кирочная ул.
1-ya Krasnoarmeyskaya ulitsa	1-я Красноармейская ул.
Kuznechniy pereulok	Кузнечный переулок
Ligovskiy prospekt	Лиговский проспект
Liteyniy prospekt	Литейный проспект
ul. Marata	ул. Марата
ul. Mayakovskovo	ул. Маяковского
ul. Pestelya	ул. Пестеля
ploshchad Rastrelli	площадь Растрелли
Shpalernaya ul.	Шпалерная ул.
Solyanoy pereulok	Соляной переулок
Tavricheskaya ul.	Таврическая ул.
Vladimirskiy prospekt	Владимирский проспект
ploshchad Vosstaniya	площадь Восстания
Zagorodniy prospekt	Загородный проспект

Metro stations

Ploshchad Aleksandra Nevskovo	Площадь Александра Невского
Chernyshevskaya	Чернышевская
Dostoevskaya	Достоевская
Ligovskiy Prospekt	Лиговский Проспект
Mayakovskaya	Маяковская
Pushkinskaya	Пушкинская
Tekhnologicheskiy Institut	Технологический Институт
Vladimirskaya	Владимирская
Ploshchad Vosstaniya	Площадь Восстания

Museums

Anna Akhmatova Museum	музей Анны Ахматовой
Arctic and Antarctic Museum	музей Арктики и Антарктики
Bread Museum	музей хлеба
Museum of Decorative and Applied Arts	музей Декоративно-прикладного искусства
Museum of the Defence of Leningrad	музей Обороны Ленинграда
Dostoyevsky Museum	музей-квартира Ф.М. Достоевского
Militia Museum	музей истории Милиции
Museum of Musical Instruments	музей Музыкальны Инструментов
Nekrasov Museum	музей-квартира Н.А. Некрасова
Rimsky-Korsakov Museum	музей-квартира Н.А. Римского-Корсакова
Suvorov Museum	музей А.В. Суворова
World of Water Museum	музей "Мир Воды"

The Southern Suburbs

The **Southern Suburbs**, largely open countryside until the mid-nineteenth century, cover a vast area beyond the Obvodniy Canal. The first buildings here were factories – some of the largest in the Tsarist empire – and the slum housing that grew up around them became home to a militant working class, which was instrumental in the revolutions of 1905 and 1917. Following the October Revolution, numerous housing projects were undertaken to replace the slum dwellings, while during the 1930s Stalin planned (and partially completed) a new city centre in these suburbs in an attempt to replace the old one, so closely associated with the *ancien régime*. Later on, during the Blockade, the front line ran close to the working-class Narva and Avtovo districts.

While it lacks the beauty of the city centre and the distances involved preclude casual sightseeing, it would be a shame to miss the dramatic **Victory Monument** and the **House of Soviets** on Moskovskiy prospekt, or the charming **Chesma Church**. Another lure is the fascinating **Literatorskie mostki** graveyard in the Volkov Cemetery, where many famous Russians are buried. If you're looking for Soviet icons and monuments, then the Constructivist buildings and elaborate **metro** stations of the Kirov district fit the bill, while train-spotters will head for the **Outdoor Railway Museum**. With the exception of the Volkov Cemetery, everywhere described is within walking distance of a metro station on the Moskovsko–Petrogradskaya or Kirovsko–Vyborgskaya lines, which intersect at Tekhnologicheskiy Institut I and II.

Moskovskiy prospekt

Moskovskiy prospekt is the city's longest avenue, a six-lane boulevard running 9km from Sennaya ploshchad in the centre out to the Victory Monument on ploshchad Pobedy. Envisaged by Stalin as the central axis of postwar Leningrad, it is laid out on a Cyclopean scale and makes an awesome introduction to the city as you drive in from the airport. While no one would suggest walking more than a block or two along the prospekt, it's worth viewing some of the vast edifices and richly appointed metro stations that once betokened a Soviet Leningrad, meant to outshine the pre-revolutionary city centre.

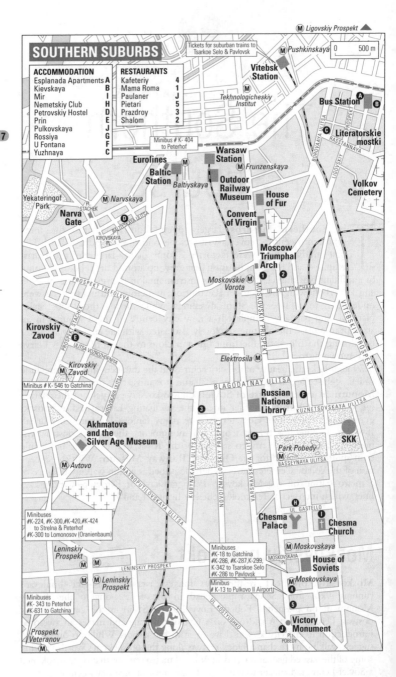

SOUTHERN SUBURBS

M Pushkinskaya   0   500 m

Vitebsk Station

ACCOMMODATION		RESTAURANTS	
Esplanada Apartments	A	Kafeteriy	4
Kievskaya	B	Mama Roma	1
Mir	I	Paulaner	J
Nemetskiy Club	H	Pietari	5
Petrovskiy Hostel	D	Prazdroy	3
Prin	E	Shalom	2
Pulkovskaya	J		
Rossiya	G		
U Fontana	F		
Yuzhnaya	C		

Tekhnologicheskiy Institut

Bus Station

Literatorskie mostki

Volkov Cemetery

Minibus # K- 404 to Peterhof

Warsaw Station

Eurolines

Baltic Station   M   Baltiyskaya

M Frunzenskaya

Outdoor Railway Museum

House of Fur

Yekateringof Park

M Narvskaya

Convent of Virgin

Narva Gate

PL STACHEK

BALTIYSKAYA ULITSA

KIROVSKIY PL

Moscow Triumphal Arch

Moskovskie Vorota M   1   2

UL KOLI TOMCHAKA

PROSPEKT TREFOLEVA

MOSKOVSKIY PROSPEKT

VITEBSKIY PROSPEKT

Kirovskiy Zavod   E

PROSPEKT STACHEK

ULITSA VOZROZHDENIYA

Kirovskiy Zavod   M

Elektrosila   M

Minibus # K- 546 to Gatchina

AVTOVSKAYA ULITSA

BLAGODATNAY ULITSA

Russian National Library   F

KUZNETSOVSKAYA ULITSA

3

Akhmatova and the Silver Age Museum

KUBINSKAYA ULITSA

NOVOIZMAILOVSKIY PROSPEKT

G

VARSHAVSKAYA ULITSA

Park Pobedy   M

BASSEYNAYA ULITSA

SKK

M Avtovo

KRASNOPUTILOVSKAYA ULITSA

Minibuses
#K-224, #K-300,#K-420,#K-424 to Strelna & Peterhof
#K-300 to Lomonosov (Oranienbaum)

UL. GASTELLO

Chesma Palace   H

I   **Chesma Church**

Leninskiy Prospekt   M   M

LENINSKIY PROSPEKT

Minibuses
#K-18 to Gatchina
#K-286, #K-287,K-299, K-342 to Tsarskoe Selo
#K-286 to Pavlovsk

M Moskovskaya

MOSKOVSKAYA PL

House of Soviets

M Leninskiy Prospekt

Minibus # K-13 to Pulkovo II Airport

M Moskovskaya   4

Minibuses
#K- 343 to Peterhof
#K-631 to Gatchina

N

UL. KOSTYUSHKO

5

J   **Victory Monument**

Prospekt Veteranov   M

PL. POBEDY

Tickets for suburban trains to Tsarkoe Selo & Pavlovsk

technology irresistible, but anyone wanting to know the facts will be stymied by the Russian-only captions and lack of brochures in any other language. There are postwar diesel locos in fetching colours and a red and green monster with the profiles of Lenin and Stalin on the front; armoured flatbeds for anti-aircraft cannons, and a massive TM-3-12 artillery train, used in the Winter War and again in 1941. While posing on the footplates is allowed, you can't enter any of the passenger carriages and there are no rides or hands-on experiences to enliven things, such as you'll find at other railway museums – for now, at least. The museum is hidden behind the derelict **Warsaw Station** on the Obvodniy Canal, set to be rebuilt as a museum extension. Hopefully, a place will be found for the forbidding **statue of Lenin** that glowers across the canal from its niche in the station's facade. See it while you can.

The museum is ten minutes' walk from Baltiyskaya metro, at the **Baltic Station**. From the square outside, minibuses run to Peterhof, and Eurolines buses depart for the West (see p.20). Otherwise there's no reason to stick around except to see the decor at **Baltiyskaya** metro, themed on the sea and maritime history. Its blue-grey marble walls and vaults resembling billowing sails are offset by bronze cameos of Russian admirals and a mosaic depicting the *Volley from the Aurora* in 1917.

Ploshchad Stachek and Yekateringof Park

Narvskaya, the next station, is equally striking, lauding the achievements of local workers in peace, revolution and war. Victory motifs and a sculpture of Lenin speaking atop an armoured car greet passengers in the vestibule, while underground there are ivory-hued marble walls and 48 columns sculpted with groups of miners, metallurgists, sailors and teachers at work, lit by crystal arcs flowing from the torches of the friezes.

You'll emerge on **ploshchad Stachek** (Strike Square), scene of the first of the many fatal clashes on "Bloody Sunday" (January 9, 1905). Tsarist troops fired without warning on the column of peaceful demonstrators heading for the Winter Palace, who were carrying portraits of the tsar and a white flag emblazoned with the message: "Soldiers! Do not fire on the people." In 1941, as the Nazis encircled Leningrad, a German motorcycle patrol managed to break through the Front and got as far as ploshchad Stachek, before it was annihilated.

At the centre of the square is the copper-plated **Narva Gate** (Narvskaya zastava), a diminutive triumphal arch erected to commemorate the Napoleonic Wars. The original arch was hastily designed by Quarenghi in wood, in order to greet the victorious Imperial armies returning from the west, but was later replaced by Stasov's present structure, crowned by a statue of Victory astride her six-horse chariot, painted a martial dark green.

The rest of the surrounding architecture dates from a redevelopment of the late 1920s, when Constructivism was still in vogue. Good examples of the genre are the convex facade of the **Gorky Palace of Culture**, beside the metro station, which was opened on the tenth anniversary of the October Revolution, and the department store opposite – not to mention the heroic **mural** on one of the buildings.

As part of the project, the nearby **Yekateringof Park** and palace founded by Peter the Great for his wife, Catherine, were given to the League of Young Communists, or Komsomol – who promptly burnt the palace down during a party. The superbly kitsch **Komsomol monument** at the park's entrance is one of the very few in St Petersburg to feature Stalin, in fading relief. Further in you'll find a small lake with pedaloes for rent, a fairground with carousels, pony rides and pensioners playing chess.

Kirovskaya ploshchad to Avtovo

To see how the plan continued, walk 200m down prospekt Stachek, to the vast megalopolis of **Kirovskaya ploshchad**, a Stalinist set piece centred on a huge, sixteen-metre-tall **statue of Kirov**, the assassinated Party boss (p.188). The southern side of the square is entirely taken up by a long **Constructivist building**, dating from 1926, which now houses a cinema at one end and the district administration offices in the eleven-storey tower at the other end. The square's other noteworthy Constructivist edifice is the first **school** to be built in the city after the Revolution, situated on the northwest corner of the square. Constructed in 1925–27, it has a convex facade and a ground plan in the vague shape of a hammer and sickle.

There's more worth seeing at the two metro stations after Narvskaya. **Kirovskiy Zavod** is named after a heavy engineering plant; the columns in its hall bear symbols of oil extraction, steel and power production, watched by a saturnine Lenin at the end of the platform. The factory was founded in 1801 as the Putilov Works, and soon became Russia's largest enterprise (employing over 40,000 people) and the cradle of the working-class movement. It was the dismissal of four *Putilovtsiy* that sparked the 1905 Revolution, while a lockout primed the overthrow of Tsarism in 1917. During the Blockade it was battered by Nazi artillery but production never ceased, though workers sometimes had to tie themselves to their benches to avoid fainting from hunger and exhaustion. After the war, the factory produced nuclear submarine turbines and other high-tech military items – a specialization that brought it to the verge of bankruptcy when the defence budget was slashed in the 1990s. Today, its finances are looking healthier thanks to arms sales to India, China and Malaysia, but much of the plant still lies idle.

The proximity of the frontline to **Avtovo** during the war might explain the lavishness of its metro station – and certainly the martial motifs that festoon the stairway to the platform, whose roof is upheld by 46 columns, thirty clad in white marble, and sixteen in cut, patterned glass, mirrored inside to conceal the concrete shafts that bear the weight. The Avtovo district makes an unlikely setting for the **Akhmatova and the Silver Age Museum** (Mon–Fri 10am–5.30pm; $1.75). Founded by admirers of the poetess Anna Akhmatova (see p.199), the display traces the lives and relationships of the poets and artists of Russia's "Silver Age", including such luminaries as Blok, Mandelstam, Roerich and Bakst. The museum is located ten minutes' walk from Avtovo station, at Avtovskaya ul. 14.

The Literatorskie mostki

Although Dostoyevsky feared that he would be buried there "beside all my enemies", few luminaries of pre-revolutionary Russian culture would have spurned a plot in the **Literatorskie mostki** (April–Oct 11am–7pm; Nov–March 11am–5pm; closed Thurs), an elite enclosure within the Volkov Cemetery. Among the better-known personalities interred here are the writers **Turgenev** and **Andreyev**, the poet **Blok**, the painter **Petrov-Vodkin** and the

Cemetery; but Stalin instead enshrined Lenin's body on Moscow's Red Square and proclaimed him a Titan. In the post-Communist era, St Petersburg considered a purge of its Soviet monuments and a special commission was established by the Mayor's office to decide which were of intrinsic value and which were too offensive to remain. All the major Lenin statues were spared. Besides this one, the most striking are at Moskovskya ploshschad and Warsaw Station, in the southern suburbs (see Chapter 7).

Kresty Prison

From the embankment beside ploshchad Lenina you can survey a bleak arc of the Neva between the most infamous buildings in the city. Across the river looms the headquarters of the secret police, the Bolshoy dom (p.205), while beyond the Arsenal on the Vyborg Side is Kresty Prison. During the 1930s and 1940s, the two "processed" scores of thousands of people, whose relatives traipsed between the buildings day after day, trying to discover the victims' fate. While the Bolshoy dom has lost its terrible grip on the population, ending up in Kresty is still to be feared by anyone arrested and charged by the Militia, for the conditions there are atrocious.

When **Kresty Prison** was first built in the reign of Catherine the Great, it was considered a model of its kind, taking its name – "Crosses" – from its double cross-shaped configuration. Here, Trotsky and other revolutionaries awaited trial in 1905, and the Bolsheviks incarcerated the entire Provisional Government except Kerensky in October 1917. During the mass **purges** of 1934–36, the poet Akhmatova queued for 21 months outside Kresty, with a host of other women, all seeking news. One day, she was recognized by a stranger, who sidled up and whispered, "Can you describe this?" Akhmatova obliged with *Requiem*, a series of prose poems that opens with an account of the episode and concludes:

> And from my motionless bronze-lidded sockets,
> May the melting snow like teardrops slowly trickle.
> And a prison dove coo somewhere over and over
> As the ships sail softly down the flowing Neva.

Nowadays, it is a pre-trial prison for "non-politicals" who spend up to two years awaiting trial. As Kresty was built to hold 3000 prisoners and currently has over ten thousand, they sleep ten or fifteen to a cell, occupying triple bunk beds in shifts. The daily sum budgeted to feed each prisoner ($0.20) would mean an exclusive diet of pearl barley soup, were it not for vegetables from Kresty's rooftop gardens. As once happened at the Peter and Paul Fortress and Shlisselburg – both now museums to Tsarist tyranny – prisoners receive their rations through hatches whose lids drop down to make tiny tables, called *kormushki* (swill troughs). The filthy, overcrowded cells are an ideal vector for tuberculosis, which is rife in the Russian penal system, where 90,000 prisoners are thought to be infected, one fifth of them with multi-drug-resistant TB.

Despite visits by Putin, Yakovlev and human rights NGOs, conditions are so abysmal that many prisoners beg to plead guilty just to be moved to a labour camp where things aren't so bad. The authorities make little attempt to prevent communications between prisoners and their loved ones, who send messages back and forth by slingshot or blowpipe from their cell windows or by semaphoring from the embankment. Bizarrely, Kresty's Preliminary Investigations Department offers a guided tour of the prison **chapel** – previously turned into a warders' club with a portrait of "Iron Felix" and the motto "Do as Dzerzhinsky would have done!" where the altar used to be – and in-house **museum**, with exhibits on famous prisoners and items crafted by others, such as a cops 'n' robbers chess set made from bits of chewed, dried, glazed bread. Visitors are cat-called by prisoners and the whole **tour** ($8.30 per person) reeks of voyeurism. Tours start on Saturday and Sunday at noon, 1.30pm and 5pm; groups of ten or more can visit any time by arrangement with Mr Zhitinov, of Investigations Dept. 1; the fax (ⓕ 248 89 49) should state when and how many people, and their willingness to pay in cash. Better to donate your money to organizations trying to improve conditions at Kresty, such as the Russian NGO Prison and Freedom (ⓦ www.prison.org) or the UK-based International Prison Studies Group (ⓦ www.prisonstudies.org).

St Samson's Cathedral

Behind the prison and the station is a hinterland of freight yards and factories. One of the earliest plants on the Vyborg Side was the Russian Diesel Factory, founded in 1824 by the Swedish immigrant **Emmanuel Nobel**, whose son, Ludwig, began producing pig iron here in 1862. Ludwig's son, Alfred, famously went on to invent dynamite and expiate his guilt by founding the Nobel prizes. Though most factories were nationalized soon after the Revolution, the economic demands of the Civil War meant that few benefits accrued to the proletariat until the early 1930s, when a Constructivist **workers' club** was built on the corner of Bolshoy Sampsonievskiy prospekt and Grenedarskaya ulitsa.

Across the road, **St Samson's Cathedral** (Sampsonievskiy sobor) is an anachronism amid the smokestacks, being one of the oldest buildings in the city.

Lenin's last secret address

A faded scarlet **mural** on the side of a tenement block is a mute reminder of **Lenin's last secret address**, Serdobolskaya ul. 1, where he stayed in the apartment of Party member Margarita Sofanova after returning from Finland. While the Central Committee procrastinated, Lenin feared that the moment for a coup would pass: on the night of October 24, he quit the flat, leaving a note reading, "I've gone where you didn't want me to go. Goodbye. Ilyich", and boarded a tram for the Smolniy. He and his companion, Eino Rahja, managed to bluff their way through several checkpoints and into the Smolniy, to join their colleagues. While the rest may be history, the idea that Lenin instantly assumed control of a well-planned coup owes much to Soviet propaganda. Though every textbook states that it occurred on October 25, 1917, the exact **date of the Bolshevik Revolution** is by no means certain. A 1962 conference of distinguished Soviet historians ended in violent disagreement – with one faction asserting the Revolution was on the morning of October 24, another, the afternoon of the same day, and a third, October 22. The implications are that the coup may have been well under way – if not virtually over by the time that Lenin arrived, unannounced – although the mural naturally emphasizes his central role and even includes a map of his route to the Smolniy. Should you fancy seeing the mural, it's near the corner of Bolshoy Sampsonievskiy prospekt, about 2km from St Samson's Cathedral (take minibus #K-262), or twenty minutes' walk from Chernaya Rechka metro, via Torzhkovskaya ulitsa.

A voluptuous sea-green edifice with a Muscovite-style gate-belfry, completed in 1740, it is thought to have witnessed the **secret wedding of Catherine the Great and Potemkin** in 1774, which was attended only by Potemkin's nephew, a lady-in-waiting and a chamberlain. Secret marriages weren't uncommon among the Romanovs: Peter the Great privately wed his mistress before he felt it wise to do so publicly; Empress Elizabeth plighted her troth with Razumovsky, but didn't acknowledge it; while Nicholas I never found out that his daughter Maria had secretly wed a Stroganov. The interior is notable for its Baroque **iconostasis**, which can be seen only on a pre-arranged **tour** (☏315 43 61; $8.50 group rate) or during **services** (Fri, Sat & Sun at 5pm). As the main gates are locked at other times, you can't even enter the grounds to view the **graves** of three courtiers executed on the orders of Empress Anna's paranoid lover, Count Biron, who was said to treat "Men like horses and horses like men". On the other side of the street stands a swashbuckling **statue of Peter the Great**.

Piskarov Memorial Cemetery

Until 1990 the **Piskarov Memorial Cemetery** (Piskaryovskoe memorialnoe kladbishche; daily 10am–5/6pm) in the city's northern suburbs used to be the first stop on Intourist excursions – a pointed reminder to visitors of the city's sacrifices in the war against fascism. Today, few tour groups visit the cemetery, but the grounds are still tidily kept and wreaths are laid every May 9 – Victory Day. Should you wish to pay your respects to the 670,000 citizens who died during the Blockade, the cemetery lies way out along prospekt Nepokoryonnykh – the "Avenue of the Unconquered". Take the metro to Lesnaya station and then bus #123, or catch bus #107 from the

---

Life during the Blockade

The Blockade may not have lasted for a full nine hundred days of popular legend, but the agonies associated with it defy exaggeration. Between early September 1941 – when the Germans cut off rail links to the city and began bombarding it – and February 7, 1944, when the first train-load of food pulled into Finland Station, Leningrad was dependent on its own resources and whatever could be brought across Lake Ladoga on the icy "Road of Life" in winter. The result was slow **starvation**, as daily rations shrank to 500–600 calories per person. In November 1941, the bread ration was 250 grammes per day for factory workers and 125 grammes for the other two-thirds of the population; the "bread" constituted fifty percent rye flour, the rest being bran, sawdust or anything else to hand. People boiled leather or wallpaper to make broth, and ate cats and dogs. Some even resorted to cannibalism so that citizens feared to walk past alleyways, lest they be garrotted and butchered; if discovered, cannibals were generally executed on the spot.

Although **bombardments** killed seventeen thousand people, far more deaths were caused by starvation and the cold. In winter there was no heating, no water, no electricity and no public transport; amidst blizzards, Leningraders queued for bread, drew water from frozen canals, scavenged for firewood and dragged their dead on sledges to the cemeteries. Eventually, the living grew too weak and the dead too numerous for individual funerals, and corpses were left at designated spots to be collected for burial in mass graves.

Finland Station to the end of the line and then ride two stops on bus #123; ask to be let off at the cemetery.

The cemetery's **origins** lie in the mass burials that took place near the village of Piskarovka from February 1942 onwards. As nobody had the strength to dig the frozen ground, sappers blasted pits into which the unidentified bodies were tipped; some 470,000 people were interred like this. After the war, it took five years of grisly labour to transform the burial ground into a memorial cemetery, which was solemnly opened in 1960. Some might find its poignancy diminished by the regimented layout and cheery flowerbeds, but its sad power is palpable on rainy days and, above all, in winter.

At the entrance are two **memorial halls** containing grim photo-montages and personal effects, such as a facsimile of the diary of 11-year-old Tanya Savicheva, whose entire family starved to death (she was later evacuated, but also died). On display, too, is the cemetery register, open at a page bearing the entries: "February, 1942: 18th – 3,241 bodies; 19th – 5,559; 20th – 10,043". Further into the cemetery, beyond the trees, an **eternal flame**, kindled by a torch lit from Marsovo pole, flickers on a terrace above the necropolis.

Flanking its 300-metre-long central avenue are 186 low, grassy mounds, each with a granite slab that simply records the year of burial and whether the dead were soldiers (marked by a red star) or civilians (with a hammer and sickle). At the far end, a six-metre-tall, bronze **statue of Mother Russia** by Vera Isayeva and Robert Taurit holds a garland of oak and laurel leaves, as if to place it on the graves of the fallen. The **memorial wall** behind is inscribed with a poem by the Blockade survivor Olga Bergholts, which asserts:

> We cannot remember all their noble names here,
> So many lie beneath the eternal granite,
> But of those honoured by this stone,
> Let no one forget
> Let nothing be forgotten.

Chernaya rechka and Novaya Derevnya

Chernaya rechka – or "Black Stream" – is an appropriate name for what is now a high-rise, industrialized zone; its only claim to fame is that it was in a meadow in this locality that **Pushkin's duel** with D'Anthès took place, on January 27, 1837. On the centenary of Pushkin's death a granite **obelisk** was erected on the spot, in what is now a park alongside Kolomyazhskiy prospekt, and a statue of the poet was installed in Chernaya Rechka metro station. Lermontov, too, fought a duel here with the son of the French ambassador, de Barantes, but escaped alive, only to be killed in another duel the following year in the Caucasus (where, ironically, he had been exiled for fighting the duel with Barantes).

To the west of the metro station lies the residential **Novaya Derevnya** (New Village) district, which sprawls along the highway opposite the Kirov Islands; the only real reason to make it out this far is to visit the Buddhist Temple.

The Buddhist Temple

Novaya Derevnya's star attraction lies way out at Primorskiy prospekt 91, near the bridge over to Yelagin Island (see p.194). St Petersburg's **Buddhist Temple**, or *datsan*, is smaller than the city's mosque, synagogue and cathedrals, yet expresses its faith and cultural heritage no less vividly. Sadly, the facade has been under scaffolding for years, so you can't admire its Tibetan-style sloping walls, pagoda spire and red-and-gold portico surmounted by totemic statues, but the joss-stick-scented **prayer hall** is lovely. Besides daily **services** at 9am, the sixteen-day New Year festival (late Feb/early March) and other holy days are celebrated here by the city's Buddhist community. Most of Russia's Buddhists are Mongols from the Buryat region of central Siberia that was taken into the Tsarist Empire centuries ago. Buddhism was recognized as a "traditional" religion of the empire like Orthodoxy, Islam and Judaism, and the Soviets treated it less harshly than the others until a Buryat revolt in 1929 led Stalin to kill 35,000 Mongols and shut all the monasteries and temples – this *datsan* became an entomology institute. Since it was handed back to the Buryat Republic in 1991, Russia's Duma has restored the status of the four "traditional" religions and obliged all other faiths to register with the local police as "cults".

The *datsan* belongs to the Gelugpa or Yellow Hat sect of Tibetan Buddhism whose spiritual leader is the Dalai Lama. Its ownership is sporadically disputed by two Buddhist groups; one controls the temple (☎430 0341; ⓦwww .datsan.spb.ru) and the other has a renegade website (ⓦhttp://snark .ptc.sbpu.ru/~use/datsan). The building itself was constructed in 1900–15 at the instigation of Nicholas II's Buddhist physician Pyotr Badmaev, who had long urged the annexation of Manchuria to bring all Buddhist Mongols into the empire, and was thus partly responsible for the war with Japan that began four years after work started on the temple – unlike the Lhasa scholar Agwan-Khamba, who helped Badmaev get the details right.

You can reach the temple (and Yelagin Island) by **minibus** #K–411 or #K–416 from Chernaya Rechka metro; any bus or minibus heading south along Lipovaya alleya from Staraya Derevnya metro; or by #K-400 from the Finland Station.

Vyborg Side

Streets and squares

Arsenalnaya nab.	Арсенальная наб.
Bolshoy Sampsonievskiy prospekt	Большой Сампсониевский пр.
Kolomyazhskiy prospekt	Коломяжский пр.
ul. Lebedeva	ул. Лебедева
Lesnoy prospekt	Лесной пр.
Lipova alleya	Липова аллея
prospekt Nepokoryonnykh	пр. Непокорённых
Primorskiy prospekt	Приморский пр.
Serdobolskaya ul.	Сердобольская ул.
Sverdlovskaya nab.	Свердловская наб.

Metro stations

Chernaya Rechka	Чёрная речка
Lesnaya	Лесная
Ploshchad Lenina	площадь Ленина
Ploshchad Muzhestva	площадь Мужества
Staraya Derevnya	Старая Деревня
Vyborgskaya	Выборгская

Sights and monuments

Buddhist Temple	Буддийский храм
Finland Station	Финляндский вокзал
Piskarov Memorial Cemetery	Пискарёвское мемориальное кладбище
St Samson's Cathedral	Сампсониевский собор

Out of
the City

Out of the City

The Imperial palaces

The Russian Imperial court was the largest and most extravagant in Europe, and the **Imperial palaces**, established outside St Petersburg during the eighteenth century, are its most spectacular legacy. During the golden age of autocracy, these estates grew ever more ostentatious, demonstrating the might of the Romanov dynasty through the sheer luxuriance of its residences. Largely designed by foreign architects, but constructed by Russian craftsmen using the Empire's vast natural resources of gold, marble, malachite, porphyry, lapis lazuli and amber, the palaces now count among the most important cultural monuments in Russia.

The peripatetic nature of **court life** meant that each ruler divided his or her time between several palaces, remodelling them as they saw fit. Initially, the palaces functioned as magnificent stage sets, against which scenes of murder, passion and intrigue were played out, but as St Petersburg grew ever more politically volatile, they became a place of refuge for the country's rulers. After the Revolution, the palaces were opened and ordinary citizens were invited to feast their eyes on the awesome facades and opulent interiors – the fruits of centuries of exploitation.

During **World War II**, all of the palaces except Oranienbaum lay within Nazi-occupied territory. Peterhof and Strelna bore the brunt of artillery barrages from Soviet-held Kronstadt, and were systematically looted by the Germans, who dynamited, burned and booby-trapped the other palaces as they fell back before the Soviet advance in 1944. This "cultural destruction" was one of the charges brought against the Nazis at the Nuremburg Trials by Soviet prosecutors who set up a special commission to assess the damage. It was years before any of the palaces were reopened to the public, and the fact that they were reconstructed at all seems even more incredible than their creation.

Peterhof and **Tsarskoe Selo** are the most elaborate and popular of the palaces, followed – roughly in order of merit – by **Pavlovsk**, **Gatchina**, **Oranienbaum** and **Strelna**. All the palaces (but not all the towns in which they stand) have reverted to their pre-revolutionary **names** (as used in this chapter), but the Soviet titles of three of them are still often used by Russians: Petrodvorets (Peterhof), Pushkin (Tsarskoe Selo) and Lomonosov (Oranienbaum). These replaced the original names, which were considered to be too reactionary or too Germanic, while Gatchina was once briefly called Trotsk (after Trotsky).

Visiting the palaces

Minibuses are the easiest way to reach the palaces: the points of departure for services to Stelna, Peterhof, Tsarskoe Selo, Pavlovsk, Oranienbaum and Gatchina are all located close to metro stations, and shown on our map of the

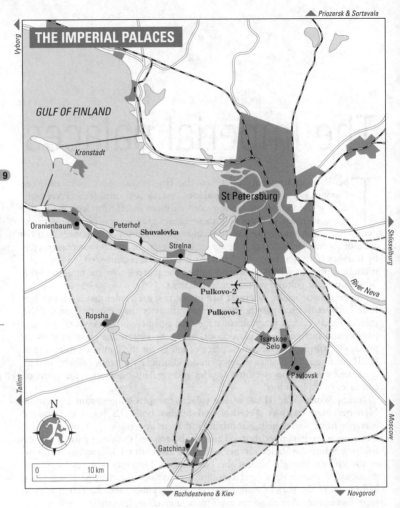

THE IMPERIAL PALACES

▲ *Priozersk & Sortavala*

◄ *Vyborg*

GULF OF FINLAND

Kronstadt

St Petersburg

► *Shlisselburg*

Oranienbaum   ● *Peterhof*   **Shuvalovka**

Strelna

Pulkovo-2

Pulkovo-1

Ropsha

Tsarskoe Selo ●

Pavlovsk ●

◄ *Tallinn*

► *Moscow*

N

Gatchina

0 ————— 10 km

▼ *Rozhdestveno & Kiev*   ▼ *Novgorod*

River Neva

Southern Suburbs (p.224). Services run every ten to twenty minutes, and since you buy a ticket on board, there's no need to queue or worry about finding the right ticket kiosk – which isn't the case with the **suburban train** system (*prigorodniy poezd* or *elektrichka*). Though trains are nearly as frequent as minibuses at weekends, they don't run at all between 10am and noon on weekdays, and foreigners are liable to be confused by the fact that the ticket kiosks (*prigorodniy kassy*) for these services are in a separate side hall, or outside the station. Last but not least are the **hydrofoils** that zoom across the Gulf to Peterhof during the summer – a highly scenic approach, but an expensive one. Full transport details appear in the "Practicalities" boxes accompanying each account.

It's also possible to visit the more popular palaces on **organized tours**, which range from upmarket excursions offered by the international hotels ($30 per person and upwards) to inexpensive trips on tour buses which depart from outside the Winter Palace and Gostiniy dvor ($5–7, payable in rubles; tickets available from kiosks outside Gostiniy dvor). As the latter cater to locals, the commentary is in Russian only; admission tickets aren't included in the price.

At all the palaces, dual **ticket prices** apply: low for Russians; much higher for foreigners, ranging from $3 to $13 and payable in rubles. Since a separate ticket is required for each palace or pavilion, the entrance fees soon mount up (**students** get a fifty-percent discount); if you wish to take **photographs** or use a **video camera** indoors, you'll need to buy a permit. The *kassa* will often be away from the palace itself, in a wooden booth or kiosk. On entry, many of the palaces require you to put on felt overshoes (*tapochki*) to protect their parquet floors.

Guided tours are on offer at most palaces, though invariably only in Russian; although you're expected to join a group, it's easy enough to catch up with the one in front, or fall behind to enjoy the rooms in peace. If you really want a tour in English it's sometimes possible to tack onto a pre-paid group and listen to their guide. Keep an eye out, too, for the palaces' various **temporary exhibitions**, featuring anything from Fabergé eggs to hitherto neglected aspects of Tsarist history.

Strelna

Only 23km from St Petersburg along the Gulf of Finland, **Strelna**, built on land wrested from Sweden during the Northern War, was the site of Peter the Great's original attempt to create a seaside palace to rival Versailles. In 1715, the **Wooden Palace** was built for Peter to live in while overseeing work on the great stone **Konstantin Palace** and its grounds, criss-crossed with canals and girdled by reservoirs. After five years' work, however, he realized that it was impossible to create the high-spurting fountains he desired without installing pumps, and that the palace's sea canal was prone to silt up – and therefore turned his attention to another site further east, which became Peterhof.

Thereafter, the Wooden Palace served as an overnight halt for journeys along the Gulf, while the stone palace remained unfinished until the reign of Empress Elizabeth. The home of grand dukes up until the Revolution, it later became a training school for the "Conquest of the North" and was pulverized during World War II. Whereas the Wooden Palace was restored under the aegis of the Peterhof Museum Reserve in the 1990s, fixing up the Konstantin Palace was beyond anyone's budget until Putin decided to make it the Russian equivalent of Camp David and the venue for the G8 Summit in 2003. Since then it has been grudgingly open to visitors, but its anodyne interior doesn't compare with the other palaces; its interest lies in its status as a head of state's residence – unlike the Wooden Palace, which is a genuine curiosity. And for those with kids or a love of kitsch, there's the recently opened **Shuvalovka Village**, 3km down the road.

The Konstantin Palace

Externally, the **Konstantin Palace** (Konstantinovskiy dvorets; 11am–5pm; closed Wed) is impressive: a vast buff, brown and khaki edifice on a lofty terrace overlooking a park stretching to the shores of the Gulf, enclosed by a high fence topped with gilded eagles and security cameras. Don't even think about getting inside without booking an **excursion**, which entails faxing (Ⓕ438 58 84) the names and passport details of everyone involved, the time and language of the tour and a contact phone number. Besides the group fee of $85 (for up to fifteen people), there's an entrance charge of $4.30 per person; opening hours may be curtailed at short notice owing to state events (Ⓣ438 53 51 for information).

Rigorous security checks and rude tour guides rub in the lacklustre interior, whose decor and furnishings hardly seem worth the $300 million spent on the palace, "donated" by LUKoil and other companies. Visitors see the mirrored **ballroom** designed by Stackenschneider – used for the G8 Summit – and three **exhibitions** drawn from the collections of the Hermitage, Peterhof and the Naval Museum. A guide relates the history of the palace since Tsar Paul gave it to his second son, Konstantin, and its heyday under several grand dukes with similar forenames or patronymics – the last, Dmitri Konstantinovich, renounced the palace after the February Revolution and moved into a house in the grounds, but was nonetheless shot by the Bolsheviks. Strelna is best known, however, for its association with his brother, **Konstantin Konstantinovich** (1858–1915), a poet, translator and playwright under the *nom de plume* of "K.R." (Konstantin Romanov), who fathered nine children but was also a secret homosexual, as his diaries posthumously revealed. Tours conclude with a wander through the **park**, bisected by a great canal choked with waterlilies.

The Wooden Palace

Further west, on a ridge overlooking the Gulf, Peter's **Wooden Palace** (Derevyanniy dvorets; 10.30am–5pm; closed Mon & the last Tues of each month; $3) is a charming, two-storey building painted yellow and white. While its decor is largely of the Petrine era – when wallpaper was a fashionable novelty – the palace's furnishings span almost two hundred years, since it was also used by later rulers. One of the finest exhibits is the weighty travel chest of Alexander III, incorporating a slide-out bed, folding desk, chairs, washstand, kitchen and homeopathic pharmacy, plus all kinds of implements including a device for stretching gloves.

Another room is devoted to pastimes: Peter loved chess and draughts, while his female successors preferred cards (playing for money was forbidden, so courtiers gambled for diamonds instead). In the **dining room**, with its beautiful tiled stove, notice the unique samovar with two taps belonging to Catherine the Great, who drank her tea with milk in the English fashion. Peter's **bedroom** has a four-poster curtained in green felt, with a patchwork quilt sewn by his wife, Catherine I, while his **study** contains a device for warming his feet while he worked at the desk. The final rooms are more formal, presaging the second-floor **Upper Hall**, adorned with Chinese vases, Japanese bronzes and European paintings.

Outside, the **garden** sports flowerbeds, glazed urns and fountains on its seaward side, and an apiary and vegetable plots to the rear which once supplied the palace with food. It was here, during the reign of Empress Anna, that potatoes were first grown in Russia – initially just for their flowers, which were worn at balls as a fashionable accessory. A little further on, a wooden cross and shrine mark the site of a church and bell tower, destroyed during the war. Sadly, nothing remains of Peter the Great's treehouse, where he used to enjoy smoking a pipe and watching ships on the Gulf in the evenings.

Practicalities

Strelna is easily reached from St Petersburg or Peterhof by **train** (alight at Strelna station and follow Frontovaya ulitsa to the Petersburg highway, then turn right and keep going till you cross the canal – the Wooden Palace lies across the road); any of the **minibuses** (#K-224, #K-300, #K-420 & #K-424) that shuttle between Peterhof and Avtovo metro station in St Petersburg; or by **tram** #36 from Avtovo, which terminates 500m short of the Konstantin Palace. Minibuses can drop you at the Wooden Palace or Shuvalovka, on request. There are a few nondescript **cafés** in Strelna, but the nearest proper **restaurant** is at Shuvalovka. While Strelna isn't an obvious place to **stay**, it would be churlish not to mention the *Baltic Star Hotel* (☎438 57 00, ⓦwww.balticstar-hotel.ru; ❼). Unveiled for the G8 Summit, in a former naval academy just along from Putin's palace, it epitomizes exclusivity and high security. A room here, though, is nothing as to what oligarchs in need of seclusion with the president are prepared to pay for palatial "Cottages" near the Gulf – rented for $5000 a day.

Shuvalovka Village

Another attraction in this neck of the woods is **Shuvalovka Village**, a theme park of "traditional" Russian life, midway between the Wooden Palace and Peterhof. Named after a village owned by Count Shuvalov that existed in the eighteenth century, it consists of photogenic log-buildings in the vernacular style of the north, with deep porches and eaves, carved gables, window-frames and shutters. Masquerading as farmhouses, the largest are really a hotel with a *banya* for guests; a **restaurant** serving Russian cuisine (dishes $4–25) and flavoured vodkas; and a crafts-cum-souvenir emporium. A **windmill**, an exact replica of a well-to-do peasant's house and a **pottery** and blacksmith's **forge** where you can watch craftsmen at work, provide a fig leaf for naked commercialism – but any pretence at authenticity is cast aside at the **beerhouse**, resembling a sixteenth-century Novgorod longship. **Folklore festivals** are staged on the meadow: singing and round dances from mid-December through to New Year, with more of the same plus heaps of pancakes on *Maslenitsa* (see p.52). For details call ☎427 53 93 or visit ⓦwww.russian-village.ru. There are plans afoot to turn the nearby Znamenka and Mikhailkovka estates into tourist attractions and create other "folk" theme parks along the Peterhof road.

Peterhof (Petrodvorets)

As the first of the great Imperial palatial ensembles to be established outside St Petersburg, **Peterhof** embodies nearly three hundred years of Tsarist self-aggrandizement. As you'd expect from its name (meaning "Peter's Court" in German, and pronounced "Petergof" in Russian), its founder was **Peter the Great**. Flushed with triumph from the Northern War against Sweden, he decided to build a sumptuous palace and town beside the Gulf, following the construction of his island fortress of Kronstadt, which secured the seaborne approaches to the city.

After an abortive attempt at Strelna, Peterhof was selected as the site owing to its more favourable hydrography and coastline, which permitted the great fountains and access by water that Peter desired. Architects scrambled to keep

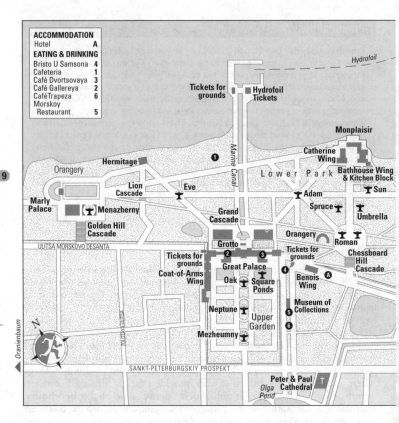

ACCOMMODATION	
Hotel	**A**
EATING & DRINKING	
Bristo U Samsona	4
Cafeteria	1
Café Dvortsovaya	3
Café Gallereya	2
CaféTrapeza	6
Morskoy Restaurant	5

up with the stream of projects issuing from his pen, while visiting ambassadors were often obliged to join the tsar in labouring on the site. Even so, Peterhof's existing Great Palace wasn't built until the reign of **Empress Elizabeth**, when court life became more opulent, reaching its apogee during the reign of **Catherine the Great**, whose acquaintance with Peterhof dated back to her loveless marriage to Peter III (see p.255). Although Catherine's immediate successors preferred other palaces, **Nicholas I** returned the court to Peterhof, building the Cottage Palace in the Alexandria Park, where the Imperial family lived with minimal pomp, reflecting the later Romanovs' creeping embourgeoisement.

In 1944, after Peterhof had been liberated from Nazi occupation, the authorities decided that its Germanic name was no longer appropriate and replaced it with its Russian equivalent, "Petrodvorets" (pronounced "Petrodvaryets"). In 1992, however, the palace officially reverted to its former name, Peterhof – although the **town** itself is still called **Petrodvorets**.

Unsurprisingly, the palace and park are the setting for several **festivals**, including the opening and closing of the "fountain season" (see opposite) and concerts and ballet in the grounds and the throne room of the palace during the White Nights in June. The latter are held under the aegis of the "Palaces of St Petersburg" festival, which also involves Tsarskoe Selo and Pavlovsk. For

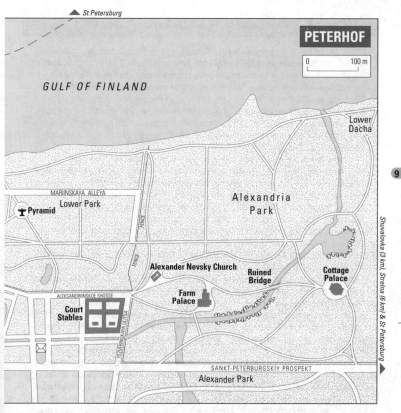

details, see the *St Petersburg Times* or *Where St Petersburg*. To whet your appetite for Peterhof, visit the Museum Reserve's **website**, Ⓦ www.peterhof.org.

The Marine Canal and Grand Cascade

The **grounds of Peterhof** are open daily from 9am to 8pm. You can walk through the Upper Garden free of charge, but a **ticket** ($8.50) is required to enter the Lower Park and gain access to the palaces – though admission is free once the fountains have been turned off at 5pm (6pm at weekends), and the daytime charge is reduced to $6 in the winter, when the fountains don't work at all. Peterhof's fountains were described by Alexandre Benois as "the symbolic expression of the sea's dominion, the mist that rises from the waves as they surge towards its shore", and the **fountain season** (mid-May to early Oct) is glorified by opening and closing **ceremonies** on the first Saturday or Sunday of June, and in the first or second week of October, with concerts, ballet and fireworks.

Approached by hydrofoil, the Great Palace rises like a golden curtain at the far end of the **Marine Canal** (Morskoy kanal), which flows through Peterhof's Lower Park and once formed an approach route for yachts. The granite-banked canal is flanked by 22 marble basins spurting water, whose splashing mingles with the oom-pah of a brass band dressed in Petrine-era costumes. Follow the

Practicalities

When to go is a tricky question. Although Peterhof's grounds are open daily (9am–8pm), its fountains operate only from June to October (11am–5pm; till 6pm at weekends), and most of its palaces are closed on Monday (the Great Palace also on the last Tues of each month). Two, however, shut on other days, namely Monplaisir (Wed) and the Catherine Wing (Thurs). This makes Fridays and weekends – when it is predictably the most crowded – the only time when everything is sure to be open. Opening days in winter are further limited: Monplaisir is closed from October to May and the Catherine Wing, Marly Palace and Cottage Palace are open only at weekends from October to April.

Getting there from St Petersburg is fairly straightforward. From late May to mid-September (weather permitting), **hydrofoils** (30–40min; $13.50 one way) speed across the Gulf of Finland to Peterhof, a trip that offers a splendid first glimpse of the Great Palace and a distant view of Kronstadt. Three firms run hydrofoils: Russian Cruises, from the Hermitage jetty (every 30min, 10am–6pm); Davranov Travel, from Universitetskaya nab. by the Academy of Sciences (hourly, 10.30am–1.30pm); and Alien, from the jetty by the Senate (hourly, 11am–6pm). Vessels and fares are identical, but tickets aren't interchangeable. If you're planning to return by hydrofoil, don't leave it too late, as long queues start forming from 4pm; the last hydrofoil leaves Peterhof at 6pm.

Alternatively, you can get there by public transport for about $2. **Minibuses** from outside the Baltic Station (#K-404) and Avtovo (#K-224, #K-300, #K-420 & #K-424) and Prospekt Veteranov (#K-343) metro stations take about an hour if traffic isn't bad, and can drop you right outside Peterhof's Upper Garden. **Suburban trains** from the Baltic Station (5.45am–midnight every 15–30min; 40min) aren't affected by traffic, but when you get off at Noviy Petergof station (not Stariy Petergof) you'll need to catch a #350, #351, #352, #353, #354, #355 or #359 bus to the palace grounds (10min). Or you can opt for one of the daily **coach tours** run by Davranov Travel and other firms with kiosks outside Gostiniy dvor; the cost per person ($4–5) doesn't include admission tickets.

Visitors need separate **tickets** to enter Peterhof's grounds (sold near the jetty, the Benois Wing and on ul. Morskovo Desanta) and each palace (sold *in situ*). If you haven't got much time, the highlights are the Great Palace, Monplaisir, the Lower Park and the Cottage Palace. The Grand Cascade, the jewel in Peterhof's crown, can be enjoyed for free, though you have to pay to visit the Grotto.

Eating and accommodation

The cheap *Bistro U Samsona* (daily 10am–9pm) near the Benois Wing serves soup, hot snacks and cakes, superior to the junk food on offer at the crowded cafeteria (daily 10am–7pm) to the west of the Marine Canal. Foreign tour groups are usually fed at the *Café Dvortsove* (daily 10am–8pm) or the fancier *Café Gallereya* (same hours) on the ground floor of the Great Palace, facing the Grand Cascade – both take credit cards. Just outside the palace grounds are two dearer options: the quaint non-smoking *Café Trapeza* (noon–10pm, closed Mon), serving such delicacies as grilled prawns, and the nautically themed *Morskoy Restaurant* (daily noon–midnight; ☏427 52 25), by the Museum of Collections, which specializes in seafood and game dishes.

Given the regular transport between Peterhof and St Petersburg, there's no need **to stay** overnight unless you fancy hitting the sights before the day-trippers arrive. At the time of writing, the hostel next door to the Benois Wing was being converted into a three-star **hotel** similar to the *Catherine Hotel* at Tsarskoe Selo (see p.265), so you'll have to make enquiries on the spot.

canal southwards from the hydrofoil jetty and you'll come to the **Voronikhin Colonnades**, named after the architect who designed this pair of Neoclassical pavilions that flank the enormous circular basin below the Grand Cascade.

The **Grand Cascade** (Bolshoy kaskad) is the pride of Peterhof, with water cascading over the blue-and-yellow ceramic steps and 142 jets spurting from 64 sources, including gilded **statues** and bas-reliefs. In the circular basin at the bottom, the glittering muscular figure of Samson rending the jaws of a ferocious lion symbolizes Russia's victory over Sweden in the Northern War: the lion is the heraldic beast of Sweden and the decisive battle of Poltava occurred on St Samson's Day (June 27) in 1709.

If you're curious about Peterhof's waterworks it's worth visiting the split-level **Grotto** beneath the Cascade (closed in winter; $3). The uppermost grotto is lined with tufa rocks and was used for informal parties, while in the lower grotto jets of water are triggered to squirt anyone tempted by the fruit on the table. The giant pipes that feed the fountains were originally made of wood and were maintained by a special Fountain Corps of men and boys – the latter being employed to crawl through the pipes to repair them. Tickets are sold from a hatch in the side of the Great Palace, overlooking the cascade.

The Great Palace

The yellow, white and gold **Great Palace** (Bolshoy dvorets; 10.30am–5pm; closed Mon & the last Tues of each month; $12) is far removed from that originally designed for Peter by Le Blond in 1714–21. Peter's daughter, Empress Elizabeth, employed Bartolomeo Rastrelli to add a third storey and two wings terminating in pavilions with gilded cupolas, while much of the interior was later redesigned by Vallin de la Mothe and Yuri Felten, with further alterations made in the mid-nineteenth century. Yet there's a superb cohesion at work, a tribute both to the vision of the palace's original creators and to the skills of the experts who rebuilt Peterhof after World War II.

The palace's popularity is such that in summer you may have to **queue** outside for up to an hour. Inside, you must put on *tapochki* and stash your camera (unless you're going to buy a photo permit). The set **itinerary** leads from the "public" state rooms into the Imperial Suite, as if you were a courtier granted intimate access to the monarch, but your route might differ slightly from the one described below, depending on how crowded the palace gets.

The State Rooms

Visitors ascend to the **State Rooms** via Rastrelli's **Ceremonial Staircase**. Aglow with gilded statues and vases, beneath a ceiling fresco of Aurora and Genius chasing away the night, it rivals the Jordan Staircase in the Winter Palace for sheer splendour. Once upstairs, you pass through an exhibition on the restoration of Peterhof before reaching the silk-papered **Blue Reception Room**, where the Imperial secretary once vetted visitors to the rooms beyond.

The **Chesma Room** takes its name from the Russian naval victory against the Turks at Chesma Bay in 1770, scenes from which decorate the walls. When Count Alexei Orlov, commander of the Russian squadron, saw Philippe Hackert's preliminary sketches, he criticized the depiction of a ship exploding in flames as unrealistic and arranged for a frigate to be blown up before the artist's eyes, as a model. Off to the right, you can gaze into the **Ballroom**, glittering with mirrors and gilded candelabras – Empress Elizabeth nicknamed it the Merchants' Hall because "they love gold", and had her favourite architect, Rastrelli, create a similar hall in the Catherine Palace at Tsarskoe Selo. You may walk around the **Throne Room**, the largest hall at Peterhof, once used for gala receptions and balls. Designed by Felten,

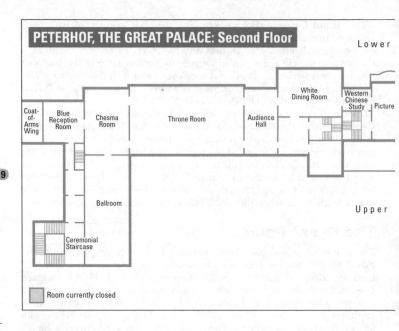

its white-and-turquoise mouldings are offset by scarlet curtains, crystal chandeliers and a magnificent parquet floor. Amidst all this opulence, the throne at the far end is an almost humble addendum, overlooked by a portrait of Catherine the Great in the green uniform of the Preobrazhenskiy Guards, astride her horse Brilliant.

Ladies-in-waiting once primped and preened in the mirrored **Audience Hall** (Audientszal) next door, where gilded cherubs and garlands festoon every frame and cornice. Beyond lies the **White Dining Room** (Belaya stolovaya), its dazzling stucco work garnished with touches of mint green; the long table is set with the 196-piece Catherine Dinner Service, made in Staffordshire, England, for the empress.

Next comes the **Western Chinese Study**, one of a pair of rooms designed by de la Mothe in the 1760s, when chinoiserie was all the rage. Sumptuously decorated in red, green and gold lacquer, with a floor inlaid with thirteen kinds of wood, it contains a suitably Oriental tea service. From here, you pass into the **Picture Hall** (Kartinny zal) at the centre of the palace, overlooking the park and gardens. It is also dubbed the "Room of Fashion and Graces", and its walls are lined with 368 portraits of eight young court ladies wearing national costumes.

The **Eastern Chinese Study** (Vostochniy Kitayskiy kabinet) originally looked quite different, its walls and furniture covered in white satin rather than the existing lacquer work (notice how the parquet clashes with the pseudo-Ming stove). Conversely, the **Partridge Drawing Room** (Kuropatochnaya gostinaya) next door is a meticulous re-creation: its partridge-spangled curtains and wall coverings use original fabric dating from the 1840s (itself patterned on eighteenth-century Lyons silk); there's also a harp and a Meissen porcelain figurine, typical features of noble Russian households of the period.

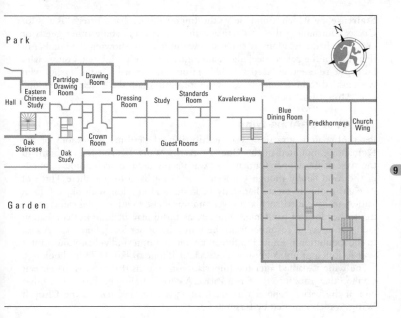

Park

Garden

Hall | Eastern Chinese Study | Partridge Drawing Room | Drawing Room | Dressing Room | Study | Standards Room | Kavalerskaya | Blue Dining Room | Predkhornaya | Church Wing

Oak Staircase | Oak Study | Crown Room | Guest Rooms

N

The Imperial Suite

The transition to the **Imperial Suite** is accomplished by an opulent **Drawing Room** (Divannaya) flaunting Chinese silk paintings and an outsized Ottoman divan. Notice the porcelain statue of Catherine's greyhound, Zemira, lying on a pillow. Her **Dressing Room** (Tualetnaya) and **Study** (Kabinet) are both tastefully furnished in French Empire style, with the latter containing portraits of Empress Elizabeth, the youthful Alexander I, Catherine and a bust of Voltaire, her favourite philosopher. From here you're channelled out of the Imperial Suite into the **Standards Room**, where the Peterhof garrison formerly displayed its regimental banners, and Rastrelli's adjacent **Equerries Room** (Kavalerskaya), where aides-de-camp once reclined on the Chippendale chaises longues. The **Blue Dining Room** was commissioned by Nicholas I for banquets of 250 people, who dined from the so-called "**Cabbage Service**" of 5550 pieces (most of which is on display), watched over by portraits of Maria Fyodorovna and Catherine the Great.

Beyond lies the **Predkhornaya** or Choir Anteroom, leading to the Court Church of SS Peter and Paul in the east wing, which is still under restoration. Consequently, the tour does a U-turn via some guest rooms to the Imperial bedchamber, a joyous mismatch of gilded swags and chinoiserie wallpaper, with the bed ensconced in a curtained alcove. Its sobriquet, the **Crown Room**, derived from Paul I's habit of mounting his crown on a stand in the room, as if to derive reassurance from the sight.

The last room visited is one of the oldest in the palace. Designed by Le Blond at Peterhof's inception, the **Oak Study** of Peter the Great reflects his enthusiasms, carved with nautical, military and festive motifs. Only eight panels survived the war, the rest being modern reproductions which took up to eighteen months' work apiece to complete. At the top of the **Oak**

Staircase, by which visitors leave the Imperial Suite, hang Peter's "Rules for Guests", forbidding them to arrive without invitation, abuse other guests or take their bedding. Nobody could stay without a card showing the number of their bed in the palace; sleeping in any other bed was prohibited. Visitors who broke the rules either faced a drubbing from the tsar or his jester, Washo (who was entitled to buffet anyone), or were forced to drain the "Great Eagle Cup" (see "Monplaisir", below).

The Coat-of-Arms Wing

Peterhof's latest attraction is an **exhibition** of personal possessions of the Romanovs, mounted in the **Coat-of-Arms Wing** (Korpus za Gerbom) to the west of the Upper Garden. This was mainly used to accommodate guests of the royal family, though Catherine the Great liked to stay there. Three of its eight rooms re-create her study, bedroom and boudoir with objects she is known to have used, such as a silver samovar incised with playing cards, attesting to her love of gambling. Other items on display include her coronation saddle and several costumes from the wardrobe of her lover, Potemkin. Access to the exhibition is limited to fifteen people at a time; individual visitors must wait to join a group. Admission costs $3.30. Phone ☎ 420 00 73 for bookings.

The wing is named after the Imperial coat-of-arms that crowns the elegant pavilion that joins it to the Great Palace. A corresponding pavilion at the other end of the palace, topped with an Orthodox cross and named the **Church Wing**, was also created by Rastrelli.

Monplaisir and the Catherine Wing

Peter the Great's favourite haunt, **Monplaisir** (French for "my pleasure"), is the major attraction at Peterhof after the Great Palace. Situated beside the Gulf of Finland, with a distant view of St Petersburg, it is both homely and extravagant, its modest facade hiding a roisterous past. If you come on Wednesday, when Monplaisir is closed, the adjacent **Catherine Wing** affords some consolation. Both are on the edge of the Lower Park, an easy walk from the Great Palace, past the Roman Fountains (see p.258).

Monplaisir

Designed by the tsar himself (with the assistance of several architects), the low, brick **Monplaisir** palace (June–Sept 10.30am–5pm; closed Wed, all winter and on rainy days; $6) reflects the influence of Holland, where Peter learned shipbuilding in 1697. Even after the Great Palace was finished, he lived and entertained at Monplaisir whenever possible. Here, too, he interrogated his son Alexei before confining him to the Peter and Paul Fortress on suspicion of treason. The main wing, on the seafront, is discreetly shuttered, and visitors have to buy tickets from a kiosk on the seaward side. Admission is restricted to groups before noon, and individual visitors from noon until 3.30pm (which is when the last tour departs).

Starting with Peter's **art collection** (the first in Russia), you progress through the **Eastern Gallery**, with its sixteen glazed doors, into the extraordinary **Lacquered Study**. A feast of black, gold and red, its 94 lacquered panels were originally created by icon painters who spent months studying Chinese techniques but couldn't resist imparting a Russian flavour to their work. The originals were chopped up and used as firewood by the Nazis; what you see today was re-created from the evidence of three surviving panels.

In the **State Hall** beyond, the ceiling fresco of Apollo surrounded by figures from the *commedia dell'arte* must have swum before the eyes of those guests forced to drink from the dreaded Great Eagle Cup, holding 1.25 litres of fortified wine, which had to be drained in one gulp by anyone who broke Peter's rules. Envoys who passed out were roused next day and either issued with axes and ordered to join him in a bout of tree felling or taken for a bracing sail on the Gulf. Peter's wife, Catherine I, entered into the spirit of things by cooking meals in the Dutch-tiled **Pantry**, and inviting guests to help themselves to *zakuski* in the **Buffet**.

On the other side of the State Hall is Peter's small **Naval Study**, with its tile-inlaid wainscotting and inspirational view of the Gulf. Their **Bedroom** is equally small and homely, and Peter's nightcap can be seen on the bedside table on the far side of the four-poster. The tour concludes in the **Western Gallery**, decorated with an allegorical fresco and seascapes (including one of Zaandam, where Peter lived with a Dutch carpenter while working at the local shipyards).

Thirty years after Peter's death, Monplaisir was home to the future Empress Catherine the Great during her loveless marriage to Peter III. When he took a mistress, Catherine started an affair with Stanislaw Poniatowski (later to become the last king of Poland) and soon the royal couple were living apart: Peter at Oranienbaum and Catherine in a pavilion beside Monplaisir, called the Tea House. There, on July 28, 1762, she learned from Alexei Orlov that the coup against her husband was under way and hastened to Petersburg to rally her supporters. By nightfall she had become Empress of All the Russias.

The Catherine Wing

The **Catherine Wing** (Yekaterininskiy Korpus; May–Sept 10.30am–5pm, closed Thurs; Oct–April Sat & Sun 10.30am–5pm; $3.30) was added to Monplaisir by Empress Elizabeth in the 1740s to accommodate court balls and masquerades, and remodelled by Quarenghi for Catherine the Great in the 1780s. Its simple Baroque exterior defers to Monplaisir's, while the interior is plush but not overly opulent. **Access** during opening hours is largely restricted to groups, with individuals admitted only between noon and 3pm. Tickets are sold from a window facing the garden courtyard.

Tours usually begin in the **Blue Drawing Room**, which dates from the same period as Alexander I's **Study**. The latter is ornamented with knick-knacks relating to the 1812 Napoleonic invasion and a portrait of Alexander's murdered father, Paul. Next you enter Alexander's **Bedroom**, which contains a magnificent "boat" bed with candelabras mounted on the headboard; some ivory piquet cards belonging to Catherine the Great are preserved in a case by the far wall. Next door is the **Heating Room** – easily mistaken for a kitchen – where plates were kept warm during banquets. The blue-and-gold dinner service comes from Ropsha, where Catherine's husband, Peter III, was murdered. Proceeding through the **Green Drawing Room**, full of walnut furniture, and the stuccoed, mirrored **Blue Hall**, you enter the glittering **Yellow Hall**, its table set for a banquet of 45 guests. The red-and-gold Guryev Service comprises several thousand pieces and was made in St Petersburg early last century. Portraits of Alexander I and Catherine the Great are accompanied by a giant tapestry depicting Peter the Great at the helm of a storm-wracked dinghy, his companions cowering astern (based on a real event).

△ The Lower Park, Peterhof

Other sights

Between the Catherine Wing and Monplaisir lies a **garden**, centred on the **Wheatsheaf Fountain**, whose 25 jets of water resemble heads of grain. A composition designed by Peter himself flanks the Wheatsheaf Fountain on four sides, consisting of gilded fountain-statues of Psyche, Apollo, Bacchus and a faun with a kid – collectively dubbed "the Bells". He also commissioned a **joke fountain** that squirts anybody who treads on a certain part of its gravel plot – always good for a laugh. The austere **Bathhouse Wing** (Baniy Korpus) and **Kitchen Block** that Catherine I added to Montplaisir give an idea of how royalty washed themselves and food was prepared, but aren't anything special (June–Sept 10.30am–5pm, closed Wed; Oct–May Sat & Sun 10.30am–4pm; $4).

The Upper Garden and the Lower Park

Having visited the Great Palace and Monplaisir, you'll have seen something of Peterhof's grounds and will probably have been tempted to stray by the **fountains** (*fontany*) glimpsed down every path. There are five in the formal Upper Garden – behind the Great Palace – and dozens in the wooded Lower Park. While the Upper Garden rates a brisk circumambulation, the Lower Park deserves a longer ramble, though most of its best fountains are either clustered between the Chessboard Hill Cascade and Monplaisir, or ennoble the approaches to the Marly Palace. Providing you keep this in mind, it doesn't matter which of the many routes you take – the account below is one of many possibilities.

In Catherine's day the gardens were used for all-night festivities, illuminated by 10,000 candles. Her successors were less addicted to such revels, but gala garden parties remained a fixture of the court and diplomatic calendar until the 1900s.

The Upper Garden

Framed by borders and hedges, the ornamental ponds of the expansive **Upper Garden** (Verkhniy sad) commence with the so-called **Square Ponds** near the Great Palace, sporting marble statues of Venus and Apollo. Next comes the **Oak Fountain**, a complete misnomer for a statue of Cupid donning a tragic mask in a circular pool ringed by allegorical figures. The garden's focal point is the **Neptune Fountain**, made in Nuremberg in 1650–58 to mark the end of the Thirty Years' War. The fountain turned out to require too much water to operate and spent years in storage until it was snapped up by Tsarevich Paul for 30,000 rubles in 1782. Stolen by the Nazis, it was tracked down in Germany and reinstalled in 1956. Lastly there's the **Mezheumny**, whose strange name (meaning "a bit of this, a bit of that") alludes to the many alterations it's undergone over the years, resulting in a plump dragon and four dolphins; an alternative translation has it meaning "neither here nor there", and refers to its location.

The Lower Park

Stretching down to the sea, the 102-hectare **Lower Park** (Nizhniy park) is laid out with symmetrical avenues linking the lesser palaces and fountains, the latter gravity-fed by water from the Ropsha Hills, 22km away. In total, Peterhof's **hydraulic system** has 50km of pipes, 22 locks and 18 lakes, discharging 100,000 cubic metres of water every day during summer. In the winter, the fountains are turned off and the statues encased in insulated boxes, to prevent them from cracking in the sub-zero temperatures.

East of the Grand Cascade's Samson statue stands the **Triton Fountain**, which honours the Russian naval victory over Sweden at Hangö, while further along the path is a piazza dominated by two **Roman Fountains**, like giant cake stands. The **Chessboard Hill Cascade** (Shakhmatnaya gorka) to the south boasts three dragons from which water spouts down a chequered chute flanked by statues of Greek and Roman deities. Between the Roman Fountains and Monplaisir are several more **joke fountains** (*shutikhi*), still primed to soak but too leaky to surprise anyone. The **Umbrella Fountain** starts raining when you sit underneath it, as does the **Spruce Fountain**, disguised as a tree. To the east of the Umbrella is the **Pyramid Fountain**, whose 505 jets rise in seven tiers to form an apex.

Heading west towards the Marly Palace you'll first encounter the **Adam Fountain**, with Adam gazing soulfully over the rooftops of two Greco-Chinese pavilions, followed by the **Eve Fountain** – Eve with apple and fig leaf in hand – beyond the Marine Canal. From there you can detour northwards to the Hermitage or press on past the grey and white marble **Lion Cascade** (resembling a Greek temple) to the Marly Palace. The southern side of the park is flanked by the **Triton Bells Fountain**, named after the fish-tailed Triton boys who hold cups full of sculpted bells amidst clouds of spray. These precede the **Menazherny Fountains**, which use less water than their powerful jets suggest – their name derives from the French word *ménager*, meaning "to economize". Beyond rises the **Golden Hill Cascade** (Zolotaya gorka), a flight of waterfalls issuing from gilded orifices. Like the Chessboard Hill Cascade, it is flanked by allegorical statues and offers a ravishing view of the park.

The Hermitage and Marly Palace

En route between Monplaisir and the Marly Palace you can visit the **Hermitage** (Ermitazh; 10am–5.30pm; closed Mon; $3.30) near the shore, a moated, two-storey pavilion with round-headed windows and Corinthian pilasters gracing its sand-coloured facade. Designed for Peter the Great, but completed only after his death, it was intended for dining *sans* servants: guests ate upstairs, with a lovely view of Peterhof and the Gulf, and ordered dishes by placing notes on the table, which was lowered by pulleys to the kitchen below and then returned laden with delicacies. In 1797, the pulley chair by which guests were hoisted upstairs was replaced by a flight of stairs after a cable snapped, stranding Tsar Paul between floors. The upstairs **Dining Room** is hung with paintings, while the **Buffet** downstairs displays Japanese and Chinese porcelain and Russian crystal.

Nearby, a raised terrace shelters from the wind what used to be an **Orangery**, overlooking the Gulf, and the large pond that fronts the **Marly Palace** (May–Sept 10.30am–5pm, closed Mon; Oct–April Sat & Sun 10.30am–5pm; $3.30). Built around the same time as Monplaisir, this takes its name and inspiration from the French royal hunting lodge at Marly le Roi, which Peter saw during his Grand Tour of Europe. More of a cosy country house than a palace, it backs on to **fishponds** where Catherine fed her pet goldfish, nowadays stocked with sturgeon and trout, which visitors are invited to catch. Tickets for the Marly are sold at the wooden hut nearby and visits are by **guided tour** only, lasting about fifteen minutes.

In keeping with Peter's no-nonsense character, the Dutch-tiled **Kitchen** connects directly with the **Buffet**, so that dishes arrived hot at the table – an innovation that he was especially proud of. As usual, the four-poster in his

Bedroom is far too short – Peter was 2.3 metres tall – and there's a small den where he drew plans and fiddled with instruments. Upstairs are guest rooms exhibiting Petrine memorabilia and a **Dining Room** with a superb view of the avenues converging on the palace.

The Benois Wing and beyond

Several low-profile sights outside the palace grounds can be seen as you leave, or en route to the Alexandria Park. The closest to the Great Palace is the **Benois Wing** (Korpus Benoua; May–Oct 10.30am–6pm, closed Mon & the last Tues of each month; Nov–April Sat & Sun 10.30am–4pm; free), the former summer home of the Benois family. Its connection with Russia dates back to 1794, when Louis Benois arrived from France to work as a chef for Tsar Paul, and married a Russian woman who bore eighteen children (seventeen of whom died when very young). Their only surviving son Nikolai was "adopted" by Empress Maria Fyodorovna; he trained as an architect and fathered six children, all of whom became artists or architects. The house proudly exhibits evidence of their talents, with displays ranging from architectural plans to surrealist paintings. Surprisingly, there are also cinema posters and photographs of the late British actor **Peter Ustinov** – a grandson of Leonty Benois, who designed the annexe of the Russian Museum – and a number of architectural sketches by Ustinov's son Igor. There may be other, temporary exhibitions, for which a small charge is levied.

Nikolai Benois was responsible for several buildings at Peterhof, including one by the Upper Garden that now houses a **Museum of Collections** (10.30am–6pm; closed Mon & the last Tues of each month; $3.30) donated by Ezrakh Moiseevich in 1991. Paintings by Roerich, Nesterov, Petrov-Vodkin and other leading artists of the "Silver Age", and porcelain from Tsarist and Soviet times, make it worth a visit. By carrying on to the far end of Pravlenskaya ulitsa and crossing Sankt-Peterburgskiy prospekt, you can see the **Peter and Paul Cathedral** (sobor Petra i Pavla) before you catch a minibus back to the city. It looks nothing like its namesake in St Petersburg, resembling instead a medieval Russian church, embodying the Slavophilism of the 1890s. It was turned into a cinema after the Revolution and returned to the Orthodox Church only a decade ago; its interior has now been refurbished and its acoustics are superb.

Alternatively, walk eastwards along Aleksandiiskoe shosse past the Benois Wing to reach the **Court Stables**, a sprawling complex modelled by Benois on Hampton Court in England. The building now houses a sanatorium and can't be entered, but makes a fitting curtain-raiser for the Anglophile follies in the Alexandria Park, beyond the stables.

The Alexandria Park

Landscaped in a naturalistic English style by Adam Menelaws, the **Alexandria Park** surrounds the Cottage Palace of Nicholas I and Alexandra Fyodorovna (after whom the park is named). Finding Peterhof's Great Palace "unbearable", she pressed Nicholas to build a home suited to a cosier, bourgeois lifestyle, where they lived *en famille* with few servants and no protocol, but heavily guarded. The Cottage Palace is definitely worth the fifteen-minute walk through the overgrown park (no ticket required). As the gates from Peterhof's Lower Park are locked, you must enter via the road alongside the Court Stables (see above); keep your ticket if you intend to return to the main buildings at

Peterhof. Just inside the park is a spiky neo-Gothic **Alexander Nevsky Church**, which was used by the court as a private chapel.

The **Farm Palace** (Fermerskiy dvorets), further east, is past saving, but remains picturesquely derelict. Built as a combined stables, stud farm and hothouse, it appealed to Nicholas and Alexandra's son, Alexander II, a keen weekend farmer. The path carries on to a whimsical **Ruined Bridge** beside a gully that once fed the park's lake. Having scrambled down and up the other side, you'll see the Cottage Palace straight ahead.

The Cottage Palace

The **Cottage Palace** (dvorets Kottedzh; May–Sept 10.30am–5pm, closed Mon & the last Tues of each month; Oct–April Sat & Sun 10.30am–4pm; $5) is a two-storeyed gingerbread house designed in 1826–29 by Adam Menelaws in the then-fashionable pseudo-Gothic style. As you enter the lobby, notice the stone carved with Arabic script: a trophy from the fortress of Varna in Bulgaria, captured during the Russo-Turkish War of 1828–29. The **Tsaritsa's Study** has a stained-glass screen and a sensuous frieze around the window bay, while the adjacent **Grand Drawing Room** (Bolshaya gostinaya) boasts a starburst ceiling as intricate as lace, and a clock modelled on the facade of Rouen Cathedral. In the burgundy-coloured **Library** (Biblioteka) are a mother-of-pearl and ivory model of a castle near Potsdam and a screen decorated with German knights – reminders that Empress Alexandra was born Charlotte, princess of Prussia, while Nicholas I had a German mother. From the **Grand Reception Room**, you pass into a **Dining Room** (Stolovaya) bisected by Gothic pillars and flanked by pew-like chairs. Its long table is set with Alexandra's dinner service of 314 porcelain and 353 crystal pieces, specially commissioned for the cottage.

The **Staircase** is a triumph of *trompe l'oeil* by G.B. Scotti, who painted Gothic arches, vaults and windows all over the stairwell in subtle tones of grey and blue. On the floor above are the **family rooms**, modestly sized and decorated by Tsarist standards. First comes the suite of rooms belonging to Tsarevich Alexander, comprising a bathroom (Vannaya), classroom (Uchebnaya komnata) and a valet's room. In the tsar's **Dressing Room** scenes from the Russo-Turkish War hang alongside a marble-topped washstand and a screened-off shower. Next door is the **Tsar's Study**, followed by the **Blue Room** (Golubaya gostinaya), which belonged to Nicholas I's daughter, Maria Nikolayevna. The room is furnished with Sèvres and Meissen porcelain and also contains a clock with 66 faces, one for each province of Russia (including "Russian America", as Alaska was known until 1867).

Entering the next room you skip a generation, for after Alexander II's assassination, the crown passed to his son, Alexander III, whose wife, Maria Fyodorovna, made this her **Drawing Room**. A sad tale lies behind the **Nursery** (Detskaya), beyond. Prepared decades earlier during Maria Nikolayevna's pregnancy, it was sealed up after she died in childbirth, its fabulous Doll's Tea Service left there for the baby that died with her.

Before leaving, nip upstairs to Nicholas I's **Naval Study**, a garret with a balcony overlooking the Gulf, from where he observed exercises off Kronstadt through a spyglass and gave orders to the fleet by telegraph or speaking trumpet.

On the anniversary of the 1918 massacre of the royal family at Yekaterinburg (July 16), admirers light candles and say prayers for them at the **site of the Lower Dacha** near the seashore. This was their favourite residence at Peterhof, where Nicholas II took two of the most fateful decisions of his reign, signing the October Manifesto of 1905 that granted a Duma (parliament), and mobilizing the Russian army in 1914. The *dacha* was totally destroyed during World War II and is unlikely to be rebuilt.

Oranienbaum (Lomonosov)

Peter the Great's cohort, Prince Menshikov, began work at **Oranienbaum** in 1713, shortly after his master started Peterhof, 12km to the east. Typically, Menshikov set out to build a palace which would surpass Peterhof, planting orange trees in the lower park ("Oranienbaum" is German for "orange tree") – the ultimate in conspicuous consumption, given the local climate. The building of Oranienbaum bankrupted Menshikov and in 1728 the whole estate passed into the hands of the Crown, whereupon it was used as a naval hospital until Empress Elizabeth gave it to her nephew, the future Tsar Peter III and husband of Catherine the Great.

Catherine hated life at Oranienbaum – "I felt totally isolated, cried all day and spat blood," she wrote in her memoirs. Conversely, Peter had a wonderful time, putting his valets through military exercises or spending hours playing with lead soldiers on the dining tables. He was also fond of inflicting his violin-playing on those around him, although, according to Catherine, "He did not know a single note . . . for him the beauty of the music lay in the force and violence with which he played it."

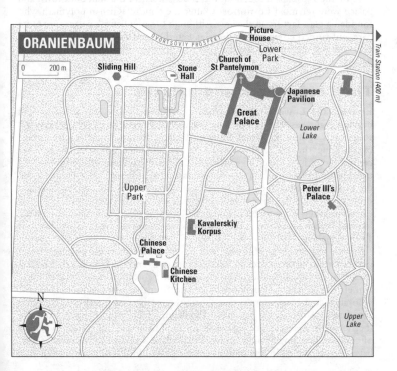

ORANIENBAUM

0 — 200 m

DVORTSOVIY PROSPEKT

Sliding Hill

Stone Hall

Picture House

Lower Park

Church of St Pantelymon

Japanese Pavilion

Great Palace

Lower Lake

Upper Park

Peter III's Palace

Kavalerskiy Korpus

Chinese Palace

Chinese Kitchen

Upper Lake

N

▶ Train Station (400 m)

Practicalities

Oranienbaum can be reached by minibus from Avtovo metro (#K-300) in St Petersburg, or from Peterhof (#K-348). Alternatively, you can catch a suburban train from the city's Baltic Station, alighting four stops after Noviy Peterhof. Sit at the front of the train to be sure of seeing the platform sign; the station also serves as the terminus for minibuses. To reach the palace grounds, cut across the small park towards the grey-domed Church of Archangel Michael; the entrance to the Lower Park is just across the road beyond the church. There are several **snack stands** near the station, and a **market** near the church sells fresh produce. Within the palace grounds there's an old-fashioned, Soviet-style **café** in the Kavalerskiy Korpus near the Chinese Palace.

Tickets and opening hours

It's worth phoning (℡423 16 27) to ask which of the palaces and pavilions at Oranienbaum are open, to avoid a wasted journey. When last heard, three were open and the others could be viewed only from outside. There's no entrance fee for the grounds, but visitors need separate tickets for each building (sold on the spot). The grounds are open all year (daily 7am–7pm), but as none of the buildings is heated they are open only from May to mid-September. All have the same **opening hours** (11am–5pm; closed Tues and last Mon of each month).

Unlike the other Imperial palaces, Oranienbaum never fell into the hands of the Germans, although it suffered constant bombardment as a tiny enclave held by the Russians throughout the Blockade. After the war, both town and palace were renamed **Lomonosov**, after the famous Russian polymath who founded a glass factory in the area. Although Oranienbaum's palaces are quite bare and ruined compared to those at Peterhof and Tsarskoe Selo, the site is peaceful and uncrowded and the parks are lovely, with meadows full of wild flowers.

The Lower Park and palaces

Entering the **Lower Park** (Nizhniy park) from Dvortsoviy prospekt and bearing right past the Lower Lake (with boats for rent in summer), you'll soon catch sight of the **Great Palace** (Bolshoy dvorets; $5) on a lofty terrace overlooking the sea. Built in 1713 by the architect Schnadel, its concave central block is upstaged by the massive domed pavilions at either end; the one on the western end previously contained the Church of St Pantelymon; the one on the eastern end is the so-called Japanese Pavilion. Menshikov had only a few years to enjoy it before he was arrested for treason in 1727 and exiled to Siberia; the following year the crown took possession of the estate, but not before his enemies, the Golitsyns, had stripped the colossal palace of all its valuables.

Anyone expecting lavish decor will be disappointed, as the palace is more impressive for its sheer size and presence than its interiors: rooms that hosted royalty in the nineteenth century now lie bare beneath damp-stained ceilings. A melancholy array of **portraits** of Oranienbaum's owners includes Peter III, who abdicated here under duress shortly before he was murdered (see box). The latest casualty is the **Japanese Pavilion**, which took its name from the shelves of Japanese ceramic figures that it used to house, but is now in danger of collapse. The lengthy side wings of the palace, screened by wooden fences, have been occupied by the military ever since World War II.

Peter III's Palace

A more rewarding sight is **Peter III's Palace** (dvorets Petra III; $7), in the southeast corner of the Lower Park. In keeping with his fetish for the military, it was once surrounded by fortifications and a moat, though all that remains of them now is a decrepit ceremonial archway. The palace itself is a modest two-storey structure built by Rinaldi for Peter before his marriage to Catherine, hence the small size of his bachelor apartments on the upper floor. One of the few memorable rooms is the **Picture Hall** (Kartinniy zal), covered in a patchwork of 58 paintings by eighteenth-century European masters. Chinese elements are also present, in the silk hangings, lacquer paintings and dress cabinets. Scenes of life in Peter's military encampment appear on the stucco-work ceiling of his **Boudoir**. On a more personal note, evidence of Peter's diminutive physique can be seen in his uniform **dress coat**, which looks the right size for a 12-year-old.

The Upper Park

Beyond the Great Palace lies the **Upper Park** (Verkhniy park), whose intricate network of minor paths is now lost in undergrowth, although the basic grid remains. It was Catherine's favourite part of the estate and is still by far the loveliest stretch of the park to wander through, with canals, bridges and ponds scattered about the mixed woodland of firs, limes, oaks and silver birch. After Peter's death, Catherine commissioned Rinaldi to build the two finest buildings at Oranienbaum here: the Sliding Hill and the Chinese Palace. En route from the Great Palace to the Sliding Hill you'll pass the **Stone Hall**, whence Catherine would sally forth in a chariot for costume balls, dressed as Minerva.

The Sliding Hill

A little way west of the Stone Hall stands the extraordinary **Sliding Hill** (Katalnaya gorka), resembling an oversized slice of wedding cake. This ice-blue

---

Peter III

Peter III inherited his love of military affairs from his father, the duke of Holstein. Happiest in the company of men, he couldn't cope with assertive, cultured women – least of all his wife, the future Catherine the Great – and the marriage wasn't consummated for several years. "When he left the room the dullest book was a delight," she recalled in her memoirs. In the first months of his reign, Peter managed to offend the Russian clergy by his continued adherence to Lutheranism and the military by introducing Prussian uniforms and spending more time with his Holstein bodyguards than with the Imperial Guards. It became common knowledge at court that he was planning to send Catherine to a nunnery and enthrone his mistress, the slatternly Countess Elizabeth Vorontsova.

In June 1762, just seven months into Peter's reign, Catherine launched a preemptive **coup**, marching on Oranienbaum with her lover, Grigori Orlov, and twenty thousand Imperial Guards. Peter tried to flee to Kronstadt, but the garrison there had already defected and he was forced to return to Oranienbaum, where, in the words of his idol, Frederick the Great, he abdicated "like a child who is sent to bed". Stripped of his Prussian uniform, Peter fainted from shock and was carted off to the palace at Ropsha, where he soon met his **death**. The announcement blamed "apoplexy", but his demise was universally ascribed to the Orlov brothers, who reputedly strangled him after he refused to drink poisoned wine. As a final humiliation, Peter was interred at the Alexander Nevsky Monastery rather than the Peter and Paul Cathedral, until his son Paul became tsar and had him reburied with the other Romanov monarchs.

and white, three-storey pleasure pavilion is all that remains of a wooden **roller-coaster** that once stretched for over 500m along the Upper Park. In winter, Catherine and her guests rode sledges; in summer, wheeled carts, offering a unique sensation of height and speed in a flat landscape, where nothing else moved faster than a horse could gallop. Such constructions were very popular in eighteenth-century Russia and were a regular feature in public fairgrounds, later spreading to Europe and America and giving rise to the mechanized versions seen today.

While the Hill is closed for repairs, you won't be able to see a scale model of the rollercoaster nor any of the top-floor rooms. The **Porcelain Room** (Farforoviy kabinet) features gilded stucco sprouting animalistic sconces that provide niches for some outrageously kitsch Meissen pottery, depicting "Chinese" and mythological scenes symbolizing Russia's victory over Turkey. The **White Room** (Beliy kabinet) – actually duck-egg blue and white – was Rinaldi's first venture into Neoclassicism after working in the Rococo style for many years. Its windows afford a distant view of Kronstadt Island: the curators claim they can forecast the weather from the visibility of Kronstadt's Naval Cathedral.

The Chinese Palace

The **Chinese Palace** (Kitayskiy dvorets; $9) boasts the snazziest interiors at Oranienbaum – but check that it isn't closed for repairs before trekking to the far end of the Upper Park. Catherine nicknamed it "Her Majesty's private *dacha*", though she spent only 48 days here in the course of her 34-year reign. Unlike the Chinese follies at Tsarskoe Selo, Rinaldi's palace shows only a few traces of the Orient. The weathered exterior is a quietly understated Baroque, while the luxurious yet intimate **interior** is decorated in a more fanciful Rococo style, with pink, blue and green *faux marbre*, ceiling frescoes by Venetian painters and ornate parquet floors. The decor is completely European until the **Buglework Room** (Steklyarusniy kabinet) with its touch of Oriental exotica – the walls depict peacocks, pheasants and other birds fashioned from beads produced at the Lomonosov factory.

Only in the last two rooms of the west wing do Chinese elements emerge clearly. Despite the proximity of Russia to the East, "Chinese Rococo" reached St Petersburg via Europe, where it had become a passion in the mid-eighteenth century. The first signs are in the **Small Chinese Room** (Maliy Kitayskiy kabinet), though even here they are confined to the wallpaper and a handful of Oriental vases. The **Large Chinese Room** (Bolshoy Kitayskiy kabinet) shows no such restraint: its walls are covered with Chinese landscapes of wood and walrus-ivory marquetry, large Chinese lanterns hang in two of its corners, and a fresco of the union of Europe and Asia (represented as a bride surrounded by warriors and mandarins) adorns the ceiling. The wonderfully carved full-sized billiard table was made in England.

East of the pond outside the palace lies a small pavilion known as the **Chinese Kitchen**. Like the Chinese Palace, the pavilion conceals a smattering of chinoiserie behind a Baroque facade.

Tsarskoe Selo (Pushkin)

Of all the Imperial palaces, none is more evocative of both the heyday and twilight years of the Romanovs than those at **Tsarskoe Selo** (Royal Village),

There's no point in coming on Tuesday (or the last Mon of the month), when the Catherine and Alexander palaces and the Lycée are closed, as are several of the museums (which are also closed on either Mon or Wed). Any day from Thursday to Sunday is fine unless you're planning to combine Tsarskoe Selo with a visit to Pavlovsk, whose palace is closed on Friday.

Tsarskoe Selo is accessible by minibus (#K-286, #K-287, #K-299 or #K-342) from Moskovskaya ploshchad (every 10–20min; 45min), or suburban train from Vitebsk Station (every 20–30min; 30min). (In the station, look out for a replica Tsarist-era steam train off the concourse, and the ex-Imperial Waiting Room in the main building, decorated with scenes of Tsarskoe Selo before the Revolution.) Minibuses terminate outside the town's train station, still named Detskoe Selo.

From there, local minibuses run to the Catherine Palace: K-#370 or #K-378 drops you at the end of Oranzhereynaya ulitsa; #K-382 stops on Leontyevskaya ulitsa, slightly nearer the palace; #K-371 follows a longer route via the Egyptian Gates, terminating near the Church of the Sign; and #K-545 runs to Tsarskoe Selo and then on to Pavlovsk. Minibuses may not even be numbered, but simply bear the Cyrillic legend ДВОРЦЫ ПАРКИ (parks & palaces).

Orientation and tickets

Starting at the Catherine Palace, it's easy to orientate yourself in relation to everything else. It takes several hours to do justice to the Catherine Park and Palace, and you should plan on spending the whole day here if you want to visit the Lycée and the Alexander Palace as well. If you're intending to combine Tsarskoe Selo with Pavlovsk, there won't be time to see more than the main palaces at each and something of the grounds.

During the summer, you need to buy an admission ticket for the Catherine Park as well as a ticket for the palace once you're inside the grounds. No tickets are required for the Alexander Park; tickets for the Alexander Palace are sold on the spot.

Eating and accommodation

Places to eat near the palace are poor value for money, whether you're talking takeaway pizzas or burgers from the *Café Tsarskoe Selo* (11am–midnight; closed Tues) opposite the Lycée; soup, pastries and beverages in the *Catherine Café* (noon–8pm) in the palace; or meals in the lacklustre *Admiralty* (noon–11pm) by the Great Pond. If you're economizing, the *Café Kolobok* (daily 9am–9pm) at Oranzhernaya ul. 29 serves tasty, cheap *bliny*, soup, salad and cutlets, or there's a 24-hour *shwarma* outlet a few doors along. For a full meal costing up to $20 a head, try the *Café Raut* (daily noon–1am) on Parkovaya ulitsa or the *Tsarskoe Selo* restaurant (noon–11pm) at the train station – both of which take credit cards – while really to push the boat out, you can enjoy *haute cuisine* and courtly service at the ultra-pricey *Staraya Bashnya* (☎466 66 98; noon–10pm) in a corner tower of the Fyodorovskiy Gorodok, on the edge of the Alexander Park.

Staying in town enables you to hit the sights before the crowds arrive. The best option is the newly opened *Catherine Hotel* (☎466 80 42; ❾) behind the palace, whose comfy en-suite rooms have unbeatable views. On the other side of the park is the less welcoming *Kochubey Dacha* (☎465 21 55; ❸), which has guarded parking. Breakfast is included at both places. The *Catherine Hotel* takes credit cards.

25km south of St Petersburg. This small town flanks two gigantic palaces, set amidst parkland: the glorious **Catherine Palace**, beloved of Catherine the Great, and the **Alexander Palace**, where the last tsar and tsaritsa dwelt. Tsarskoe Selo is also associated with the great poet Alexander Pushkin, who studied at the town's **Lycée**; and with Rasputin, a frequent visitor who was

TSARSKOE SELO & PUSHKIN

KUZMINSKOE SHUSSE

ACCOMMODATION
Catherine Hotel A
Kochubey Dacha B

EATING AND DRINKING
Admiralty 8
Café Kolobok 3
Café Raut 7
Café Tsarskoe Selo 5
Catherine Café 6
Staraya Bashnya 1
Tsarskoe Selo
 Restaurant 2
24-hour Shwarma 4

AKADEMICHESKI

St Fyodor's Cathedral

Alexander Park

Arsenal

FENCE

VOLKHONSKOE SHUSSE

N

Mount Parnuss

TREBLE ALLEY

Chinese Theatre

0   500 m

Chinese Village

FENCE

FENCE

Agate Rooms

Cameron Gallery

Great Caprice

FENCE

Kagul Obelisk

Kitchen Ruin

RAMPOVAYA ALLEYA

Chinese Pavillion

Concert Hall

Granite Terrace

Grotto

FENCE

Gates

PARKOVAYA

Great Pond

Ferry

Chesma Column

Hall on the Island

8

Admiralty

Marble Bridge

Pyramid

Turkish Bath

Tower Ruin

PARKOVAYA ULITSA

0   100 m

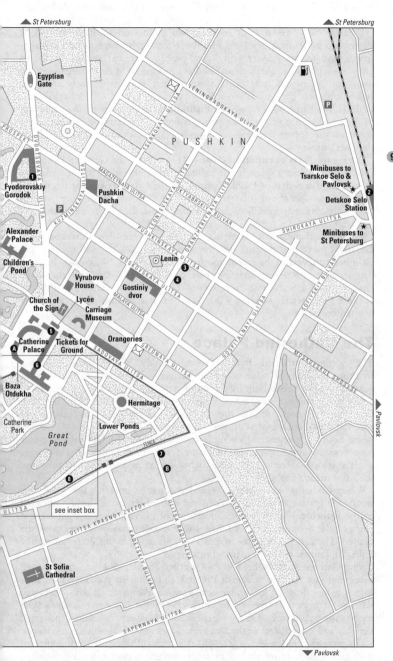

Egyptian
Gate

PUSHKIN

**Minibuses to
Tsarskoe Selo &
Pavlovsk** ★

2

**Detskoe Selo
Station**

**Minibuses to
St Petersburg** ★

LENINGRADSKAYA ULITSA

PROSPEKT

DVORTSOVAYA ULITSA

ISEROVSKAYA ULITSA

MAGAZEYNAYA ULITSA

KUZMINSKAYA ULITSA

DMITRIYEVSKAYA ULITSA

OKTYABRSKIY BULVAR

ORANZHEREYNAYA ULITSA

PUSHKINSKAYA ULITSA

SHIROKAYA ULITSA

SOFIYSKIY BULVAR

MOSKOVSKAYA ULITSA

GOSPITALNAYA ULITSA

MOSKOVSKOE SHOSSE

1
**Fyodorovskiy
Gorodok**

**Pushkin
Dacha**

**Alexander
Palace**

**Children's
Pond**

**Vyrubova
House**

⊙ **Lenin** **3**

4

**Gostiniy
dvor**

**Church of
the Sign**

Lycée

**Carriage
Museum**

MALAYA ULITSA

5

**Catherine
Palace**

Ⓐ

**Tickets for
Ground**

Orangeries

SREDNAYA ULITSA

SADOVAYA ULITSA

6

**Baza
Otdukha**

Catherine
Park

*Great
Pond*

Hermitage

Lower Ponds

FENCE

7

Ⓑ

8

see inset box

ULITSA

ULITSA KRASNOY ZVEZDY

ULITSA RADISHEVA

KADETSKIY BULVAR

PAVLOVSKOE SHOSSE

**St Sofia
Cathedral**

SAPERNAYA ULITSA

▼ Pavlovsk   ► Pavlovsk

buried here for a short time. Lenin, too, came here several times before the Revolution, and once spent hours in the park, evading Tsarist agents.

Tsarskoe Selo was once a model town connected to Pavlovsk and St Petersburg by Russia's first train line (built for the Imperial family's convenience), and featuring electric lighting, piped water and sewage works. Its chessboard plan incorporates a scaled-down version of St Petersburg's Gostiniy dvor and numerous villas that were turned into orphanages after the Revolution, when the town was renamed Detskoe Selo – "Children's Village". In 1937, the name was changed to **Pushkin**, to commemorate the centenary of the poet's death; although the palace is now called Tsarskoe Selo again and the main streets bear their pre-revolutionary names, the **town** itself still bears the poet's name.

During the **Nazi occupation** (Sept 1941–Jan 1944) the Germans looted the palaces and left not a single house habitable. After liberation, the first window to be glazed was that of Pushkin's room in the Lycée. Following decades of **restoration** work, both palaces appear to be their old selves again (at least externally), but many pavilions are still unrestored, such is the effort and cost involved.

Visitors can enjoy two **festivals** in June: the one-day **Tsarskoe Selo Carnival** procession through the streets of town, and a series of operatic and chamber **concerts** in the throne room of the Catherine Palace – for the exact dates, see the *St Petersburg Times* or *Where St Petersburg*, or check out the municipal **website** Ⓦ www.pushkin-town.net. The Catherine Palace and Park are covered in detail on the Tsarskoe Selo Museum Reserve's site, Ⓦ www.eng.tzar.ru.

The Catherine Palace

The existing **Catherine Palace** (Yekaterininskiy dvorets) owes everything to Empress Elizabeth, who made the village of Tsarskoe Selo her summer residence, had a palace built by three different architects and then decided to scrap it for another one, fit to rival Versailles. Her new Italian architect, Bartolomeo Rastrelli, rose to the challenge, creating a Baroque masterpiece that the delighted empress named after her mother, Catherine I. Despite being nearly a kilometre in circumference, its blue-and-white **facade** avoids monotony by using a profusion of atlantes, columns and pilasters, which were covered with gold leaf in Elizabeth's day, causing villagers to think that the roof itself was made of solid gold.

When Catherine the Great inherited the palace in 1762, she found the weathered gilding an eyesore and ordered it to be removed. She also objected to the **interior** – a continuous succession of interconnecting rooms – and engaged the Scottish architect Charles Cameron to make the alterations she desired. Thereafter, Catherine stayed every summer, living quite informally unless diplomatic protocol required otherwise.

After Catherine's death, her son Paul spurned Tsarskoe Selo and appropriated many items for his own palaces at Pavlovsk and Gatchina. Although the palace gained a new lease of life under her grandson, Alexander I, who celebrated Russia's victory over Napoleon by employing Viktor Stasov to redesign several rooms and repair fire damage after 1820, subsequent monarchs preferred Peterhof's Cottage Palace or the nearby Alexander Palace as summer residences.

The palace's grandest sweep faces the Alexander Park across a vast courtyard with gilded gates, through which courtiers and guests once entered. Nowadays, only large tour groups enter the palace from this direction; individual visitors now display **temporary exhibitions**. On the upper level, the **Agate Room** proper sports a magnificent parquet floor from the palace that Catherine was building for her last lover, Lanskoy, before his untimely death. The **Great Hall** beyond features malachite columns and a bronze coffered ceiling, and was originally lit by candelabras held by four marble maidens. A door leads directly to Catherine's private **Hanging Garden**, on a level with her private apartments and the upper storey of the Cameron Gallery.

The **Cameron Gallery** (10am–5pm; closed Wed & the last Tues of each month; $6.75) is a perfect Neoclassical foil to the Baroque palace. Cameron reputedly doffed his hat to Rastrelli's Catherine Palace every time he passed it on the way to work, and continuously modified his own design of the gallery to harmonize with Rastrelli's creation. Among the antique statues installed beneath the arcades was a bust of Charles James Fox, arch enemy of British Prime Minister Pitt the Younger, whom the empress despised. Nowadays the gallery is used for **temporary exhibitions**, and accessible from the park by a grand flight of steps.

The Catherine Park

The 566-hectare **Catherine Park** (Yekaterininskiy park; daily 6am–11pm; ticket office closes at 5pm; summer $2.50; winter admission free) is characterized by three styles of landscape gardening: French, English and Italian. Directly behind the Catherine Palace, the original nucleus of the park – commissioned by Elizabeth – was laid out geometrically in the French fashion, with pavilions and statues at the intersections. Sadly, you can't see inside the **Upper Bath**, which was reserved for royalty, or the **Lower Bath**, used by the courtiers. Nor can you enter the derelict **Hermitage** pavilion, whose Baroque facade echoes that of the Catherine Palace at the opposite end of the avenue. Between the baths and the **Fish Canal** (which once supplied food for banquets) are marble statues of **Adam** and **Eve**, similar to those at Peterhof.

Around the Great Pond

One of the more alluring sights in the park is the **Great Pond**, the focal point of the romantic "English Park" below the Cameron Gallery. Here, the court floated on gilded boats, watching regattas of gondolas and sampans, or pyrotechnic battles between miniature warships. Its designer, John Bush, exploited the hilly terrain to create ravishing perspectives that Catherine's architects embellished with pavilions and follies. The island amid the lake is accessible by a **ferry** (Mon–Fri noon–6pm, Sat & Sun 11am–6pm; $6.75) pulled by an underwater cable, which enables you to visit the **Hall on the Island**, where musicians once played, and the **Chesma Column**, honouring the Russian naval victory at Chesma Bay and modelled on the Rostral Columns in St Petersburg.

A clockwise circuit of the pond takes about thirty minutes, starting with the so-called **Grotto** (no entry), a domed blue and white pavilion once decorated inside with 250,000 shells. Beware of drunken youths diving into the pond from the terrace, who sometimes push passersby into the water. Further on, you can wander off to the **Lower Ponds** and the marble **Column of Morea** (commemorating Russian victories in Greece in 1770), or head straight for the **Admiralty** – two Dutch-style boathouses flanking a tower (now a café). Further along are a former **Turkish Bath**, resembling an Ottoman mosque, the stone **Pyramid** where Catherine buried her favourite dogs, and Cameron's **Marble Bridge**, a copy of the Palladian bridge at Wilton House in England.

Towards the Chinese Village

West of the Great Pond lies the "**Italian Park**", whose canals and hillocks are interlaced with paths meandering from one folly to another. Catherine liked to stroll here with her dogs, unaccompanied by courtiers; in *The Captain's Daughter*, Pushkin relates how the heroine of the tale, Maria Ivanovna, unknowingly encountered the empress and interceded for her betrothed. Even more fancifully, Catherine is supposed to have once told a sentry to stand watch over a violet that she wanted to pick, but then forgot about it. As the order was never revoked, a guard was posted on the spot for decades afterwards.

A zigzag trail taking in the park's highlights starts either at the **Granite Terrace** above the Great Pond, or the **Kagul Obelisk** beyond the Cameron Gallery. On an island further south are a small **Concert Hall** and **Kitchen Ruin**, the latter designed to look picturesque rather than for cooking pur-poses. On another islet, visible from the bridge, stands a **Chinese Pavilion** flying metal flags. Also known as the "Creaking Pavilion" because it was designed to creak whenever someone entered, it is now derelict and closed.

Heading west, you'll soon spot the colourful **Chinese Village** (Kitayskaya derevnya), a series of Oriental pavilions in an overgrown corner of the park – though you can't reach them unless you climb over the fence beside the main avenue. Originally a whimsical folly, the village was later turned into a home for serfs who had run away from cruel masters. Ravaged during World War II, the pavilions have now been restored and turned into luxury apartments; the rental income is used to repay the restoration costs. Their upturned roofs are as gaudy as circus tents and crowned with dragons. From here, a path continues on to the **Great Caprice**, a massive humpback arch topped by a pagoda.

Around the Lycée

Across Sadovaya ulitsa from the Catherine Palace stands the famous Imperial **Lycée** (10.30am–5pm; closed Tues; $2.75) where **Alexander Pushkin** once studied. Established to provide a modern education for the sons of distinguished families, it proved more attractive to the poorer nobility than to great aristocrats, who refused to send their children away to boarding school. The 12-year-old Pushkin was a member of the first class presented to Alexander I at the inauguration ceremony on October 19, 1811. During his six years at the Lycée, he grew bold and lyrical, drank punch and wrote poetry, culminating in a bravura recital of his precocious *Recollections of Tsarskoe Selo* in the assembly hall, on June 9, 1817.

Guided tours show you around the classrooms, music room and the physics laboratory – all equipped as in Pushkin's day. Upstairs in the dormitories, the cubbyhole labelled *No. 14. Alexander Pushkin* is reverentially preserved. If you understand Russian, you'll hear much about the influence of his favourite teacher, Kunitsyn (to whom he dedicated several poems), and his crafty valet, Sazanov, who secretly committed several murders and robberies in the two years that he was employed by Pushkin.

Most visitors then head north to see the **statue of Pushkin** daydreaming on a bench, created in 1900 by Robert Bach – it's just beyond the **Church of the Sign** (tserkov Znameniya) of 1734, the oldest building in Tsarskoe Selo. South along Sadovaya ulitsa, a sign directs visitors into a courtyard containing the royal stables, now a **Carriage Museum** (11am–5pm; closed Wed & the last Tues of each month in summer; open Sat & Sun only in winter; $3.30). Further on are the **Orangeries**, a vast sea-green complex now used by the Horticultural Faculty of St Petersburg University.

Practicalities

Pavlovsk is 30km south of St Petersburg, a 35-minute journey by **suburban train** (departures every 20–30min) from Vitebsk Station, or an hour by minibus #K-286 from Moskovskaya ploshchad. Since Pavlovsk is only 5km south of Tsarskoe Selo, it's possible to visit both in succession if you choose the right day, but to do justice to either really requires a full day each. Whatever you decide, bear in mind the opening times for the Great Palaces at Pavlovsk (see p.276) and Tsarskoe Selo (see p.269).

Orientation and tickets

From outside Pavlovsk Station – one stop after Detskoe Selo – it's either a short ride on bus #370 or #383 to right outside the Great Palace, or a twenty-minute walk southeast through the park. If you're planning on seeing Pavlovsk only, it's probably best to take the bus, view the Grand Palace and then do the grounds on the way back to the station. If you're intending to combine Pavlovsk with Tsarskoe Selo, you could walk through the grounds to the Great Palace, then catch a minibus #K-299 or #K-545 to Tsarskoe Selo.

With over 607 hectares of woodland and few signposts, it's easy to get lost in Pavlovsk Park. Tickets ($1.60) are sold at the entrance opposite the train station, and beside the Great Palace, but the fee is waived in wintertime (except during Christmas and Easter festivals). You'll also need separate tickets for the Great Palace and any of the pavilions that happen to be open, which are sold on the spot.

Eating

If you want to eat cheaply, it's best to bring your own picnic and head off into the park – or maybe grab a *shashlyk* and a beer at the outdoor *Café Snezhanka* (daily 11am–5pm) near Druzheskaya alleya. For more substantial fare, try *Podvorye* (daily noon–11pm; ☏466 85 44 to be sure of a table; ⊛www.podvorye.ru) on Sadovaya ulitsa, a fancy restaurant in the style of an *izba* (traditional wooden peasant cottage), 400m from the station (turn left as you come off the platform), which serves traditional Russian food with a flourish and includes Prince Charles and President Chirac among its satisfied customers. You can eat well for $25; there's also sometimes a fun folk ensemble playing. In the palace itself there's a posh self-service café (10am–6pm; closed Fri) in the Columned Hall in the south wing, serving expensive drinks, cakes and sandwiches.

by Charles Cameron, who transformed Tsarskoe Selo's Catherine Palace. Cameron was one of the few architects to win Catherine the Great's lasting admiration, and she therefore foisted his talents upon her son as well. Pretty soon, however, Cameron's Palladian fixation and concern for minutiae began to clash with Paul's and Maria Fyodorovna's tastes, and he was eventually dismissed, his assistant, Vincenzo Brenna, being employed to extend the palace into a much larger, more elaborate complex. Some of the best architects in St Petersburg were recruited to decorate its interior – Quarenghi, Rossi and Voronikhin among others – and the overall Neoclassical effect is surprisingly homogenous.

Life at Pavlovsk was conducted according to the whims of Paul and Maria. While he drilled his troops all day, she painted and embroidered. Guests generally found the social life extraordinarily dull, consisting of interminable gatherings where only banalities were exchanged. The palace was meant to be approached from the east, from where you get the best overall view off the great sweep of Brenna's semi-circular wings. At the centre of the courtyard is a **statue of Paul** dressed in the Prussian military uniform he loved so much.

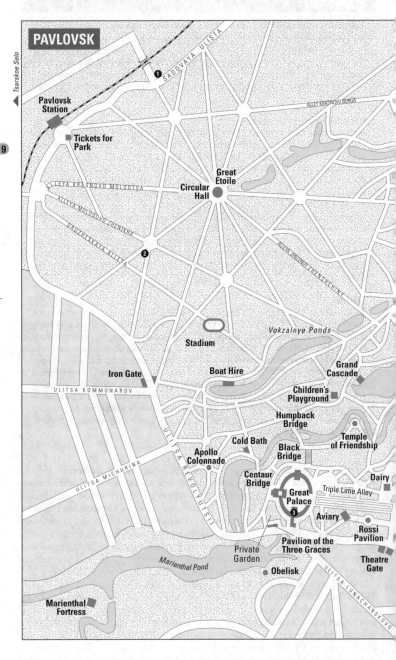

PAVLOVSK

Tsarskoe Selo ▲

Pavlovsk Station

SADOVAYA ULISTA

ALLEY KRASNOVO BORGA

Tickets for Park

ALLEYA KRASNOVO MOLODTSA

ALLEYA MOLODOVO ZHENIKHA

DRUZHESKAYA ALLEY

Circular Hall

Great Etoile

ALLEYA ZHELENDY ZHENISTCHINY

Vokzalnye Ponds

Stadium

Iron Gate

ULITSA KOMMUNAROV

Boat Hire

Grand Cascade

Children's Playground

Humpback Bridge

Cold Bath

Apollo Colonnade

Black Bridge

Temple of Friendship

ULITSA REVOLYUTSII

Centaur Bridge

ULITSA MICHURINA

Great Palace

Triple Lime Alley

Dairy

Aviary

Rossi Pavilion

Pavilion of the Three Graces

Private Garden

Theatre Gate

Marienthal Pond

Obelisk

ULITSA LUNACHARSKOVO

Marienthal Fortress

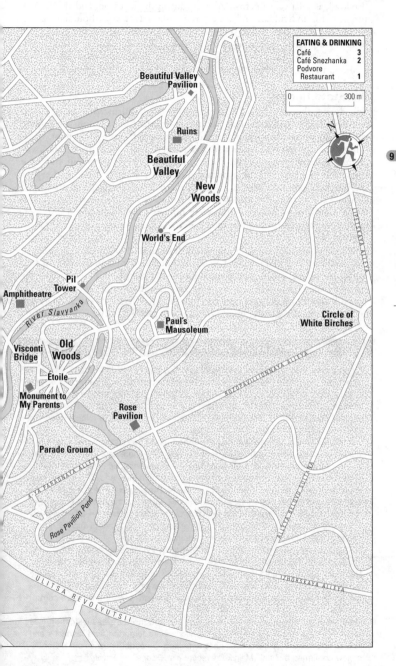

EATING & DRINKING
Café 3
Café Snezhanka 2
Podvore
Restaurant 1

0   300 m

N

Beautiful Valley Pavilion

Ruins

Beautiful Valley

New Woods

World's End

Pil Tower

Amphitheatre

River *Slavyanka*

Paul's Mausoleum

Circle of White Birches

Visconti Bridge

Old Woods

Étoile

Monument to My Parents

Rose Pavilion

ROZOFAVILIONNAYA ALLEYA

Parade Ground

TA PARADNAYA ALLEYA

Rose Pavilion Pond

ALLEYA

IZHORSKAYA ALLEYA

ULITSA REVOLYUTSII

Pavlovsk is relatively uncrowded even during high season, and the separate entrances for individuals and tour groups mean that you shouldn't have to queue for more than a few minutes; tickets are sold inside the palace. The **itinerary** described below may not always be followed in practice, but most of the rooms are permanently open; each contains a black-and-white photograph documenting its ruination during the war.

The State Rooms

Built during the era of the European Grand Tour and the first great archeological digs, the palace contains numerous motifs from antiquity, beginning with the **Egyptian Vestibule** (Yegipetskiy vestibyul) on the first floor, which is lined with pharaonic statues and zodiac medallions. From here, visitors are ushered upstairs to the second-floor **State Rooms** via the main **staircase**, designed by Brenna and using martial motifs to pander to Paul's pretensions. The northern parade of rooms reflect his martial obsessions, the southern ones the more domesticated tastes of Maria Fyodorovna. The striking thing about all the rooms, though, is their relatively human scale – you could just about imagine living here – unlike those of the Great Palaces of Peterhof and Tsarskoe Selo.

At the top of the stairs is the domed **Italian Hall** (Italyanskiy zal), rising up into the palace's central cupola. The decor, intended by Cameron to evoke the atmosphere of a Roman bathhouse, is uniformly Neoclassical, with rich helpings of *trompe l'oeil* and stucco, and a fine collection of candelabras shaped like French horns. From here you pass through the small Valet's Room and Dressing Room into **Paul's Study**, hung with a portrait of Peter the Great and lined

Tsar Paul – the "Russian Hamlet"

Given the oddities of many of the Romanovs, it's rather unfair that **Paul** (1754–1801) should be the only one tagged "the mad tsar". Rumours of illegitimacy plagued him throughout his life, though his boorish temperament and obsession with all things military suggest that Peter III might have been his real father after all. However, his mother, Catherine the Great, had already taken Sergei Saltykov as a lover when she became pregnant, so people drew the obvious conclusion.

Paul saw little of Catherine during **childhood**, and was just eight years old when his father was deposed with her consent. Although she immediately designated Paul as her successor, he never forgave her for his father's murder. A sickly child, Paul suffered from digestive problems, vomiting and diarrhoea, and in later life from insomnia, tantrums and paranoia. His first **marriage** was a disaster: his wife was seduced by his best friend and died in childbirth; but the second one proved happier, despite the fact that Maria Fyodorovna reputedly had an affair with her Scottish physician, Dr Wilson, who may have been the real father of Tsar Nicholas I (his face was strikingly like Wilson's and utterly unlike Paul's).

After Catherine's death, Paul sought to destroy everything she had stood for, sacking those who had enjoyed her favour and elevating those whom she had disgraced. Besides those embittered by their fall, he caused widespread resentment among the nobility by attempting to curtail their abuses of power. He abolished the 25 years' military service that oppressed the peasantry; planned to reform Russia's corrupt financial institutions; and almost acquired Malta as a Russian naval base – to the alarm of England, whose ambassador was involved in Paul's **assassination** (see p.90). After his death, Paul's worthy intentions were forgotten, and his faults and foibles emphasized. As he himself once remarked, "Anecdote pushes out History" – a view confirmed by Vitaly Melnikov's recent film, *Poor, Poor Pavel*.

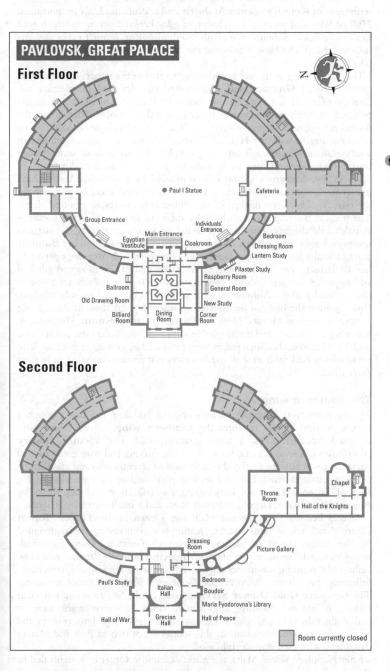

PAVLOVSK, GREAT PALACE

First Floor

N

● Paul I Statue

Cafeteria

Group Entrance

Individuals' Entrance

Main Entrance

Egyptian Vestibule

Cloakroom

Bedroom

Dressing Room

Lantern Study

Pilaster Study

Raspberry Room

General Room

New Study

Corner Room

Ballroom

Old Drawing Room

Billiard Room

Dining Room

Second Floor

Chapel

Throne Room

Hall of the Knights

Dressing Room

Picture Gallery

Paul's Study

Italian Hall

Bedroom

Boudoir

Maria Fyodorovna's Library

Hall of War

Grecian Hall

Hall of Peace

Room currently closed

with busts of Roman emperors. At the far end is Paul's modestly proportioned **Hall of War** (Zal voyny), an explosion of gilded *objets de guerre*, in which even the candlesticks symbolize war spoils – although Paul himself never saw any military action. The bas-reliefs below the ceiling represent the Trojan Wars and *The Odyssey*.

The palace wing of the tsar is connected to that of the tsaritsa by Cameron's green-coloured **Grecian Hall** (Grecheskiy zal), designed to resemble the interior of a Greek temple. It's undoubtedly the most ornate room in the palace, featuring a set of exquisite jasper urns and series of wooden divans; the fireplaces were taken from the Engineers' Castle after Paul's death. Maria's suite of rooms begins with the **Hall of Peace** (Zal mira), the perfect antidote to Paul's Hall of War, though no less gilt-laden, the symbols of war replaced instead by floral motifs, musical instruments and images of fecundity.

Maria Fyodorovna's Library is considered by many to be Voronikhin's masterpiece, not the least of whose treasures is the desk chair he designed for the tsaritsa, its back rest flanked by two fluted horns containing potted plants. The parquet flooring, inlaid with twelve different varieties of wood, is exceptional, while the bay study is surrounded by books on botany, the tsaritsa's favourite hobby. Though you can't hear it in action, the table in her **Boudoir** plays melodies from Bach and Beethoven whenever its drawers are opened. In her **Bedroom**, two golden putti stand at the end of the canopied gilt bed and opposite is a glass cabinet containing the 64-piece toilette set given to the tsaritsa by Marie Antoinette, with whom she got on famously while in Paris. Neither the bed nor the toilette set was ever used, their function being merely to impress visitors. Next is Maria's **Dressing Room** (Tualetnaya), featuring an unusual steel dressing table with matching accessories, all studded with "steel diamonds". Such pieces were produced by craftsmen from the state armouries at Tula, who were allowed to carry out private commissions in their spare time.

The southern wing

At this point, you leave the palace's original building and pass through a couple of tiny lobbies to enter the **southern wing**, whose rooms were designed by Brenna on a much grander scale. The **Picture Gallery** (Kartinnaya galereya) is a case in point: a long, curving hall with green ruched curtains, it was built to display the collection of seventeenth- and eighteenth-century paintings which Paul and his wife purchased on their grand shopping tour of Europe. Whilst not outstanding, the collection includes works by Angelica Kauffmann, Tiepolo, Salvatore Rosa and a small sketch by Rubens.

Beyond lies the Great Dining Hall, also known as the **Throne Room** (Tronniy zal), whose most arresting feature is a giant ceiling fresco, designed by the Russo-Italian set designer Pietro di Gottardo Gonzago, which struggles to achieve some sort of false perspective from the flat and rather low ceiling (the painting was in fact only executed during the postwar renovation, following the chance discovery of Gonzago's plans by Soviet restorers). The 606-piece **Gold Dinner Service**, made by the St Petersburg porcelain factory, is laid out on three large dining tables – otherwise the room is barely furnished. On special occasions, an orchestra used to play in the adjacent room which contains marble sculptures of two of Paul and Maria's daughters, who died during childhood.

After Napoleon seized Malta, the island's Chivalric Order of Knights fled to Russia, where they promptly deposed the current Grand Master and elected

Paul in his place. Paul was a wise choice in terms of position and wealth, but as an Orthodox believer, his election wasn't recognized by the pope. Nevertheless, he built the lime-green **Hall of the Knights** (Kavalerskiy zal) to receive his charges. The hall contains lashings of lapis lazuli and a collection of Classical sculptures, but the only reference to the knights themselves is the small Maltese cross on the ceiling.

From here, you enter the **Imperial Chapel**, which is totally non-Orthodox in its design, with sculptural decoration and no icons. The paintings are copies of seventeenth- and eighteenth-century Western European works in the Hermitage. Paul's throne stands in the corner of the gallery.

Back through the Picture Gallery, you come to a staircase up to the **top floor**, which contains an interesting exhibition of furniture and interiors from the 1800s to the Revolution. Rooms typical of each period have been re-created to give a real sense of how people actually lived – unfortunately this part of the palace is often closed owing to staff shortages.

The private apartments

Returning down the staircase to the **first floor** of the north wing brings you to the tsar and tsaritsa's **private apartments**, on a cosier scale than the State Rooms, though no less ornate. First is the **Raspberry Room** (Malinoviy kabinet), so called for the colour of the upholstery and draperies, followed by the **General Room** (Obshchiy kabinet), where Paul and his family used to gather. Such gatherings were seldom happy for, as Chancellor Rostopchin observed, "Alexander hates his father, Konstantin fears him, the daughters, under their mother's influence, loathe him, and they all smile and would be glad to see him ground to powder."

Beyond lies Paul's formal **New Study** (Noviy kabinet), designed on simple, Neoclassical lines by Quarenghi and hung with a series of engraved copies of Raphael's frescoes for the papal chambers of the Vatican. Next comes the **Corner Room** (Uglovaya gostinaya), sporting lilac-tinted false marble walls and Karelian birch furniture. The room was designed by Carlo Rossi, who began his illustrious career here in 1803, redesigning fire-damaged rooms. The largest room on the first floor is the Cameron-designed **Dining Room** (Stolovaya), whose austerity was in keeping with Paul's liking for simple food – his favourite dish was cabbage.

Passing through the Billiard Room, whose table was destroyed during the war, you reach the **Old Drawing Room** (Staraya gostinaya). Its pale blue walls are adorned with tapestries given to Paul by Louis XVI following his visit to Paris, which originally hung in Paul's palace at Gatchina (see p.288). Altogether more satisfying, though, is the cheerful sky-blue and gold **Ballroom** (Tantsevalniy zal), restored to Cameron's original design after the war and dominated by two huge scenes of Rome by the French artist Hubert Robert. The procession of private apartments in the **southern wing** is currently being renovated.

Pavlovsk Park

The walk from the train station to the Great Palace gives only the briefest of glimpses of **Pavlovsk Park** (Pavlovskiy park; daily all year-round 9am–8pm; $1.60), which stretches for several kilometres either side of the River Slavyanka. The park was laid out by Cameron and Brenna, with help from the stage designer Gonzago; Voronikhin and Rossi also contributed, and some say that Capability Brown actually devised the original plan. Whatever the truth, the park's distinguishing feature is its naturalistic landscaping, with gently slop-ing hills, winding paths, a meandering river and hectares of wild forest – it's especially lovely in the autumn, owing to its richly coloured and variegated foliage. Russians come here to harvest mushrooms in June and August and berries in September.

Most of Cameron's and Rossi's **architectural diversions** are concentrated in the more formal gardens around the palace and in the immediate vicinity of the river, which flows through the middle of the park. You could cover a large number of these fairly comfortably in an afternoon; a more thorough explo-ration of the park would take the best part of a day. There are no hard-and-fast rules about which route you should take through the park; the following account is a guide to the highlights.

From the Private Garden to the Marienthal Fortress

Southwest of the Great Palace, separated from the rest of the park by a high iron railing, the tsar and tsaritsa's **Private Garden** was laid out by Cameron in a formal Dutch style, with flowerbeds that explode with colour in summer-time. At the far end of the garden, by the main road, Cameron's Greek-style **Pavilion of the Three Graces** takes its name from the central statuary group representing Joy, Flowering and Brilliance.

On the other side of the road, the upper section of the River Slavyanka forms the large **Marienthal Pond**, in an area once known as the "Russian Switzerland" (various other sections of the park were landscaped in emulation of France, Italy and England – a popular conceit of the time). Cameron's **Obelisk** on the southern shore of the pond commemorates the foundation of Pavlovsk in 1782, while at the far western end of the water stands the "Bip" or **Marienthal Fortress**, a toy Gothic castle built by Brenna in 1795 to flatter the new tsar's military pretensions.

North of the Slavyanka

From the terrace behind the Great Palace, you can view the wide sweep of the Slavyanka valley. High up on the opposite bank, Cameron's **Apollo Colonnade** was left a picturesque ruin after being struck by lightning and then damaged by a landslide during a storm in 1817. Down to the right, steps descend to the **Centaur Bridge**, guarded by four centaurs, which leads to a **Cold Bath** (Kholodnaya banya) that occasionally serves as a venue for small exhibitions. From here, there's a superb view uphill to the palace.

Several more bridges cross the Slavyanka downstream from the Cold Bath – including the **Humpback Bridge** and the **Black Bridge** – with a monu-mental staircase running down from the palace to meet them. Beyond, set in a sharp bend in the slow-moving river, lies the largest and most eye-catching of Cameron's pavilions, the circular **Temple of Friendship** (Khram Druzhby), the first building in Russia to use the Doric order. Commissioned as a diplomatic gesture in an effort to cement the shaky relationship between Maria Fyodorovna and Catherine the Great, it is studded with medallions illustrating the themes of platonic and romantic love.

On the plateau to the north of the Slavyanka valley, the **Vokzalnye Ponds** are a popular spot for a bit of lazy **boating**, with boats available for rent on the north shore. In Tolstoy's time, day-trippers arrived at a train station (*vokzal*) on the site of what is now a small stadium; there are plans to re-lay the track and rebuild the station if enough money can be raised. Beyond lies a web of leafy avenues, radiating from the **Great Étoile**, with its **Circular Hall**.

Along the Triple Lime Valley

Immediately to the east of the palace, the **Triple Lime Alley** stretches for 300m through a more formal section of the park. The north side of the avenue is designed as a parterre, made up of two **Great Circles**, with early eighteenth-century marble statues of Peace and Justice at their centres. To the south, Cameron built an **Aviary** (Voler), used for small receptions and meals, and now prettily strewn with vines. On the other side of the ornamental box-hedge maze stands the **Rossi Pavilion**, designed by Rossi but erected only on the eve of World War I, and within which lurks a statue of Maria Fyodorovna. At the far end of the alley lies a common **grave** for the Soviet soldiers killed clearing Pavlovsk of mines.

Towards the Old and New Woods

Paul's favourite hobby was drilling his regiments in the **Parade Ground** laid out to the northeast of the Triple Lime Alley, which was later transformed into parkland. In his bid to Germanize and "civilize" Russia's upper classes, the police were ordered to scour the park, destroy all the traditional round Russian hats they could find and cut the lapels off coats and cloaks – as the English ambassador was mortified to discover.

North of the Parade Ground is the area known as the **Old Woods**, where a circle of twelve paths forms an **Étoile**. At its centre stands Apollo, chief patron of the Muses, while a bronze statue of a muse or mythological figure marks the start of each path. One leads to the **Monument to My Parents**, a pavilion erected by Maria Fyodorovna in memory of her father and mother, the duke and duchess of Württemburg, whose profiles appear on the marble pyramid within.

To the northeast of the Étoile stands **Paul's Mausoleum**, built by Thomas de Thomon on the tsaritsa's instruction. Despite the difficulties of their marriage, she always took her husband's side in the intrigues of Catherine's last years, and the dedication – "To My Husband and Benefactor" – is probably sincere. Not that Paul is actually buried here – he lies with the other Romanovs in the Peter and Paul Cathedral.

From here you can turn south towards the **Rose Pavilion** (May–Sept daily 10am–5pm) where **concerts** of classical music are held on summer evenings (tickets sold on the spot), or forge deeper into the park. Gonzago's **Circle of White Birches** is one of the loveliest, most isolated areas, or there are more romantic vistas in the **Beautiful Valley** and the **New Woods**, north of Paul's mausoleum. A few scattered monuments serve as points of orientation – the "ruined" **Pil Tower**, the **World's End** column and the **Beautiful Valley Pavilion** – though none is architecturally outstanding.

Gatchina

In 1776, Catherine the Great gave **Gatchina** and its neighbouring villages to her lover, Grigori Orlov, as a reward for helping her to depose (and dispose of) her husband, Peter III. Its enormous palace wasn't completed by Rinaldi until 1781; by then Orlov – tormented by visions of Peter's ghost – was on the verge of insanity and had only two miserable years to enjoy it before he died, whereupon Catherine promptly passed it on to her son, Paul, who thus inherited Gatchina from his own father's murderer. Paul had Vincenzo Brenna remodel

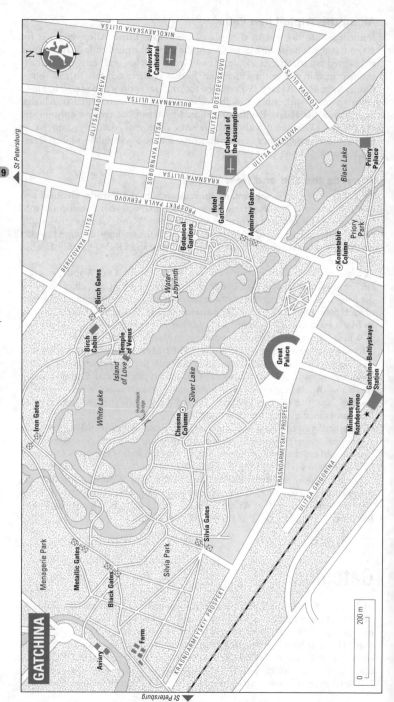

GATCHINA

St Petersburg

St Petersburg

N

NIKOLAEVSKAYA ULITSA

Pavlovskiy Cathedral

ULITSA RADISHEVA

BULVARNAYA ULITSA

ULITSA DOSTOEVSKOVO

SOBORNAYA ULITSA

Cathedral of the Assumption

KRASNAYA ULITSA

ULITSA CHKALOVA

LEONOVA ULITSA

Hotel Gatchina

PROSPEKT PAVLA PERVOVO

Admiralty Gates

Black Lake

Priory Palace

BEREZOVAYA ULITSA

Botanical Gardens

Water Labyrinth

Konnetable Column

Priory Park

Birch Gates

Birch Cabin

Temple of Venus

Island of Love

Great Palace

Iron Gates

White Lake

Hunchback Bridge

Silver Lake

Chesma Column

Gatchina-Baltiyskaya Station

Minibus for Rozhdestveno

KRASNOARMEYSKIY PROSPEKT

ULITSA GRIGORINA

Menagerie Park

Metallic Gates

Black Gates

Silvia Park

Silvia Gates

Farm

Aviary

KRASNOARMEYSKIY PROSPEKT

200 m

0

Practicalities

Located about 50km south of St Petersburg, Gatchina is accessible by **minibus** from Moskovskaya (#K-18), Kirovskiy Zavod (#K-546) or Prospekt Veteranov (#K-631) metro stations; they take about 45 minutes and terminate at Gatchina-Baltiyskaya train station, two minutes' walk from the palace. Alternatively, catch a **suburban train** (every 40min; 6.30am–midnight) from St Petersburg's Baltic Station to the same destination – though beware that some stop instead at the Tatyanino and Gatchina-Varshavskaya stations on the other side of town from the palace, which entails a much longer walk.

Besides a café in the palace itself, there are several nondescript places **to eat** on Sobornaya ulitsa, ten minutes' walk from the palace in the centre of town. In the unlikely event that you want **to stay**, the *Hotel Gatchina* (℡271/1 14 58; ❶) on the corner of Krasnaya ulitsa and ulitsa Chkalova has basic rooms and shared bathrooms. It lacks hot water, but has a sauna for guests ($10 per hour). Another, fully equipped new hotel was under construction at the time of writing.

the palace during the 1790s, raising the height of its semi-circular galleries and side blocks, and installing cannons and sentry boxes to make it look even more like a feudal castle or a barracks – which suited Paul's interests perfectly.

During its heyday, five thousand people were employed at Gatchina (most from families that had served the Romanovs for generations), while its kennels included every breed of dog from borzois to bulldogs (used for bear-hunting). Some thirty years after Paul's murder, Gatchina became the residence of Nicholas I, who had both side blocks reconstructed and his own living quarters installed on the first floor of the Arsenal Block, while the late eighteenth-century State Rooms in the central block were restored. The next Romanovs to spend much time here were Alexander III and his wife Maria Fyodorovna, who fled here for security reasons immediately after Alexander II's funeral, and henceforth left Gatchina only for official engagements in the Winter Palace. Finding Gatchina "cold, disgusting and full of workmen", with drawing rooms large enough to hold a regiment and ceilings too high for an intimate atmosphere, they occupied the servants' quarters, but their English governess refused to bring up their baby under such conditions, so the nursery was installed upstairs in a vast drawing room hung with tapestries. For almost two years after his accession, Alexander lived in seclusion, dressing like a peasant, shovelling snow and cutting wood. When a visitor expressed surprise, the tsar retorted: "Well, what else can I do till the Nihilists are stamped out?"

In October 1917, Gatchina witnessed the ignominious "last stand" of the Provisional Government, whose leader **Kerensky** fled here in an American embassy car on the morning of October 25, thus escaping arrest at the Winter Palace. After lunch he drove on to Pskov and persuaded a cavalry unit to return with him to Gatchina, whose curator lamented that "the prospect of lodging an entire Cossack division in the palace was not a happy one". In the event, Kerensky refused to accompany them into battle, remaining in his room "lying on the couch, swallowing tranquillizers," until he slipped away disguised as a sailor (*not* a female nurse, as alleged by the Soviets) on October 31.

His nemesis **Trotsky** was made of sterner stuff. In July 1919, Red Guards halted the final advance of White forces from Estonia (the "kennel of the dogs of the counter-revolution") at Gatchina, where Trotsky led them into battle waving a walking stick. To commemorate his heroism, the town was renamed Trotsk – but reverted to its old name after Trotsky became synonymous with "deviationism" in Stalin's Russia.

Like the other palaces, Gatchina was ravaged by the Nazis in World War II, though its staff managed to evacuate four train-loads of treasures before the Germans arrived. It was turned into a naval college after the war, and restoration work didn't begin until 1985, and even then it was accorded a far lower priority than Peterhof or Tsarskoe Selo – hence the small number of rooms that have been restored and the fact that work is still continuing. Restorers have been helped, however, by a collection of 1870s watercolours by Edward Hau and Luigi Premazzi, which illustrated many rooms in meticulous detail. Check out the examples on the **website** Ⓦwww.alexanderpalace.org/gatchina.

The palace

The semi-circular palace flanks a courtyard where regiments once drilled, fronted by a dry moat and a thigh-booted **statue of Paul**. His fervent militarism and admiration for German ways endeared him to Gatchina's Nazi occupiers, who posted a sentry to protect the statue from being vandalized – till 1944, when they tried to destroy the palace before retreating. Its two-metre-thick walls withstood the blast, but the interior was gutted.

Built of weathered limestone, the **Great Palace** (10am–6pm; closed Mon & the first Tues of each month; $5.50) is in stark contrast to its counterparts at Pavlovsk, Peterhof and Tsarskoe Selo, whose decorative stucco facades are painted in bright colours. Restoration work has been confined to the central section, and the interiors of the Arsenal and Kitchen blocks will probably never be renewed, since paintings and photographs of their decor perished at the same time as the originals – though an idea of what they looked like can be gained from a historical exhibition on the first floor. Here you'll also find an **Exhibition of Weaponry**, with 1100 items that were either brought back as booty, received as gifts or purchased by the tsars, displaying extraordinary crafts-manship and a generous use of gold, silver, ivory and coral. A circular **Church** (11am–6pm) with a skylight in its cupola lies further along the corridor and up some backstairs, built into a corner tower of the Kitchen Block.

To dispel the dour impression left by the first floor, visitors are greeted by staff in eighteenth-century livery, at the foot of the **Grand Staircase** to the second floor of the central block. Like guests of old, you approach the State Rooms via an **Antechamber** decorated with armorial mouldings and a ceiling fresco of the Virgin and infant Jesus, illuminated by chandeliers in drum-like casings. Paul's love of the military is also echoed by the trumpet-shaped candelabras within the columned **Marble Dining Room**, which Nicholas I's wife later used as a bathroom. Beyond lies Paul's **Throne Hall**, with its huge red velvet and gilt throne and pistachio-coloured walls hung with Gobelin tapestries presented by Louis XVI of France – one represents Asia and depicts a lion savaging a zebra; the other Africa, showing a tribal chieftain in a litter.

The **Crimson Drawing Room** was once adorned by three Gobelin tapestries illustrating scenes from *Don Quixote,* of which only one – showing Sancho Panza's arrival on the isle of Baratana – now hangs *in situ,* the other two being held at Pavlovsk, and unlikely to return soon. (In an episode worthy of Gogol's satires, the director of Gatchina wrote to the Ministry of Culture requesting the tapestries' return. Shortly afterwards he was appointed director of Pavlovsk, in which capacity he received his own request, and rejected it.) In Paul's **State Bedroom**, gilded mirrors create the illusion of a corridor receding to infinity, while a disguised door beside his bed leads to the secret passage beneath the palace.

Finest of all is the **White Hall**, or ballroom. Its parquet floor is inlaid with nine kinds of rare wood and its ceiling festooned with stucco garlands. Notice

Palaces and parks

Strelna	Стрельна
Konstantin Palace	Константиновский дворец
Shuvalovka	Шуваловка
Wooden Palace	Деревянный дворец
Peterhof	Петергоф
Petrodvorets	Петродворец
Alexandria Park	Парк Александрия
Bathhouse Wing	Банный корпус
Benois Wing	Корпус Бенуа
Catherine Wing	Екатерининский корпус
Cottage Palace	Коттедж
Great Palace	Большой дворец
Hermitage	Эрмитаж
Lower Park	Нижний парк
Marly Palace	Марли дворец
Monplaisir	Монплезир
Upper Garden	Верхний сад
Oranienbaum	Ораниенбаум
Lomonosov	Ломоносов
Chinese Palace	Китайский дворец
Great Palace	Большой дворец
Japanese Pavilion	Японский павильон
Lower Park	Нижний парк
Peter III's Palace	дворец Петра III
Sliding Hill	Катальная горка
Upper Park	Верхний парк
Tsarskoe Selo	Царское село
Pushkin	Пушкин
Alexander Palace	Александровский дворец
Alexander Park	Александровский парк
Catherine Palace	Екатерининский дворец
Catherine Park	Екатерининский парк
Pavlovsk	Павловск
Great Palace	Большой дворец
Pavlovsk Park	Павловский парк
Gatchina	Гатчина
Birch Cabin	Береовая изба
Great Palace	Большой дворец
Priory Palace	Приоратский дворец

the lion and the lobster above the doorways, representing the astrological symbols for the months of July and August, when the palace was used as a Imperial residence. Half-a-dozen rooms on the floor above exhibit **paintings** of historical rather than artistic merit, such as the scenes of life at Gatchina during Nicholas I's reign; portraits of Catherine the Great as a young bride and an old woman; and Paul's daughter Anna, who was wooed by Napoleon – whom Maria Fyodorovna dismissed as "that Corsican show-off" – and later married into the Greek royal family (making her an ancestor of Britain's current Prince of Wales).

To go back downstairs, you may end up using a spiral stairway within the **Signal Tower** – originally one of 150 such towers, which were capable of transmitting messages all the way from St Petersburg to Warsaw in twenty minutes using a heliographic relay system. Lastly, you can go in search of the dank **subterranean passage** that runs from the palace to the Silver Lake – it's not, as you might imagine, a product of Paul's fear of assassination, but was created during Orlov's time as a kind of romantic folly. Its acoustics are such that a word spoken at one end clearly echoes back from the far end, 200m away.

The park and town

The wildest of all the palace grounds, Gatchina's **park** is what draws most visitors, particularly in the autumn, when its sense of uncontrolled nature reclaiming a man-made setting is most vivid. From the formal **Dutch Garden** near the palace, paths wend across a chain of islands between the **White and Silver lakes**. The former never freezes over, and provided a testing ground for the first Russian submarine in 1879. On its far side, a decrepit **Temple of Venus** stands on the Island of Love, where pleasure boats once docked, while on the mainland is a postwar replica of another folly. The **Birch Cabin** (Berozavaya izba; May–Sept 10am–6pm; closed Mon; $2) resembles a stack of logs from the outside, but contains a palatial suite of mirrored rooms within. Admission tickets for the cabin are sold at the *kassa* in the Great Palace.

Besides the geometric **Silvia Park**, there are two ex-hunting grounds: to the north, **Menagerie Park** is where Alexander III took his children to follow animal tracks in summer and dig paths through the snow during winter; in the other direction lies the **Priory Park**, named after the **Priory Palace** (10am–6pm; closed Mon & Tues; $0.30) overlooking the **Black Lake**. This Germanic-looking edifice was built for Prince Conday, Prior of the Maltese Knights of St John, who never actually lived there. Its architect, Nikolai Lvov, pioneered the use of rammed earth as a building material, which proved robust enough to withstand a bomb landing nearby during World War II. An exhibition upstairs features plans for many buildings in the German style, annotated by Paul with the order "Let it be!" – but they were never realized due to his murder.

Finally, the town itself boasts two imposing buildings: the Baroque **Pavlovskiy Cathedral** and the pseudo-medieval **Cathedral of the Assumption**, plus some folksy **wooden houses** along ulitsa Chkalova.

Kronstadt, the Gulf coast and Vyborg

The island fortress and naval base of **Kronstadt** was established soon after St Petersburg was founded. Sited on Kotlin Island in the Gulf of Finland, the fortress was the linchpin of the city's defences against seaborne invasion and the home port of the Baltic Fleet, yet would later become the state's Achilles heel when its forces revolted against tsar and commissar alike. Off-limits to foreigners for decades, this curiously time-warped town

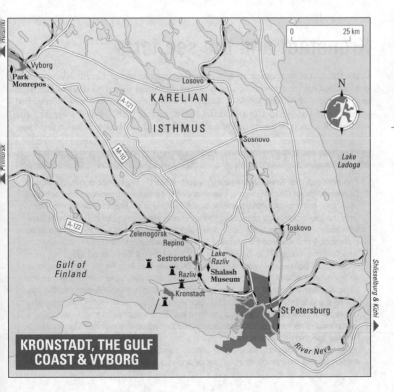

now welcomes tourists, but is likely to appeal mainly to those keen on maritime history or bizarre urban landscapes.

A more mainstream attraction is the **Karelian Isthmus** between the Gulf of Finland and Lake Ladoga, where Petersburgers relax at their *dachas* between bouts of sunbathing, swimming and mushroom-picking. It's a soothing landscape of silver birches and misty hollows, with spectacular sunsets reflected in limpid water, the mosquitoes being the only drawback. You'll need a car, however, really to explore the region. Relying on public transport, you're limited to the towns along **the Gulf coast**: namely **Razliv**, where Lenin hid out in 1917; **Repino**, which houses the delightful memorial house of the artist Repin; and historic **Vyborg**, with its castle, Nordic houses and romantic Park Monrepos.

Historically, the Karelian Isthmus has been a bone of contention between Russia and its Baltic neighbours since medieval times. In 1812 it passed to the Grand Duchy of Finland (then a semi-autonomous part of the Tsarist Empire), with the frontier drawn to the east of Kronstadt. In 1917, during the turmoil of revolution, the Finns seized the opportunity to declare independence and the isthmus remained Finnish territory until the Winter War of 1939–40, when Stalin annexed Karelia to form a buffer zone to protect Leningrad. To regain Karelia, Finland allied itself with Nazi Germany in World War II and the Red Army was driven out; when it returned in 1944, Stalin claimed even more territory in the far north (now the Karelian Republic), which Russia retains to this day, insisting that the matter is non-negotiable.

Kronstadt and the sea forts

Peter the Great was quick to grasp the strategic value of Kotlin Island, 30km out in the Gulf: the waters to the north of the island were too shallow for large ships to pass through, while a sandbank off the southern shore compelled vessels to sail close to the island. In the winter of 1703–4 Peter erected the offshore Kronschlot Fort, followed by a shipyard on Kotlin Island; the large

The Kronstadt sailors' revolt

The eighteen-day **Kronstadt sailors' revolt** of March 1921 went under the slogan "Soviets without Communism". Their manifesto demanded freedom of speech and assembly, the abolition of Bolshevik dictatorship and an end to War Communism. Only the ice-locked Gulf prevented the rebel cruisers *Sevastopol* and *Petropavlovsk* from steaming into the Neva basin and holding St Petersburg hostage. With a thaw imminent, Trotsky warned the rebels: "Only those who surrender unconditionally can count on the mercy of the Soviet Republic" – but few of them responded.

Two hours before dawn on March 8, 45,000 white-clad Red Army troops advanced on Kronstadt, across the frozen Gulf, unnoticed until they were within 500m of the fortress, when a third of them drowned after Kronstadt's cannons ruptured the ice. The next assault was spearheaded by volunteers from the Tenth Party Congress, who laid ladders between the ruptured ice floes and then swarmed across to establish a beachhead. The fortress was subsequently stormed on the night of March 16–17. Besides the thirty thousand killed on both sides in the battle, 2000 sailors were executed on the spot and many more sent to the Gulag (though 8000 managed to escape across the ice to Finland). The sailors were posthumously pardoned in 1994.

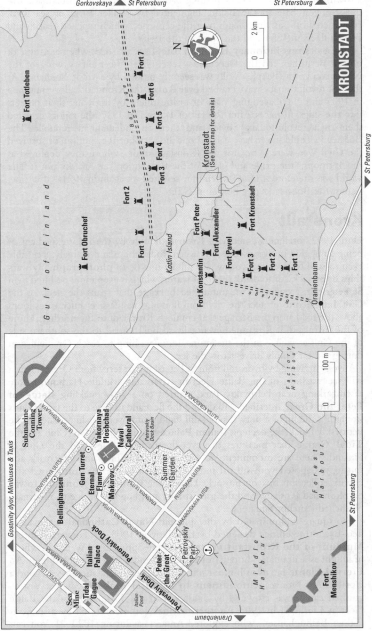

KRONSTADT

Gorkovskaya ▲ St Petersburg

St Petersburg ▲

N

0   2 km

Gulf of Finland

Fort Totleben

Fort 7
Fort 6
Fort 5
Fort 4
Fort 3
Fort 2
Fort 1

Fort Obruchef

Kronstadt
(See inset map for details)

Kotlin Island

Fort Peter

Fort Konstantin

Fort Alexander
Fort Pavel

Fort Kronstadt

Fort 3
Fort 2
Fort 1

St Petersburg ▲

Oranienbaum

St Petersburg ▼

Inset map

▲ Gostiniy dvor, Minibuses & Taxis

Submarine
Conning
Tower

UL ITSA ROSHALYA

Gun Turret

Yakornaya
Ploshchad

Eternal
Flame

Naval
Cathedral

Makarov

KOMMUNISTICHESKAYA ULITSA

PROSPEKT LENINA

ULITSA KARLA MARKSA

Bellinghausen

SOVETSKAYA ULITSA

KRASNAYA ULITSA

Petrovskiy
Dock Basin

Summer
Garden

PETROGRADSKAYA ULITSA

ULITSA KONSOMOLA

*Factory
Harbour*

0   100 m

Sea
Mine

Tidal
Gague

Italian
Palace

Italian
Pond

Petrovskiy Dock

Peter
the Great

MAKAROVSKAYA ULITSA

Petrovskiy
Park

*Forest
Harbour*

▼ St Petersburg

*Middle
Harbour*

Fort
Menshikov

Oranienbaum ▼

293

colony that developed around them took the name Kronstadt (City of the Crown) in 1723. Its defences, floating batteries and naval harbour made this the strongest base in the Baltic, augmented by smaller *forty*, or sea forts, constructed on outlying islands over the centuries, which repelled British and French fleets in 1854, and the Nazis in the 1940s.

Kronstadt's **revolutionary tradition** dates back to 1825, when a Kronstadt officer, Bestushev, led the Decembrist rebels; later, the military wing of the Narodnaya Volya (People's Will) was secretly headed by a sailor, Sukhanov. As the first revolutionary wave crashed over Russia, the Kronstadt sailors mutinied in 1905 and 1906, avenging years of maltreatment by throwing their officers into the ships' furnaces. After the fall of Tsarism in 1917, the sailors declared their own revolutionary Soviet and then an independent republic. The Bolsheviks could never have carried out the October Revolution, or survived the Civil War, were it not for the Kronstadt sailors, whom they deployed as shock troops: "the pride and glory of the Revolution", as Trotsky put it. The world was therefore stunned when they revolted yet again in 1921 – this time, against the Bolsheviks (see box on p.292).

Kronstadt

Until 1992, foreigners could visit **Kronstadt** only by the risky expedient of being smuggled in disguised as a Russian. Today the island is freely accessible even to solo tourists, but you would still be unwise to **photograph** any war-ships or barracks, or to drink the local **water**, which is even more polluted than St Petersburg's owing to an unfinished **barrage** that spans the neck of the Gulf. Intended to protect the city from flooding, its massive sluice gates loom above the road atop the barrage that connects Kronstadt to the northern shore of the mainland. It is planned eventually to built a road to the southern side of the Gulf as well – in the meantime, locals wishing to reach Oranienbaum during winter simply drive across the ice.

Anyone arriving by hydrofoil from St Petersburg or ferry from Oranienbaum will see warships of the Baltic Fleet in Kronstadt's Middle Harbour, before disembarking near Petrovskiy Park, centred on a swashbuckling **statue of Peter the Great**, inscribed: "To defend the fleet and its base to the last of one's strength is the highest duty." Sailors still stand guard over the sluice gates of the Petrovskiy Dock, the decrepit **Italian Palace** housing the Sailors' Club and the **Tidal Gauge** that measures the ever-fluctuating sea level in the Gulf of Finland. There are monuments to sailors or submariners in every park and square, juxtaposed with surreal installations such as the **sea-mine** used as a charity collection box on prospekt Lenina, the **submarine conning tower** on ploshchad Roshalya and the **gun turret** guarding the bridge to Yakornaya ploshchad (Anchor Square).

The square is dominated by the splendid **Naval Cathedral** – a massive neo-Byzantine edifice designed by Kosyakov in 1903–13, converted into a **Museum of the Kronstadt Fortress** (11am–5pm; closed Wed; $2), whose highlight is a dramatic diorama of the town under Nazi bombardment. An **Eternal Flame** burns in honour of the fallen defenders' memory, beyond a glorious Art Nouveau **monument to Admiral Makarov**, whose distin-guished career was crowned by disaster with the decimation of the Baltic Fleet at Tsushima in 1905. Another mariner commemorated by a statue is Faddei Bellinghausen, who explored Antarctica during 1820–21. You can also see a stretch of the eighteenth-century **fortifications** along the northern shore.

The remainder of the town (pop. 50,000) consists of decaying factories, barracks and oily eighteenth-century canals and dock basins that criss-cross the centre, their names redolent of faraway lands. In Petrine times these were lined with taverns and brothels where sailors caroused; long afterwards, the preacher Father **John of Kronstadt** made his name here by crusading for 53 years against drunkenness, vice and poverty – founding workshops, a refectory, pharmacy and primary school. After his death in 1908 he was buried in the St Petersburg convent that now bears his name (see p.189), mourned by a crowd of 60,000 and "sung out" by a weeping Imperial Choir.

Practicalities

Tour firms outside St Petersburg's Gostiniy dvor run coach **excursions** (4–5hr; $5–8) to Kronstadt most days. In summer, there are also excursions by **hydrofoil** from the Hermitage dock (Wed, Sat & Sun; $33), run by Russian Cruises (☎325 61 20, ✉travel@russian-cruises.ru), which can supply an English-speaking guide for groups of thirty people or more. Alternatively, it's forty minutes by **minibus** #K-510 or a shared taxi from outside Staraya Derevnya metro station, reaching Kronstadt via the barrage from the northern mainland, and stopping in the centre, on Yakornaya ploshchad or prospekt Lenina. There is also a **car ferry** (every 1–2hr) from Oranienbaum on the southern shore of the Gulf; bus #6 runs from Oranienbaum train station to the ferry (*parom*) landing stage, from where the crossing takes 45 minutes. When it comes to the **return journey**, minibuses and taxis leave from the Gostiniy dvor on the corner of Grazhdanskaya ulitsa, a few blocks north of *Skazka*, the best of a handful of **cafés** along prospekt Lenina. On weekdays, there's a **currency exchange** in the cinema on the corner of Sovetskaya ulitsa and ulitsa Roshalya.

The sea forts

Aficionados of maritime life or naval history might consider visiting some of the old *forty* – or **sea forts** – built on man-made islands in the Gulf, which last saw active service during World War II. The so-called **Numbered Northern Forts** were constructed in the 1800s and upgraded just in time for the Crimean War, when they repulsed an Anglo-French fleet under Admiral Napier, which lost two ships to sea mines (their first ever use in warfare) before withdrawing. Two of the forts are accessible on foot from the tidal barrage between Kronstadt and the mainland, but their crumbling casements are hardly worth the effort.

Fort Konstantin, on the southernmost tip of the island (a taxi from town costs $2–3) is a larger complex of stone ravelins where visitors may fire a small naval cannon into the Gulf ($14) – ask to *vystrel iz pushki* if you're interested. Two café-bars complete the amenities of its grandly named International Customs Terminal, though a tourist marina and other developments are on the cards.

Here, you can hire a motorboat (at $50 an hour not cheap, unless there's a group of you to split the cost or you manage to join a Russian excursion group) to reach **Fort Alexander**, 600m offshore. Built with great difficulty by the military engineer Van der Veide (1838–45), this kidney-shaped bastion had four gun decks and 103 cannon ports, which Napier dared not engage. It developed a sinister reputation, acquiring the nickname "**Plague Fort**" (*Chumnoy*), when research into a vaccine for bubonic plague was conducted here from 1897 to 1917. The fort had a laboratory, a menagerie, stables and lodgings for the scientists and their families, whose only link to St Petersburg was a steamship called *Microbe*. Those who died in lab accidents were cremated at the fort. Having reverted to a naval role after the Revolution, it was finally decommissioned in the 1960s; cannons, blast doors and fittings were removed and the shell was left to rot until rave organizers began staging **all-night parties** there – advertised in *Pulse* and on ⓦwww.fortdance.com – with a chartered boat and buses to carry ticket-holders from St Petersburg and back next morning.

If you have the time and money, it's possible to hire a yacht with crew to reach **Obruchef** or **Totleben**, two large forts with concrete casements and harbours built in the 1900s between Kotlin Island and Sestroretsk, that served as anti-aircraft gun platforms in World War II. Visits involve an overnight stay with a *shashlyk* barbecue. Compare quotes from Sunny Sailing and the River Yacht Club in St Petersburg (see p.397).

The Gulf coast

The **Gulf coast** of the Karelian Isthmus begins on the edge of St Petersburg, from where a ribbon of urban development extends northwest along the water as far as Zelenogorsk. Happily, for most of the way high-rise buildings are less in evidence than clapboard *dachas*, painted in bold colours and decorated with intricate fretwork gables. Although rocky headlands and sandy coves can be glimpsed through the pine trees, Russian holidaymakers are equally fond of the birch woods and lakes that lie inland. There are bathing lakes near Dubki and Lisiy Nos, en route to Razliv, 30km from the city.

With a **car** you can stop wherever looks promising along the coast, or venture into the interior. Public transport is less flexible, but enables visitors to see a fair amount. *Elektrichka* **trains** from Finland Station (Ploshchad Lenina metro) run every thirty minutes. There are two lines, the direct, inland Vyborg line, and the Krugovoy or round-coast line. Bear in mind, however, that not all trains stop at all stations.

Razliv and Repino are both accessible by **minibuses** that terminate at Zelenogorsk – namely #K-400 from outside Ploshchad Lenina metro/Finland Station, or #K-305б from Staraya Derevnya metro (a shorter journey). Other minibuses from Chernaya Rechka metro run only as far as Sestroretsk (#K-417 & #K-425).

Razliv

In Soviet times, tourists and schoolchildren were regularly bussed into **Razliv** to view two hideouts used by Lenin before the Revolution, both reverentially preserved as memorial museums. Now, only true believers and curiosity-seekers bother to come, and Razliv is otherwise just a residential satellite of Sestroretsk, further up the road. Of the two, the Shalash Museum is hard to reach without a car, though the Sarai Museum is easily accessible by public transport – mini-buses and buses stop at several points along the road through Razliv, or you can come by *elektrichka* train, getting off at the Tarkhovka halt. Either way, the journey from St Petersburg takes about 45 minutes. It's wise to phone ahead to check that the Lenin museums are open – the numbers are given below.

The Sarai Museum

The **Sarai Museum** (11am–7pm; closed Wed; ☏434 61 45; $0.75) is at ul. Yemelyanova 2, a signposted ten-minute walk from the *elektrichka* stop. Lenin arrived here by train on the night of July 10, 1917, a fugitive from Petrograd, where the Provisional Government had begun cracking down on the Bolsheviks. His host was a local munitions worker and secret Party member, Nikolai Yemelyanov, whose family were then living in a small barn (*sarai*) while their house was being repaired. Lenin was installed in the loft, reached by a steep ladder, until he found other quarters (see below).

The year after Lenin's death in 1924, the barn was given concrete underpinning, impregnated with protective resins and later shielded from the elements by a glass screen, resulting in the surreal building that you see today. On the first floor are the family's possessions; in the loft above, copies of the chairs and samovar which Lenin used (the originals were formerly displayed in the main Lenin Museum in Leningrad). The **house** opposite the barn exhibits photographs of various Bolsheviks in disguise and copies of the articles that Lenin wrote while staying here.

The Shalash Museum

Four kilometres north of the main road through Razliv, the turn-off to the lakeside **Shalash Museum** (11am–6pm; closed Wed; ☎ 437 30 98; $0.30) is signposted by a large Soviet monument. In 1917, the far shore of Lake Razliv was accessible only by boat and offered greater concealment than the barn, where Lenin was liable to be spotted by government spies. Yemelyanov told his neighbours that he planned to raise a cow and had hired a Finn to cut the hay. Under this pretext, Lenin moved into a hut (*shalash*) made of branches and thatch, built in a clearing by the lake. In this "green study" he wrote articles such as *On Slogans* and *The Answer*, and began *The State and Revolution*. After a fortnight, however, even this hideout seemed too risky, and on August 8 Lenin was smuggled into Finland disguised as a steam-engine fireman (see p.233).

What used to be a meadow is now laid out with paths and features a granite **monument** with a stylized representation of the hut. Being made of perishable hay – and occasionally set alight by vandals – the **hut** itself is rebuilt every year. In the nearby glass-and-concrete **pavilion** you can see copies of the peasant's smock and scythe that Lenin used, a blue notebook containing his notes for *The State and Revolution*, and Vladimir Pinchuk's statue, *Lenin in Razliv*. Ironically, all the surrounding land has now been sold to rich Russians who have built luxury **villas** there, restricting access to the lake.

Between Razliv and Repino

Lake Razliv (which means "flood") was actually created as a reservoir for Russia's first armaments factory, founded by Peter the Great at **Sestroretsk**, 33km from St Petersburg. Like the city's Vyborg Side, the township was once noted for its working-class militancy, though its factory now produces nothing more dangerous than television screens (though in Russia even these can be fairly lethal, since certain models are liable to explode). Between here and the next settlement, **Solechnoe**, the *Dyuny* sanatorium has a **golf** course (☎ 437 38 74; Tues–Sun 10am–9pm) where the National Cup is held in the first week of August.

Repino

Repino, 47km northwest of St Petersburg, is what Russians call a *poselok*, or small urban-type settlement, named after the eminent painter **Ilya Repin** (1844–1930), who built a house near what was then the village of Kuokkala and lived there permanently from 1900. Repin showed no inclination to leave even after Kuokkala became Finnish territory in 1917, but continued to receive visitors and honours from Soviet Russia until his death. Turned into a museum after the Soviet annexation of Karelia, the house was burned to the ground by the Nazis in 1944 and then painstakingly re-created in the postwar era. If you arrive **by train**, head from the station down towards the sea and then, after 600m, turn left onto ulitsa Repina – the brightly coloured gates of Repin's estate are 500m further along. **Minibuses** #K-305Б and #K-400 from St Petersburg stop right outside: ask to get off at Penaty. To avoid a wasted journey, phone (☏231 68 34) to check that the house is open.

Repin's house: Penaty

Repin's house (May–Sept 10.30am–5pm; Oct–April 10.30am–4pm; closed Tues; $2) is named **Penaty** after the household gods of ancient Rome, the Penates, a title that suits its highbrow domesticity. The picturesque wooden building has a steep glass roof and an abundance of windows, while the **interior** reflects the progressive views of Repin and his wife, Natalya Nordman. A sign in the cloakroom advises: "Take off your own coats. Don't wait for servants – there aren't any." On Wednesdays, when the Repins held open house, guests were expected to announce their own arrival by ringing a gong.

Only intimates were admitted to Repin's **study**, which contains a huge jasper paperweight and statues of Tolstoy and the critic Stasov. The drawing room is hung with autographed pictures of Gorky and Chaliapin, and there's a painting of the Repins' artist son, Yuri. Repin himself also dabbled in sculpture: his statue of Tolstoy occupies the glassed-over winter veranda. The dining room features a round table with a revolving centre. Guests had to serve themselves (without asking others to pass anything) and stow the dirty dishes in the drawers underneath; anyone who didn't was obliged to mount the lectern in the corner of the room and deliver an impromptu speech. Only vegetarian food was served.

The best room in the house is Repin's **studio**, upstairs, filled with light and cluttered with *objets* and sketches. Notice the metre-long brushes and the special palette-belt, which the ageing artist used to compensate for his long-sightedness and atrophying muscles. Beside the stove are various props used in his famous painting of *The Zaporozhe Cossacks Writing a Mocking Letter to the Sultan*, and Repin's last self-portrait, painted at the age of 76. Finally, you go up to the top floor to view a touching home movie of Repin and his friends throwing snowballs in the grounds of Penaty.

The grounds behind the house contain two follies, the **Temple of Osiris and Isis** and the **Tower of Scheherazade**, both built of wood. **Repin's grave** is on top of a hillock by an oak tree, as stipulated in his will – follow the path leading off to the right to reach it.

Vyborg

After decades of Soviet neglect, the historic town of **Vyborg**, 174km northwest of St Petersburg and just 30km from the Finnish border, is looking to Finland to revive its fortunes – an ironic reassertion of past leanings, given that the Finns regard Vyborg (which they call Viipuri) as theirs by right. Architecturally, at least, they have a point, as its old quarter consists of Baltic merchants' houses and Lutheran churches, while the centre is defined by Finnish Art Nouveau and Modernist architecture, interspersed with Soviet eyesores. Demographically, however, Vyborg is definitely Russian, not least because most of its Finnish population fled in 1944 (those that stayed were sent to the Gulag) – though Russians have lived here since the town's earliest days. In Soviet times, Vyborg's port, paper mills and optics factory employed half the population; today, its economy is heavily dependent on cross-border tourism, smuggling and prostitution, and is in a parlous state – many outlying settlements are without gas and hot water in the depths of winter. This partly explains a spate of **crimes** against Finnish tourists, from pickpocketing and muggings to the robbery of whole tourist coaches. Despite Militia crackdowns, it's worth being more than usually cautious here.

With luck, your visit might coincide with one of Vyborg's annual **festivals**: the Sonorous Nightingale children's festival in May; the Knight's Tournament historical pageant in June (see p.301); the yacht regatta in July; or the "Window of Europe" film festival in August.

The Town

The town is spread out over the series of rocky peninsulas that enclose Vyborg Bay, on the Gulf of Finland. Ignoring the industrial suburbs, basic **orientation** is fairly simple; from the **train** and **bus stations** on the northern mainland, a grid of streets spreads around Park Lenina and west to the old quarter, huddled on the peninsula's cape. The castle, situated on an island off the end of the peninsula, is easily recognizable by its lofty tower, visible from all around the bay. Vyborg itself is compact enough for visitors to see everything on foot in a couple of hours except for Park Monrepos, outside town, for which you'll need to take a taxi. You can catch a **bus** (#1, #6 or #12) directly from the train station to Vyborg Castle.

From Krasnasya ploshchad to the old town

A five-minute walk from the station will bring you to **Krasnaya ploshchad**, notable for its unusually corpulent **statue of Lenin**. Carry on to prospekt Lenina and across the park to reach the **Alvar Aalto Library**, an early work by the famous Finnish architect, fronted by a bronze bull elk. Completed in 1935, when Aalto was in his thirties, its boxy, light simplicity established him as a Modernist. Sadly, in Soviet times the library was clumsily "renovated" and a granite facade reminiscent of Lenin's mausoleum added – Aalto himself, revisiting the library shortly before his death in 1976, disclaimed the building as his own work.

Head northwest along prospekt Lenina to reach **Rynochnaya ploshchad** (Market Square), where stalls selling clothes, souvenirs, and binoculars and sniper-scopes from the optics factory presage an orange-brick, neo-Gothic **Market Hall** (Mon–Sat 9am–7pm). Nearby stands the squat, sixteenth-century **Round Tower** (Kruglaya bashnya), crowned by an iron cupola and spike – formerly part of a belt of fortifications girdling the entire peninsula, it now contains a restaurant and bar (see p.303).

From here you can head into the picturesquely decrepit old quarter, known as the **Stone City**, where Krepostnaya ulitsa leads eastwards to the yellow Lutheran **SS Peter and Paul Cathedral**, built in the 1790s, and the pink, blue-domed Orthodox **Transfiguration Cathedral** that catered to Vyborg's Russian population during its Finnish era. Beside the nearby cinema, ulitsa

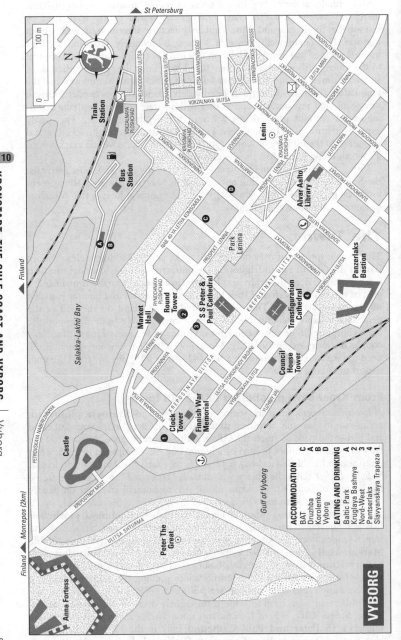

▲ St Petersburg

N

0   100 m

Train
Station

Bus
Station

▲ Finland

Salakka-Lakhti Bay

VOKZALNAYA ULITSA

POGRANICHNAYA ULITSA

ZHELENDOOROGO ULITSA

VOKZALNAYA PLOSHCHAD

LENINGRADSKOE SHOSSSE

ULITSA MAYAKOVSKOGO

BULVAR KUTUZOVA

ULITSA MIRA

MOSKOVSKY PROSPEKT

PROSPEKT LENINA

SEVERNAYA

DMITROVA

KRASNAYA
PLOSHCHAD

PROSPEKT LENINA

KRASNAYA
PLOSHCHAD

SUVOROVSKY PROSPEKT

SLOBODSKY PROSPEKT

Lenin

Alvar Aalto
Library

ULITSA KEPPA

SOVETSKAYA ULITSA

LENINGRADSKAYA ULITSA

Park
Lenina

Panzerlaks
Bastion

VYBORGSKAYA ULITSA

KREPOSTNAYA ULITSA

NAB. 40-YA LETIYA KOMSOMOLA

PROSPEKT LENINA

LENINGRADSKY PROSPEKT

Market
Hall

Round
Tower

RYNOCHNAYA
PLOSHCHAD

S S Peter &
Paul Cathedral

Transfiguration
Cathedral

SEVNYI VAL

PROGONNAYA

KREPOSTNAYA ULITSA

ULITSA STOROZHEVOY BASHNI

Council
House
Tower

VYUZHNYI VAL

VODNAYA ULITSA

VYBORGSKAYA ULITSA

PODGORNAYA ULITSA

Clock
Tower

Finnish War
Memorial

Castle

PETROVSKAYA NABEREZHNAYA

▲ Finland   ▲ Monrepos (2km)

KREPOSTNOY MOST

ULITSA SHTURMA

Peter The
Great

Anna Fortress

Gulf of Vyborg

ACCOMMODATION
BAT   C
Druzhba   A
Korolenko   B
Vyborg   D

EATING AND DRINKING
Baltic Park   A
Kruglaya Bashnya   2
Nord-West   3
Pantserlaks   4
Slavyanskaya Trapeza   1

VYBORG

Titova leads downhill towards the octagonal **Council House Tower** (Bashnya Ratushi) – another remnant of the medieval fortifications – or you can walk along ulitsa Storozhevoy bashni to the massive seventeenth-century **Clock Tower**. On a ledge above the Sea Terminal stands a **Finnish war memorial** erected in 2001; an earlier version was vandalized by Russians affronted by any tribute to what they saw as Fascist invaders. Soon afterwards you'll reach the bridge leading to Vyborg Castle.

Vyborg Castle and other fortifications

Vyborg Castle (summer 10.30am–5pm; winter 10.30am–4pm; closed Mon; $2) – known as the *zamok* or *krepost* – occupies an island in the bay below the Stone City. Protected by five-metre-thick walls and numerous bastions, it was founded in 1293 by Torgils Knutsson after the Swedes took what had been a Russian trading port during the third crusade in Southern Karelia ("Wiborg" means "holy fortress" in Swedish). In 1701 the castle fell to Peter the Great after a month's bombardment, and the Russians began additional fortifications to safeguard their hard-won prize. Vyborg's military role declined after 1812, when the city was transferred to the Grand Duchy of Finland, and the castle served as a prison until its reversion to active service between 1939 and 1944, when it was captured by the Soviets, retaken by the Finns and recaptured again by the Red Army. Today, it makes an ideal setting for **mock battles** and sieges during the **Knights' Tournament** (Rytsarskiy turnir) on the last weekend in July. For details phone ☏ 81278/21 515 or email ✉ castle@vyborg.ru.

The castle boasts Russia's only **Underwater Archeology Museum**, displaying cannons and other relics from a Swedish warship sunk in a battle during Petrine times; the curator reckons that around forty boats lie at the bottom of the Gulf of Vyborg. Military maps and weapons comprise the rest of the exhibits in the citadel, and the real attraction is the 48-metre-high **tower**, which affords a stunning **view** of the whole town and far out into the Gulf of Finland.

If you're into military history – or photographing the Gulf – there are other neglected fortifications on the seaward approaches. The peninsula on the far side of Vyborg Castle is crowned by the **Anna Fortress** (Anninskaya krepost), whose star-shaped ravelins – typical of the Vauban-style fortifications of the eighteenth century – are named after Empress Anna Ivanova. Near the docks below the Stone City, the three-storey **Panzerlaks** (Shield of the Lakes) **bastion** was once part of the Swedish "Horned Fortress" constructed at the end of the sixteenth century, and now contains a studio–gallery. Further east is **Battery Hill** (Batareynaya gora), whose sunken galleries were laid out in the 1860s by the military engineer Totleben; the front line ran across it at the end of the Winter War in 1940. For more on these and other fortifications throughout Karelia, check out ⓦ www.nortfort.ru.

Park Monrepos

Vyborg's final and perhaps finest attraction is **Park Monrepos** (daily 10am–6pm; $1), beside the Gulf of Finland, 2km beyond the castle. Though not accessible by public transport, you can take a taxi there ($2) and arrange for it to pick you up again later. Entered by a massive wooden neo-Gothic gateway, the park uses the mossy, red granite crags and boulders of the Karelian shoreline to stunning effect, enhanced by dwarf firs and spruces that give it something of the look of a Japanese garden, embellished by Classical pavilions and Gothic follies – though sadly it's rather run-down owing to lack of funds. Laid out in 1759 by Commandant Stupishin, the park attained its apotheosis under Baron Nikolai, whose family is buried in a mock castle on the rocky **Isle of the Dead** (accessible by rowing boat). The isle lies off to the left beyond the boarded-up wooden **palace** of Count Wurtemburg – currently being restored by Finns – while further to the west, a spring gushes pure water. You can learn more about the park's history on Ⓦ www.oblmuseums.spb.ru/eng/museums/20/info.html.

Practicalities

Aside from signing up for a coach **excursion** (9–10hr; $10–15) at a kiosk outside Gostiniy dvor, the easiest way of reaching Vyborg from St Petersburg is by *elektrichka* **train** from Finland Station – preferably one of the *komerchiskaya* expresses (1hr 45min) rather than a regular train (3hr). Trains depart more or less hourly. Or you can book a seat as far as Vyborg on any of the Finnord or Ardis **buses** to Helsinki, Tampere or Sortavala, leaving from their office at Italyanskaya ul. 37 or the bus station by the Obvodniy Canal – though most of these depart in the evening and arrive at Vyborg in the small hours. **Motorists** have a choice of three routes: the M-10 "Scandinavia" highway, the coastal A-122, or the A-121, which runs furthest inland.

Vyborg doesn't have a tourist office and **information** can be hard to come by – try asking at reception in the *Druzhba Hotel*. Nor are **websites** much help at present: Ⓦ www.vyborg.net is largely in Russian and Finnish; Ⓦ www .travel.vbg.ru is out of date, but can provide tourist services for a fee; and Ⓦ www.vbg.ru merely offers a live-cam view of the city and weather reports. There's a 24-hour **currency exchange** in the *Druzhba*, and an ATM upstairs in the train station.

Accommodation

BAT ul. Nikolaev 3 ☎ & ℱ **81278/34 537,** Ⓦ **www.bathotel.ru**. Decent-value mini-hotel on the top floor of an old building in the centre. Cosy en-suite rooms (some non-smoking) with cable TV. Internet access. Takes Maestro, MC, Visa. Reduction of 70 percent if you book 3 to 7 days ahead. ➍

Kronstadt the Gulf Coast and Vyborg	
Kronstadt	Кронштадт
Razliv	Разлив
Repino	Репино
Sestroretsk	Сестрорецк
Solnechnoe	Солнечное
Vyborg	**Выборг**
Krasnaya ploshchad	Красная площадь
Krepostnaya ul.	Крепостная ул.
prospekt Lenina	пр. Ленина
Leningradskiy prospekt	Ленинградский проспект
Luzhskaya ul.	Лужская ул.
ul. Nikolaev	ул. Николаев
ul. Storozhevoy bashni	ул. Сторожевой башни
Rynochnaya ploshchad	Рыночная площадь
ul. Titova	ул. Титтова
ul. Yuzhniy val	ул. Южний вал
Zheleznodorozhnaya ul.	Железнодорожная ул.

Druzhba Zheleznodorozhnaya ul. 5 ☎ &
Ⓕ 81278/25 744, ⓔ druzba@vbg.spb.ru.
Overlooking the bay near the station, this
pyramid-shaped complex run by the Best
Eastern chain has en-suite rooms with
satellite TV, video channel and minibar
(suites have private saunas); a good restaurant and beer garden; sauna (free for
guests) and tennis courts. Search accommodation websites for big discounts. Amex,
DC, MC, Visa. ❺

Korolenko Sakkala-Lakhti Bay ☎ & Ⓕ 81278/34
478. Old-fashioned boat-hotel moored near
the *Druzhba*. Its dinky, spick-and-span cabins are tolerable and the staff friendly, but
the 24-hour bar can be noisy. ❸
Vyborg Leningradskiy pr. 19 ☎ 81278/22 383,
Ⓕ 81278/26 196. Slightly shabby three-star
Soviet-style establishment on a busy road
in the centre, that costs midway between
the *BAT* and the *Druzhba*. Restaurant,
sauna. ❹

Eating and drinking

Baltic Park Druzhba Hotel. Frequented by
local moneybags and hookers, Finnish
tourists and businessmen, this relatively
posh restaurant serves French and Russian
cuisine. Amex, DC, MC, Visa. Daily
noon–1am.
Kruglaya bashnya Rynochnaya pl. ☎ 81278/30
600. Atmospheric restaurant on the top floor
of the Round Tower, popular for its delicious, reasonably priced, Russian and
Finnish dishes, with a downstairs bar that's
open till the small hours. MC, Union, Visa.
Daily noon–11pm.

Nord-West Rynochnaya ul. 17 ☎ 81278/25 893.
Just behind the Round Tower, this slick,
Finn-friendly bar-restaurant does great
salmon cream soup and seafood entrées.
MC, Visa. Daily 10am–midnight.
Pantserlaks Luzhskaya ul. 1. Low-key café-
bar near the Panzerlaks Bastion. No credit
cards. Daily 9am–11pm.
Slavyanskaya Trapeza ul. Yuzhniy val 4/2
☎ 81278/93 299. This folksy cellar-restaurant
in the Stone City serves hearty Russian
soups, stews and fish dishes. No credit
cards. Daily noon–2am.

Shlisselburg, Valaam and Kizhi

The eastern shore of the Karelian Isthmus is craggier than the Gulf coast, reflecting the stormy nature of **Lake Ladoga** (Ladozhskoe ozero). Covering 17,872 square kilometres, Ladoga is Europe's largest lake and the source of the River Neva. Frozen over for up to six months of the year, it became famous during World War II for the **"Road of Life"**, which enabled Leningrad to survive the Blockade. Whenever the ice was thick enough, convoys drove across the lake through the night, hoping to avoid the Luftwaffe. In this way, 1,500,000 tonnes of supplies and 450,000 troops reached the city, and 1,200,000 civilians were evacuated.

Near the lake's outflow into the Neva, the Tsarist prison fortress of **Shlisselburg** makes an interesting day-trip in summer (the fortress is closed from November to April). At the other end of Ladoga, the **Valaam** archipelago is renowned for its hermitages and natural beauty, and is a popular destination for **cruises** (see box on p.311). Some cruises continue further north to **Lake Onega** (Onezhskoe ozero) and the fabulous wooden churches of **Kizhi** island, within 100km of the infamous **White Sea Canal**. Valaam and Kizhi can also be reached independently, entailing a night's stay in Sortavala or an overnight train journey to Petrozavodsk. This will allow you more time to explore the islands and may work out cheaper than the cost of a cruise during high season, but will inevitably take longer – say two days for either site and its associated town, or a week for both.

Shlisselburg (Schlüsselburg)

The island fortress of **Shlisselburg** was born of rivalry between the medieval rulers of Novgorod and Sweden, who realized that the River Neva's outflow from Lake Ladoga held the key to the lucrative trade route between Russia and the Baltic. First fortified in 1323 by Prince Yuri of Novgorod, the island known to the Russians as **Oreshek** ("little nut") and to the Swedes as Noteborg constantly changed hands until its definitive recapture in 1702 by Peter the Great, who renamed it Schlüsselburg (meaning "Key Fortress" in German).

Having lost its military significance after Peter's victory over Sweden in the Northern War, the fortress became a **prison** for anyone threatening autocracy, becoming synonymous with Tsarist oppression as the Lubyanka would be in Soviet times. In the February 1917 Revolution it fell without a shot being

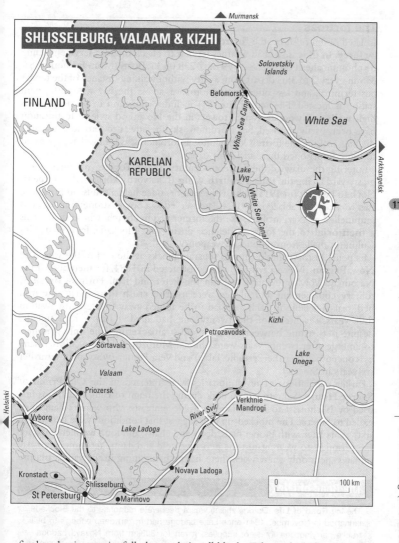

fired, and prisoners joyfully burnt their cell blocks. When asked if it should be preserved as a monument to tyranny, they replied: "We have suffered enough, let the foul place crumble to ruin!"

Nonetheless, the Bolsheviks turned it into a **museum** devoted to the infamies of Tsarism a few years after Ladoga became the gateway to a chain of waterways and penal camps reaching to the Solovetskiy Islands within the Arctic Circle, where uncounted thousands perished building the White Sea Canal (see p.312). Although the town fell to the Nazis in 1941, the fortress held out for 500 days until the Blockade of Leningrad was broken. In honour of this feat, the town was renamed Petrokrepost (Peter's Fortress) – a name that's still used in everyday speech, notwithstanding its official reversion to Shlisselburg (a Russified form of the original name) in 1990.

The fortress

Isolated 600m offshore, the **fortress** (May–Oct daily 10am–5pm) is accessible by **ferry**. In the case of bad weather it's best to check there's a service running by phoning ahead on ☎238 06 79 or ☎238 05 11. Boats (Mon–Fri hourly; Sat & Sun every 2 to 3hr) depart from a jetty within walking distance of the town's bus terminal, and less often from Morozova, across the bay where the train station is located. The return fare ($1) includes admission to the fortress. Its high **walls** and wooden-roofed towers in the Novgorod style of fortification have been partly restored, but its ruinous skyline attests to ferocious wartime shelling, making the fortress look almost as forbidding as it must have appeared to those imprisoned there in Tsarist days.

Entering the maw of the sixteenth-century **Tsar's Tower**, you emerge in a grassy yard facing the ruined **Fourth Wing** (Chetvortiy korpus), the last penal block to be built (in 1911), whose three floors once held a thousand prisoners, two to a cell. Set ablaze in 1917, it later served as a Soviet strongpoint and was pummelled by Nazi artillery, like the former prison church, whose shell forms a **memorial** to the fortress's defence during the Blockade, festooned with sculptures made from redundant weaponry.

Its penal history unfolds in two separate blocks at the end of the yard. The **New Prison** (Novaya tyurma) was constructed in 1884, for members of the Narodnaya Volya previously held in the Peter and Paul Fortress. Brutality, solitary confinement and silence were used to crush their spirits; the iron bed, seat and table in each cell had to be folded away between use. Within four years, seventeen of the twenty-one had died – many from suicide, despite nets strung between landings and straitjacketing. The only prisoners to emerge after twenty years were Nikolai Morozov (who kept himself sane by conceptualizing the Periodic Table) and Vera Figner (who spent a further six years in Siberia).

Earlier generations of revolutionaries were interred in the Old Prison or **Secret House** (Sekretny dom) built during the reign of Paul, which was first used by Nicholas I to incarcerate those Decembrists who weren't hanged or exiled to Siberia. The mocked-up cells suggest that conditions were better than sixty years later, with proper beds, desks and chairs, and long woollen coats for the prisoners to wear against the pervasive cold and damp. Yet some latter-day inmates spent only a few weeks here, before being hung in the yard; a **plaque**

The Road of Life

The icy **Road of Life** (Doroga zhizni) was a desperate response to the Blockade, launched in November 1941 once Lake Ladoga had frozen deep enough to bear trucks carrying one tonne of supplies. It ran for 308km from Novaya Ladoga – beyond the Nazi encirclement – through forests and swamps and across 30km of ice, to deliver the first supplies on the eighty-third day of the siege. By mid-December there were sixty trails across the ice, used by 3500 trucks, that allowed an increase in the bread ration when morale was at breaking point, preserving Leningrad through the first winter of the siege. During the second winter the Road was their only lifeline for supplies and the evacuation of tens of thousands of non-combatants. On February 7, 1943, the first train from newly liberated Shlisselburg arrived at Finland Station on the 526th day of the siege – signifying that the Blockade had been broken, though it wasn't lifted until January 1944. The event is depicted by a diorama in the **Breakthrough of the Blockade Museum** (10am–6pm; closed Mon; free) at **Marinovo**, off the road to Shlisselburg – taxi drivers can stop over on the way there or back for a few dollars extra.

marks the spot where Lenin's brother, Alexander Ulyanov, was executed for attempted regicide in 1887.

Still earlier there was the (no longer extant) **Tower of Cells**, where VIPs were confined. Peter the Great's half-sister Maria was lucky to spend only three years for "encouraging disaffection"; Prince Golitsyn languished until the overthrow of Count Biron – who ended up in Shlisselburg himself. The cruellest fate was that of Anna Leopoldovna's son, Ivan VI, whom Empress Elizabeth spared as a mercy, but was deprived of any education or enjoyment so that he would grow up unfit to be a tsar – and he was ultimately murdered after trying to escape. Even Catherine the Great saw fit to imprison the publisher and Freemason Novikov and the Chechen rebel leader Sheikh Mansur, who died in prison in 1793.

To dispel the grim mood, exit by a portal near Ulyanov's execution place, to find a rocky **beach** where you can sunbathe and even swim in the lake – just beware of broken glass and the strong currents only 5m offshore.

Practicalities

From May to October, the Eclectica agency by Gostiniy dvor (see p.40) runs popular weekly coach **excursions** to Shlisselburg ($9), while Russian Cruises sails there from the Hermitage pier (Sun 2pm; 3hr 30min one way; $33 return). Otherwise you can get there without trouble by taking the metro to Ulitsa Dybenko and then an unofficial **taxi** for $4–5 (group rate), which takes about forty minutes – less time than sporadic, irregularly numbered **buses** (usually #575 but ask to be sure) – and with the option of a stopover at Marinovo (see box on p.306). Shlisselburg's bus and taxi terminus is just across the sluice gates from the jetty for ferries to the fortress, which makes this a far more convenient approach than by **train** from Finland Station to the railway halt at Morozova, on the far side of Shlisselburg Bay, whence ferries are less frequent.

A couple of beer and *shashlyk* dens by the town jetty and in the park near the bus terminal can satisfy your need for **food**, but there's nowhere to stay – nor any reason to. Buses back to St Petersburg are less frequent after 5pm; the last one leaves shortly before 11pm.

Valaam

The islands of the **Valaam** archipelago at the northern end of Ladoga have a unique history and society, shaped by mystics, exiles and nature. Despite being icebound for five months of the year, Valaam is blessed with a favourable micro-climate, enjoying twice the sunshine of St Petersburg and abounding in berries, mushrooms, wild flowers, butterflies and songbirds. It remains almost as quiet as it was when Avram of Rostov – the founder of Valaam's hermetic tradition – arrived in 960, and heard a leaf fall in the forest.

For Orthodox believers, Valaam is a **holy isle** of saints and hermits, whose shrines echo Christ's Passion in the Holy Land; a "Jerusalem of the North", offering redemption to the sinful and miracles to the faithful. The monastery's own resurrection has been remarkable, for until six monks returned in 1989 there had been none on Valaam since 1940, when its brethren and treasures were evacuated to Finland as Stalin occupied Karelia. In the meantime, Valaam had served as a dumping ground for disfigured war veterans, isolated from Soviet society until 1967, when it became a tourist destination for Leningrad's intelligentsia, and both sides were shocked by the gulf in living standards and horizons.

Over the past fifteen years the **monastery** has recovered its former de facto sovereignty over Valaam. The restoration of the monastery is the only building

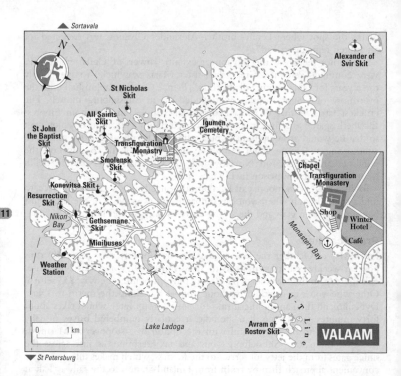

Alexander of
Svir Skit

St Nicholas
Skit

All Saints
Skit

Igumen
Cemetery

St John
the Baptist
Skit

Transfiguration
Monastery
See
inset box

Smolensk
Skit

Chapel

Transfiguration
Monastery

Konevitsa Skit

Resurrection
Skit

Shop

Winter
Hotel

Nikon
Bay

Gethsemane
Skit

Monastery Bay

Café

Minibuses

Weather
Station

0   1 km

Lake Ladoga

Avram of
Rostov Skit

V T Line

VALAAM

work allowed on the island, whose six hundred inhabitants are disgruntled that their promised new housing hasn't materialized and would probably leave if the monastery banned liquor and tobacco, as in Tsarist times. Locals also complain of being excluded from moneymaking activities such as trout farming, and of the monks erecting roadblocks to impede traffic. The Patriarch of the Russian Orthodox Church (who was once a monk on Valaam) has even ensured that the local army garrison consists of true believers, with leave to fast and attend holy festivals.

The monastery

The origins of the **Monastery of the Transfiguration of the Saviour** (Spaso–Preobrazhenskiy Valaamskiy monastyr) are obscure, but there seems to have been a cloister here even before Avram's arrival. Legend attributes the conversion of the pagans of Valaam to none other than the Apostle Andrew, the "First Called", who is said to have smashed their sacrificial altars. From the fourteenth century onwards the monastery was often sacked by the Swedes, and served as a fortress against them. Laid waste in 1611, it was rebuilt a century later with funds from Peter the Great, and reached its zenith in the late nineteenth century, when the existing cathedral and residential blocks were built, hermitages were rebuilt or founded, and there were nearly a thousand monks in residence. Although six hundred were conscripted and all but two hermitages closed during World War I, the monastery had the good fortune to end up on Finnish territory and escape the scourging of the Church in Russia – while monks who fled Karelia in 1940 were able to establish the New Valaam Monastery in Finland, whose rejection of Patriarchal authority during the

Religious processions at Valaam

For monks and pilgrims, **processions** affirm the true faith and its unity with the rocks and waters of Valaam. Icons are borne forth and liturgies sung in slow procession from one shrine to another. Tourist spectators are tolerated, but expected to observe the proprieties of dress and behaviour, including not photographing the monks.

May 19 A procession by water from Monastery Bay to the Nicholas Skit on the day of the transportation of St Nicholas's relics.

All Saints' Day A procession from the monastery to the All Saints' Skit, and a celebration in its lower church.

July 11 A procession around the monastery in memory of SS Sergei and German.

August 14 From the monastery to the bay, for the consecration of the water.

Soviet era was reciprocated by the Russian Church. Recently, however, relations have improved to the point that each monastery's website now features a link to the other's.

The hundred-odd monks on Valaam maintain their own **"time zone"**, synchronized to Jerusalem and the Holy Land rather than Moscow. Among the **monks** are an ex-Moscow DJ, a Socialist Realist artist turned icon painter and an actor who found God through a stage adaptation of Dostoyevsky's *The Possessed*. Rising at 5.30am, they spend up to ten hours a day praying in the **cathedral**, whose lower church contains the relics of St German and St Sergei, and the icon *Our Lady of Valaam*. The huge upper church is still under repair, but its blue cupola and the red and white crosses that emblazon its facade are visible all around Monastery Bay. Tall service blocks surround the compound, housing monks' cells and local families with nowhere else to live. Controllers ensure that nobody enters the holy precincts improperly dressed, and monks speed around the island's dirt roads in jeeps like an occupying army.

Visitors are told not to photograph the monks and that entry to churches is conditional on men wearing long trousers and women full-length skirts and headscarves. Women in trousers may be offered a wraparound skirt to pass muster, but shouldn't count on it – the monks would prefer that only pilgrims disturbed their sanctuary. The monastery's **website** (ⓦ www.valaam.ru) is one of many devoted to Valaam and its saints – the movement is also strong in America, where eighteenth-century missionaries from Valaam made converts and founded churches and monasteries as far afield as Alaska. **Chants** by Valaam's brethren are available on CD, or can be heard at ⓦ http://193229.204.8:8080/ramgen/valamo/agni.smi.

The skits

The **skit** (pronounced "skeet") or hermitage – the domicile of a few monks living under stricter vows than their monastic brethren, such as continual silence and prayer or a vegan diet – is a leitmotif of Valaam's landscape and religious life. The first skits were founded by Abbot Nazary in the 1790s, with rock-cut cells in emulation of bygone, solitary hermits such as Avram or Alexander of Svir, but these proved so harmful to the health that Abbot Damaskin (known for sleeping in a coffin) built brick living quarters, so that the larger skits came to resemble miniature monasteries.

The **Resurrection Skit**, overlooking Nikon Bay, was built during the 1890s where a hermit of the previous century had lived in a cave with snakes, and where St Andrew is said to have raised a stone cross only 28 years after the death of Christ. Its tidy quadrangle of brick dwellings could be mistaken for a private school, but for the monastery guides who greet visitors disembarking from cruise ships in the bay.

Ten minutes' walk inland, the **Gethsemane Skit** is a simple cream-coloured wooden church near a picturesquely dark lake, offset by the sky-blue roofs and the spires of surrounding cabins where the monks live. From here you can follow a path through the woods to the **Konevitsa Skit** – a wooden chapel, used only on holy days, in a wonderful location atop the sheer cliffs of a narrow bay. A trail with stretches of timber baulks circumvents **Lake Igumen** and the **Black Lake**, with one route returning to the main road between the Resurrection Skit and the monastery, and the other forging on towards Saints' Island.

The smallest of the three main islands in the archipelago, this has now been declared **off limits** so that the five monks at the **All Saints' Skit** may adhere to their rule of continuous prayer, abjuring the sight of women and the consumption of flesh. This is the oldest, most romantic-looking of Valaam's hermitages, with a stone church and cells on the spot where St Alexander of Svir once lived, amid a sheltered clearing whose shallow soil is quickly warmed by the sun, enabling the monks to grow water melons as well as vegetables.

The other hermitages are accessible only by boat. Visitors who sign up for the organized trip from Nikon Bay to the monastery will get a distant view of the **John the Baptist Skit** – which is likewise **off limits** – and a closer one of the **Nicholas Skit** at the mouth of Monastery Bay, whose monks formerly acted as customs officials, searching incoming vessels for booze and tobacco. But you'll need to charter your own boat to reach the remote mini-archipelagos where the **Alexander of Svir** and **Avram of Rostov** hermitages are sited. The latter also hosts an observation tower, a bunker with naval guns and other relics from the **V-T Line** of **fortifications** that the Finns built in 1942 to stop the Soviets from outflanking the Mannerheim Line. This outpost's garrison withdrew to avoid being cut off after the Red Army breached the V-T Line in June 1944. A boat trip and tour of the site takes about three hours.

Practicalities

Valaam is situated 170km north of Shlisselburg and about 250km from St Petersburg. Most tourists come on a **cruise** (see box on p.311), which limits you to a day on Valaam. To stay longer entails **getting there via Sortavala**, which can be reached from St Petersburg by **bus** (daily except Tues; 12hr) from the Finnord office, arriving late enough to mean an overnight stay before sailing to Valaam next day – the *Galjot* hotel-ship by the jetty (☎81430/40 504; ❸) and the *Seurahuone Hotel* at Karelskaya ul. 22 (☎81430/22 338; ❹) are both within walking distance of the bus station. There may be more than one **hydrofoil** a day if enough passengers materialize, but services are replaced by a **boat** (3hr; 1hr by hydrofoil) when the weather turns rough. When the lake is frozen, adventurous Finns reach Valaam on snowmobiles.

Accommodation on Valaam is limited to grungy single-sex hostels for pilgrims and the all-year *Winter Hotel* (☎ & ℻81430/38 248, ✉tweltour @foxline.ru; ❹) near the monastery, which has clean, simple triple rooms and shared bathrooms with hot water. There are basic **cafés** serving *shashlyk* at Nikon Bay and below the monastery; a **shop** outside the latter sells tinned food, booze and cigarettes; or you can buy delicious smoked fish, berries, mushrooms and honey at **stalls** near the minibus stop above Nikon Bay. There are no exchange offices, but you might be able to change dollars or euros with cruise boat staff or locals.

From May to September, **cruise boats** depart for Valaam and Kizhi every day or so from St Petersburg's River Terminal (Rechnoy vokzal) at pr. Obukhovsoy obornony 95, near Proletarskaya metro. East German-built boats such as the *Kronstadt* and *Sankt Petersburg* have en-suite cabins, a restaurant and bar-disco, and are used by foreign tour operators and local firms alike – the only difference being the quality of the meals and the cost of the cruise. Older Russian vessels such as the *Popov* and *Rodina* have been refitted and are now rated the same standard – though, to be honest, all the boats are past their prime.

You can buy **tickets** in St Petersburg from the operator Russian Cruises (Nevskiy pr. 51 ☎325 61 20, ⓦwww.russian-cruises.ru) or agents such as Sindbad Travel (3-ya Sovetskaya ul. 28 ☎327 83 84, ⓦwww.sindbad.ru) or Infinity Travel (Bolshaya Morskaya ul. 39 ☎313 50 85, ⓦwww.infinity.ru). **Prices** per person depend on the month (July & Aug are dearest; May & Sept cheapest), the type of cabin and the duration and itinerary of the cruise. A two-night cruise that gives you the best part of a day on **Valaam** (and nowhere else) costs from $65 to $116 in low season and $80 to $130 in high season (according to the type of cabin); weekend trips cost $15 more. Of the two cruises to **Kizhi**, the three-day, four-night version runs only in July and August, but it's not worth paying more for an extended cruise via Petrozavodsk (any month), as both give passengers just two hours on Kizhi, and actually spend longer at Valaam and Verkhnie Mandrogi (see p.312). The three-day, four-night cruise costs from $175 to $275, depending on the cabin. On top of this, there's a **surcharge** for foreigners of $25 for Valaam and $40 for Kizhi. **Children** up to the age of 12 get a fifteen-percent discount on tickets but pay the full surcharge.

While a cruise to Valaam seems too brief, the long **journey** to Kizhi and back can pall unless you bring books or other entertainments. Packages include all **meals** except dinner the first night (which isn't served till 10pm) and breakfast on return to Petersburg (which isn't provided at all); vegetarians need to bring alternatives to the meaty, Soviet canteen-style fare. Passengers are assigned a shift (*smena*) for meals and excursions. **Alcohol**, soft drinks and cigarettes are dear by Russian standards, so you may wish to bring your own – not that this deters people from making merry at the **disco**. As there are no facilities for exchanging **money** or using credit cards, you should bring enough rubles to cover expenses.

Cruise boats offer passengers a free **guided walk** from the Resurrection to the Konevitsa Skit to ensure that nobody gets lost, while after lunch there's a motorboat ride around the coast to visit the monastery. There's nothing to stop you exploring the island for yourself, however: local **minibuses** leaving from the stalls uphill from the landing stage run to and from the monastery (6.5km) 8–9am, 1–3pm and 6–8pm ($1.25 per person). Skippers offer private **boat trips** to beaches, lakes or islands for $40–50 an hour (group rate); boats seat ten to fifteen people. Minibus driver Dmitri Soshkin (mobile ☎7921/220 4802) owns the *Maksim*, which he'll happily **charter** for trips of several days exploring the remoter islands.

From Ladoga to Lake Onega

If you're cruising to Kizhi, you'll sail from Ladoga into Lake Onega up the **River Svir**. This 230-kilometre waterway is partly canalized, with two huge **locks** that form the final stage of the Baltic–White Sea Canal (see box on p.312), but looks quite wild for much of its length, lined with pine and birch forests. In early May and September, its estuary on Ladoga supports vast numbers of **birds**: 200,000 ducks, 150,000 geese and up to 5000 swans, plus cranes,

The White Sea Canal

The notion of linking the White Sea to the Baltic originated in Petrine times, but remained a pipe dream until 1930, when Stalin made it a goal of the First Five-Year Plan. To avoid importing costly machinery, the task was assigned to **Gulag** slave workers; the required specialists were simply arrested by the NKVD. For twenty months, up to 180,000 **prisoners** at a time toiled with shovels, picks and barrows to cut through 37km of solid granite. Perhaps 100,000 died hewing the first few kilometres of deep excavations; some put the total work force at 300,000 and death toll as high as 200,000 – but nobody really knows, as the survivors were set to work on subsequent canal projects that were equally fatal.

Inaugurated in March 1933, the canal was extolled for "re-forging" criminals into honest citizens. A "brigade" of **writers** led by Gorky took a cruise on the waterway and produced a book entitled *A Canal Called Stalin* (as it was originally named). One author had a brother in the canal camps and kept silent to protect him, but it seems most of the others were fooled by the staged normality (as US senators would later be at other camps). Henceforth, forced labour became the norm for all major construction projects in Stalin's Russia.

The canal's human cost was underscored by its futility. Ice-bound for half the year and too small for maritime vessels, it fulfilled neither its economic nor strategic rationale. Only a few barges carrying timber or fuel pass through its locks each day. Yet as a feat of **engineering** it once had a place in the record books: its 227 kilometres feature seven locks that raise boats 70m to Lake Vyg, and twelve along the River Vyg, rising 102m – not including the locks on the Svir that handle the 30m difference between Onega and Ladoga. Bizarrely, the canal is still commemorated by a brand of cigarettes, *Belomor* (short for *Belomorkanal*), whose packet bears a map of the waterway.

warblers, snipes and rarer species such as White-winged Black Terns. The isthmuses on either side of Ladoga are under the White Sea–Baltic Flyway, the route along which millions of birds from northern Russia migrate to and from their wintering grounds in Western Europe and Africa.

In the late 1990s a St Petersburg entrepreneur capitalized on the river's tourist traffic by creating **Verkhnie Mandrogi** – a Disneyesque version of a "traditional" Russian village of the nineteenth century. Instead of decrepit cottages, muddy tracks and drunken peasants, there are extravagantly carved and painted houses, neat paths and a community of craftspeople that moves in over summer to produce handicrafts for sale. During his televised visit in 2001, Putin was shown painting a *matryoshka* and throwing a clay pot; as thanks for the publicity the village received, he was given a house there. The largest building in the settlement is full of **workshops** making dolls, carved figures, lace and ceramics. Other diversions include a **vodka museum** ($20 for a 2hr visit with unlimited sampling), pony rides, and photo opportunities with a bear cub. Several *bliny* bars and rustic-style eateries feed up to 2000 visitors a day at the height of the season.

Kizhi

The northern half of **Lake Onega** is characterized by low-lying peninsulas and islands termed *Zaonezhe* ("Beyond the Onega"), that were the domain of the pagan Ves and Saami peoples of Karelia until their absorption by the kingdom of Novgorod in the twelfth century. At the heart of the archipelago lies the small island of **Kizhi**, whose name (pronounced "*Kee*-zhi") is thought to derive from the ritual games (*kizhat*) that were once held there. Kizhi remained the religious and commercial centre of the region under Russian rule: its domain numbered 130 villages by the sixteenth century and was rich in timber, furs and foodstuffs, though it was repeatedly invaded by Swedes, Poles and Lithuanians until Russia's victory in the Northern War brought peace, and an upsurge in construction across the region gave rise to some of the finest **wooden architecture** in Europe, exemplified by Kizhi's *pogost* complex.

Owing to Kizhi's remoteness, both the buildings and the folk culture that sustained them survived into the twentieth century, but were deteriorating as a result of the declining, ageing population (the custom that elder daughters had to marry first didn't help) and the impact of modernization. From 1948 onwards, Soviet ethnographers studied the villages, purchased outstanding buildings and began moving them to Kizhi to create what is now the **Open-air Museum of History, Architecture and Ethnography** (daily: May 25 to mid-Oct 8am–8pm; mid-Oct to May 24 11am–3pm; $10) – a folklore reservation of both indigenous and reconstructed villages. Their thirty-odd inhabitants have a lifestyle that isn't so different from their grandparents' but their aspirations are higher, influenced by Petrozavodsk and the summer influx of tour guides (who stay with local families). While tourism offers an economic lifeline, the number of visitors has been limited to 130,000 a year to minimize damage to the environment.

Disembarking tourists are filtered through the museum's entrance to buy a ticket that covers all the buildings designated as museums and to be assigned a **guide** speaking English, French or German – the entrance charge and guide fee ($1.25) are usually included in the price of cruises or excursions from Petrozavodsk. It's worth staying with a guide since they are well informed, but there's nothing to stop you from wandering off. Sadly, cruise schedules limit visitors to a mere two hours on Kizhi, which is enough **time** to explore the *pogost* and the nearby village, but not the rest of the island – day-trippers from Petrozavodsk get longer (see p.315). It is strictly **forbidden** to stay on Kizhi – offenders may be arrested and "deported" to the mainland – and for fear of fire, smoking is permitted only in designated areas.

If you can, time your visit to catch one of the local **festivals**. The Festival of Kizhi Volost (Aug 23) features folk music, dancing and handicrafts, while other events are mainly religious, but still end in feasting and drinking – such as the Easter gatherings, the festivals of Christ's Transfiguration (Aug 19) and the Intercession of the Virgin (Oct 14) and the chapel feast of the Dormition at Vasilevo (Aug 28). For a preview of Kizhi, check out the museum's **website** Ⓦ http://kizhi.karelia.ru.

The pogost

Built over three centuries by local carpenters, the *pogost* comprises an extraordinary ensemble of disparate wooden structures enclosed by a dry-stone stockade. The *pogost* was begun in 1714 with the 37-metre-high **Church of the Transfiguration** – a magnificent edifice twice as tall as St Basil's in Moscow, with 22 onion domes upon tiers of *bochka* (barrel) roofs, inset one above another to form a cascade of shingles reaching almost to the ground. Its dramatic silhouette is enhanced by the contrast between its dark fir timbers and the shingles (called *cheshui* – or "fish scales" – in Russian) carved from moist gles were designed to channel rainwater away, and there was also an inner flush roof to catch any leaks and carry them into a drain, these precautions didn't prevent rot from affecting its beams over the centuries; the interior is now supported by a metal cage and off limits to visitors, pending restoration by 2014.

Despite the legend that, after its completion, master carpenter Nestor cast his axe into the lake, vowing, "There has not been, nowhere is and never will be a church like this!", the inhabitants of Kizhi had another go fifty years later, erecting the **Church of the Intercession**, whose boxy, nine-domed silhouette offsets the pyramidal Church of the Transfiguration. Meant for winter use, it became the only place of worship after 1937, till services were banned entirely after World War II, when the open-air museum was established. They resumed in 1997 under Father Nikolai, a French-born priest who still runs the parish. Among the diverse icons from the Onega region is a splendid *Last Judgement* from the Chapel of St Nicholas Tomskiy. A tall, freestanding **bell tower** of 1874 completes the *pogost*. Its existence today is owed to a Finnish pilot, who was ordered to bomb the *pogost* as a "partisan centre" in 1944 but flew away without doing so.

The villages

Afterwards you can make a circuit of a reconstructed village nearby. There are two large farmsteads that once belonged to middling-affluent peasants, combining home and barn under one roof, with spacious, functional living quarters full of artefacts. The **Oshevnev house**, built in 1876, features a baby-walker and a faceless doll (for superstitious reasons), and is used for demonstrating weaving and pearl embroidery (locals used to collect pearls from the lake), while the **Yelizarov house** from Seredeka contains an array of boats and sleighs. The latter was inhabited until the 1950s, and its living room boasts a family tree going back to the seventeenth century. Further along are a rustic *banya* and an octagonal tent-roofed **Chapel of the Archangel Michael**, from Lelikozero in the Kizhi skerries, whose bells toll melodiously. Drying racks, a threshing barn and a windmill are followed by the **Church of the Resurrection of Lazarus** from the Muromskiy Monastery in northern Karelia. The oldest wooden church extant in Russia (1390), it was reputedly built by a monk, Lazarus, whom the pagans decided not to kill after he cured a child of blindness.

If time allows, you can press on to the **Chapel of St Veronica's Veil** on Naryina Hill, whose picturesque witch's hat belfry adorns the highest point on Kizhi. From there, the trail diverges towards two villages indigenous to Kizhi (though some of the buildings in them have been transplanted from other sites) and still inhabited. **Vasilevo**, on the western side of the island, boasts the finest secular building on Kizhi: the enormous, rambling **Sergin house** that once accommodated a family of 22. Taken from the village of Munozero, it now shares the limelight with the **Sergeeva house** from Lipovitsy, the abode of the Vasilevs, one of the most prosperous local families a century ago. Nearby is the earliest native church on the island, the seventeenth-century **Assumption Church**, whose large octagonal bell tower originally doubled as a watchtower.

Across the island, **Yamka** lacks any outstanding houses but epitomizes the traditional Zaonezhne village, with dwellings running along the shore facing the lake, fields and kitchen gardens out back, barns and granaries nearby, and a windmill, threshing barn and wayside cross further on. As with all Kizhi's timber structures, the logs were felled in the late autumn after the final ring of the tree had hardened, and left on the ground until late spring. By using axes instead of saws, the grain of the wood was closed rather than left open to moisture; and nails were dispensed with in favour of notches or mortise and tenon joints, which are better suited to the climate.

Kizhi	Кижи
Marinovo	Мариново
Petrozavodsk	Петрозаводск
Shlisselburg	Шлиссельбург
Sortavala	Сортавала
Valaam	Валаам

Practicalities

As an alternative to cruising, you can **get to Kizhi via Petrozavodsk** on the Karelian mainland. Overnight **train** #657 from St Petersburg arrives at Petrozavodsk shortly before 7am, giving you time to get to the waterfront to catch the 9am **hydrofoil** that runs from June to August if enough people have booked tickets (☎8142/007), or the regular daily noon service that operates throughout the navigation season; both take an hour and a half to make the 66km crossing. Foreigners pay $20 for the return trip plus $10 admission before they've set foot on the island. As hydrofoils **leave** Kizhi at 12.15pm and 4.25pm, you may be able to stay there for up to five hours – twice as long as cruise passengers. Two snags are the lack of anywhere to **buy food** on Kizhi (bring supplies), and the need to catch a train back to St Petersburg that night (which needs pre-booking) or stay on in **Petrozavodsk**. Fortunately, the Karelian capital (pop. 280,000) offers a range of **accommodation**: central hotels include the *Maski* (pr. Marksa 3a ☎8142/761 478, @mrteatr@karelia.ru; ❷), *Metro* (ul. Dzerzhinskovo 11 ☎8142/769 291; ❹) and *Severnaya* (pr. Lenina 21/6 ☎8142/762 224, @severnaja@onego.ru; ❺) – the last has a sauna and Jacuzzi. For more **information** and a **map** of the city, see the online magazine *KomArt* (@http://komart.karelia.ru), which has some info in English and lots more in Russian.

Novgorod

Centuries before St Petersburg was dreamt of, **Novgorod** was the lodestar of northern Russia, a beacon of civilization that some Russian historians have characterized as the first (or only) democracy in Russian history. Today, its medieval **Kremlin** and **churches** draw Russian tourists in droves, while the **Museum of Wooden Architecture** and **monasteries** outside town enshrine folk customs and religious faith. A beach and leafy promenades contribute to the mellow ambience of the city centre, where there are plenty of places to eat and drink cheaply, and folklore events and music **festivals** throughout the year. Although it's possible to see Novgorod on a long day excursion from St Petersburg, you'd do better to stay overnight; local accommodation is also good value, and there's even a tourist office that really knows its job and is keen to help.

Despite its name, meaning "New Town", Novgorod is Russia's oldest city, founded, according to popular belief, by the Varangian (Scandinavian) Prince Rurik in 862 AD. By the end of the tenth century it had developed into an important commercial centre thanks to its position on the River Volkhov, which flows north into Lake Ladoga and on to the Gulf of Finland – part of an ancient trade route in amber and furs, from Scandinavia to Greece. Originally ruled by the eldest son of the prince of Kiev, Novgorod was later governed by popular **assemblies** (*veche*) dominated by wealthy landlords whose attitude was "if the prince is no good, into the mud with him". As the only major city in Russia to withstand the Tatar invasion, and the seat of a principality that stretched to Poland and the White Sea, it became known as **Velikiy Novgorod** (Great Novgorod) – a title still used today to distinguish it from Nizhniy Novgorod on the Volga. Its wealth and status were reflected by over a hundred churches and a score of monasteries that formed their own school of icon painting, while the level of **literacy** amongst the population was unmatched by anywhere else in Russia, as attested by over 750 texts inscribed on birch bark that have been found during excavations since 1951.

Novgorod remained proudly independent until Ivan III brought it under the administrative control of Muscovy in 1478. Yet its free spirit was so persistent that **Ivan the Terrible** suspected the city of forging a secret deal with Poland. In 1570 he surrounded it with a high timber wall to prevent anyone from leaving. Every day for five weeks, hundreds of citizens were put to death in front

Novgorod's **phone prefix** varies according to the number of digits in the subscriber's number – namely ☎8162 for 6-digit numbers and ☎81622 for 5-digit numbers. This applies to all calls from abroad or elsewhere in Russia, or using a mobile phone in Novgorod.

of the tsar and his depraved son Ivan: stories tell of dozens being fried alive in a giant metal pan, and estimates of the number slaughtered range from 15,000 to 60,000. So many bodies were thrown into the Volkhov that "the river overflowed its banks", and for years afterwards, citizens were ordered to gather in the centre to conceal the extent of the depopulation from foreign visitors. After Ivan's death, the Kremlin was strengthened at Boris Godunov's bidding, but occupied by the Swedes from 1611 to 1617. After their eviction, Novgorod's inhabitants rebuilt it and restored the fortifications, which played a vital role in the defence against Swedish attack for decades afterwards.

Things remained relatively peaceful until **World War II**, during which 98 percent of Novgorod's buildings were ruined and its population decimated as the front rolled back and forth over the city. As a matter of patriotic pride the Soviets determinedly rebuilt the Kremlin walls, the churches and the rest of the town from scratch. Today, Novgorod seems genteel and crime-free in comparison to St Petersburg, despite being on a major smuggling route. Its administration has cultivated foreign ties and investment; Novgorod belongs to the **Hanseatic League** of northern European cities and is twinned with Strasbourg under the TACIS programme for encouraging convergence with the **European Union** – Novgorod in fact won an EU award for exemplary performance in 1997.

Orientation and information

The factories and tower blocks that you see on arrival account for much of this city of 240,000, but are easily ignored once you cross the dry moat encircling the **old town**, divided neatly in two by the sweep of the River Volkhov. The

---

Festivals in Novgorod

Try to time your visit to coincide with one of the festivals staged throughout the year. Towards the end of February there's the Shrovetide festival of **Maslenitsa**, with pancakes galore and traditional entertainments such as "storming the ice fortress". The **Day of Slav Culture** (May 24) honours saints Kyril and Methodius – who brought Christianity to the Slavs and invented the Cyrillic alphabet – with liturgies and bell-ringing in the Kremlin, concerts and folklore performances in churches and at the Museum of Wooden Architecture (see p.325). On the first Sunday in June the museum hosts an **international folklore festival**, featuring traditional games and sideshows and lots of handicrafts and musical instruments for sale, followed by **City Day**, on the second weekend in June, with floats, concerts, sporting events, contests and fireworks, in the Kremlin and Yaroslav's Court, on Sofiyskaya ploshchad and at the beach. Novgorod's pagan roots are revived on the **Night of Ivana Kupala** (July 6), when merrymakers jump over bonfires and go swimming in Lake Ilmen. The party is held on the far shore of the lake, some 30km from town; minibuses collect revellers at 5pm and bring them back in the small hours (℡81622/59 795 for bookings). Another raucous event is the Kremlin Cup **motor rally** (Aug 9–10), which starts on Sennaya ploshchad at noon, and continues on the city outskirts (℡8162/133 758). Novgorod's **Sacred Music** festival (late Sept) is a fine chance to hear Orthodox choirs in the Cathedral of the Sign, the St Nicholas Cathedral and other churches (℡8162/665 380), while new Russian and foreign films are presented at the *Rossiya* cinema during the "Smile, Russia!" **film festival** (Nov 4–8). The festive calendar concludes with *troika* rides and other winter entertainments at the Museum of Wooden Architecture (Dec 29–Jan 1), and a carnival featuring *Ded Moroz* (Grandfather Frost) and *Snegurochka* (the Snow Maiden), on Sofiyskaya ploshchad on **New Year**'s night (Dec 31).

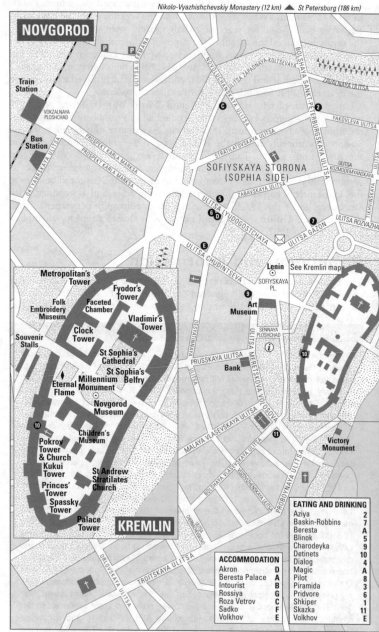

Nikolo-Vyazhishchevskiy Monastery (12 km) ▲ St Petersburg (186 km)

NOVGOROD

Train Station

VOKZALNAYA PLOSHCHAD

Bus Station

PROSPEKT KARLA MARKSA

PROSPEKT KARLA MARKSA

OKTYABRSKAYA ULITSA

ULITSA G. GERMANA

NOVOLUCHANSKAYA ULITSA

STRATILATOVSKAYA ULITSA

ULITSA ZAPADNAYA-KOLTSEVAYA

BOLSHAYA SANKT-PETERBURGSKAYA

ZAVALNAYA ULITSA

YAKOVLEVA ULITSA

ULITSA KOZMODEMYANSKAYA

ULITSA IKHVINSKAYA

ULITSA ROZVAZHA

SOFIYSKAYA STORONA (SOPHIA SIDE)

ZABAVSKAYA ULITSA

ULITSA LYUDOGOSTCHAYA

ULITSA GAZON

ULITSA CHUDINTSEVA

DESYATINNAYA

PRUSSKAYA ULITSA

ULITSA MERETSKOVA VOLOSOVA

Lenin

SOFIYSKAYA PL.

Art Museum

SENNAYA PLOSHCHAD

Bank

See Kremlin map

MALAYA VLASEVSKAYA ULITSA

BOLSHAYA VLASEVSKAYA ULITSA

VIDOVINSKAYA ULITSA

PROBOYNAYA ULITSA

Victory Monument

KREMLIN

Metropolitan's Tower

Folk Embroidery Museum

Faceted Chamber

Fyodor's Tower

Clock Tower

Vladimir's Tower

Souvenir Stalls

St Sophia's Cathedral

St Sophia's Belfry

Eternal Flame

Millennium Monument

Novgorod Museum

Pokrov Tower & Church

Children's Museum

Kukui Tower

St Andrew Stratilates Church

Princes' Tower

Spassky Tower

Palace Tower

TROITSKAYA ULITSA

ORLOVSKAYA ULITSA

ACCOMMODATION

Akron	D
Beresta Palace	A
Intourist	B
Rossiya	G
Roza Vetrov	C
Sadko	F
Volkhov	E

EATING AND DRINKING

Aziya	2
Baskin-Robbins	7
Beresta	A
Blinok	5
Charodeyka	9
Detinets	10
Dialog	4
Magic	A
Pilot	8
Piramida	3
Pridvore	6
Shkiper	1
Skazka	11
Volkhov	E

▼ Museum of Wooden Architecture & Yuryev Monastery (3 km)

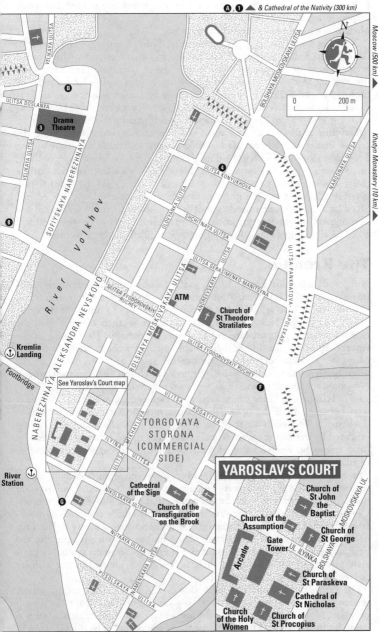

A, **1** ▲ & Cathedral of the Nativity (300 km)

N

Moscow (500 km) ▶

Khutyn Monastery (10 km) ▶

0   200 m

VELIKAYA ULITSA

ULITSA DOSLANYA

B

3 Drama Theatre

VELIKAYA ULITSA

SOFIYSKAYA NABEREZHNAYA

8

River Volkhov

ULITSA KONYUKHOVA

4

OLOVYANAYA ULITSA

SHCHITNAYA ULITSA

ULITSA GERASIMENKO-MANITSYNA

BOLSHAYA MOSKOVSKAYA ULITSA

NARODNAYA ULITSA

ULITSA PANKRATOVA – ZAPOLSKAYA

ULITSA FYODOROVSKIY RUCHEY

BOLSHAYA MOSKOVSKAYA ULITSA

ANDREYEVSKAYA

ATM

Church of St Theodore Stratilates

ULITSA FYODOROVSKIY RUCHEY

F

Kremlin Landing

NABEREZHNAYA ALEKSANDRA NEVSKOVO

Footbridge

See Yaroslav's Court map

ULITSA ROGATITSA

MIKHAYLOVA

ILYINA

ULITSA

TORGOVAYA STORONA (COMMERCIAL SIDE)

River Station

G

NIKOLSKAYA ULITSA

Cathedral of the Sign

Church of the Transfiguration on the Brook

NUTNAYA ULITSA

POSOLSKAYA ULITSA

ZNAMENSKAYA ULITSA

YAROSLAV'S COURT

Church of St John the Baptist

Church of the Assumption

Gate Tower

UL. ILYINKA

BOLSHAYA MOSKOVSKAYA UL.

Church of St George

Arcade

Church of St Paraskeva

Cathedral of St Nicholas

Church of the Holy Women

Church of St Procopius

left bank, known as the **Sophia Side** (Sofiyskaya storona), is focused on the walled Kremlin, where the prince and later the archbishop resided. This oval-shaped fortress, which predates its more famous namesake in Moscow, is the obvious place to begin a tour of Novgorod.

On the opposite bank is the **Commercial Side** (Torgovaya storona), site of the old marketplace and once home to the city's rich merchants. Much of the present layout of the city dates from the reign of Catherine the Great, when the existing medieval network of narrow streets was replaced by a series of thoroughfares radiating out from the Kremlin on the left bank and running at right angles to the river on the right bank. The two sides are linked by a pedestrian footbridge from the Kremlin and a road-bridge further north.

Arriving at the bus or station on the Sophia Side, walk 800m along the central boulevard, prospekt Karla Marksa, until you reach the main square, Sofiyskaya ploshchad, with its landmark Lenin statue. One block south of there, on Sennaya ploshchad, you'll find Novgorod's excellent **tourist office** (Mon–Fri 9am–6pm, Sat & Sun 10am–5pm; ☎81622/73 074, ℱ8162/137 142, ⒺRedizba@novline.ru, Ⓦhttp://eng.tourism.velikynovgorod.ru), named the "Red Izba" (cottage) after the design of its premises. Its friendly staff can tell you anything you might want to know and may phone around on your behalf if asked nicely; a lot of info is featured on their regularly updated **website**.

The Kremlin

Novgorod's **Kremlin** (known locally as the *Detinets* or citadel) looks almost as mighty as Moscow's. Indeed, Muscovite architects supervised the construction of its red-brick walls at the end of the fifteenth century to supersede the stone ones raised by the Novgorodians in 1302, which in their turn replaced the original wooden ramparts erected by Prince Vladimir in 1044. Most of the **towers** date from the 1480s; their steeply pitched wooden roofs show how Moscow's Kremlin might look without the spires that were added in the seventeenth century, while a wide, overgrown ditch that encircles the centre of Novgorod marks the course of its medieval outer ring of **earthworks** (called a *val* in Russian). In olden times, as many as eighteen churches and 150 houses were crammed inside the citadel, though much of the Kremlin now consists of open space. The **walls** are best seen from the east, along the river, being obscured by trees on the western side. **Access** to the territory of the Kremlin (6am–midnight; free) is unrestricted, though the museums within observe regular opening hours.

St Sophia's Cathedral (Sofiyskiy sobor; daily 8am–1pm & 2–8pm; free) is the earliest and by far the largest of all the churches in Novgorod and has been the Kremlin's main landmark since its completion in the mid-eleventh century. Commissioned by Yaroslav the Wise, this Byzantine edifice resembles its namesake in Kiev, which Yaroslav had erected a decade earlier – it may in fact have been constructed by the same Greek master builders. As such it represents the peak of princely power in Novgorod and afterwards became a symbol of great civic pride: "Where St Sophia is, there is Novgorodo" mused Prince Mstislav as Novgorod held out against the Tatars.

The cathedral's five silver bulbous domes cluster around a slightly raised, golden helmet dome topped by a stone pigeon. Legend has it that if the pigeon ever falls, Novgorod will suffer a calamity; so far the worst fate to befall it was being hit by a bullet shortly before the town was occupied by the Germans in 1942. In Soviet times the cathedral was classified as a museum and worship forbidden; like many such buildings, it was returned to the Orthodox Church in 1991. Though the exterior has long been plastered and whitewashed, it was once bare brick, as can be seen on a small patch on the northern side. The only original decorative features that survive are on the western facade, which sports a faded fresco and the splendid bronze twelfth-century **Magdeburg Doors**, made in Germany and covered with little figures in high relief (the sculptors themselves are depicted in the bottom left-hand corner).

Inside, on the far side of the nave, a framed fragment of eleventh-century fresco survives – a portrait of the Byzantine emperor Constantine and his mother Helen. Here you can also see part of the original floor, nearly 2m below the level of the current one. Other minor patches of frescoes can be seen in the cupola and on the embrasures, but most of these date from the end of the nineteenth century. The well-preserved iconostasis is one of the oldest in Russia and includes works from the eleventh to seventeenth century; to the right of the altar, encased in a box, is the famous **Icon of the Sign**, with its damaged eye (see p.324). Note also the vast chandelier, which was a present from Tsar Boris Godunov, and the ornately carved wooden chapel where Ivan the Terrible used to pray before he ravaged Novgorod. **Services** are held at 10am and 6pm every day.

To the east of the cathedral stands **St Sophia's Belfry** (10am–1pm, 1.30–5.30pm; closed Tues; $0.30), constructed during the fifteenth to seventeenth century, but drastically altered in the nineteenth century. The giant bells which once tolled from its arched upper gallery are now displayed outside in their dismantled state, but a score of smaller ones are still working, and can be seen from the rooftop, which also affords a fine **view** of the river with the Cathedral of the Nativity visible to the north.

On the other side is an octagonal **Clock Tower**, erected by Archbishop Evfimii in the fifteenth century, whose famous bell, that summoned citizens to meetings of the *veche*, was carried off to Moscow by Ivan III after he revoked Novgorod's charter of self-government. Evfimii was also responsible for the **Faceted Chamber** (Granovitaya palata), whose nondescript exterior conceals a rib-vaulted, fifteenth-century reception hall, now a high-security exhibition of ecclesiastical treasures (labelled in English) within a **Museum of Applied, Decorative and Jewellers' Art** (10am–6pm, closed Wed; $2.75), that includes life-sized embroidered "portrait shrouds" of Varlaam Khutynskiy, Anthony the Roman and other local saints. This is complemented by a **Folk Embroidery Museum** (10am–6pm; closed Thurs & the last Wed of each month; $1.30) in another wing, by the Kremlin ramparts.

From the Millennium Monument to the Kukui Tower

At the centre of the Kremlin stands the vast, bell-shaped **Millennium Monument**, cast in iron by an English company and unveiled in 1862 on the thousandth anniversary of Rurik's arrival in Novgorod. Figures representing Mother Russia and the Orthodox Church crown the monument's giant globe, while around it (clockwise from the south) stand Rurik, Prince Vladimir, the tsars Mikhail (the first Romanov), Peter the Great and Ivan III, and lastly Dmitri Donskoy trampling a Tatar. A frieze around the base of the monument contains more than a hundred smaller figures, including Catherine the Great, Alexander Nevsky, Pushkin, Lermontov and Glinka, as well as sundry other military and artistic personages. The Nazis dismantled the 65-tonne monument during World War II, intending to transport it to Germany, but never got around to doing so. West of the monument, an **eternal flame** commemorates those who died during the fight to liberate Novgorod from Nazi occupation. Like the Tomb of the Unknown Soldier by the Kremlin walls in Moscow, it is a traditional spot for newlyweds to lay flowers and have their photographs taken.

Behind the Millennium Monument is an E-shaped administrative block where the radical writer Alexander Herzen worked in the 1840s during one of his many periods of internal exile. Now home to the **Novgorod Museum** (10am–6pm; closed Tues & the last Thurs of each month; $2.75), its first floor is devoted to historical artefacts, ranging from birch-bark texts and an original segment of tree-trunk pavement from the fifteenth century to a bullet-holed bust of Tolstoy that received its wounds during the Nazi occupation. On the upper floor you'll find a splendid collection of **icons** from the Novgorod school, including *The Battle Between Novgorod and Suzdal*, which dates from the 1560s – somewhat later than the version in the Russian Museum in St Petersburg.

Beyond this, a tiny **Children's Museum** (10am–4pm; closed Tues; $0.50) mounts temporary exhibitions aimed at kids – but they'll have more fun climbing the **Kukui Tower** (10am–2pm & 3–6pm; closed Mon & Thurs; $0.75), which has a splendid **panoramic view** of the Kremlin and the Sophia Side. The last of the Kremlin towers to be built (in the seventeenth century), it embodies the lessons that Muscovite fortress builders had learned from Italian experts two centuries previously.

Outside the Kremlin

On Sovetskaya ploshchad, outside the Kremlin, Novgorod's **Art Museum** (10am–6pm; closed Mon & the first Thurs of each month; $2) musters a good showing by many of the artists featured in St Petersburg's Russian Museum. Paintings to look out for include Ge's Catherine the Great smirking over the coffin of Empress Elizabeth, and a copy of his famous *Peter the Great Interrogating Tsarevich Alexei at Peterhof*; nocturnal landscapes by Aivazovsky; Repin's *Last Supper*; an orgy scene by Svedomsky; set designs by Golovin and other luminaries of the World of Art, and a vibrant *Peasant Woman* by Malevin. The top floor is devoted to work by artists from the Soviet era, including Nepromyanashchiy's illustrations for Gogol's tales and Zhuravlev's Cubist *Novgorod Kremlin*.

Numerous stalls by the path from the Kremlin to Sennaya ploshchad sell souvenirs and artworks. Besides the usual *matryoshka* dolls, icons and Palekh lacquer-ware, there are traditional local **handicrafts** as well as boxes and platters made from birch-bark; linen tablecloths, blouses and dresses; "bears on a seesaw" and other amusing toys – all at far lower prices than in St Petersburg or Moscow.

In summertime, residents flock to the sandy **beach** beside the Kremlin to tan themselves and bathe in the River Volkhov. Ask at the Kremlin landing stage about two-hour **river cruises** which are sometimes scheduled to the lovely wetlands at the mouth of Lake Ilmen ($1–2).

The Commercial Side

From the river bank on the east side of the Kremlin, there's a great view of the **Commercial Side** (Torgovaya storona), site of Novgorod's medieval market. More than any other Russian city, Novgorod developed a middle class of artisans and merchants thanks to its unique access to trade routes with the rest of northern Europe. During the city's medieval heyday, numerous wooden and masonry churches were built on this side of the river, funded increasingly by the rich mercantile class, and the market once boasted 1500 stalls selling everything from silver and bone to honey and fur – though all that remains now is a long section of the old seventeenth-century **arcade**, and beyond it, from the same period, a **gate tower**.

The foundation of St Petersburg in 1703 dealt a major blow to Novgorod's commercial prosperity, and the final straw came in 1851, when the new railway linking Moscow and St Petersburg bypassed the town entirely. By the mid-nineteenth century, an English traveller found "no life left in the bazaar; customers are so rare. The principal trade seems to be that of icons."

Yaroslav's Court

The densest cluster of surviving medieval buildings is to be found immediately behind the arcade, where the palace of Yaroslav the Wise once stood in a grassy area still known as **Yaroslav's Court** (Yaroslavovo dvorishche). Its most important surviving building is the **Cathedral of St Nicholas** (Nikolskiy sobor; 10am–noon & 1–6pm; closed Mon, Tues & the last Fri of each month; $1.30), which once enshrined an icon that reputedly cured Yaroslav of an illness. Built in 1113 in a Byzantine style that was a deliberate challenge to St Sophia's, it originally sported a full complement of five domes, which unfortunately received a bashing in World War II. The only interior feature worth mentioning is a graphically gruesome but severely damaged fresco of Job afflicted with boils.

The neighbouring **Church of St Paraskeva** (Tserkov Paraskevy Pyatnitsi) was commissioned a century later by the newly ascendant local merchants and dedicated to the patron saint of commerce, but was then rebuilt in 1345. Its distinctive style – large, round-arched porches flanked by clusters of thin columns supporting a single-domed, gabled roof – was probably executed by craftsmen from Smolensk and represented a dramatic shift in the Novgorodian style. Nowadays, sadly, it has fallen into a state of disrepair and is closed to the public.

On the other side of the Cathedral of St Nicholas are two sixteenth-century *trapeznie* churches – churches that included a refectory (*trapezna*) at the west end – which heralded the beginning of a new period of building by the Muscovite merchants who controlled Novgorod following Ivan III's occupation. The wooden-roofed **Church of the Holy Women** (Tserkov Zhon-mironosits), built in 1510 by the merchant Ivan Syrkov, and now a children's centre, is a classic example, with an arcaded refectory and a series of *kokoshniki*, or decorative wooden gables. Next door the smaller **Church of St Procopius** (Tserkov Prokopiya), begun by Syrkov's son in 1529, likewise departed from the austere norm of Novgorod, reflecting the more fanciful tastes of its Muscovite patron.

North of St Paraskeva, the former **Church of St George** houses an exhibition called "A Walk Around Old Novgorod", with sepia photos and merchants' wares from Tsarist times (Mon, Tues & Fri 10am–5pm, Sat & Sun 11am–6pm; $1.25). The nearby **Church of St John the Baptist** and **Church of the Assumption** were begun by Prince Vsevolod some years before he and his family were hounded out of Novgorod by the local nobility in 1137. Neither is open.

Beyond Yaroslav's Court

One of Novgorod's finest creations stands 500m east of Yaroslav's Court, on ulitsa Ilyina. The **Church of the Transfiguration on the Brook** (Tserkov Spasa Preobrazheniya na Ilyine; 10am–5pm; closed Mon, Tues & the last Thurs of each month; $2) was built in 1374 by the *ulichani*, or street community, which kept its bank vault on the upper floor. A standard single-domed structure with a tall drum (the steeply pitched roof is modern), the church has a facade notable for a mix of pagan and Christian symbolism – sun signs and anthropomorphic crosses, either indented or in relief – while the interior contains fragmentary fourteenth-century **frescoes**, the only documented paintings in Novgorod by Theophanes the Greek, Andrei Rublev's teacher. The best preserved are on the upper levels, depicting the Trinity, the saints David, Daniel, Semyon the older and younger, and Olympus, all seated on pillars. During the war, Germans used the church as a machine-gun nest.

Across the road stands the **Cathedral of the Sign** (Znamenskiy sobor; April–Oct 10am–5pm; Nov–March 10am–4pm; closed Wed & the first Thurs of each month; $1.30), built in the seventeenth century's state-approved Muscovite style, although its surrounding outbuildings make it look more like a monastic complex. It is now used as a concert hall, owing to its superb acoustics, but visitors can go inside to view the wonderful frescoes in hues of russet, pink and blue. To the right of the doorway, between two windows, look out for the one of Peter the Great (in a green suit) awaiting judgement for his reforms of the Orthodox Church. The cathedral's predecessor on this site was built to house the famous **Icon of the Sign**, which was carried to the walls of Novgorod's Kremlin when the town was besieged by the Suzdalians in 1169. Legend has it that when one of the enemy's arrows pierced the icon's right eye, the Virgin turned her face away to weep and the Suzdalian soldiers went blind and started killing each other in a frenzy. It is now displayed in St Sophia's Cathedral (see p.321).

Both churches stand at the crossroads of ulitsa Ilyina and **Znamenskaya ulitsa**, which is lined with the sort of picturesque **wooden houses** that characterized the majority of towns and villages in Russia before 1917, though the ones that you see here were built shortly after World War II. There are too many other churches scattered around the Commercial Side to describe them all, but two deserve special mention. On the north side of ulitsa Fyodorovskiy ruchey stands the **Church of St Theodore Stratilates** (tserkov Fyodora Stratilata; 10am–5pm; closed Thurs, Fri & the last Wed of each month; $1.30), the prototype for the Church of the Transfiguration on Ilyina, built by the widow and son of a wealthy merchant. It's a classic example of fourteenth-century Novgorodian architecture, a single-domed cubic structure, modestly decorated on the outside and containing fourteenth-century frescoes within.

Last but not least is the **Cathedral of the Nativity** (Rozdenstvenskiy sobor; 10am–5pm; closed Wed & the first Thurs of each month; $1.30), located at the far northern end of Bolshaya Moskovskaya ulitsa, 500m beyond the *Beresta Palace* (bus #1, #4 or #5). This was once the centrepiece of the Antonov Monastery (whose buildings are now occupied by Novgorod University), founded in 1125 by St Anthony the Roman, who is said to have floated all the way from Rome to Novgorod on a rock. Most of the frescoes in the cathedral date from the nineteenth century; those in the refectory hall depict the life of Anthony, whom the Russians call Antonni Rimylani.

Outside town

If you want to explore further afield, it's only a three-kilometre journey south to the shores of **Lake Ilmen**. Here you'll find the **Yurev Monastery** – the largest surviving complex of its kind in Novgorod – and the wonderful **Museum of Wooden Architecture**, which is also the site of several festivals (see box on p.317). To get there, take bus #7 or #7a from ulitsa Meretskova-Volosova, across the road from the tourist office. Two **convents** to the north of town are less readily accessible, but worth visiting if you're around for longer. At these religious establishments, visitors must **dress** appropriately: long trousers for men, and headscarves and full-length skirts for women.

The Yurev Monastery

Once there were over twenty monasteries and convents around Novgorod, some with hundreds of monks or nuns. Forcibly suppressed in Soviet times, a few have been revived since the early 1990s, starting with the **Yurev Monastery** (Yuryev monastyr; daily 10am–8pm; $1) that was founded by Prince Vsevolod in 1117, and used as a barracks by the Spanish Fascist Blue Division in World War II. Surrounded by massive white walls and with a 52-metre-high bell tower above the entrance, the complex has now been partially restored by ten resident monks.

At its heart is the majestic **Cathedral of St George** (Georgievskiy sobor), built in 1119 by a "Master Peter" who is renowned as the first truly Russian architect. As one of the final great churches to be built by the Novgorod princes, it was a last-ditch attempt to surpass St Sophia, which was by then in the hands of the archbishop. During his rape of Novgorod, Ivan the Terrible personally wrenched the icons from its iconostasis. Although twelfth-century frescoes survive here and there, most date from the nineteenth century. On the west wall is a splendid *Last Judgement*, with the Devil seated on the Beast of the Apocalypse and the dead being raised from their graves; another fresco depicts a crocodile and an elephant from Noah's ark.

The Museum of Wooden Architecture

In the woods 500m back down the road to Novgorod, the **Museum of Wooden Architecture** (muzey Derevyannovo Zodchestva; daily: April–Oct 10am–6pm; Nov–March 10am–5pm; $1.50) was established on the site of the ancient village of Vitoslavlitsy in the 1960s to display old timber buildings from the Novgorod region. Wood was the most practicable and readily available building material in northern Russia – from the earliest times the Novgorodians were derided by others as mere "carpenters".

The oldest buildings here date from the sixteenth century, including a wonderful **Church of the Nativity from Peredeiki** encircled by a raised gallery where the villagers would gossip after services. Most of the houses feature large lean-to barns, although the actual living quarters were much smaller, with benches on opposite sides of the room for the adults to sleep on, men on one side and women on the other. As the children slept just below the roof and grandparents above the stove, opportunities for procreation were limited to the weekly visit to the *banya* (bathhouse).

The museum hosts an annual **folk festival** and **events** marking Maslenitsa, the Day of Slav Culture, City Day and New Year (see box on p.317).

The Nikolo-Vyazhishchevskiy and Khutyn convents

Another architectural gem in a sylvan setting is the **Nikolo-Vyazhishchevskiy Monastery** (Nikolo-Vyazhishchevskiy monastyr; daily 8am–8pm; free). First recorded in 1391, it became one of the richest monasteries under the patronage of Archbishop Evfimii, who had once been a monk there. The existing complex epitomizes the florid Muscovite style of the late seventeenth century – particularly the **Church of St John the Baptist**, linked to its belfry by a long refectory with bands of polychrome **tiles** in high relief. Across the way stands the smaller **Church of St Nicholas**, built fourteen years earlier, in 1685, with an upper summer church reached by a two-storey gallery. Since being restored a decade ago, Nikolo-Vyazhishchevskiy has been a **convent**. Located 12km north of town, it can be reached only by **taxi** ($5 per hour).

The older **Khutyn Monastery of the Transfiguration of the Saviour** (Khutinskiy Spaso-Preobrazhenskiy monastyr; daily 10am–5pm; free) was reputedly founded in the twelfth century on a site controlled by evil spirits, which were exorcised by monks led by Varlaam Khutynskiy (whose portrait shroud is in the Faceted Palace museum). Although the monastery was patronized by the rulers of Muscovy from the fifteenth century, its **Cathedral of the Transfiguration** – built in 1515 – is closer to the Novgorod style of the previous century, with rounded apses, blind arches and an austere white facade. Like Nikolo-Vyazhishchevskiy, it has been re-consecrated as a nunnery. **Bus** #121 from Novgorod's terminal (at 6.30am, 9am, 10.20am and 6pm daily – plus 1.30pm at weekends and 2.30pm on weekdays) runs all the way to the convent, 10km east of town – the journey takes half an hour, and the bus heads back to town thirty minutes later.

Practicalities

Novgorod is 186km south of St Petersburg, a three-and-a-half-hour journey by road. If you don't mind the restrictions of an **organized tour**, it's probably easiest to take your pick of the rival companies whose kiosks stand outside Gostiniy dvor, offering day-trips by coach to Novgorod (11–13hr; $10–17). The price doesn't include admission charges to the museums and churches, and commentary will be in Russian only, but it's far cheaper than the car-plus-interpreter deals offered by tourist agencies and top hotels. Just be sure to check which sites are featured on the itinerary.

Buses from St Petersburg ($4.50) leave roughly every two hours from the bus station by the Obvodniy Canal (see map on p.224). The first departs at 7.30am; the last bus back leaves Novgorod at 6.30pm. Buses aren't air-conditioned, so the journey is unpleasantly hot during summer, with only one halt at a filthy roadside toilet. **Trains** from St Petersburg are comfier but less convenient, with a slow train (5hr) from Vitebsk Station at 8.30am and a fast service (3hr) from Moscow Station at 5.20pm. Novgorod is also accessible **from Moscow** by bus (Mon & Sat; 10hr 30min) or overnight train (arriving at 5.15am), and **from Rīga** by bus (Tues, Wed, Sat & Sun; 11hr 30min).

You can change **money** at *Sberbank* (Mon–Fri 10am–2pm & 3–7pm, Sat 10am–6pm) on the corner of Prusskaya ulitsa, or use the **ATMs** on Bolshaya Moskovskaya ulitsa or in the *Rossiya* and *Beresta Palace* hotels. There's **Internet** access at the *Skazka* café on Bolshaya Vlasevskaya ulitsa (see 328).

If you haven't tried a *banya* in St Petersburg, there's a decent public **bathhouse** at Velikaya ul. 4, that charges $3 per person, or $17 to rent a private cabin for three hours (fun for a group of friends). You can order in food and drink, and rent birch twigs to lash yourself, if so inclined.

Accommodation

If you fancy staying with a local English-speaking family, very pleasant **B&B** in a quiet area of the inner city off Malaya Vlasevskaya ulitsa ($49 for one; $85 for two) can be pre-booked in St Petersburg through HOFA (see p.332).

Otherwise, you can take your pick of local **hotels**, which are unlikely to be all booked up whatever the time of year – though it's worth reserving a room if you're set on staying somewhere in particular:

Akron Predtechenskaya ul. 24 ☎8162/136 908. Centrally located, but quite noisy, this hotel has homely rooms nicer than the lobby and stairways suggest, with bathrooms and TV; "lux" ones have a lounge with a sofa, cups, saucers and an electric kettle. ❷

Beresta Palace Studentcheskaya ul. 2a ☎8162/158 010, ℉8162/158 025, eberesta @novtour.ru, ✉http://novtourinvest .vnovgorode.ru. Located 1km north of the Commercial Side, this four-star hotel has disabled access, a largish swimming pool, sauna and tennis courts (free for guests), a restaurant, nightclub, DHL office and ATM. Buffet breakfast included. Takes Amex, DC, MC and Visa. ❹

Intourist Velikaya ul. 16 ☎81622/74 236, f81622/74 157, ✉hotel@intourist.natm.ru, ✉http://intourist.natm.ru. This 1970s behemoth overlooking the river has clean rooms with TV and basic bathrooms, one step up

from – and a few dollars dearer than - the *Akron* or *Rossiya*. Breakfast not included. Amex, DC, MC, Visa. ❸

Rossiya nab. Aleksandra Nevskovo 19/1 ☎81622/34 185, ℉81622/36 086. Moribund, threadbare Soviet hotel with fantastic views of the river, feasible as a cheapo option in summer, but too chilly in winter. Some rooms have been renovated and its suites have fridges. There's a 25 percent reservation fee for the first night. Breakfast not included. ❷

Roza Vetrov Novoluchanskaya ul. 27a ☎81622/74 795. The cheapest place in town, a shabby but clean hostel on a quiet backstreet beside the *val*; rooms with shared or private bathrooms – "lux" ones have a fridge, TV, sofa, and crockery, and there's a kitchen and an ironing board on each floor. Little English is spoken. No credit cards. ❷

Novgorod	Новгород
Streets and squares	
Bolshaya Moskovskaya ul.	Большая Московскя ул.
Bolshaya Vlasevskaya ul.	Большая Власьевская ул.
ul. Fyodorovskiy ruchey	ул. Фёдоровский ручей
ul. Gazon	ул. Газон
ul. Ilyina	ул. Ильина
Lyudogoshaya ul.	Людогошая ул.
ul. Meretskova-Volosova	ул. Мерецкова-Волосова
Novoluchanskaya ul.	Новолучанская ул.
Predtechenskaya ul.	Предтеченская ул.
prospekt Karla Marksa	проспект Карла Маркса
Sennaya ploshchad	Сенная площадь
Sofiyskaya ploshchad	Софийская площадь
Studencheskaya ul.	Студенческая ул.
Velikaya ul.	Великая ул.
Yakovleva ul.	Яковлева ул.
Znamenskaya ul.	Знаменская ул.
Sights	
Faceted Chamber	Грановитая палата
Khutyn Monastery	Хутынский монастырь
Museum of Wooden Architecture	музей Деревянного Зодчества
Nikolo-Vyazhishchevskiy Monastery	Николо-Вяжишевский монастырь
St Sophia's Cathedral	Софийский собор
Yurev Monastery	Юрьевский монастырь

Sadko ul. Fyodorovskiy ruchey 16 ☎81622/94 382, ℻8162/663 017, Ⓔsadko@novline.ru, Ⓦwww.veliky-novgorod.ru. Clean, quiet, old-fashioned Soviet-style hotel on the Commercial Side. Rooms are carpeted, with TV, short beds and tiny bathrooms. No credit cards. ❷

Volkhov Predtechenskaya ul. 24 ☎8162/115 505, ℻8162/115 526, Ⓔvolkhov@novtour.ru, Ⓦhttp://novtourinvest.vnovgorode.ru. Round the corner from the *Akron*, on a quieter street, this recently refurbished, Best Eastern-run hotel has an inviting ambience, and its "half-lux" suites are superior to and cost less than a standard room at the *Beresta Palace* – though the only amenities are a restaurant and a casino. Amex, EC, MC, Visa. ❹

Eating, drinking and nightlife

Aziya Yakovleva ul. 22/1 ☎81622/72 227. Cosy basement café on the Sophia Side, serving tasty Uzbek, Korean and Russian cuisine; in the summer it has a *shashyk* grill on the square across the road. No credit cards. Daily noon–2am.

Baskin-Robbins ul. Gazon 52. Sells most of the chain's range of ice creams. No credit cards. Daily noon–10pm.

Beresta Beresta Palace Hotel ☎8162/158 010. Chintzy restaurant whose menu runs the gamut from bear medallions with cranberries to Vienna schnitzel, rounded off by a strawberry flambé dessert – but not so good as other, less expensive places. Accepts Amex, DC, MC and Visa. Daily 7–11am, noon–4pm & 6–11pm.

Blinok Lyudogoshaya ul. 10. Serves tasty pancakes with sweet or savoury fillings, and also beer in the sit-down section. Daily 9am–9pm.

Charodeyka ul. Meretskova-Volosova 1/1. Chrome and glass, indoor-outdoor café with a Euro-oriented menu of pizzas, steaks, chicken dishes, salads and ice cream sundaes, catering to hip, weight-watching locals. Service is slow. No credit cards. Daily 10am–11pm.

Detinets in the Pokrovskaya Tower of the Kremlin ☎81622/74 624. Medieval-style restaurant specializing in ancient Russian recipes and drinks such as baked carp, beef-in-the-pot, *medovukha* (honey mead) and *sbittern* (a herbal concoction, served warm). Tables outdoors in the summer; live music in the evenings. EC, Union, Visa. Daily noon–5pm & 7–11pm.

Dialog Bolshaya Moskovskaya ul. 37/9 ☎8162/662 822. This Chinese restaurant at the northern end of the Commercial Side is well regarded by locals and cheaper than its equivalents in St Petersburg. No credit cards. Daily 7pm–6am.

Magic Beresta Palace Hotel. Its $7 admission charge keeps this nightclub the haunt of hotel guests, hookers and wealthier Novgorodians. Can be quite dead, despite the floor show and DJ. Thurs–Sun 9pm–7am.

Pilot Velikaya ul. 3. Relaxed Sophia Side bar with a DJ most nights and live music on Sun. No credit cards. Daily 11am–1am.

Piramida Velikaya ul. 14. Up the road from *Pilot*, on the sixth floor of the Drama Theatre (with its own entrance), this all-night billiards club offers a choice of pool and Russian billiards, and has a sweeping view of the river. Tues–Fri 3pm–6am, Sat & Sun 11am–6am.

Pridvore Lyudogoshaya ul. 3 ☎81622/74 333, Ⓔpridvore@mail.ru. Excellent Russian food, but you'd do best to eat in the bar rather than the restaurant, where the service is a bit slapdash. Does a cut-price weekday lunch. EC, MC, Visa. Noon–midnight, closed Sun.

Shkiper Studencheskaya ul. Regular guests at the *Beresta Palace* slip across the hotel car park to this inexpensive roadhouse, which has tasty *shashlyk*, live Georgian music some evenings, and dancing if customers are in the mood. No credit cards. Daily noon–1am.

Skazka Bolshaya Vlasevskaya ul. 1. Cheery, kid-centred café with slot machines and Internet. Hosts summer barbeques and live music in the evenings. Children's menu from $3. MC, Union, Visa. Daily noon–midnight.

Volkhov Volkhov Hotel ☎8162/115 509. Better value for money than the *Beresta* if you're going to splurge on *haute cuisine* and fancy service. Try the salmon appetizer, the veal medallions with mushroom sauce or stuffed pike-perch from Lake Ilmen, with a chocolate and coffee mousse to follow. Amex, EC, MC, Visa. Daily noon–midnight.

Listings

Listings

13

Accommodation

There has long been a shortage of good, inexpensive to middle-range places in St Petersburg and **accommodation** is likely to be by far the largest chunk of your daily expenditure, with most half-decent hotels charging $100 upwards for a double room. The situation, however, is beginning to improve. In the past, the system was biased towards package tourists, but independent travellers can at last hope for a fair deal. Would-be visitors can now compare rates on hotel websites with those being quoted by accommodation **agencies** (see overleaf), and the range of accommodation is opening up, helping to bring down prices across the board: an increasing number of apartments are available for rent, and small, well-run mini-hotels have appeared on the scene, offering better **value** than the aged Soviet hotels that used to be the only option for those who couldn't afford de luxe establishments.

While the supply of accommodation has improved enormously, though, it still falls short of demand in June, July and August, making **reservations** essential at this time. Most hotels charge more in **high season**, though what constitutes high season varies from place to place (some raise rates as early as April or May). You may be able to get a peak period **discount** by booking in winter or spring, and are sure to pay less if you visit off season (roughly, November to May). The acceptability of **credit cards** in listings below is indicated by the abbreviations: Amex = American Express; DC = Diners Club; EC = EuroCard; JCB = Japanese Credit Bank; MC = MasterCard. Russia's central bank levies a three-percent **surcharge** on card transactions initiated abroad, and some mini-hotels prefer bank transfers instead.

Visas and registration

While **visas and registration** (see p.25) are taken care of for package tourists, independent travellers require visa support and must be registered once in St Petersburg. Large **hotels** can register guests for the duration of their hotel stay, however they obtained their visa support – a few places have a sideline in registering "virtual" guests on behalf of mini-hotels that aren't legally able to. Depending on their legal status, some mini-hotels offer visa support for a fee per person; registration may cost extra, if handled by an agency. Visa support is also available online for tourists booking hotel rooms and maybe also **homestay or flat rental**. In the case of the last two, only the company that issued your visa invitation is legally allowed to register you, so it's vital that they have an office (or accredited partner) in St Petersburg. Similarly, **hostels** may only register guests who got their visa support from the hostel (or its partner). Beware of staying somewhere that can do neither, as this will leave you liable to a hefty fine if you can't find somebody to register you – the Tais agency (see p.26) or the *Morskaya*, *Neva* and *Rus* hotels (see listings) are probably your best hope in this fix. These expedients depend on how zealously the Militia are enforcing the regulations, which periodically change – if you arrive just after a crackdown, they may be unable to help until a way round the impasse has been found. The Way to Russia website (Ⓦhttp://waytorussia.net) spells out the **current regulations** in all their Kafkaesque complexity.

The **cost of visa support** cited for accommodation agencies or individual hotels listed below refers to visa support for a single person for a regular tourist visa, unless specified otherwise.

Accommodation agencies

Accommodation agencies and the Internet are revolutionizing the market, allowing tourists to shop around for **discounts** at hotels, far below their walk-in rack rates. This applies equally to de luxe hotels such as the *Astoria*, old Soviet behemoths, and the many new mini-hotels that market themselves online while staying invisible at street level. As a rule, the prices in our listings refer to rack rates, and you should be able to save anything from $20 to $200 by booking through an agency rather than the hotel itself. That said, there are dodgy agencies and hotels about, and the consequences of a foul-up are potentially worse than not being happy with the room – such as spending days trying to sort out your registration. A few of the agencies below have **walk-in offices** in St Petersburg that can arrange a room on the spot; others only do business **online** and may need several days' notice if visa support is required.

All Hotels in Russia Ⓦwww.all-hotels.ru. One of Russia's leading online agencies, offering discounts at over a dozen hotels in St Petersburg, apartments from $550 per week in the centre, or $300 in the suburbs. Their website has a currency converter and reassuring comments from past users.
All Russian Hotels Ⓦwww.hotels.msk.ru. Online bookings agency with a wide range of hotels in St Petersburg and throughout Russia.
Arent ☏311 13 97, Ⓦhttp://apartment-rentals-russia.com. A locally based Russian-American agency which rents Euro-standard and luxury apartments in the centre from $40 to $300 a night, and provides visa support ($40) and registration for clients. Payment by Western Union.
Host Families Accommodation (HOFA) Tavricheskaya ul. 5, apt. 25 ☏ & ℻275 19 92 or 323 18 48, Ⓦwww.hofa.ru. No walk-in office, but very reliable if you book in advance. Homestay B&B (single $36; double $48), full board ($48; $85) and apartment rental (from $60 a night) in the centre of the city. Offers transfers, tours, excursions and language tuition in St Petersburg, and the

same plus homestay in other cities. Visa support and registration $35. Payment by bank transfer, MC, Visa or Western Union.
Hotels on Nevsky Association (HON) ☏103 38 61, Ⓦwww.hon.ru. Besides owning two mini-hotels (see p.339), HON rents luxury apartments with a sauna and Jacuzzi, sleeping three ($200 nightly/$3000 monthly) or four ($300/$4850) people, mostly within a few blocks of Nevskiy. Also airport transfers ($25) and other services such as visa support/registration, excursions and tickets for the ballet.
Lodging.ru Ⓦwww.lodging.ru. Russian online agency offering discounts at a dozen or so three- and four-star hotels in St Petersburg, and similarly in many other cities. No visa support service, but registration shouldn't be problematical for hotel guests.
Ost-West Kontaktservice Nevskiy pr. 105 ☏327 34 16, ℻327 34 17, Ⓦwww.ostwest.com. Their office (Mon–Fri 10am–6pm) in the yard a few blocks south of Ploshchad Vosstaniya metro can arrange B&B and flat rental. Online visa support ($35) includes registration, which otherwise costs $30. Homestay B&B from $35 daily,

apartments from $50 to $145 per day (reduced monthly rates). Also books rooms in hotels at discount rates, and offers airport transfer ($35 for up to three people), excursions to the Hermitage, Imperial palaces and Novgorod, theatre booking and other services.

Russian Guide Network ⓦwww.russian-guidenetwork.com. This website features links to several local hotel and apartment booking agencies, with visa support and registration ($40), but is chiefly notable for its warts-and-all reviews of over 130 hotels and guesthouses in St Petersburg.

Russian St Petersburg Tours (RST) Zvenigorodskaya ul. 3 ⓣ974 03 73, ⓕ320 01 81, ⓦwww.russian-st-petersburg.com; Pushkinskaya metro. Tourist agency (Mon–Fri 10am–6pm) that runs a Russian language school (ⓦwww.educacentre.net), and can arrange B&B (from $27 in the centre, $17 in the suburbs), discount hotel rooms, hostel beds, visa support for guests ($40) and students ($65 for three months), airport transfers ($30), city tours and excursions. They also sell ISIC student cards.

St Petersburg Bed and Breakfast Bolshaya Konyushennaya ul. 3, office #15 (daily 10am–10pm) ⓣ315 19 17 or 315 04 95; Malaya Morskaya ul. 16, office #34 (Mon–Fri 11am–7pm) ⓣ318 41 96 or 315 56 35,

ⓦwww.bednbreakfast.sp.ru; both Nevskiy Prospekt metro (to which the first office is much nearer). With two branches downtown, this agency is even handier than Ost-West for walk-in clients. Central B&B and apartment rental $35–150 a day, $300–3000 a month. Visa support ($35) and airport transfers ($35; $50 group). Payment by bank transfer or in cash; no cards.

St Petersburg Hotels Guide ⓦwww.hotels.spb.ru. Discount bookings at diverse hotels, plus homestay from $20 (not including breakfast). Visa support ($30), registration ($30) and airport transfers ($40). Excursions to the Imperial palaces and Novgorod.

Way to Russia ⓦhttp://waytorussia.net. Russia-based information portal with links to providers of apartments (from $50 a night in the centre), visa support ($30) and registration ($20). Their website has a regularly updated section on the ever-changing rules governing visas and registration.

Windows on Nevsky ⓣ272 07 11, ⓦwww.w-o-n.ru. Local agency (daily 9am–7pm) that rents apartments on or just off Nevskiy from $75 a night, each located on a map and illustrated with photos. Its partner agency can provide visa support and registration for clients ($40).

Hotels and guesthouses

St Petersburg now has a huge array of **hotels**, from multinational chains to chic mini-hotels or guesthouses with real character. While medium-sized and large hotels are highly visible, **mini-hotels** and **guesthouses** keep a low profile – and may not even be licensed. Many occupy former flats within apartment blocks, which are typically arranged round an inner **courtyard** (*dvor*), accessible from the street via an archway, with several public **stairways** to separate parts of the complex. These are often dirty and gloomy, but some fabulous places exist in run-down buildings. The **security** of these communal areas may be non-existent, or depend on a code being inputted into the outer door; a few *dvor* are gated, with a bell to ring for access and CCTV. Identifying the right entrance can be difficult; many have only a tiny **sign** or no sign at all. If any doubt exists or you need to know the current door-code (they change at intervals), call ahead to obtain the exact details.

When selecting a hotel, consider its **location**. With lots of options within the Fontanka, off Liteyniy prospekt or the lower end of Nevskiy, and the "central" areas of Vasilevskiy Island and the Petrograd Side, there's no need to stay in the suburbs unless you're on an especially tight budget or leave finding somewhere till the last moment. Proximity to a **metro** station is certainly advantageous, but some places are relatively far from one while still being in **walking** distance of many sights, in atmospheric quarters of the inner city. Check our chapter maps for locations.

Rooms overlooking major roads will suffer from traffic **noise** unless they have sound-proofing or are at least four floors above street level, and from **air pollution** if you have to open the windows to cope with the sultry heat of summer. At this time of year, **mosquitoes** are a serious pest – especially near canals and rivers (which means much of the city centre) – making **air-conditioning** (A/C) a real plus. If it doesn't exist, the room's *fortochka* (small ventilation window) should be screened to keep mosquitoes out (if not, buy an Ezalo device, see p.28).

The system of **rating** hotels with stars should be taken with a pinch of salt. When a hotel was built (or last refurbished) is more important. Whereas two-star hotels are 1950s low-rises with matchbox rooms, often without en-suite facilities, three-star hotels may be recently refitted 1970s complexes with restaurants and nightclubs, or brand-new mini-hotels that can be as stylish as four- and five-star hotels, which come closest to matching the standards of their Western counterparts. While the cheapest rooms at old hotels may lack en-suite **bathrooms**, these are generally mandatory for three-stars upwards. **Decor** is age-related, too; places basically unchanged since Soviet times (described in our reviews by the shorthand *sovok*, a slang term for Soviet that literally means "dustpan") have ugly wallpaper, stained carpets, shoddy furniture and beds that are too short. Conversely, de luxe hotels or classy guesthouses may have antiques or artworks in the rooms.

At larger hotels you'll receive a **guest card** that enables you to pass the security guards and claim your room key – don't lose it. Top hotels have electronic card keys for improved security. Most big hotels have a **service bureau**, which can obtain theatre tickets and suchlike. In older hotels, each floor is monitored by a **concierge** or *dezhurnaya*, who will keep your key while you're away and can arrange to have your laundry done.

Within the Fontanka

If you're looking for a location near the major sights, this is it. Here are some of the city's premier hotels – but also a fair number of reasonably priced mini-hotels and guesthouses, many in the atmospheric quarters between St Isaac's Cathedral and the Fontanka, marked on the maps on pp.60–61, pp.62–63, p.79 and p.98, as appropriate.

Admiral Inn nab. kanala Griboedova 33 ℡319 44 62, ⓕ319 43 28, ⓦwww.admiralhotel.ru (in

Russian); 15min walk from Nevskiy Prospekt/Gostiniy Dvor metro. In an excellent location beside a canal not far off Nevskiy, this mini-hotel is reached by a grotty communal stairway. Shared showers and toilets. Breakfast included. Amex, Maestro, MC, Visa. ❹

Angleterre Bolshaya Morskaya ul. 39 ☎313 51 43, ⒻF313 51 58, ⓦwww.rfhotels.com; 15min walk from Nevskiy Prospekt/Gostiniy Dvor metro. A stone's throw from St Isaac's Cathedral, and famous as the site of Yesenin's suicide (see p.100), this historic four-star annexe to the *Astoria* shares its facilities and is inexplicably more expensive. Breakfast not included. All major credit cards. ❾

Arcadia nab. reki Moyki 58A ☎311 61 73, ⓦwww.arkadia.allcafe.info; 15min walk from Sadovaya/Sennaya Ploshchad metro. On the Moyka, not far from St Isaac's. Enter the yard and bear right to reach this small purpose-built hotel, A/C and en-suite throughout (the attic suites are especially stylish) and with a sauna. Breakfast included. Cirrus, Maestro, MC, Visa. ❺

Astoria Bolshaya Morskaya ul. 39 ☎313 57 70, toll-free from UK ☎0800 181123, ⒻF313 51 33, ⓦwww.rfhotels.com; 15min walk from Nevskiy Prospekt/Gostiniy Dvor metro. Five-star big brother to the *Angleterre*, round the corner, with a guestbook featuring such names as Lenin, Thatcher and Chuck Norris. Rooms are light and airy but without A/C; the decor is a mix of Art Nouveau and Classical. Breakfast not included. All major credit cards. ❽

Bed N Breakfast Kazanskaya ul. 11 ☎315 56 35; 15min walk from Nevskiy Prospekt/Gostiniy Dvor metro. Low-budget option within walking distance of many sights; eleven second-floor rooms, sharing four toilets and showers. New and clean but not at all stylish. Breakfast included. No cards. ❸

Central ul. Yabubovicha 2, apt. #14 ☎117 45 16, ⒻF346 86 36; 20min walk from Nevskiy Prospekt/Gostiniy Dvor metro. Just around the corner from St Isaac's. Four rooms with separate bathrooms, overlooking a yard – available for just a few hours, if desired. There's a small sign outside but no English is spoken. Breakfast included. No cards. ❹

Columb Kazanskaya ul. 41☎315 70 93, ⒻF314 09 96, ⓦwww.columbhotel.com; 10min walk from Sadovaya/Sennaya Ploshchad metro.

Three comfy A/C en-suite rooms near Voznesenskiy prospekt, on the edge of *Crime and Punishment* territory. Look for the steel door with a sign in the yard (door code required). Internet. Visa support and registration. Amex, DC, EC, JCB, MC, Visa. ❺

Comfort Bolshaya Morskaya ul. 25 ☎318 67 00, ⒻF314 65 23, ⓦwww.comfort-hotel.spb.ru; 15min walk from Nevskiy Prospekt metro. Look for a tiny sign on the street door and ring to enter this mini-hotel on the corner of Gorokhovaya ulitsa, within walking distance of St Isaac's, the Hermitage and other sights. Nice en-suite rooms with A/C, satellite TV and phone. Internet access. Breakfast included. Visa support $40; free registration. Amex, DC, Maestro, MC, Visa. ❺

Grand Hotel Europe Mikhailovskaya ul. 1/7 ☎329 60 00, ⒻF329 60 05, toll-free ☎0800 86 8588 (from UK), ☎800 426 3135 (from US), ⓦwww.grandhotel-europe.com; near Nevskiy Prospekt/Gostiniy Dvor metro. Arguably the finest and certainly the best-situated five-star hotel in St Petersburg, a brief stroll from the Hermitage. All rooms have huge bathrooms and A/C; the fancier suites are virtual Art Nouveau museum pieces. Clinton, Kohl and Sharon Stone have enjoyed its marbled magnificence and impeccable service. Non-smoking floor. Sauna, solarium and gym. Amex, DC, MC, Visa. ❼

Korona Malaya Konyushennaya ul. 7 ☎117 00 86, ⒻF314 38 65, ⓦwww.korona-spb.com; 5min walk from Nevskiy Prospekt metro. Just off Nevskiy, unmarked at street level (press the "call" button beside door #8 to the left of the main arch) and with only a crown logo outside flat #68 on the second floor, this mini-hotel's discretion is matched by its comfort. All rooms en-suite with hair-dryers, A/C and satellite TV; Jacuzzis in the suites. Breakfast. Visa support $30, registration $25. EC, Maestro, MC, Visa. ❻

Matisov Domik nab. reki Pryazhka 3/1 ☎318 54 45, ⒻF318 74 19; minibus #K-180 from Gostiniy Dvor metro. This pleasant villa-type hotel is within walking distance of the Mariinskiy Theatre but not much else, in a decrepit locality plagued by mosquitoes. Clean en-suite rooms with fridge, phone and satellite TV; the suites have kitchens. Sauna. Breakfast. MC, Visa. ❹

Nevsky B&B (aka Nevsky Inn or Nevsky Prospekt) Nevskiy pr. 11, flat #8 ☎325 93 98, ⓦwww.russiabnb.com; 10min walk from Nevsky Prospekt metro. Accessible from Kirpichniy pereulok via a dark stairwell in the yard, this is like a *kommunalka*, full of clutter and scruffy furniture, with five noisy rooms and a single toilet. Overpriced, despite its central location. No cards. ❹

Polikoff Nevskiy pr. 64/11, apt. 24–26 ☎314 79 25, ⓦwww.polikoff.ru; 10min walk from Gostiniy Dvor metro. A pleasant mini-hotel on the corner of Karavanaya ulitsa, where its unmarked street door is located. Its en-suite non-smoking rooms on the fourth floor (no lift) are soon to be augmented by A/C, noise-insulated rooms and a Jacuzzi two floors down. Buffet breakfast. Visa support. ❹

Premier ul. Soyuz Pechatnikov 4 ☎114 18 77, ⓦwww.spbhotel.com; 20min walk from Sadovaya metro. Sited near the Mariinskiy and the Synagogue, this inexpensive mini-hotel (reached by a communal stairway) has OK en-suite rooms with TV and fridge, and a bar in the lobby. Breakfast. ❹

Pushka Inn nab. reki Moyki 14 ☎312 09 13, ⓕ312 09 57, ⓦwww.pushkainn.ru; 15min walk from Nevskiy Prospekt metro. On one of the loveliest canals in the city, in a house built for a friend of Pushkin's, beside the poet's own apartment (see p.81). Two floors of chic rooms, all en-suite with satellite TV, phone and Internet access (some also have fitted kitchens and dishwashers), above a restaurant decorated with an artillery theme (*Pushka* means "cannon"). ❻

Renaissance Pochtamtskaya ul. 4 ☎380 40 00, ⓕ380 40 01, ⓦwww.marriott.com/ledbr; 20min walk from Gostiniy Dvor or Sadovaya metro. This four-star Marriott near St Isaac's looks set to rival the *Astoria*. Fabulous lobby and atrium; A/C rooms with all mod cons (some designed for wheelchair users); gym and sauna. All major cards. ❽

Turgenev Bolshaya Konyushennaya ul. 13 ☎314 45 29, ⓕ311 51 80; 5min walk from Nevskiy prospekt/Gostiniy dvor metro. Near the Church of the Saviour on the Blood off Nevskiy, this cosy, family-run guesthouse is furnished with antiques, and will bring you breakfast in bed. Guests are met at the airport for free and don't have to pay for visa support until they arrive. As there are only four rooms it's essential to book months ahead. No cards. ❺

Vasilevskiy Island

Location is everything on Vasilevskiy Island. The low-numbered *linii* (see p.155) have decent amenities and are within walking distance of a metro, whereas Gavan and Primorskiy are bleak high-rise zones, where you have to rely on minibuses to reach Primorskaya metro or "mainland" St Petersburg. Fortunately, the nicest hotels are all in the vicinity of Vasileostrovskaya metro station (which gets ridiculously crowded in rush hour) and Sportivnaya metro on the Petrograd Side (which doesn't). See the map on pp.156–157.

Morskaya pl. Morskoy Slavy 1 ☎322 60 69, ⓕ322 60 55; 25min by minibus #K-129 from Gostiniy Dvor metro. A concrete monstrosity above the Sea Terminal; its soulless character and location (far from anything except the D-2 submarine) make it the least desirable choice on the island. Bowling and billiards. Breakfast included. Amex, DC, JCB, Maestro, Visa. ❺

Prestige 3-ya liniya 52, block 4H ☎ & ⓕ328 53 38, ⓦwww.prestigehotel.spb.ru; 10min walk from Vasileostrovskaya/Sportivnaya metro. Perhaps the best option on the island, this chic mini-hotel has a decor that's pure Austin Powers. Very comfy en-suite rooms with satellite TV, phone and modem plug; it's worth paying $20–30 extra for a suite with a Jacuzzi. Visa support $20; room rates thirty percent lower from mid-July till mid-May. Breakfast included. Amex, DC, Maestro, MC, Visa. ❻

Pribaltiyskaya ul. Korablestroiteley 14 ☎356 30 01, ⓕ356 00 94, ⓦwww.pribaltiyskaya.ru; minibus #K-62 from Vasileostrovskaya metro, or #K-162 from Primorskaya metro. Gigantic, Swedish-built hotel beside the Gulf of Finland, mainly used by Finns on booze-cruises, but also for sport and ballroom-dancing competitions. Rooms are on the small size, but have A/C, TV, phone and minibar. Facilities include a sauna and bowling alley. Breakfast included. All major cards. ❻

Rinaldi Maliy pr. 6 ☎ & ⓕ323 32 55, ⓦwww.rinaldi.ru; 10min walk from Vasileostrovskaya metro. Cramped, clean mini-hotel facing a courtyard; turn left once through the arch. Four en-suite rooms with a budget feel, and a small kitchen. The same firm runs another hotel on Moskovskiy prospekt (see p.339). Visa support $25, registration $15 (free if you stay three nights). Breakfast included. DC, EC, MC, Union, Visa. **④**

Shelfort 3-ya liniya 26 ☎ 328 05 05, Ⓦ www.shelfort.e-spb.ru; 10min walk from Vasileostrovskaya metro. Mini-hotel on two floors of an ornate 1900s building. Look for the door in the yard with a yellow sign. All rooms with shower, toilet, TV and phone; a de luxe one has an antique stove with a fireplace. From October to April rates are $20 lower. Breakfast included. **⑤**

SpbVergaz 6–7-ya liniya 70 ☎ 327 88 83, Ⓔ hotel@vergaz.spb.ru; 5min walk from Vasileostrovskaya metro. An excellent mid-range hotel, with a stylish lobby and modern en-suite rooms. Bar/café and sauna. Almost as good as the *Prestige* and considerably cheaper. Breakfast included. **④**

Petrograd Side and the Kirov Islands

Petrograd Side is an interesting location, with fewer hotels than you'd expect. Besides the ones listed below, there is the excellent *Prestige-Sport Hostel* (see p.343). All are shown on the map on pp.174–175.

Avrora Malaya Posadskaya ul. 15 ☎ 233 30 21, Ⓕ 233 36 41, Ⓦ www.hostel.com.ru; 10min walk from Gorkovskaya metro. On a quiet street a few blocks from the mosque, this discreet mini-hotel in flat #76 has bright, cheerful rooms overlooking a leafy courtyard. En-suite rooms are $20 extra; both kinds cost $30 less in low season. Satellite TV. English and German spoken. No credit cards. **④**

Eurasia Gatchinskaya ul. 5 ☎ 323 95 55, Ⓕ 230 44 32, Ⓦ www.eurasia.allcafe.info; 10min walk from Chkalovskaya metro. Not as near the sights as the *Avrora*, *Iskra* or *Piter*, this mini-hotel in the backstreets north of Bolshoy prospekt is quiet and comfy nonetheless, with a sign outside. Rooms on four floors with nice bathrooms and TV. English spoken. Breakfast included. Visa support. EC, Visa. **④**

Gyot ul. Professora Popova 23 ☎ 347 56 28; 15min walk from Petrogradskaya metro. This low-key, business-class hotel has quite a classy interior, with a sauna and *banya*, but feels rather marooned in a backwater of

Apetarskiy Island. Rooms $30 cheaper from November to April. Breakfast included. **⑥**

Iskra Malaya Posadskaya ul. 10/1 ☎ 230 60 27, Ⓦ www.iskrahotel.ru; 5min walk from Gorkovskaya metro. Named after the Bolshevik newspaper, this nice ground-floor mini-hotel in a residential block on the corner of Bolshaya Posadskaya ulitsa has seven en-suite rooms with underfloor heating. Internet for only $1 an hour. Breakfast included. No cards. **⑤**

Krestovskiy Ostrov Deputatskaya ul. 34 ☎ 235 02 36; 10min walk from Krestovskiy Ostrov metro. The most distant and primitive option on Krestovskiy Island, this Soviet youth hotel (still known to locals as the *Sportivnaya*) hasn't been upgraded for ages, and standards are awful, which doesn't stop it being promoted online. No English spoken. No cards. **②**

LDM (Leningradskiy Dvorets molodezhi) ul. Professora Popova 47 ☎ 234 06 96, Ⓕ 234 98 18, Ⓦ www.ldm.ru (in Russian only); bus #25 from Petrogradskaya metro. A 1960s high-rise youth hotel with a jungly atrium and fun-oriented facilities (billiards, bowling, mini golf, disco, pool with waterslides, 24hr bars and a tacky nightclub). Rooms are smallish and *sovok*, even the renovated ones on the sixth floor. Breakfast included. No cards. **④**

Piter pr. Dobrolyubova 5/1 ☎ 325 15 18; 10min walk from Sportivnaya metro. Close to the Peter and Paul Fortress and within walking distance of the Strelka and the Hermitage, this is one of the best options on the Petrograd Side. Seven rooms, all en-suite and A/C. Sauna, solarium, billiards, bar and restaurant with European cuisine. DC, MC, JCB, Visa. **④**

Liteniy, Smolniy and Vladimirskaya

There are many new mini-hotels on, or just off, Nevskiy, which complement the three-star megaliths that have been around since the 1970s, plus the new luxury piles that cater to business travellers. Other options exist in the agreeable residential area east of Liteyniy prospekt – but beware of staying too near Smolniy, a relatively isolated district with zero amenities. See the map on pp.200–201.

Arbat Nord Artilleriyskaya ul. 4 ☎ 103 18 99, Ⓕ 103 18 98, Ⓦ www.arbat-nord.ru; 10min walk from Chernyshevskaya metro. Inviting new hotel on a quiet street near Liteyniy prospekt. Very pleasant en-suite rooms with satellite TV and A/C, double or twin beds. Bar and restaurant; secure parking. Registration fee $7. Buffet breakfast. Amex, DC, Maestro, MC, Visa. ❻

Austrian Yard Furshtatskaya ul. 45 ☏ & ℻ 279 82 35, @ www.austrianyard.com; 5min walk from Chernyshevskaya metro. Cool mini-hotel in a gated yard near the Austrian consulate and the Tauride Garden. Ring the bell to the left of the arch. Comfy rooms with satellite TV, and bathrooms decorated with Egyptian hieroglyphs, goddesses and sea creatures. Kitchen; billiards. Rooms $30 cheaper off-season. Visa support and registration $50. Breakfast included. No cards. ❺

Bubyr's Guesthouse Stremyannaya ul. 11, apt. #10 ☏ 310 66 15, @ www.bubyrs.ru; 5min from Ploshchad Vosstaniya/Mayakovskaya metro. Classy guesthouse in a shabby building behind the *Nevsky Palace Hotel*. Its sixth-floor location could be bad news if the lift is broken, and guests must book well ahead since there are only three bedrooms (all en-suite). Antiques and contemporary art create a stylish yet homely ambience. Free fruit, a library of books about the city, and a bar and kitchen. Free registration for guests using *Bubyr's* visa support ($35) – otherwise it costs $30. As we went to press, they'd just opened a larger place at ul. Marata 22–24, near the Arctic and Antarctic Museum. ❹

Comfort na Chekhova ul. Chekhova 2 ☏ & ℻ 272 54 08, @ comfort2@yandex.ru; 10min walk from Mayakovskaya/Ploshchad Vosstaniya metro. A cut-price offshoot of the *Comfort* (see p.335), on the fourth floor of a residential building (no lift) one block off Nevskiy and Liteyniy prospekts, this six-room mini-hotel has shared toilets and showers, a kitchen and Internet access. Visa support $40; free registration for guests. Amex, Maestro, MC, Visa. ❸

Dostoyevsky Vladimirskiy pr. 19 ☏ 331 32 00, ℻ 331 32 01, @ www.vladimirskiy.ru; by Dostoyevskaya metro. Located near its namesake's last residence, this plush new hotel wrapped around the Vladimirskiy Passage mall is rated three-stars but deserves four – and charges accordingly. Rooms are A/C and insulated against noise; some overlook the mall's atrium or the St Vladimir Church, and a few are designed for disabled guests. Rates $100,

lower off season. Buffet breakfast included. Amex, MC, Visa. ❼

Fifth Corner Zagorodniy pr. 13 ☏ & ℻ 380 81 81, @ www.5ugol.ru (in Russian); 5min walk from Vladimirskaya/Dostoevskaya metro. Entered via a jeans shop in a building overlooking "Five Corners" (see p.220), this mini-hotel has spacious en-suite rooms whose decor is a mixture of minimalist chic and 1950s retro. Breakfast included. Slightly cheaper in low season. ❼

Grand Hotel Emerald Suvorovskiy pr. 18 ☏ 140 50 00, @ www.grandhotel.emerald.com; minibus #K-147 or #K-180 from Mayakovskaya metro. This new five-star hotel is somewhat removed from the centre, but looking to poach customers from its de luxe rivals by offering online discounts and packages. Amenities include a sauna, *banya* and fitness centre. All major cards. ❽

Helvetia Hotel Suites ul. Marata 11 ☏ 311 88 30, ℻ 110 65 46, @ www.helvetia-suites.ru; 5min walk from Ploshchad Vosstaniya/Mayakovskaya metro. On a busy road just off Nevskiy, this comfy apartment-hotel beside the Swiss consulate is set around a gated courtyard. All rooms en-suite with fans, modem plugs and kitchens; some have washing machines and A/C. DC, MC, Visa. ❼

Marshal Shpalernaya ul. 41 ☏ 279 99 55, @ marshal.hotel@tpark.spb.ru; 15min walk from Chernyshevskaya metro. Best Eastern mini-hotel in a former Household Cavalry barracks where Field Marshal Mannerheim, the wartime Finnish president, was once an ensign. Pleasant en-suite rooms with A/C and Internet plugs. Sauna, bar and restaurant. Breakfast included. Rates 15 percent lower from September till mid-June. DC, MC, Visa. ❻

Mercury Tavricheskaya ul. 39 ☏ 325 64 44, ℻ 276 19 77; 15min walk from Chernyshevskaya metro. Opposite the Tauride Palace, this former apparatchiks' hotel – where Gorbachev once stayed – preserves its discretion (there's no sign outside) and boasts three banqueting halls, but is otherwise nothing special. Its single rooms have showers, the doubles, baths. No breakfast. Maestro, MC, Visa. ❹

Moskva pl. Alexandra Nevskovo 2 ☏ 274 00 22, ℻ 274 21 30, @ www.hotel-moscow.ru; beside Ploshchad Alexandra Nevskovo I metro. Enormous 1970s hotel that's been refurbished. Front-facing rooms are insulated against traffic noise and may overlook the Alexander Nevsky Monastery. Facilities include a sauna. Reservation fee of 25 percent for the first night (even for online booking); rates 30 percent cheaper in low season. All major cards. **⑥**

Neptun nab. Obvodnovo kanala 93A ☏324 46 91, ℻324 46 11, ⓦwww.neptun.spb.ru or ⓦwww.bestwestern.com; 15min walk south of Pushkinskaya metro. Part of the Best Western chain, this 1990s business-class hotel has decent facilities, including a pool, bowling and billiards, but a fairly grim location on the Obvodniy Canal. Rooms with baths instead of showers cost $30 more. Breakfast included. All major cards. **⑤**

Neva ul. Chaykovskovo 17 ☏278 05 09, ℻273 25 93; 5min from Chernyshevskaya metro. This old-fashioned hotel in a nineteenth-century townhouse that was once a brothel doesn't deserve its three-star rating, but is near a metro and a 15–20min walk from the Summer Garden and the Hermitage. The only facilities are a bar and sauna. Breakfast included. Maestro, MC, Visa. **④**

Nevsky 90 & 91 Nevsky pr. 90/92 ☏273 73 14 and 91 ☏103 38 60, ℻103 38 61, ⓦwww.hon.ru; 5–10min walk from Mayakovskaya/Ploshchad Vosstaniya metro. Two stylish A/C mini-hotels owned by the Hotels on Nevsky Association. No. 90 is across the road from the *Nevsky Palace*, in the block behind *Café Max*; enter the yard and bear left. Located on the third floor (no lift), its en-suite rooms overlook the yard and share a small kitchen. No. 91 is nearly 1km down the prospekt, in the block with a rooftop Coca-Cola sign on ploshchad Vosstaniya. It's hard to find the right entrance in an inner yard, and the communal stairway isn't inviting, but the hotel is delightful, with all mod cons including a sauna. Airport transfers ($25). Breakfast included. Rates $50 lower off season. Accepts Visa. **⑥**

Nevsky 150 Nevsky pr. 150 ☏277 12 19, ℻277 06 40, ⓦwww.oksanas.net/NevskyProspect150.htm; 15min walk from Ploshchad Vosstaniya or Ploshchad Aleksandra Nevskovo metro. Ideal for a group of friends and fantastic value, this stylish, spacious fourth-floor apartment has three bedrooms, a dining room, fitted kitchen, washing machine, VCR and even a piano. Available only in summer. Visa support $35. MC, Visa, Western Union. For this price, you get the entire place to yourself. **⑥**

Nevsky Palace Nevsky pr. 57 ☏380 20 01, ℻380 19 37, ⓦwww.corinthia.ru; 5min walk from Mayakovskaya metro. Formerly a Sheraton and now part of the Corinthia chain, this five-star hotel is characterless compared to its downtown rivals the *Astoria* and *Grand Hotel Europe*, but popular with business travellers. Secure parking, sauna, solarium and small gym. All major cards. **⑦**

Oktyabrskaya Ligovskiy pr. 10 ☏277 63 30, ℻315 75 01, ⓔhotel@spb.cityline.ru; near Ploshchad Vosstaniya/Mayakovskaya metro. A large, recently refurbished three-star hotel on a busy junction near Moscow Station. Favoured by low-budget tour groups but not such good value for independent travellers as the *Filial* (see below). All rooms en-suite with satellite TV; some suites have views of ploshchad Vosstaniya. Bar, billiards, Internet. Visa support. Breakfast included. All major cards. **④**

Oktyabrskiy Filial Ligovskiy pr. 43/45 ☏277 72 81, ℻315 75 01, ⓔhotel@spb.cityline.ru; Ploshchad Vosstaniya/Mayakovskaya metro. This cheaper offshoot of the *Oktyabrskaya* nearer Moscow Station has freshly renovated rooms of all shapes and sizes. Don't be deterred by the grubby exterior or the streetwalkers outside at night – the interior is fine and security is good. If emailing or faxing a reservation, be sure to specify "Filial". **④**

Radisson SAS Royal Nevsky pr. 49/2 ☏322 50 00, ℻322 50 02, toll-free ☏00 800 3333 3333 (from UK) or 1-800 333 3333 (from US), ⓦwww.radissonsas.com; 10min from Mayakovskaya or Gostiniy Dvor metro. Medium-sized, four-star business hotel within walking distance of many sights. A/C rooms with satellite TV and Internet plugs. Fitness centre. All major cards. Breakfast not included. **⑨**

Rinaldi Moskovskiy pr. 20 ☏973 51 40, ℻316 05 79, ⓦwww.rinaldi.ru; 5min walk from Tekhnologicheskiy Institut metro. Quiet, clean, mini-hotel off a noisy avenue (turn right as you enter the yard, go through the arch on the right and ring the bell by the yellow-framed door). All rooms en-suite with TV and phone. Breakfast included. Visa support $25, registration $15 (free if you stay three nights). DC, EC, MC, Union, Visa. **④**

Rus Artillereyskaya ul. 1 ☎273 46 83, ℱ279 36 00; 5min walk from Chernyshevskaya metro. This 1970s eyesore facing the *Arbat Nord* (see p.337) is half given over to a business centre, and the hotel side seems a bit indifferent. All rooms have cable TV, VCR and fridge; ones with bathrooms cost $40 extra. Excellent sauna, a café and bar, but no breakfast. Amex, JCB, MC, Visa. ❹

Sonata ul. Mayakovskovo 50 ☎380 40 90, ⓦwww.hotel-sonata.com; 10min walk from Chernyshevskaya metro. A clean, well-lit communal stairway leads to this pleasant mini-hotel above the *Red Fox Jazz Club*, with en-suite rooms, a café and bar. Guests are urged to visit the Russian Vodka Museum, which is run by the same company. ❹

Vesta Nevskiy pr. 90/92 ☎272 13 22, ℱ279 55 40; ⓦwww.vestahotel.spb.ru; 5min walk from Mayakovskaya metro. In the same residential complex as *Nevsky 90* (see p.339), but much further back into the *dvor*, to the left of a playground, this cheaper mini-hotel is en-suite and attractively furnished throughout, with a café and Internet access. Visa support $35. Breakfast included. ❺

The Southern Suburbs

The Southern Suburbs are far from attractive as a rule, but some parts are well served by metro, making it more convenient than you'd think. Park Pobedy and Moskovskaya ploshchad are a fifteen-to-twenty-minute ride from the centre; both localities are quite leafy, with a mixture of high-ceilinged Stalinist apartments and later matchbox low-rises. Some hotels here were built decades ago; others are new mini-hotels, inside residential blocks. See the map on p.224 for locations.

Esplanada Apartments Ligovskiy pr. 130, flat #41 ☎ & ℱ166 38 97, ⓦhttp://esplanada.chat.ru/index.html; 10min walk from Ligovskiy Prospekt metro. Strictly a cheapo last resort: tiny rooms sharing a shower, and a larger one with private facilities, on the sixth floor of a dingy block on a polluted thoroughfare. No visa support or registration. No cards. ❷

Kievskaya Dnepropetrovskaya ul. 49 ☎ & ℱ166 56 95, ⓔinfo@kievskaia.spb.ru; trams #10 and #16 or trolleybus #42 from Ploshchad Vosstaniya or Ligovskiy Prospekt metro. Near the intercity bus station but nothing else, this 1960s low-rise hotel has small, clean rooms, some en-suite. Inferior to the *Mir* and *Nemetsky Club* (see below) in almost all respects, but charges the same. Internet. Breakfast included. No cards. ❹

Mir ul. Gastello 17 ☎108 51 66; 15min walk from Park Pobedy metro. Off Moskovskiy prospekt, 10min drive from Pulkovo airport and 20min metro ride from the centre, this refurbished 1960s hotel has matchbox rooms with bathrooms and phones; ask for one at the back overlooking the Chesma Church. Breakfast included. No cards. ❹

Nemetsky Club ul. Gastello 20 ☎371 51 04, ℱ371 56 90; 15min from Park Pobedy metro. On the same street as the *Mir* but much better value for the same price – a stylish mini-hotel within an old house with a garden, facing the Chesma Palace. Established by a German (its name means "German Club"), and equipped with good security and a solarium. Breakfast included. DC, JCB, MC, Visa. ❹

Prin ul. Vozrozhdeniya 4 ☎324 49 49, ℱ324 49 70, ⓦwww.prin.bc.ru; 10min walk from Kirovskiy Zavod metro. Award-winning hotel-business centre near the Kirov Works. En-suite rooms with cable TV; café-bar. Rooms $20–30 cheaper in low season, and heavily discounted online. Breakfast included. All major cards. ❺

Pulkovskaya pl. Pobedy 1 ☎140 39 00, ℱ140 39 48, ⓦwww.pulkovskaya.ru; 10min walk south of Moskovskaya metro. Clean but slightly shoddy 1980s hotel, overlooking the Victory Monument en route to the airport. Facilities include a sauna, gym and tennis courts; rooms have A/C and voicemail. Breakfast included. About $30 cheaper in low season. All major cards. ❻

Rossiya pl. Chernyshevskovo 11 ☎329 39 00; 5min walk from Park Pobedy metro. A gloomy Stalinist pile with 1970s additions such as a pool and sauna; all rooms with showers and toilets, TV, and phone. Internet. Breakfast included. All major cards. ❹

U Fontana ul. Sevastyanova 14 ☎388 12 78, ℱ388 12 78, ⓔufontana@comset.net; 10min walk from Park Pobedy metro. In a high-rise zone one block north of the park, this mini-hotel has clean, light singles and doubles with TV and phone; en-suite facilities cost $15 extra. Reservation fee $10. ❸

Yuzhnaya Rasstannaya ul. 2Б ☎166 10 88, ⓕ166 10 87, ⓦhttp://yuzhnaya.all-hotels.ru; minibus #K-170 from Ligovskiy Prospekt metro or #K-139 from Vladimirskaya/Dostoyevskaya metro. High-ceilinged *sovok* rooms with shower, fridge, phone, TV, far from everywhere but the Volkov Cemetery. No cards. ❸

Vyborg Side

Vyborg Side is the district with the least going for it in terms of ambience, although the *St Petersburg Hotel* has the saving grace of being near the cruiser *Aurora*, with great views of the Neva. The high-rise Okhta district to the east of the Neva has assumed new importance with the opening of Ladoga Station, where trains from Finland terminate. Though some hotels here charge low rates and have good amenities, you might be deterred by their surroundings or distance from a metro (see map on p.233).

Deson Ladoga pr. Shaumyana 26 ☎528 56 28, ⓕ528 52 20, ⓦwww.deson.lek.ru; 10min walk from Novocherkasskaya metro. A pleasant, modern hotel catering to business travellers, in a seedy location a few stops from the centre by metro. All staff speak English and the restaurant offers European and Chinese cuisine. A morning sauna as well as breakfast is included in the price. All major cards. ❺

Nautilus Inn Rizhskaya ul. 3 ☎449 90 00, ⓦwww.nautilus-inn.ru; 15min walk from Novocherkasskaya metro. An attractive, new, nautically-themed hotel on a quiet street in a grotty neighbourhood. All rooms en-suite with cable TV and phone. Solarium, saunas, gym, billiards, restaurant. Breakfast included. All major cards. ❹

Okhtinskaya Victoria Bolsheokhtinskiy pr. 4 ☎222 86 01, ⓕ227 25 14, ⓦwww .okhtinskaya.spb.ru; tram #7, #23 or #46, or trolleybus #7 from Novocherkasskaya metro. A decent three-star hotel with a fine view of the Smolniy Convent across the Neva, A/C rooms with minibar and VCR, and a sauna and Italian deli on the premises. On the downside, there are no baths, only showers, and the hotel is awkward to reach. Breakfast included. Amex, Maestro, MC, Visa. ❹

St Petersburg Pirogovskaya nab. 5/2 ☎380 19 19, ⓕ380 19 06, ⓦwww.hotel-spb.ru; 15min walk from Ploshchad Lenina metro. The best features of this renovated 1970s eyesore are the magnificent view of the Neva from the front-facing rooms and a colossal split-level dining hall. All rooms en-suite with TV and phone; sauna and business centre. Breakfast included. All major cards. ❺

Sputnik Staro-Pargolovskiy pr. 34 ☎552 56 32, ⓕ552 80 84; minibus #K-123 or #K-221 from Ploshchad Muzhestva metro. Difficult to reach and plagued by traffic noise, its rooms are clean, with a shower, phone and MTV, but marred by narrow beds and unreliable plumbing. Reduced rates Sept–April. No cards. Breakfast included. ❹

Vyborgskaya Torzhovskaya ul. 3 ☎ & ⓕ246 91 94 or 246 81 87, ⓔvyb@mail.linkey.ru; 5min walk from Chernaya Rechka metro. Accessible, cheap, 1950s hotel in the Novaya Derevnya district, whose claim to fame is that Vladimir Mashkov – star of the film *The Thief* – once stayed there. Clean rooms with phones, TV, fans and fridges; some have showers. Café; billiards. No cards. ❸

Zanevskiy Zanevskiy pr. 32-2 ☎528 7655, ⓕ528 76 55, ⓦwww.hotel-zanevsky.narod.ru (Russian only); 15min walk from Ladozhskaya metro. Basic mini-hotel on the second floor of an Okhta high-rise. Clean, cramped doubles and triples with shared toilets and showers. Breakfast included. No cards, visa support or registration. ❸

Homestay accommodation

Agencies in St Petersburg and abroad can arrange homestay accommodation in the city. **Staying with a Russian family**, you'll be well looked after and experience the cosy domesticity that is the obverse of brusque public life. Your introduction to this homely world will be a pair of *tapochki* – the slippers which Russians wear indoors to avoid tramping in mud – followed by a cup of tea or a shot of vodka. Your room will be clean and comfortable, though it can be disconcerting to discover, in small apartments, that it belongs to one of the family, who will sleep elsewhere for the duration of your stay.

Another, more disagreeable, surprise might be that the district **hot water** supply has been cut off, as happens for up to two weeks during the summer, so that the utilities company can clean the water mains. Don't blame your hosts should this happen – it's not their fault. All you can do is put up with it, or move to another district of the city that isn't affected at the time. The water company gives only a week's notice that supplies will be cut off, so a flat with its own boiler is highly desirable.

Booking through a **local agency** (see p.332) you can pay as little as $20 per person (without breakfast), but most charge from $30 for B&B. Companies **abroad** (see "Getting There" in Basics) may charge up to $60 a head per night – which for two travelling together is dearer than some hotels. Try to ascertain the exact location, and judge if it's worth the price. If you book through an agency or tour company that also provides visa support, your **registration** should be handled automatically – but be sure to verify that this is so. There have been instances where agencies failed to follow through with the paperwork, landing their clients in a bureaucratic nightmare.

This being Russia, there's also an **unregulated alternative** – namely people touting for guests at Moscow Station and other mainline terminals. Most are genuine widows or pensioners with a room or flat to let, but inevitably there are tricksters too. You'll have to depend on your instincts as to whom to trust, and shouldn't agree to anything without them showing you the flat's location on a map – let alone part with cash before seeing it. They're extremely unlikely to be able to register you, so anyone using this option faces a registration problem if they stay more than three days. Rates for "unofficial" B&B can be as low as $15 a day.

Flat rental

If you're going to be in town longer than a week, or are coming as a group of friends or a family, you should consider renting a self-contained **apartment** (*kvartira*) to save money and enjoy more privacy than a hotel or B&B allows. This can be done before you arrive through agencies such as Arent, HOFA, Ost-West Kontaktservice, St Petersburg Bed and Breakfast, and others (see p.332). Some charge on a per person basis, others according to the size and quality of the apartment. Rates for a single person can be as low as $35–50 daily for a short-term letting (try any of the firms above, or Way to Russia). Two or more people should look for flats being rented at a set price, which makes it easier to compare what's being offered by different agencies. Broadly speaking, flats come with Soviet fittings, or **refurbished** to "Euro Standard" (a new kitchen and bathroom at least), but in either category there are some places that are superlative and others that are disappointing. An apartment sleeping three costs $100–200 a night, which can get you a really cool de luxe pad with a Jacuzzi and plasma TV if you're lucky – the author once had a flat with a columned ballroom. For longer stays, weekly rates should drop to $450–600, monthly rent to $700–1200, while if you don't mind living in a high-rise block outside the centre, a flat can cost as little as $300 a month.

Aside from the price, location and decor, the things to look for are a **boiler** (*kolonka*), so you won't be deprived of hot water if the district supply is cut off, a **bed** that's long enough to be comfortable, and a **door** that provides good security. Many apartments have a sturdy outer door, whose lock is operated by pushing in and then retracting a notched metal strip; the inner door is unlocked by conventional keys; while the door from the apartment building onto the street or yard may be locked by a device which requires you to punch in a code. **Door codes** usually consist of three digits; you have to push all three buttons simultaneously to make it work; alternatively, if there's a metal ring, press the numbers in order and pull upwards.

Hostels

Ever since the Russian Youth Hostel Association (RYHA) and the first international hostel were set up by a Californian and his Russian partners in 1992, St Petersburg's **hostels** have faced the dilemma that not enough backpackers visit the city outside summer to balance their books without raising prices so high that their clientele decides that homestay or cheapo hotels offer better value for money. Another constraint is that, by law, hostels may register only guests who've obtained their visa support through the hostel or its partner agency – which means that guests who didn't and stay longer than three days risk being in breach of registration rules (see p.331). Yet new hostels open each year and the general standard is improving. Hot water in the bathrooms is standard, and some places have mosquito-screens or coils in the rooms, Internet access, a café or other facilities.

If saving money is your chief priority, the *Petrovskiy Hostel* has by far the cheapest daily rates, while the *Prestige-Sport* offers the best value for money in terms of amenities and visa support. The *City Guide* and *Herzen* hostels are right in the heart of the city and charge accordingly, while the other three places are in residential areas beyond the Fontanka. There are no age limit or membership restrictions, but a Hostelling International (HI), RYHA or ISIC student card may get you a few dollars discount on a dorm bed. RYHA cards ($3) are also valid for discounts at hostels in Moscow and Latvia.

City Guide Hostel nab. kanal Griboedova 29, ☎ & ℻ 112 69 28, ⓦ www.spbcityguide.com; 5min walk from Nevskiy Prospekt/Gostiniy Dvor metro (see map on pp..62–63). Only 200m off Nevskiy, by a lovely bridge over the Griboedov Canal, this attractive mini-hostel has a few singles and doubles with cheery Ikea decor, shared bathrooms and a well-equipped kitchen. Enter the yard, turn left and look for the metal door of flat #9 – there's no sign to identify the hostel. English, German, French and Italian spoken.

Herzen University Hostel Kazanskaya ul. 6 ☎ 314 74 72, ℻ 314 76 59, ℮ hotel@herzen.spb.ru; 5min walk from Nevskiy Prospekt/Gostiniy Dvor metro (see map on pp.62–63). Equally central, just 100m behind the Kazan Cathedral, this trainee teachers' hostel has good security and clean rooms with en-suite showers or baths; a café on one floor and a karaoke-bar and Internet ($1.25/hr) upstairs. On the

downside, they can't provide visa support or register guests, and a single or double room costs $63

Petrovskiy Hostel Baltiyskaya ul. 26 ☎ & ℻ 252 53 81; 10min walk from Narvskaya metro (see map on p.224). Sited in the southern suburbs, 15min from the centre by metro, this Russian students' hostel affiliated to the RYHA has the cheapest rates ($10 per person, year round) for its simple double and triple rooms with shared bathrooms. Cafeteria and sauna. Little English spoken. Can provide visa support through a tourist agency for $35, and register guests for $7.

Prestige-Sport Hostel pr. Dobrolyubova 14 ☎ 328 53 38, ⓦ www.youth-hostel.ru; 5min walk from Sportivnaya metro (see map on p.174). Located in a 1980s complex facing the Yubileyniy Sports Palace, within walking distance of the Peter and Paul Fortress, this swanky new hostel has bathrooms, phones and satellite TV in all its rooms, sleeping two ($42), three ($64) or four ($96) in bunk beds, and mostly without windows. Breakfast $4.50. Visa support and registration $20. Run by the same firm as the *Prestige Hotel* on Vasilevskiy Island (p.336). Amex, DC, Maestro, MC, Visa.

Puppet Theatre Hostel ul. Nekrasova 12 ☎272 54 01, ⓦhttp://hostel-puppet.ru; 15min walk from Mayakovskaya or Chernyshevskaya metro (see map on p.201). Just off Liteyniy prospekt, within walking distance of the Engineers' Castle, this fourth- and fifth-floor RYHA hostel is reached via the trade entrance of the puppet theatre next door. Security is OK but the premises are shabby, washrooms pong, and the only amenity is a pay phone. It has high (April–Oct), low (Nov–March) and Christmas (mid-Dec to mid-Jan) rates for double rooms ($48; $38; $42) and dorm beds ($19; $15; $16), with $1 discount for HI or ISIC card holders. Breakfast included, plus free tickets to the puppet theatre. Visa support and registration $25.

RST Hostel Sinopskaya nab. 22 ☎327 03 73, ⨍327 03 73, ⓦwww.russian-st-petersburg.com or ⓦwww.educacentre.net; 5min walk from Ploshchad Aleksandra Nevskovo I metro (see map on p.201).

Currently closed for refurbishment. When it reopens in 2005, facilities and rates are likely to be on a par with the *St Petersburg International Hostel* (see below). Meantime the parent company, Russian St Petersburg Tours, does visa support ($40), homestay, or rooms in the *Prestige-Sport Hostel* (see p.343).

St Petersburg International Hostel 3-ya Sovetskaya ul. 28 ☎329 80 18, ⨍329 80 19, ⓦwww.ryh.ru; 10min from Ploshchad Vosstaniya metro (see map on p.201). On a quiet street north of Moscow Station, this long-established, clean and friendly hostel has Internet ($2/hr), laundry service ($5), a useful notice board, cable TV in the common room and salubrious washrooms. High (March–Oct), low (Nov–March) and Christmas (mid-Dec to mid-Jan) rates for double rooms ($52; $42; $44) and dorm beds ($21; $15; $16) – with $2–3 discount for HI members and a $10 child's rate in the dorm. Breakfast included. Provides visa support ($35) and has its own travel agency, Sindbad travel (ⓦwww.sindbad.ru/en). Reservations can be made through STA in Britain and the USA or at any Hostelling International IBN (International Booking Network) location.

Eating and drinking

When I eat pork at a meal, give me the whole pig; when mutton, give me the whole sheep; when goose, the whole bird. Two dishes are better than a thousand provided a fellow can devour as much of them as he wants.

Dead Souls, Gogol.

A s the above quotation suggests, quantity rather than variety has long characterized the Russian appetite. Especially under Communism, when *haute cuisine* was wiped out, citizens made a virtue of the slow service that was the norm in Soviet restaurants by drinking, talking and dancing for hours. The Western notion of a quick meal was unthinkable.

Nowadays, the gastronomic scene has improved enormously, with hundreds of new **cafés** and **restaurants** offering all kinds of cuisine and surroundings, aimed at anyone with a disposable income – from mega-rich New Russians and expense-account expatriates to fashion-conscious wealthy teenagers. While some places at the top end of the market can rightfully boast of their *haute cuisine*, there are lots whose decor and pretensions surpass their cooking, where the clientele's main aim seems to be to flash their money around.

While all bars, cafés and restaurants take **payment** in rubles, more tourist-oriented places may list prices on their menus in dollars or so-called "Standard Units" (using the Cyrillic abbreviation УЕ), which amounts to the same thing. In that case, the total is converted into rubles at the current central bank rate or the rate of exchange advertised on the premises (which may be less favourable). It's often (though not invariably) true that a menu in dollars is an indication that the establishment is overpriced by local standards.

Credit cards are accepted by most top-range or foreign-managed restaurants – we've indicated in our listings which ones are accepted using the relevant abbreviations (Amex = American Express, DC = Diners Club, MC = MasterCard, EC = EuroCard, JCB = Japanese Credit Bank) – but you shouldn't take it for granted. As for paying with traveller's cheques, forget it.

Breakfast, bakeries and snacks

At home, most Russians take **breakfast** (*zavtrak*) very seriously, tucking into calorific dishes such as pancakes (*bliny*) or buckwheat porridge (*kasha*), with curd cheese (*tvorog*) and sour cream (*smetana*), although some settle simply for a cup of tea and a slice of bread. Hotels will serve an approximation of the "Continental" breakfast, probably just a fried egg, bread, butter and jam; the flashier joints, however, provide a *Shvedskiy stol*, or "Swedish table", a sort of smorgasbord.

Pastries (*pirozhnoe*) are available from cake shops (*konditerskaya*) and some grocers (*gastronom*). Savoury pies (*pirozhki*) are often sold on the streets from late morning; the best are filled with cabbage, curd cheese or rice. It's advisable to steer clear of the meat ones unless you're buying from a reputable café.

Bread (*khleb*), available from bakeries (*bulochnaya*), is one of the country's culinary strong points. "Black" bread (known as *chorniy* or *rzhanoy*) is the traditional variety: a dense rye bread with a distinctive sourdough flavour and amazing longevity. *Karelskiy* is similar but with fruit; *surozhniy* is a lighter version, made with a mixture of wheat and rye. French-style baguettes (*baton*) – white, mixed-grain or plaited with poppy seeds – are also popular. For wholegrain, focaccia or fruit breads, check out the Baltic Bread chain of bakeries.

Like other Eastern Europeans, the Russians are very fond of **cakes** (*tort*). The Sladoezhka chain of patisseries sells all kinds of freshly made fruit or chocolate gateaux, while supermarkets stock various cakes whose main ingredients are sponge dough, honey and a distinctive spice such as cinnamon or ginger or lots of cream and jam. Whatever the season, Russians are always happy to have an **ice cream** (*morozhenoe*), available from kiosks all over town. Much of the locally produced ice cream is cheaper and of better quality than the imported brands; try the popular crème-brûlée or eskimo, a sort of choc-ice. Alternatively, there are a few Baskin-Robbins outlets around town.

Department stores, theatres and major museums feature a stand-up *bufet*, offering open **sandwiches** with salami, caviar or boiled egg as well as other nibbles. Less appealing buffets can be found in train and bus stations, and around metro stations and markets.

Zakuski

Despite the popularity of Western fast food, Russian culinary traditions are still strong, especially with regard to *bliny* (pancakes), one of the best-loved of Russian **zakuski** – small dishes or hors d'oeuvres, which are often a meal in themselves. *Zakuski* traditionally form the basis of the famous *Russkiy stol*, or "Russian table", a feast of awesome proportions, in which the table groans under the weight of the numerous dishes while the samovar steams away. Among the upper classes in Tsarist times, *zakuski* were merely the prelude to the main meal, as foreign guests would discover to their dismay after gorging themselves on these delights. Salted fish, like sprats or herrings, are a firm favourite, as are gherkins, assorted cold meats and salads. Hard-boiled eggs and *bliny*, both served with **caviar** (*ikra*), are also available. Caviar is no longer as cheap as during Brezhnev's era, when people tired of eating so much of it, but it's still cheaper than in the West. There are two basic types: red (*krasnaya*) and black (*chornaya*), with the latter having smaller eggs and being more expensive.

Meals

Russians usually eat their main meal at lunchtime (*obed*), between 1pm and 4pm, and traditionally have only *zakuski* or salad and tea for supper (*uzhin*). Restaurants, on the other hand, make much more of the evening, though many now offer a set-price business lunch to attract extra customers.

Menus are usually written in Russian only, although more and more places offer a short English version. But beware, because the Russian menu is usually typed up every day, whereas the English version will give only a general idea of what might be available. In such cases, you'd probably be better off asking what they recommend (*shto-by vy po rekomendovali?*), which can elicit some surprisingly frank replies.

If your main concern is price, you'll need to stick to **fast-food** outlets or **cafés**, the latter providing some of the best **ethnic food** in the city, including Armenian (*Armyanskiy*), Georgian (*Gruzinskiy*), and Korean (*Koreyskiy*), as well as traditional Russian cooking.

Russian cuisine owes many debts to Jewish, Ukrainian and Caucasian cooking, but remains firmly tied to its peasant origins. In former times, the staple diet of black bread, potatoes, cabbages, cucumber and onions made for bland eating – *Shchi da kasha, pishcha nasha* ("cabbage soup and porridge are our food") as one saying goes – with flavourings limited to sour cream, garlic, vinegar, dill and a few other fresh herbs. These strong tastes and textures – salty, sweet, sour, pickled – remained the norm, even among the aristocracy, until Peter the Great introduced French chefs to his court in the early eighteenth century.

Most menus start with a choice of soup or *zakuski*. **Soup** (*sup*) has long played an important role in Russian cuisine (the spoon appeared on the Russian table over four hundred years before the fork). Cabbage soup, or *shchi*, has been the principal Russian dish for the last thousand years, served with a generous dollop of sour cream; beetroot soup, or *borsch*, originally from Ukraine, is equally ubiquitous. Soups, however, are often available only at lunchtime and Russians do not consider even the large meaty soups to be a main meal; they will expect you to indulge in a main course afterwards. Chilled soups (*okroshki*) are popular during the summer, made from whatever's available.

Main courses are overwhelmingly based on **meat** (*myaso*), usually beef, mutton or pork, and sometimes accompanied by a simple sauce (mushroom or cheese). Meat may also make its way into *pelmeni*, a Russian version of ravioli, usually served in a broth. As far as regional meat dishes go, the most common are Georgian barbecued **kebabs** (*shashlyk*), or pilau-style Uzbek rice dishes called *plov*.

A wide variety of **fish and seafood** is available in St Petersburg. Pickled fish is a popular starter (try *selyodka pod shuby*, herring in a "fur coat" of beetroot, carrot, egg and mayonnaise), while fresh fish often appears as a main course – salmon, sturgeon and cod are the most common choices, though upmarket restaurants may boast lobster and oysters as well.

In cafés most main courses are served with boiled potatoes and/or sliced fresh tomatoes, but more expensive restaurants will serve a full selection of accompanying **vegetables**. These are called *garnir* and often have to be ordered and paid for separately. Where the meat is accompanied by vegetables, you may see an entry on the menu along the lines of 100/25/100g, which refers to the respective weight in grams of the meat (or fish) portion, and its accompanying servings of rice/potatoes and vegetable *garnir*. In ethnic restaurants, meat is almost always served on its own. Other vegetables are generally served boiled or pickled, but seldom appear separately on the menu.

Desserts (*sladkoe*) are not a strong feature of Russian cuisine. Ice cream, fruit, apple pie (*yablochniy pirog*) and jam pancakes (*blinchikiy s varenem*) are restaurant perennials, while in Caucasian restaurants you may get the flaky pastry and honey dessert, *pakhlava* (like Greek or Turkish baklava).

The influence of diverse culinary traditions on Russian food is epitomized by *pelmeni* (ravioli). Originating as *dim sum* in pork-eating China, they spread as *manty* to the mutton-eating cultures along the Silk Road and westwards with the Tatars to Crimea, before being adopted by Russian peasants in Siberia – whence the recipe spread to European Russia. Closer to home, Jewish, Russian and Ukrainian cooking were so entwined that the only dishes not claimed by all three traditions are ones using pork. The cuisines of the Caucasus were also a lasting influence; most Russian restaurants have *shashlyk*, the Georgian kebab, or *tolma*, Armenian stuffed vine leaves, on the menu. Yet each ethnic cuisine is distinctive and deserves to be experienced in a proper "national" restaurant.

In Soviet times **Georgian** restaurants were the most esteemed, and Caucasian entrepreneurs supplied Russian cities with fruit, wine and flowers. Georgians have a legend that God took a meal break from Creation, tripped over the Caucasus range and spilled his food onto the land below – their cuisine was "scraps from Heaven's table". Its distinctive ingredients include ground walnuts and walnut oil for cooking; condiments such as *khmeli-suneli* (dried coriander, chili, garlic, pepper and marigold petals), *adzhika* (tomato, red pepper and chili sauce) and *tkemali* (plum sauce); and lashings of fresh dill, coriander, parsley and cilantro, which are also eaten raw, to cleanse the palate between courses, and used to garnish cheeses made from sheep's or goat's milk. Traditionally, dishes of aubergines, tomatoes, garlic and beans were the staple diet, but feast days were marked by banquets of meaty soups, stews and kebabs, with repeated toasts in wine or brandy, orchestrated by a *tamada* (toast master). Favourites include *satsivi*, a cold dish of chicken

in walnut sauce; *chikhirtmi*, lemon-flavoured chicken soup; *kharcho*, spicy beef soup; and *khinkali*, dumplings stuffed with lamb or a mixture of pork and beef. *Khachapuri*, a delicious, cheesy soft bread that's served hot, is a filling starter.

Armenian and **Azerbaijani** cuisine is closer to Middle Eastern cooking (with the addition of dried nuts, saffron and ginger), while **Uzbek** features *khinkali* (a spicier kind of *pelmeni*) and sausages made from pony meat (*kazy*). Ginger and garlic also feature prominently in **Korean** food, originally introduced by Korean railway workers exiled to Kazakhstan in the 1930s. Marinaded beef dishes such as *bulkogi* are fried at your table, accompanied by raw vegetables and hot pickled garlic relish (*kimichi*). One dish often found even in non-Korean eateries is spicy carrot salad (*morkov po-koreyskiy*). More recently, Russians have fallen in love with **Japanese** food – though arguably sushi and sashimi aren't far removed from smoked fish *zakuski*, or the salmon and crab diet of Russia's Far Northern peoples. **Thai** food is also currently chic, while a decade's exposure to **Indian** and **Chinese** cuisine has acclimatized sophisticated locals to curries and spicy dishes that were previously toned down to suit Russian tastes.

Among the **other cuisines** represented by at least one restaurant in St Petersburg are Brazilian, French, German, Hungarian, Italian, Japanese, Jewish, Latvian and Mexican.

Although the situation for **vegetarians** has improved a lot with the spread of salad bars and health- (or at least weight-watching) awareness, meat still takes pride of place in the nation's cuisine. While fish eaters will find plenty to sustain them, strict vegetarians often have to fall back on *bliny* stuffed with mushrooms or cabbage, *griby s smetanoy* (mushrooms cooked with onions and sour cream), or the cold summer soup *okroshka*, if there aren't any vegetarian dishes from other ethnic cuisines, such as Korean carrot salad, Caucasian aubergine puree or the Georgian bean dish *lobio*. You could also try asking for *postniy shchi* (meatless, literally "fasting", *shchi*, or cabbage soup) or *ovoschnoy plov* (vegetable pilaf). If you're obliged to spell things out, the crucial phrases are *ya vegetarianets/vegetarianka,* I'm a vegetarian (masculine/feminine), and *Kakiye u vas yest blyuda bez myasa ili ryby?* Is there anything without meat or fish? For emphasis you could add *ya ne yem*

myasnovo ili rybnovo (I don't eat meat or fish).

In general, **ethnic restaurants** (Georgian, Lebanese, Korean, Indian or Chinese) have the most interesting vegetarian options, though many pizzerias run to veggie pizzas and salad bars. For those **self-catering**, fresh vegetables are widely available in markets (see p.385) and on the streets, and many supermarkets sell beans, grains and pulses. Locally produced fruit and vegetables are available only from June to October; at other times of the year everything is imported and therefore pricier.

Drinking

The story goes that the tenth-century Russian prince Vladimir, when pondering which religion to adopt for his state, rejected Judaism because its adherents were seen as weak and scattered; Catholicism because the pope claimed precedence over sovereigns; and Islam because "Drinking is the joy of the Russians. We cannot live without it."

A thousand years on, **alcohol** remains a central part of Russian life, and the prime cause of falling life expectancy of Russian males. It's a sobering experience to visit provincial towns where almost every man is stumbling drunk by midday, or villages where dozens have died from toxic hooch. In St Petersburg, alcoholics congregate in parks and around kiosks; virtually all cafés serve alcohol, and it seems as if every fourth pedestrian is swigging from a bottle of beer. As the price of drinks in **cafés** and **bars** is at least double that charged by the **street kiosks**, many Russians still prefer to buy booze from kiosks and drink it at home, or on the nearest bench. Partly owing to the prevalence of bootlegging (see overleaf), the City Council prohibits the sale of spirits from kiosks, though many continue to sell vodka under the counter, and cans of ready-mixed gin and tonic or vodka and cranberry don't count as spirits anyway. It is **illegal** to drink spirits on the streets or in parks (though the law is flouted by alcoholics), but beer drinking is not an offence.

Drinking spirits in a bar, the usual **measures** are 50 or 100 grams (*pyatdesyat/sto gram*), which for those used to British pub measures seem extremely generous. If you're invited to eat with Russians, it can be difficult to avoid drinking a succession of **toasts** in vodka, each glass tossed back *do dna* – to the end – as refusal may cause offence. The only ironclad excuse is to pretend that you have a liver problem, or suffer from alcoholism. If you do submit to a drinking session, be sure to eat something after each shot – Russians say that even the smell of a crust of bread is better than nothing.

Vodka and other spirits

Vodka is the national drink – its name means something like "a little

drop of water". Normally served chilled, vodka is drunk neat in one gulp, followed by a mouthful of food, such as pickled herring, cucumber or mushrooms; many people inhale deeply before tossing the liquor down their throats. Drinking small amounts at a time, and eating as you go, it's possible to consume an awful lot without passing out – though you soon reach a plateau of inebriated exhilaration.

Taste isn't a prime consideration; what counts is that the vodka isn't **bootleg liquor** (*podelnaya*, *falshivaya* or *levnaya* in Russian). At best, this means that customers find themselves drinking something weaker than they bargained for; at worst, they're imbibing diluted methanol, which can cause blindness or even death. To minimize the risk, familiarize yourself with the price of a few brands in the shops; if you see a bottle at well below the usual price it's almost certainly bootleg stuff. Among the hundreds of native brands on the market, Smirnov and the varieties produced under the

Liviz and Dovgan labels are probably the best, though many drinkers regard imported vodkas such as Absolut, Finlandia or Smirnoff as more prestigious. To play extra safe, buy vodka from a branded outlet, or *firmeny magazin* – the Liviz distillery has several stores in the city. Otherwise, check that the bottle's seal and tax label are intact, and don't hesitate to pour its contents away if it smells or tastes strange. A litre of decent vodka costs about $5 in the shops.

In addition to standard vodka you'll also see **flavoured vodkas** such as *pertsovka* (hot pepper vodka), *limonaya* (lemon vodka), *okhotnichaya* (hunter's vodka with juniper berries, ginger and cloves), *starka* (apple and pear-leaf vodka) and *zubrovka* (bison-grass vodka). Some Russians make these and other variants at home by infusing berries or herbs in regular vodka.

Vodka folklore

Russians have a wealth of phrases and gestures to signify drinking vodka, the most common one being to tap the side of your chin or windpipe. The story goes that there was once a peasant who saved the life of Peter the Great and was rewarded with the right to drink as much vodka as he liked from any distillery. Fearing that a written *ukaz* would be stolen while he was drunk, the man begged the tsar to stamp the Imperial seal on his throat – the origin of the tapping gesture.

Fittingly, the Russian word for drunk – *pyany* – comes from an incident where two columns of drunken soldiers advancing on either side of the Pyany River mistook each other for the enemy and opened fire. Given its long and disreputable role in Russian warfare, it's ironic that the Tsarist government's prohibition of vodka for the duration of World War I did more harm than good, by depriving the state of a third of its revenue and stoking class hatred of the aristocracy, whose consumption of cognac and champagne continued unabated. Stalin knew better during World War II, when soldiers received a large shot of vodka before going into battle.

In Soviet society, vodka was the preferred form of payment for any kind of work outside the official economy and the nexus for encounters between strangers needing to "go three" on a bottle – a half-litre bottle shared between three people was reckoned to be the cheapest and most companionable way to get a bit drunk. Whereas rationing vodka was the most unpopular thing that Gorbachev ever did, Yeltsin's budgets categorized it as an essential commodity like bread or milk. Despite Yeltsin's notorious fondness for vodka, one would rather not believe Shevardnadze's claim to have found him lying dead drunk in the White House during the 1991 putsch, though at the time Shevardnadze told the crowd outside that "I have met the President and he is standing firm in defence of democracy". At least Yeltsin never lent his name and face to his own brand of vodka – unlike Zhirinovsky (who professes not to drink the stuff) – while Putin is well known to prefer beer.

Other domestic liquors include **cognac** (*konyak*), which is pretty rough compared to French brandy, but easy enough to acquire a taste for. Traditionally, the best brands hail from Armenia (Ararat) and Moldova (Beliy Aist), but as both states now export these for hard currency, bottles sold in Russia are often fakes. More commonly, you'll find Georgian or Daghestani versions, which are all right if they're the genuine article, but extremely rough if they're not. Again, it's best to buy from Liviz or the specialist Daghestani shop on Nevskiy (see p.386). Otherwise, you can find imported spirits such as whisky, gin and tequila in many bars and shops, along with Irish Cream, Amaretto and sickly Austrian fruit brandies.

Beer, wine and champagne

Beer is the preferred drink of younger Russians if only because it's widely available – and consumed – at any time of day or night, and hardly regarded as alcohol, but simply as a refreshing drink. Some of Russia's best-selling beers come from St Petersburg breweries. **Baltika** beers come in 50cl bottles, numbered from 1 to 12 (mainly in order of their strength). The most popular are #3, "Classic" lager (ask for *Troika*), #4, "Original" brown ale, and #5, "Porter" stout; #6 and #7 are often found on tap in pool bars and discos; #9 is the strongest; #10 has an aroma of almond and basil, and Medovoe supposedly tastes of honey. **Stepan Razin** (named after the peasant rebel hero) produces eleven different beers, including Spetsialnoe (only 3.6 percent alcohol), the light pilsner Admiralteyskoe, the potent Kalinkin (7 percent), and Zolotoe, with a fine aroma of malt and hops. The **Vena** brewery is best known for Nevskoe Originalnoe (which won second prize at a beer festival in Britain) and Porter (which won a gold medal in Denmark); it also makes Svetloe, a

light beer, and Kronverk, without alcohol. More recent newcomers are **Bochkarev**, whose Svetloe (light) and Tyomnoe (dark) are very popular, and **Tinkoff**, which bottles some of the unfiltered beers available on tap at its microbrewery near the Kazan Cathedral (see p.356). Other Russian brands include Afanasy, a mild ale brewed in Nizhniy Novgorod, and Sibirskaya Korona (Siberian Crown) lager. You're bound to find some of these on tap (*razlivnoe*) in bars, together with foreign imports such as Tuborg, Carlsberg, Holsten, or Guinness, which may also come in bottles or cans in shops.

The **wine** (*vino*) on sale in St Petersburg is either imported from the European Union or California, or from the vineyards of Moldova, Georgia and the Crimea, Russia's traditional source of wine. Georgian and Moldovan wines are made from varieties of grapes that are almost unknown abroad, so it would be a shame not to sample them, but since the cheapest generic brands in shops are either bootlegs or simply disgusting, you should stick to the dearer versions ($6 and upwards). The ones to look out for are the dry reds Mukuzani and Saperavi, or the sweeter full-bodied reds Kindzmarauli and Khvanchkara, drunk by Stalin. Georgia also produces some fine white wines, such as the dry Gurdzhani and Tsinandali (traditionally served at room temperature), as well as the **fortified wines** Portvini (port) and Masala, which are also produced in the Crimea and known in Russian as *baramatukha* or "babbling juice", the equivalent of Thunderbird in the States.

Despite notice from France that Russia's concession to use the word **champagne** has expired (it was granted after World War II in gratitude to the Soviet Union), not all local manufacturers have relabelled their product "Soviet Sparkling" (*Sovietskoe Igristoe*), and consumers

△ Vodka – Russia's joy and curse

still request "Soviet champagne" (*Sovetskoe shampanskoe*, or *shampanskoe* for short). Besides being far cheaper than the French variety, some of it is really pretty good if properly chilled. The two types to go for are *sukhoe* and *bryut*, which are both reasonably dry; *polusukhoe* or "medium dry" is actually very sweet, and *sladkoe* is like connecting yourself to a glucose drip. It's indicative of Russian taste that the last two are the most popular.

Tea, coffee and soft drinks

Traditionally, Russian **tea** (*chay*) was brewed and stewed for hours, and topped up with boiling water from an ornate tea urn, or samovar, but nowadays even the more run-of-the-mill cafés use imported teabags. Quite a few places also offer herbal or fruit-flavoured teas, which were tradition-ally prepared at home using herbs and leaves from the forest (*travyanoy chay*), or ginseng and ginger from the east. Most Russians drink tea without milk and you need to ask for it in cafés. **Milk** (*moloko*) itself is sold in stores alongside **kefir**, a sour milk drink that's something of an acquired taste for foreigners. There are full cream and low-fat versions of both.

Coffee (*kofe*) is sold all over the place and varies enormously in quality. Kiosks and cheap cafés use vile powdered stuff; avoid places with automats and look for a proper coffee maker on the premises. Seattle-style coffee houses are all the rage in St Petersburg, with chains such as Idealnaya Chaska offering espresso, cappuccino, lattes, mocca, flavoured coffees and alcoholic coffee cocktails. A few old-fashioned cafés prepare Turkish or Arabic coffee by heating it in hot sand, a method used in Soviet times.

Pepsi and Coca-Cola jostle for sales with cheaper brands of **fizzy drinks** imported from Eastern Europe, or manufactured in Russia. Besides generic colas, lemonades and orangeades, you'll see such distinctly Russian drinks as **kvas**, an unusual but delicious thirst-quencher made from fermented rye bread; **myod**, or honey-mead, which is seen as a soft drink but contains alcohol; and **tarkhun**, a bright green, sickly sweet drink made from tarragon – all of which have made a comeback since they fell out of fashion with the demise of the Soviet Union.

The days when the only **mineral water** (*mineralnaya voda*) available was Narzan and Borzhomi from the Caucasus (both a bit salty and sul-phurous for most Western tastes, but worth persevering with) are long over. Kiosks and shops are full of Evian, Vittel and Perrier, and diverse Russian brands of spring water, which may be carbonated (*gazirovanaya voda*) or without gas (*negazirovanaya*). The brand Svyati Istochik (Sacred Spring) even comes with a blessing from the Orthodox Patriarch.

Fast-food chains

Fast-food chains have become hugely popular in Moscow and St Petersburg, offering a variety of food and standards of hygiene and service infinitely superior to the grimy *stolovaya* (canteens) that were the lot of gener-ations of citizens during Soviet times, but which younger Russians now take for granted. Besides such worldwide giants as *McDonald's*, *Pizza Hut* and *KFC*, there's the Scandinavian burger chain *Carrol's*, and various Russian chains serving Russian food – *bliny* (pancakes), salads and kebabs – that's far tastier and healthier than the food of the burger chains. There are also some awful ones, dishing up half-defrosted *bliny* and other inedible junk. **Avoid** *Blin Donalds*, *Fiesta*, *Galeo*, *Hannover Bistro*, and anywhere named simply

The chain gang

Carrol's *Burgers, soups, fries, salads, milkshakes and dessert.* Gostiniy dvor, Gostiniy Dvor metro (daily 9am–11pm); Nevskiy pr. 45, Mayakovskaya metro; ul. Vosstaniya 5, Ploshchad Vosstaniya metro; Kamennoostrovskiy pr. 31, Petrogradskaya metro; Grazdanskiy pr. 41, Akademicheskaya metro; Zanevskiy pr. 71/1, Ladozhskaya metro (all daily 9am–11pm).

Idealnaya Chashka (Ideal Cup) *Russia's own Starbucks. All kinds of coffees, coffee cocktails and desserts. No smoking. No cards.* Nevskiy pr. 15, 112 & 130, Nevskiy Prospekt/Gostiniy Dvor, Mayakovskaya/Ploshchad Vosstaniya or Ploshchad Aleksandra Nevskovo metro; Vladimirskiy pr. 1, Mayakovskaya metro; Sadovaya ul. 25, Sennaya Ploshchad or Gostiniy Dvor metro; Kirochnaya ul. 19, Chernyshevskaya metro; ul. Nekrasova 1, Chernyshevskaya metro; Moskovskiy pr. 6, Sadovaya/Sennaya Ploshchad metro; Kamennoostrovskiy pr. 2, Gorkovskaya metro; Bolshoy pr. 82, Petrogradskaya metro; Sredniy pr. 46, Vasileostrovskaya metro (all daily 7am–11pm).

Laima *One of the best Russian chains. Salads, soups, stuffed peppers, chicken, fish, kebabs, fresh juices, milkshakes and beer. No smoking. No cards.* Nab. kanala Griboedova 14, Nevskiy Prospekt/Gostiniy Dvor metro; Bolshoy pr. 88, Petrogradskaya metro (both daily 24hr).

McDonald's Bolshaya Morskaya ul. 11/6, Nevskiy prospekt metro (daily 24hr); Kamennoostrovskiy pr. 39, Petrogradskaya metro (daily 8am–11pm); Moskovskiy pr. 195a, Moskovskaya metro (daily 24hr); Sennaya pl. 4/1, Sennaya Ploshchad/Sadovaya metro (daily 8am–11pm); Sredniy pr. 29a, Vasileostrovskaya metro (daily 24hr); ul. Savushkina 119a, minibus #K-132 from Chernaya Rechka metro (daily 24hr); Zagorodniy pr. 45a, Pushkinskaya metro (daily 24hr).

Orient *Similar to* Laima *but not quite as good. Sells alcohol. No smoking. No cards.* Bolshaya Morskaya ul. 25, Nevskiy Prospekt/Gostiniy Dvor metro; Suvorovskiy pr. 18, Ploshchad Vosstaniya metro (both daily 24hr).

Patio Pizza *Thin-crust wood-oven pizzas, salad bar, alcohol. Business lunch Mon–Fri noon–4pm. Amex, DC, JCB, MC, Visa.* Nevskiy pr. 30, Nevskiy Prospekt/Gostiniy Dvor metro; Nevskiy pr. 182, Ploshchad Aleksandra Nevskovo I metro (both daily 24hr).

Pizza Hut *Regarded by locals as classy restaurants, with takeaway slice bars. Discounts before 4pm. Amex, DC, EC, MC, Visa.* Gorokhovaya ul. 16, on the corner of the Moyka embankment, Sadovaya/Sennaya Ploshchad metro (daily 10am–11pm); Nevskiy pr. 96, Mayakovskaya/Ploshchad Vosstaniya metro (daily 11am–11pm).

Sladkoezhka (Sweet Tooth) *Patisserie chain with good coffee, cakes, sundaes, cocktails, wine and spirits. No smoking. No cards.* Nevskiy pr. 88, Mayakovskaya metro; Gorokhovaya ul. 11, Sadovaya/Sennaya Ploshchad metro; Sadovya ul. 60, Sadovaya/Sennaya Ploshchad metro; ul. Marata 2 & 11, Mayakovskaya metro; Zakharevskaya ul. 25, Chernyshevskaya metro (all daily 10am-11pm).

Teremok *These brown-and-yellow kiosks sell delicious freshly made* bliny *with savoury or sweet fillings to eat standing at outdoor tables. No cards.* Located on Manezhnaya pl. downtown and outside several mainline train and suburban metro stations (all daily 11am–11pm).

U Tyoshi na blinakh (At Mother-in-Law's for Pancakes) *Rustic-style Russian chain with salads, chicken Kiev,* bliny, *stuffed cabbage, soups and alcohol. No cards.* Ligovskiy pr. 20, Ploshchad Vosstaniya metro; Zagorodniy pr. 18, Dostoyevskaya/Vladimirskaya metro; Gorokhovaya ul. 43, on the corner of Sadovaya ul., Sadovaya/Sennaya Ploshchad metro (all daily 24hr).

"Bistro". The outlets listed in the box on p.354 are reliable, but not reviewed under cafés or included on maps in this book.

Cafés and bars

Cafés and **bars** in St Petersburg run the gamut from humble eateries to slick establishments, and since most places serve alcohol (beer, if not spirits too) the distinction between them is often a fine one. With some exceptions (mostly places in top-class hotels) cafés are generally cheaper than fully fledged restaurants, making them popular with Russians who have some disposable income, but don't ride around in a Mercedes.

Though all cafés are private ventures nowadays, some retain the surly habits of Soviet days, when customers counted themselves lucky if they were served at all, and even where they aim to please, you sometimes find inexplicable lapses in standards or decorum. However, you can also find some delicious meals and friendly watering holes if you know where to look, and the number of acceptable places is rising all the time.

Another phenomenon is **street cafés** (usually open from May to late Sept), where you can have a coffee, beer or hamburger, while watching the world go by. There are several on Malaya Sadovaya ulitsa, just off Nevskiy, and along the prospekt itself, outside the Lutheran Church at no. 24, by the Portico opposite the *Grand Hotel Europe* (no. 33) and the beer garden in the yard of no. 86 – but you'll find them all around the centre and in residential districts too.

The following selection is listed in alphabetical order under area headings corresponding to the chapters in the Guide section. We've provided phone numbers for bars and cafés where it's advisable to phone ahead and reserve a table, particularly if you are planning to eat.

Within the Fontanka

The listings in this section are marked on the map on pp.60–61. Some places also appear on the maps on pp.62–63, p.79 and p.98.

Adzhika Moskovskiy pr. 7; Sadovaya/Sennaya Ploshchad metro. Friendly, homely, nicely decorated café serving great Georgian food at low prices, just off the "Haymarket" (see p.104). *Adzhika* is tomato and red pepper condiment used in Georgian kitchens and as a relish during meals. No cards. Daily 24hr.

Aprikosov (Apricots) Nevskiy pr. 40; Gostiniy Dvor/Nevskiy Prospekt metro. This nineteenth-century *kofeynya* (coffee house) is one of the oldest still extant, with an elegant Chinoiserie decor. Its cakes, sundaes and coffee are fairly pricy, but worth it. Full of tourists by day, it attracts a Russian crowd at night. Maestro, MC, Visa. Daily 9am–3am.

Atrium Café Nevskiy pr. 25; Nevskiy Prospekt/Gostiniy Dvor metro. Lots of light and space, fresh juices, tasty soups and crusty bread make the *Atrium* a popular spot to take a break from shopping or the office, amid a mall by the Kazan Cathedral. Not cheap, but then neither is its clientele. MC, Visa. Daily 10am–11pm.

Idiot Café nab. reki Moyki 82 ☎315 16 75; Sadovaya/Sennaya Ploshchad metro. Named after the Dostoyevsky novel, this cosy basement is furnished with divans and period junk, and beloved by foreigners. Its (mainly) vegetarian menu is strongest on *borsch, pelmeni, bliny* and pickled nibbles. Hangover-sufferers should try the "Gentleman's Lunch" of cold snacks with 100g of vodka – all orders come with a shot in any case. They also have backgammon and a library of foreign-language books (mostly rubbish). No cards. Daily 11am–midnight.

La Cucaracha (The Cockroach) nab. reki Fontanki 39 ☎110 40 46; Gostiniy Dvor metro. Tex-Mex cantina where the food is tasty and filling, if not as authentic as purists might wish. The bill can be reasonable if you don't splurge on margaritas or aged tequila. Reserve a table to avoid queuing after 7pm. Happy hour 6–8pm; live music Tues, Thurs & Fri. DC, JCB, Maestro, MC, Visa. Mon–Thurs & Sun noon–1am, Fri & Sat noon–5am.

Lenin's Mating Call Kazanskaya ul. 34; Sadovaya/Sennaya Ploshchad metro. A Commie-theme bar with gilded Lenin busts like stalactites, bar girls in sexed-up Komsomol uniforms and Soviet newsreels inter-cut with porn on the monitors (under-18s aren't allowed in). Unlike most such places, the food is tasty, portions are generous and prices reasonable. Quiet by day; popular with tour groups at night. Daily 1pm–2am.

Macco Club Nevskiy pr. 27; Gostiniy Dvor/Nevskiy Prospekt metro. The latest incarnation of a coffee shop and patisserie that has been around forever, and is currently themed on Kalahari Bushmen in a bid to attract hip "urban warriors". Its coffee and cakes are fine anyhow. Daily 9am–11pm.

Sadko Grand Hotel Europe ul. Mikhailovskaya 1–7; Gostiniy Dvor/Nevskiy Prospekt metro. No longer the exclusive haunt of a decade ago, *Sadko's* still enjoys the finest street-level view on Nevskiy. A $16 business lunch (noon–4pm) is the cheapest way to sample its Russian and European cuisine. Amex, EC, DC, MC, Visa. Daily 10am–10pm.

Shamrock ul. Dekabristov 27; 20min walk from Sadovaya metro. Themed Irish bar opposite the Mariinskiy Theatre, serving draught and bottled foreign beers ($7–8) and hearty pub fare. Can be pretty empty despite live music in the evenings, but sure to be heaving for English premier league football on Sat (6pm) and Sun (7pm), or party nights shared with *Mollie's Irish Bar* (see p.358). Daily noon–2am.

Stroganov Yard Nevskiy pr. 17; Gostiniy Dvor/Nevskiy Prospekt metro. A glassed-in café in the courtyard of the Stroganov Palace, where each table has a phone for calling diners at other tables, if one is lulled into a flirty mood by the live music in the evenings. Popular for its salad buffet ($5) and spaghetti ($3) during daytime. Accepts major cards; bureau de change in the yard. Daily 10am–1am.

Tinkoff Kazanskaya ul. 7; Nevskiy Prospekt/Gostiniy Dvor metro. Russia's first micro-brewery won Putin's seal of approval and made Oleg Tinkov a household name. His trendy hangout features ten varieties of freshly brewed beer (some unfiltered), a stylish sushi bar, a restaurant with Euro cuisine, TV sports and live music (Wed–Sun). The sushi is good value but drinks are costly. MC, Visa. Daily noon–2am.

Zhili Byli (Once Upon a Time) Nevskiy pr. 50; Gostiniy Dvor/Nevskiy Prospekt metro. St Petersburg *Sex and the City* babes' hangout with a terrace that's almost too close to street life for comfort. Wide range of salads, hot snacks, cakes and sundaes, at affordable prices. Daily 24hr.

Vasilevskiy Island

The listings in this section are marked on the map on pp.156–157.

Bogemus Birzhevoy proezd 1/10; Vasileostrovskaya or Sportivnaya metro. A good place for lunch on the Strelka if you're not a vegetarian, this maritime-themed Czech pub has lots of hearty pork and dumpling dishes and six brands of Czech beer. Its nocturnal alter ego has beer parties every Fri, a dance hall and DJ. All major cards. Daily: pub 11am–1am; disco 1am till the last customer leaves.

Café Rotunda 5-ya liniya 42; Vasileostrovskaya metro. If you can't stomach the fast-food joints near the metro station, this chi-chi Russian take on a Parisian bistro does steaks, seafood, soups and salads, with wine as well as beer and vodka to drink, and is also good for coffee and cakes. No cards. Daily 11am–11pm.

Cheburechnaya 6-ya liniya 19; Vasileostrovskaya metro. A *cheburechnaya* is a Soviet greasy spoon café specializing in *chebureki* (a kind of Caucasian samosa). When meat was hard to obtain in the late 1980s, this particular one drew people from all over with its tasty Georgian soups and stews. It's still good and cheap, but looks uninviting. Try the *chanaxhi* soup. No cards. Daily 10am–8pm.

Petrograd Side

The listings in this section are marked on the map on pp.174–175.

Baltic Bread on Bolshoy Bolshoy pr. 80; Petrogradskaya metro. A wonderful bakery and confectioner's selling over 200 types of loaves, puff-pastry savouries, gateaux and pastries, to be enjoyed with coffee. Great for breakfast. No cards. Daily 10am–10pm.

Kamini pr. Dobrolyubova 7/2; **Sportivnaya metro.** Not far from the Peter and Paul Fortress, this friendly café serves *bliny* with mushrooms and sour cream, cabbage soup and pies, buckwheat *kasha*, stews and steak dishes, all at low prices. No cards. Daily 11am–11pm.

Mama Roma Bolshoy pr. 70/72; **Petrogradskaya metro.** An inexpensive pizza-pasta place with over a dozen salads and focaccia bread on the menu. Does breakfast (9am–noon) for $2 and a $5 business lunch (Mon–Fri noon–4pm). Discounts on pizza 4–6pm, and at any time for take-aways. No cards. Daily 9am–2am.

Petrovskie Shatry behind the Peter and Paul Fortress; **Gorkovskaya metro.** Handy for a break from sightseeing, this glass pavilion offers fresh trout, perch and other fish from a tank in the Kronverk Canal, grilled on the spot, plus alcoholic and hot drinks. In summer, customers may be invited to catch their fish, as at *Russkaya rybalka* (see p.363) – *Petrovskie Shatry* is cheaper and without frills. No cards. Daily 24hr.

Tiblisi Sytninskaya ul. 10 ☎232 93 91; **Gorkovskaya metro.** One of the oldest Georgian cafés in the city, near Petrograd Side's food market. Its decor is quite gloomy, but their homemade cheese, *khachapuri* and meaty stews make a good, inexpensive introduction to Caucasian cuisine, if you can't afford to eat at *Salkhino* (see p.363). It's worth booking in the evening. No cards. Daily noon–11.30pm.

Troitskiy most Malaya Posadskaya ul. 2; **Gorkovskaya metro.** No longer the Hare Krishna place that it was for decades, but still a cheap and cheerful source of veggie burgers, soya dishes, salads and potato cutlets. No cards. Daily 9am–11pm.

Liteyniy, Smolniy and Vladimirskaya

The listings in this section are marked on the map on pp.200–201.

Aziya (Asia) ul. Ryleeva 23 ☎272 01 68; **Chernyshevskaya metro.** Wonderfully fresh and tasty Uzbek and Russian cuisine at amazingly low prices – even locals are impressed. Try the spicy vegetable or lamb *cheburek*, and a soup or a kebab and you'll be stuffed. Be sure to book in the evening (ask for the booth by the aquarium). No cards. Daily 11am–11pm.

Bagration Bistro Liteyniy prospekt 8/19; **Chernyshevskaya metro.** Named after a Georgian-born Tsarist general who beat Napoleon, this tiny, chic cellar serves tasty, inexpensive Georgian dishes from the kitchen of a de luxe restaurant around the corner. Don't miss their *lobio*, spicy beef *chashashuli* and cheesy *khachapuri*. No smoking. No cards. Daily 10am–11pm.

Baltic Bread Grechiskiy pr. 25; tram #5 or #7 from Ploshchad Vosstaniya metro. Sells all kinds of bread, pastries and savouries, with a few tables for drinking tea or coffee. A good breakfast spot if you're staying at the *St Petersburg International Hostel* and don't mind walking six blocks to get here. There's another branch on the Petrograd Side (see p.356). No cards. Daily 10am–9pm.

Bliny domik (Pancake Cottage) Kolokolnaya ul. 8; **Dostoevskaya/Vladimirskaya metro.** This cosy place near Dostoyevsky's flat and the Arctic and Antarctic Museum not only serves *bliny* with all kinds of fillings, but spicy aubergine salad, cheese or meat fondue, herbal teas and a full breakfast menu – all very tasty, healthy (they use low-cholesterol oil) and affordable. No cards. Daily 8am–11pm.

Café Club Che Poltavskaya ul. 3 ☎277 76 00; **Ploshchad Aleksandra Nevskovo or Ploshchad Vosstaniya metro.** Looks and feels like an Amsterdam Brown Café. A peaceful place for coffee, cakes, soup and hot snacks, which turns into an all-night club with live Cuban music and an element of face control, frequented by trend-setters, promoters and hangers-on. Cigar smoking is encouraged. Daily 9am–7am.

Café Rico Pushkinskaya ul. 1/3. Pleasant ethno-funk café with Arabic coffee, coffee cocktails and lattes, cakes, ice cream and fresh juices. A tiny fountain, a community notice board and the aromatic atmosphere make it popular with chic couples taking a break from shopping at local boutiques. No smoking. No cards. Mon–Fri 9am–midnight, Sat & Sun 10am–midnight.

Café Vienna *Nevsky Palace Hotel*, Nevsky pr. 57; **Mayakovskaya metro.** Certainly not cheap but easily the best cakes in town, and its scrumptious cream and chocolate Viennese creations are half-price after 10pm. All major cards. Daily 10am–midnight.

Green Cross Salad Bar Vladimirskiy pr. 5/7; **Mayakovskaya, Dostoevskaya or Vladimirskaya metro.** A decent pit stop for refuelling with salads (not all veggie), *borsch*, steak or chicken, with Tinkoff beer on tap. Customers share tables. No smoking. No cards. Daily 9am–11pm.

Khuratok (The Farm) 3-ya Sovetskaya ul. 26; Ploshchad Vosstaniya metro. Kitsch rustic basement café two doors along from the *St Petersburg International Hostel*, where you can sample Russian cuisine on the cheap; try the *borsch* or mushroom soup. No cards. Daily noon–11pm.

Kolobok ul. Chaykovskovo 40; Chernyshevskaya metro. Named after the roly-poly doughy hero of Russian folklore, this clean self-service place has tasty sweet and savoury *pirozhki* (pies) at ridiculously low prices, plus hot meals and salads. Its early-morning opening makes it ideal for breakfast, and there's a discount before 11am. No smoking inside. No cards. Daily 7.30am–9pm.

Metekhi ul. Belinskovo 3; Gostiniy Dvor/Nevskiy Prospekt metro. One of the oldest Georgian cafés in town, it wins no prizes for decor or service, but the *khachapuri*, *lobio* and *satsivi* are all spot-on, though the choice gets thin towards the evening. No cards. Daily 11am–9pm.

Mollie's Irish Bar ul. Rubinshteyna 36; Vladimirskaya or Mayakovskaya metro. Generally livelier than the *Shamrock* (see p.356), *Mollie's* boasts 19 draught beers, 50 cocktails, pub grub, and Irish music (Tues–Thurs & Sun) or TV sports. Amex, DC, JCB, MC, Visa. Daily noon–5am.

Propaganda nab. reki Fontanki 40; Mayakovskaya or Gostiniy Dvor metro. Worth a drink purely for its decor – a hybrid of Constructivist chic and Soviet High Command bunker, with Meccano-style furniture and toilets like airlocks – but the burgers and Russian food are pricy and inferior to that of its rival theme-bar, *Lenin's Mating Call* (see p.356). No cards. Daily 3pm–3am.

Russkie bliny (Russian Pancakes) ul. Gagarinskaya 13; 15–20min from Nevskiy Prospekt metro. Very popular, cheap lunchtime spot. Traditional *bliny*, both savoury and sweet – the *bliny* with red caviar or the *blinchiki* (folded deep-fried *bliny*) with mushrooms or puréed salt fish are wonderful. No smoking or alcohol. Come before 1pm or after 2.30pm to avoid the queues. No cards. Mon–Fri 11am–6pm.

Shwarma Liteyniy pr. 64; Mayakovskaya metro. Perhaps the best *shwarma* outlet in the city, attracting a diverse clientele (if you can say that about a basement nook with room for six customers to stand) and selling draught Baltika. No smoking. No cards. Daily 24hr.

Stariy dom (Old House) ul. Nekrasova 27; Chernyshevskaya metro. Smoky basement dive serving authentic Azerbaijani cuisine. You can't reserve and may have to share a table. Go for the marinated nibbles with vodka, then a meatball and chervil soup or a kebab – there's even ram's balls if you fancy them – before finishing up with a pot of smoked black tea. No cards. Daily 11am–11pm.

Sunduk (The Chest) Furshtatskaya ul. 42 ☏272 31 00; Chernyshevskaya metro. Cosy, funky art café with a Spanish/jazz orientation. The inexpensive food (mostly Russian) is less noteworthy than the ambience, with nightly Spanish, blues or jazz music after 8.30pm, and outdoor tables for people watching during the day. No cards. Daily noon–11pm.

Wooden Pub ul. Chaykovskovo 36; Chernyshevskaya metro. Small, friendly basement bar with tables outside in summer. Draught Irish, Danish and Russian beers and a wide range of spirits and French wines, as well as seafood snacks. Saxophonist and fiddler (Fri & Sat night). No cards. Daily 11am–2am.

The Southern Suburbs

The listings in this section are marked on the map on p.224.

Kafeteriy Moskovskiy pr. 216; Moskovskaya metro. Spacious, two-floor confectioner's with a wide choice of inexpensive cakes, ices, savoury pastries, soups and coffee – good for breakfast if you're staying in the area, or feel hungry after coming back from Tsarskoe Selo (the minibus stand is right outside). No cards. Daily 10am–10pm.

Mama Roma Moskovskiy pr. 120; Moskovskie Vorota metro. Rises above other Italian pizza chains with its range of salads and foccacia breads. Does breakfast (9am–noon), a business lunch (Mon–Fri noon–4pm) and fifty-percent discount on pizzas in the restaurant (daily 4–6pm) or takeaways (any time). No cards. Daily 9am–2am.

Prazdroy **pr. Stachek 57; Kirovskiy Zavod metro**. Cosy pub with traditional Czech cuisine (vegetarians needn't bother), twelve Czech beers, an extended business lunch (Mon–Fri 11am–5pm) and billiards. All major cards. Daily 11am–1am (Fri & Sat till 2am).

Restaurants

St Petersburg's **restaurants** are as diverse as the food they serve. At the top end of the scale, you'll probably feel uncomfortable if you're not dressed to the hilt – though not many places impose a formal dress code (a jacket and tie for men, a skirt or dress for women). At present, relatively few places include a **service charge** in the bill, so you can tip (or not) as you like. Some places feature **floorshows** consisting of "folk music" (or belly dancing) and maybe some kind of striptease act (which Russians regard with equanimity), for which there may or may not be a surcharge. At most restaurants it's customary to consign your coat to the *garderob* on arrival; if you are helped to put it back on later, a small tip is warranted.

As in Moscow, more and more places offer a "**business lunch**", a set lunch consisting of three or four courses at lower prices than you'd pay dining *à la carte*. Such deals are advertised by signboards outside with the Cyrillic words бизнес ланч (pronounced *biznes lanch*), and in the city's foreign-language press, where you may also find details of **food festivals** being held, most frequently at the *Nevsky Palace Hotel*.

We've given **telephone numbers** for all the restaurants listed, as reserving in advance is always a good idea, particularly to eat after 9pm. Most places now have at least one member of staff with a rudimentary grasp of English. If not, a useful phrase to get your tongue around is *Ya khochu zakazat stol na . . . cheloveka sevodnya na . . . chasov* (I want to reserve a table for . . . people for . . . o'clock today).

Within the Fontanka

The listings in this section are marked on the map on pp.60–61 and some are also marked on the inset maps later in the chapter.

Cheap

Mekong **Malaya Sadovaya ul. 1/25** ☎314 39 65; **Nevskiy Prospekt/Gostiniy Dvor metro**. Sited just off Nevskiy, this funky basement restaurant features a mix of Japanese, Thai and Vietnamese dishes, with a daily buffet (noon–6pm) and live music from 7pm. Just the place to satisfy a craving for spicy food, and great value for its location. No cards. Daily noon–11pm.

The restaurant listings are divided into geographical areas that correspond to the chapters, and into price categories, too – cheap, inexpensive, moderate, expensive and very expensive. You should be able to get a soup, a main course, a dessert plus a couple of beers in the price bracket indicated:

Cheap up to $10 a head
Inexpensive $11–20 a head
Moderate $21–50 a head

Expensive $51–100 a head
Very expensive over $100 a head

These categorizations refer to dining *à la carte*, but many restaurants offer a business lunch or Sunday brunch that costs a lot less than this. Generally, beer and vodka are cheap enough to **drink** a lot without hugely increasing the final bill – but wine or imported liquors are another matter, especially in restaurants with de luxe cellars. Never order wine without verifying the price.

Inexpensive

Dinastiya (Dynasty) Gorokhovaya ul. 11 ☎315 07 54; Gostiniy Dvor/Nevskiy Prospekt metro. Charming, family-run Russian restaurant whose lengthy menu includes such intriguingly named dishes as "St Petersburg's Secrets" (beef stuffed with apricots and prunes) and "Babushka cake" (sponge cake with hazelnut butter-cream or wild blueberry purée). Maestro, MC. Daily noon–11pm.

La Strada Bolshaya Konyushennaya ul. 27 ☎312 47 00; Gostiniy Dvor/Nevskiy Prospekt metro. A glass-roofed Italian restaurant designed to resemble a pavement café, with a wood-fired oven turning out the best pizzas in town; they also serve Italian nibbles with baked potatoes, a terrific vegetarian lasagne and wonderful tiramisu. No cards. Daily from noon till the last customer leaves.

Peking Opera ul. Dekabristov 27 ☎314 11 73; Sadovaya/Sennaya Ploshchad metro. Contemporary-style Chinese restaurant facing the Mariinskiy Theatre, with a business lunch for under $5 (noon–5pm), cut-price *pelmeni* and beer before 7pm, and feasting on recipes from the Imperial Chinese court after the ballet has finished. All major cards. Daily noon–midnight.

Tandoor Voznesenkiy pr. 2 (by St Isaac's) ☎312 38 86; Gostiniy Dvor/Nevskiy Prospekt metro. The oldest Indian restaurant in St Petersburg. Its decor and atmosphere are fine, but the food is slightly disappointing if you're seeking a curry that bites back, although vegetarians will be heartened by the choice of dishes. Business lunch. Amex, Visa, DC, MC, JCB. Daily noon–11pm.

Moderate

Brasilia Kazanskaya ul. 24 ☎320 87 77; Nevskiy Prospekt or Sennaya Ploshchad metro. A cosy, stylish place to enjoy Brazilian food, with an open fire for grilling the house speciality, *rodisio*, consisting of nine kinds of charbroiled meat and fish brought to your table impaled on swords, with a choice of dressings. Try one of the rum-based long drinks, such as a *majito* or *calerini*. Most cards. Mon–Thurs & Sun noon–3am, Fri & Sat noon–6am.

Kalif (Caliph) Millionnaya ul. 21/6 ☎312 22 65; Gostiniy Dvor/Nevskiy Prospekt metro. Delicious Uzbek food, with plenty of salads if you don't fancy specialities such as *kazy* (horse sausage), while the colourful decor, waitresses in silk gowns, Uzbek musicians and beguiling belly dancers (8.30pm & 10pm) make for a memorable evening. Finish up with a yummy *Badrok halva*. MC, Union, Visa. Daily noon–midnight.

Kavkaz Bar Karavannaya ul. 18 ☎312 16 55; Gostiniy Dvor/Nevskiy Prospekt metro. The most tourist-oriented of St Petersburg's many Caucasian restaurants, with an interior styled like a Georgian courtyard, waitresses in national costume and live music after 8pm. Rather overpriced, especially drinks. Maestro, MC, Union, Visa. Daily: café 11am–8pm; restaurant 11am–1am.

Le Francais Galernaya ul. 20 ☎315 24 65, ⓦwww.lefrancais.spb.ru; bus #22 from Nevskiy pr. A French chef produces fine bistro cuisine from Russian ingredients such as sturgeon and crayfish, accompanied by French cheeses and wines. Finish up with a Grand Marnier mousse. Piano music in the evenings. Free secure parking. Amex, DC, EC, MC, Visa. Daily 11am–1am.

Senat Bar Galernaya ul. 1–3 (by the Bronze Horseman) ☎314 92 53, ⓦwww.senat-bar.spb.ru; bus #5 or #22 from Nevskiy pr. A popular haunt for suits in a stylishly refurbished basement of the Senate building that once played host to Clinton, offering good Euro-Russian cuisine and an endless selection of beer and wine. Business lunch noon–5pm. Amex, MC, Visa. Daily noon–5am.

St Petersburg nab. kanala Griboedova 5 ☎314 49 47; Gostiniy Dvor/Nevskiy Prospekt metro. Does fine seafood (try the marinated salmon flavoured with juniper and saffron) and a great beef stroganoff. After 9pm there's a variety show with Peter the Great surrounded by nubile showgirls, or a Russian folk ensemble on Sun. Amex, DC, MC, Visa. Daily noon–2am.

Expensive

Caviar Bar *Grand Hotel Europe*, Mikhailovskaya ul. 1–7 ☎329 60 00; Gostiniy Dvor/Nevskiy Prospekt metro. An aristocratic haunt before the Revolution, it now panders to the merely wealthy with delicacies such as Kamchatka crab, Siberian *pelmeni* in champagne sauce, sturgeon and salmon mousse, and *bliny* with caviar – all accompanied by champagne or de luxe vodkas. Amex, Visa, MC, DC. Daily 5–11pm.

Chopsticks *Grand Hotel Europe*, Mikhailovskaya ul. 1–7 ☎329 60 00; Gostiniy Dvor/Nevskiy Prospekt metro. Prestigious Chinese restaurant specializing in Szechuan and Cantonese cuisine, served mild or spicy as desired. The hot and sour soup and Szechuan chicken are especially good, while the service is so attentive that it borders on the slavish. Amex, DC, EC, MC, Visa. Daily noon–11pm.

Europe *Grand Hotel Europe*, Mikhailovskaya ul. 1–7 ☎329 60 00; Gostiniy Dvor/Nevskiy Prospekt metro. Heavily sauced European and Russian dishes, impeccably served in a sumptuous Art Nouveau setting. Jacket and tie required. Amex, EC, DC, MC, Visa. Open for breakfast (daily 7–10.30am) and dinner (Mon–Sat 7–11pm), with a champagne jazz brunch on Sun (noon–4pm).

Nikolay Bolshaya Morskaya ul. 52 ☎311 59 00; bus #22 from Nevskiy pr. Recipes from the era of Nicholas I, with silver service, in the magnificent walnut-panelled dining room of the House of Architects near St Isaac's. Guests might be given a tour of the fabulous rooms upstairs (see p.108). Smart dress required. All major cards. Daily noon–11.30pm.

1913 god Vosnesenskiy pr. 13/2 ☎315 51 48; bus #22 from Nevskiy pr. Its name refers to Russia's "best ever year", before the outbreak of war, revolutions and terror. Looks nothing special from outside, but rated one of the best Russian restaurants, popular with cultural figures. Generous portions of simple rural dishes like potato pancakes with bacon and sour cream (*draniky*), and richer foreign dishes such as lobster fricassée. Guitar, accordion and violin music after 8pm. MC, Visa. Daily noon–1am.

Sakura nab. kanala Griboedova 10/12 ☎315 94 74; Gostiniy Dvor/Nevskiy Prospekt metro. Mouthwatering sushi, *nabe*, seafood and meat soups, prepared by a Japanese chef and served by kimono-clad waitresses in *shoji*-screened rooms. Arguably the best Japanese restaurant in the city, and certainly the costliest. MC, Visa. Daily noon–11pm.

Very Expensive

Dvoryanskoe Gnezdo (The Noble Nest) ul. Dekabristov 21 ☎312 32 05; Sadovaya/Sennaya Ploshchad metro. Housed in the summer pavilion of the Yusupov Palace, near the Mariinskiy Theatre, the *Dvoryanskoe*

Gnezdo draws on European, Russian and Asian culinary traditions to create arguably the finest *haute cuisine* in St Petersburg. Formal dress and reservations essential. Music from 7pm. Amex, Visa, MC, DC, JCB. Daily noon–midnight.

Graf Suvorov ul. Lomonosova 6 ☎315 43 28; Gostiniy Dvor metro. Gourmet Russian and European food served in surroundings of fake luxury. Try the bear fillet or deer carpaccio and the extensive range of salads, but beware of the stunningly expensive wine list. Also features musical evenings ranging from Gypsy to jazz or Soviet retro, depending on the day of the week. Amex, DC, JCB, MC, Visa. Daily from noon till the last customer leaves.

Hermitage Dvortsovaya pl. 8 (in the General Staff building) ☎314 47 72; Nevskiy Prospekt metro. Its prestigious location, cool decor and obsequious greeters set unwitting guests up for average Russian food at crazy prices (beware of being suavely offered bottles of wine costing $600), with special menus for foreigners and slow service to add insult to injury. All major cards. Daily 9am until the last customer leaves.

Taleon Club nab. reki Moyki 59 ☎312 53 73; Nevskiy Prospekt metro. Housed in the splendid mansion of the merchant Yeliseev (p.67), latterly the Institute of Marxism Leninism, this award-winning establishment is the place to go if you've money to burn. Its menu runs from Escoffier classics to tilapia with rock lobsters and chanterelle mushrooms; the princely wine list has two pages of cognacs; and the decor is utterly amazing. Poker tournaments are held in a Baroque casino with a Socialist Realist painting on its ceiling. *Taleon*'s $34 Sun brunch (noon–4pm) is an entry ticket for the merely affluent, but it goes without saying you should dress to the hilt and make reservations. Major cards. Daily: casino 24hr; restaurant 7pm–3am.

Vasilevskiy Island

The listings in this section are marked on the map on pp.156–157. Some places are nearer to Sportivnaya metro on the Petrograd Side than to Vasileostrovskaya metro on Vasilevskiy Island; others are best reached by minibus from the city centre.

EATING AND DRINKING | Restaurants

Inexpensive

Csardas nab. Makarova 22 ☎ 323 85 88;
Sportivnaya metro. Overlooking Tuchkov
most, this stylish Hungarian bistro-restau-
rant is the place to try cold cherry soup and
richly sauced meat or fish dishes. No cards.
Restaurant: Sun–Wed noon–midnight, Fri &
Sat till 2am. Bistro: daily 9am–11.30pm.
Swagat Bolshoy pr. 91 ☎ 322 21 11,
ⓦ www.swagat.restaurant.ru; minibus #K-129
from Nevskiy pr. It's worth a journey to the
far end of Bolshoy prospekt to enjoy the
mouthwatering northern Indian cuisine here
– but they'll deliver for free. Very friendly
service, sitar music and Indian dancing after
8pm, and hookahs with a choice of
flavoured tobaccos. Business lunch for $10
(noon–4pm). Amex, Visa, MC, DC, JCB.
Daily noon–11pm.

Moderate

Byblos Maliy pr. 5 ☎ 325 85 64; **Sportivnaya**
metro. A welcome addition to the culinary
scene, this Phoenician-style Lebanese
restaurant serves tasty *kibbe*, *tabuli*,
humus, stuffed vine leaves and yogurt-rich
salads. Lebanese wines, hookahs with
flavoured tobaccos, and live music with
belly dancing (Fri & Sat). Maestro, MC, Visa.
Daily 11am–11pm.
Ketino 8-ya liniya 23 ☎ 326 01 96,
ⓔ katino@mail.ru; **Vasileostrovskaya metro**.
The finest Georgian food in the city is
served at this spacious, air-conditioned
"café restaurant" and its sibling *Salkino* on
the Petrograd Side, run by Ketino and Eka.
Everything is fantastic – the *suluguni*
cheese starters, *lobio*, *satsivi* and main
courses – and the Georgian wines can be
sublime. There are Georgian songs every
other night, and Georgian art on the walls
(for sale). You can spend a lot, but won't
regret it. No cards. Daily 11am–11pm.

Expensive

Restoran (The Restaurant) Tamozhniy per. 2
☎ 327 89 79; minibus #K-187 from Nevskiy pr.
Located opposite the Kunstkammer. This
restaurant's classical decor is so minimalist
that when the owners came to inspect the
premises, they asked the designer "Is that
it?" The food is traditional Russian and
made from the finest ingredients, but it
takes ages to arrive and the security goons
have been known to be aggressive towards

guests who protested about the delay. All
major cards. Daily noon–midnight.
Staraya Tamozhnya (Old Customs House)
Tamozhniy per. 1 ☎ 327 89 90; minibus #K-187
from Nevskiy pr. Just up the road from the
Kunstkammer, this classy cellar conversion
with an open kitchen and a doorman
dressed as a Tsarist customs official has
Russian and European dishes such as lobster, steak and caviar *bliny* – all OK but not
spectacular. MC, Visa. Daily 1pm–1am.

Petrograd Side

The listings in this section are marked
on the map on pp.174–175.

Inexpensive

Evropa (Europe) pl. Leva Tolstovo 2 ☎ 346 22
73; **Petrogradskaya metro**. An agreeable
restaurant with European cuisine and live
music. Portions are huge and tasty. There
are some veggie options, but meat and
seafood dishes are its forte. No cards. Daily
noon–midnight.

Moderate

Austeria in the Ioanavskiy ravelin of the Peter
and Paul Fortress ☎ 230 03 74; **Gorkovskaya**
metro. In an old officers' mess, with an
eighteenth-century Dutch decor and an
antique music box, this restaurant specializes in recipes from the time of Peter the
Great. The sauces involve combinations
such as cranberry and horseradish, and
there are all sorts of flavoured vodkas. Peter
would have also appreciated its billiard
room and evening concerts of classical
music or *chansons*. All major cards except
MC. Daily noon–midnight.
Demyanova Ukha (Demyan's Ukha)
Kronverkskiy pr. 53 ☎ 232 80 90; **Gorkovskaya**
metro. *Ukha* is the Russian equivalent of
bouillabaisse, and one of the specialities of
the house, whose menu features every kind
of fish dish in the Russian culinary lexicon –
be sure to start with the red caviar *bliny*.
Bookings advisable after 7pm. Major cards.
Daily 11am–11pm.
Fujiama Kamennoostrovskiy pr. 54 ☎ 234 49
22; **Gorkovskaya metro**. Delectable sushi
combo platters (up to $50), sashimi and
miso soup served with ceremony in vari-
ously sized rooms, including one where you
can dine seated on *tatami* matting. MC,

Visa. Mon–Thurs & Sun noon–11pm, Fri & Sat noon–1am.

Russkaya rybalka (Russian Fishing) Yuzhnaya Doroga 11 ☎323 98 13; Krestovskiy Ostrov metro. Fishing is very popular in Russia, and this pond-side theme-restaurant lets diners hook their own trout, sturgeon or sterlet, and watch it being grilled. Nearby is a fake windmill housing the *Karl and Friedrich* brewery-restaurant (☎320 79 78), under the same management, which has a Bavarian brewer and a French chef. Both places are hard to find after dark and you may have to take a taxi back. No cards. *Russkaya rybalka*: daily noon–9am; *Karl and Friedrich*: daily noon–2am.

Salkhino Kronverkskiy pr. 25 ☎232 78 91, ✉katino@mail.ru; Gorkovskaya metro. This cosy "café restaurant" hung with colourful paintings by Georgian artists living in St Petersburg is a lot smaller than *Ketino* (see p.362) and doesn't have air-conditioning, but the Georgian food and wine are equally wonderful. Booking is advisable at any time of day. No cards. Daily 11am–11pm.

U Gorchakova (At Gorchakov's) Bolshaya Monetnaya ul. 19 ☎233 93 72; Petrogradskaya metro. Russian and Ukrainian *haute cuisine* (try the roast veal with cherries, or sterlet in mushroom sauce), a lavish wine cellar, flavoured vodkas, *medovukha* (mead) and *sbiten* (a herbal liquor) complimented by a theatrical decor and nostalgic piano music. Major cards. Daily noon–midnight.

Liteniy, Smolniy and Vladimirskaya

The listings in this section are marked on the map on pp.200–201.

Cheap

Planet Sushi Nevskiy pr. 94 ☎275 75 33; Mayakovskaya/Ploshchad Vosstaniya metro. Sushi for the masses, with an all-you-can-eat buffet of sushi, sashimi and salads, with green tea or coffee and dessert (Mon–Fri noon–5pm). Purists might sniff at the quality, but the prices are as low as you'll get for Japanese food in St Petersburg. All major cards. Daily noon–6am.

Inexpensive

Gino-no-Taki pr. Chernyshevskovo 17 ☎272 09 58; opposite Chernyshevskaya metro. Stylish, traditionally designed Japanese restaurant

with 180 dishes on its menu – sushi, sashimi, salads, you name it. Japanese beers and sake. Rarely busy in the daytime, so you get the full benefit of the attentive service. Children's menu $10. All major cards except Amex. Daily 11am–6am.

Jamoneria Liteyniy pr. 11 ☎327 34 77; Mayakovskaya or Gostiniy Dvor metro. Move over Almodóvar – every single dish here is made from *jamón*, with Spanish wines and *finos* to wash them down. You can sample different kinds in the tasting room or try a business lunch ($4) in lieu of a full-blown dinner. Maestro, MC, Visa. Mon 1pm–11pm, Tues–Sun 11am–11pm.

Karavan-Saray (Caravanserai) ul. Nekrasova 1 ☎273 42 05, ⊛www.caravan-saray.ru; trolleybus #3, #8 or #15 from Mayakovskaya metro. Attractive Uzbek restaurant with waitresses in traditional costume, whose specialty is *plov* (pilaf). If you can't afford *Kalif* (see p.360), this makes a good substitute. No cards. Daily noon–2am.

Rigas Seta (Riga Courtyard) ul. Mayakovskovo 34/4 (entrance on Baskov per.) ☎273 11 49, ⊛www.rigasseta.ru; 15min walk from Mayakovskaya or Chernyshevskaya metro. A cosy Latvian restaurant serving such native specialties as cold strawberry soup, mutton on the bone with prunes and apricots, or venison with prunes in wine sauce. Czech beer. No cards. Daily noon–midnight.

Ulitsa Razbitykh Fonarey (Street of Broken Lamp Posts) ul. Radisheva 34 ☎275 99 35, ✉menty@tvorchestvo.spb.ru; Chernyshevskaya metro. Owned by Alexander Polovtsev, one of the stars of the popular TV cop series after which the restaurant is named, its Russian and European cuisine is great value for money. Live music Wed, Fri & Sat, but otherwise quiet. All cards except Amex. Daily noon–midnight.

Moderate

Arirang 8-ya Sovetskaya ul. 20 ☎274 04 66; tram #5 or #7 from Ploshchad Vosstaniya metro. Tailor-made for RTW travellers missing Asia, this basement Korean restaurant five blocks from the *St Petersburg International Hostel* features lots of spicy, garlicky dishes, plus a sushi and sashimi bar (11am–11pm) and nightly karaoke (6pm–5am). All major cards. Daily 11am–11pm.

Imperial *Nevsky Palace Hotel*, Nevskiy pr. 57 ☎380 20 01; Mayakovskaya metro. Enjoy a wonderful view of Nevskiy as you tuck into the buffet of Japanese, Mexican, Thai and Indian appetizers (noon–4pm) or the caviar bar, or choose from the Continental menu. Jazz brunch Sun noon–4pm. Children's menu and playroom. All major cards. Mon–Sat 7–11pm.

Kolkhida (Colchis) Nevskiy pr. 176 ☎274 25 14; Ploshchad Aleksandra Nevskovo I metro. The restaurant's name refers to the ancient land (nowadays Georgia) where Jason sought the Golden Fleece. Being close to the *Moskva Hotel*, it's geared for tour groups and feels impersonal compared to other Georgian places, but the food is tasty and reasonably priced. All major cards. Daily from noon till the last guest leaves.

Matrosskaya Tishina (Sailors' Silence) ul. Marata 54/34 ☎164 44 13, ⓦ www.tishina.ru; Ligovskiy Prospekt metro. Self-styled "fish fashion restaurant" with portholes, oysters on ice and aquariums brimming with giant perch, crab and lobsters. First-rate French-style seafood and an affluent clientele. MC, Visa. Daily noon–midnight.

Rasputin Nevskiy pr. 163 ☎277 31 41; Ploshchad Aleksandra Nevskovo II metro. A goat-legged statue of the Mad Monk welcomes guests to this kitsch cellar restaurant decorated with erotic mermaids and stained glass. Come at lunch to enjoy its superb smoked fish *zakuski*, or join the New Russians for a lusty night out, with pole dancing, a beachwear show and DJ ($6 surcharge). No cards. Daily noon–11pm.

Rioni ul. Shpalernaya 24 ☎273 32 61; trolleybus #3 or #8 from Nevskiy pr. or 15min walk from Ploshchad Lenina metro. Named after Georgia's main river, this friendly basement place at the back of an alley opposite the Bolshoy dom isn't so great as it used to be, but still one of the better Georgian options east of Liteyniy. Children welcome. No cards. Mon–Sat noon–11pm.

Shinok (Puppy) Zagorodniy pr. 13 ☎311 82 67; Dostoevskaya/Vladimirskaya metro. Unlike its Moscow counterpart, this faux-Ukrainian tavern doesn't have a captive cow and milkmaid for diners to gawp at, but its menu similarly lists two kinds of *borsch*, four varieties of *vareniki* (dumplings) and five types of *salo* (lard) as starters, with suckling pig, chicken or rabbit to follow, accompanied by *gorilka* (Ukrainian vodka) and folk music after 7pm. Amex, DC, MC, Visa. Daily 24hr.

Expensive

Landskrona *Nevsky Palace Hotel*, Nevskiy pr. 57 ☎380 20 01; Mayakovskaya metro. Top-floor restaurant with superb views of the city skyline, and a summer terrace. Known for its gourmet Mediterranean specialities and silver service, it matches the *Europe* on food, but can't compete on the interiors. Live music in the evenings. Amex, DC, MC, Visa. Daily 6.30pm–midnight.

The Southern Suburbs

The listings in this section are marked on the map on p.224.

Inexpensive

Paulaner *Pulkovskaya Hotel*, pl. Pobedy 1 ☎140 39 00; Moskovskaya metro. With seating for 600, this brewery-restaurant serving Paulaner beer and hearty Bavarian food is chiefly aimed at groups staying in the hotel, but good for a meal or a drink if you're in the vicinity of the Victory Monument. Major cards. Daily noon–1am.

Shalom ul. Koli Tomchaka 8 ☎327 54 75; Moskovskie Vorota metro. This kosher restaurant celebrates the bond between Russia and Israel by offering Russian, Ashkenazi (matzo soup, *farshmak*, gefilte fish) and Israeli (salads, *falafel* and *shwarma*) cuisine. Seder meals and other events catered for. Live music. No cards. Noon–11pm; closed Sat.

Moderate

Pietari Moskovskiy pr. 222 ☎373 18 09; Moskovskaya metro. Finnish-style venture ("Pietari" is the Finnish name for St Petersburg) with pasta dishes, reindeer steaks, tiger-prawn salad, sturgeon *solyanka* and pork with prunes on the menu. There's no need to reserve for the restaurant (live music 8–11pm) or the beer hall next door. Amex, JCB, Maestro, MC, Visa. Daily 11am till the last customer leaves.

Vyborg Side

The listings in this section are marked on the map on p.233.

Inexpensive

7.40 Bolshoy Samsonievskiy pr. 108 ☎246 34 44; minibus #K-262 from Ploshchad Lenina

metro. Jewish home cooking (not all kosher) amid photos and ephemera of the Jewish heritage in Russia, with live music in the evenings. The restaurant is harder to reach than *Shalom* (see opposite), but it doesn't close on Saturdays. Don't miss the nearby Lenin mural (p.236). Major cards except Amex. Mon 3–11pm, Tues–Sun noon–11pm.

Schwabski Domik (Swabian Cottage) Novocherkasskiy pr. 28/19 ☏528 22 11; Novocherkasskaya metro. This sprawling wood-panelled bar-restaurant-cum-bistro features hearty German and Czech fare served by waitresses in Swabian costume, and twenty different beers, including some from the Black Forest. Each section has a slightly different menu. Amex, DC, MC, Visa. Daily: restaurant 11am–1am; bistro 9am–9pm; pub 11am–11pm.

Moderate

Kavkaz (Caucasus) ul. Stakhanovtsev 5 ☏444 43 09; Novocherkasskaya metro. Like its downtown offshoot, the *Kavkaz Bar*, it serves Georgian specialities such as *khachapuri*, *shashlyk* and marinated meat

basturma, not to mention a restorative *khásh* (tripe soup – reckoned a cure for hangovers) on Sun morning. Its café (daily 10am–9pm) has a more limited menu. MC, Visa. Daily noon–midnight.

Staraya Derevnya (Old Village) ul. Savushkina 72 ☏431 00 00; three stops by tram #2 or #31 from Chernaya Rechka metro. Excellent, family-run restaurant with a cosy interior and traditional Russian home-cooking, accompanied by piano and accordion music (Sun–Thurs) or Gypsy, Russian and French songs (Fri & Sat). The beef with plum and nut sauce is a winner. Be sure to reserve. No cards. Daily 1–11pm.

Expensive

U Petrovicha (At Petrovich's) Sredneokhtinskiy pr. 44 ☏227 21 35; tram #7 or bus #174 from Novocherkasskaya metro. The crummy neighbourhood is forgotten once you're settled in this cosy den, with its eighteenth-century decor and traditional Russian festive dishes, such as elk, wild boar, rabbit or suckling pig. Musical duets 7–11pm. Reservations required. No cards. Daily noon–11pm.

Clubs and live venues

St Petersburg isn't a city that goes to bed early. With alcohol on sale 24 hours, Russian youths wander the streets from one *tsusovka* (event) to another, playing guitars in parks or the subways on Nevskiy. During the White Nights, even families with young children come to watch the bridges rise along the Neva embankments and enjoy the music and party atmosphere. Winter may force parties indoors, but there's no let-up on the club scene. Whether it's jazz-fusion, trance, grunge, S&M or gender bending, there are **clubs** for all tastes. Local DJs and foreign guests perform at most of these, and there are lots of one-off raves and theme parties (advertised by flyers). Many also double as **live music venues**, hosting indigenous acts, spanning the range of tastes from Russian reggae to thrash, plus alternative and world music bands from abroad – big-name acts are likely to stage concerts in one of the city's sports palaces or stadiums.

The term *klub* can cover anything from an arthouse café with a spot of live music to a dance warehouse, or a fancy nightclub with a restaurant and casino. Most cater to a certain crowd, whether it's creative professionals, students, shell-suited flatheads or designer-draped models. While formal dress codes are rare, **face control** (*feys kontrol*) is widespread. Russians distinguish between "democratic" face control (aimed at keeping out hooligans and bandits), and the kind that favours the rich (never mind how they behave). It's unwise to rile club security staff, however rude they might be. If you end up in a club full of **flatheads**, be careful not to flash your money around but don't be too nervous; they are out for a good time and unlikely to be looking for trouble. Men should be aware that most of the tourist-oriented clubs are full of **prostitutes**, for whom dancing with guys is just a prelude to business – though there are also lots of girls simply out for a good time, which can lead to misunderstandings. Striptease or pole-dancing acts are a feature of quite a few clubs and generally not regarded as sleazy by Russians – and cabaret shows can be even raunchier.

Admission charges and **drinks** prices are modest in most places, but a few clubs are pricy on both counts – see the reviews below. To find out the latest on up-and-coming events, check the **listings** sections in the Friday edition of the *St Petersburg Times* or the current month's issue of *Pulse*, or drop into any Titanik music store (see "Shopping", p.387) to browse through the flyers for gigs and parties. In the case of clubs or events on Vasilevskiy Island, Petrograd Side or Vyborg Side, guests can find themselves stranded on the wrong side of the Neva when the **bridges** are raised during the small hours (see p.39).

Pop, dance, rock and world music

Russian pop music is something of a joke to foreigners. The only act to get worldwide fame in recent years was the "lesbian" duo TaTu, while before then, the only performer that anyone outside Russia could identify was Alla Pugachova, who resembles a contestant in a drag ball. MTV-Russia is dominated by bland boy bands and Britney wannabes such as Zemfira and Glucosa; the only indie bands to get any exposure are Mumiy Troll from Vladivostok (led by the androgynous, intellectual Ilya Lagushenko), and the multi-instrumental Chiz (whose fusion of Celtic, Russian and Soviet roots music fits the prevailing mood of retro-patriotism). However, a far wider range of bands play in St Petersburg's clubs, particularly during SKIF, a three-day **festival** of DJs, performance artists and bands from all over Russia and abroad, in mid-April. **Bands** to look out for include Dva Samolota, Tequilajazz, Markscheider Kunst and Spitfire. Foreign acts have included David Byrne, Nick Cave and Bjork. Otherwise, dance music rules the day and the big names at clubs are **DJs** such as Vadim, Kefir and Pushkin – often joined by DJs from Britain, Holland, Ibiza, Finland or the Baltic States, such as Leeroy Thornhill (ex-Prodigy) or Lottie (from BBC Radio 1).

City Club Apraksin dvor, korpus 13 (enter via Sadovaya ul. and veer slightly right) ☎310 05 49, ⊛www.moneyhoney.org/cityclub/; Nevskiy Prospekt/Gostiniy Dvor metro. A mellow hangout for thirtysomethings, above the raucous *Money Honey* (see p.368). Three bars, pool tables and real fireplaces, plus live rock, pop, blues or Latin music Wed–Sun at 8.30pm ($1.75 for gigs). Beware of the thuggish security.

Cynic per. Antonenko 4 ☎312 95 26, ⊛www.cynic.spb.ru; Sadovaya/Sennaya Ploshchad metro. Peripatetic grunge club popular with students, the boho crowd and foreign residents. Hosts occasional free concerts by leading underground bands. Watch your belongings on the premises. Sun–Thurs 10am–3am, Fri & Sat 10am–7am.

Fish Fabriqué Ligovskiy pr. 53 ☎164 48 57, ⊛www.fishfabrique.spb.ru (Russian only); Ploshchad Vosstaniya metro. Legendary alternative club that's become more of a café for musicians and artists since it moved out into the courtyard of Pushkinskaya 10 (see p.381). Concerts start 7.30pm ($2–3), but regulars come for the table-football, cheap food and cult foreign movies. Daily 3pm till the last person leaves.

Golden Dolls Nevskiy pr. 60 ☎110 55 70; Gostiniy Dvor/Nevskiy Prospekt metro. The most in-your-face erotic nightclub on Nevskiy, with bar-girls and whores primed to milk customers for every buck. Russian and European food; all cards accepted. Daily 3am–6am.

Griboedov Club Voronezhskaya ul. 2a ☎164 43 55; Ligovskiy Prospekt metro. Run by the band Dva Samolota, this club is a magnet for avant-garde groups, trendsetters and poseurs, set in a deep bomb shelter with a darkened chill-out room and music ranging from jazz-hop to goth rock; gigs start at 10pm, DJs at midnight. Cover $2–3; free entry 6–8pm. Sun–Thurs 6pm–6am, Fri & Sat 6pm–7am.

Hollywood Nites Nevskiy pr. 46 ☎325 74 74; Nevskiy Prospekt/Gostiniy Dvor metro. Faux American-style nightclub and casino with a strip club next door. Food and drinks are pricy, the clientele and security intimidating. Thursday offers "events and surprises" (anything from erotic shows to competitions); while on Friday to Sunday there are pop concerts and discos. Daily 10pm–6am; casino & restaurant 24hr.

Jumpin' Jack Gagarinskaya ul. 6a ☎27506 11; Chernyshevskaya metro. This small rock and roll club features relatively unknown bands, with rock and roll parties on Fri and jazz and blues on weekdays. Cheap drinks and hot meals. Concerts start at 8pm ($1.50–2.50 entry). Daily 11am till the last customer leaves.

Konyushenniy dvor (aka Marstall) nab. kanala Griboedova 5 ☎315 76 07, ⊛www.kondvor.ru; Nevskiy Prospekt/Gostiniy Dvor metro. A hassle-free strip joint (after 11pm) and disco thronged with foreigners and local girls looking for fun. Drinks are inexpensive, and trouble is rare. It's packed at weekends;

quieter during the week. Entry free for foreigners with their passports. Daily noon–6pm.

La Plage pr. Kosygina 17 ☎525 63 13; tram #10 or #64 from Ladozhskaya metro. Way off the expat circuit, this "Beach Club" in the high-rise suburbs caters to fun-loving New Russians. Eurodance, house and Latin American, enlivened by stripping and bottle-spinning barmen and appearances from "the cream of Russian pop". All cards except Amex. Entry $3–12; free to women in bikinis. Thurs–Sun 10pm–6am.

Luna Vosnesenskiy pr. 46 ☎310 16 16; Sadovaya or Tekhnologicheskiy Institut metro. Typical New Russian hybrid of cheese, sleaze and flashiness, with a casino and floorshow. Fashion shows on Wed; male striptease Thurs; erotic super-show Fri & Sat. Cover $7–12; women free till 11pm except Fri & Sat. Daily 9pm–6am.

Magrib Nevskiy pr. 84 ☎275 12 55; Mayakovskaya metro. Voted the city's best restaurant-club in 2002, *Magrib* has a Moroccan-style interior with divans and hookahs, a restaurant with Oriental, Japanese and European cuisine, belly dancing, DJs and fashion shows. Accepts EC, Maestro, MC, Visa. Restaurant: Mon & Tues from 6pm, Wed–Sun noon–6am. Café: daily 9am–6am.

Mama Malaya Monetnaya ul. 3b ☎232 31 37; Gorkovskaya metro. Minimalist, split-level club in an old house; look for the "Centre for Youth" sign in Russian. Packed with affluent teenagers in the latest club wear, dancing to jungle, drum 'n' bass, house, techno and acid jazz. Arrive early or late to avoid queuing outside. Cover $4–5. Fri & Sat 11.50pm–6am.

Metro Ligovskiy pr. 174 ☎166 02 04, ⊛www.metro.club.ru; Ligovskiy Prospekt metro, then any tram south. Huge, mainstream club with Russian and Eurodance music on the first floor, techno and house on the second, and parties on the third level (Mon, Wed, Fri & Sat), frequented by teenagers from the Southern Suburbs (hence the ban on chewing gum).Cover $3–4 Sun–Thurs, $4–7 Fri, Sat & holidays. Daily 10pm–6am.

Moloko (Milk) Perekupnoy per. 12 ☎274 94 67, ⊛www.molokoclub.ru (Russian only); Ploshchad Aleksandra Nevskovo metro. One of St Petersburg's best venues for live music – from funk-hop to post-punk – with a friendly bohemian ambience, cheap drinks

and no pretensions. Their website features band biographies and MP3s. Gigs start at 8pm; $2–5. Daily 7–11pm.

Money Honey Apraksin dvor, korpus 13 (enter via Sadovaya ul. and veer slightly right) ☎310 05 49, ⊛www.moneyhoney.org; Nevskiy Prospekt/Gostiniy Dvor metro. A sprawling Texan saloon for local rockabillies to strut their stuff. Rowdy but relaxed; don't forget your leather jacket and quiff. Nightly live music at 8pm & 12.30am ($2 entry from 7pm). Mon 10am–midnight, Tues–Sun 10am–5.30am.

Orlandina il. Mira 36a ☎110 65 36, ⊛www.caravanrecords.spb.ru (Russian only); Gorkovskaya metro. An art rock club owned by the local music label Caravan Records, with decor by the artist Kopeikin, who works with the band NOM-Zhir. With space for only 150, you need to turn up before gigs start to be sure of getting in. Nightly concerts of alternative, folk-rock, reggae or Brit pop, from 7pm. Cheap drinks. Cover Mon–Thurs $2.50, Fri–Sun $3.50.

Ostrov (Island) nab. Leytenanta Shmidta 37 ☎328 46 49; minibus #K-129 from Nevskiy pr. to 16-ya & 17-ya liniya, then walk to the Neva embankment. Entertainments complex with a dance floor that rises, falls and revolves, while showering dancers with artificial rain and snow; erotic and dance shows, live vocal music; a chill-out room with hammocks; three bars and a restaurant. Beware of being stranded by the bridges. Entry from $6. Wed–Sun 10pm–6am.

Par.spb Alexander Park 5B ☎233 33 74, ⊛www.par.spb.ru (Russian only); Gorkovskaya metro. Sprawling, industrial-chic club in an old hospital laundry (*par* means "steam") diagonally opposite the metro. There are several rooms hosting up to a dozen DJs a night, plus occasional cult film screenings, style parties and underground jazz bands ($5–10 entry), an indoor lounge and patio. Democratic face control. Lounge: daily noon–8am. Club: Fri, Sat & Sun 11pm–7am.

Pla.Styl.Inn 2-ya Krasnoarmeyskaya ul. 5 ☎316 72 02; Tekhnologicheskiy Institut metro. Occupying the premises of the now defunct gay club *69*, this is a (mainly) straight dance club that often hosts theme parties starting at 11pm ($7). *Plastylin* is the Russian for Plasticine and a slang term for hashish. Sun–Thurs 10am–midnight, Fri & Sat 10am till the last person leaves.

Popugai (Parrot) Fonarniy per. 1 ☎311 59 71; Sennaya Ploshchad metro. The only reggae bar in St Petersburg plays non-stop Bob Marley and occasionally has live music (no entry charge), but reggae stars like Dva Samoleta play at other venues, and the cheap beer and eclectic international menu are otherwise the main attractions. Daily noon–midnight.

Purga (Blizzard) nab. reki Fontanki 11☎312 41 23 and 13 ☎311 23 10; Gostiniy Dvor metro. Two arty basement clubs run in tandem. At no. 11 they celebrate New Year every midnight with champagne, the Soviet anthem and Brezhnev and the Kremlin Clock on TV, before the disco ($1 entry). No. 13 resembles the sperm bank in Woody Allen's *Everything You Always Wanted to Know about Sex*, and stages mock weddings between members of the audience, with live music on Tues & Thurs ($1.50). Hot meals and snacks at the former, cold

zakuski at the latter. If you book a table ($10) the entry fee is waived. Both daily: no. 11, 4pm–6am; no. 13, 8pm–8am.

Tribunal Bar pl. Dekabristov 1 ☎311 16 90; Nevskiy Prospekt metro. Customers are outnumbered by hookers at this passé New Russian den, opposite the Bronze Horseman. Mon ladies night with male strippers; Thurs "Russian party" with prizes; Fri & Sat cabaret, transvestite show and female striptease. Euro and Latin dance music. No cover charge, but drinks are pricy. Daily 4pm–6am.

Tunnel corner of Zverinskaya ul. and Lyubyanskiy per. ☎233 40 15, @www.tunnel-club.ru; Sportivnaya or Gorkovskaya metro. Russia's oldest techno club, in a former nuclear bunker whose concrete corridors reverberate with drum 'n' bass, house or hip hop. Stoned under-20s crowd and cheap drinks; admission $5–8. Thurs–Sat 10am–8am.

Occasional live venues

The following places are sometimes used for **concerts** by major Russian pop stars or foreign bands – look out for flyers in music shops, or in the *St Petersburg Times* or *Pulse* magazine for details.

Bolshoy Concert Hall Oktyabrskiy (Bolshoy kontsertniy zal, or BKZ) Ligovskiy pr. 6 ☎275 13 00; Ploshchad Vosstaniya metro. Used by pop stars such as Pugachova, the Eifman and Male Ballet companies, and visiting foreign acts. Box office Mon–Fri 11am–8pm, Sat & Sun 11am–7pm.

Ice Palace (Ledovy dvorets) pr. Pyatiletok 1 ☎118 41 17, @www.newarena.spb.ru; Prospekt Bolshevikov metro. With seating for 14,000, and the finest lighting, sound and televisual facilities in the city, the Ice Palace hosts concerts by the likes of Bjork.

Lensoviet Palace of Culture Kamennoostrovskiy pr. 42 ☎346 04 38;

Petrogradskaya metro. A popular venue for veteran bands such as Akvarium, or schlock-rock acts from Moscow. Box office daily noon–3pm & 4–8pm.

SKK pr. Yuriya Gagarina 8 ☎378 17 10; Park Pobedy metro. Used for concerts by big-name bands. Box office daily 10am–6pm.

Yubileyniy Sports Palace pr. Dobrolyubova 18 ☎323 93 15; Sportivnaya metro. An occasional venue for big-name bands during summer, not to mention all-night ice-skating discos. The box office is open daily noon–7pm.

Cabaret and comedy clubs

Brodyachaya Sobaka (Stray Dog) pl. Iskusstv 5 ☎312 80 47; Nevskiy Prospekt metro. From 1912 to 1915, this basement club was the nexus of St Petersburg's avant-garde. Artists got in for free, while celebrity-spotters paid heavily to watch Akhmatova, Diaghilev, Meyerhold and Mayakovsky

holding court. Its 2001 reincarnation hoped to do the same for the contemporary scene, but soon found that creative types preferred hanging out at *Che*, and tour groups paid the bills, so its concerts and performances ($5–7) are more burlesque than avant-garde. Daily 11am–midnight.

If you were looking for somewhere to stage a rave, an abandoned plague laboratory and naval fort way out in the Gulf of Finland wouldn't spring to mind – unless you were from the inventive crowd that held "pool parties" at St Petersburg swimming baths in the 1990s. While these ended after someone drowned, the **Fort Dance** has evolved since 2000 into a sponsored annual event with tight security to disarm the flathead influx drawn by the original art-house venture. The main action is at Fort Alexander, off the coast of Kronstadt (see p.292), which has all-night DJ programmes in two "arenas" (one VIP); there's a third one at the on-shore Fort Konstantin. Video streams of previous Fort Dances can be seen on the Russian-language website Ⓦ www.fortdance.com. The one-day event occurs in the last week of July; tickets are available from Aisberg and Titanik stores or online at Ⓦ www.kassir.ru. A shuttle-bus for ticket-holders runs from Chernaya Rechka metro to Fort Konstantin from 3pm onwards. The Fort Dance may or may not coincide with the **Love Parade**, an annual event modelled on its Berlin namesake, that usually takes the form of a procession of floats and DJs along Nevskiy prospekt towards the end of July, but in 2003 took to the water for a cruise around the canals and Neva basin, winding up at Fort Alexander for a rave, before sailing back at 1am. A similar cruise may be scheduled sometime in September, depending on how the July event goes. See *Pulse* or flyers in music shops for details.

Chaplin Club ul. Chaykovskovo 59, ☏272 66 49; Chernyshevskaya metro. A cosy comedy club with evening shows by Yuri Galtsev, Gennady Vetrov and other actors from clown-mime troupes, that can be enjoyed without much or any knowledge of Russian ($8–10; table reservations essential). Otherwise it's just a place to eat and drink. Major cards. Daily noon–1am.

Hali Guli Lanskoe shosse 15 ☏246 38 27; Vyborgskaya metro. Famous bad-taste club aimed at affluent Russians with no inhibitions: waitresses are encouraged to swear and smoke; patrons, to engage in drinking contests ($15 to sink a metre of beer, with a prize at the end) or lewd acts (participants in the penis-measuring event get one percent discount on drinks for each centimetre). You need to understand Russian to get the smutty cabaret, but might come just for the debauched atmosphere. Beware of being stranded by the bridges. Arrive before the show starts at 9pm ($27) or they may not let you in; the disco begins at midnight ($7). Accepts MC, Visa. Daily 6pm–4am.

Gay and lesbian clubs

Although homosexuality is no longer illegal in Russia, society remains extremely homophobic. Attitudes in St Petersburg are more liberal than anywhere else in the country, but many local gays are still in the closet. In recent years several gay clubs have folded after trouble with gay-bashers and police raids. If you can read Russian, the local website Ⓦ www.Xs.gay.ru features more up-to-date gay **listings** than you'll find in English on Ⓦ www.gay.ru (a nationwide umbrella site) or the otherwise informative site of the St Petersburg gay rights NGO, Krilija (Ⓦ www.krilija.spb.ru) – perhaps because they want tourists to hire a guide through their travel agency, which could be a wise move if this is your first visit to Russia.

Cabaret ul. Dekabristov 34 ☏114 50 56; Sennaya Ploshchad metro. Due to move once the new Mariinskiy Theatre gets under way, this gay disco in the First Five Year Plan Palace of Culture (for now) has a cheap bar, and transvestite shows with impersonations of Soviet pop stars (entry $1.25–10). Thurs–Sun 11am–6pm.

Greshniki (Sinners) nab. kanala Griboedova 28/1 ☏318 42 91, ⓦwww.greshniki.gay.ru; Nevskiy Prospekt/Gostiniy Dvor metro. Its S&M dungeon decor, staff dressed as angels or demons, and leather-clad strippers, carry on where the former *69* club left off. There are four floors and a roof for cooling off, with great view of the canal. Men free till 9pm, then $1.50; women $3–6. Daily 6pm–6am. Tri El 5-ya Sovetskaya ul. 45 ☏110 20 16, ⓦwww.triel.hotmail.ru; Ploshchad Vosstaniya

metro. Russia's only full-time lesbian club (all the others are gay clubs with lesbian nights) features striptease and gender-bending shows (Fri & Sat), occasional concerts (Thurs) and dance parties, and pool on weekdays. Women only except on Thurs & Fri. Free entry Mon & Tues; other days $1–5. Mon & Tues 5pm–midnight, Wed 9pm–6am, Thurs 7pm–midnight, Sat 9pm–6am; closed Sun.

Jazz and blues

St Petersburg has an indigenous jazz tradition going back to the 1930s, and its clubs lure talent from across Russia and the Baltic States, plus musicians from elsewhere during the **Jazz Guitar** (early March), **White Nights Swing** (early July) and **Autumn Rhythms** (mid-November) festivals. Besides the clubs listed below there are **jazz cruises** on the River Neva from June to September, sailing from the Hermitage jetty every Saturday at 6pm. There's swing and trad jazz on one deck, free-form on the other. Tickets are available from theatre ticket kiosks around the city; phone ☏315 90 46 or 153 40 20 for information. **Blues**, Cuban, flamenco and *fado* music also have their admirers. Two useful **websites** with audio links are "Jazz in Russia" (ⓦwww.jazz.ru) – whose text in English includes a section on festivals – and "Blues" (ⓦwww.blues.ru), in Russian only.

Café-Club Che Poltavskaya ul. 3 ☏277 76 00; Ploshchad Aleksandra Nevskovo or Ploshchad Vosstaniya metro. An Amsterdam Brown Café by day (see p.357); its nighttime vibe is sultry with Cuban music and cigars, as goateed webmasters mingle with drunken fashionistas. Democratic face control. Live music nightly 10pm–3am. Daily 9am–7am.
812 Jazz Club Bolshoy pr. 98 ☏346 16 31; Petrogradskaya metro. This bunker-style club in the courtyard of the Dom Mod goes in for jazz-funk, ragtime, jazz vocal and blues acts; gigs from $3–5 starting at 8pm, followed by jam sessions. Daily from 8pm till the last customer leaves.
Jazz-i-Phrenia Nevskiy pr. 91 ☏277 51 30; Ploshchad Vosstaniya metro. Jazz, blues, funk and rock bands perform at this basement club, which has a restaurant serving European and Caucasian food, and billiards. Concerts nightly except Mon, with two acts on Fri & Sat. Cover $2 Sun–Thurs, from $3 Fri & Sat. Mon–Fri 2pm till the last customer leaves, Sat & Sun 2pm–5am.
Jazz Philharmonic Hall Zagorodniy pr. 27 ☏164 85 65, ⓦwww.jazz-hall.spb.ru; Vladimirskaya/Dostoevskaya metro. A rather formal venue founded by the veteran jazz

violinist David Goloshchokin, who often plays here. The Bolshoy zal is used for mainstream and Dixieland jazz, while the smaller Ellington Hall hosts intimate, candlelit concerts. Advance tickets from the box office (2–8pm) $3–6; student discount for the Bolshoy zal. Daily 7–11pm; Ellington Hall 8–11.30pm.
Jazz Time Bar Mokhovaya ul. 41 ☏273 53 79; Chernyshevskaya metro. A smaller, three-room offshoot of the *JFC Jazz Club* (see below), that has jazz, blues and Latin concerts Wed–Sun at 9pm. Daily from 11am till the last person leaves.
JFC Jazz Club Shpalernaya ul. 33 ☏272 98 50, ⓦwww.jfc.spb.ru; Chernyshevskaya metro. Directed by Andrei Kondakov, voted Russia's best jazz musician in 2002, this is a relaxed venue for all styles of jazz and Latin nights with cut-price Bacardi. Table reservations for gigs essential, as the club is tiny and very popular. Follow the signs the back of the courtyard. Concerts $3–5. Daily 9am–11pm.
Jimi Hendrix Blues Club Liteyniy pr. 33 ☏279 88 13; Chernyshevskaya metro. One of the hottest venues in the city for jazz, blues, rock and country; gigs start at 7.30pm and

cost $2–3. Does decent Armenian food but the service is awful. Daily 24hr.

Palitra Art Café Malaya Morskaya ul. 5 ☎312 34 35; Nevskiy Prospekt metro. A small café beside the Palitra gallery, that hosts photographic exhibitions and concerts of jazz, blues and occasionally rock or country, from 9pm ($1 entry). Daily 10am–11pm.

Red Fox Jazz Club ul. Mayakovskovo 50 ☎275 42 14, ⊛www.rfjc.ru; Chernyshevskaya metro.

Agreeable jazz/blues café with live music of the 1930s and 1940s 8–10pm nightly ($2 entry) except Mon. Café opens 10.30am on weekdays, 2pm on Sat & Sun.

Sunduk Furshtatskaya ul. 42 ☎272 31 00; Chernyshevskaya metro. Another cosy art café, with nightly Spanish, blues or jazz music after 8.30pm ($1 entry). Daily noon–11pm.

16

The Arts

For well over a century, St Petersburg has been one of the world's great centres of **classical music and ballet**, most famously represented by the Mariinskiy opera and ballet company – formerly called the Kirov, the name by which it's still marketed abroad – and also by its fine orchestras and choirs. Although many suffered from the withdrawal of state funding and the exodus of talented artists in the early 1990s, the Mariinskiy has retained its world-class reputation for classical ballet, and acquired new laurels as an opera house.

Despite small drama troupes springing up all over, **theatre** has had a harder time, largely because of the language barrier, which prevents it from attracting richer, foreign audiences. Nevertheless, there are performances that don't require much (if any) knowledge of Russian, such as **mime** and **puppetry**. Sadly, **film**, which once flourished through the local studio Lenfilm, has all but disappeared as a home-grown art form. Most cinemas screen Hollywood blockbusters or Italian soft-porn; nearly all the Russian films made nowadays are produced and financed in Moscow; Lenfilm's studios and film crews are employed on TV dramas. But the **visual arts** are thriving, with dozens of exhibitions, multi-media and performance events every month – though they're not always widely advertised.

If you're lucky (or you've planned ahead), you'll be able to catch specific **festivals** or annual events – see pp.52–53 for a full rundown.

Tickets and information

For most concerts and theatrical performances, you can buy **tickets** from the venue's box office (*kassa*), the many theatre-ticket kiosks (*teatralnaya kassa*) on the streets and in metro stations, or from the **central box office** at Nevskiy pr. 42 (opposite Gostiniy dvor). Buying tickets from **touts** outside venues is fraught with risks – if you do buy a ticket this way, check the date and the seats specified on the ticket. In Russian, the stalls are *parter*; the first or second tier of balconies are the *beletazh* and all the rest are *balkon* seats; *ryad* means row, and *mesto*, seat. Seating plans of the major venues can be found in the *Traveller's Yellow Pages* (see p.30). Be sure to keep your ticket if you leave the auditorium during the intermission; some places won't let you back in without it.

Unfortunately for visitors, a **two-tier price system** whereby foreigners are charged far more than Russians applies at the Mariinskiy, Maliy Opera and Ballet, Hermitage and Maliy theatres, as well as the circus. While a local acquaintance can obtain you tickets at the Russian price, it's almost impossible

theatre	театр	balcony	ъалккон
cinema	кино-театр	beletazh	ъел Этаж
theatre-ticket		stalls	партер
kiosk	театральная касса	seat	место
box office	касса	row	ряд

to get past the vigilant *babushki* at the Mariinskiy, who send foreigners back to pay the premium charge – though at other venues you might manage to sneak through if you speak Russian or really look the part. Even so, prices are reasonable by world standards: a halfway decent seat at the Mariinskiy can be had for $50, and elsewhere you'll rarely pay more than $10.

Music lovers planning to be in town for some time might buy **abonimenty**, batches of tickets to about ten concerts – by a specific composer, or in a genre such as chamber music – performed at one concert hall or different venues over the course of a month or two. There are various *abonimenty* available, and besides saving you money they can also save you the hassle of queuing for popular concerts if you choose them carefully beforehand.

The *St Petersburg Times* (Fri edition) and *Pulse* both carry **English-language listings** of events at the main concert halls and theatres, although the listings in Russian-language newspapers such as *Chas Pik* (especially its weekly supplement, *Pyatnitsa*) are more comprehensive. You can also look out for posters around town, or ask about current events at the hotels' service bureaux, which can reserve tickets for a fee. Some hotels, such as the *Grand Hotel Europe*, organize prestigious concerts in places like the Hermitage Theatre or the Yusupov Palace, in which case you can be certain of the quality, though it will come at a price. Lastly, bear in mind that some (though by no means all) theatres and concert halls are **closed in July or August**.

Ballet, opera and classical music

Due to the demand by visitors, tickets for **ballet** at the Mariinskiy can be hard to obtain, but don't despair if you have no luck, as there are several other respected venues for ballet and opera, and the Mariinskiy isn't the only star act in town. The Eifman Company has won rave reviews for its modern gloss on classical ballet styles and even performs at the Mariinskiy during the August break, though it's now so popular that getting tickets can be difficult. Another well-known company is Valery Mikhailovsky's Male Ballet, which performs *Swan Lake* and other classics with more than a *soupçon* of irony. Conversely, the Stars of the St Petersburg Ballet festival at the Hermitage Theatre in June and

Folklore shows

A spectacle that might appeal to some are **folklore shows**, featuring Russian folk songs and high-kicking Cossack dancers, with a bit of ballet thrown in for good measure. The "Feel Yourself Russian" bash in the ballroom of the Nikolaevskiy Palace on pl. Truda (☎312 55 00) includes a vodka, champagne and *zakuski* buffet, and is held daily at 6.30pm and 9pm. Or there's the show in the concert hall of the Anichkov Palace on Nevskiy pr. (☎310 99 88), featuring the Song and Dance Ensemble of the Leningrad Military District, which starts at 7.30pm daily. Tickets for both are available on the spot, from $11.

July purports to feature leading dancers at the Mariinskiy, but tends to be performed by little-known understudies.

Under director Valery Gergiev the Mariinskiy has not only nurtured a new generation of great dancers, but has inaugurated a new golden age of **opera**, unseen since the era of Chaliapin. Besides inviting the film director Konchalovsky to stage Prokofiev's *War and Peace*, he has risked disapproval by introducing Wagner to the Mariinskiy's repertoire – a composer never liked in Russia, whose works now take precedence over the Italian and French operas traditionally beloved of Russians. The only negative aspect to this success is that Gergiev, along with star singers such as Olga Borodina and Nikolai Putilin, are often abroad – which is great for attracting sponsorship to the Mariinskiy, but means that they're not in St Petersburg as often as their fans – and visiting tourists – would like.

Classical music concerts take place throughout the year, with the largest number during the Stars of the White Nights Festival. In addition to the main venues listed below, there are also concerts in churches and palaces – including Peterhof, Tsarskoe Selo and Pavlovsk, outside St Petersburg. For news and links to local orchestras, check out the website Ⓦ www.classicalmusic.spb.ru.

You should definitely try to hear some **Russian Orthodox Church music**, which is solely choral and wonderfully in keeping with the rituals of the faith. Splendid choirs perform at the Preobrazhenskiy Church near Liteyniy prospekt (daily at 10am & 6pm) and the Alexander Nevsky Trinity Cathedral (6pm daily except Wed). The choir at the former is composed of professional singers from the Kapella Choir. Orthodox services are also held at the St Nicholas Cathedral at 6pm, and less regularly at other churches. Musically speaking, the best services are those on Saturday evening and Sunday morning. **Military bands** are also worth hearing: they often play in the Alexander Garden at lunchtime on Sundays during summer, and come out in force on Victory Day, Navy Day and the Defenders of the Motherland Day.

Concert halls, opera houses and other venues

Beloselskiy-Belozerskiy Palace Nevskiy pr. 41 ☎ 315 52 35; Gostiniy Dvor metro; box office noon–6pm. The palace's mirrored ballroom hosts performances by the St Petersburg City Concert Orchestra, and occasional folklore shows.

Bolshoy Concert Hall Oktyabrskiy (Bolshoy kontsertniy zal, or BKZ) Ligovskiy pr. 6 ☎ 275 13 00; Ploshchad Vosstaniya metro; box office Mon–Fri 11am–8pm, Sat & Sun 11am–7pm. One of the city's largest and most modern concert halls, with comfy seating and unobstructed views of the stage. Used by pop stars such as Alla Pugachova, the Eifman and Male Ballet companies, as well as visiting international acts. Ballet performances are to recorded music.

Eifman Ballet Theatre ul. Liza Chaykinoy 2 ☎ 230 78 91, Ⓦ www.eifmanballet.spb.ru; Sportivnaya metro. When not appearing at the Mariinskiy or the BKZ, this world-renowned company may perform at their own studio-theatre. Boris Eifman's reinterpretations of classical ballets are superb, but his own choreography can sometimes be embarrassingly self-obsessed, so be careful to check what's on the bill.

Hermitage Theatre Dvortsovaya nab. 32 ☎ 279 02 26 or 272 96 82; Nevskiy Prospekt/Gostiniy Dvor metro; box office Tues–Sun 10.30am–5pm. Between May and October, Catherine the Great's private theatre is an exquisite venue for evening concerts by chamber groups from the Philharmonia, and gala performances by Mariinskiy soloists and dancers. It also has its own resident orchestra, the St Petersburg Kamerata. Tickets aren't numbered, so be sure to arrive early to claim a decent seat.

Kapella nab. reki Moyki 20 ☎ 314 10 58; Nevskiy Prospekt/Gostiniy Dvor metro; box office daily noon–3pm & 4–7pm. The oldest concert hall in St Petersburg, to the east of the Winter Palace, with its own internationally renowned choir and the State Kapella Orchestra, drawn from students at the Conservatory, who join forces to perform music of varying styles and ages, from Baroque to twentieth century. The Kapella hosts the international Prokofiev Young Violinists contest (early March) and an Early Music festival (late Sept till mid-Oct).

Kannon Dance ul. Dekabristov 34 ☎ 114 20 27; bus #22 or #43 from Nevskiy pr., or tram #5 from Sennaya Ploshchad/Sadovaya metro. Modern jazz-dance school near the Mariinskiy, whose *Stansiya* theatre is used by local contemporary dance troupes. The school organizes the Open View (or Open Look) international festival of modern dance in July – staged at venues and outdoor stages around the city.

Male Ballet (Muzhskoy balet) Gorokhovaya ul. 71 ⊛ www.maleballet.spb.ru; Pushkinskaya metro. Valery Mikhailovsky was principal dancer for the Eifman company for fourteen years, before founding his acclaimed all-male ballet company in 1992. It performs "Classical Transformations" of Tchaikovsky ballets, and modern compositions such as *Ecce Homo*, with music by Vangelis, Sinck and Albinoni. When not abroad, it appears at venues such as the BKZ, as advertised in the local press and by posters outside their rehearsal studio.

Maliy Opera and Ballet Theatre (Maliy operniy teatr, aka the Mussorgsky or Mikhailovsky Theatre) pl. Iskusstv 1 ☎ 595 42 82, ⊛ www.mikhailovsky.ru; Nevskiy Prospekt/Gostiniy Dvor metro; box office 11am–3pm & 4–8pm. Though the ballet and opera at the Maliy aren't as good as at the Mariinskiy, its apricot-and-silver auditorium is no less beautiful and its repertoire includes mainstream ballets such as *Giselle*, *Les Sylphides* and *Swan Lake*, and Russian operas like *Prince Igor* and *Khovanshchina*. A small museum on the third floor displays designs for the first productions of Prokofiev's *War and Peace* and Shostakovich's *The Nose*. Tickets are easy to come by, except in August when the Mariinskiy is closed and tour groups come here instead.

Mariinskiy Theatre (Mariinskiy teatr) Teatralnaya pl. 2 ☎ 114 43 44, ⊛ www .mariinsky.spb.ru; bus #22 or #43 from Nevskiy prospekt, or tram #5 from Sennaya Ploshchad/Sadovaya metro; box office 11am–7pm. A sumptuous nineteenth-century ballet and opera house, better known by its old Soviet title, the Kirov. Unlike the Bolshoy in Moscow, its reputation for ballet

is undiminished – but the price of success is that the company is obliged to tour for much of the year, leaving lesser dancers behind. The best time to catch the company is during winter, when ballerinas such as Yuliana Lopatkina, Diana Vishneva and Altinai Asilmuratova are around, hopefully accompanied by Farukh Ruzimantov or Igor Zelensky. At this time of the year the Mariinskiy also stages *The Golden Cockerel* for kids, performed by junior members of the Vaganova ballet school. As for opera, Wagner rules at present, but Verdi, Bizet, Mozart and Rossini are still staged. Look out for the baritones Victor Chernomortsev and Nikolai Putilin, or even a rare appearance by Olga Borodina, who's more of a fixture at La Scala, the Met or Covent Garden nowadays. At the Mariinskiy, Russian operas are staged with English surtitles, and foreign operas with Russian ones. The company doesn't perform in August. Tickets sell out fast, so it's worth booking before you arrive in Russia. This can be done on the Mariinskiy's website up to sixty days in advance. You can pay by MasterCard or Visa and get an email voucher to exchange for tickets at the *kassa* just before the performance, or pay cash upon collection, in which case the tickets must be collected within 72 hours of booking. If you leave things till the last moment, you should see what (if anything) is available at the theatre's downtown box office (daily 11am–7pm) on the mezzanine level of the Haute Couture Gallery on Dumskaya ulitsa, or the central ticket office at Nevskiy pr. 42, before trying hotel service bureaux or hoping to get a cheap standby seat at 6pm on the night of the performance. You may want to dress up to the nines, quaff champagne and promenade with your companion around the Great Hall during the intermission – since that's what everyone else does.

Peter and Paul Cathedral in the Peter and Paul Fortress ☎ 238 05 03; Gorkovskaya metro. Hosts concerts of choral music (religious and secular) and bell-ringing during the summer months.

Philharmonia (Filarmoniya) Mikhaylovskaya ul. 2 ☎ 110 42 57, ⊛ www.philharmonia.spb.ru; Nevskiy Prospekt/Gostiniy Dvor metro; box office 11am–3pm & 4–8pm. The grand Bolshoy zal, named after Shostakovich, is home to the St Petersburg Philharmonic Orchestra, whose concerts vary depending on the conductor; Mariss Jansons or Yuri Temirkanov are sure to please and sell out fast. The hall is also used by visiting foreign artists and an orchestra called Klassika that specializes in Strauss waltzes and other lowbrow favourites. The smaller Maliy zal (named after Glinka) has better acoustics and a separate entrance (at Nevskiy pr. 30) and phone number (☎ 311 83 33). It's used for solo and chamber recitals, which are usually excellent.

Rimsky-Korsakov Museum Zagorodniy pr. 28 ☎ 113 32 08; Vladimirskaya/Dostoevskaya metro. Weekly chamber music perform-ances and recitals in the composer's former apartment, every Wed from Oct till May. Book ahead as seating is limited.

Rimsky-Korsakov Opera and Ballet Theatre (Teatr Opery i Baleta Konservatorii imeni Rimskovo-Korsakova) Teatralnaya pl. 3 ☎ 312 25 19; bus #22 from Nevskiy prospekt or tram #5 from Sennaya Ploshchad/Sadovaya metro; box office 11am–7pm. The St Petersburg Conservatory's own company of students and teachers stages some fine opera and ballet performances, but the lack of star performers means that tickets are fairly easy to come by.

Smolniy Cathedral pl. Rastrelli ☎ 311 36 90; minibus #K-46 or #K-136 from Chernyshevskaya metro. Regular performances of orchestral and choral music in what is outwardly one of the most striking buildings in St Petersburg (see p.209). Its bare, white-washed interior is a let-down, but the acoustics are wonderful.

St Petersburg Opera Chamber Music Theatre Galernaya ul. 33 ☎ 314 09 55, ⓦ www.opera.spb.ru; trolleybus #5 or #22 from Nevskiy prospekt. Having finally found a permanent home in a former baronial mansion, the company is set to build upon the success of Yuri Alexandrov's staging of the Pushkin-based operatic trilogy The Queen of Spades, Eugene Onegin and Boris Godunov. Its repertoire also includes Offenbach's operetta La Belle Hélène.

Yubileyniy Sports Palace pl. Dobrolyubova 18 ☎ 323 93 15; Sportivnaya metro. Sports com-plex on the Petrograd Side with an ice rink that stages "ballet on ice" shows during the winter.

Theatre

St Petersburg prides itself on its dramatic tradition and boasts several sumptu-ously appointed **theatres**, but at present can't honestly claim superiority over Moscow – unlike with ballet and opera – although a couple of companies are deservedly acclaimed. Though the fact that shows are invariably in Russian limits its appeal to foreigners, you don't need to understand much to appreciate some of the more experimental productions, puppetry, musicals, mime or the circus. The main events in the theatrical calendar are the **Festival of Russian Theatres**, with performers from all the CIS countries (mid-April), and the **Baltic House Festival** of drama from northern Russia and the Baltic States (Oct). Both are held at the Baltiyskiy dom.

Drama theatres

Akimov Comedy Theatre Nevskiy pr. 56 ☎ 312 45 55; Nevskiy Prospekt/Gostiniy Dvor metro; box office open daily noon–3pm & 4–8pm. If your Russian is up to it, this is the place to catch such comic classics as The Importance of Being Earnest, Bulgakov's adaptation of Molière's works, and an acclaimed production of Shakespeare's Twelfth Night. Closed during the first half of Aug.

Aleksandriinskiy Theatre pl. Ostrovskovo 2 ☎ 312 15 45; Gostiniy Dvor metro; box office daily 11am–3pm & 4–8pm. A beautiful Neoclassical theatre designed by Rossi, with no fewer than four venues, used for opera and ballet as well as drama. Most of the forty-odd plays in its repertoire are by the nineteenth-century dramatist Alexander Ostrovsky, but you can also see Gogol's The Marriage and Wilde's Lady Windermere's Fan, while the St Petersburg Theatre of Classical Ballet stages favourites such as The Nutcracker and Swan Lake.

Baltiyskiy dom (Baltic House) Alexander Park 4 ☎ 232 335 39, ⓦ www.baltichouse.spb.ru; Gorkovskaya metro; box office daily noon–3pm &

4–7pm. The Baltiyskiy dom's Farce Theatre is the main crowd-puller, while the Small Stage puts on romances and comedies. However, the real attraction is the wealth of talent at the two international drama festivals held here (see p.377).

BDT (Bolshoy dramaticheskiy teatr) nab. reki Fontanki 65 ☏310 92 42; Gostiniy Dvor metro; box office daily 11am–3pm & 4–7pm. The city's most heavyweight theatre, whose actors' talents have long been wasted on leaden stagings of Chekhov, Gogol and other Russian classics. More recent productions have included Stoppard's *Arcadia* and Strindberg's *The Father*. At the *malaya stena* (studio theatre) you can see works in progress, drama competitions and festival shows. In July and August, the main auditorium often hosts performances of *Swan Lake* and *Giselle* by soloists from the Mariinskiy.

Interior Theatre (Interierniy teatr) Nevskiy pr. 104 ☏273 14 54; Mayakovskaya metro. Stories and legends from the history of St Petersburg imaginatively enacted for audiences of 5–12-year-olds, plus productions of plays for adults, such as *Hamlet*. Worth visiting just to see the costumes and models, like Madame Tussaud's redone in the style of *Frankenstein*. Closed mid-July to mid-Sept.

Komissarzhevskiy Drama Theatre (Teatr imeni V.F. Komissarzhevskoy, or KDF), Italyanskaya ul. 19 ☏315 53 55; Nevskiy Prospekt/Gostiniy Dvor metro; box office noon–3pm & 4–7pm. Known for intense realist dramas that are particularly inaccessible to non-Russian speakers, the KDF has tried to widen its appeal by staging farces such as Woody Allen's *A Midsummer Night's Sex Comedy*. Closed Mon & Tues.

Lensoviet Theatre Vladimirskiy pr. 12 ☏113 21 91; Vladimirskaya/Dostoyevskaya metro. The performances on its second, smaller stage are especially good. Their repertoire includes *Waiting for Godot*, Pinter's *The Lover*, Bruckner's *Voychek*, and Nabokov's *King, Queen, Knave*.

Maliy Dramatic Theatre (Maliy dramaticheskiy teatr), ul. Rubinshteyna 18 ☏113 20 78, ⓦwww.mdt-dodin.ru; Mayakovskiy metro; box office daily noon–7.30pm. Under director Lev Dodin, this formerly provincial troupe has gained an international reputation and numerous prizes, including an Olivier Award, for its coruscating productions of

the classics – though its performances of contemporary works are often less assured. Repertoire includes *The Seagull*, *Uncle Vanya*, *Play Without a Name*, *Gaudeamus*, *The Master and Margarita* and a nine-and-a-half-hour version of Dostoyevsky's *The Possessed*.

Priyut komedianta (Comedians' Refuge) Sadovaya ul. 27 ☏310 33 14; Sadovaya/Sennaya Ploshchad metro. Renowned for Yuri Tomoshevsky's adaptations of prose and poetry readings from the "Silver Age" of Russian literature, but also stages the alcoholic epic known abroad as *Moscow Stations*, Fassbinder's *I Only Want to be Loved*, and Capek's *Uneasy Tango*. Closed June 25–Aug 1.

Theatre on Liteyniy (Dramaticheskiy teatr na Liteynom), Liteyniy pr. 51 ☏273 53 35; Mayakovskaya/Ploshchad Vosstaniya metro. This company features some of St Petersburg's best actors, and won a prize in the 1998 Golden Mask awards for O'Neill's *Moon for the Misbegotten*. Shakespeare, Molière, Tolstoy and Sophocles feature in its diverse classical repertoire. The only theatre in the city with wheelchair access. Closed July.

Yusupov Palace Theatre nab. reki Moyki 94 ☏314 98 83. This gorgeous private theatre occasionally hosts concerts and light opera.

Puppetry, musicals and circus

Bolshoy Puppet Theatre (Bolshoy teatr kukol), ul. Nekrasova 10 ☏273 66 72; 15min from Chernyshevskaya/Mayakovskaya metro; box office daily 10.30am–3pm & 4–6pm. Programmes aimed at kids aged 3–10, which don't always involve puppets. Its repertoire includes *Snow White*, *Little Red Riding Hood* and *The Tale of Yemelya*.

Children's Ice Theatre (Detskiy Ledoviy teatr) Ligovskiy pr. 148 ☏112 86 25, ⓦwww .Russian-theater-on-ice.com; Ligovskiy Prospekt metro. Dramas and spectacles on ice, appealing to children of all ages.

Circus at Avtovo (Tsirk na Avtovo) Avtovskaya ul. 1 ☏184 68 43; Avtovo metro; box office daily 10am–7pm. Traditional circus performances and spectacles on specific themes, including a "Rhapsody on Ice" show with all the performers on iceboards or skates. Shows start at noon, 3pm & 6pm every day except Mon.

Demmi Marionette Theatre (Teatr marionetok imeni Demmeni) Nevskiy pr. 52 ☎ 311 21 56; Nevskiy Prospekt/Gostiniy Dvor metro; box office daily 10.30am–2pm & 3.15–6pm. Founded in 1918, this marionette (stringed puppet) theatre has won a bunch of awards at international puppet festivals.

Fairytale Puppet Theatre (Kukolniy teatr skazki) Moskovskiy pr. 21 ☎ 388 00 31; Moskovskie Vorota metro; box office Tues–Sun 10.30–noon & 1.30–4pm. Performances aimed at children aged 5 and over, including *Pinocchio*, *Thumbelina*, *The Nutcracker and the Mouse King* and *The Tale of Lazy Ivan*. Closed Mon.

Mimigranty Clown-Mime Theatre Rizhskiy pr. 23, Block 2 ☎ 251 63 28; tram #28; box office Mon–Fri & Sun 1–5pm. When they're not clowning around on the streets, Mimigranty can be found in their theatre on the seedy side of the Fontanka. Their repertoire includes *The Circus of Shardam-S*, by the cult writer Daniil Kharms, Pinter's *The Caretaker* and an improvisation for clowns entitled *Comedy with Murder*.

Music Hall (Myuzik Holl) Alexander Park 4 ☎ 232 92 01; Gorkovskaya metro; box office daily noon–3pm & 4–6pm. In the same complex as the Baltiyskiy dom and the Planetarium, it stages *Dr Dolittle from Zverinskaya Street* for children, and a Busby Berkley-style musical, *St Petersburg*

Crescendo, besides hosting visiting circus troupes from abroad.

State Circus (Tsirk) nab. reki Fontanki 3 ☎ 314 84 78, ⊛ www.circus.spb.ru; Nevskiy Prospekt/Gostiniy Dvor metro; box office daily 11am–7pm. Russia's oldest circus, two blocks north of Anichkov most. Trapeze artists, acrobats, illusionists, performing bears and seals – a real old-style show that you'll either love or hate. Tickets can usually be bought on the spot; foreigners pay $9 surcharge, children are admitted for free. Performances at 7pm on Tues, Wed & Fri, and at 11.30am, 3pm & 7pm on Sat & Sun. Closed mid-July to mid-Sept.

Theatre of Young Spectators (Teatr yunykh zriteley, or TYuZ) Pionerskaya pl. 1 ☎ 310 18 18; Pushkinskaya metro; box office Tues–Sun 11am–2pm & 4–6pm. Musicals and dance shows aimed at children and teenagers, including Saint-Exupéry's *The Little Prince*. Performances start at 11am & 6pm. Also hosts the international festival of modern dance in July.

Zazerkalye (Through the Looking Glass) ul. Rubinshteyna 13 ☎ 112 51 35; Vladimirskaya/Dostoevskaya metro; box office daily noon–3pm & 4–7pm. Colourful opera and ballet "for children", that's also enjoyable for adults. Recent productions include an opera-musical based on *The Hobbit*, and Puccini's *La Bohème*. Around New Year, they sometimes do English-language shows.

Film

Although local director Andrei Balabanov wowed Russian audiences with his brutal thrillers *Brat* (Brother) and *Brat 2*, the vast majority of **films** screened in the city are Hollywood blockbusters or Euro B-movies, dubbed into Russian with varying degrees of sophistication – a practice that's even applied to foreign films at the city's one remaining arthouse cinema, Dom kino. More positively, many long-neglected local cinemas have been refurbished, with comfy seating, Dolby Digital sound and sometimes also air-conditioning. All cinemas are non-smoking; none takes credit cards or phone bookings.

To find out **what's showing**, see the Friday edition of the *St Petersburg Times*. If you understand Russian you can peruse a weekly list posted outside the Avrora Cinema on Nevskiy prospekt (where several cinemas are located), or obtain film schedules at any cinema by calling ℡064, 050 or 089. The **Festival of Festivals** in June is the best time to catch new Russian and foreign movies. Other film festivals are held in Vyborg (May) and Novgorod (early Nov).

Avrora Nevskiy pr. 60 ℡064, ⓦwww.avrora.spb.ru; **Gostiniy Dvor metro**. The city's oldest cinema, founded in 1913, has now been fully modernized. Besides the main feature in the auditorium, they sometimes show other films in the café. Tickets $2.50–13.

Barrikada Nevskiy pr. 15 ℡312 53 86; **Nevskiy Prospekt metro**. One of the smaller, older downtown cinemas, whose sound system has been improved, but little else. Tickets $1.50–7.

Dom kino Karavannaya ul. 12 ℡314 06 38; **Nevskiy Prospekt/Gostiniy Dvor metro**. This wonderful Style Moderne building is the professional clubhouse for the city's filmmakers, and occasionally screens retrospectives. It has a bar and restaurant. Tickets $2–3.

Kolizey Nevskiy pr. 100 ℡272 87 75; **Mayakovskaya metro**. New, very comfortable two-screen cinema whose amenities include VIP boxes and divans for partying or horizontal viewing, and three bars. Tickets $1–7.

Kristall Palace Nevskiy pr. 72 ℡272 23 82; **Mayakovskaya metro**. The first cinema in St Petersburg to be upgraded, it mostly screens blockbusters – either Russian or American. Tickets $1–6.50.

Mirazh Bolshoy pr. 35 ℡238 07 58; **Petrogradskaya metro**. The best-equipped cinema on Petrograd Side. Tickets $2–8.

Molodyozhniy Sadovaya ul. 12 ℡311 05 45; **Gostiniy Dvor metro**. A run-down complex with two screens, which sometimes features retrospectives based on the oeuvre of a single director or actor. Tickets $2–3.

Pariziana Nevskiy pr. 80 ℡273 48 13; **Mayakovskaya metro**. Untouched by modernization, it offers a Soviet-style film-going experience. Tickets $2–3.

The visual arts

St Petersburg has dozens of **private galleries** and **exhibition halls**, in addition to the temporary displays which can be seen in its museums and state galleries. Most of the private galleries cater for the tourist market and are stuffed to the gills with picture-postcard paintings of the city, alongside *matryoshka dolls*, balalaikas and other folk objects. However, if you search hard enough there's some decent art on display, too, while at the city's best-known exhibition spaces you're guaranteed to find something interesting at most times of the year – look out especially for temporary exhibitions at the Benois Wing of the Russian Museum (p.142), or in the Engineers' Castle. In addition, there are countless **street artists** showing off their talents along Nevskiy prospekt and outside the major tourist attractions.

Borey Liteyniy pr. 58 ℡273 38 37; **Mayakovskaya metro; Tues–Sat noon–8pm**. Hosts excellent exhibitions, including shows by experimental artists and work by cult figures such as David Byrne. There's a fabulous art bookshop at the back.

Centre of National Cultures Nevskiy pr. 166 ℡277 12 16; **Ploshchad Vosstaniya metro; Tues–Sun 11am–7pm**. Solo exhibitions by independent artists, ranging from batiks to handmade toys or plastic carvings. Accepts Visa, MC.

Golubaya gostinaya (Blue Hall) Bolshaya Morskaya ul. 38 ℡315 74 14; **Nevskiy Prospekt/Gostiniy Dvor metro; daily noon–7pm**. Outlet for members of the St Petersburg Artists' Union, that also deals in Socialist Realist artworks (export documentation and a framing service is available on site). All major cards.

Manège (Manezh) pl. Dekabristov ☎ 314 82 53; Nevskiy Prospekt metro; 11am–6pm, closed Thurs. Used for temporary exhibitions by the Artists' Union and others, including an annual showcase of contemporary art in August, and an international Biennale in late July.

Masters' Guild Nevskiy pr. 82 ☎ 279 09 79; Mayakovskaya metro; daily 11am–7pm. High-quality, long-established gallery specializing in well-known artists formerly involved in the Stergovlitsi and LOSKh movements. Export documentation available.

Palitra Malaya Morskaya ul. 5 ☎ 272 48 80, ℮ palitra-gallery@solaris.ru; Nevskiy Prospekt metro; Tues–Fri 11am–7pm, Sat noon–6pm. One of the best-known galleries for painting, graphic art and sculpture by local artists, many of whom were "underground" figures in Soviet times. The Palitra art café (☎ 312 34 35), next door, has live jazz and blues every evening.

Pechatnya (Printing Press) in the Peter and Paul Fortress ☎ 238 07 42; Gorkovskaya metro; daily 11am–6pm. Besides the woodcuts, etchings and linocuts on display, you can see artists at work in this refurbished Petrine-era printer's. All major cards.

Pushkinskaya 10 entry through arch of Ligovskiy pr. 53; Ploshchad Vosstaniya metro. A longstanding artists' squat that's become part of the mainstream art world (see p.215). Diverse exhibitions at the KINO-FOT film gallery (Wed–Sun 3–7pm) on the seventh floor of block A; FOTOimage gallery (Sat 4–7pm) on the second floor of block C; and the Techno-Art Centre (Tues–Sat 3–8pm) and Gallery of Experimental Sound on the first and third floors of block D.

Sol-Art Stolyanoy per. 15 ☎ 327 30 82; Gostiniy Dvor or Mayakovskaya metro; daily 10am–6pm. Gallery dealing in contemporary St Petersburg artists, whose paintings and prints are stacked alongside Palekh boxes, *matryoshka* dolls and other souvenirs, in the lobby of the Museum of Decorative and Applied Arts (see p.204). Amex, DC, Visa.

Shopping

O lder Russians conditioned by decades of queuing and carrying an *avoska* ("just in case" bag) find the notion of **shopping** for pleasure strange, but those with money revel in the diversity of products and today's teenagers are as label-conscious and shopping-happy as any in Europe. While the mall-culture that's such a feature of Moscow is still in its infancy here, suburban mega-stores are accustoming families to the joys of pushing a trolley round Ikea. For visitors, it's never been easier to buy foodstuffs, souvenirs and gifts; the main bargains are CDs, porcelain, lacquer-ware, Soviet memorabilia, caviar and vodka. If you're going to visit Novgorod, traditional handicrafts are far cheaper there than in St Petersburg. Shop assistants in Soviet times were famously rude, and it's still unusual to be treated courteously unless you're a big-spender in a ritzy salon. Some former state stores still insist on the infuriating system where customers pay at the *kassa* before collecting their goods, which entails queuing at least twice, but most new shops use the one-stop system.

Antiques and icons

Antiques are loosely defined in Russia; anything pre-1960 can be deemed part of the national heritage and needs an **export licence** from the Ministry of Culture (see p.26). Lovely as they are, bronze and silver **samovars** (tea urns) are probably not worth the hassle of exporting legally (you can find them in flea markets abroad), and impossible to get past the scanners at the airport. The same goes for **icons** – although contemporary icons which can look as fine as antiques, yet aren't subject to controls, are sold at the *lavka* (church shop) in the Alexander Nevsky Monastery and various churches in the city. However, the samovars made today aren't worth buying at all.

Apraksin dvor off Sadovaya ul.; **Gostiniy Dvor metro**. Two antiques shops and an outlet for Lomonosov porcelain factory seconds make this seedy old commercial arcade worth a visit, while you can occasionally find wonderful 1930–1960s tea and coffee services in the flea market in the yard. Beware of pickpockets.

Peterburg Nevskiy pr. 54; **Gostiniy Dvor metro**. A salon to window-shop antique furniture, statuettes, icons and porcelain, even if you can't afford their prices. Major cards. Daily 10am–8pm.

Rapsodiya (Rhapsody) Bolshaya Konyushennaya ul. **13**. Expensive furniture, silverware, bronzes and ceramics. Major cards. Daily 11am–8pm.

Russian Icon Gallery Bolshaya Konyushennaya ul. **15**; **Nevskiy Prospekt metro**. Contemporary icons, and the restoration of antique ones. Export documentation arranged. Tues–Sat 10am–6pm.

Staraya Kniga (Old Book) Kamennoostrovskiy pr. **17**; **Gorkovskaya metro**. Icons, old books, furniture, bronzes, porcelain and antique Soviet memorabilia. No cards. Mon–Sat 10am–7pm, Sun 11am–4pm.

Books, maps and prints

Books about the Hermitage, the Russian Museum and the Imperial palaces are widely available in English and other languages (the Russian version of the same book is usually cheaper). If you can read Russian, bookshops offer a feast of literature and non-fiction at low prices (hardbacks especially), whereas the selection of imported books in other languages (on Russian history and society, or foreign fiction) is inevitably limited. The same is true of **maps**; locally produced ones in Cyrillic script are far more up-to-date than foreign maps. Glossy **calendars** featuring views of the city or the Imperial palaces, Russian icons or Old Masters, cost $4–5, and reproduction posters and **prints** (on Soviet themes or historic lithographs of the city) even less. An original litho or etching will set you back anything from $10 upwards. Legally, a **licence** is required to take books or prints more than twenty years old out of the country.

Angliya (England) nab. reki Fontanki 40; Gostiniy Dvor metro. Stocks all kinds of books in English, with a good selection on Russia (including guidebooks, maps and dictionaries), and the city's widest range of bestsellers. It has a relaxed, Anglophile ambience, and hosts art exhibitions and literary events in collaboration with the British Council. Major cards. Daily 10am–7pm.

Bukvoed (Pedant) Nevskiy pr. 13 & 20, Nevskiy Prospekt metro; ul. Pestelya 23, Chernyshevskaya metro; Kirochnaya ul. 23, Chernyshevskaya metro. Hot on the heels of Snark (see below), this new book and stationery chain has plenty of art books and a fair selection of history and fiction in foreign languages, plus posters, calendars and repro prints and posters. All major cards. Mon–Sat 9am–10pm, Sun 10am–10pm.

Dom knigi (House of Books) Nevskiy pr. 28 & 62, Nevskiy Prospekt/Gostiniy Dvor metro. The historic bookstore in the Singer building has a great range of maps, art books, posters and calendars on the second floor, and a smattering of cheap novels in English downstairs, where you'll also find stationery, CD-ROMs and software. There's a new branch opposite the Anichkov Palace. All major cards. Mon–Sat 9am–10pm, Sun 9am–9pm.

Dom knigi na Liteynom (House of Books on Liteyniy) Liteyniy pr. 30; Chernyshevskaya metro. Russian and secondhand foreign books;

prints, maps, calendars and stationery. No cards. Mon–Sat 10am–9pm, Sun 11am–7pm.

Dom voennoy knigi (House of Military Books) Nevskiy pr. 20, Nevskiy Prospekt metro. Despite its name it stocks everything from trashy romances and blockbusters to art books, posters, CD-ROMs and model kits. No cards. Mon–Sat 9am–10pm, Sun 10am–10pm.

Mir pechati (World of Print) Sadovaya ul. 25, Sennaya Ploshchad metro; ul. Chaykovskovo 65, Chernyshevskaya metro. Two stores with a wide range of antique, reproduction and contemporary prints, postcards and posters. No cards. Daily 9am–8pm.

Pechatnya (Printing Press) in the Peter and Paul Fortress; Gorkovskaya metro. A Petrine-era printing house that sells a fantastic range of woodcuts, etchings and linocuts – some repro antiques, others limited editions by contemporary artists. All major cards. Daily 11am–6pm.

Snark Nevskiy pr. 87/2, Ploshchad Vosstaniya metro; Zagorodniy pr. 21, Vladimirskaya metro; pr. Chernyshevskovo 17, Chernyshevskaya metro; and other locations. Browser-friendly chain with a full range of Russian and some foreign books, helpful staff, discounts for members, and plenty for kids. The flagship branch on pl. Vosstaniya is open 24hr, most of the others 9am–9pm daily.

Clothing and accessories

While the city is awash with stores selling Italian, French and US designer clothing, prices are higher than abroad, and Russians with money to travel often restock their wardrobes in Paris or London. For visitors, the only bargains are Russian **linen** and **fur** hats and coats (if you've no moral scruples about fur). Fake fur **hats** are a popular souvenir, but if you're going to wear a real fur *ushanka* here, avoid cheap rabbit-fur versions, as Russians look down on people wearing "road kill". If you've money to burn or an interest in fashion you should check out some boutiques devoted to Russian designers.

Alexander Petrov ul. Dekabristov 34; Sennaya Ploshchad metro. All Petrov's clothes involve either fish skin (sazan, carp, trout and salmon) or fur. If fish skin clothing and accessories sounds weird, the peoples of the far Russian North have been using such materials for centuries. Major cards. Daily 10am–8pm.

Lilla Kisselenko Nevskiy pr. 3 and Malaya Sadovaya ul. 4; Nevskiy Prospekt metro. Two outlets for one of St Petersburg's trendiest women's couturiers. Kisselenko's Malaya Sadovaya salon is in a yard, and open Mon–Sat 11am–8pm, the Nevskiy emporium Mon–Fri 11am–6pm. No cards.

Slavyanskiy Stil (Slav Style) Pushkinskaya ul. 5, Ploshchad Vosstaniya metro; Nevskiy pr. 151, Aleksandra Nevskovo metro; Ⓦwww.linorusso.ru. These two shops sell fine linen products – blouses, skirts, shirts, tablecloths, sheets and duvet covers – for far less than you'd pay back home. The clothes are updates of traditional Russian designs: waist-less shirts buttoned at the collar and ankle-length sleeveless *sarafan*

dresses (with or without embroidery). Maestro, Union, Visa. Mon–Fri 10am–8pm, Sat & Sun 11am–8pm.

Tatyana Parfionova Nevskiy pr. 51; Mayakovskaya metro; Ⓦwww.parfionova.ru. Parfionova was the first St Petersburg designer to start her own fashion house, and her salon also sells *haute couture* by other designers. Amex, DC, Maestro, MC, Visa. Mon–Sat noon–8pm.

Voyentorg Nevskiy pr. 67; Mayakovskaya metro. A Soviet-era store catering to the armed forces, police and security guards, that stocks peaked caps, fake fur hats, Airborne Forces vests, parade uniforms, combat fatigues, badges and insignia (repro Soviet, today's military, Militia and OMON). Most items are sold to anyone who asks. No cards. Mon–Fri 10am–6pm.

Yelena Tsvetkova Nevskiy pr. 53; Mayakovskaya metro. A local designer whose salon is a few doors along from Parfionova's, her striking women's clothes and accessories use a lot of fur. Maestro, MC, Visa. Daily 10am–9pm.

Department stores

The city's **department stores** are a varied bunch. Passazh is great for window-shopping and the Grand Palace rules for fashion victims. Whether it's souvenirs, an item of clothing or some gadget that's required, the labyrinthine Gostiniy dvor offers an endless array of specialized shops; DLT is easier to find your way around but doesn't have the same scope; while the Moskovskiy stores in the Southern Suburbs are for those seeking bargains or a quasi-Soviet shopping experience.

DLT (Dom Leningradskoy Torgovli) Bolshaya Konyushennaya ul. 21–23; Nevskiy Prospekt metro. This store once catered to Tsarist officers and civil servants. Its lower floor has a vast range of toys (mostly imported, but there are some Russian ones hidden away) and cosmetics; head upstairs for lingerie, sportswear and shoes – there's even an outlet for Doc Martens. EC, MC, Visa. Mon–Sat 10am–9pm, Sun 11am–9pm.

Gostiniy dvor Nevskiy pr. 35, Gostiniy Dvor/Nevskiy Prospekt metro. An eighteenth-

century shopping bazaar divided into countless little stores selling CDs, lingerie, cosmetics, pet supplies, stationery and much else. There's an entire mini-store for kids with a play area, and several ATMs near the stairs. Beware of conmen on Dumskaya ulitsa. Maestro, Visa Electron. Daily 10am–10pm, Thurs till 10.30pm.

Grand Palace Nevskiy pr. 44; Gostiniy Dvor/Nevskiy Prospekt metro. Opened in 2003, this four-floor mall is devoted to fashion and fripperies, with exclusive outlets for Escada, Pal Zileri, Roccobarocco, Machiavelli, Femme Etoile, Christian Dior, Christian Lacroix and others, plus a chocolate boutique and jeweller's. Major cards. Daily 11am–9pm.

Moskovskiy univermag Moskovskiy pr. 205–207 & 220–222; Moskovskaya metro. Situated on the way to the airport, on both sides of the prospekt, these Soviet megastores sell souvenirs, fur hats, clothes, porcelain, chocolates, caviar and booze. Finding the right section and then the correct

kassa to pay can be a nightmare – or a taste of the old days to be savoured. MC, Visa. Mon–Sat 10am–9pm, Sun 11am–9pm.

Passazh Nevskiy pr. 48; Gostiniy Dvor/Nevskiy Prospekt metro. A few doors along from the Grand Palace, this stately nineteenth-century arcade has shops selling repro antiques, porcelain, glassware, shoes and cosmetics, with a well-stocked supermarket in the basement. Maestro, MC, Visa. Mon–Sat 10am–9pm, Sun 11am–9pm; supermarket till 10pm.

Lacquered boxes and tableware

After *matryoshka* dolls (see "Toys") the commonest souvenirs are **lacquered boxes**, varying in size and shape from pillboxes to jewellery caskets. Traditionally they were produced by four villages where the poor soil made handicrafts a better source of income than agriculture, each of which developed their own style, but nowadays imitations are widely produced and only connoisseurs know the differences between the Palekh, Fedosino, Khuly and Mstyora styles – which most people would lump together as lush, minutely detailed depictions of Russian fairytales, medieval cities or rural scenes. A smudgy machine-printed "Palekh" box costs $1–5, depending on the vendor or shop; quality, hand-painted boxes start at $5 and can exceed $100 for large compositions. Other "folk" products sold all over are birch-wood **bowls**, **spoons** and **platters** from Khokloma, painted with floral patterns in red, black and gold. Finally there are objects made from supple **birch-bark** – purses, handbags, slippers, lampshades, tablemats, coasters and fruit baskets – manufactured in Novgorod. All are widely available at wildly differing prices – shop around.

Lakir (Lacquer) Muchnoy per. 2; Sennaya Ploshchad metro. This shop on a side street near the Economics University sells nothing but lacquered boxes of all shapes, sizes and designs. No cards. Mon–Fri noon–5pm.

Russian Traditional Souvenirs ul. Chekhova 5; Ploshchad Vosstaniya metro. Manufactures and stocks a wide range of hand-painted nesting dolls, boxes, Easter eggs, bottle cases and decorative panels. Quite pricy

but the quality is good. Visa. Daily 10am–7pm.

Vernissazh nab. kanala Griboedova; Nevskiy Prospekt metro. The city's main outdoor tourist market, beside the Church of the Saviour on the Blood, has an infinite variety of boxes, *matryoshky*, Khokloma bowls, fur hats and watches. Some stalls take credit cards; haggling is acceptable at most of them. Daily 8am–9pm (or later).

Markets and food and drink stores

While local groceries stock a range of Russian and foreign products, the freshest produce is found at **markets** (*rynok*), where vendors tempt buyers with nibbles of fruit, cheese, sour cream, ham, pickles and other homemade delights. Although large stores may accept credit cards, it's wiser to assume that you'll need to pay cash. Shopping for gifts, the best buys are **caviar** and **vodka**. Caviar should be bought in a delicatessen or supermarket rather than a market, where the stuff on sale is almost certainly of illicit origin and may be unsafe to eat. You can take out as much red caviar as you wish, but no more than 250 grams of black. Vodka and other spirits are best purchased in a *firmeny magazin* such as Liviz.

Markets

Kuznechniy Kuznechniy per. 3; **Vladimirskaya/Dostoevskaya metro**. The best-stocked and most expensive market hall in the city, up the road from Dostoyevsky's last apartment (see p.217). Worth a visit just for the atmosphere. Mon–Sat 8am–7pm, Sun 8am–4pm.

Maltsevskiy ul. Nekrasova 52; tram #16 or #25 from Ploshchad Vosstaniya. Still better known by its former name, Nekrasovskiy, this is good for beans, fruit 'n' veg and oriental spices, but the "fresh" butter and cream can be rancid. Potatoes are sold in the basement, reached by steps behind the market. Mon–Sat 8am–7pm, Sun 8am–4pm.

Sennoy Moskovskiy pr. 4–6; Sennaya Ploshchad metro. This outdoor market just off Sennaya ploshchad is good for seasonal produce in the summer, but rather thin at other times of the year. Mon–Sat 8am–7pm, Sun 8am–4pm.

Sytniy Sytninskaya pl. 3–5; Gorkovskaya metro. Another rewarding market for Caucasian food produce, where the chefs of some of the best Georgian restaurants in town do their shopping. Mon–Sat 8am–7pm, Sun 8am–4pm.

Vasileostrovskiy Bolshoy pr. 14/16; Vasileostrovskaya metro. Also known as the Andreevskiy, after the Church of St Andrew across the road, this eighteenth-century market hall was closed for modernization at the time of writing, but you may still find a small outdoor flea market along 6-ya liniya, around the corner.

Specialist food and drink stores

Baltic Bread Grechiskiy pr. 25, tram #5 or #7 from Ploshchad Vosstaniya metro; Bolshoy pr. 80, Petrogradskaya metro. These two outlets sell over 200 types of freshly baked loaves, rolls, sweet and savoury pastries and gateaux, and serve tea and coffee, too. No cards. Grechiskiy pr. branch: daily 10am–9pm; Bolshoy pr. branch till 10pm.

Chocolate Museum Nevskiy pr. 17 (in the passage of the Stroganov Palace yard), Gostiniy Dvor/Nevskiy Prospekt metro; ul. Zhukovskovo

18, Ploshchad Vosstaniya metro. Two outlets for handmade dark and milk chocolates – liquors and other soft-centres sold by weight. There are also individually moulded pieces; a tiny St Isaac's costs $2, a bust of Lenin $10, a chess set $20. Amex, DC, JCB, Maestro, MC, Visa. Daily 11am–9pm.

Dagestan Nevskiy pr. 172; Ploshchad Aleksandra Nevskovo 1 metro. Specializes in Dagestani cognacs (some extremely costly, in cut-glass presentation bottles), plus vodka, French wines and liquors. Electron, MC, Visa. Mon–Sat 9am–9pm.

Gino-no-Taki pr. Chernyshevskovo 17; Chernyshevskaya metro. Japanese mini-market attached to the *Gino-no-Taki* restaurant, which sells tofu, dried seaweed, green tea, Japanese household goods and clothing. All major cards except Amex. Daily 9am–8pm.

Kalinka Stockmann Finlyandskiy pr. 1; Ploshchad Lenina metro. Finnish supermarket with a galactic range of imported food – from avocados and broccoli to Worcester sauce – at jaw-dropping prices. All major cards. Daily 10am–9pm.

Liviz Nevskiy pr. 21 & 43, Nevskiy Prospekt or Ploshchad Vosstaniya metro; ul. Chaykovskovo 13, Chernyshevskaya metro; ul. Zhukovskovo, Mayakovskaya metro; Sinoptskaya nab. 56, Ploshchad Aleksandra Nevskovo metro. A chain of outlets for the entire range of Liviz vodkas, plus Moldavian, Georgian and French wines and other alcohol, all guaranteed not to be bootlegs. No cards. Daily 9am–8pm.

Pchelovodstvo (Bee-Keeping) Liteyniy pr. 42; Mayakovskaya metro. All kinds of fresh honey from the Rostov region, plus creams and remedies made from bee pollen and royal jelly, and honey-flavoured herbal teas. No cards. Mon–Sat 10am–6pm.

Siva Bolshaya Zelenina ul. 14/18; Chkalovskaya metro. One of two huge supermarkets on the Petrograd Side, stocking Russian and imported products. The store is nearer to Chkalovskaya metro than *Super Babylon*. All major cards. Mon–Thurs & Sun 10am–9pm, Fri & Sat 10am–10pm.

Super Babylon Maliy pr. 54/56; Chkalovskaya metro. Siva's rival superstore sells everything from groceries and household goods through to DIY materials, and has a fantastic bakery. All major cards. Daily 24hr.

Yeliseyev's Nevskiy pr. 56; Gostiniy Dvor metro. St Petersburg's equivalent of Harrod's (see p.67), this specialist Russian food store in a gorgeous Style Moderne building stocks an above-average range of caviar, smoked fish, alcohol and chocolates. The left-hand hall has the grandest decor. Amex, MC,

Visa. Mon–Fri 10am–9pm, Sat & Sun 11am–9pm.

Zhar-Pititsa pr. Bakunina 2; Ploshchad Vosstaniya metro. One of many retail outlets for the Krupskaya Confectionery Factory (named after Lenin's wife), a well-known Soviet manufacturer that's still going strong. No cards. Mon–Fri 10.30am–6.30pm.

Music, videos and CD-ROMs

Hollywood and Microsoft may fume, but Russia remains the world's largest market for **pirate** CDs, DVDs, videos, cassettes and CD-ROMs. Kiosks in the Nevskiy prospekt underpasses near Gostiniy dvor and in metro stations all over town sell bootlegs, while chain stores stock them alongside licensed products – and will happily tell you which is which. The quality of pirated products varies from abysmal to indistinguishable from the real thing, but prices are so much lower ($3–4 for a CD, $5–10 for a CD-ROM) that Russians are willing to risk the odd dud – especially when they can buy the entire recorded works of almost any top artist on a single CD-ROM. The same goes for computer games and software – even though it's said that three out of four programmes have some kind of defect or virus.

Aisberg (Iceberg) Nevskiy pr. 38, 67 & 87, Nevskiy Prospekt, Mayakovskaya or Ploshchad Vosstaniya metro; Kamennoostrovskiy pr. 38, Petrogradskaya metro. Music and video chain with thousands of CDs, DVDs and CD-ROMs. No cards. Daily 24hr.

Kinomir (Film World) Nevskiy pr. 88, Ploshchad Vosstaniya metro; Vladimirskiy pr. 18/2, Vladimirskaya metro. Sells videos and DVDs of all kinds of films in Russian, and a selection of blockbusters and art movies in other languages. No cards. Mon–Sat 11am–10pm, Sun 11am–9pm.

Klassica Mikhaylovskaya ul. 2; Nevskiy Prospekt metro. The city's oldest music shop is still one of the best places to buy classical, opera, folk and church music on CDs, tapes and vinyl; books and videos about music, and scores. Major cards. Daily 11am–3pm & 4–7.30pm.

Otkryty Mir (Open World) Malaya Morskaya ul. 16; Nevskiy Prospekt metro. Stocks a wide range of classical, jazz and ethnic music on CD, DVD, VHS, cassettes and vinyl. No cards. Mon–Sat 11am–8pm, Sun noon–7pm.

Titanik Nevskiy pr. 158, Ploshchad Aleksandra Nevskovo metro; Liteyniy pr. 57, Mayakovskaya metro; Kirochnaya ul. 17, Chernyshevskaya metro; Zagorodniy pr. 10, Vladimirskaya/Dostoevskaya metro. Chain with a vast array of music CDs, Hollywood and Soviet movies and cartoons (some in English), and CD-ROM games. No cards. Daily 24hr.

Severnaya Lira (Northern Lyre) Nevskiy pr. 26; Nevskiy Prospekt/Gostiniy Dvor metro. Sheet music, CDs, music books and musical instruments. Major cards. Mon–Sat 10am–8pm, Sun 11am–7pm.

Porcelain, glass and crystal

St Petersburg has a long tradition of manufacturing **porcelain** (*farfor*), glass and crystal ware; most of the factories producing them today were founded to supply the court and nobility with settings for their banquets. Russian Futurists leapt at the chance to turn these status symbols into utensils for the masses – the first Soviet ceramics bore the Romanov seal, over-painted with revolutionary imagery. Today, such porcelain is highly prized and requires an export licence (as does anything pre-revolutionary), but high-quality reproductions are easily found and freely exportable. Among the most popular are Empire Style blue, gold and white patterns from Tver and Novgorod; Constructivist motifs from the 1920s, and sets celebrating the Moscow metro or Soviet feats in space. You can buy a single cup and saucer for $4–6, a dinner plate for $7–8, a teapot for $15–50, and a full tea or dinner service for $50–300 (the more gilding the dearer). Gizhel ceramic figurines aren't nearly such good value: a lot of what's on offer is rubbish, or wildly overpriced (like the novelty figures of New Russians at play). Cut **glass** (*steklo*) or **crystal** (*khrustal*) glasses, bowls, ornamental vases and knick-knacks are a feature of most Russian homes, but the designs tend to be very 1970s – which may be to your taste or not.

Lomonosov Porcelain Grand Hotel Europe, Nevskiy Prospekt metro; Nevskiy pr. 160, Ploshchad Aleksandra Nevskovo metro; Vladimirskiy pr. 7, Vladimirskaya metro; pr. Obukhovskoy Oboroniy 151, Lomonosovskaya metro; ⓦ www.lomonosovporcelain.ru.
Europe's third-oldest porcelain factory (est. 1744) has over 500 items in its catalogue. Prices are marked up at the *Europe*; do your shopping at Nevskiy pr. 160 (daily 10am–8pm), or the factory showroom (Mon–Fri 10am–7pm, Sat & Sun 11am–5pm). To reach this from Lomonosovskaya metro, head towards the Neva embankment and turn left (north). Packing and export service

available. Amex, DC, JCB, Maestro, MC, Visa.
Russian Museum Inzhenernaya ul. 4; Gostiniy Dvor/Nevskiy Prospekt metro. The museum shop sells reproductions of some of the Futurist crockery in its storerooms, with designs by Malevich, Rodchenko, Popova and El Lissitsky. Major cards. Mon 10am–5pm, Wed–Sun 10am–6pm.
World of Crystal ul. Sedova 69; Lomonosovskaya metro. The showroom of the Gus Khrustalniy factory is in the same district as the Lomonosov factory, and offers a big choice of crystal tableware, vases and curios. No cards. Mon–Fri 10am–8pm, Sat & Sun 11am–6pm.

Soviet memorabilia

Soviet memorabilia is as popular with tourists as it was when the USSR still existed, but most of the posters, uniforms and watches on sale today are **reproductions** rather than originals; vintage posters fetch $100 at auctions, and embroidered banners are heading that way. About the only genuine items that are ubiquitous are **lapel pins** (*znachki*). In Soviet times, every sports club, factory or hobby society had its own and collectors traded them – *Pravda* once rebuked the Plumbers' Union for producing a badge shaped like a toilet. Nowadays, *znachki* made of semi-precious metals, or featuring Trotsky or Beria, are rare enough to be valuable – but there are millions of enamelled alloy or plastic badges around. Repro **posters** ($2–5) are sold in many bookshops besides the one below and are currently popular with Russians who never experienced Soviet life – whereas military fur hats, peaked caps or pointy felt Budyonny hats (named after the Civil War cavalry commander) are strictly for tourists (or conscripts). They're sold at street stalls near all the major tourist sites, and at the Voyentorg (see "Clothing and accessories").

Main Post Office Pochamtskaya ul. 9; trolleybus #5 or #22 from Nevskiy pr.
Cosmonauts, collective farms and Marxism-Leninism are among the themes celebrated by Soviet commemorative stamps, sold at the philately booth (#11) in the Main Post

Office (see p.108). Many of the designs are exquisite, and stamps cost only $0.20 each. No cards. Mon–Sat 9am–7pm, Sun 10am–4pm.
Mint Shop in the Peter and Paul Fortress; Gorkovskaya metro. Sells certified replicas of

△ Soviet memorabilia – reproductions outnumber originals

military, anniversary and commemorative medals bearing the visages of tsars, Lenin, Stalin, marshals or cosmonauts, issued by the Mint over three centuries. Major cards. Daily 10am–6pm.

Knizhniy Salon Nevskiy pr. 94 & 114; Mayakovskaya/Ploshchad Vosstaniya metro. This bookstore and stationery chain

stocks a variety of cheap repro posters and fridge magnets extolling the Communist Party or agitating against alcoholism – the one of a guy refusing a glass of vodka adorns the ice box in many a Russian home. No cards. Mon–Fri 10am–11pm, Sat & Sun 10am–10pm.

Sports equipment

Hunting and fishing are widely popular in Russia (obliging every cabinet minister to claim that their summer vacation was spent doing one or the other), while the younger generation is into inline skating, skateboarding or martial arts. For visitors invited to go camping in the wilderness – or spend a weekend at someone's *dacha* – the following specialist stores may prove useful.

Frankardi nab. Bolshoy reki Nevki 124; Chernaya Rechka metro. Everything for skiing, snowboarding, ice-skating and jet-skiing. No cards. Daily 10am–8pm.

Motolyubitel Apraksin dvor, korpus 1, lock-ups 50-63 ☏310 01 54; Sadovaya metro. Sells German, Italian and Hungarian racing and mountain bikes, helmets and other gear, plus a range of spares. No cards. Daily 11am–9pm.

Soldat Udachi (Soldier of Fortune) ul. Nekrasova 37, Cheryshevskaya metro; Bolshoy pr. 17, Vasileostrovskaya metro. Two macho outlets for camping, hunting and fishing gear, Swiss Army knives, Maglite torches,

GPS devices, martial arts equipment, reproduction antique weapons and modern military firearms, right up to anti-tank rockets. No cards. Mon–Sat 10am–6pm.

Sportmaster Moskovskiy pr. 10; Sadovaya metro. Skis and skiwear, swimwear, tennis racquets, trainers and camping equipment. Major cards. Daily 10am–9pm.

Techno Sport Centre Morskaya Hotel, pl. Morskoy Slavy 1; minibus #K-129 from Primorskaya metro. Devoted to clothing and gear for yachting, surfing, scuba diving, fishing, bird watching and other outdoor pursuits. Major cards. Daily 10am–10pm.

Toys

Nesting dolls or *matryoshky*, are a cliché souvenir and symbol of Russia. Invented in 1890 at the children's workshop of the Abramtsevo artists' colony, the original design of a headscarfed peasant woman was subverted during perestroika, when Gorby, Lenin *et al* appeared – since followed by Putin, Bush and Bin Laden. A recent version panders to Islamophobia with Bin Laden, Arafat, a Chechen suicide bomber and a miniature Koran. All these are sold at stalls, shops and museums throughout the centre. You may also see traditional wooden toys from Novgorod, such as **dancing bears** and **bears on a see-saw**, which are also produced in joke forms such as two bears taking it in turns to work on a computer, or one bear spanking the other with a broom. Young children will also like the wooden building blocks in the style of Petersburg palaces or medieval kremlins, and the cut-out paper dolls in antique Russian costumes, sold on the lower floor of the DLT (see "Department Stores").

Doll Museum Kamskaya ul. 8 ☏327 72 24, ⓦ www.russiandolls.ru; tram #1 or minibus #K-249 from Vasileostrovskaya metro. Sells handmade dolls by local designers, perhaps better treated as art than consigned to the

playroom. If you're bringing your kids along, phone to check that the museum isn't mounting an adults-only show (see p.171), and come on Sunday, when children can make their own dolls and the admission charge doesn't seem unjust. MC, Visa. Tues–Sun 11am–6pm.

Toy Museum ul. Vsevoloda 22/32; Petrogradskaya metro. This private museum also charges you to look around, and sells artistic handmade toys at collectors' prices. Open 11am–6pm; closed Mon & the last Tues of each month.

Yuri Lesnik ⓒylesnik@hotmail.com. Yuri is an avant-garde artist and toy-maker, who specializes in handmade bath toys in the form of sponge cubes (*kyubiki*) that turn into dragons or tortoises when squeezed inside out. They make lovely presents for kids up to the age of 6 or 7, and cost about $5. Giant versions that are more like soft furniture can be carved to order. Contact him by email to arrange a meeting (he doesn't have a permanent address, but moves from art squat to art squat).

18

Children's St Petersburg

A lthough Russians dote on **children**, St Petersburg is not a child-friendly environment, especially for toddlers: parks and playgrounds are littered with broken glass or even syringes, and slides and swings are often unsafe. However, in compensation, there are many attractions for kids to see and enjoy. Circuses, puppet shows, musicals and spectacles on ice are detailed under "The Arts" (Chapter 16). Russians have high expectations of their children's attention span and behaviour; you'll see 6-year-olds sitting through three-hour ballets at the Mariinskiy or Maliy theatres (where the minimum age is 5 for matinees, 8 for evening performances). Sports facilities aren't so readily accessible to visitors, but children are welcome to accompany adults to the *banya* (bathhouse), a football or ice hockey match – and anyone with a skateboard will find lots of company (see Chapter 19, "Sports"). For toys and souvenirs, see "Shopping" (Chapter 17).

Children up to the age of 7 ride free on all public **transport** (including minibuses, if they sit on a parent's lap). Baby food and disposable nappies are available at most supermarkets and pharmacies, though you may wish to bring a small supply to tide you over. Russians regard breastfeeding in public as something that "only Gypsies do". Outside summer, Russians **dress** their children in hats, scarves and layers of clothing – when foreign parents might simply pop a sweater on – and do their best to ensure that Russian kids never sit on the ground, for fear of catching cold, or developing maladies in later life. Russian grannies feel free to admonish strangers who allow their own kids to go "undressed".

Attractions

Museums that might interest children of all ages are the bizarre Kunstkammer and Museum of Anthropology (p.162), the Railway Museum (p.106) and the Arctic and Antarctic Museum (p.218). If they're unfazed by the language barrier, they can join Russian kids to try their hand at printmaking, weaving or pottery at the Children's Centre (Sat & Sun 11am–5pm) of the Russian Ethnographic Museum (see p.92). The World of Water Museum has a collection of antique toilets and a beguiling illuminated fountain in its atrium (see p.208). Children going through a bellicose phase might also enjoy the *Narodovolets* submarine (p.169), the cruiser *Aurora* (p.186), the Naval Museum (p.160) and the Artillery Museum (p.183). Young girls are more likely to enjoy the Doll Museum (p.171) or Toy Museum (p.189).

While the twin exhibitions in the Beloselskiy-Belozerskiy Palace on Nevskiy (p.64) are the most lifelike and historically accurate of the **waxworks** exhibitions doing the rounds, kids may prefer the Mysteries of History show in the Peter and Paul Fortress (p.182), with its melodramatic tableaux of Tsar Paul's assassination, and Princess Tarakanova's miserable fate.

Of the **Imperial palaces** outside the city (see Chapter 9), Peterhof, Tsarskoe Selo and Pavlovsk are the most enjoyable for kids, with huge parks, truly fabulous interiors and the odd amusement park or boating lake. Peterhof is especially rewarding, as children love to try their luck with the "joke" fountains in Lower Park (see p.258). A trip to the woods and beaches of the **Karelian Isthmus** is also recommended in the summer; Zelenogorsk has the best beach for bathing (see Chapter 10).

St Petersburg's run-down **Zoo** (p.182) is enjoyable only for the really young or totally insensitive, though there is the odd pony ride to enliven proceedings. It's within walking distance of the city's **Planetarium** in the Alexander Park, whose rota of shows includes footage from the Mir space station besides the usual astronomical projections (Tues–Sun 10.30am–6pm; tickets $1), and the Alisa amusement park (see below). Additionally, there's a **Dolphinarium** (*delfinarium*) with an hour-long performance by dolphins and a sea lion (with which kids can be photographed) – though the conditions they're kept in will dismay adults. It's at Konstantinovskiy pr. 19 ☎235 46 31; Krestovskiy Ostrov metro. Shows are Wed–Fri 2pm, Sat & Sun noon, 1pm, 2pm, 4pm & 6pm. Tickets cost $1–2; children under 5 get in free.

If you're settling in St Petersburg with children, they may like to join the **Small Academy of Arts** (Malaya Akademiya Iskusstv) in the courtyard of nab. reki Fontanki 2 ☎273 20 62 (see p.204), across the Fontanka from the Summer Garden. The academy takes children from 5 years upwards for twice-weekly crafts' days (ceramics, sculpture, murals, etc), and one day a week visiting museums to study under master restorers and curators. Adults are welcome to participate, too; all the teachers and helpers are volunteers, and the academy is free of charge. The only snag is, it's closed over summer.

Eating

Kids demanding to eat something familiar can be pacified with a visit to *McDonald's*, *Pizza Hut* or *Patio Pizza*, while the Russian chain *Laima* has tasty salads, burgers, chips and other childish favourites – for addresses see the box on p.354. But it would be a shame not to give Russian food a try. Pancakes (*bliny*) usually go down well with kids, once they've found a filling to their taste: salted fish is probably a no-no, but pancakes with condensed milk (*bliny so sgushchenkoy*) go down a treat. You can get *bliny* at almost any Russian café or restaurant. For a **special occasion**, there's the *Mary Poppins Café*, ul. Nekrasova 23 ☎275 51 44; Chernyshevskaya metro. Themed around the children's classic of the same name, it can lay on clown shows, live music and parties for children.

Parks, playgrounds, boat trips and bike rides

Young children are sure to enjoy **parks** such as Mikhailovskiy Gardens (p.93) behind the Russian Museum, which has lots of room to dash about; the

Tauride Gardens (p.203) which has an old-fashioned funfair and several play areas; the Yusupov Garden (p.106) on Sadovaya ulitsa, where you can paddle in the pool; and the Summer Garden, with its picturesque statues (though you can't touch them). Most of the city's **playgrounds** (often in the courtyards of residential blocks) are poorly maintained, but there are two excellent public facilities on the Petrograd Side: on Kamennoostrovskiy prospekt, 100m south of Petrogradskaya metro, and at the corner of Bolshaya Pushkarskaya and ulitsa Lenina. In the city centre, you could get away with using the playgrounds for residents in the gated block at Italyanskaya ul. 27 (leading through to Malaya Sadovaya ul. 4), or the block between Gagarinskaya ulitsa and the River Fontanka, where the Small Academy of Arts is located (see p.393).

Older kids should head for one of the city's **amusement parks**. Alisa (daily 11am–9pm) in the Alexander Park near Gorkovskaya metro is close to the Peter and Paul Fortress and the Planetarium, with bouncy castles, dodgems, carousels and scarier rides ($2–4). The city's newest and best-equipped fun park is **Wonder Island** (Mon 3–10pm, Tues–Fri noon–10pm, Sat & Sun 11am–10pm), near Krestovskiy Ostrov metro, which has rollercoasters and waterchutes ($1–3). There are other funfairs at Park Pobedy (p.227) and Yekateringof Park (p.229).

A **boat trip** is a good way to pass an hour or so. In addition to the guided tours of the city's river and canals, you can hire a motorboat with a driver and set your own itinerary. A **hydrofoil** ride to Peterhof (p.250) is a pricier but unforgettable experience; children pay half the adult rate. Or you can go **rowing** on the serpentine ponds of Yelagin Island (see p.194); the boat depot also has a few **bicycles** to rent.

Street entertainment

There are often **buskers and street performers** along Nevskiy prospekt and outside major tourist spots. Don't miss the guy who plays tunes on a saw by the Church of the Saviour on the Blood. At the Peter and Paul Fortress and Peterhof, kids can be photographed with actors wearing eighteenth-century period costumes, and hire crinolines or frock coats to dress up for the shot.

Crossing the panoramic Neva Basin is fun, too: **trams** #2 and #54 from Sadovaya ulitsa cross the river within sight of the Peter and Paul Fortress, and during summer antique trams run from Finland Station into the centre, in view of the cruiser *Aurora*. For those children who can keep awake until the early hours, the spectacle of the **bridges** on the Neva opening to let ships through is a memorable one (see p.39 for times).

Sports

I n Soviet times, **sport** was accorded high status: a carefully nurtured elite of Olympic medal-winning athletes were heralded as proof of Communism's superiority, while ordinary citizens were exhorted to pursue sporting activities to make them "ready for labour and defence". Consequently, there's no shortage of sports facilities in St Petersburg, though most are for club members only; visitors can either try striking some kind of deal with the staff, or settle for paying much higher rates to use hotel facilities. If you're doing any outdoor activities, including sports such as horse riding and yachting, be sure that they're covered by your **insurance** policy.

For the slothful majority, however, the most popular activity remains visiting the **bathhouse**, or *banya*. Russian bathhouses are a world unto themselves and are the preferred cure for the malady known locally as "feeling heavy" – which encompasses everything from having flu to being depressed. For a truly Russian experience, a visit to the *banya* is an absolute must.

Bathhouses

The Russian **banya** is as much a national institution as the sauna in Finland. Traditionally, peasants stoked up the village bathhouse and washed away the week's grime on Fridays; Saturdays were for drinking and Sundays for church – "a *banya* for the soul". Townspeople were equally devoted to the *banya*: the wealthy had private ones, while others visited public bathhouses, favoured as much for their ambience as the quality of their hot room. In Russia's favourite romantic comedy, *Irony of Fate*, the hero gets so drunk at the *banya* celebrating his stag night in Moscow that he ends up in Leningrad by mistake, and meets his true love there. Although bathhouses are more associated with heterosexual than gay sexuality, foreign neophytes can feel differently. Some US Marines were once invited by their Russian counterparts to an unmarked basement where, to their dismay, the Russians undressed and mimed beating each other before vanishing into a room. When grunts and lashing sounds were heard, the Marines formed a circle and prepared for unarmed combat....

So here's the procedure when **visiting a banya**. Some have separate floors for men and women, while others operate on different days for each sex, but whatever the set-up, there's no mixed bathing, except in the section available for private rental (where anything goes). The only thing the *banya* will definitely provide (for a modest price) is a sheet in which to wrap yourself. You should **bring** a towel, shampoo, some plastic sandals and possibly a hat to protect your head (towels, flip-flops and weird mushroom-shaped felt hats can be rented at some *banyas*). Expect to pay $3–5 to use a standard *banya*; more at de luxe establishments. At the entrance, you can buy a *venik* – a leafy bunch of birch twigs (or prickly juniper twigs for the really hardy) – with which bathers fan and flail themselves (and each other) in the steam room, to open up the skin's pores and enhance blood circulation. This isn't obligatory, but it feels great afterwards.

Hand your coat and valuables to the cloakroom attendant before going into the changing rooms. Beyond these lies a washroom with a **cold plunge pool** (*basseyn*); the metal basins are for soaking your *venik* to make it supple. Finally you enter the **hot room** – or *parilka* – with its tiers of wooden benches – the higher up you go, the hotter it gets. Unlike in a Finnish sauna, it's a damp heat, as from time to time water is thrown onto the stove to produce steam. Five to seven minutes is as long as novices should attempt in the *parilka*. After a dunk in the cold bath and a rest, you can return to the *parilka* for more heat torture, before cooling off again – a process repeated several times, with breaks for tea and conversation. Two hours is the usual time allowed in the public baths and the rental period for private sections (*individualnoe nomer*) – though you can reserve a *nomer* for longer if desired.

Many *banya*-goers cover their heads with hats to protect them from the heat, while others take advantage of traditional health cures and beauty treatments: men rub salt over their bodies in order to sweat more copiously, and women coat themselves with honey, to make their skin softer – you can also throw beer on the stove for a wonderful yeasty aroma. As *banya*-going is a dehydrating experience, it's advisable not to go drunk, with a bad hangover or on a full stomach. Beer is usually on sale in the men's section, but women should bring their own drinks. The traditional farewell salutation to fellow *banya*-goers is "*S lyogkim parom*" – "May the steam be with you".

Lastly, a word of **warning**: Russian mobsters love partying at the *banya*. They usually rent a private section and bring their girlfriends or call girls along; drunken quarrels may occur, followed by murders next day (so Militia detectives say). This tends to happen on Thursday nights, at baths that stay open late. By day, the clientele is far more respectable as a rule.

In addition to those *banya*s listed below in the city, there are several around the lakes in **Ozerki**, to the north of the city (take bus #38 from Ozerki metro). At these, you can try the Russian custom of leaping through the ice into freezing water in winter rather than just into a cold plunge pool. The *banya* at Bolshaya Ozyornaya ul. 84 (☎553 23 96) is open 24 hours a day and has a sauna, *parilka*, pool, gym and massage.

Hamam Zastavskaya ul. 19 ☎380 08 37; **Moskovskie Vorota metro.** A Turkish steam bath, Finnish sauna, wood-fired *banya* and swimming pool in one complex, with billiards, karaoke, Turkish, classical and erotic soap massage, plus apartments for rent by the hour. Daily 24hr.

Kruglye bani ul. Karbesheva 29a ☎550 09 85; **Ploshchad Muzhestva metro.** Favoured by expatriates who rent the de luxe *banya* on Wednesday nights, it occupies a round building opposite the metro – hence its name, the "Round Baths". Mon, Tues & Fri–Sun 8am–10pm.

Marshal Hotel Shpalernaya ul. 41 ☎279 99 55; **Chernyshevskaya metro.** If it's privacy you want, this spanking-new hotel sauna with a Jacuzzi can be booked by non-residents for only $14 (group rate). Be sure to order in advance, as they have to fire up the boilers. No set hours.

Mytninskie Bani ul. Mytninskaya 17/19 ☎271 71 19; **trolleybus #10 from pl. Vosstaniya.** One of the few wood-stoked *banya*s still operating in town, its public section is quite shabby, but the private sauna is fine, with a whirlpool plunge bath ($17 group rate). Mon, Tues & Fri–Sun 8am–10pm.

Neptun 17-ya liniya 38 ☎321 81 54; **Vasileostrovskaya metro.** Sauna, *parilka*, pool and private cubicles. Mon & Thurs–Sun 8am–10pm.

Pushkarskie bani Bolshaya Pusharskaya ul. 22 ☎237 02 94; **Petrogradskaya metro.** District *banya* for the Petrograd Side, with a public and private sauna and *parilka*. Wed–Sun 8am–9pm.

VIP Sauna Gavanskaya ul. 5 ☏ 325 55 64; minibus #K-129 from Gostiniy Dvor metro. Its amenities include a Russian *banya*, Finnish sauna, swimming pool and billiards.Thursday nights are best avoided, unless you want to mix with Goodfellas. Daily 24hr.

Yamskie bani ul. Dostoevskovo 9 ☏ 312 58 36; Vladimirskaya metro. Frequented by the *banya* cognoscenti and well kept by local standards. Thursday is cheap day for pensioners, so there are huge queues. Also has a de luxe section, with private rooms and a gym. Daily 8am–10pm.

Boating and yachting

A relaxing way to spend a couple of hours is to go **boating** on the serpentine lakes of Yelagin Island. Rowboats are rented for about $5 an hour on the lake near the bridge to Vyborg Side, but it's best to avoid weekends and public holidays, when facilities are oversubscribed. More ambitiously, you could go **yachting** on the Gulf of Finland, where strong winds make for fast, exciting sailing, especially during the **St Petersburg Sailing Week** (mid-Aug) and **Vyborg regatta** (July). If you plan to sail your own boat to St Petersburg, details of navigation channels, ports, customs bureaucracy and maritime charts can be found on ⓦ http://sailing.dkart.ru, while ⓦ http://home.clara.net /rayglaister/Russia/htm covers inland river journeys as far north as the White Sea. Charter trips range from a couple of hours to overnight expeditions to uninhabited islands or sea forts (see p.295) out in the Gulf. Most yachts sleep six to eight people. Prices depend on the firm or club and what you want to do, so it's definitely worth comparing quotes.

Neva Yacht Club Martynova nab. 94 ☏ 235 27 22; Krestovskiy Ostrov metro. Favoured by non-sailors who enjoy partying with babes and booze aboard a yacht or power-cruiser, but also used by real enthusiasts. Enquires to Tatyana Bykova ☏ 966 26 01. Daily 24hr.

River Yacht Club (aka Tsentralniy Yacht Club), Petrovskaya Kosa 9, Petrovskiy Island ☏ 235 66 36; trolleybus #7 from Nevskiy pr. to the end of the line. This club once produced teams for the Olympics and was founded as long ago

as 1858. Contact English-speaking Vladimir Ivankiv ⓔ vliv@medport.ru. Morozov Yachts (☏ 237 06 02 Mon–Fri 10am–6pm) build powerboats and yachts at the same site, and can do repairs.

Sunny Sailing ul. Vosstaniya 55 ☏ 327 35 25, ⓦ www.sailing.spb.ru; Ploshchad Vosstaniya metro. An upmarket agency with a down-town office, chartering all kinds of boats moored at Stelna, near Peterhof; for trips to Valaam they use yachts out of Priozersk.

Bowling and billiards

The city has several well-equipped **bowling** alleys and hundreds of places with **billiards** or pool tables ($2–10/hr, depending on the venue and time of day or night). The main difference between Russian billiards and the English game is that there are no cannons – you can score points only by straightforward pots.

Akademiya Bilyarda ul. Ryleeva 5 ☏ 279 74 39; Chernyshevskaya metro. If you want to improve your game, this billiards academy beside the *Arbat Nord Hotel* is the place – owner Yakov Aloev holds several championship medals. Tables cost $5 per hour by day, $7 at night. If you're going to spend a whole evening there, Armenian meals can be arranged. Daily 24hr.

Aquatoria Vyborgskaya nab. 61 ☏ 245 20 30, ⓦ www.aquatoria.ru; Lesnaya metro. Mega entertainment complex near Kantimirovskiy most, with nine "Brunswick" lanes, "Cosmic Bowling" and lanes for kids, Russian and American billiards, and a disco (Wed–Sun 10pm–6am) with go-go dancers and strippers. Bowling daily noon–6am.

Billiards Blues-Style ul. Professora Popova 47 ☏234 44 48; bus #25 from Petrogradskaya metro. Billiards, pool and darts, with live blues music and a bar, in the *LDM* – a hotel-cum-entertainment centre on Petrograd Side (see "Accommodation", p.337). There's also a Q-Zar laser-gun labyrinth that can be rented in 15-minute blocks by groups of up to forty shooters. Daily 10am–7am.

5th Avenue pl. Konstityutsi 2 ☏123 08 09; **Moskovskaya metro**. Two blocks west of Moskovskaya ploshchad, with seven lanes for US tenpin bowling, plus Russian and American billiards. Mon–Fri from noon, Sat & Sun from 10am, till the last customer leaves. **Fartver pl. Morskoy Slavy 1** ☏322 69 39, ⓦwww.bowling.spb.ru; minibus #K-128 from

Nevskiy pr. A well-equipped six-lane bowling club in the *Morskaya Hotel* on Vasilevskiy Island. Maestro, MC, Visa. Mon–Fri from noon, Sat & Sun from 10am till the last customer leaves.

M11 Moskovskiy pr. 111 ☏320 44 00, ⓦwww.m111.ru; **Moskovskie Vorota metro**. Sixteen bowling lanes, plus kids' lanes, Russian billiards and pool tables. Discounts for children under 14 Mon–Fri noon–8pm. Fri & Sat live music from 11pm, cabaret after midnight. Daily noon–6am.

Tuborg Club Kirochnaya ul. 36 ☏272 18 32; **Chernyshevskaya metro**. Comfy café-bar with a garden and a full menu, and billiards tables upstairs. Daily 24hr.

Cycling, rollerblading and go-karting

Cycling for pleasure is trendy among affluent, health-conscious under-30s. While potholes, cobbles and heavy traffic make cycling in the centre hazardous, residential backwaters and the leafy Kirov Islands are perfect for cycling. For a longer ride you could cycle to the Imperial palace of Tsarskoe Selo, outside the city; the road is fairly free of traffic once you get beyond the airport. You can buy imported mountain bikes, helmets and spare parts at Motolyubitel (see "Shopping", p.389).

Rollerblading (inline skating) is widely popular among Russian youth. The flat expanse of Dvortsovaya ploshchad and the bumpy granite embankments along the Neva are hot sites in the centre; traffic-free avenues and bags of space around the Kirov Stadium are just a metro ride away on Krestovskiy Island. It's even possible to take a package holiday that features blading tours of the city and Tsarskoe Selo, led by the 2003 European Rollerblade Slalom champion, Katya Voronicheva (see "The Beetroot Bus", p.22). To learn more about rollerblading in St Petersburg, visit ⓦhttp://inlineskating.about.com/library /weekly/aa010728.htm.

Or you can say nuts to the environment and head for the motor-racing circuit near the Kirov Stadium, where **Formula 1600 races** are held on the first Sunday in July at 12.30pm (admission free). At other times, the track is used for driving racing cars and **go-karting**. To arrange driving and/or lessons, contact Nevsky Ring in the stadium (office #420 ☏235 54 35, ⓦwww.nr.spb.ru; Mon–Fri 11am–6pm).

Gyms

While many **gyms** in St Petersburg require expensive membership, the less prestigious set-ups will let you pay a one-off fee of a few dollars, and most of the top hotels have gyms open to non-residents for a fee.

Angleterre Fitness Centre Angleterre Hotel, Bolshaya Morskaya ul. 39 ☏313 58 69; **bus #22 or #43 from Nevskiy pr**. Always phone first as

hotel guests have priority. Swimming pool, training hall, sauna, massage and health-bar. Major cards. Daily 7am–10pm.

Galactika Petrovskiy Stadium, Petrovskiy Island ☎ 328 89 41; Sportivnaya metro. Sports club with a gym and aerobics room, offering individual computerized programmes for increasing or reducing body mass. Mon–Fri 8am–11pm, Sat & Sun 10am–10pm.

Planet Fitness Grand Hotel Europe ☎ 329 65 97, Nevskiy Prospekt metro; Kazanskaya ul. 37 ☎ 315 62 20, Nevskiy Prospekt metro; Petrogradskaya nab. 18 ☎ 332 00 00, Gorkovskaya metro; nab. Robespera 12 ☎ 275 13 84, Chernyshevskaya metro; and other locations ⊛ www.fitness.ru. A chain of gyms with various membership deals – check the website for special offers and opening hours.

Sampsonievskiy Maliy Sampsonievskiy pr. 4 ☎ 324 77 27, ⓔ dominion@sampsonievskiy.ru; Vyborgskaya metro. Besides aerobics and training machines there's squash, target shooting, a solarium and sauna. Daily 7am–11pm.

Zdorovie ul. Gagarinskaya 32 ☎ 279 02 26; Chernyshevskaya metro. Aerobics, "shaping" (low-impact aerobics) and oriental meditation. Daily 8am–11pm.

Horse riding

If you're looking for more than a ten-minute ride at speed around Dvortsovaya ploshchad or ploshchad Iskusstv, you need to pay in the region of $17–20 an hour at a proper riding club. Brief pony rides for young children can be had by the funfair in the Alexander Park near Gorkovskaya metro.

Proster Equestrian Centre Krestovskiy Island ☎ 230 78 73; tram #34 from Gorkovskaya metro. Riding lessons, plus *troika* and sleigh rides in winter.

Yumax ul. Tankistov 5 ☎ 437 70 17; train from Finland Station to Solechnoe. Out-of-the-city equestrian club with thoroughbreds and trekking ponies for hire, and lessons. Tues–Sun 10am–1pm & 4–8pm.

Ice hockey

Ice hockey (*khokkey*) runs soccer a close second as Russia's most popular sport, and SKA St Petersburg is one of the country's best teams, despite an exodus of top strikers to foreign clubs. Matches are fast and physical, cold yet compelling viewing – the season starts in September and culminates in the annual world championships the following summer, when the Russians strive to defeat Sweden, Canada and the US. The club trains and plays friendly matches at the SKA Palace of Sports, but league games are held at the Yubileyniy Sports Palace, while for internationals the action shifts to the high-tech Ice Palace, built for the World Ice Hockey Championship 2000. Matches are played throughout the year, as listed in *Chas Pik* and *Sport Ekspress*; the latter is the best source of information on all spectator sports.

Ice Palace (Ledovy dvorets) pr. Pyatiletok 1 ☎ 118 41 17, ⊛ www.newarena.spb.ru; Prospekt Bolshevikov metro. With seating for 14,000, and the finest lighting, sound and televisual facilities in the city, the Ice Palace hosts championship matches and major pop concerts.

SKA Palace of Sports Zhdanovskaya nab. 2 ☎ 237 00 73; Sportivnaya metro. SKA's home ground is smaller and old-fashioned compared to the other two venues. When not being used for training it's a public skating rink.

Spartak Palace of Sports ul. Butlerova 36 ☎ 535 28 55; Udelnaya metro. Distant venue for matches in the local St Petersburg Cup league.

Yubileyniy Sports Palace pr. Dobrolyubova 18 ☎ 323 93 15; Sportivnaya metro. The main venue for Russian league games, that's also an indoor skating rink. The box office is open daily noon–7pm.

Rock climbing, bungee jumping and skydiving

Given St Petersburg's flat topography, local **rock climbing** enthusiasts are obliged to go to the Karelian Isthmus, where participants of any nationality may attend the "Climbing for Everybody" **festival** in early May, held 150km north of St Petersburg; trains from Finland Station run to Kuznechnoe, 15km from the site. For details, contact Sergei Mikheev (©s.mikheev@actor.ru) well ahead of time, and check out the website ⓦwww.citycat.ru/skala. To get the adrenalin really flowing, there's a **bungee jump** at Ozerki, on the northern edge of the city (near Ozerki metro), from a cabin suspended 50m above a lake (daily 2–11pm).Or you can go **skydiving** with Baltic Air (Nevskiy pr. 7/9, office #12 ⓣ238 50 18) at Rzhevka Airfield to the east of the city.You jump strapped to an instructor so no experience is needed; a jump costs $150. For more possibilities and contacts, visit ⓦwww.risk.ru – an online magazine for Russian hazardous sports enthusiasts.

Skating, skiing and snowboarding

During winter, Russians dig out their ice skates or skis and revel in the snow. If you can borrow or buy a pair of skates, some picturesque places to go **ice-skating** are the frozen straits between the Peter and Paul Fortress and the Kronverk, the Krasnaya Zarya open-air rink on Lesnoy prospekt, or the lake in the Tauride Gardens. Alternatively, you can rent skates and use the indoor **rinks** at the Yubileyniy Sports Palace or the SKA Palace of Sports (see "Ice Hockey") for $3 an hour; both are near Sportivnaya metro. In addition, both the Tauride Gardens and the park behind the Russian Museum are popular nursery slopes, where children learn to ski.Russia's terrain dictates that cross-country rather than downhill **skiing** is the norm; two popular destinations are Toskovo on the Karelian Isthmus (accessible by train from Finland Station) and the park surrounding Pavlovsk Palace (see p.283). **Snowboarding** enthusiasts make do with any steep bank or slope going.You can buy skates, skiing and snowboarding gear at Frankardi or Sportmaster (see "Shopping", p.389).

Soccer

While the Russian oligarch Roman Abramovich is feted in Britain for buying Chelsea football club, Russian **soccer** (*futbol*) is under-funded compared to its European competitors. Though the nation was enthralled when Russia qualified for the 2004 European Championship finals (which had seemed impossible when Georgy Yartsev took over as coach), hopes have been raised – and dashed – before, and few would bet on a Russian victory. Meanwhile, clubs from Moscow dominate the domestic league, and while St Petersburg's **Zenit** (see p.192) has kept its hard-won place in the premier division, its historic cup victory over Spartak in 1999 has yet to be repeated.Yet the club has undoubtedly benefited from its move to the all-weather Petrovskiy Stadium, which allows the team to train on a full-sized pitch throughout the winter, rather than indoors, as at the old Kirov Stadium.Their **fan club**, Nevsky Front, has its clubhouse at ul. Nekrasova 3–5 (ⓣ275 03 30, ⓦwww.soccer.ru/zenit; Mayakovskaya metro; Mon–Fri 9.30am–6pm). Other websites include the Russian football union's ⓦwww.rfs.ru and ⓦwww.russianfootball.com, which features a schedule of matches for the year.

There are two national competitions: the Russian **Championship**, running from spring to autumn, and the Russian **Cup**, which starts in the summer and ends in the summer of the next year. Games usually begin at 6.30pm and tickets ($2–10) can be obtained from any theatre-ticket kiosk in the city (see p.373), or the stadium box office.

Kirov Stadium Krestovskiy Island ☎235 54 52; bus #71 or a 15min walk from Krestovskiy Ostrov metro. Vast, windswept and neglected now that Zenit have forsaken it, the stadium still hosts Cup matches, starting at 4pm. There's a motor-racing circuit nearby. **Petrovskiy Stadium** Petrovskiy Island ☎233

17 52; Sportivnaya metro. The city's premier soccer venue for Championship and international matches has seating for 30,000 and under-field heating. During the Blockade, soldiers were trained here in unarmed combat and there was an anti-aircraft battery in the centre of the stadium.

Swimming

Locals take pride in the so-called "**walruses**" (*morzhi*), who swim in the polluted Neva by the Peter and Paul Fortress all year round, breaking holes in the ice during winter. This rugged tradition has produced some great swimmers – Alexander Popov has won the 100-metres race at two Olympics and three world championships – but unsurprisingly most people just swim in the summer, at Yelagin Island, the parks surrounding the Imperial palaces, or along the coast or inland on the Karelian Isthmus (see Chapter 10). Few people are deterred by algae in the water or broken glass on the shore; littering is appalling. Yet public **swimming pools** are only supposed to admit bathers with a health certificate (*spravka*) from a Russian doctor. They tend to limit bathers to only half an hour in the water and insist that **children** are accompanied to the changing room by an adult of the same sex (even if the adult isn't going to swim). And some close from July to September anyway. Hotel pools don't have the same restrictions, but it can be difficult for non-residents to gain access to them, as pools are small and guests get priority.

BMF Pool Sredniy pr. 87 ☎322 45 05; Vasileostrovskaya metro. Has children's pools, a sauna and training hall. Daily 7am–10pm. **Dinamo Sports Cente** pr. Dinamo 44 ☎235 47 17; Krestovskiy Ostrov metro. Two swimming pools, and indoor and outdoor tennis courts. Some English spoken. Mon–Thurs 9am–6pm, Fri 9am–5pm.

LDM Water Centre ul. Professora Popova 47 ☎234 97 72; bus #25 from Petrogradskaya metro. Fun pool with slides and waterfalls, next to *Billiards Blues-Style* and the *LDM* hotel (see p.337). A certificate is required in theory, but seldom asked for in practice. There's also a solarium and hydro-massage. Daily 8am–11pm.

Tennis

Disdained in Soviet times as an aristocratic sport, tennis was popularized in Russia by Boris Yeltsin and imbued with fame and glamour by Anna Kournikova. Russia's premier international fixture is the Kremlin Cup, held in Moscow (though prizes aren't as lavish now under Putin). St Petersburg's **Tennis Open** hasn't the cash to lure major foreign players, and is held indoors at the SKK in September. If you want to play yourself, **courts** can be rented at the following places. Fees vary widely, from $10 per hour upwards.

Dinamo pr. Dinamo 44 ☎235 47 17; Krestovskiy Ostrov metro. Clay, synthetic and indoor courts (booking essential), plus a swimming pool. Mon–Thurs 9am–6pm, Fri 9am–5pm.

Governor's Tennis Club nab. Martynova 40 ☎235 80 88; Krestovskiy Ostrov metro. As its name suggests, the clientele aren't short of a bob. It has seven indoor and seven outdoor courts. There's also a fitness centre, sauna, children's playground, bar and restaurant.

Molniya Primorskiy pr. 50 ☎430 68 34; Staraya Derevnya metro. Book well in advance for their clay courts. Also runs shaping, judo,

aikido and dance fitness courses. Daily 9am–11pm.

Neptun nab. Obvodnovo kanal 93a ☎324 46 96; Pushkinskaya metro. Courts at the *Neptun Hotel* (see p.339), which also has billiards, bowling and a sauna. Daily 7am–midnight.

SKK (Sportivniy-Kulturniy Kompleks) pr. Yuriya Gagarina 8 ☎298 12 11; Park Pobedy metro. Indoor venue for the Tennis Open championship in September, otherwise used for concerts and trade shows.

Yelagin Tennis Club near the palace on Yelagin Island ☎430 11 21; Staraya Derevnya metro. Floodlit outdoor courts. Daily 9am–11pm.

Windsurfing and scuba diving

Windsurfing is becoming a popular sport at resorts on the Gulf coast – particularly Zelenogorsk, whose Golden Beach hosts the annual **Baltic Cup** championship in the second half of July. There aren't hire shops at resorts yet, but you can buy boards and wetsuits at the Techno Sport Centre on Vasilevskiy Island (see "Shopping", p.390).

Scuba diving in the murky waters of the Neva and the Gulf isn't so inviting, but there's a wealth of historical remains and sunken wrecks to explore around the sea forts of Kronstadt and the offshore waters of Vyborg (see Chapter 10). Excursions are organized by Red Shark Divers, 5-ya Sovetskaya ul. 3 ☎110 27 95, ⓦwww.redshark.ru, which also runs PADI open water courses, ice diving, family trips, and rents and sells diving equipment.

Directory

Airlines Unless stated otherwise, all the following offices are within walking distance of Nevskiy Prospekt metro. Aeroflot, Kazanskaya ul. 5 ☎327 38 72. Air France, Bolshaya Morskaya ul. 35 ☎325 82 52. Austrian Airways, Nesvkiy pr. 57, *Nevsky Palace Hotel* ☎325 32 60; Mayakovskaya metro. British Airways, Malaya Konyushennaya ul. 1/3a, office #B-23 ☎329 25 65. CSA, Bolshaya Morskaya ul. 36 ☎315 52 59. Delta, Bolshaya Morskaya ul. 36 ☎311 58 20. Finnair, Kazanskaya ul. 44 ☎326 18 70. KLM, Malaya Morskaya ul. 23 ☎346 68 68. Lufthansa, Nevskiy pr. 32 ☎320 10 00. Malév, Pulkovo-2 airport ☎324 32 43; minibus #K-13 from Moskovskaya metro. SAS, Nesvkiy pr. 25 ☎326 26 00. Swissair, Malaya Konyushennaya ul. 1/3a ☎329 25 25.

American Express Malaya Morskaya ul. 23 ☎326 45 00, ✪www.americanexpress.ru; Nevskiy Prospekt metro. Holds mail for Amex card or traveller's cheque holders for 30 days (address to: c/o American Express St Petersburg, PO Box 87, SF-53501, Lappeenranta, Finland). Card replacement in 24hr, cheques take 1–3 days. Mon–Fri 9am–5pm.

Consulates

Australia Italyanskaya ul. 1 ☎325 73 33, ✉oz@concoulteast.com; Nevskiy Prospekt metro. Mon–Fri 9.30am–5pm.

Austria Furshtatskaya ul. 43 ☎275 05 02; Chernyshevskaya metro. Mon–Fri 9am–1pm.

Britain pl. Proletarskoy diktatury 5 ☎320 32 45, ✪www.britain.spb.ru; minibus #K-129 or #K-147 from Nevskiy pr. Mon–Fri 9.30am–1pm & 2–5.30pm.

Canada Malodetskoselsky pr. 32 ☎325 84 48; Frunzenskaya metro. Mon–Fri 9am–noon.

China nab. kanala Griboedova 134 ☎114 76 70; Sadovaya metro. Visa section Mon & Wed 9.30–11.30am.

Czech Republic Tverskaya ul. 5–7 ☎271 46 12; Chernyshevskaya metro. Mon–Thurs 9am–12.30pm & 1.30–4pm, Fri 9am–2pm.

Denmark Bolshaya alleya 13, Kamenniy Island ☎103 39 00; Chernaya Rechka metro. Mon–Wed & Fri 10am–noon.

Estonia Bolshaya Monetnaya ul. 14 ☎102 09 24; Gorkovskaya metro. Tues, Thurs & Fri 9am–noon, Wed 9–11am.

Finland ul. Chaykovskovo 71 ☎273 73 21, ✪www.pietari.com; Chernyshevskaya metro. Mon–Fri 8.30am–4.15pm.

France nab. reki Moyki 15 ☎312 11 30; Nevskiy Prospekt metro. Mon–Fri 9.30am–12.30pm & 2–5pm.

Germany Furshtatskaya ul. 39 ☎320 24 00, ✪www.german-consulate.spb.ru; Chernyshevskaya metro. Mon–Thurs 8am–noon & 1–3pm, Fri 10am–1pm.

Italy Teatralnaya pl. 10 ☎312 32 17; bus #22 from Nevskiy pr. Mon–Fri 10am–noon.

Japan nab. reki Moyki 29 ☎314 14 18; Nevskiy Prospekt metro. Mon–Fri 10–11.30am.

Latvia 10-ya liniya 11 ☎327 60 55; Vasileostrovskaya metro. Mon–Thurs 9am–noon.

Lithuania Gorokhovaya ul. 4 ☎314 58 57; trolleybus #5 or #22 from Nevskiy pr. Mon–Thurs 9am–noon.

Netherlands nab. reki Moyki 11 ☎312 03 38; Nevskiy Prospekt metro. Mon–Thurs 9.30am–12.30pm.

Norway Nevskiy pr. 25 ☎326 26 50; Nevskiy Prospekt metro. Mon–Fri 9.30am–noon.

Poland 5-ya Sovetskaya ul. 12/14 ☏274 41 70; Ploshchad Vosstaniya metro. Mon–Fri 9am–1pm.

Spain ul. Rubinshteyna 38 ☏325 84 70; Vladimirskaya metro. Mon, Wed & Fri 10am–1pm.

Sweden Malaya Konyushennaya ul. 1/3 ☏329 14 30; Nevskiy Prospekt metro. Mon–Fri 9am–noon.

Switzerland ul. Marata 11 ☏325 62 71; Mayakovskaya metro. Mon–Fri 9am–noon.

USA Furshtatskaya ul. 15 ☏331 26 00, ⓦwww.usconsulate.spb.ru; Chernyshevskaya metro. Mon–Fri 9.30am–1.30pm.

Contraceptives Turkish-made condoms (*prezervativiy*) are available in all pharmacies and many 24-hour shops and kiosks, but are generally untrustworthy.

Cultural Institutes

American Center Millionaya ul. 5 ☏325 80 50; Nevskiy Prospekt metro. Aside from US newspapers and TV news there isn't much to attract tourists, as it's mainly aimed at Russians and promoting business. Mon–Fri 9am–7.30pm.

British Council nab. reki Fontanki 46 ☏118 50 60, ⓦwww.britishcouncil.ru/spb; Gostiniy Dvor metro. Newspapers, magazines and a lending library ($17 annual membership; passport and two photos required) on the third floor of the Mayakovsky State Library, near the Anichkov Bridge. Tues–Fri 12.30–7pm, Sat noon–5pm.

Institut Francais nab. reki Moyki 20 ☏117 09 95, ⓦwww.ifspb.com; Nevskiy Prospekt metro. Has a lending library (free membership; passport and two photos required), and organizes all kinds of cultural events, from French films at dom Kino and concerts at the Philharmonic and Kapella to Bastille Day celebrations. Mon & Wed 2–6.30pm, Tues & Thurs 2–8pm, Fri noon–5pm.

Goethe Institut nab. reki Moyki 58 ☏314 40 15, ⓦwww.goethe.de; Sadovaya/Sennaya Ploshchad metro. Organizes film showings and lectures, and diverse extramural events. Also responsible for a German library (Mon–Sat noon–7pm) in the Mayakovsky State Library (see the British Council, above). Mon–Thurs 3–6pm.

Prince Galitzine Memorial Library nab. reki Fontanki 46 ☏311 13 33; Vladimirskaya

metro. In the same building as the British Council, this charitable foundation has an extensive collection of books about Russia in English. It is not a lending library, but tourists are welcome to use the reading room. Mon–Fri noon–7pm, Sat 1–5pm.

Drugs Grass (*travka*) and cannabis resin (*plastylin*) from the Altay Mountains are commonplace on the club scene, as are acid, ecstasy and heroin (which, at only $1 a wrap, is responsible for the soaring addiction rate). At some clubs, the merest whiff will draw the bouncers; at others, dope-smokers are stolidly ignored. While simple possession of dope may incur only a caution, hard drugs – and smuggling – are still punishable, in theory at least, by the death penalty. The safest policy is to avoid all drugs entirely.

Electricity A standard Continental 220 volts AC; most European appliances should work as long as you have an adaptor for Continental-style, two-pin round plugs. North Americans will need this plus a transformer.

Feminist contacts The best places to start looking are the Russian Feminist Resources website ⓦwww.geocities.com/Athens/2533 /russfem.html, which has a lot of links and material in English; the Women Information Network has a regularly updated news site in Russian (ⓦwww.womnet.ru) and a database of women's organizations throughout Russia in English (ⓦwww.womnet.ru/db /English/English.html. For informal contacts, visit the *Art-Buffet* café in block D of Pushkinskaya 10 (see p.215), a hangout for the city's self-styled "cyber feminists".

Film and photos Outlets for imported film and one-hour processing services can be found all over the city centre, Agfa, Fuji and Kodak Express all being represented. Do not take photos of foreign consulates – you might have your film confiscated. When leaving the country put films in your pocket, as Russian filmsafe X-rays do not always live up to the name.

Gay and lesbian contacts The St Petersburg Human Rights Centre for Gays and Lesbians, PO Box 108, St Petersburg 191186; ☏312 31 80 ⓦwww.krilija.sp.ru. Their website features articles about gay life and history in Russia, links and listings (the latter rather out of date). See p.370 for gay and lesbian clubs in St Petersburg.

Language Russian-language courses in St Petersburg can be arranged through EducaCentre, Zvenigorodskaya ul. 3 ☎974 03 73, ⊛www.educacentre.net; Language Link, Kazanskaya ul. 5 ☎311 39 48, ⓔinfo@ll.spb.ru; or the Swiss-run Liden & Denz School, Transportniy per. 11, 4th floor ☎325 22 41, ⊛www.lidenz.ru. All these centres can provide visa support for their students. Don't expect the diversity of teaching materials that you'd get on language courses in your own country.

Laundries Landromat, 11-ya liniya 46, Vasileostrovskaya metro (daily 8am–10pm) is the only self-service laundry in the city; a machine load costs $5. There's a laundry service for guests at the *St Petersburg International Hostel*. Clothes can be washed, ironed and delivered in three days by Stirka-Servis, Udelniy pr. 51 ☎553 53 00 (Mon–Fri 9am–9pm, Sat 9am–5pm).

Left luggage Most bus and train stations have lockers and/or a 24-hour left-luggage office, but you would be tempting fate to use them.

Lost property Anything you might lose is unlikely to end up at the lost property depots (*stol nakhodok*) at Sredniy pr. 70 and ul. Zakharyevskaya 19, or the centre for lost documents at Bolshaya Monetnaya ul. 6 (Mon–Fri 10am–6pm), though there's slightly more chance of lost property being recovered at Pulkovo-2 airport (☎324 37 87).

Marriage agencies The foreign-language press is full of advertisements by agencies offering to supply Russian brides for foreign males. A lot of them are purely aimed at extracting money from hapless foreigners, and even where "genuine", many of the women are simply planning to divorce their spouses as soon as they gain a foreign residency permit or passport. For a real relationship, find someone yourself.

Religious worship Anglican, Lutheran Church of St Peter, Nevskiy pr. 22/24 ☎327 08 14 (Sun 11am); Baha'i, Bolshaya Morskaya ul. 53/8, apt. #17 ☎311 45 58; Baptist, International Baptist Church, Novocherkasskiy pr. 47, korpus 1, staircase 12 ☎442 01 07 (Sun 11am & Wed 7.30pm); Buddhist, Buddhist Temple, Primorskiy pr. 91 ☎239 03 41 (daily 9am & 5pm); Catholic, St Catherine's Church, Nevskiy pr. 32/34 ☎311 71 70 (Mon–Fri 8am & 6.30pm in Russian, Sun 9.30am in English); Hindu, Hare Krishna Temple, Bumazhnaya ul. 17 ☎186 72 59 (7pm daily & Sun 4pm); Jewish, Small and Great synagogues, Lermontovskiy pr. 2 ☎114 11 53 (9am & 7.45pm daily, Sat 10am); Muslim, Mosque, Kronverkskiy pr. 7 ☎233 98 19 (daily 10am–7pm); Russian Orthodox, Preobrazhenskiy Church, Preobrazhenskaya pl. 1 ☎272 36 62 (daily 10am & 6pm).

Smoking Nearly all Western brands of cigarettes are available, though many of the packets sold at kiosks are made under licence (or counterfeited) in Russia or Turkey. It is normal to be approached by strangers asking for a light (*Mozhno pokurit?*) or a cigarette. While museums and public transport are no-smoking (*ne kurit*) zones, Russians puff away everywhere else, and see nothing wrong with it. However, many fast-food chains have a no-smoking policy.

Student cards ISIC cardholders get a fifty percent reduction on museum and palace admission charges, and free entry to the Hermitage. Student cards issued in Russia entitle you to Russian student rates, which are even lower. You can buy an ISIC card without proof of student status at the EducaCentre (see "Language" above) and at the *RST Hostel*, once it reopens (see p.344).

Superstitions Russians consider it bad luck to kiss or shake hands across a threshold, or return home to pick up something that's been forgotten. Before departing on a long journey, they gather their luggage by the door and sit on it for a minute or two, to bring themselves luck for the journey. When buying flowers for your hostess, make certain that there's an odd number of blooms; even-numbered bouquets are for funerals. It's considered unlucky to whistle indoors, or to put a handbag on the floor.

Tampons These are widely available all over town. Local chemists sell Ukrainian-made Tampax, while imported ones can be found in large supermarkets.

Time St Petersburg uses Moscow Time, which is generally three hours ahead of Britain and eight hours ahead of US Eastern Standard Time, with the clocks going forward on the last Saturday of March and back again on the last Saturday of October.

Tipping In taxis, the fare will usually be agreed in advance so there's no need to tip; in restaurants, no one will object if you leave an extra ten percent or so, but in most places it's not compulsory. Check, too, that it hasn't already been included. In those places where a service charge is compulsory, it ranges from ten to fifteen percent; the exact figure will be stated on the menu.

Toilets It's generally acceptable for non-customers to use the toilets in restaurants and hotels, since public toilets (*tualet* or *WC*) are few and far between – despite efforts to boost numbers by locating Portaloo-type cabins in parks and squares. There is a small charge, which includes a wad of toilet paper given out by the attendant. Otherwise, make for the nearest *McDonald's*. Men's facilities are marked М; ladies, Ж. You can buy toilet paper (*tualetnaya bumaga*) in any supermarket or pharmacy.

Contexts

Contexts

A history of St Petersburg

For a city barely three hundred years old, St Petersburg has experienced more than its fair share of upheaval. Founded by Peter the Great as a "window on the West", and steeped in culture and bloodshed, it was admired and despised in equal measure as the Imperial capital of the Romanov dynasty and the most European of Russian cities. As the cradle of three revolutions, St Petersburg has a history inseparable from that of modern Russia, whose own travails are reflected in the city's changing names: from Tsarist St Petersburg to revolutionary Petrograd, and from Soviet Leningrad back to post-Communist St Petersburg. The city celebrated its tercentenary in 2003.

Peter the Great

The foundation of St Petersburg was the work of Tsar Peter I, a giant in body and spirit better known as **Peter the Great** (1682–1725), one of the three "great despots" of Russian history (the other two being Ivan the Terrible and Stalin). After a disturbed and violent childhood – at the age of 10 he witnessed the murder of many of his closest relatives by the Kremlin Guards – he became obsessed with all things military and nautical, drilling regiments during his early teens and learning the art of shipbuilding at first hand in Dutch shipyards during his famous "Great Embassy" to Western Europe in 1697.

Following his tour, where he had been gripped by what he saw, Peter embarked upon the forced **westernization** of his backward homeland. He changed the country's name from Muscovy to Russia and proceeded to violate many of the most cherished traditions of Old Muscovy and the

---

Names and dates

Slightly confusingly for those unfamiliar with Russian history, the city has been known by several names throughout its existence. In this book we have used whichever one is chronologically appropriate, namely:

Prior to August 31, 1914 – **St Petersburg**

August 31, 1914 to January 26, 1924 – **Petrograd**

January 26, 1924 to September 1991 – **Leningrad**

From September 1991 to present day – **St Petersburg**

Russia has been chronologically out of sync with other parts of Europe for much of this time. In 1700, Peter the Great forced Russians to adopt the **Julian calendar** that was then in use in Western Europe, in place of the old system dictated by the Orthodox Church. Ironically, Western Europe changed to the Gregorian calendar not long afterwards, but this time the Russians refused to follow suit. However, the Julian calendar was less accurate and by the twentieth century lagged behind the Gregorian by almost two weeks. The Soviet regime introduced the **Gregorian calendar** in February 1918 – in that year January 31 was followed by February 14 – which explains why they always celebrated the Great October Revolution on November 7. In this book we have kept to the old-style calendar for events that occurred before February 1918.

Orthodox Church. His courtiers were ordered to wear Hungarian or German dress instead of their familiar kaftans, and the tsar personally cut off their flowing beards – a symbol of pride for Orthodox believers, whose religion held that only the unshorn had a chance to enter heaven. When Peter extended the ban on beards throughout society and decreed the substitution of the Julian calendar for the Orthodox one, he was denounced as the Antichrist for imperilling Russians' salvation and perverting time itself. In response, he replaced the self-governing Patriarchate with a Holy Synod (essentially a secular ministry of religion subordinate to the tsar), but permitted devout believers to keep their beards, providing they paid a "beard tax".

Of more lasting import was Peter's creation of the **Table of Ranks**, or *chin*. This abolished the hereditary nobility and recast a new aristocracy based on service to the state, extending across the civil service and the armed forces to include engineers and specialists at every level. In theory, promotion was based on merit rather than birth, and the system was meant to dissolve snobbish distinctions between those who served the greater good of the nation. It did see able men of humble origin elevated to the highest ranks of the state – such as Mikhail Shafirov, a Jew who became Peter's foreign secretary – but in practice, the *chin* soon became a self-interested bureaucracy. The *chinovnik*, or bureaucrat, would be a stock character in the plays of Gogol and Chekhov a century and a half later.

To impose his vision on Russia, Peter relied on repressive measures characteristic of Old Muscovy and introduced new ones that his Tsarist or Communist successors would exploit to the hilt. It was Peter who invented the internal passport system, and who organized forced labour gangs to build his great projects. When faced with opposition or rebellion, he was ruthless, even overseeing the torture and death of his own son, Alexei, whom he suspected of conspiring against him. War characterized much of Peter's reign and many of his reforms were fashioned simply to keep Russia's military machine running smoothly. The quest for a seaport dominated his military thinking and in 1700 a peace treaty with Turkey left Peter free to pursue his main objective: the foundation of a new capital with trading access to the West via the Baltic Sea.

The major Baltic power of the day was Sweden and the war between the Russians and Swedes, known as the **Great Northern War**, lasted from 1700 to 1721. In 1700, at **Narva**, 150km west of present-day St Petersburg, the 18-year-old Swedish king, Charles XII, put the Russians to flight in blizzard conditions, but failed to follow up his victory with a march on Moscow, concentrating instead on subduing the rebellious Poles. Peter took advantage of the break in hostilities to strengthen his position around the Gulf of Finland.

The foundation of St Petersburg

Although popular legend has it that prior to the foundation of St Petersburg the Neva delta was an uninhabited wilderness, in fact there already existed a Swedish trading town, **Nyen**, in what is now the Okhta district, which had to be overrun before Peter could establish his new capital. Nonetheless, the site he chose was so exposed that it can fairly be termed a settlement in the wilderness – a fetid marshland chronically prone to flooding, with few natural or human resources nearby. On May 16, 1703, Peter is said to have snatched a halberd from one of his soldiers, cut two strips of turf, laid them across each other, and declared, "Here there shall be a town!"; though, of course, Pushkin's version of Peter's speech – "By nature we are fated here to cut a window through to Europe" – is more famous. Either way, **Sankt Pietr Burkh** (as it was originally called in the Dutch fashion) soon became known as the "city built on bones". Thousands of Swedish prisoners-of-war were press-ganged into work, joined by numerous other non-Russians from the far reaches of the Empire. Conditions were dire: there was a shortage of basic tools; earth had to be carried in the workers' clothing; and thousands died of starvation, cold, disease and exhaustion.

Nevertheless, in less than five months, a wooden fortress had been built on a small island. Next a wooden church was erected, along with a modest wooden cottage, which served as Peter's residence, and an inn, the *Four Frigates*, which doubled as the town hall. Within a year, there were fifteen houses on nearby Petrograd Island, where Peter first intended to base his new city, and the beginnings of the Admiralty on the mainland, then little more than a shipyard.

In the summer of 1706, with St Petersburg barely on the map, Charles XII invaded Russia from Poland. Again, within an ace of victory, he made the fateful decision not to march on Moscow, but to concentrate his efforts on Ukraine. Charles's supply and baggage train was attacked and defeated en route from Estonia in October 1708. The Russian winter inflicted yet more casualties on the Swedes and on June 27, 1709, at the **Battle of Poltava**, Peter trounced Charles, forcing him to flee to Turkey. The Great Northern War dragged on for another twelve years, but, as Peter put it, "Now the final stone has been laid in the foundation of St Petersburg."

Russia's victory at Poltava greatly strengthened the position of St Petersburg. In 1710, the Imperial family moved to the new city, together with all government institutions, and in 1712, Peter declared St Petersburg the Russian capital. Owing to the shortage of masons, a decree was issued forbidding building in stone anywhere in the Empire outside St Petersburg; forty thousand workmen a year were sent from the provinces, while small landowners and nobles were obliged to resettle in the city and finance the building of their own houses. Encampments larger than the city itself rose up to absorb the incoming labour force. Floods still plagued the islands – at one point Peter himself nearly drowned on Nevskiy prospekt – and wolves roamed the streets after dark, devouring anyone foolish enough to go outside.

Peter's successors

Having killed his only natural heir, Peter was forced to issue a decree claiming the right to nominate his successor, but when he died in 1725, he was so ill that he was unable to speak. Initially his wife, **Catherine I** (1725–27), was hailed as tsaritsa but she died after a reign of less than two years. Peter's grandson, **Peter II** (1727–30), then became tsar and moved the capital and the court back to Moscow in 1728, leaving St Petersburg in decline.

Peter II's sudden death from smallpox in 1730 left the throne wide open. In desperation, the Supreme Privy Council turned to a German-born niece of Peter the Great. Empress **Anna Ivanova** (1730–40) re-established St Petersburg as the capital and brought with her an entourage of unpopular German courtiers. Her ten-year reign was characterized by cruelty and decadence, best illustrated by the Ice Palace that she ordered to be built on the River Neva (see p.78). Affairs of state were handled by her favourite, Ernst-Johann Buhren, a Baltic German baron who executed or exiled thousands of alleged opponents – a reign of terror known as the *Bironovshchina*, after his Russified name, Biron.

Anna died childless in 1740, leaving the crown to her great-nephew, **Ivan VI**, who – because of his youth – was put under the regency of his mother, **Anna Leopoldovna**. However, real power remained in the hands of the hated Biron, until a coup, backed by the Preobrazhenskiy Guards and financed with French money, elevated Peter the Great's daughter Elizabeth to the throne, whereupon Biron and Ivan were imprisoned at Shlisselburg (see p.307).

Elizabeth and Peter III

Like her father, Empress **Elizabeth** (1741–61) was stubborn, quick-tempered and devoted to Russia, but, unlike him, she detested serious occupations and "abandoned herself to every excess of intemperance and lubricity". Elizabeth was almost illiterate and her court favourite, Razumovsky (a Cossack shepherd turned chorister whom she secretly married), couldn't write at all. She liked dancing and hunting, often stayed up all night, spent hours preening herself and lived in chaotic apartments, the wardrobes stacked with over fifteen thousand dresses, the floors littered with unpaid bills. Her peregrinations from palace to palace and from hunting parties to monasteries resulted in a budget deficit of eight million rubles by 1761.

Although Elizabeth hated the sight of blood, she would order torture at the slightest offence – or throw her slipper in the offender's face. Yet she abolished the death penalty and was sensible enough to retain as one of her principal advisers the enlightened Count Shuvalov, who encouraged her in the foundation of Moscow University and the St Petersburg **Academy of Arts**. Indeed, the spectacular achievements of Catherine the Great were based more than Catherine liked to admit on the foundations laid in Elizabeth's reign. In foreign affairs, Elizabeth displayed a determined hostility towards Prussia, participating in both the War of Austrian Succession (1740–48) and the Seven Years' War (1756–63), during which Russian troops occupied Berlin.

On Elizabeth's death in 1761, the new tsar – her nephew, **Peter III** – adopted a strongly pro-Prussian policy, forcing the army into Prussian uniforms and offending the clergy by sticking to the Lutheran faith of his Holstein homeland. The one concession to the nobility during his six-month reign was the abolition of the compulsory 25-year state service. It was a decree of great consequence, for it created a large, privileged leisured class, hitherto unknown in Russia. Childish, moody and impotent, Peter was no match for his intelligent, sophisticated wife, Sophia of Anhalt-Zerbst, who ingratiated herself with her subjects by joining the Orthodox Church, changing her name to Catherine in the process. Their marriage was a sham, and in June 1762 she and her favourite, Grigori Orlov, orchestrated a successful **coup** with the backing of the Imperial Guards. Peter was imprisoned in the palace of Ropsha, and soon murdered by the Orlov brothers.

Catherine the Great

The reign of Catherine the Great spanned four decades (1762–96) and saw the emergence of Russia as a truly great European power. Catherine was a woman of considerable culture and learning and a great patron of the arts. Many of St Petersburg's greatest architectural masterpieces – including the Winter Palace, the Smolniy Cathedral and the Tauride Palace – were completed during her reign, while Catherine's art collection still forms the core of the Hermitage. Inevitably, however, she is best known for her private life; her most prominent favourite, Count Potemkin, oversaw one of the most important territorial gains of her reign – the annexation of Crimea in 1783, which secured the Black Sea coast for Russia.

After consolidating her position as an autocrat – after all, she had no legitimate claim to the throne – Catherine enjoyed a brief honeymoon as a liberal. French became the language of the court, and with it came the ideas of the **Enlightenment**. Catherine herself conducted a lengthy correspondence with Voltaire, while the first great Russian polymath, Lomonosov, was encouraged to standardize the Russian language. However, the lofty intentions of her reforms were watered down by her advisers to little more than a reassertion of "benevolent" despotism. When it came to the crucial question of the emancipation of the serfs, the issue was, not for the first or last time, swept under the carpet. And when writers like Radishchev began to take her at her word and publish critical works, she responded by exiling them to Siberia.

Catherine's liberal leanings were given a worse jolt by the **Pugachev Revolt**, which broke out east of the River Volga in 1773, under the leadership of a Don Cossack named Pugachev. Encouraged by the hope that, since the nobility had been freed from state service, the serfs would likewise be emancipated, thousands responded to Pugachev's call for freedom from the landowners and division of their estates. For two years, Pugachev's Cossack forces conducted a guerrilla campaign from Perm in the Urals to Tsaritsyn on the Volga, before being crushed by Imperial troops. The French Revolution of 1789 killed off what was left of Catherine's benevolence and in her later years she relied ever more heavily on the powers of unbridled autocracy.

Paul and Alexander I

On Catherine's death in 1796, her son **Paul** became tsar. Not without reason, he detested his mother, and immediately set about reversing most of her policies: his first act was to give his father, Peter III, a decent burial. Like his father, Paul was a moody and militarily obsessed man, who worshipped everything Prussian. He offended the army by forcing the Guards back into Prussian uniforms, earned the enmity of the nobility by attempting to curtail some of the privileges they had enjoyed under Catherine, and reintroduced the idea of male hereditary succession that had been abandoned by Peter I.

Paul was strangled to death in March 1801 (see p.90), in a palace coup that had the tacit approval of his son, **Alexander I** (1801–25). Alexander shared Catherine's penchant for the ideas of the Enlightenment, but also exhibited a strong streak of religious conservatism. His reign was, in any case, dominated by foreign affairs and, in particular, the imminent conflict with Europe's dictator, Napoleon. His anti-Napoleonic alliance with Austria and Prussia proved a dismal failure, producing a series of Allied defeats that prompted Alexander to switch sides and join with Napoleon – an alliance sealed by the Treaty of Tilsit in 1807, but which proved to be only temporary.

The Patriotic War

In June 1812, Napoleon crossed the River Niemen and invaded Russia with his Grand Army of 600,000 men – twice the size of any force the Russians could muster. Progress was slow, with the Russians employing their famous "scorched earth" tactics to great effect, while partisans harassed the French flanks. Patriotic fervour forced the Russian general, **Kutuzov**, into fighting a pitched battle with Napoleon, despite having only 100,000 men at his disposal. The **Battle of Borodino**, which took place outside Moscow, resulted in horrific casualties on both sides, but produced no outright victor. Napoleon continued on his march, entering Moscow in September; the following day, the city was consumed in a fire. The popular Russian belief at the time was that the French were responsible, though the governor of Moscow – determined to avoid the capture of his city – was actually the culprit.

Despite abandoning Moscow to the French, Alexander steadfastly refused to leave St Petersburg and meet with Napoleon, leaving the latter no choice but to forget his conquest and begin the long retreat home. Harassed by Russian regulars and partisans, and unprepared for the ferocity of the Russian winter, the Napoleonic Grand Army was reduced to a mere 30,000 men when it finally recrossed the Niemen. The Russians didn't stop there, but pursued Napoleon all the way back to Paris, which they occupied in 1814. At the Congress of Vienna, the following year, Russia was assured of its share of the spoils of the post-Napoleonic carve-up of Europe.

The Decembrists

Another result of the war was that it exposed thousands of Russians to life in other countries. The aristocracy and gentry noted parliaments and constitutional monarchies, while peasant foot soldiers saw how much better their lot could be without serfdom. As the tsar and his chief minister, Count Akracheev, were sure that any reforms would endanger autocracy, opposition festered underground. Guards officers and liberal aristocrats formed innocuously named groups such as the "Southern Society", under the leadership of Colonel Pavel Pestel, whose aim was to establish a classless utopia; and the "Northern Society", which favoured a constitutional monarchy. Both conducted secret propaganda and recruitment from 1823 onwards, and planned to assassinate the tsar.

When Alexander conveniently died in November 1825, without leaving a male heir, the plotters sought to take advantage of the dynastic crisis that ensued. The Imperial Guards initially swore allegiance to Alexander's brother, Konstantin, who was next in line for the throne, but who had secretly renounced his right to the succession. The plotters hurriedly devised a coup, to be staged on December 14, the day the soldiers were to swear a new oath of allegiance to Alexander's younger brother, Nicholas. Word got out about the **Decembrists**, as they became known, and on the day, their nerve failed. For six hours, loyalist troops and Decembrists faced one another across what is now ploshchad Dekabristov, with neither side prepared to fire the first shot. As dusk fell, Nicholas gave the order to clear the square: within two hours the revolt was crushed and hundreds of corpses were tipped into the River Neva.

Nicholas I

In the aftermath of the revolt, **Nicholas I** (1825–55) personally interrogated many of the plotters. Five ringleaders were executed and more than a hundred exiled to Siberia. Though no mention of this "horrible and extraordinary plot" (as he called it) was allowed in public, the fate of so many aristocrats inevitably resulted in gossip – especially when Countess Volkonskaya followed her husband into exile, inspiring other wives to do likewise. Although the Decembrists themselves failed, their example would be upheld by future generations of Russian revolutionaries.

Nicholas's reign was epitomized by the slogan "Orthodoxy, Autocracy, Nationality", coined by one of his ministers. The status quo was to be maintained at all costs: censorship increased, as did police surveillance, carried out by the infamous **Third Section** of the tsar's personal Chancellery. A uniformed gendarmerie was created and organized along military lines, while an elaborate network of spies and informers kept a close watch on all potential subversives. The most intractable problem, as ever, was **serfdom**, "the powder-magazine under the state", as Nicholas's police chief put it. Serfs accounted for four-fifths of the population, and during the late 1820s there were several abortive serf rebellions, though none approached the scale of the Pugachev revolt. The economic position of Russia's serfs remained more or less stagnant throughout Nicholas's reign, and hampered the industrialization of the country, which was mostly confined to developments in the cotton and beet-sugar industries.

Perhaps the greatest social change in Russia took place in the upper echelons of society. In the 1840s, the deferential admiration in which the educated classes normally held the tsar was replaced by scorn and dissent. The writer Dostoyevsky was among those drawn to the clandestine **Petrashevsky Circle** of utopian socialists, who dreamt of a peasant rebellion. In 1849, over a hundred of them were arrested as Nicholas clamped down in the wake of revolutions in Poland and Hungary, which his armies suppressed, earning him the nickname the "Gendarme of Europe" abroad (at home, he was known as *Palkin*, or "The Stick").

In early 1854, the **Crimean War** broke out and Russia found itself at war with Britain, France and Turkey. The war went badly for the Russians and served to highlight the flaws and inadequacies inherent in the Tsarist Empire: Russian troops defending Sebastopol faced rifles with muskets; Russian sailing ships had to do battle with enemy steamers; and the lack of rail-lines meant that Russian soldiers were no better supplied than their Allied counterparts, who were thousands of miles from home. The Allied capture of Sebastopol in 1855 almost certainly helped to accelerate the death of the despondent Nicholas, whose last words of advice to his son and successor were "Hold on to everything!"

The Great Reforms

In fact, the new tsar, **Alexander II** (1855–81), had to sue for peace and initiate changes. The surviving Decembrists and Petrashevsky exiles were released, police surveillance eased and many of the censorship restrictions lifted. The most significant of the so-called **Great Reforms** was the **emancipation of the serfs**, which earned him the sobriquet of "Tsar Liberator". Although two-thirds of the land worked by serfs was handed over to village communes, the ex-serfs were saddled with "redemption payments" to the former landowners over 49 years, and neither side was happy with the deal. Other reforms were more successful. Obligatory military service for peasants was reduced from twenty-five years to six; appointed regional *zemstva* (assemblies) marked the beginning of limited local self-government; trial by jury and a trained judiciary were instituted; and Jews were allowed to live outside the Pale of Settlement.

Yet Alexander baulked at any major constitutional shift from autocracy, disappointing those who had hoped for a "revolution from above". The 1860s saw an upsurge in peasant unrest and a radicalization of the opposition movements coalescing among the educated elite. From the ranks of the disaffected intelligentsia came the amorphous **Populist** (Narodnik) movement, which gathered momentum throughout the late 1860s and early 1870s. Its chief ideologue, **Nikolai Chernyshevsky**, was committed to establishing a socialist society based on the peasant commune, without the intervening stage of capitalism – but there were widely differing views on how to do this. Initially, the **Nihilists** – as the writer Turgenev dubbed them in his novel *Fathers and Sons* (1862) – led the charge, most famously with the first attempt on the tsar's life, carried out in April 1866 by the clandestine organization, "Hell".

The other school of thought believed in taking the Populist message to the people. This proselytizing campaign climaxed in the "**crazy summer**" of 1874, when thousands of students, dressed as simple folk, roamed the countryside attempting to convert the peasantry to their cause. Most of these exhortations fell on deaf ears, for although the peasants were fed up with their lot, they distrusted townspeople and remained loyal to the tsar. The state was nevertheless sufficiently nervous to make mass arrests, which culminated in the much publicized trials of "the 50" and "the 193", held in St Petersburg in 1877–78.

Following what was probably Russia's first political demonstration, outside St Petersburg's Kazan Cathedral in 1876, a new organization was founded, called **Land and Liberty**, which soon split over the use of violence. Land redistribution was the major aim of the "Black Partition", one of whose leaders, Plekhanov, went on to found the first Russian Marxist political grouping; while the **People's Will** (Narodnaya Volya) believed that revolution could be hastened by spectacular terrorist acts – "propaganda of the deed" – culminating in the assassination of the tsar himself in March 1881 (see p.82).

Reaction and industrialization

But regicide failed to stir the masses to revolution, and the new tsar, **Alexander III** (1881–94), was even less inclined than his father to institute political change. Assisted by his ultra-reactionary chancellor, Pobedonostsev, the tsar shelved all constitutional reforms, increased police surveillance and cut back the powers of the *zemstva*. The police stood by during a wave of **pogroms** in 1881–82, Pobedonostsev subsequently promulgating anti-Semitic laws that reversed the emancipation of the Jews instituted by Alexander II. Though hated by Russian liberals, the regime succeeded in uprooting the terrorist underground, which wouldn't pose a danger until a decade hence.

Yet despite turning the clock back in many ways, social and economic change was inexorable. The emancipation of the serfs had led to ever more peasants seeking work in the cities. **Industrialization** increased with breakneck speed – Russia's rate of growth outstripped that of all the other European powers, and foreign investment more than doubled during Alexander III's reign. In St Petersburg, huge factories sprang up in the suburbs, where the harsh conditions and exposure to new ideas and ways of life gradually forged an urban working class. Although it didn't begin to make an impact on politics until the late 1890s, this influx transformed St Petersburg, whose population swelled to almost half a million (making it the fourth largest city in Europe), with all the desperate poverty, child beggars and prostitution described in *Crime and Punishment*. Ministers were keenly aware that the urban poor were a potential threat to the regime, but industrialization was essential if Russia was to compete with other European powers, and legislating factory conditions seemed a slippery slope to wider reforms.

One problem that nobody anticipated was the death of Alexander III, at the age of 49. Immensely strong (he used to bend steel pokers for fun and once held up the roof of a carriage which had derailed), he had been expected to reign for at least another decade. His heir, Nicholas, had barely begun to be initiated into the business of government and was "nothing but a boy, whose judgements are childish" (as Alexander described him). Nobody was more shocked and unprepared than the tsarevich when Alexander died in October 1894, worn out by overwork and nephritis (he loved vodka and defied his doctors' orders by swigging from flasks hidden in his thigh-boots).

The gathering storm

If ever there was a ruler unfit to reign at a critical time (1894–1917), it was **Nicholas II**. Obsessed by trivia, he hated delegating authority, yet was chronically indecisive, consulting "grandparents, aunts, mummy and anyone else" and adopting "the view of the last person to whom he talks". His wife, the German-born princess Alexandra of Hesse, was a fervent convert to Orthodoxy who shared his belief in divinely ordained autocracy and a mystic bond between tsar and peasantry. Painfully shy at receptions and appalled by the lax morals of high society, she was scorned by the aristocracy and urged Nicholas to "stand up" to his ministers. At their Moscow coronation in May 1896, 1300 people were killed in a stampede – an inauspicious start to a doomed reign.

By rejecting the constitutional reforms proposed by the *zemstvo* of Tver as "senseless dreams", Nicholas dismayed liberals and turned moderate Populists into militants. The late 1890s saw a resurgence of underground activity by the **Socialist Revolutionary Party**, or SRs, whose terrorist wing, the SR Fighting Section, assassinated the interior minister, and the tsar's chief minister, Plehve (see p.225), but still failed to attract the mass of the peasantry to its cause. Meanwhile, some of the intelligentsia had shifted its ideological stance towards **Marxism**, which pinned its hopes on the urban proletariat as the future agent of revolution. A Russian Marxist organization was founded as early as 1883 by ex-Populist exiles in Switzerland, but its membership was so tiny that, when out boating on Lake Geneva, the "father of Russian Marxism", **Georgy Plekhanov**, once joked, "Be careful: if this boat sinks, it's the end of Russian Marxism."

Yet its ideas spread back home, disseminated by study groups and underground newspapers. In 1898, Plekhanov was joined by Vladimir Ilyich Ulyanov – better known as Lenin – and founded the Russian Social Democratic Labour Party

(RSDLP). At its 1902 congress in Brussels, the RSDLP split into two factions over the nature of the party and its membership. Lenin wanted it restricted to active militants, obeying orders from the leadership, while his rival Martov desired a looser, mass membership. Adroitly, Lenin provoked half of Martov's supporters to walk out, thereby claiming for his own faction the description Bolsheviks ("majority") and casting his opponents as Mensheviks ("minority").

In Russia, meanwhile, the tsar continued to ignore pleas from the *zemstvo* and business groups to legalize moderate parties and establish a parliamentary system and civil rights. This failure to broaden his base of support and bring new talent into government while Russia was relatively stable would leave the regime perilously isolated when events took a turn for the worse.

The 1905 Revolution

In 1900, Russia's economic boom ended. Unemployed workers streamed back to their villages, where land-hunger and poverty fuelled unrest. The interior minister, Plevhe, organized anti-Semitic pogroms to "drown the revolution in Jewish blood", and urged a "short victorious war" with Japan. But the **Russo-Japanese War** soon led to disaster at Port Arthur, sending shockwaves across Russia. In the capital, a strike broke out at the giant Putilov engineering plant and quickly spread to other factories that encircled the city.

On January 9, 1905 – **Bloody Sunday** – 150,000 strikers and their families converged on the Winter Palace to hand a petition to the tsar, demanding civil rights and labour laws. Led by Father Gapon, the head of a police-sponsored union, the crowd marched peacefully from different parts of the city, carrying portraits of the tsar and singing hymns. In a series of separate incidents, the Imperial Guards fired on the crowd to disperse the protesters, killing as many as one thousand demonstrators and wounding several thousand others. For the rest of his reign, the tsar would never quite shake off his reputation as "Bloody Nicholas".

When the first wave of strikes petered out, the tsar clung to the hope that a reversal of fortune in the Far East would ease his troubles. However, the destruction of the Baltic Fleet at **Tsushima Bay** in May 1905, and the mutiny of the crew of the battleship *Potemkin*, forced the reluctant tsar to make peace with Japan and concede the establishment of a consultative assembly – the **Duma** (from the Russian word *dumat*, "to think"). However, this last-minute concession was insufficient to prevent a printers' strike in St Petersburg in late September from developing into an all-out general strike. Further mutinies occurred among the troops and the countryside slid into anarchy.

By the middle of October, Nicholas had little choice but to grant further concessions. In the **October Manifesto**, he gave a future Duma the power of veto over any laws, promised basic civil liberties and appointed Count Witte as Russia's first prime minister. Meanwhile, in the capital, the workers seized the initiative and created the **St Petersburg Soviet**, made up of some 500 delegates elected by over 200,000 workers (Soviet meaning "council" in Russian). Under the co-chairmanship of **Trotsky** (who had yet to join the Bolsheviks), the Soviet pursued a moderate policy, criticizing the proposed Duma, but not calling for an armed uprising – but still the middle classes took fright.

With the opposition divided over the issue of participation in the Duma, Nicholas seized the chance to arrest the leaders of the Soviet in December, and crushed a belated Bolshevik-inspired uprising in Moscow. During 1906, there were further mutinies in the army and navy, and mayhem in the countryside, but the high point of the revolution had passed. Notwithstanding isolated terrorist successes by the SR Fighting Section, the workers' movement began to decline, while the revolutionary elite languished in prison or, like Lenin, was forced into an impotent exile in Europe.

The only joy for Nicholas and Alexandra during these years was the birth of a son, **Alexei** – and even this soon became a source of pain, for the tsarevich was afflicted by haemophilia, an incurable condition that put him at constant risk of death, a fact they dared not admit to the nation.

The Duma

Of the parties formed in the wake of the October Manifesto, the largest was the Constitutional Democratic, or Kadet, Party, founded by Professor Milyukov to represent Russia's liberal bourgeoisie, whose aims were shared by many of Nicholas's officials. Although the first nationwide elections in Russian history (on a broad-based franchise, though far from universal suffrage) propelled the Kadets to the forefront, the inauguration of the First Duma at the Tauride Palace (May 10, 1906) saw an unprecedented confrontation of courtiers and peasants' and workers' deputies, whose faces impressed the Dowager Empress with their "strange, incomprehensible hatred". After ten weeks of debate, the issue of land distribution reared its head, prompting the tsar to surround the palace with troops and dissolve the Duma. The succeeding Second Duma suffered a similar fate.

Witte's successor as prime minister, **Pyotr Stolypin**, sent nearly 60,000 political detainees to Siberia or the gallows (nicknamed "Stolypin's necktie"), but knew that repression alone was not enough. The **Third Duma**, elected on a much narrower franchise, duly ratified a package of reforms that let peasants leave the village communes to farm privately. Stolypin envisaged a new class of rural entrepreneurs as a bulwark against revolution, so that the state could wager its security "not on the needy and the drunken, but on the sturdy and the strong". However, vested interests and the peasants' reluctance to leave the security of the commune ensured that this new class grew far slower than he had hoped. Stolypin was also frustrated by Nicholas and Alexandra's increasing dependence on the debauched "holy man", **Rasputin**, whom they believed held the key to the survival of their son, Alexei. Stolypin's assassination by a secret police double agent in 1911 deprived Nicholas of his ablest statesmen only a few years before the regime would face its sternest test.

The most positive post-revolutionary repercussions took place within **the arts**. From 1905 to 1914, St Petersburg (and Moscow) experienced an extraordinary outburst of artistic energy: Diaghilev's Ballets Russes dazzled Europe; Chekhov premiered his works in the capital; poets and writers held Symbolist seances in city salons; while Mayakovsky and other self-proclaimed Futurists toured the country, shocking the general public with their statements on art.

World War I

By 1914, Europe's Great Powers were enmeshed in alliances that made war almost inevitable, once the fuse had been lit. The assassination of the Habsburg

Archduke Ferdinand in Sarajevo, Austria-Hungary's ultimatum to Serbia and German mobilization left Russian public opinion baying for war in defence of its "Slav brothers". In the patriotic fervour accompanying the outbreak of **World War I**, the name of the capital, St Petersburg, was deemed too Germanic and replaced by the more Russian-sounding **Petrograd**. Yet grave deficiencies in the structure of the army and in military production were barely acknowledged, let alone tackled. The first Russian offensive ended in defeat at Tannenberg in August 1914, with estimated casualties of 170,000. From then onwards, there was rarely any good news from the front; in the first year alone, around four million soldiers lost their lives. In an attempt to prove that everything was under control, the tsar foolishly assumed supreme command of the armed forces – a post for which he was totally unqualified – and left his wife in charge of the home front.

By 1916, even devout monarchists were angry. Empress Alexandra, the "German woman", was openly accused of treason, and Rasputin was assassinated by a group of aristocrats desperate to force a change of policy. Ensconced with his son in the General Staff headquarters at Mogilev, Nicholas refused to be moved. As inflation spiralled and food shortages worsened, strikes began to break out once more in Petrograd. By the beginning of 1917, everyone from generals to peasants talked of an imminent uprising.

The February Revolution

On February 22, 1917, there was a lockout of workers at the Putilov works in Petrograd. Next day (International Women's Day), thousands of women and workers thronged the streets attacking bread shops, singing the *Marseillaise* and calling for the overthrow of the tsar. Soldiers and Cossacks fraternized with the demonstrators and when the Volhynia Guards obeyed orders and fired on the crowds, the Petrograd garrison mutinied. On February 27, prisons were stormed and the Fourth Duma was surrounded by angry demonstrators and mutinous troops. The Duma, which the tsar had formally prorogued, approved the establishment of a Provisional Committee "for the re-establishment of order in the capital", while Trotsky and the Mensheviks quickly revived the Petrograd Soviet. On March 2, en route to the capital, the tsar was finally persuaded to abdicate in favour of his brother, Grand Duke Michael, who gave up his claim to the throne the following day: the Romanov dynasty had ended.

Out of the ferment arose what Russians called "**dual power**" (*dvovlastie*). The **Provisional Government**, under the liberal Count Lvov, tried to assert itself as the legitimate successor to Tsarist despotism. Freedom of speech and a political amnesty were immediately decreed; there were to be elections for a Constituent Assembly, but there was to be no end to the war. This last policy pacified the generals, who might otherwise have attempted to suppress the Revolution, but quickly eroded the Provisional Government's popularity. The other power base was the **Petrograd Soviet**, dominated by Mensheviks, which was prepared to give qualified support to the "bourgeois revolution" (they were less enthusiastic about the war) until the time was ripe for the establishment of socialism. The Soviet's chief achievement was the effecting of "Order No. 1", authorizing the formation of Soviets throughout the army, whose existence rapidly undermined military discipline.

After ditching some of its more right-wing elements, the Provisional Government cooperated more closely with the Petrograd Soviet. **Alexander**

Kerensky became minister of war and toured the front calling for a fresh offensive against the Germans, which commenced in late June. It began well, but soon turned into a retreat, while discontent in Petrograd peaked again in a wave of violent protests known as the **July Days**. Soldiers and workers, egged on by the city's Anarchists and some Bolsheviks, marched on the Soviet, calling for the overthrow of the Provisional Government. However, Lenin, who had returned from exile in April, felt that the time was not right for an armed uprising, and the Soviet was unwilling to act. In the end, troops loyal to the government arrived in Petrograd and restored order. Trotsky and others were arrested, Lenin was accused of being a German spy and forced once more into exile, and the Bolsheviks as a whole were branded as traitors.

Kerensky used the opportunity to tighten his grip on the Provisional Government, taking over as leader from Count Lvov and making the fateful decision to move into the Winter Palace. If the July Days were a blow to the Left, the abortive **Kornilov Revolt** was an even greater setback for the Right. In late August, the army's commander-in-chief, General Kornilov, attempted to march on Petrograd and crush Bolshevism once and for all. Whether he had been encouraged in this by Kerensky remains uncertain, but in the event, Kerensky turned on Kornilov, denouncing the coup and urging the Bolsheviks and workers' militia to defend the capital. Kerensky duly appointed himself commander-in-chief, but it was the Left who were now in the ascendance.

The October Revolution

During September, the country slid into chaos: soldiers deserted the front in droves; the countryside was in turmoil; and the "Bolshevization" of the Soviets continued apace. By mid-month, Lenin, who was still in hiding in Finland, urged a coup against the Provisional Government, but didn't win over the Bolshevik leadership until mid-October, whereupon Trotsky used the Military Revolutionary Committee which had been established by the Petrograd Soviet to defend the city against the threat of counter-revolution, to ready the Bolshevik Red Guards for action, from their headquarters at the Smolniy Institute.

The **October Revolution** is thought to have begun in the early hours of the 25th, with the occupation of key points in Petrograd by Red Guards. Kerensky fled the city, ostensibly to rally support for the government; it was in fact his final exit. Meanwhile, posters announcing the overthrow of the Provisional Government appeared on the streets at 10am, though it wasn't until 2am the following day that the government's ministers were formally arrested in the Winter Palace. It was an almost bloodless coup (in Petrograd at least), but it unleashed the most bloody civil war and regime in Russia's history.

It had been planned to coincide with the Second All-Russian Congress of Soviets, which convened at the Smolniy on the night of the coup. At the congress the Bolsheviks had a majority, enhanced when the Mensheviks and right-wing SRs walked out in protest at the coup. Lenin delivered his two famous decrees, calling for an end to the war and approving the seizure of land by the peasants. An all-Bolshevik **Council of People's Commissars** was established, headed by Lenin, with Trotsky as Commissar for Foreign Affairs. A spate of decrees was issued, the most important of which were those calling for the institution of an eight-hour working day, the abolition of social classes and the nationalization of all banks and financial organizations.

Conditions in Petrograd deteriorated further. Food was scarcer than ever; rumours of anti-Bolshevik plots abounded. As early as December 1917, Lenin created a new secret police, the "All-Russian Extraordinary Commission for Struggle against Counter-Revolution, Speculation and Sabotage", or **Cheka** (aptly meaning "linchpin" in Russian). Although the Bolsheviks had reluctantly agreed to abolish the death penalty in October, the Cheka, under "Iron" **Felix Dzerzhinsky**, reserved the right to "have recourse to a firing squad when it becomes obvious that there is no other way".

Following elections, the long-awaited **Constituent Assembly** met for the first and only time on January 5, 1918, in the Tauride Palace. As the first Russian parliament elected by universal suffrage, this was meant to be "the crowning jewel in Russian democratic life", but Lenin already privately regarded it as "an old fairytale which there is no reason to carry on further". Having received only a quarter of the vote, the Bolsheviks surrounded the palace next day, preventing many delegates from entering; Red Guards eventually dismissed those inside with the words, "Push off. We want to go home."

Civil War

More pressing than the internecine feuds of the socialist parties was the outcome of the peace negotiations with Germany. In mid-February 1918, talks broke down and the Germans launched a fresh offensive. On March 3, Trotsky signed the **Treaty of Brest-Litovsk**, which handed over Poland, Finland, Belarus, the Baltics and – most painfully of all – Ukraine, Russia's bread basket. Following the treaty, the Bolsheviks transferred the **capital** from Petrograd to **Moscow** – leaving the city more exposed than ever to foreign attack. Within two years, Petrograd's population had shrunk by 65 percent, to 799,000.

At the Seventh Party Congress, at which the RSDLP was renamed the **Communist Party**, the Left SRs walked out in protest at the treaty. On July 6, an SR member assassinated the German ambassador, and the next day the SRs staged an abortive coup in Moscow, followed by the assassination of the Petrograd Cheka chief, Uritsky, and an unsuccessful attempt on Lenin's life in August. The Bolsheviks responded with a wave of repression called the **Red Terror**. Declaring "an end to clemency and slackness", the Cheka immediately shot 512 "hostages" in Petrograd and 500 at Kronstadt. Dzerzhinsky's deputy pronounced that one look at a suspect's hands would suffice to determine his class allegiance.

By this time a **Civil War** was raging across Russia, fuelled by **foreign intervention**. In a vain attempt to force Russia back into the war against Germany, but also from fear of Bolshevism spreading, the Western powers sent troops to fight the Reds. A Czech Legion seized control of much of the Trans-Siberian Railway; British troops landed in Murmansk and Baku; US, Japanese, French and Italian forces took over Vladivostok; while the Germans controlled the vast tracts of land given to them under the Brest-Litovsk treaty. Fearing that the **Imperial family** would be freed from captivity in Yekaterinburg, Lenin ordered their **execution**, carried out by local Bolsheviks on July 16–17.

With the end of World War I, foreign troops began to return home, leaving the Reds and the **Whites** (anti-Soviet forces) to fight it out. What the Reds lacked in military experience they made up for in ideological motivation and iron discipline. The disparate anti-Soviet forces, on the other hand, represented every type of political movement from monarchists to SRs. The sides were evenly matched in numbers and rivalled each other in ferocity when it came to exacting revenge on collaborators. Ultimately, the Reds prevailed, though not without a few close calls: during the autumn of 1919, a White force of 20,000 was prevented from capturing Petrograd only by the personal intervention of Trotsky, who rallied the Red Army and turned the tide of the battle at Gatchina.

Besides costing the lives of millions, the Civil War promoted the militarization of Soviet society, under the rubric of "**War Communism**". Workers' control in the factories and the nationalization of land had plunged the economy into chaos just as the Civil War broke out. To cope, the Bolsheviks introduced stringent economic centralization, replacing workers' control with labour discipline of a kind unseen since the pre-trade union days of Tsarism. With inflation spiralling and the currency almost worthless, the peasants had little incentive to sell their produce in the cities, so Red Guards were sent into the countryside to seize food, and "committees of the poor" were set up to stimulate class war against the richer peasantry, or *kulaks*.

The Kronstadt revolt and the NEP

By 1921, Russia was economically devastated – in Petrograd alone, the population shrank by two-thirds. The Communists found themselves confronted with worker unrest and, for the first time, serious divisions appeared within the Party. The most outspoken faction was the **Workers' Opposition**, led by Alexandra Kollontai and Alexander Shlyapnikov, whose main demands were the separation of the trade unions from the Party and fewer wage differentials. In February 1921, even the Kronstadt sailors – who had been among the Bolsheviks' staunchest supporters – turned against the Party. The **Kronstadt sailors' revolt** precipitated a general strike in Petrograd when troops once more refused to fire on the crowds. Rejecting calls for negotiations, the Bolsheviks accused the Kronstadt sailors of acting under the orders of a White general and, after a bloody battle, succeeded in crushing the rebellion (see p.292).

Whilst the revolt was under way, Lenin was presiding over the **Tenth Party Congress**, at which he banned factions and declared a virtual end to democratic debate. Those SRs still at large were rounded up and either exiled or subjected to the first Soviet show trial, in 1922. From now on, real power was in the hands of the emerging party bureaucracy, or **Secretariat**, whose first General Secretary was the Georgian Communist, **Iosif Stalin**.

At the congress, Lenin unveiled his **New Economic Policy** (NEP), a step back from the all-out confrontation with the peasantry that had been the hallmark of War Communism. The state maintained control of the "commanding heights" of the economy, but restored a limited free market for agricultural produce and consumer goods, giving peasants an incentive to increase productivity, and stimulating trade. It was a formula that favoured the peasantry (who still formed the majority of the population) and speculators of all kinds (known as "Nepmen") rather than the urban working class, who dubbed the NEP the "New Exploitation of the Proletariat".

Stalin and Collectivization

Lenin's death on January 24, 1924 inaugurated an all-out power struggle. Trotsky, the hero of the Civil War, and Bukharin, the chief exponent of the NEP, were by far the most popular figures in the Party, but it was **Stalin**, as head of the Secretariat, who held the aces. Stalin organized Lenin's funeral and was the chief architect in his deification, which began with the renaming of Petrograd as **Leningrad**. Using classic divide-and-rule tactics, Stalin picked off his rivals one by one, beginning with the exile of Trotsky in 1925, followed by the neutralization of Zinoviev, the Leningrad Party boss, and Bukharin in 1929.

Abandoning the NEP, in the first Five-Year Plan (1928–32), Stalin ordered the forced **collectivization** of agriculture and industrialization on an unprecedented scale. Declaring its aim to be "the elimination of the *kulak* as a class", the Party waged open war on a peasantry who were overwhelmingly hostile to collectivization. This conflict has been dubbed the "Third Revolution" – for it transformed Russian society more than any of the country's previous revolutions. The peasants' passive resistance, the destruction of livestock and the ensuing chaos all contributed to the **famine of 1932–33**, which resulted in the death of as many as five million people from starvation and disease.

Realizing that some retrenchment was unavoidable, Stalin ascribed the consequences to Party cadres "dizzy with success" and advocated more realistic goals for the second Five-Year Plan (1933–37). In 1934, at the Seventeenth Party "**Congress of Victors**", Stalin declared that the Party had triumphed, pronouncing that "Life has become better, Comrades. Life has become gayer". While the 2000-plus delegates cheered, there were many who privately thought that, with Soviet power assured, Stalin should make way for a new General Secretary and a return to collegial decision-making. The likeliest candidate was the Leningrad Party boss, **Sergei Kirov**, who had popular appeal, yet lacked the urge to dominate his colleagues.

The Great Terror

Whether there was ever a chance of unseating Stalin is among the many "what ifs" of Russian history. In reality, **Kirov's assassination** at the Smolniy on December 1, 1934, gave Stalin the pretext for a **purge of Leningrad** that saw 30,000–40,000 citizens arrested in the spring of 1935 alone, and perhaps as many as a quarter of the city's population within a year – the majority destined for the **Gulag**, or "Corrective Labour Camps and Labour Settlements".

This was merely the prelude to a nationwide frenzy of fear and denunciation. At the first of the great Moscow **show trials** in the summer of 1936, Lenin's old comrades, Kamenev and Zinoviev, "confessed" to Kirov's murder and were shot along with fourteen others (Zinoviev begged, "For God's sake, tell Stalin … he'll say it's all a dreadful mistake!"). In early 1937, the head of the NKVD (secret police), Genrikh Yagoda, was arrested and succeeded by the dwarfish Nikolai Yezhov, who presided over the darkest period in Russian history, the *Yezhovshchina*, or **Great Terror**, of 1937–38. Exact figures are impossible to ascertain, but the total number of people arrested during the purges is thought to have been in the region of eight million, of whom at least a million were executed, while countless others died in the camps. Besides the lives lost or blighted, the loss of engineers, scientists and skilled workers wrought havoc on industry, research and the railways – there came a point beyond which terror was self-defeating, even for the most ruthless regime. So in December, 1938, Yezhov was replaced by Lavrenty Beria – a signal from Stalin that the worst was over, for the time being.

Few realized that purges within the Red Army had left it gravely weakened. From the defence minister Marshal Tukhachevsky downwards, the majority of senior officers had been either shot or sent to camps, and their hastily promoted successors were under-qualified and afraid to display any initiative. As Anglo-French appeasement allowed Nazi Germany to invade Austria and Czechoslovakia, and to set its sights on Poland, Stalin feared that the USSR would be next on its *Drang nach Osten* (Drive to the East) and authorized Foreign Minister Molotov to negotiate with his Nazi counterpart. The Molotov-Ribbentrop pact of August 1939 bound both parties to non-aggression, and the Soviets to supply food and raw materials to the Nazis. It also contained secret clauses relating to the division of Poland and the Soviet occupation of the Baltic States, which was put into practice in the first weeks of World War II. In October, Stalin demanded the moving of the Finnish frontier further from Leningrad, and in November, attacked the Karelian Isthmus. But the Winter War (1939–40) exposed the flaws of the Red Army, and although it eventually prevailed – taking Karelia - Stalin's act ensured that Finland would join the Nazi invasion to recover its lost territory.

The Great Patriotic War

On June 22, 1941, Hitler's forces invaded the Soviet Union, starting what Russians call the **Great Patriotic War**. Despite advance warnings from numerous sources, Stalin was taken by surprise and apparently suffered a nervous breakdown, withdrawing to his *dacha* outside Moscow while his subordinates attempted to grapple with the crisis. In the first days of the war, over a thousand Soviet aircraft were destroyed on the ground; whole armies were encircled and captured; and local Party officials fled from the advancing *Blitzkrieg*. In some regions the population welcomed the Germans as liberators – until Nazi brutality flung them back into the arms of Stalin.

The position of **Leningrad** soon became critical. By September 1941, it was virtually surrounded by German forces, whose operational directive read: "The Führer has decided to wipe the city of Petersburg off the face of the earth. It is proposed to tighten up the blockade of the city and level it to the ground by shelling and continuous bombing from the air." So began the terrible "900 Days" of starvation and bombardment, known to Russians as the **Blockade** (*blokada*). No preparations had been made for a siege: indeed, shortly before it began, food had actually been sent out of Leningrad to the forces at the front. The only supply line lay across Lake Ladoga, to the east of the city, where trucks could cross the icy **Road of Life** (see p.306) when the lake was frozen in winter. Yet, despite heroic improvisations, Leningrad came close to collapse in the winter of 1941–42, when 53,000 people died in December alone. By the second winter, supplies were better organized and the population had developed a powerful sense of solidarity, but even so, 670,000 citizens died before the Blockade was finally broken in January 1944. In recognition of its sacrifices, Leningrad was proclaimed a "**Hero City**" of the Soviet Union; its shops were supplied with the best food in the country and every child born in the city received a special medal.

Stalin's final years

After the enormous sacrifices of the war – in which 27 million Soviet citizens had perished – people longed for a peaceful, freer life. But any liberalization was anathema to Stalin, whose suspicion of rivals and subversive trends was stronger than ever. It seems likely that he planned to purge the Politburo of all those who had served him since the 1930s, and install a new generation of lackeys. As ever, he used others to pick off his victims and script the show trials. Beria and Malenkov united against **Andrei Zhdanov**, who had been promoted to the Politburo for leading Leningrad through the Blockade. Criticized for a "lack of ideological vigilance" in his home city, Zhdanov responded with a crackdown on "anti-patriotic elements" among the intelligentsia, launching a vitriolic attack on two local journals and vilifying the city's beloved poet, Akhmatova, as "half-nun, half-whore".

When Zhdanov died (or was poisoned) in 1948, Beria fabricated the "**Leningrad Affair**", in which Zhdanov's closest allies were accused of trying to seize power and were executed. Thousands of Leningraders fell victim to the witch-hunt that followed and wound up in the Gulag. Stalin's final show trial was the notorious "**Doctors' Plot**", where eminent physicians "confessed" to murdering Zhdanov and plotting to kill others in the Politburo. It was "no coincidence" (a phrase beloved of Stalin) that the doctors were mostly Jewish, nor that the list of their intended victims omitted Beria. The stage was being set for a nationwide pogrom and the deportation of all Jews to a remote region of Siberia for "their own protection", while Beria would be cast as the villain in future show trials. Thankfully, two months into the charade, the **death of Stalin** (March 5, 1953) brought an end to proceedings and charges were subsequently dropped.

Khrushchev

Stalin's successors jockeyed for power. The odious Beria was the first to be arrested and executed, in July 1953; Malenkov lasted until 1955, before he was forced to resign; Molotov hung on until 1957. The man who emerged as the next Soviet leader was **Nikita Khrushchev**, who, in 1956, when his position was by no means unassailable, gave a "**Secret Speech**" to the Twentieth Party Congress, in which Stalin's name was for the first time officially linked with Kirov's murder and the sufferings of millions during the Great Terror. So traumatic was the revelation that many delegates had heart attacks on the spot. In the same year, thousands were rehabilitated and returned from the camps. Yet for all its courage, Khrushchev's **de-Stalinization** was strictly limited in scope – after all, he himself had earned the nickname "Butcher of the Ukraine" during the *Yezhovshchina*.

The cultural **thaw** that followed Khrushchev's speech was equally selective, allowing the publication of Solzhenitsyn's account of the Gulag, *One Day in the Life of Ivan Denisovich*, but rejecting Pasternak's *Doctor Zhivago*. Khrushchev emptied the camps, only to send dissidents to psychiatric hospitals. In **foreign affairs**, he was not one to shy away from confrontation, either. Soviet tanks spilled blood on the streets of Budapest in 1956, while Khrushchev oversaw the building of the Berlin Wall and, in October 1962, took the world to the edge of the nuclear precipice during the Cuban Missile Crisis. He also boasted that the Soviet Union would surpass the West in the production of consumer goods within twenty years, and pinned the nation's hopes on developing the so-called "Virgin Lands" of Siberia and Kazakhstan.

By 1964, Khrushchev had managed to alienate all the main interest groups in the Soviet hierarchy. His emphasis on nuclear rather than conventional weapons lost him the support of the military; his de-Stalinization was unpopular with the KGB; while his administrative reforms struck at the heart of the Party apparatus. As the Virgin Lands turned into a dust bowl, his economic boasts rang hollow and the Soviet public was deeply embarrassed by his boorish behaviour at the United Nations, where Khrushchev interrupted a speech by banging on the table with his shoe. In October 1964, his enemies took advantage of his vacation at the Black Sea to mount a bloodless coup, and on his return to Moscow, Khrushchev was presented with his resignation "for reasons of health". It was a sign of the changes since Stalin's death that he was the first disgraced Soviet leader to be allowed to live on in obscurity, rather than being shot.

Brezhnev and the Era of Stagnation

Khrushchev's ultimate successor, **Leonid Brezhnev**, made an about-turn. Military expenditure rose, attacks on Stalin ceased and the subject of the Great Terror became taboo again. The show trial of the writers, Sinyavsky and Daniel, in February 1966, marked the end of the thaw and was followed by a wave of repression in major cities, including Leningrad, while the crushing of the Prague Spring in August 1968 showed that the new Soviet leaders were as ruthless as their predecessors in stamping out dissent abroad. Owing to press censorship and public indifference, most Russians knew little of **Alexander Solzhenitsyn** when he was exiled to the West in 1974, and even less of **Andrei Sakharov**, the nuclear physicist sentenced to internal exile for his human-rights campaigns.

Despite Party and KGB control of society, the Brezhnev era is now remembered in Russia as a rare period of peace and stability. With many goods subsidized, citizens could bask in the knowledge that meat and bread cost the same as they had done in 1950 (even if you did have to queue for it), while those with money had recourse to the burgeoning black market. The newfound security of the Party cadres (subject to fewer purges than at any time since the Soviet system began) led to unprecedented corruption. As sclerosis set in across the board, industrial and agricultural output declined to new lows. By 1970, the average age of the Politburo was over 70 – embodying the geriatric nature of Soviet politics in what would later be called the **Era of Stagnation** (*zastoy*). Amongst the Politburo members tipped to succeed Brezhnev was **Grigori Romanov**, the Leningrad Party secretary who let the city fall into decay and, it was (falsely) rumoured, once borrowed a priceless dinner service from the Hermitage for his daughter's wedding.

Brezhnev died in November 1982 and was succeeded by **Yuri Andropov**, the former KGB boss, who had hardly begun an anti-corruption campaign when he too expired (February 1984). Brezhnev's clique took fright at the prospect of yet more change and elected the 73-year-old **Konstantin Chernenko** as General Secretary, but when he also died barely a year later, it was clear that the post required some new blood.

The Gorbachev years

Mikhail Gorbachev – at 53, the youngest of the Politburo – was chosen with a brief to "get things moving". The first of his policies to send shock waves through society – a campaign against alcohol – was the most unpopular, abortive initiative of his career, followed shortly afterwards by the coining of the two famous buzz words of the Gorbachev era: **glasnost** (openness) and **perestroika** (restructuring). The first took a battering when, in April 1986, the world's worst nuclear disaster – at **Chernobyl** – was hushed up for a full three days, before the Swedes forced an admission out of the Soviet authorities. Similarly, Gorbachev denied the existence of political prisoners right up until Sakharov's release from exile in the "closed" city of Gorky, in December 1986.

Regardless, Gorbachev pressed on, shaking up the bureaucracy and launching investigations into numerous officials who had abused their positions in the Brezhnev era. One of the most energetic campaigners against corruption was the new Moscow Party chief, **Boris Yeltsin**, whose populist antics, such as exposing black market dealings within the *apparat*, infuriated the old guard. In October 1987, Yeltsin openly attacked Gorbachev and the hardline ideologist, Yegor Ligachev, and then dramatically resigned from the Politburo; shortly afterwards, he was sacked as Moscow Party leader.

Yeltsin's fate was a foretaste of things to come, as Gorbachev abandoned his balancing act and realigned himself with the hardliners. In the summer of 1988, radicals within the Party formed the **Democratic Union**, the first organized opposition movement to emerge since 1921. Gorbachev promptly banned its meetings and created a new security force – the **OMON** – while in the Baltic republics, nationalist **Popular Fronts** emerged, instantly attracting a mass membership. Estonia was the first to make the break, declaring sovereignty in November 1988 and raising the national flag in place of the hammer and sickle in February the following year.

1989 and all that

In the **elections** for the Congress of People's Deputies of March 1989, Soviet voters were, for the first time in decades, allowed to choose from more than one candidate, some of whom were even non-Party members. Despite the heavily rigged selection process, radicals – including Yeltsin and Sakharov – managed to get elected. At the congress in May, a Latvian deputy started the proceedings with a call for an enquiry into events in Georgia, where Soviet troops had recently killed 21 protesters. When Sakharov urged an end to one-party rule, his microphone was switched off – a futile gesture by Gorbachev, since the sessions were being broadcast live on Russian TV.

Gorbachev's next crisis came with the **miners' strike** in July, when thousands walked out in protest at shortages, safety standards and poor wages. Gorbachev managed to entice them back to work with various promises, but the myth of the Soviet Union as a workers' state had been shattered for ever. The events which swept across the satellite states in Eastern Europe throughout 1989, culminating with the **fall of the Berlin Wall** and the Velvet Revolution in Czechoslovakia, were another blow to the old guard, but Gorbachev was more concerned with holding together the Soviet Union itself. That Communism now faced its greatest crisis at home was humiliatingly made plain by unprecedented counter-demonstrations during the October Revolution celebrations on November 7, 1989: one of the banners read: "Workers of the World – we're sorry."

The year 1990 proved no better for Gorbachev or the Party. On January 19, Soviet tanks rolled into the Azerbaijani capital, Baku, to crush the independence movement there – more than a hundred people were killed that night. In February, Moscow witnessed the largest **demonstration** since the Revolution of 1917, calling for an end to one-party rule and protesting against the rising anti-Semitic violence that had resulted in several murders in Leningrad. Gorbachev attempted to seize the initiative by agreeing to end one-party rule and simultaneously electing himself president, with increased powers to deal with the escalating crisis in the republics.

The voters registered their disgust with the Party at the March **local elections**. In the republics, nationalists swept the board and declarations of independence soon followed, while in Russia itself, the new radical alliance, **Democratic Platform**, gained majorities in the powerful city councils of Leningrad and Moscow. Gavril Popov became chairman of the Moscow council, while an equally reformist law professor, **Anatoly Sobchak**, was eventually elected to the leading post in Leningrad. May Day was another humiliation for Gorbachev, who was jeered by sections of the crowd in Red Square. By the end of the month Yeltsin secured his election as chairman of the Russian parliament and, two weeks later, in imitation of the Baltic States, declared **Russian independence** from the Soviet Union (June 12, 1990).

In July, the Soviet Communist Party held its last ever congress. Yeltsin tore up his Party card in full view of the cameras – two million had done the same by the end of the year. The economic crisis, spiralling crime and chronic food shortages put Gorbachev under renewed pressure from Party hardliners. The first ominous signs came as winter set in, with a series of leadership reshuffles that gave the Interior Ministry and control of the media back to the conservatives. On December 20, the liberal Soviet foreign minister, Edvard Shevardnadze, resigned, warning that "dictatorship is coming".

The effects of Gorbachev's reshuffle became clear on January 13, 1991, when thirteen Lithuanians were killed by Soviet troops as they defended – unarmed – the national TV centre. Yeltsin immediately flew there and signed a joint declaration condemning the violence. A week later in Latvia, the OMON stormed the Latvian Interior Ministry in Rīga, killing five people. Hours before this attack, Moscow witnessed its largest ever demonstration – 250,000 people came out to protest against the killings. The Russian press had a field day, going further than ever before, mocking Gorbachev and backing the Balts. Gorbachev responded by threatening to suspend the liberal press laws, while adding more hardliners to the Politburo and giving wider powers to the security forces.

In June, the citizens of Leningrad narrowly voted in a referendum to rename the city **St Petersburg**, to the fury of Gorbachev, who refused to countenance it (the decision was ratified by parliament only after the putsch). At the same time, both Moscow and St Petersburg voted in new radical mayors (Popov and Sobchak) to run the reorganized city administrations.

Popular disgust with Party rule was manifest in the overwhelming majority of votes cast for Yeltsin in the **Russian presidential election** of June 12, 1991. As Russia's first ever democratically elected leader, he could claim a mandate for bold moves and within a month had issued a decree calling for the removal of Party "cells" from factories. It was the most serious threat yet to the dominance of the Party in Soviet life. Three days later, leading hardliners published a lengthy appeal for action "to lead the country to a dignified and sovereign future". Another indication of what might be in store came at the end of July, when seven Lithuanian border guards were shot dead in one of the continuing Soviet army attacks on Baltic customs posts.

The end of the USSR

On Monday August 19, 1991, the Soviet Union awoke to the soothing sounds of Chopin on the radio and *Swan Lake* on television. A **state of emergency** had been declared, Gorbachev had resigned "for health reasons" and the country was now ruled by a self-appointed "State Committee for the State of Emergency in the USSR". Its members included many of Gorbachev's recently appointed colleagues, under the nominal leadership of Gennady Yenayev, whose election as vice-president Gorbachev had obtained only after threatening his own resignation. Gorbachev himself, then on holiday in the Crimea, had been asked to back the coup the previous night, but had refused (to the surprise of the conspirators) and was consequently under house arrest. So began what Russians call the **putsch**.

In Moscow, tanks appeared on the streets from mid-morning onwards, stationing themselves at key points, including the Russian parliament building, known as the **White House**. Here, a small group of protesters gathered, including Yeltsin, who had narrowly escaped arrest that morning. When the first tank approached, he leapt aboard, shook hands with its commander and appealed to the crowd (and accompanying radio and TV crews): "You can erect a throne using bayonets, but you cannot sit on bayonets for long." The Afghan war hero, Alexander Rutskoy, turned up and started organizing the defence of the building, making it harder for regular troops to contemplate attacking it. Actually, the role of storming the White House had been allocated to the crack KGB Alpha Force, but, for reasons unknown, they never went into action. News of the standoff – and Yeltsin's appeal to soldiers not to "let yourselves be turned into blind weapons" – was broadcast around the world and beamed back to millions of Russians via the BBC and the Voice of America.

In Leningrad, the army stayed off the streets and Mayor Sobchak kept his cool, quoting the constitution to the local coup commander at Military District headquarters. He warned them, "If you lay a finger on me, you will be put on trial like the rest of the Nazis." It was pure bravado, but it worked: the local commander agreed to keep his forces in their barracks. The putsch had been badly planned from the start, with no preparatory round-up of opponents, nor any effort to sever international and domestic telephone lines. By Monday evening, Sobchak had appeared on local television and denounced the putsch – in Leningrad, it was effectively over on day one, though the citizens who gathered to defend City Hall had an anxious night awaiting tanks that never materialized. The following day, 200,000 Leningraders massed on Palace Square in protest against the putsch, while the eyes of the world were on Moscow.

On Tuesday, the defenders of the White House were heartened by the news that one of the coup leaders had resigned due to "high blood pressure" (he had been drinking continuously) and the crowd grew to 100,000 in defiance of a curfew order. Around midnight, an advancing armoured column was stopped and firebombed on a Moscow ring road and three civilians were shot dead. Next morning it was announced that several military units had decamped to Yeltsin's side and on Wednesday afternoon the putsch collapsed as its leaders bolted. One group flew to the Crimea in the hope of obtaining Gorbachev's pardon and was arrested on arrival. Yenayev drank himself into a stupor and several others committed suicide.

Gorbachev flew back to Moscow, not realizing that everything had changed. At his first press conference, he pledged continuing support for the Communist Party and Marxist-Leninism, and openly admitted that he had trusted the conspirators as men of "culture and dialogue". He was, by now, totally estranged from the mood of the country and marooned by the tide of history. The same day, jubilant crowds toppled the giant statue of Dzerzhinsky which stood outside the Lubyanka in Moscow. On Friday, Gorbachev appeared before parliament and was publicly humiliated by Yeltsin in front of the television cameras. Yeltsin then decreed the Russian Communist Party an illegal organization, announced the suspension of pro-coup newspapers such as *Pravda* and had the Central Committee headquarters in Moscow sealed up.

The failure of the putsch spelt the **end of Communist rule** and the **break-up of the Soviet Union**. Any possibility of a Slav core remaining united was torpedoed by loose talk of re-drawing the border between Russia and Ukraine, and the newfound goodwill between Russia and its former satellites quickly evaporated. In December, Ukraine voted overwhelmingly for independence; a week later the leaders of Russia, Belarus and Ukraine formally replaced the USSR with a **Commonwealth of Independent States** (CIS), whose nominal capital would be Minsk; the Central Asian republics declared their intention of joining. On December 25, Gorbachev resigned as president of a state which no longer existed; that evening the Soviet flag was lowered over the Kremlin and replaced by the Russian tricolour.

New Russia

On January 2, 1992, Russians faced their New Year hangovers and the harsh reality of massive price rises, following a decree by Yeltsin that lifted controls on a broad range of products. The cost of food rose by up to 500 percent and queues disappeared almost overnight. According to the Western advisers shaping Russia's new economic policy, this would stimulate domestic production and promote the growth of capitalism in the shortest possible time. Initially, **inflation** was limited by keeping a tight rein on state spending, in accordance with the monetarist strategy of Prime Minister **Yegor Gaidar**, but despite Yeltsin's defence of his painful and unpopular measures the policy soon came unstuck after the Central Bank began printing vast amounts of rubles to cover credits issued to state industries on the verge of bankruptcy. Inflation soared.

St Petersburg also had other concerns. On March 25, an accident at the nuclear reactor at **Sosnovy Bor**, on the Gulf of Finland, caused concern around the world. The reactor was of the same type as the one that blew up at Chernobyl and initial reports suggested that St Petersburg had been contaminated. In fact, no radiation was released, but the accident highlighted environmental worries, including the **pollution** of the city's water supply by industrial effluents discharged into Lake Ladoga and the Neva, exacerbated by the half-finished tidal barrage across the Gulf. While Mayor Sobchak toured the West to raise funds to invest in St Petersburg, unscrupulous foreign companies tried to take advantage: one firm offered to build the city a free ring road if only they could bury rubbish beneath it, neglecting to mention that they had highly toxic waste in mind.

By the autumn of 1992, Russia's economic policy was in dire straits and Yeltsin was forced to replace Gaidar with the veteran technocrat **Viktor Chernomyrdin**, in December 1992. He surprised parliament by immediately reneging on earlier promises to increase subsidies to industry and to restore them for vital foodstuffs (including vodka). For much of 1993 there was a "**War of Laws**" between the government and parliament, with each flouting or repealing the other's decrees and budgets. Parliament's speaker, **Ruslan Khasbulatov**, exercised such influence over the deputies that articles in the press suggested he had them under some form of hypnosis – although as a leader Khasbulatov suffered the political handicap of being a non-Russian (born in Chechnya), and few believed that his defence of parliamentary privilege was anything but self-serving. Another erstwhile Yeltsin ally who now found himself in opposition was Vice-President **Alexander Rutskoy**, who denounced Gaidar's team as "boys in pink pants", and railed against the government as "scum" and "faggots".

In March 1993, Congress reneged on its earlier promise to hold a **referendum** on a new constitution. Yeltsin declared that he would hold an opinion poll anyway, which he hoped would provide evidence of popular support for himself, although it would have no legal force. On March 20, Yeltsin appeared on TV to announce the introduction of a special rule suspending the power of Congress and called for new elections. In the meantime, there was a nation-wide vote of confidence in the president and vice-president, plus a referendum on the draft constitution, and new electoral laws were passed. At this point Congress and Rutskoy attempted to impeach Yeltsin. The impeachment was narrowly avoided and a referendum was held. Yeltsin claimed to have been vindicated by 55 percent of those who voted (32 percent of the electorate), but the count took place in secret and the ballot papers were incinerated afterwards, so his opponents saw no reason to back down.

The uneasy stalemate lasted until September, when Yeltsin brought things to a head by dissolving Congress under a legally dubious decree. In response, **deputies occupied the White House**, refusing to budge as Yeltsin cut off their electricity and finally blockaded them in. The crisis deepened as Rutskoy gathered an armed force around the building and appeared on TV handing out guns. Who fired the first shot is still disputed, but the result was a series of battles, which lasted two days and left more than a hundred people dead. Snipers picked people off on the streets, Rutskoy ordered his supporters to storm the Moscow council building and the TV centre, and national television went off the air. Yeltsin responded by ordering tanks to shell the White House into submission on the morning of October 4.

With his parliamentary foes behind bars Yeltsin turned on the local councils who had supported Congress out of sympathy for their policies or simply as elected representatives. Councils all over Russia were abolished and new elections declared, leaving power concentrated in the hands of local mayors and their bureaucrats. While Yeltsin was determined to be re-elected and rewrite the constitution, he bewildered many supporters by distancing himself from the party created to represent his government in the forthcoming elections, which bore the presumptuous name of **Russia's Choice** and campaigned as if its triumph was a foregone conclusion.

Zhirinovsky and Chechnya

The result of the December 1993 elections to the new parliament or Duma was a stunning rebuff for Russia's Choice, which won only 14 percent of the vote, compared to 23 percent for the so-called Liberal Democratic Party of **Vladimir Zhirinovsky**, an ultra-nationalist with a murky past who threatened to bomb Germany and Japan and to dump radioactive waste in the Baltic States. His success owed much to a superbly run TV campaign, whose effects lasted just long enough to get the LDP into parliament, beside the "red-brown" alliance of other ultra-nationalists and Communists.

While Russian liberals and world opinion were aghast, evidence later emerged of systematic voting fraud in Zhirinovsky's favour, which could only have been organized at the highest level. For Yeltsin, the crucial point was that Zhirinovsky supported the new **Constitution**, giving unprecedented powers to the president, and backed Yeltsin's government in the Duma, despite his aggressive rhetoric. Even so, it seemed a humiliating rebuff when the Duma promulgated an amnesty for the participants in the October "events", and the organizers of the 1991 putsch too.

In the wake of the elections, the government backpedalled on further economic reforms and tried to improve its nationalist credentials by taking a sterner stand on the rights of Russians in the ex-republics, or "Near Abroad". Resurgent **nationalism** was evident across the board in foreign policy, from warnings against expanding NATO into Eastern Europe or the Baltics to arguments with Ukraine over Crimea, and increasingly blatant interventions in civil wars in the Caucasus and Central Asia. The Russian Army's new strategic doctrine identified regional wars as the chief threat to national security and defending the old borders of the USSR as a top priority.

In **St Petersburg**, the election of a new city council in March 1994 returned only half the required number of deputies, as apathetic and confused voters stayed at home. This allowed Sobchak to take sole command and pursue his strategy of boosting St Petersburg's international reputation by hosting conferences and the **Goodwill Games** and attracting state visits by Prince Charles and Queen Elizabeth: his fondness for ceremonies and VIPs led to him being dubbed "**Tsar Anatoly** the First". Although further elections finally produced a new council at the end of 1994, it was so divided that most of its energies went on feuding. Sobchak himself spent much of his time on foreign trips, and his reputation also suffered from rumours that members of his family had profited from shady property deals – factors that would contribute to his electoral defeat less than two years later.

In December, 1994, the Kremlin embarked on a **war in Chechnya** to subdue the breakaway Caucasian republic. The Chechens put up fierce resistance in their capital Grozny, which Defence Minister Grachev had boasted could be taken by a regiment of paratroops in two hours, but in fact fell only after weeks of bombardment, leaving the city in ruins and up to 120,000 dead – including tens of thousands of Russian conscripts. Back home, the debacle was attributed to the so-called "**Party of War**", a shadowy alliance of figures within the military, security and economic ministries, whose geopolitical or personal interests coincided. It was even said that Grachev and other commanders deliberately sacrificed their own troops to write off hundreds of armoured vehicles, in order to cover up the illicit sale of 1600 tanks from the Soviet Army in East Germany.

As the war dragged on throughout 1995, there was a huge protest vote for the Communists in the December parliamentary elections, which boded ill for Yeltsin's chances in the **Presidential election** of June 1996. Fearing the consequences of a victory by the Communist leader **Gennady Zyuganov**, Russia's financiers and journalists gave unstinting support to Yeltsin, with television, in particular, demonizing Zyuganov and denying the Communists any chance to state their case. Yeltsin's campaign was masterminded by Deputy Prime Minister **Anatoly Chubais**, who banked on the anti-Yeltsin vote being split between Zyuganov and the ex-paratroop general **Alexander Lebed** – as indeed happened. Having gained half the vote, Yeltsin co-opted Lebed by offering him the post of security overlord, and subsequently ordered him to end the war in Chechnya. Lebed duly negotiated the withdrawal of Russian forces – leaving the issue of Chechen independence to be resolved at a future date – only to be sacked from the government soon afterwards, having served his purpose.

Yeltsin's second term

With the Communist threat dispelled, the **oligarchs** behind Yeltsin's re-election soon fell out over the remaining spoils. **Vladimir Potanin** acquired thirty percent of the world's nickel reserves for a mere $70 million and a controlling stake in the telecom giant Svyazinvest owing to the intervention of Chubais – enraging **Boris Berezovsky**, whose TV station ORT aired a 29-minute diatribe against Potanin during a news show. Along with the banking and media moguls **Vladimir Gusinsky** and **Mikhail Khodorkovsky**, and oil or gas barons such as **Roman Abramovich** (later famous abroad for buying Chelsea football club), they became synonymous with a series of scandals – including "book advances" to Chubais and his privatization chief Alfred Kokh which were patently bribes. After Chubais had to resign as a sop to public opinion (he became boss of the electricity monopoly), Berezovsky's influence in the Kremlin grew even greater, and he was widely seen as the "kingmaker" of Russian politics.

Meanwhile, St Petersburg's 1996 mayoral election saw Sobchak ousted by his own deputy, **Vladimir Yakovlev**, following a bitter campaign dominated by allegations of corruption and nepotism. Though it didn't seem important at the time, one of Sobchak's protégés – an ex-KGB officer, **Vladimir Putin** – reacted to this by leaving St Petersburg politics to work in the Kremlin, where he would soon become noticed and destined for greater things. At the time, however, all eyes were on Yakovlev as he assumed the new post of governor and tried to grapple with the city's chaotic finances and decrepit infrastructure. His first year in office was marked by bungles and U-turns, but by 1997 he found the nerve to double municipal rents and service charges, paving the way for a balanced budget that helped St Petersburg to float a $300 million Eurobond issue, bringing in new funds for development.

Property was (and is) a vital issue. The privatization of municipal real estate yielded vast profits for speculators and corrupt officials, who were assumed to have ordered the 1997 assassination of St Petersburg's Vice-Governor **Mikhail Manevich**, after he began investigating fraudulent city property deals. Even more shocking was the murder of the widely admired **Galina Starovoitova** in November 1998. An outspoken democrat and human-rights campaigner, who opposed the war in Chechnya and was untainted by corruption, she was mourned by many as the last true democratic politician in Russia.

The 1998 crash

Prime ministers and cabinets changed with bewildering frequency, as Yeltsin manoeuvred to build or neutralize coalitions in the Duma and its upper house, the Federation Council (dominated by regional governors), and find scapegoats for Russia's economic problems. First he encouraged Russia's creditors by appointing the energetic reformer **Boris Nemtsov** to the cabinet – only to sacrifice him a few months later to placate Chernomyrdin and the Duma, whose featherbedding of the gas, industrial and collective farm lobbies ensured that the state budget went into deficit, obliging it to rely on short-term "hot" loans. By April, 1998, Russia's foreign debt stood at $117 billion, workers were owed $9 billion in unpaid wages, and pensioners over $13 billion. With a crisis imminent, Yeltsin stunned the world by dismissing Chernomyrdin's entire cabinet and nominating 35-year-old **Sergei Kirienko** as prime minister. A low-profile technocrat with no power base, his nomination was twice rejected by the Duma, until Yeltsin warned deputies that their Moscow flats and sinecures would be forfeit if they did so a third time.

Kirienko's rescue plan depended on a "final loan" from the International Monetary Fund, at a time when the collapse of economies across Asia raised fears of a global crash, and pushed down the price of Russia's chief exports, oil and gas. As the IMF loan stalled and hard currency reserves evaporated, the pressure to default or devalue became intolerable, until the Central Bank caved in. In August, the **ruble crashed** and many banks and businesses went into liquidation; the capitalist bubble had burst. Kirienko was promptly sacked and replaced by the veteran diplomat and spymaster **Yevgeny Primakov**, a "safe" candidate accepted across the political spectrum, and also internationally. The US sent three million tonnes of emergency food aid, to avert the possibility of food riots during the winter.

Yet the crash had some positive results. With imports so costly, shoppers switched back to domestic products, rewarding firms that survived the crisis with a larger share of the market. It also cut a few of the oligarchs down to size – though others seized the chance to snap up rivals' assets or dump all their own liabilities. By the end of the decade, these changes combined with arms sales and the rising price of gas and oil to produce a modest economic revival, which would contribute to the groundswell of support for Russia's next leader.

Yeltsin's endgame

While his government grappled with governing, Yeltsin was preoccupied with ensuring his own future – if not by running for president again in 2000, then by choosing a successor who would safeguard "**the Family**" – a term widely used to describe his inner circle of advisers and relatives, whose backroom deals with Berezovsky were the source of constant speculation in parts of the media they didn't control. With his health so uncertain that even Prime Minister Primakov expressed doubts as to whether Yeltsin could function as president – for which Primakov was sacked in January 1999 – Yeltsin had no alternative but to find a successor whom he could trust to guarantee the Family's security after they left the Kremlin. There would be no mercy if the Communists won, nor any sympathy from Lebed, while Moscow's Mayor Luzhkov and the recently dismissed Primakov offered little hope either – but any of them could win the next election.

Yeltsin's chosen successor emerged as suddenly and mysteriously as the apartment-block **bombings** that killed over 300 people in Moscow and other cities in September. Coming only a month after a Chechen warlord seized thousands of hostages in Daghestan, most Russians believed the government's claim that Chechen terrorists were responsible (though foreign journalists speculated that the FSB was behind the bombings), and demanded action.

It was then that the new acting prime minister, **Vladimir Putin**, made his name by pledging, "We will wipe the terrorists out wherever we find them – even on the toilet." Within weeks Russia launched a **second war in Chechnya**, using overwhelming firepower from the start. By December eighty percent of Grozny was in ruins and the plight of its besieged civilians was an international issue, but in Russia most greeted the city's fall as just revenge for Russia's defeat five years earlier. Berezovsky's media went into overdrive, casting Putin as the resolute, honest leader that Russia required, while tarring Luzhkov as hand-in-glove with the mafia, and Primakov as old and sick. A new party nicknamed "Bear" materialized overnight to back Putin's candidacy, and was soon riding high in the polls.

The final masterstroke was **Yeltsin's surprise resignation** during his New Year message to the nation on the last night of the old millennium, when Russians would be more inclined to raise a rueful toast than ponder how power had so swiftly passed to Putin. His first decree as acting president was to grant Yeltsin and his family lifelong immunity from arrest, prosecution or seizure of assets, and confer on Yeltsin the title of "First President" in perpetuity.

President Putin: 2000–

Ensconced in the Kremlin as acting president, Putin enjoyed every advantage in the forthcoming election, which most of his opponents tacitly conceded was a foregone conclusion. His **inauguration** on May 5, 2000, was heralded as the first peaceful democratic transfer of power in Russian history, replete with ceremonial trappings harking back to Tsarist times, invented for the occasion. His pledge to restore Russia's greatness was followed by decrees doubling military spending, increasing the powers of the security agencies, and appointing seven "Super Governors" to oversee the regions. Five of these were army or ex-KGB officers, while twenty percent of the new regional governors were from the military or navy. The FSB took control of the Border Guards and bugging agency that Yeltsin had made into separate entities, regaining all the powers of the KGB in Soviet times. Putin spoke openly of the need to create a "**strong vertical**" power in Russia – the *vertikal* became as much a mantra of his presidency as "all power to the Soviets" had been in the days of his grandfather (who had been a cook for

Lenin and Stalin). Putin's view of Russian history embraced the Soviet, Tsarist and post-Soviet eras as equally worthwhile – symbolized by his decision to restore the Tsarist eagle as the state symbol, and the old Soviet national anthem (with revised words).

For those who feared that totalitarianism was creeping back, an early sign was the **campaign against NTV** and other elements of the Media-MOST group, which had infuriated the Kremlin by revealing human-rights abuses in Chechnya and casualties among Russian troops. Media-MOST's boss, Gusinsky, was arrested and spent several days in Moscow's notorious Butyurka prison, in what was seen by liberals as a warning to other media moguls, but welcomed by most Russians as a blow against the hated oligarchs. Putin then convened a meeting of the oligarchs that pointedly excluded Gusinsky, Berezovsky and Abramovich, where the invitees reportedly pledged to pay more taxes and quit meddling in state affairs. Gusinsky prudently left Russia, soon to be followed by Berezovsky. Besides alleging that millions of dollars had been embezzled to finance Putin's election campaign, Berezovsky also implied that he had paid the Chechen warlord to invade Daghestan and thus set the stage for a new war in Chechnya and Putin's rise to power.

However, Putin's reputation suffered more from a spate of high-profile **disasters** – a bomb in a Moscow subway that killed twelve and injured scores; a fire in Moscow's Ostankino TV Tower that blacked out national television for several days; and the loss of 118 men aboard the submarine *Kursk*, a tragedy which cast both navy and Kremlin in the role of villains after they had rejected offers of foreign help at a time when it was still possible to save some survivors.

Nonetheless, his objectives were broadly accepted by the Duma, and foreign heads of state queued up to meet him. On the **foreign agenda** were the prospect of NATO forces on Russia's borders, once Poland and the Baltic States joined the alliance; the status of the Russian enclave of Kaliningrad within the European Union; and whether to ratify the Kyoto Treaty on climate change. On the first issue Putin could only register objections; the others allowed more scope for bargaining, but Russia's prestige had been so dissipated in the Yeltsin years that it no longer commanded respect. If foreign leaders were bothered by Russia's systematic human-rights abuses in **Chechnya**, it was barely mentioned in public, while Russian TV viewers had no difficulty in believing that the situation was being "normalized". Putin's claim to be fighting Islamic terrorism became even easier to sell after **September 11**, 2001, when the US needed Russian help to sweep the Taliban from power in Afghanistan. The Northern Alliance was rearmed with Russian munitions and spares; US Special Forces were launched and supplied from an airbase in Tajikistan (whose ruler was equally quick in seizing the chance to whitewash his own human-rights abuses).

At home, Putin's popularity remained sky high. Brewers and bar owners named their wares and premises after the president, whose self-confessed love of beer "in moderation" compared favourably with Yeltsin's habits and especially appealed to women voters, all-too-familiar with alcoholic men. Whereas Yeltsin boasted of his prowess at tennis but could sometimes barely stand, Putin had a black belt in judo and looked a convincing tough guy when he posed on the deck of a nuclear submarine or flew over Chechnya in a jet fighter. Although he professed to dislike his own personality cult and occasionally made his displeasure plain (a Muscovite who created a larger-than-life statue of Putin was told, "We are sure that this work will not be displayed anywhere but the courtyard of the sculptor's house"), he clearly reaped its benefits and hardly needed to orchestrate it when there were so many media lackeys to do the job. In the run-up to the 2003 parliamentary elections, every radio station played a pop song that was rated number one overnight, despite existing only in the form of a tape, delivered to the stations the night before. Its refrain ran:

A man like Putin
Full of strength.
A man like Putin
Who doesn't drink.
A man like Putin
Who won't hurt me.
A man like Putin
Who won't run away.

Among the achievements that Putin claimed for his first term was **reviving the economy**. Since 1999, growth has averaged more than five percent a year and inflation has stayed low. Revamped light industries cater to a growing middle-class who find local products in no way inferior to imported foodstuffs and aren't ashamed to buy Russian clothes any more. New sectors such as telecoms and advertising are thriving, while industries that have traditionally earned Russia hard currency – such as arms sales – have bounced back since their sharp decline in the 1990s. Yet many economists argue that Putin's successful record depends on the windfall of high world prices for Russia's major natural resource. Official figures claim oil and gas provide only 9 percent of Russia's GDP, but the World Bank puts it as high as 25 percent, suggesting that a slump in oil and gas prices would endanger the stability of the whole economy.

Even now, **poverty** is endemic. About a third of Russia's population live below the official poverty line ($53 a month, less than the $73 that independent experts reckon is needed). Income inequality is grotesque; the top ten percent have 23 times more than the bottom ten percent (the same ratio in Britain is twelve, in Poland, seven). Alcoholism, a collapsing health system, unemployment and despair have sent male life expectancy plummeting – the average is now 59 years, less that what it was in the late nineteenth century. Having children is simply too expensive for many Russians (the weekly state child benefit is only $2.70) and it's estimated that for every ten live births, thirteen pregnancies are terminated. Since the Soviet Union's collapse, Russia's population has shrunk by 3.3 million to about 145 million – an unprecedented decline for an industrialized nation in peacetime – and is falling at a rate of about a million a year, leading Putin to warn that it could drop to 123 million in a decade. While the Orthodox Church applauded moves to curb abortions in 2003, St Petersburg's governor hit upon another way to rectify the declining birthrate, by offering parents of babies born on the city's anniversary day the chance of a free apartment.

Putin's ability to manage the tensions arising from these contradictions rests on a tripod of power, whose most "vertical" leg consists of senior or ex-officers of the security services and armed forces, installed at the highest levels of government across the Federation – known as the *silovki* (from the Russian word *sil*, meaning "force"). The second is the Kremlin's control of most of the media, which is used to undermine any party that might crystallize discontent. This needs the cooperation of Russia's oligarchs, for whom the *quid pro quo* is a veil drawn over how they acquired their wealth in the Yeltsin years. The rules of this *modus vivendi* were demonstrated to all when the billionaire Mikhail Khodorkovsky, chairman of the Yukos oil conglomerate, was arrested in his private jet on a Siberian runway in October 2003. Khodorkovsky had been funding the liberal Yabloko party and looked set to challenge the Kremlin. His arrest aroused a storm of protest from foreign governments and business interests, some of whom denounced it as an act of anti-Semitism or a violation of civil liberties. But Russian voters were delighted, rewarding Putin's United Russia party with 222 seats in the parliamentary elections of December 2003. The Communists, meanwhile, were reduced to only 53 seats in the Duma.

In February 2004, Putin dismissed his long-serving prime minister, Kasyanov, and the entire cabinet, seen by some as retribution for Kasyanov's public criticism of the jailing of Khodorkovsky. Others interpreted the sackings as a move to cast Putin as the only personality in government, or to inject some drama into the March presidential election that everyone knew would be a walkover. TV channels gave endless airtime to United Russia and starved the other parties of publicity, while the tabloids did their bit by comparing one challenger to Hitler and accusing him of fathering four illegitimate children; another claimed to have been drugged and filmed in compromising positions, before fleeing to London and withdrawing from the race. Putin received 71 percent of votes cast; his nearest rival, the Communist candidate, 13.7 percent, and the only liberal just 3.9 percent. "Russia's choice: the end of democracy", was the verdict of one (pro-Kremlin) newspaper – for with both chambers of the legislature under Putin's control, the formal checks and balances of the constitution are nullified, making him an absolute sovereign in all but name. (His hero is Peter the Great.) Yet to Russians he's patently a "man of the people" – to make it from a *kommunalka* to the Kremlin is the Russian equivalent of going from a log cabin to the White House.

Meanwhile, in St Petersburg...

As a local boy made good, Putin pulled out all the stops for St Petersburg's **tercentenary anniversary** in 2003. A staggering $1.7 billion was budgeted to cover street repairs and the face-lifting of monuments. Extra police were drafted in from Ingushetia and the homeless were swept off the streets. In addition, a two-metre high, ten-kilometre-long fence was erected to hide the cottages and allotments between Pulkovo airport and the Konstantin Palace at Strelna; the palace had been refurbished at a cost of $300 million to host the G8 Summit of 45 world leaders, who were serenaded on the terrace by Pavarotti. Ordinary citizens fumed about the oppressive security restrictions and felt that the vast expenditure was unjustifiable, when St Petersburg had so many social and environmental problems needing to be tackled.

HIV is spreading faster here than anywhere else in Europe; it's estimated that half the city's prostitutes are HIV-positive, and there has been a sixteen-fold increase in HIV among street children. The single hospital that treats people with HIV doles out antibiotics to treat opportunistic infections, but has no anti-retroviral drugs that could hinder the virus's proliferation. **Heroin addi-ction** is spiralling; a wrapper costs only $1 – as cheap as or cheaper than a bottle of vodka. The number of children diagnosed with an alcohol, drug or substance abuse problem has more than trebled since 1993. **Alcoholism** and homelessness among adults are longstanding, intractable, problems. **Crime** is – statistically – falling, but cynics say that this is simply because corruption is so entrenched that crimes go unreported or are covered up; it's thought that virtually all businesses either pay for "protection" (known as a *krysha*, or "roof") or are owned by organized crime. The exposure of a local extortion racket run by senior detectives led to the arrest of dozens more "Werewolves" in Moscow, including a junior minister.

Small wonder that Petersburgers were indifferent to the gubernatorial election, required after Yakovlev was "promoted" to the Kremlin (where his future insignificance was signalled by the award of a fourth-class medal). United Russia's candidate, **Valentina Matvienko**, was Putin's "Special Envoy" in St Petersburg, and opponents claimed that she used her state job to promote her campaign. Since being elected on a low turn-out in the autumn of 2003, Matvienko's battle to improve her image hasn't been helped by the presidential administration that she previously headed, which caused an uproar by laying claim to buildings around St Isaac's Square and on the Neva embankment, housing scientific and literary institutes. It looks like a dispute that's set to run and run....

Books

The number of books available about Russia and the old Soviet Union is vast. We have concentrated on works specifically related to St Petersburg and on useful general surveys of Russian and Soviet history, politics and the arts. Publishers are detailed below in the form of British publisher/American publisher, where both exist. Where books are published in one country only, UK or US follows the publisher's name. Out-of-print books are designated o/p; University Press is abbreviated UP. Books tagged with the ✶ symbol are particularly recommended.

General accounts, guides and illustrated books

Baedeker's Handbooks (Baedeker, o/p). The 1914 *Handbook to Russia* was a stupendous work that almost bankrupted the company, with dozens of maps and reams of information that were soon rendered irrelevant by the Revolution. A facsimile edition was produced in the 1970s, but today this, too, is almost as rare as the original, copies of which sell for up to £500 in antiquarian bookshops.

Marshall Berman *All That is Solid Melts into Air: The Experience of Modernity* (Verso/Penguin). A wide-ranging study of modernism with a superb chapter on St Petersburg, covering Pushkin, Gogol, and Chernyshevsky amongst others. Thought-provoking stuff.

Kathleen Berton Murrell *St Petersburg: History, Art and Architecture* (Troika, Moscow/Flint River Press, UK). Informative text by a long-term resident in Russia, although the photographs follow no apparent logical order.

James H. Billington *The Icon and the Axe* (Vintage, US). Dated in many of its perceptions, but still the most comprehensive and readable study of Russian culture from medieval to Soviet times.

Robert Byron *First Russia, Then Tibet* (Penguin, UK). A classic travel account of the 1930s with a well-honed chapter on Leningrad (though it is the Tibetan section that really shines).

✶ **Marquis de Custine** *Empire of the Czar* (Anchor). Another vintage masterpiece, and the first book by a Westerner to get to grips with Russia, which de Custine visited during the 1830s. Waspish, cynical and indignant by turns, many of its observations are still uncannily true today.

Michael Dohan (ed) *St Petersburg Traveller's Yellow Pages* (Infoservices International, US). Annual listings book on sale all over St Petersburg in its Cyrillic edition, and less widely in the English one. Also accessible online at ⓦ www.infoservices.com.

Duncan Fallowell *One Hot Summer in St Petersburg* (Vintage, UK). Sex, drugs and tears during the torrid White Nights, as an English writer gets into the St Petersburg demi-monde and falls in love with a naval cadet. Some good descriptions, amidst a lot of hyperbolic waffle.

Prince George Galitzine *Imperial Splendour* (Viking, UK). Palaces and monasteries of old Russia, presented by a member of the Russian nobility who lived most of his life in London, but made regular trips back to St Petersburg from the early 1960s.

Katya Galitzine *St Petersburg: The Hidden Interiors* (Hazar Publishing, UK). Written by the Prince's British-born daughter (who also founded a library in his name, see p.404), its title is a bit of a misnomer, since most of the buildings featured are well known, but Leonid Bogdanov's photographs make this an irresistible coffee-table book.

Vadim Gippenreiter & Alexei Komech *Old Russian Cities* (Laurence King, o/p). Colour photos of the loveliest towns and cities in Russia, carefully staged to exclude any Soviet architecture. Among the dozens of places featured are St Petersburg, Novgorod and the Imperial palaces.

Mikhail Iroshnikov et al *Before the Revolution: St Petersburg in Photographs 1890–1914* (Abrams, o/p). Evocative black-and-white photographs (many never published before) of the city in the last decades of its Tsarist incarnation, with a historical text by four eminent St Petersburg academics.

Ian Jack (ed) *Russia: the Wild East* (Granta, UK). A disturbing anthology of pieces on Russian life by writers such as Orlando Figes, Colin Thubron and Vitaly Vitaliev, ranging from St Petersburg to Siberia, and vodka to the war in Chechnya.

Pavel Kann *Leningrad: A Guide* (Planeta, Moscow). The last in a classic Soviet series of city guides, giving pride of place to Lenin memorial sites and the like; the 1988 edition is blissfully impervious to perestroika. You may still find copies in the city's bookshops.

Lawrence Kelly *St Petersburg: A Traveller's Anthology* (Constable & Atheneum, o/p). Amusing descriptions of court life, eyewitness accounts of historic events and excerpts from books long out of print. Stops short of Petrograd and the Revolution, though.

Evgenia Kirichenko & Mikhail Anikst *The Russian Style* (Laurence King, UK). A coffee-table book of Russian interiors, ranging from the palatial to the humble, including famous writers' homes, amazing Style Moderne mansions and glittering palace halls.

Prince Michael of Greece *Imperial Palaces of Russia* (IB Tauris/St Martin's Press). Lavishly illustrated survey of all the major palaces in and around St Petersburg, by the "heir" to a royal family that the Greeks rejected in 1974.

★ **Suzanne Massie** *Land of the Firebird*; *Pavlovsk: The Life of a Russian Palace* (both Hearttree Press, US). The first is a colourful tour of pre-revolutionary Russian culture; the second sweeps over three centuries of history as embodied by Pavlovsk Palace, its inhabitants and its restorers, accompanied by wonderful illustrations.

★ **John Nicholson** *The Other St Petersburg*. Absurdity, drinking and courtyards loom large in these amusing character sketches of Leningrad as it was before capitalism changed everything. Nicholson still lives in St Petersburg and now owns *Bubyr's Guesthouse* (see p.338), where copies of this self-published book are sold. You can read excerpts online at ⓦ www.other.spb.ru.

Anthony Ross *By the Banks of the Neva* (Cambridge UP, UK). A history of the British community in eighteenth-century St Petersburg and their contribution to the city as engineers, artists, governesses, soldiers and sailors – the list is endless.

★ **Colin Thubron** *Among the Russians* (Penguin, UK); *In Siberia* (Chatto & Windus, UK). The first includes a chapter on

Leningrad, a visit to which formed part of Thubron's angst-ridden journey around the USSR in the early 1980s; the second is as lapidary and insightful and even more gloom-inducing, given such locales as Kolyma and Vorkuta, the worst hells of the Gulag.

Solomon Volkov *St Petersburg: A Cultural History* (Free Press). A scholastic *tour de force*, ranging from

architecture and music to fashion and philosophy.

Various *St Petersburg: A Guide to the Architecture* (Bibliopolis, St Petersburg). A compact guide to who built what and where, illustrated with black-and-white photographs. Though widely available in Nevskiy prospekt bookshops, it's worth buying only if you're especially interested in architecture.

History, politics and society

John T. Alexander *Catherine the Great: Life and Legend* (Oxford UP, UK). Just what the title says, but it gives rather more credence to some of the wilder stories than Cronin's biography (see below).

Anne Applebaum *Gulag: A History of the Soviet Camps* (Penguin). This Pulitzer Prize-winning tome emphasizes the human cost and economic futility of the Gulag, drawing on extensive archival material, but its assertion that only fellow travellers on the left had a soft spot for Stalinism is wrong, since *Time* magazine made Stalin its man of the year in 1939 and 1941, and many European conservatives lauded him as a "splendid fellow".

⭐ **Antony Beevor** *Stalingrad* and *The Fall of Berlin 1945* (both Penguin). Military history told from the standpoint of ordinary soldiers on both sides and the civilians caught in the middle. Stalingrad was one of the decisive battles of World War II, its epic scale matched by its ferocity. In 1945, the Red Army took revenge on the German capital, where isolated acts of decency were submerged in an orgy of rapine, licensed by Stalin's order and Soviet propaganda.

⭐ **Bruce Clark** *An Empire's New Clothes* (Vintage, UK). A provocative assessment of the *realpoli-*

tik behind the dramas of the 1990s by *The Times*'s man on the spot, who argues that Yeltsin's "democrats" did more to lay the foundations of a resurgent Russian empire than those who accused them of selling out to the West.

⭐ **Robert Conquest** *Stalin: Breaker of Nations* (Weidenfeld & Nicolson/Viking Penguin); *The Great Terror: A Reassessment* (Pimlico/Oxford UP). The first is a short, withering biography of the Soviet dictator; the second, perhaps the best study of the Terror. In 1990, this was revised after new evidence suggested that Conquest's tally of the number of victims of the Terror was an underestimate; previously he had been accused of exaggeration.

Steve Crawshaw *Goodbye to the USSR: The Collapse of Soviet Power* (Bloomsbury, UK). A clear and insightful account of the Gorbachev era by *The Independent*'s Eastern European editor, covering the period from 1985 up to Gorbachev's resignation in the aftermath of the putsch.

Vincent Cronin *Catherine, Empress of all the Russias* (Harvill/HarperCollins). Salacious rumours are dispelled in this sympathetic biography of the shy German princess who made it big in Russia.

Isaac Deutscher *Stalin* (Penguin, UK). Classic political biography, criticized for being too sympathetic towards its subject.

Harold Elletson *The General Against the Kremlin* (Little, Brown). An intriguing biography of the maverick soldier-turned-politician Alexander Lebed, that stops short of his career's downward trajectory after 1996 and his death in a helicopter crash in 2002.

Marc Ferro *Nicholas II: The Last of the Tsars* (Oxford UP, UK). A concise biography of Russia's doomed monarch, by a French historian who argues that some of the Imperial family escaped execution at Yekaterinburg. Most scholars reckon that the sole survivor was the family spaniel, Joy.

★ **Orlando Figes** *A People's Tragedy: The Russian Revolution 1891–1924* (Pimlico/Viking Penguin). Vivid, detailed, anecdotal, closely argued and sure to infuriate Marxists and monarchists alike, it sees the Feburary and October revolutions and the Civil War as a continuum. A *tour de force*.

★ **Stephen Handleman** *Comrade Criminal: The Theft of the Second Russian Revolution* (Yale UP). Fascinating study of how organized crime spread through every level of Russian society and how Communist *apparatchiki* transformed themselves into gangster-capitalists.

★ **Adam Hochschild** *The Unquiet Ghost: Russians Remember Stalin* (Serpent's Tail/Penguin). A searching enquiry into the nature of guilt and denial, ranging from the penal camps of Kolyma to the archives of the Lubyanka. Hochschild concludes that the road to hell is paved with good intentions and that few people living under the Terror would have behaved any better.

Andrew Jack *Inside Putin's Russia* (Granta, UK). Written by the

Financial Times's correspondent in Moscow during Putin's first term as president, it epitomizes the consensual view of Russia as a "managed democracy" of authoritarian, oligarchic rule over an impoverished majority, groping towards prosperity, legality and human rights.

★ **John Kampfner** *Inside Yeltsin's Russia* (Cassell, UK). Racy account of Yeltsin's presidency, focusing on political crises, crime and corruption, with vignettes of the highlights and leading characters up to 1994. Best read in conjunction with Bruce Clark's book, for a somewhat different view and conclusions.

★ **Dominic Lieven** *Nicholas II* (St Martin's Press, US). Another, especially insightful post-Soviet study of the last tsar that draws comparisons both between the monarchies of Russia and other states of that period, and the downfall of the Tsarist and Soviet regimes.

★ **Robert Massie** *Peter the Great* (Abacus/ Ballantine); *Nicholas and Alexandra* (Indigo/Dell). Both the boldest and the weakest of the Romanov tsars are minutely scrutinized in these two heavyweight, but extremely readable, biographies – the one on Peter is especially good, and contains much about the creation of St Petersburg.

★ **Andrew Meier** *Black Earth: Russia After the Fall* (HarperCollins). Like Jack's book, this focuses on Putin's efforts to restore "vertical power" and Russia's prestige abroad, but also stresses the cultural tradition and the vastness of the country as crucial to an understanding of its politics and economics. Meier used to be *Time* magazine's reporter in Moscow.

William Millinship *Front Line* (Methuen, o/p). Interviews with diverse women in the new Russia by the erstwhile Moscow correspondent of Britain's *Observer*. By turns vivid, gripping, moving and appalling – a fascinating slice of Russian life.

Edvard Radzinsky *Rasputin: The Last Word* (Weidenfeld, UK). The most recent and comprehensive biography of the "mad monk" who hastened the fall of tsarism, using newly discovered files from the archives of the Provisional Government.

John Reed *Ten Days that Shook the World* (Penguin). The classic eyewitness account of the 1917 Bolshevik seizure of power, which vividly captures the mood of the time and the hopes pinned on the Revolution. The book of the film *Reds*.

Anna Reid *The Shaman's Coat: A Native History of Siberia* (Weidenfeld & Nicholson, UK). Only peripherally related to St Petersburg, but a sobering account of the havoc wrought on the indigenous peoples of Siberia that's a corrective to the Russo-centric perspective of painters such as Surikov and the Soviet "Conquest of the North". Written by the former Kiev correspondent of Britain's *Daily Telegraph* and *Economist*.

⭐ **David Remnick** *Lenin's Tomb* (Penguin/Random House); *Resurrection: The Struggle for a New Russia* (Picador, UK). Written by the *Washington Post*'s correspondent in Moscow in the early 1990s, *Lenin's Tomb* remains the most vivid account of the collapse of the Soviet Union, though some of its judgements seem simplistic with hindsight. *Resurrection* is also riveting, but the jury is still out on Remnick's analysis of the Yeltsin era.

⭐ **Harrison Salisbury** *Black Night, White Snow* and *The Nine Hundred Days* (both Da Capo Press, US). The events of the 1905 and 1917 revolutions and the wartime siege of Leningrad are vividly related in these two heavyweight, but extremely readable, books by an American journalist, who first visited Leningrad shortly after the lifting of the Blockade.

⭐ **Robert Service** *History of Modern Russia from Nicholas II to Putin* (Penguin, UK); *Russia: Experiment with a People* (Macmillan, UK). The first is a magisterial survey of twentieth-century Russian history; the second focuses on the corruption, authoritarianism and missed opportunities of the Yeltsin era. Service is a professor of Russian history at London's School of Slavonic Studies.

⭐ **Jonathan Steele** *Eternal Russia: Yeltsin, Gorbachev and the Mirage of Democracy* (Faber/Harvard UP). *The Guardian's* former Moscow correspondent provides a thought-provoking, incisive look at the evolution of the new Russia, which he sees very much as a product of a deep-rooted authoritarian tradition.

Henri Troyat *Alexander of Russia* (Dutton, US). Study of the "Tsar Liberator", Alexander II, sympathetically profiled by a French historian.

Peter Truscott *Putin's Progress* (Simon & Schuster). Whilst adhering to the consensual view of Putin's Russia (see Jack's and Meier's books, above), this one contains more biographical detail about Russia's judo-loving president than the others.

John Ure *The Cossacks* (Constable, UK). A lively history of the free-booting warriors who rocked the Romanov dynasty but also served as its most faithful instrument of repression, by a former British diplomat who began his career in Russia.

Dmitri Volkogonov *Stalin: Triumph and Tragedy* (Prima Publishing, US). Weighty study of the Soviet dictator, drawing on long-withheld archive material, by Russia's foremost military historian.

Edmund Wilson *To the Finland Station* (Penguin). A classic appraisal of Lenin's place in the Russian revolutionary tradition, first published in 1940, combining metaphysics and political analysis with waspish characterization.

The arts

Anna Benn & Rosamund Bartlett *Literary Russia: A Guide* (Picador, UK). A comprehensive guide to Russian writers and places associated with their lives and works, including such famous Petersburgers as Dostoyevsky and Akhmatova, along with figures who are less well known abroad, such as the cult author Daniil Kharms.

Alan Bird *A History of Russian Painting* (Phaidon/Macmillan). A comprehensive survey of Russian painting from medieval times to the Brezhnev era, including numerous black-and-white illustrations and potted biographies of the relevant artists.

John E. Bowlt (ed) *Russian Art of the Avant Garde* (Thames & Hudson/Penguin). An illustrated volume of critical essays on this seminal movement, which anticipated many trends in Western art that have developed since World War II.

Leslie Chamberlain *The Food and Cooking of Russia* (Penguin). An informative and amusing cookbook, full of delicious – if somewhat vague – recipes.

★ **William Craft Brumfield** *A History of Russian Architecture* (Cambridge UP). The most comprehensive study of the subject, ranging from early Novgorod churches to Olympic sports halls, by way of Baroque palaces and Style Moderne mansions. Illustrated by hundreds of photos and line drawings.

★ **Matthew Cullerne Brown** *Art Under Stalin* (Phaidon/Holmes & Meier); *Contemporary Russian Art* (Phaidon, UK). The former is a fascinating study of totalitarian aesthetics, ranging from ballet to sports stadia and films to sculpture; the latter covers art in the Brezhnev and Gorbachev eras.

John Drummond (ed) *Speaking of Diaghilev* (Faber). What may prove to be a definitive work, given that it consists of over twenty interviews with Diaghilev's few remaining contemporaries. Dancers, conductors, choreographers and contemporary observers give their thoughts and memories of the impresario behind the Ballets Russes.

★ **Camilla Gray** *The Russian Experiment in Art 1863–1922* (Thames & Hudson). A concise guide to the multitude of movements that constituted the Russian avant-garde, prior to the imposition of the dead hand of Socialist Realism.

★ **George Heard Hamilton** *The Art and Architecture of Russia* (Yale UP). An exhaustive rundown of the major trends in painting, sculpture and architecture in Russia, from Kievan Rus to the turn of this century.

★ **Geir Kjetsaa** *Fyodor Dostoyevsky: A Writer's Life* (Macmillan, UK). Readable yet scholarly, this is the best one-volume biography of Russia's most famous writer, by a Finnish academic.

Jay Leyda *Kino* (Princeton UP). A weighty history of Russian and Soviet film to the early 1980s.

Geraldine Norman *The Hermitage: The Biography of a Great Museum* (Pimlico, UK). An affectionate and engrossing history of the acquisitions, dramas and personalities that have made the Hermitage a museum in a league of its own.

Roberta Reeder *Anna Akhmatova: Poet and Prophet* (Allison & Busby, UK). Comprehensive and well-researched biography of one of the greatest poets of Russia's "Silver Age", with accounts of the artists, poets and events that influenced her life and work.

Artemy Troitsky *Back in the USSR: The True Story of Rock in Russia* and *Tsusovka: Who's Who in the New Soviet Rock Culture* (both Omnibus, UK). Two first-hand account of thirty years of rock music in Russia, by the country's leading

music journalist and critic, who later edited the Russian edition of *Playboy* magazine and is now a director at state television.

⭐ **A.N. Wilson** *Tolstoy* (Penguin). Heavyweight but immensely readable biography of the great novelist and appalling family man.

Russian fiction and poetry

⭐ **Anna Akhmatova** *Selected Poems* (Penguin). Moving and mystical verses by the doyenne of Leningrad poets, whose *Requiem* cycle spoke for a generation traumatized by the purges. Essential reading.

Boris Akunin *The Winter Queen* (Random House). Wildly popular in Russia at present, Akunin's detective stories set in Pushkin's time are being promoted abroad in translation, but have yet to inspire the same rapture, and are slated at home by some critics as shallow pastiches.

Andrei Bely *Petersburg* (Penguin, US). Apocalyptic novel set in 1905, full of *fin-de-siècle* angst and phantasmagorical imagery, by St Petersburg's equivalent of Kafka. One of the characters is a time bomb.

Andrei Bitov *Pushkin House* (Harvill/Random House). A bittersweet tale about growing up in Leningrad during the post-Stalin years, partly based on the author's own experiences at university.

⭐ **Fyodor Dostoyevsky** *Poor Folk and Other Stories*; *The Brothers Karamazov*; *The Gambler*; *The House of the Dead*; *The Idiot* (all Penguin); *Crime and Punishment* (Penguin/Random House); *Notes from the Underground* (Penguin/Bantam); *The Possessed* (Vintage/NAL-Dutton). Pessimistic, brooding tales, often semi-autobiographical (particularly *The Gambler*

and *The House of the Dead*). His masterpiece, *Crime and Punishment*, is set in Petersburg's infamous Haymarket district.

Daniil Kharms *Incidences* (Serpent's Tail, UK). Literary miniatures by the legendary St Petersburg absurdist. In his home city you can find other works in Russian, including Kharms's irreverent "Pushkin stories", illustrated with his own cartoons.

⭐ **Vladimir Nabokov** *Invitation to a Beheading*; *Laughter in the Dark*; *Look at the Harlequins!*; *Nabokov's Dozen*; *Speak, Memory* (all Penguin/Random House). Though best known abroad for his novel of erotic obsession, *Lolita*, Nabokov is chiefly esteemed as a stylist in the land of his birth. His childhood home stands just off St Isaac's Square, and is vividly recalled in his autobiographical *Speak, Memory*.

⭐ **Boris Pasternak** *Doctor Zhivago* (HarperCollins/Ballantine). A multi-layered story of love and destiny, war and revolution, chiefly known in the West for the film version. Russians regard Pasternak as a poet first and a novelist second.

⭐ **Victor Pelevin** *A Werewolf Problem in Central Russia and Other Stories*; *Omon Ra*; *The Blue Lantern: Stories* (all New Directions, US); *Buddha's Little Finger* (Viking, US); *The Life of Insects* (Penguin); *The Clay Machine-Gun* (Faber, UK).

Digital-age fables by the literary voice of Russia's "Generation P", for whom Pepsi, not the Party, set the tone.

Nina Sadur *Witch's Tears and Other Stories* (Harbord Publishing, UK). Strikingly original tales of late Soviet times and afterwards, by one of the best writers in Moscow today. Pain and loss are at the heart of them, whether it's the legacy of Chernobyl, emigration to Israel, or Gagarin's mother, talking to her long-dead son.

Aleksandr Solzhenitsyn *August 1914* (Penguin); *Cancer Ward* (Vintage/Random House); *First Circle* (Harvill/Northwestern University Press); *The Gulag Archipelago* (HarperCollins); *One Day in the Life of Ivan Denisovich*

(Vintage/Knopf). Russia's most famous dissident – the last two books listed here constitute a stunning indictment of the camps and the purges, for which Solzhenitsyn was persecuted by the state in Brezhnev's time and feted in the West (at least before he lambasted its decadence).

★ **Lev Tolstoy** *Anna Karenina* and *War and Peace* (Penguin). The latter is the ultimate epic novel, tracing the fortunes of dozens of characters over decades. Its depiction of the Patriotic War of 1812 cast common folk in a heroic mould, while the main, aristocratic characters are flawed – an idealization of the masses that made *War and Peace* politically acceptable in Soviet times.

Foreign fiction

Malcolm Bradbury *To The Hermitage* (Overlook Press, US). A witty and intriguing story interweaving St Petersburg in the time of Catherine the Great and in 1993, with French *encyclopédiste* Diderot as the central character.

Celia Brayfield *White Ice* (Penguin, UK). A tale of passion and greed involving a diamond necklace and four disparate characters, in a story that ranges from pre-revolutionary St Petersburg to Thatcher's Britain, via Leningrad and London in the 1960s.

★ **Alan Brien** *Lenin: The Novel* (Paladin & Morrow, o/p). A masterly evocation of Lenin's life and character, in the form of a diary by the man himself, every page exuding his steely determination and sly irascibility.

Anthony Burgess *Honey for the Bears* (Norton, US). An amusing tale of misadventure, sexual discovery and black-marketeering in 1950s Leningrad. An early work by the

prolific British polymath, whose interest in Russia ran deep.

Bruce Chatwin *What Am I Doing Here* (Picador/Penguin). A memorable account of visiting Russia with the art collector George Ortiz and a lively essay on Russian Futurism are only two of the gems in this collection of travel pieces and *pensées*.

J. M. Coetzee *The Master of Petersburg* (Minerva/Penguin). A brooding novel centred on Dostoyevsky, who gets drawn into the nefarious underworld of the St Petersburg Nihilists after the suspicious suicide of his stepson.

★ **Helen Dunmore** *The Siege* (Penguin). This acclaimed novel follows the love affairs of two generations through the awful hardships of the Blockade. Harrowing, moving and uplifting by turns.

Tom Hyman *Seven Days to Petrograd* (Penguin & Bantam, o/p). A thriller about an attempt to avert the Bolshevik Revolution by killing

Lenin aboard the "sealed train", featuring an unlikely romance between the would-be assassin and Lenin's soul mate, Inessa Armand.

Michael Ignatieff *The Russian Album* (Vintage & Penguin, o/p). An evocative family history dating back to before the Revolution by the émigré scion of an old Russian family with roots in St Petersburg.

Philip Kerr *Dead Meat* (Vintage/Bantam). An edgy, atmospheric thriller set in a mafia-infested St Petersburg, where the lugubrious detective Grushko tries to uncover the truth behind a journalist's murder. Made into a three-part BBC television series.

John le Carré *The Russia House* (Hodder/Knopf). A well-intentioned but overlong attempt to exorcize the ghosts of the Cold War by the world's best-known spy novelist. His snapshots of Leningrad and Moscow in the days of perestroika are less illuminating than the author's own perspective as a former spy.

I Allan Sealy *The Brainfever Bird* (Picador, UK). An intriguing romantic thriller that moves between St Petersburg and Old Delhi, replete with deadly viruses, international espionage and neo-Nazi thuggery.

★ **Gillian Slovo** *Ice Road* (Little, Brown). Not, as you might imagine, about the wartime Road of Life, but about Kirov's assassination, that plunged Leningrad into a vortex of fear and suffering. Slovo's intrepid narrator is an unforgettable creation.

Language

Language

Language

The official language of the Russian Federation is Russian (russkiy yazik), a highly complex eastern Slav tongue. Any attempt to speak Russian will be appreciated, though don't be discouraged if people seem not to understand, as most will be unaccustomed to hearing foreigners stumble through their language. English and German are the most common second languages, especially among the younger generation. Bilingual signs and menus are fairly common in the heart of the city, but being able to read the Cyrillic alphabet makes life a lot easier. For a fuller linguistic rundown than the one below, buy the *Rough Guide Russian Phrasebook*, set out dictionary-style for easy access, with English-Russian and Russian-English sections, cultural tips for tricky situations and a menu reader.

The Cyrillic alphabet

The Cyrillic alphabet – derived from a system invented by Saints Cyril and Methodius, the "Apostles of the Slavs" – is an obstacle that's hard to get around, and is worth trying to learn if you're going to be in Russia more than a few days. Seven of the thirty-three letters represent approximately the same sound

Cyrillic characters

Аа	a	Ии	y	Уу	u	Ьь	a silent
Бб	b	Кк	k	Фф	f		"soft sign"
Вв	v	Лл	l	Хх	kh		which softens
Гг	g*	Мм	m	Цц	ts		the preceding
Дд	d	Нн	n	Чч	ch		consonant
Ее	e*	Оо	o	Шш	sh	Ъъ	a silent "hard
Её	e	Пп	p	Щщ	shch		sign" which
Жж	zh	Рр	r	Ыы	y*		keeps the
Зз	z	Сс	s	Ээ	e		preceding
Ии	i	Тт	t	Яя	ya		consonant hard*

*To aid pronunciation and readability, we have introduced a handful of **exceptions** to the above transliteration guide:

Гг (g) is written as v when pronounced as such, for example Горкого – Gorkovo.

Ее (e) is written as Ye when at the beginning of a word, for example Елагин – Yelagin.

Ыы (y) is written as i, when it appears immediately before й (y), for example Литейный – Liteyniy.

To confuse matters further, **hand-written Cyrillic** is different again from the printed Cyrillic above – although the only place you're likely to encounter it is on menus. The chief differences are:

б which looks similar to a "d"

г which looks similar to a backwards "s"

и which looks like a "u"

т which looks similar to an "m"

as they do in the Roman alphabet; others are taken from the Greek alphabet, or are unique to the Slavonic languages. It's often possible to decipher the names of streets or metro stations by focusing on the letters you can recognize, but this won't get you far in other situations. Where signs are bilingual, you'll notice variations in **transliterating** Cyrillic into Latin script (for example "Chajkovskogo" or "Chaykovskovo" for Чайковского). In this book, we've used the English System, with a few modifications to help pronunciation. All proper names appear as they are best known, not as they would be transliterated; for example "Tchaikovsky" not "Chaykovskiy".

The list on p.453 gives the Cyrillic characters in upper and lower case form, followed simply by the Latin equivalent. In order to pronounce the words properly, you'll need to consult the pronunciation guide below.

Pronunciation

English-speakers often find Russian difficult to pronounce, partly because even letters that appear to have English equivalents are subtly different. On the other hand, Russian spelling is more phonetically consistent than English and the vast majority of words contain no silent letters. The most important factor that determines pronunciation is stress; if you get this wrong, even the simplest Russian words may be misunderstood. Attuning your ear to how stress affects pronunciation is more useful than striving to master Russian grammar (which shares many features with Latin).

Vowels and word stress

Unlike some Slavonic languages, the **stress** in a word can fall on any syllable and there's no way of knowing simply by looking at it – it's something you just have to learn, as you do in English. If a word has only one syllable, you can't get it wrong; where there are two or more, we've placed accents over the stressed vowel/syllable, though these do not appear in Russian itself. Once you've located the stressed syllable, you should give it more weight than all the others and far more than you would in English. We've marked the syllable to be stressed with an accent.

Whether a **vowel** is stressed or unstressed sometimes affects the way it's pronounced, most notably with the letter "o" (see below).

а – a – like the *a* in father

я – ya – like the *ya* in yarn, but like the *e* in evil when it appears before a stressed syllable

Э,э – e – always a short *e* as in get

е – e – like the *ye* in yes

и – i – like the *e* in evil

й – y – like the *y* in boy

о – o – like the *o* in port when stressed, but like the *a* in plan when unstressed

ё – e – like the *yo* in yonder. Note that in Russia, this letter is often printed without the dots

у – u – like the *oo* in moon

ю – yu – like the *u* in universe

ы – y – like the *i* in ill, but with the tongue drawn back

Consonants

In Russian, **consonants** can be either soft or hard and this difference is an important feature of a "good" accent, but if you're simply trying to get by in the language, you needn't worry. The main features of consonants are:

б – b – like the *b* in bad; at the end of a word like the *p* in dip

в – v – like the *v* in van but with the upper teeth behind the top of the lower lip; at the end of a word, and before certain consonants like *f* in leaf

г – g – like the *g* in goat; at the end of a word like the *k* in lark

д – d – like the *d* in dog but with the tongue pressed against the back of the upper teeth; at the end of a word like the *t* in salt

ж – zh – like the *s* in pleasure; at the end of a word like the *sh* in bush

з – z – like the *z* in zoo; at the end of a word like the *s* in loose

л – l – like the *l* in milk, but with the tongue kept low and touching the back of the upper teeth

н – n – like the *n* in no but with the tongue pressed against the upper teeth

р – r – trilled as the Scots speak it

с – s – always as in soft, never as in sure

т – t – like the *t* in tent, but with the tongue brought up against the upper teeth

х – kh – like the *ch* in the Scottish loch

ц – ts – like the *ts* in boats

ч – ch – like the *ch* in chicken

ш – sh – like the *sh* in shop

щ – shch – like the *sh-ch* in fresh cheese

There are of course exceptions to the above pronunciation rules, but if you remember even the ones mentioned, you'll be understood.

Words and phrases

Basics

Yes	da	да
No	net	нет
Please	pozháluysta	пожалуйста
Thank you	spasíbo	спасибо
Excuse me	izviníte	извините
Sorry	prostíte	простите
That's OK/it doesn't matter	nichevó	ничего
Hello/goodbye (formal)	zdrávstvuyte/do svidániya	здравствуйте/до свидания
Good day	dóbriy den	добрый день
Good morning	dóbroe útro	доброе утро
Good evening	dóbriy vécher	добрый вечер
Good night	spokóynoy nochi	спокойной ночи
See you later (informal)	poká	пока
Bon voyage	schastlívovo putí	счастливого пути
Bon appetit	priyátnovo appetíta	приятного аппетита
How are you?	kak delá?	как дела?
Fine/OK	khoroshó	хорошо
Leave me alone!	ostavte menya!	оставте меня!
Help!	na pómoshch!	на помощь!
Today	sevódnya	сегодня
Yesterday	vcherá	вчера
Tomorrow	závtra	завтра
The day after tomorrow	poslezávtra	послезавтра
Now	seychás	сейчас
Later	popózzhe	попозже

This one	*éta*	это
A little	*nemnógo*	немного
Large/small	*bolshóy/málenkiy*	большой/маленький
More/less	*yeshché/ménshe*	ещё/меньше
Good/bad	*khoróshiy/plokhóy*	хороший/плохой
Hot/cold	*goryáchiy/kholódniy*	горячий/холодный
With/without	*s/bez*	с/без

Pronouns, names and introductions

Normally, you should use the **polite form** вы (*vy*, "you" plural) in conversation. The informal ты (*ty*, "you" singular) is for children, close friends and relatives (before the Revolution, the ruling classes also used it to serfs, servants and conscripts). Older Russians often introduce themselves and address others using their first name and **patronymic**, eg Maria Fyodorovna (Maria, daughter of Fyodor) or Anton Ivanovich (Anton, son of Ivan). At some stage they may suggest that you use their first name only, or begin using *ty* to each other. This is usually a good sign, but remember that such informality isn't appreciated at a business meeting (a Russian boss might call his colleagues by their first names, but they would certainly use his patronymic, too).

I	*ya*	я
you (singular)	*ty*	ты
we	*my*	мы
he, she, it	*on, oná, onó*	он, она, оно
you (plural)	*vy*	вы
they	*oní*	они
What's your name?	*kak vas zovút?*	как вас зовут?
My name is…	*menya zovút…*	меня зовут
Pleased to meet you	*óchen priyátno*	очень приятно

Getting around

Over there	*tam*	там
Round the corner	*za uglóm*	за углом
Left/right	*nalévo/naprávo*	налево/направо
Straight on	*pryámo*	прямо
Where is. . . ?	*gde?*	где?
How do I get to Peterhof?	*kak mne popást v Petergof?*	как мне попасть в Петергоф?
Am I going the right way for the Hermitage?	*ya právilno idú k Ermitazhu?*	я правильно иду к Эрмитажу?
Is it far?	*etó dalekó?*	это далеко?
By bus	*avtóbusom*	автобусом
By train	*póezdom*	поездом
By car	*na mashine*	на машине
On foot	*peshkóm*	пешком
By taxi	*na taksi*	на такси
Ticket	*bilét*	билет
Return (ticket)	*tudá i obrátno*	туда и обратно
Train station	*vokzál*	вокзал

Bus station	*avtóbusniy vokzal*	автобусный вокзал
Bus stop	*ostanóvka*	остановка
Is this train going to Novgorod?	*étot póezd idét v Nóvgorod?*	этот поезд идёт в Новгород?
Do I have to change?	*núzhno sdélat peresádku?*	нужно сделать пересадку?
Small change (money)	*méloch*	мелочь

Questions and answers

Do you speak English?	*Vy govoríte po-anglíyski?*	вы говорите по-английски?
I don't speak German	*ya ne govoryú po-nemétski*	я не говорю по-немецки
I don't understand	*ya ne ponimáyu*	я не понимаю
I understand	*ya ponimáyu*	я понимаю
Speak slowly	*govoríte pomédlenee*	говорите помедленее
I don't know	*ya ne znáyu*	я не знаю
How do you say that in Russian?	*kak po-rússki?*	как по-русски?
Could you write it down?	*zapishíte éto pozháluysta*	запишите это пожалуйста
What . . .	*chto*	что
Where	*gde*	где
When	*kogdá*	когда
Why	*pochemú*	почему
Who	*kto*	кто
How much is it?	*skólko stóit?*	сколько стоит?
I would like a double room	*ya khochú nómer na dvoíkh*	я хочу номер на двоих
For one night	*tólko sútki*	только сутки
Shower	*dush*	душ
Are these seats free?	*svobódno?*	свободно?
May I . . . ?	*mózhno?*	можно?
You can't/it is not allowed	*nelzyá*	нельзя
The bill please	*schet pozháluysta*	счёт пожалуйста
Do you have . . . ?	*u vas yest?*	у вас есть?
That's all	*eto vsé*	это всё

Signs

Entrance	*vkhod*	вход
Exit	*výkhod*	выход
Toilet	*tualét*	туалет
Men's	*múzhskóy*	мужской
Women's	*zhénskiy*	женский
Pull (a door)	*k sebe*	к себе
Push (a door)	*ot sebya*	от себя
Open	*otkrýto*	открыто
Closed (for repairs)	*zakrýto (na remont)*	закрыто на ремонт
Out of order	*ne rabótaet*	не работает
No entry	*vkhóda net*	входа нет
Danger zone	*opasnaya zona*	опасная зона

No smoking	*ne kurít*	не курить
Drinking water	*piteváya vodá*	питьевая вода
Information	*správka*	справка
Ticket office	*kássa*	касса

Days of the week

Monday	*ponedélnik*	понедельник	Friday	*pyátnitsa*	пятница
Tuesday	*vtórnik*	вторник	Saturday	*subbóta*	суббота
Wednesday	*sredá*	среда	Sunday	*voskreséne*	воскресенье
Thursday	*chetvérg*	четверг			

Months of the year

January	*yanvár*	январь	July	*iyúl*	июль
February	*fevrál*	февраль	August	*ávgust*	август
March	*mart*	март	September	*sentyábr*	сентябрь
April	*aprél*	апрель	October	*oktyábr*	октябрь
May	*may*	май	November	*noyábr*	ноябрь
June	*iyún*	июнь	December	*dekábr*	декабрь

Numbers

L
LANGUAGE | Words and phrases

1	*odín*	один	50	*pyatdesyát*	пятьдесят
2	*dva*	два	60	*shestdesyát*	шестьдесят
3	*tri*	три	70	*sémdesyat*	семьдесят
4	*chetkre*	четыре	80	*vósemdesyat*	восемьдесят
5	*pyat*	пять	90	*devyanósto*	девяносто
6	*shest*	шесть	100	*sto*	сто
7	*sem*	семь	200	*dvésti*	двести
8	*vósem*	восемь	300	*trísta*	триста
9	*dévyat*	девять	400	*chetkresta*	четыреста
10	*désyat*	десять	500	*pyatsót*	пятьсот
11	*odínnadtsat*	одиннадцать	600	*shestsót*	шестьсот
12	*dvenádtsat*	двенадцать	700	*semsót*	семьсот
13	*trinádtsat*	тринадцать	800	*vosemsót*	восемьсот
14	*chetkrnadtsat*	четырнадцать	900	*devyatsót*	девятьсот
15	*pyatnádtsat*	пятнадцать	1000	*tksyacha*	тысяча
16	*shestnádtsat*	шестнадцать	2000	*dve tksyachi*	две тысячи
17	*semnádtsat*	семнадцать	3000	*tri tksyachi*	три тысячи
18	*vosemnádtsat*	восемнадцать	4000	*chetkre tksyachi*	четыре тысячи
19	*devyatnádtsat*	девятнадцать			
20	*dvádtsat*	двадцать	5000	*pyat tksyach*	пять тысяч
21	*dvádtsat odín*	двадцать один	10,000	*désyat tksyach*	десять тысяч
30	*trídtsat*	тридцать	50,000	*pyatdesyát tksyach*	пятьдесят тысяч
40	*sórok*	сорок			

Food and drink terms

Basics

аджика	*adzhíka*	spicy Georgian relish	рис	*ris*	rice
бутерброд	*buterbrod*	open sandwich	перец	*pérets*	pepper
чашка	*cháshka*	cup	плов	*plov*	pilau
десерт	*desért*	dessert	пирог	*piróg*	pie
фрукты	*frúkty*	fruit	рыба	*ryba*	fish
горчица	*gorchítsa*	mustard	сахар	*sákhar*	sugar
хлеб	*khleb*	bread	салат	*salat*	salad
ложка	*lózhka*	spoon	сметана	*smetána*	sour cream
масло	*máslo*	butter/oil	соль	*sol*	salt
мёд	*myod*	honey	суп	*soup*	soup
молоко	*molokó*	milk	стакан	*stakán*	glass
мясо	*myáso*	meat	тарелка	*tarélka*	plate
напиток	*napítok*	drinks	ужин	*úzhin*	supper
нож	*nozh*	knife	вилка	*vílka*	fork
обед	*obéd*	main meal/lunch	яйца	*yáytsa*	eggs
овощи	*ovoshchi*	vegetables	яичница	*yaichnitsa*	fried egg
пицца	*pizza*	pizza	завтрак	*závtrak*	breakfast
			закуски	*zakúski*	appetizers

Appetizers (*zakúski*) and salads

ассорти мясное	*assortí myasnóe*	assorted meats
ассорти рыбное	*assortí rybnoe*	assorted fish
бастурма	*bastúrma*	marinated dried meat
блины	*bliný*	pancakes
блинчики	*blinchiki*	*bliny* rolled around a filling and browned
брынза	*brynza*	salty white cheese
грибы	*griby*	mushrooms
икра баклажанная	*ikrá baklazhánnaya*	aubergine (eggplant) purée
икра красная	*ikrá krásnaya*	red caviar
икра чёрная	*ikrá chórnaya*	black caviar
хачапури	*khachapuri*	Georgian nan-style bread, stuffed with cheese
хачапури по-Мингрелский	*khachapuri po-Mingrelskiy*	*khachapuri* cooked with an egg in the middle
колбаса копчёная	*kolbasá kopchónaya*	smoked sausage
маслины	*maslíny*	olives
морков по-корейский	*morkov po-koreyskiy*	spicy carrot salad
огурцы	*ogurtsy*	gherkins
осетрина с майонезом	*osetrína s mayonézom*	sturgeon mayonnaise
пельмени	*pelmeni*	Siberian ravioli
салат из огурцов	*salat iz ogurtsóv*	cucumber salad

салат из помидоров	*salát iz pomidórov*	tomato salad
сардины с лимоном	*sardíny s limónom*	sardines with lemon
сельдь	*seld*	herring
селёдка под шубы	*selyódka pod shuby*	pickled herring with beetroot, carrot, egg and mayonnaise
шпроты	*shpróty*	sprats (like a herring)
столичный салат	*stolíchniy salát*	meat and vegetable salad
сыр	*syr*	cheese
ветчина	*vetchiná*	ham
винегрет	*vinegrét*	"Russian salad"
язык с гарниром	*yazyk s garnírom*	tongue with garnish

Soups

борщ	*borsch*	beetroot soup
бульон	*bulón*	consommé
чихиртми	*chikhirtmi*	lemon-flavoured chicken soup
харчо	*khárcho*	spicy beef or lamb soup
хаш	*khásh*	tripe soup, traditionally drunk as a hangover cure
клёцки	*klyótski*	Belorussian soup with dumplings
лапша	*lapsha*	chicken-noodle soup
окрошка	*okróshka*	cold vegetable soup
постный борщ	*póstny borsch*	borsch without meat
рассольник	*rassólnik*	brine and cucumber soup
щи	*shchi*	cabbage soup
солянка	*solyánka*	spicy, meaty soup flavoured with lemon and olives
уха	*ukhá*	fish soup

Meat dishes

азу из говядины	*azú iz govyádiny*	beef stew
антрекот	*antrekot*	entrecôte steak
баранина	*baránina*	mutton/lamb
бастурма	*bastúrma*	thinly sliced, marinated, dried meat
бифстроганов	*bifstróganov*	beef stroganoff
биточки	*bitóchki*	meatballs
бифштекс	*bifshtéks*	beef steak
булкоги	*bulkogi*	spicy, stir-fried, marinated beef
чахохбили	*chakhokhbili*	slow-cooked chicken with herbs and vegetables
казы	*kázy*	pony-meat sausages
хинкали	*khinkáli*	dumplings stuffed with lamb, or beef and pork
котлеты по-киевски	*kotléty po-kíevski*	chicken Kiev
кролик	*królik*	rabbit
курица	*kúritsa*	chicken
рагу	*ragú*	stew

сациви	satsivi	chicken in walnut sauce, served cold
шашлык	shashlyk	kebab
свинина	svinína	pork
телятина	telyátina	veal
сосиски	sosíski	frankfurter sausages
котлета	kotleta	fried meatball

Fish

форель	forel	trout	щука	shchúka	pike
карп	karp	carp	скумбрия	skúmbriya	mackerel
лещ	leshch	bream	треска	treská	chub
лососина	lososína	salmon	сёмга	syomga	salmon
осетрина	osetrína	sturgeon	судак	sudak	pike perch

Vegetables and herbs

баклажан	baklazhán	aubergine (eggplant)
чеснок	chisnok	garlic
гарниры	garniry	any vegetable garnish
горох	gorókh	peas
грибы	griby	mushrooms
грибы с сметаной	griby s smetanoy	mushrooms cooked with sour cream
капуста	kapústa	cabbage
картофель	kartófel	potatoes
кимичи	kimichi	spicy, garlicky pickled cabbage
кинза	kinza	coriander
лобио	lóbio	red or green bean stew
лук	luk	onions
мхали	mkhali	beetroot or spinach puree with herbs and walnuts
морковь	morkóv	carrots
огурцы	ogurtsy	cucumbers
петрушка	petrushka	parsley
помидоры	pomidóry	tomatoes
редиска	redíska	radishes
салат	salát	lettuce
свёкла	svyokla	beetroot
толма	tólma	tomatoes, aubergines or vine-leaves stuffed with meat and rice
укроп	úkrop	dill
зелень	zélen	fresh herbs

Fruit

абрикосы	abrikósy	apricots	банан	banan	banana
апельсины	apelsíny	oranges	чернослив	chernoslív	prunes
арбуз	arbúz	watermelon	дыня	dynya	melon

финики	*fíniki*	dates	виноград	*vinográd*	grapes
груши	*grushi*	pears	вишня	*víshnya*	cherries
инжир	*inzhír*	figs	яблоки	*yábloki*	apples
лимон	*limón*	lemon	ягоды	*yágody*	berries
сливы	*slivy*	plums			

Common terms

фаршированные	*farshiróvannye*	stuffed
фри	*fri*	fried
копчёные	*kopchonye*	smoked
маринованные	*marinóvannye*	pickled or marinated
паровые	*paróvye*	steamed
печёные	*pechónye*	baked
отварные	*ótvarnye*	boiled
овошной	*óvoshchnoy*	made from vegetables
на вертеле	*na vertele*	grilled on a skewer
с грибами	*s gribámi*	with mushrooms
солёные	*solyónye*	salted
со сметаной	*so smetánoy*	with sour cream
тушёные	*tushónye*	stewed
варёные	*varyónye*	boiled
жареные	*zhárenye*	roast/grilled/fried

Drinks

чай	*chay*	tea
кофе	*kófe*	coffee
с сахаром	*s sakarom*	with sugar
без сахара	*bez sákhara*	without sugar
сок	*sok*	fruit juice
кэфир	*kefir*	the Russian equivalent of *lassi*
квас	*kvas*	a drink made from fermented rye
мёд	*myod*	honey mead
сбитэн	*sbiten*	a herbal liquor
тархун	*tarkhun*	a tarragon-flavoured drink
пиво	*pívo*	beer
вино	*vinó*	wine
красное	*krásnoe*	red
белое	*béloe*	white
бутылка	*butýlka*	bottle
лёд	*lyod*	ice
минеральная вода	*minerálnaya vodá*	mineral water
водка	*vódka*	vodka
вода	*vodá*	water
шампанское	*shampánskoe*	champagne
брют	*bryut*	extra dry

сухое	*sukhoe*	dry
полусухое	*polusukhóe*	medium dry
сладкое	*sládkoe*	sweet
коньяк	*konyák*	cognac
за здоровье	*za zdaróve*	cheers!

A glossary of Russian words and terms

Note: the accents below signify which syllable is stressed, but they are not used in the main text of this book.

bánya bathhouse

báshnya tower

bulvár boulevard

dácha country cottage

dom kultúry communal arts and social centre; literally "house of culture"

dvoréts palace

górod town

kanál canal

kassa ticket office

kládbishche cemetery

kommunálka communal flat, where several tenants or families share the bathroom, kitchen and corridor

krépost fortress

monastyr monastery or convent; the distinction is made by specifying *muzhskóy* (men's) or *zhenskiy* (women's) *monastyr*

most bridge

muzhík before the Revolution it meant peasant; it now means masculine or macho

náberezhnaya embankment

óstrov island

ózero lake

pámyatnik monument

pereúlok lane

plóshchad square

prospékt avenue

reká river

restorán restaurant

rússkiy/rússkaya Russian

rýnok market

sad garden/park

shossé highway

sobór cathedral

storoná district

teátr theatre

tsérkov church

úlitsa street

vokzál train station

výstavka exhibition

zal room or hall

zámok castle

An architectural glossary

Art Nouveau French term for the sinuous, stylized form of architecture dating from the turn of the century to World War I, called Style Moderne in Russia.

Atlantes Supports in the form of carved male Atlas figures, used instead of columns to support an entablature.

Baroque Exuberant architectural style of the seventeenth and early eighteenth centuries that spread to Russia via Ukraine and Belarus. Characterized by heavy, ornate decoration, complex spatial arrangement and grand vistas.

Caryatids Sculpted female figures used as a column to support an entablature.

Constructivism Soviet version of modernism that pervaded the arts during the 1920s. In architecture, functionalism and simplicity were the watchwords – though many Constructivist projects were utterly impractical and never got beyond the drawing board.

Empire style Richly decorated version of the Neoclassical style, which prevailed in Russia from 1812 to the 1840s. The French and Russian Empire styles both derived from Imperial Rome.

Entablature The part of a building supported by a colonnade or column.

Faux marbre Any surface painted to resemble marble.

Fresco Mural painting applied to wet plaster, so that the colours bind chemically with it as they dry.

Futurism Avant-garde art movement glorifying machinery, war, speed and the modern world in general.

Grisaille Painting in grey or other coloured monotone used to represent objects in relief.

Icon Religious image, usually painted on wood and framed upon an iconostasis. See p.142 for more about Russian icons.

Iconostasis A screen that separates the sanctuary from the nave in Orthodox churches, typically consisting of tiers of icons in a gilded frame, with up to three doors that open during services. The central one is known as the Royal Door.

Nave The part of a church where the congregation stands (there are no pews in Orthodox churches).

Neoclassical Late eighteenth- and early nineteenth-century style of architecture and design returning to classical Greek and Roman models as a reaction against Baroque and Rococo excesses.

Neo-Russian (also known as Pseudo-Russian) Style of architecture and decorative arts that drew inspiration from Russia's medieval and ancient past, folk arts and myths.

Pilaster A half column projecting only slightly from the wall; an engaged column stands almost free from the surface.

Portico Covered entrance to a building.

Putti Cherubs.

Rococo Highly florid, fiddly but occasionally graceful style of architecture and interior design, forming the last phase of Baroque.

Sanctuary (or Naos) The area around the altar, which in Orthodox churches is always screened by an iconostasis.

Stalinist Declamatory style of architecture prevalent from the 1930s up to the death of Stalin in 1953 that returned to Neoclassical and neo-Gothic models as a reaction against Constructivism and reached its "High Stalinist" apogee after World War II.

Stucco Plaster used for decorative effects.

Style Moderne Linear, stylized form of architecture and decorative arts influenced by French Art Nouveau, which took its own direction in Russia.

Trompe l'oeil Painting designed to fool the onlooker into believing that it is actually three-dimensional.

Political terms and acronyms

Apparatchiki A catch-all term to describe the Communist Party bureaucrats of the Soviet era.

Bolshevik Literally "majority"; name given to the faction that supported Lenin during the internal disputes within the RSDLP during the first decade of this century.

Cheka (Extraordinary Commission for Combating Counter-revolution, Speculation and Delinquency in Office) Bolshevik secret police, 1917–21.

CIS Commonwealth of Independent States – loose grouping that was formed in December 1991 following the collapse of the USSR. Most of the former Soviet republics have since joined, with the exception of the Baltic States, now in the European Union.

Civil War 1918–21 War between the Bolsheviks and an assortment of opposition forces including Mensheviks, SRs, Cossacks, Tsarists and foreign interventionist armies from the West and Japan.

Decembrists Those who participated in the abortive coup against the accession of Nicholas I in December 1825.

Duma The name given to three parliaments in the reign of Nicholas II, and the lower house of the parliament of the Russian Federation since 1993 (its upper chamber is called the Federation Council).

February Revolution Overthrow of the tsar in February 1917.

Five-Year Plan Centralized masterplan for every branch of the Soviet economy. The first five-year plan was promulgated in 1928.

FSB (Federal Security Service) The name of Russia's secret police since 1993.

GIBDD Traffic police.

GPU Soviet secret police, 1921–23.

Gulag Official title for the hard labour camps set up under Lenin and Stalin.

Kadet Party (Constitutional Democratic Party) Liberal political party 1905–1917.

KGB (Committee of State Security) Soviet secret police 1954–91.

Kuptsy Wealthy merchant class, often of serf ancestry, that rose to prominence in the late nineteenth century.

Menshevik Literally "minority"; name given to the faction opposing Lenin during the internal disputes within the RSDLP during the first decade of the twentieth century.

Metropolitan Senior cleric, ranking between an archbishop and the patriarch of the Russian Orthodox Church.

MVD Soviet secret police from 1946 to 1954; now runs the regular police (Militia) and the OMON (see below).

Narodnaya Volya (People's Will) Terrorist group that assassinated Alexander II in 1881.

New Russians (*novye russkie*) Brash nouveaux riches of the post-Soviet era, mocked by countless New Russian jokes.

NKVD Soviet secret police, 1934–46.

October Revolution Bolshevik coup d'état which overthrew the Provisional Government in October 1917.

OGPU (Unified State Political Directorate) Soviet secret police 1923–34.

Okhrana Tsarist secret police.

Old Believers (Staroobryadtsy) Russian Orthodox schismatics.

Oligarchs Immensely rich and shady financiers who emerged during the Yeltsin era.

OMON Paramilitary force used for riot control and fighting civil wars within the Russian Federation.

Patriarch Head of the Russian Orthodox Church.

Petrine Anything dating from the lifetime of Peter the Great (1672–1725).

Populist Amorphous political movement of the second half of the nineteenth century advocating Socialism based on the peasant commune, or *mir*.

Purges Name used for the mass arrests of the Stalin era, but also for any systematic removal of unwanted elements from positions of authority.

RSDLP (Russian Social Democratic Labour Party) First Marxist political party in Russia, which rapidly split into Bolshevik and Menshevik factions.

SR Socialist Revolutionary.

Tsar Emperor. The title was first adopted by Ivan the Terrible.

Tsaritsa Empress; the foreign misnomer Tsarina is better known.

Tsarevich Crown prince.

Tsaraevna Daughter of a Tsar and Tsaritsa.

USSR (Union of Soviet Socialist Republics) Official name of the Soviet Union from 1923 to 1991.

Whites Generic term for Tsarist or Kadet forces during the Civil War, which the Bolsheviks applied to almost anyone who opposed them.

Rough
Guides
advertiser

Rough Guides travel...

...music & reference

inidad & Tobago

frica & Middle East
ape Town
gypt
he Gambia
rdan
enya
arrakesh
DIRECTIONS
orocco
uth Africa, Lesotho
& Swaziland
ria
nzania
nisia
est Africa
nzibar
mbabwe

avel Theme guides
rst-Time Around the
World
st-Time Asia
st-Time Europe
st-Time Latin
America
iing & Snowboarding
in North America
avel Online
avel Health
alks in London & SE
England
omen Travel

staurant guides
nch Hotels &
Restaurants
ndon
w York
n Francisco

ps
arve
sterdam
alucia & Costa del Sol
entina

Athens
Australia
Baja California
Barcelona
Berlin
Boston
Brittany
Brussels
Chicago
Crete
Croatia
Cuba
Cyprus
Czech Republic
Dominican Republic
Dubai & UAE
Dublin
Egypt
Florence & Siena
Frankfurt
Greece
Guatemala & Belize
Iceland
Ireland
Kenya
Lisbon
London
Los Angeles
Madrid
Mexico
Miami & Key West
Morocco
New York City
New Zealand
Northern Spain
Paris
Peru
Portugal
Prague
Rome
San Francisco
Sicily
South Africa
South India
Sri Lanka
Tenerife
Thailand

Toronto
Trinidad & Tobago
Tuscany
Venice
Washington DC
Yucatán Peninsula

**Dictionary
Phrasebooks**
Czech
Dutch
Egyptian Arabic
EuropeanLanguages
(Czech, French, German,
Greek, Italian,
Portuguese, Spanish)
French
German
Greek
Hindi & Urdu
Hungarian
Indonesian
Italian
Japanese
Mandarin Chinese
Mexican Spanish
Polish
Portuguese
Russian
Spanish
Swahili
Thai
Turkish
Vietnamese

Music Guides
The Beatles
Bob Dylan
Cult Pop
Classical Music
Country Music
Elvis
Hip Hop
House
Irish Music
Jazz
Music USA

Opera
Reggae
Rock
Techno
World Music (2 vols)

History Guides
China
Egypt
England
France
India
Islam
Italy
Spain
USA

Reference Guides
Books for Teenagers
Children's Books, 0–5
Children's Books, 5–11
Cult Fiction
Cult Football
Cult Movies
Cult TV
Ethical Shopping
Formula 1
The iPod, iTunes &
Music Online
The Internet
Internet Radio
James Bond
Kids' Movies
Lord of the Rings
Muhammed Ali
Man Utd
Personal Computers
Pregnancy & Birth
Shakespeare
Superheroes
Unexplained
Phenomena
The Universe
Videogaming
Weather
Website Directory

so! More than 120 Rough Guide music CDs are available from all good book
and record stores. Listen in at www.worldmusic.net

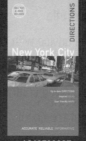

Small print
and
Index

A Rough Guide to Rough Guides

In the summer of 1981, Mark Ellingham, a recent graduate from Bristol University, was travelling round Greece and couldn't find a guidebook that really met his needs. On the one hand there were the student guides, insistent on saving every last cent, and on the other the heavyweight cultural tomes whose authors seemed to have spent more time in a research library than lounging away the afternoon at a taverna or on the beach.

In a bid to avoid getting a job, Mark and a small group of writers set about creating their own guidebook. It was a guide to Greece that aimed to combine a journalistic approach to description with a thoroughly practical approach to travellers' needs – a guide that would incorporate culture, history and contemporary insights with a critical edge, together with up-to-date, value-for-money listings. Back in London, Mark and the team finished their Rough Guide, as they called it, and talked Routledge into publishing the book.

That first *Rough Guide to Greece*, published in 1982, was a student scheme that became a publishing phenomenon. The immediate success of the book – with numerous reprints and a Thomas Cook prize shortlisting – spawned a series that rapidly covered dozens of destinations. Rough Guides had a ready market among low-budget backpackers, but soon also acquired a much broader and older readership that relished Rough Guides' wit and inquisitiveness as much as their enthusiastic, critical approach. Everyone wants value for money, but not at any price.

Rough Guides soon began supplementing the "rougher" information about hostels and low-budget listings with the kind of detail on restaurants and quality hotels that independent-minded visitors on any budget might expect, whether on business in New York or trekking in Thailand.

These days the guides – distributed worldwide by the Penguin group – offer recommendations from shoestring to luxury and cover more than 200 destinations around the globe, including almost every country in the Americas and Europe, more than half of Africa and most of Asia and Australasia. Our ever-growing team of authors and photographers is spread all over the world, particularly in Europe, the USA and Australia.

In 1994, we published the *Rough Guide to World Music* and *Rough Guide to Classical Music*; and a year later the *Rough Guide to the Internet*. All three books have become benchmark titles in their fields – which encouraged us to expand into other areas of publishing, mainly around popular culture. Rough Guides now publishes:

- Travel guides to more than 200 worldwide destinations
- Dictionary phrasebooks to 22 major languages
- History guides ranging from Ireland to Islam
- Maps printed on rip-proof and waterproof Polyart™ paper
- Music guides running the gamut from Opera to Elvis
- Restaurant guides to London, New York and San Francisco
- Reference books on topics as diverse as the Weather and Shakespeare
- Sports guides from Formula 1 to Man Utd
- Pop culture books from *Lord of the Rings* to Cult TV
- World Music CDs in association with World Music Network

Visit **www.roughguides.com** to see our latest publications.

Rough Guide credits

Text editor: Ruth Blackmore
Layout: Ajay Verma, Umesh Aggarwal
Cartography: Rajesh Chhibber, Animesh
Pathak, Jai Prakash Mishra, Rajesh Mishra
Picture research: Harriet Mills
Proofreader: Carole Mansur
Editorial: **London** Martin Dunford, Kate
Berens, Helena Smith, Claire Saunders, Geoff
Howard, Gavin Thomas, Polly Thomas,
Richard Lim, Lucy Ratcliffe, Clifton Wilkinson,
Alison Murchie, Fran Sandham, Sally Schafer,
Alexander Mark Rogers, Karoline Densley,
Andy Turner, Ella O'Donnell, Keith Drew,
Andrew Lockett, Joe Staines, Duncan Clark,
Peter Buckley, Matthew Milton; **New York**
Andrew Rosenberg, Richard Koss, Yuki
Takagaki, Hunter Slaton, Chris Barsanti,
Steven Horak
Design & Pictures: London Simon Bracken,
Dan May, Diana Jarvis, Mark Thomas, Jj
Luck, Harriet Mills; **Delhi** Madhulita
Mohapatra, Umesh Aggarwal, Ajay Verma,
Jessica Subramanian

Production: Julia Bovis, John McKay,
Sophie Hewat
Cartography: **London** Maxine Repath,
Ed Wright, Katie Lloyd-Jones, Miles Irving;
Delhi Manish Chandra, Rajesh Chhibber,
Jai Prakash Mishra, Ashutosh Bharti, Rajesh
Mishra, Animesh Pathak, Jasbir Sandhu,
Karobi Gogoi
Cover art direction: Louise Boulton
Online: **New York** Jennifer Gold, Cree
Lawson, Suzanne Welles, Benjamin Ross;
Delhi Manik Chauhan, Narender Kumar,
Shekhar Jha, Rakesh Kumar
Marketing & Publicity: **London** Richard
Trillo, Niki Smith, David Wearn, Chloë
Roberts, Demelza Dallow, Kristina Pentland;
New York Geoff Colquitt, Megan Kennedy
Finance: Gary Singh
Manager India: Punita Singh
Series editor: Mark Ellingham
PA to Managing Director: Julie Sanderson
Managing Director: Kevin Fitzgerald

Publishing information

This fifth edition published September 2004 by
Rough Guides Ltd,
80 Strand, London WC2R 0RL.
345 Hudson St, 4th Floor,
New York, NY 10014, USA.
Distributed by the Penguin Group
Penguin Books Ltd,
80 Strand, London WC2R 0RL
Penguin Putnam, Inc.
375 Hudson Street, NY 10014, USA
Penguin Books Australia Ltd,
487 Maroondah Highway, PO Box 257,
Ringwood, Victoria 3134, Australia
Penguin Books Canada Ltd,
10 Alcorn Avenue, Toronto, Ontario,
Canada M4V 1E4
Penguin Books (NZ) Ltd,
182–190 Wairau Road, Auckland 10,
New Zealand
Typeset in Bembo and Helvetica to an original
design by Henry Iles.

Printed in China

496pp includes index
A catalogue record for this book is available from
the British Library.

ISBN 1-84353-281-6

3   5   7   9   8   6   4   2

Help us update

We've gone to a lot of effort to ensure that the
fifth edition of **The Rough Guide to St
Petersburg** is accurate and up to date.
However, things change – places get
"discovered", opening hours are notoriously
fickle, restaurants and rooms raise prices or
lower standards. If you feel we've got it wrong
or left something out, we'd like to know, and if
you can remember the address, the price, the
time, the phone number, so much the better.

We'll credit all contributions, and send a
copy of the next edition (or any other Rough

Guide if you prefer) for the best letters.
Everyone who writes to us and isn't already a
subscriber will receive a copy of our full-colour
thrice-yearly newsletter. Please mark letters:
"**Rough Guide St Petersburg Update**" and
send to: Rough Guides, 80 Strand, London
WC2R 0RL, or Rough Guides, 4th Floor, 345
Hudson St, New York, NY 10014. Or send an
email to **mail@roughguides.com**

Have your questions answered and tell
others about your trip at
www.roughguides.atinfopop.com

Acknowledgements

The author would like to say a special thanks to all those in Russia: Catherine Phillips for frequent impositions; Maria Novikova for diligent research and caring for Sonia; Lena Yefimovich and Nikolai Nikolaiovich for all their kindness; Andrei Khlabystin and Alla Mitrofanova for laughs and wisdom; Alexei Larionov for many sage corrections at the Hermitage; Olga Filimonova at Tsarskoe Selo; Yelena Yefimova and Yuri Anatalovich at Gatchina; Olga Utochkina at the Yusupov Palace; Vladimir Puchkov at the Engineers' Castle; Lyubov Stepanova Petrova aboard the cruiser *Aurora*; Isaak Friedman and Alla Kvasha in Novgorod; Elena Zakharova at Russian Cruises; and the staff of the St Petersburg tourist office. In **England**, thanks to Ruth Blackmore at Rough Guides for sensitive and erudite editing; Ildar Walker at Inntel-Moscow; and Olga Scott at Scott's Tours.

The editor would like to join the author in thanking Carole Mansur for proofreading, Umesh Aggarwal for typesetting, Harriet Mills for picture research; and Manish Chandra, Jai Prakash Mishra, Rajesh Chhibber, Ashutosh Bharti, Rajesh Mishra and Animesh Pathak for cartography.

Readers' letters

Many thanks to all the readers of the last edition who took the time to write in with their comments and suggestions (and apologies to anyone whose name we've misspelt or omitted):

Benjamin Brierley & Elena Malysheva; Dorothy Cull; Wendy Scott Fletcher; R.S. Gibbs; Bo Gronningsaeter; Clive & Mary Hicks; Chad Z. Hower; Edo Huber; Andrew Jameson; Alice Jones; Viktor Kabakchi; N. Peter Knoll; Dr Igor Kotin; Lea Leatham; Zelda Chaikin Linekar; Rebecca Lindley; Alexander Mattea; Ahilleas Maurellis & Iryna Grygorenko; Simon Pizzey; Agnieszka Popisuil; Peter Romilly; Amanda Sloat; A. Stone; Sandy Tarpinian; Simon Wade; Victor Blease; Stephen Rich; and John Richard Williamson.

Photo credits

Index

Map entries are in colour.

Map symbols

Maps are listed in the full index using coloured text.

–·–··	Province boundary	♨	Monastery
– – –	Chapter division boundary	⚱	Church (regional maps)
═══	Major road	✈	Airport
═══	Minor road	)(	Bridge
▥▥▥▥	Steps	P	Parking
- - - - -	Path	⛽	Fuel station
━━━	Railway	*(i)*	Tourist office/information
— —	Ferry route	⊠	Post office
——	River	ⓒ	Phone office
——	Wall	⚓	Hydrofoil/Boat station
■—■	Fence	⊙	Statue/memorial
〰 Rocks		⊠	Gate
Ⓜ	Metro station	★	Bus stop
▲	Peak	@	Internet café
◆	Place of interest	⬭	Stadium
🏛	Monument	■	Building
🕌	Mosque	⊟	Church (town maps)
✡	Synagogue	⊞	Cemetery
♜	Fortress	▦	Park
⚘	Gardens	⬚	Beach
		🗺	Forest

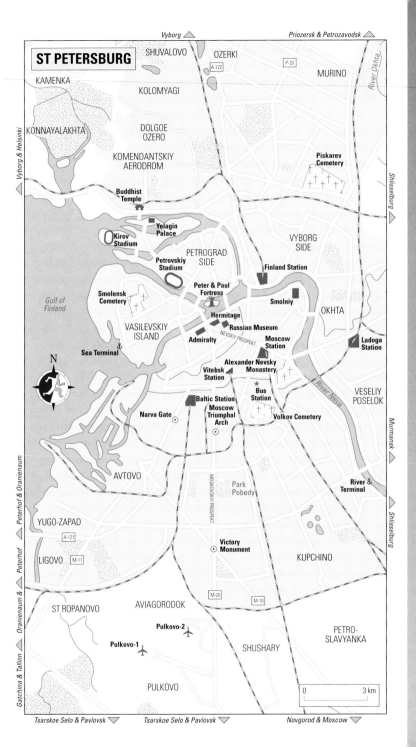

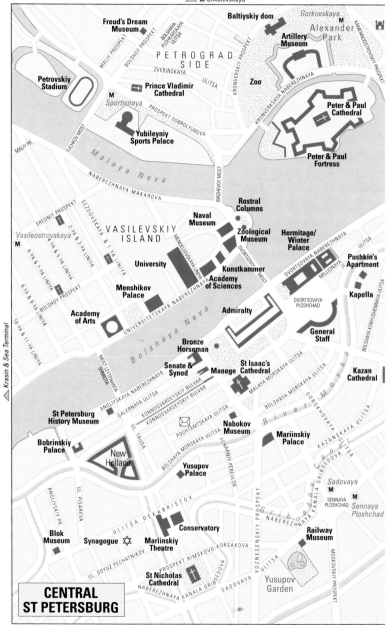

Freud's Dream Museum

Baltiyskiy dom

Gorkovskaya

M

Alexander Park

Artillery Museum

BOLSHAYA PUSKARSKAYA ULITSA

MALIY PROSPEKT

BOLSHOY PROSPEKT

KRONVERKSKIY PROSPEKT

KAMENNOOSTROVSKIY PROSPEKT

PETROGRAD SIDE

ZVERINSKAYA

Zoo

Prince Vladimir Cathedral

Sportivnaya

M

PROSPEKT DOBROLYUBOVA

ULITSA

KRONVERKSKAYA NABEREZHNAYA

Petrovskiy Stadium

Peter & Paul Cathedral

MALIY PR.

Yubileyniy Sports Palace

TUCHKOV MOST

Peter & Paul Fortress

M a l a y a   N e v a

NABEREZHNAYA MAKAROVA

BIRZHEVOY MOST

Rostral Columns

SREDNIY PROSPEKT

SEZDOVSKAYA & 1-YA LINIYA

2-YA & 3-YA LINIYA

Naval Museum

Zoological Museum

Vasileostrovskaya

M

6-YA & 7-YA LINIYA

8-YA & 9-YA LINIYA

VASILEVSKIY ISLAND

MENDELEEVSKAYA LINIYA

DVORTSOVYY MOST

Hermitage/ Winter Palace

DVORTSOVAYA NABEREZHNAYA

MILLIONAYA

ULITSA

Pushkin's Apartment

University

Kunstkammer

Academy of Sciences

Kapella

8-YA & 9-YA BOLSHOY PROSPEKT

Menshikov Palace

UNIVERSITETSKAYA NABEREZHNAYA

DVORTSOVAYA PLOSHCHAD

BOLSHAYA KONYUSHENNAYA ULITSA

Academy of Arts

Admiralty

General Staff

10-YA & 11-YA LINIYA

△ Krasin & Sea Terminal

MOST LEYTENANTA SHMIDTA

B o l s h a y a   N e v a

Bronze Horseman

Senate & Synod

Manege

St Isaac's Cathedral

Kazan Cathedral

ANGLIYSKAYA NABEREZHNAYA

GALERNAYA ULITSA

KONNOGVARDEYSKIY BULVAR

MALAYA MORSKAYA ULITSA

BOLSHAYA MORSKAYA ULITSA

GOROKHOVAYA ULITSA

R i v e r   M o y k a

KAZANSKAYA ULITSA

St Petersburg History Museum

POCHTAMTSKAYA ULITSA

Nabokov Museum

Mariinskiy Palace

Bobrinskiy Palace

UL. TRUDA

New Holland

BOLSHAYA MORSKAYA ULITSA

FONARNYY PEREULOK

Sadovaya

NABEREZHNAYA KANALA GRIBOEDOVA

M

Sennaya Ploshchad

ANGLIYSKIY PR.

UL. PISAREVA

Yusupov Palace

SENNAYA PLOSHCHAD

VOZNESENSKIY PROSPEKT

Blok Museum

Synagogue ✡

ULITSA DEKABRISTOV

Conservatory

Mariinskiy Theatre

Railway Museum

MOSKOVSKIY PROSPEKT

UL. SOYUZ PECHATNIKOV

PROSPEKT RIMSKOVO-KORSAKOVA

Yusupov Garden

St Nicholas Cathedral

NABEREZHNAYA KANALA GRIBOEDOVA

SADOVAYA ULITSA

CENTRAL ST PETERSBURG

△ Piskarov Cemetery (5km)

Mosque

Museum of Russian
Political History

Peter's
Cabin

Cruiser
Aurora

PIROGOVSKAYA NABEREZHNAYA

PETROVSKAYA NABEREZHNAYA

TROITSKIY MOST

Ploshchad
Lenina

Finland
Station

VYBORG SIDE

Lenin ⊙

Kresty
Prison

ARSENALNAYA NABEREZHNAYA

R i v e r   N e v a

NABEREZHNAYA KUTUZOVA

LITEYNIY MOST

NABEREZHNAYA ROBESPERA

Bolshoy dom

SHPALERNAYA ULITSA

ZAKHAREVSKAYA   ULITSA

ULITSA CHAYKOVSKOVO

FURSHTADTSKAYA   ULITSA

KIROCHNAYA ULITSA

PR. CHERNYSHEVSKOVO

POTEMKINSKAYA ULITSA

Tauride
Gardens

M Chernyshevskaya

Marble
Palace

Summer
Palace

Museum of
the Defence
of Leningrad

Museum of
Decorative &
Applied Arts

MOKHOVAYA

Summer
Garden

SADOVAYA ULITSA

Marsovo
Pole

ULITSA PESTELYA

MANEZHNIY PER.

ULITSA RYLEEVA

Preobrazhenskiy
Church

ULITSA

LITEYNIY PROSPEKT

ULITSA RADISHCHEVA

Suvorov
Museum

Church
of the Saviour
on the Blood

NABEREZHNAYA KANALA GRIBOEDOVA

NABEREZHNAYA KANALA GRIBOEDOVA

Russian Museum
& Ethnographical
Museum

Engineers'
Castle

NABEREZHNAYA REKI FONTANKI

Circus

UL. BELINSKOVO

BASKOV   PEREULOK

Nekrasov
Museum

ULITSA NEKRASOVA

ULITSA MAYAKOVSKOVO

ULITSA VOSSTANIYA

ULITSA ZHUKOVSKOVO

PL.
ISKUSSTV

Nevskiy
Prospekt

ITALYANSKAYA ULITSA

N E V S K I Y   P R O S P E K T

Sheremetov
Palace

LIGOVSKIY PROSPEKT

1-YA SOVETSKAYA

2-YA SOVETSKAYA

SUVOROVSKIY PROSPEKT

M
Nevskiy
Prospekt

Gostiniy
dvor

M

Gostiniy
Dvor

Beloselskiy-
Belozerskiy
Palace

Mayakovskaya
M

Ploshchad
Vosstaniya

M Vosstaniya

SADOVAYA ULITSA

ULITSA LOMONOSOVA

Aleksandriinskiy
Drama Theatre

NABEREZHNAYA REKI FONTANKI

R i v e r   F o n t a n k a

ULITSA RUBINSHTEYNA

VLADIMIRSKIY PROSPEKT

DOSTOEVSKOVO

Ploshchad
Vosstaniya M

Moscow
Station

Apraksin
dvor

Dostoevskaya
M

Arctic &
Antarctic
Museum

KUZNECHNIY PER.

Militia
Museum

NABEREZHNAYA REKI FONTANKI

ZAGORODNIY PROSPEKT

Vladimirskaya
M

Dostoyevsky
Museum

PUSHKINSKAYA ULITSA

LIGOVSKIY PROSPEKT

Bread
Museum

N

Rimsky-Korsakov
Museum

RAZEZZHAYA ULITSA

ULITSA DOSTOEVSKOVO

ULITSA MARATA

Vitebsk
Station

M Pushkinskaya

Theatre of
Young Spectators

ULITSA MARATA

BOROVAYA UL.

M Ligovskiy
Prospekt

0   500 m

▽ Bus Station

▷ Smolniy Complex

▷ Alexander Nevskiy Monastery

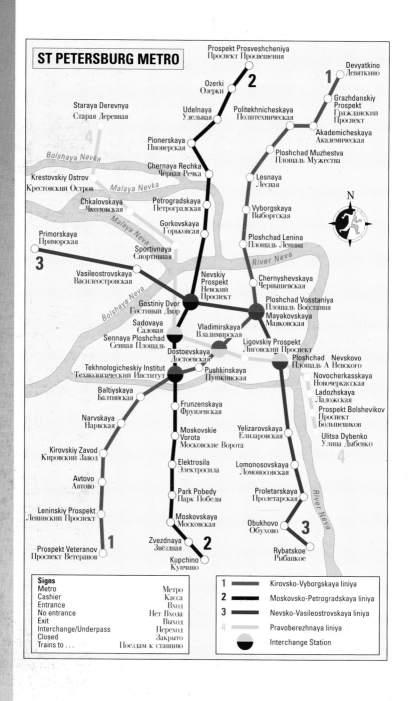

ST PETERSBURG METRO

Prospekt Prosveshcheniya
Проспект Просвещения

2

Devyatkino
Девяткино

1

Ozerki
Озерки

Staraya Derevnya
Старая Деревная

Udelnaya
Удельная

Politekhnicheskaya
Политехническая

Grazhdanskiy
Prospekt
Гражданский
Проспект

Akademicheskaya
Академическая

4

Pionerskaya
Пионерская

Ploshchad Muzhestva
Площадь Мужества

Bolshaya Nevka

Chernaya Rechka
Чёрная Речка

Lesnaya
Лесная

Krestovskiy Ostrov
Крестовский Остров

Malaya Nevka

Petrogradskaya
Петроградская

Vyborgskaya
Выборгская

Chkalovskaya
Чкаловская

Malaya Neva

Gorkovskaya
Горьковская

Ploshchad Lenina
Площадь Ленина

N

Primorskaya
Приморская

Sportivnaya
Спортивная

3

Vasileostrovskaya
Василеостровская

Nevskiy
Prospekt
Невский
Проспект

Chernyshevskaya
Чернышевская

River Neva

Bolshaya Neva

Gostiniy Dvor
Гостинный Двор

Ploshchad Vosstaniya
Площадь Восстания

Mayakovskaya
Маяковская

Sadovaya
Садовая

Vladimirskaya
Владимирская

Sennaya Ploshchad
Сенная Площадь

Ligovskiy Prospekt
Лиговский Проспект

Ploshchad Nevskovo
Площадь А Невского

Dostoevskaya
Достоевская

Novocherkasskaya
Новочеркасская

Tekhnologicheskiy Institut
Технологический Институт

Pushkinskaya
Пушкинская

Ladozhskaya
Ладожская

Baltiyskaya
Балтийская

Frunzenskaya
Фрунзенская

Prospekt Bolshevikov
Проспект
Большевиков

Narvskaya
Нарвская

Moskovskie
Vorota
Московские
Ворота

Yelizarovskaya
Елизаровская

Ulitsa Dybenko
Улица Дыбенко

Kirovskiy Zavod
Кировский Завод

Elektrosila
Электросила

Lomonosovskaya
Ломоносовская

4

Avtovo
Автово

Park Pobedy
Парк Победы

Proletarskaya
Пролетарская

River Neva

Leninskiy Prospekt
Ленинский Проспект

Moskovskaya
Московская

Obukhovo
Обухово

3

Prospekt Veteranov
Проспект Ветеранов

1

Zvezdnaya
Звёздная

2

Rybatskoe
Рыбацкое

Kupchino
Купчино

Signs	
Metro	Метро
Cashier	Касса
Entrance	Вход
No entrance	Нет Входа
Exit	Выход
Interchange/Underpass	Переход
Closed	Закрыто
Trains to . . .	Поездам к станцию

1 — Kirovsko-Vyborgskaya liniya

2 — Moskovsko-Petrogradskaya liniya

3 — Nevsko-Vasileostrovskaya liniya

4 — Pravoberezhnaya liniya

◐ Interchange Station

WORDSWORTH CLASSICS
OF WORLD LITERATURE

General Editor: Tom Griffith MA, MPhil

THE GOLDEN ASS